Crime and Society in Britain

Crime and Society in Britain

Second Edition

Hazel Croall

Glasgow Caledonian University

Longman
is an imprint of

Harlow, England • London • New York • Boston • San Francisco • Toronto • Sydney • Singapore • Hong Kong
Tokyo • Seoul • Taipei • New Delhi • Cape Town • Madrid • Mexico City • Amsterdam • Munich • Paris • Milan

Pearson Education Limited
Edinburgh Gate
Harlow
Essex CM20 2JE
England

and Associated Companies throughout the world

Visit us on the World Wide Web at:
www.pearsoned.co.uk

First published by Addison Wesley Longman Limited 1998
Second edition published 2011

ISBN: 978-1-4058-7335-2

British Library Cataloguing-in-Publication Data
A catalogue record for this book is available from the British Library

Library of Congress Cataloging-in-Publication Data
Croall, Hazel, 1947–
Crime and society in Britain / Hazel Croall. – 2nd ed.
p. cm.
Rev. ed. of: Crime and society in Britain. 1998.
Includes bibliographical references and index.
ISBN 978-1-4058-7335-2 (pbk.)
1. Crime–Great Britain. 2. Great Britain–Social conditions–1945– I. Title.
HV6947.C736 2011
364.941–dc22

2010045115

10 9 8 7 6 5 4 3 2 1
14 13 12 11 10

Typeset in 10/12.5pt Sabon by 35
Printed and bound by Ashford Colour Press, Gosport

Contents

List of figures

Acknowledgements

Many people have helped the author in completing this text. Brian Willan was the original commissioning editor, without whom the first edition and the Crime and Society series would not have existed. Anonymous reviewers provided many useful suggestions for the second edition. Gareth Addidle, Mwenda Kailemia and Lisa Kerr carried out some valuable research and made some helpful comments. Thanks are also due to the anonymous reviewers for their supporting comments to earlier drafts and for their helpful suggestions – I hope I have done them justice. Andrew Taylor at Pearson has been patient throughout long delays and has also made some invaluable comments – the book is more readable as a result. Many colleagues and students have also made their contributions, with special mention being due to Jo Buckle for his much appreciated bibliographical work. Many friends have been supportive throughout the process, putting up with long discussions about different issues covered in the book and providing much needed light relief! Finally Ailsa, Matt, Andrew and Megan have provided useful breaks and moments of sanity.

Publishers acknowledgements

The publishers would like to thank Hazel Croall for all the dedication, skill and hard work she has put into this new edition.

We would also like to thank all the reviewers who have provided invaluable comments to help improve the book.

We are grateful to the following for permission to reproduce copyright material:

Figures

Figures 3.2, 8.1 from Criminal Statistics: England and Wales 2008, http://www.justice.gov.uk/publications/docs/criminal-stats-2008.pdf; Figures 3.3, 3.4 adapted from Crime in England and Wales 2009/10: Findings from the British Crime Survey and police recorded crime, http://rds.homeoffice.gov.uk/rds/pdfs10/hosb1210.pdf; Figures 3.3, 3.4 from Crime in England and Wales 2009/10: Findings from the British Crime Survey and police recorded crime, http://rds.homeoffice.gov.uk/rds/pdfs10/hosb1210.pdf; Figure 3.4 from *Scottish Crime and Justice Survey: First Findings*, Scottish Government Social Research (MacLeod, P., Page, L., Kinver, A. and Iliasov, A., Littlewood, M. and Williams, R. 2009), The Scottish Government; Figure 3.5 from *Scottish Crime and Justice Survey: First Findings*, Scottish Government Social Research (MacLeod, P., Page, L., Kinver, A., Iliasov, A., Littlewood, M. and Williams, R. 2009) Chart 5; Figure 3.6 from *Scottish Crime and Justice Survey: First Findings*, Scottish Government Social Research (MacLeod, P., Page, L., Kinver, A., Iliasov, A., Littlewood, M. and Williams, R. 2009) 35, The Scottish Government; Figure 3.7 from *Scottish Crime and Justice Survey: First Findings*, The

Scottish Government (MacLeod, P., Page, L., Kinver, A., Iliasov, A., Littlewood, M. and Williams, R. 2009) Page 29, The Scottish Government; Figure 3.8 from Crime in England and Wales 2008/09: Wales factsheet, www.homeoffice.gov.uk/rds/pdfs09/wales09.pdf, The Office of Public Sector Information; Figure 6.1 from *Scottish Crime and Justice Survey: First Findings*, The Scottish Government (MacLeod, P., Page, L., Kinver, A., Iliasov, A., Littlewood, M. and Williams, R. 2009) 63, The Scottish Government; Figures 6.2, 7.2 from Crime in England and Wales 2008/09: Findings from the British Crime Survey and police recorded crime, http://rds.homeoffice.gov.uk/rds/pdfs09/hosb1109vol1.pdf; Figure 6.3 from Perceptions of Crime: Findings from the Northern Ireland Crime Survey, Research and Statistics Bulletin, www.nio.gov.uk, Northern Ireland Office Statistics and Research Branch; Figure 7.1 from *Scottish Crime and Justice Survey: First Findings*, The Scottish Government (MacLeod, P., Page, L., Kinver, A., Iliasov, A., Littlewood, M. and Williams, R. 2009) Page 36, The Scottish Government; Figures 9.1, 10.1 from Statistics on Women and the Criminal Justice System: A Ministry of Justice publication under Section 95 of the Criminal Justice Act 1991, http://www.justice.gov.uk/publications/docs/women-criminal-justice-system-2008-09.pdf; Figure 16.1 from 'It says 'An honest product from an honest company . . . 100% artificial'.' Farris, Joseph, Catalog Reference: jfa3029, www.cartoonstock.com

Text

Boxes 8.1, 8.2 adapted from *Young People and Crime: Findings from the 2006 Offending, Crime and Justice Survey*, Home Office (Roe, S. and Ashe, J. 2008) p. 6, http://rds.homeoffice.gov.uk/rds/pdfs08/hosb0908.pdf

Picture Credits

The publisher would like to thank the following for their kind permission to reproduce their photographs:

(Key: b-bottom; c-centre; l-left; r-right; t-top)

Alamy Images: HOBBS 153bc, ilian studio 318bl; **Corbis:** Bettmann 33bl, REUTERS / Raj Patidar 364tl; **Mary Evans Picture Library:** 68bl; **Getty Images:** 29bl, eyespy 305tl, Flying Colours Ltd 288bc, Frederick Hoare / Central Press 385tc, INDRANIL MUKHERJEE / AFP 97tl; **Mirrorpix:** 83tc; **Press Association Images:** Andrew Parsons / PA Archive 223tc, David Cheskin / PA Archive 217bl, John Stillwell / PA Archive 243bl, LIBERTY / PA Archive 389bl, LM OTERO / AP 200bl, Mahesh Kumar A 324bc, PA / PA Archive 26bc, 225tc, Peter Macdiarmid, Pool 251tl, Stefan Rousseau / PA Archive 217tc, 345bl, Stefan Rousseau / PA Archive 217tc, 345bl; **Reuters:** 168bl, Goran Tomasevic 251bc, Jeff J Mitchell 150tc, Keith Bedford 341tc, Lucas Jackson 109bl, Sean Gardner 362tl, Yiorgos Karahalis 178tc

Every effort has been made to trace the copyright holders and we apologise in advance for any unintentional omissions. We would be pleased to insert the appropriate acknowledgement in any subsequent edition of this publication.

Chapter 1
Introduction: crime and society

This chapter will introduce:

- ➜ The fear and fascination of crime
- ➜ Definitions of crime
- ➜ The relationship between crime and society
- ➜ Crime in Britain
- ➜ Issues in researching and analysing crime and victimization
- ➜ Crime and social inequalities
- ➜ Patterns of crime
- ➜ The structure of the book

Crime has become a major area of public policy and political debate, and to politicians and public commentators it is often seen as a sign of underlying problems in society. Governments, academic researchers and other commentators ask many questions about crime. Are levels of crime really rising? What affects crime rates? Why do people commit crime? What actions should be defined as criminal? How should offenders be dealt with? How can crime be reduced? These issues all arouse considerable discussion and debate and an enormous amount of information has been produced in the attempt to measure and understand crime. This book introduces readers to the academic study of crime which will enable them to better understand and critically evaluate these issues. It will examine how we find out about crime and how different theoretical approaches have sought to understand it. It will ask how crime can be related to social inequality in society, to social deprivation and socio-economic status, and to age, gender and race. It will explore different kinds of crime, from violent and sexual crimes to organized, corporate and environmental crime and the crimes of the state.

Firstly, however, it is important to look carefully at the focus of the book – at crime. What do we mean when we talk about crime? What is crime? How is it different from other kinds of behaviour? How is it related to society? This chapter will start by looking at some of the conflicting feelings aroused by crime before asking how it is defined. It will go on to explore how crime can be related to society and will finally outline the structure and scope of this book.

The fear and fascination of crime

Our attitudes to crime are complex and contradictory. Dramatic news stories of murder, rape, assault and major frauds horrify and frighten us, while at the same time exciting our curiosity about the criminals and victims involved. We are, therefore, both fascinated by and afraid of crime (Clarke 1996). Criminals can be portrayed as heroes, anti-heroes or villains. We can be appalled by accounts of sensational murders while at the same time have a grudging respect for the bank robber who outwits the police. These mixed emotions are fuelled by dramatic reports of crime in the news, which, as will be seen in Chapter 2, often distort our images of crime and criminals. Crime is often regarded as something which happens to other people – criminals are feared as strangers or outsiders and victims, too, may be seen as different by having done something to provoke a crime. Yet crime is an everyday occurrence – we are victimized every day by crimes we may not even be aware of, and many of us commit crime.

The attractions of crime are illustrated in its domination of newspapers, TV dramas and documentaries, films and literature. Some criminologists have drawn attention to the 'seductions of crime' (Katz 1988) pointing out that engaging in crimes such as gang fighting or consuming illegal drugs can satisfy desires for excitement and risk-taking, as indeed can forms of financial crime such as investing other people's money to make a financial 'killing'. Crime has long been a major theme in classical drama, literature and *film noir*. While these are dramatic and fictional accounts they reveal the abiding appeal of crime.

Fear of crime, often prompted by sensational stories, affects our everyday lives. Reports of child murders make parents more protective of their children. People avoid certain streets or areas at particular times of the day or night. Some women and children effectively live under a curfew, being scared of going out alone. We take many other precautions against crime. Every day we lock our doors and carry a bunch of keys to our home, car or workplace. We carry credit cards, identity and membership cards, all of which are designed to prevent theft and fraud. We are surrounded by crime prevention devices. We face security barriers at home, at work or in the bank and when we are shopping, travelling or walking we are under the gaze of security cameras. These not only protect us from crime, they also aim to prevent us committing it. We often feel that it is our fault for not taking sufficient precautions if we are defrauded, if our identity is 'stolen', if we are assaulted or our homes are broken into – as will be seen in Chapter 6, we also feel that some victims are more deserving of our sympathy than others.

Yet our image of crime, affected by dramatic stories of atypical crimes, may be misleading. What people tend to fear most of all is the unprovoked attack from the stranger – so much so that we avoid going to places where this might happen. In reality the risk of this is small and dangers lie elsewhere. Many crimes take place not in the public places we avoid but in the home. We are far more likely to be physically and sexually assaulted by family members than by strangers and fraud and theft can also take place within family and friendship networks. We can be harmed by pollution, unsafe working environments or the food we eat, often as a result of some neglect of criminally enforced regulations. We can be defrauded by family members, local shops or financial advisers. We are indirectly affected by many other forms of crime – we pay higher prices for goods to cover the cost of shoplifting or employee theft and pay more tax to compensate for tax evasion.

While most of us do not see ourselves as 'criminals', many of us commit 'crimes' – as motorists we break speed limits, we may be less than honest about our incomes to tax inspectors, we may 'borrow' items from work and we may avoid paying fares on the bus or train. A recent study of the 'crimes of everyday life' (Karstedt and Farrell 2006) points to the many crimes of those who consider themselves to be 'respectable' citizens such as not paying TV licence fees, avoiding taxes or making false insurance claims. We may conspire in crime by buying cheap goods without asking where they came from. Most of us would distinguish these activities from the activities of murders, rapists or hooligans. This demonstrates the very narrow borderline between what is generally regarded as 'criminal' and 'normal', legal or illegal. Crime is therefore very difficult to define.

Defining crime

As commonly understood, crime includes many different kinds of activities such as theft, fraud, robbery, corruption, assault, rape and murder. Do these activities have anything in common other than that they are all widely accepted as crime? How can crime be defined? As this section will illustrate, there is no one straightforward way of defining crime and differentiating it from other activities. At first sight it seems easy to define crime as it might, for example, be seen as doing something wrong. Crime is often, therefore, related to morality.

There are, however, many difficulties with this. Is there any agreement over what is morally right or wrong? Can, or should, all moral wrongs be crime? Lying, cheating or deliberately hurting someone might all be considered immoral, but not criminal. It could also be argued that poverty, deprivation, or racism are 'crimes against humanity' whereas these would not normally be regarded as crime. It could also be asked whether all crimes are moral wrongs. We can be prosecuted under the criminal law for parking on a yellow line but this is not generally seen as being immoral. The criminal law therefore does not necessarily reflect morality, nor do legal definitions reflect commonsense notions of crime. Furthermore, the criminal law is created in Parliament and there is a political dimension in defining crime. This section will focus on the legal, social and political elements in defining crime.

Crime and the criminal law

The simplest way of defining crime is to see it as 'something which is against the criminal law' and it could be argued that the only common characteristic of 'crimes' is that at some time they have been made subject to the criminal law. This involves using public as opposed to private enforcement and punishment. Criminal law is enforced by public agencies like the police, and involves prosecution in criminal courts, findings of guilt and sentencing, whereas private law deals with resolving conflicts between private individuals and determining appropriate remedies, which may involve financial recompense (see, for example, Davies et al 2009). Criminal law, therefore, involves a distinctive process of law enforcement. But what characterizes the activities with which it is concerned? Are they different from, or more serious than, other activities? Some of the problems of using legal definitions of crime are outlined below.

Are all crimes really 'crime'?

As has been seen, many people break the criminal law but are not seen as 'criminal'. The criminal law prohibits activities ranging from failing to pay a dog, car, or television licence to assault and murder. While some of these activities are incontestably 'crime', many others are not and the criminal law itself distinguishes different kinds of crime. In English law, for example, some offences such as murder, theft or serious assaults are described as *mala in se* or wrong in themselves. These are often seen as 'real' crimes in contrast to acts which are *mala prohibita*, prohibited not because they are morally wrong but for the protection of the public (see, for example, Lacey et al 1990). Thus the criminal law is used to enforce regulations concerning public health, pollution or the quality or quantity of goods on sale, not because neglecting these regulations is universally seen as 'crime' but because it is considered to be the most effective way of ensuring that regulations are complied with. These offences are often distinguished from 'real' crime by saying they are, for example, 'technical' offences. Criminal law is also used to enforce traffic regulations and licensing requirements where offenders would similarly not be seen as 'criminal'.

These distinctions do appear to reflect different levels of seriousness and perceptions of morality and immorality, but it is not easy to dismiss all 'technical' offences as not 'really' crime. Parking on a yellow line could be seen to be motivated by a selfish disregard for other road users and neglecting health and safety regulations endangers the lives of consumers, workers or passengers. Claiming that goods contain ingredients which they do not or that food is 'healthy' when it is full of fat and salt, amounts to defrauding consumers.

Legally defining crime – from actions to offences

What is often called 'black letter law' cannot capture the multitude of situations in which specific actions are legally or socially interpreted as crime as this so often depends on the context in which they occur. A simple example is the offence of possessing an offensive weapon. Any item, such as an umbrella, handbag or beer glass, can be offensive if a person uses it in a threatening way. Taking any action which results in someone being injured or killed might also be assumed to be wrong and criminal, yet killing someone is legitimate if that person is threatening the safety of oneself or others. The police, for example, have a legitimate right to use 'reasonable force', but the situations in which that force is reasonable are often highly contested. How much force, for example, should be used to remove someone in a demonstration?

Another set of questions surrounds the intentions of the person committing the act. Did the person intend to harm someone? The drunken driver may not intend to injure anyone, but driving while under the influence of alcohol may reflect recklessness about the consequences of such an action. Is the factory manager who neglects to ensure the safety of workers similarly reckless, making this a 'real' rather than a 'technical' offence? Actions therefore have to be defined as criminal. Howard Becker, whose work will be explored later, argued that crime is not an intrinsic property of any particular action or behaviour – it is the interpretation that others place upon it that makes it criminal (Becker 1963).

Changing legal definitions

Legal definitions of crime change over time and vary across cultures. In some countries the sale and consumption of alcohol is a crime, in others the sale and consumption of opium, heroin or cannabis is perfectly legal. While most criminal codes include murder, assault, theft and fraud, many other activities are subject to what is described as criminalization and decriminalization. In the 1960s so-called liberal legislation decriminalized aspects of homosexuality, abortion and prostitution, making many acts which were formerly criminal no longer so. It was argued, for example, that there were no direct victims and that the activities involved 'consenting adults'. Criminalizing these activities could also lead to participants becoming involved with other forms of crime, and law enforcement was expensive. The legal status of different drugs is continually contested and changes over time, with some arguing that many drugs should be decriminalized while others wish to see more punitive legislation. Recent debate has surrounded how stringently so-called Internet 'pirates' who illegally download material should be dealt with and there has been considerable criminalization of anti-social behaviour as outlined in Chapter 8. Legal definitions of crime must therefore be considered alongside social constructions and political processes.

The social construction of crime

The legal definition of crime can therefore be distinguished from commonsense definitions, and in everyday speech the words 'crime' or 'criminal' assume a commonly understood or shared meaning. This reflects what sociologists call a social construction, in which 'crime' is a distinctive category constructed around the variety of meanings which are taken for granted in the description of an event, activity or a group of events or activities as 'crime'. They are taken for granted in that they are rarely expressed but widely accepted – everyone more or less knows what they mean by crime. The social construction of crime can be revealed by 'deconstructing', or taking apart, the construct and exploring its meanings. Examples of the kinds of question which do this are outlined below and many more examples will be given throughout this book.

How is 'crime' different?

The construction of crime can be illustrated by looking at what it includes and excludes. To Mars (1982), 'crime', 'theft' and 'offence' are 'hard' words which can be differentiated from 'softer' words such as 'fiddle' or 'perk' which might be used to describe technically criminal activities in the workplace. Similarly, the word 'con' might be used to describe something which does not quite amount to 'fraud', as might phrases such as 'creative accounting' or 'fiddling the books'. The word abuse, as in for example child abuse, elder abuse or sexual abuse, is often used to describe what are in effect forms of sexual and physical violence, and it distinguishes these acts from violent crime by placing them in a different category. Incidents in which people are killed or injured in a train crash or as a result of using unsafe equipment are generally described as 'accidents' or 'disasters' rather than as 'crimes', albeit they often result from a failure of transport operators or managers to comply with safety regulations (see, for example, Tombs and Whyte 2007). These different words compartmentalize different kinds of crime, with some crimes being excluded from the social construction of crime.

Criminals and victims

Crime is associated with 'criminals' and 'victims'. It has already been seen that not all those convicted of offences would be described as 'criminal'. On the other hand, it will be seen in subsequent chapters that crime is often associated with particular groups such as young men or the unemployed, some of whom become 'folk devils' identified with different forms of crime. Criminals are also often seen as 'strangers' or 'outsiders' and subject to a process which sociologists describe as 'othering', whereas many crimes are committed by people known to their victims. It will also be seen in Chapter 6 that the concept of the victim is socially constructed. If, for example, someone is assaulted in a fight in which they themselves have participated, they would be seen as having provoked an assault and thus be distinguished from more 'deserving' victims such as a child assaulted by a stranger.

Constructing the 'crime problem'

The social construction of crime is reflected in media discussions and portrayals of crime, particularly in discussions of the 'crime problem'. When, for example, rising crime rates or policies aiming to 'crack down' on crime are discussed, the focus tends to be on burglary, violent crime or anti-social behaviour rather than on pollution, serious fraud or safety crimes. A narrow definition is therefore often used and 'the' crime problem constructed around particular kinds of crime. As will be seen in later chapters, this typically involves offences such as 'knife' or 'gang' crime involving young people from 'high crime' areas in towns and cities. Yet older, middle-class people from affluent suburbs also commit crimes, often with a more serious impact. It will also be seen in subsequent chapters that many different kinds of crime are also socially constructed.

Crime, politics and criminalization

Social constructions and legal definitions are related to political processes as laws are made in Parliament and social constructions may reflect political interests.

Criminalization and decriminalization involve challenging the way in which crime is defined through campaigns undertaken by interested groups. Homosexuals, for example, campaigned to change the criminal status of homosexuality and business groups consult with government on laws which seek to regulate their activities. These may also involve law enforcement as not all laws are enforced with equal vigour and sentences may not reflect the assumed severity of offences. The police may want more powers to enforce some laws and the leniency or toughness of sentences is a highly contested issue. Police activity against, for example, young people, suspected terrorists or motorists is often criticized as either too hard or too soft, with some arguing that young people are demonized by the police, whereas others might argue that the police 'do nothing' about disorderly behaviour in their area or about violence within the home. Some issues are outlined below, and these factors will also form a major theme in later chapters.

Political power and the law

Legal definitions of crime reflect the operation of political power. It has often been suggested, for example, that the apparently more lenient treatment of offences committed by business groups reflects their ability to affect the law and its enforcement. It has also been seen that the crime problem is often associated with young people, and recent years have involved what to some is the further criminalization of young people by successive legislation in relation to 'anti-social behaviour', in itself a term extremely difficult to define. The neglect of domestic violence which for many years was a relatively invisible crime attracting few prosecutions was also interpreted as reflecting women's relative powerlessness, and the treatment of racially motivated crimes could similarly be seen as indicating the powerlessness of minority ethnic groups. A stark indication of the relationship between political power and the criminal law is seen in relation to the difficulties of defining 'state crime' in respect of which, for example, it has been argued that the invasion of Iraq could be interpreted as a 'war crime' (see Chapter 17). Clearly, governments are not readily going to pass laws against their own activities, or accept that they themselves have broken international laws.

The ideological construction of crime

In this way, legal definitions and social constructions of crime can be seen as ideological, which means that they are supported and reinforced by a set of ideas and beliefs about crime and what constitutes the crime problem. These ideas most often reflect powerful interests. Overall, 'the crime problem' is most often associated with the crimes of young people and those of lower socio-economic status whereas the 'crimes of the powerful' are less likely to be regarded as 'crime' or their perpetrators as criminal. These definitions in themselves can also be altered depending on political and social change. People and groups once described as, for example, 'freedom fighters' or 'terrorists' can later become highly respected, legitimate governments as has happened, for example in South Africa or Northern Ireland (Chapters 11 and 17).

Crime and society in Britain

Crime and society

The phrase 'crime and society', used in the title of this book and in many sociology and criminology courses, assumes that crime is related to society. It has already been seen that crime is socially constructed and that its definition can be linked to wider structures of power. Crime is often perceived as threatening the 'fabric of society' or as symptomatic of a breakdown in social order. It is generally seen as a social problem although to some sociologists, as will be seen in Chapter 4, it is inevitable. It can also be asked whether crime is better explained by looking at individual criminals or at their environment, culture or the social structure. This involves relating crime to social and economic change and to social inequality, by looking at whether some groups commit more crime or whether their crimes are more subject to criminalization. This section will introduce these issues, all of which form a major theme of this book.

Crime, culture and social structure

A major issue in the study of crime is the relationship between individual and social problems. In many ways crime appears to be an individual problem – individual offenders choose to commit an offence. This could be related to a number of personal problems, but individual decisions are made in a social context. One sociologist, C. Wright Mills, pointed to the close relationship between individual and social problems, between personal troubles and public issues (Mills 1970). Unemployment, for example, may create personal problems such as marital breakdown, depression or suicide. The unemployment causing these problems is, however, linked to wider economic and social problems, and its solution may be beyond the individual's control. Individual choices to commit crime must therefore be seen in the context of their social environment and socio-economic situation.

This can be illustrated in a hypothetical situation in which an individual decides to commit a crime to resolve a short-term financial problem (which in itself may be caused by other problems). They must then consider what kind of crime to commit and how they can justify it. This will depend on their social environment. Within their social group, some offences might be tolerated more than others, and their social and economic situation will determine the opportunities they have for committing crime. Stealing from work or evading taxes might be seen as ways of committing crime which attract less disapproval. But not everyone has the opportunity to commit these kinds of crime – in particular they require some form of employment. Those who are unemployed would need to consider other forms of crime such as shoplifting, benefit fraud or street robbery, choices which may similarly be affected by their local culture. Some might see benefit fraud or shoplifting as preferable to street robbery as it involves less direct harm to, or confrontation with, individual victims (Chapter 13).

Crime and social change

Changes in the social and economic structure of society have often been associated with crime. Economic, social and technological changes affect the opportunities for crime and the forms of crime which are prevalent. Increasing amounts of money or goods in circulation mean increasing opportunities for crime. Placing large numbers of consumer goods on display in shops not only tempts people to commit crime but provides a greater range of opportunities. Changes in business, commerce and technology also affect patterns of crime. In pre-industrial times wealthy travellers who carried large amounts of goods and money were vulnerable to the activities of highway robbers. This form of crime subsided as people travelled with less cash and money was held in banks, which then became the target of bank robbers.

The development of cars, and then computers, also created different forms of crime which have required new laws to keep pace with them. Cars became associated with a range of crimes in relation to driving such as driving while drunk and driving without sufficient regard for other road users or the general public. They can be subject to aggressive encounters, known as 'road rage'. They also became attractive targets for the thieves who either wanted parts or accessories and for so-called 'joyriding' by young people. Culturally, they were associated with genres of film focusing on the 'car chase', and popular computer games such as 'Grand Theft Auto'. Much feared nowadays are new crimes such as cyber crime, hacking or identity theft, although some of these are essentially old forms of crime which use computer technology. Computers have, however, contributed to changes in patterns of crime – traditional style bank robberies may be a thing of the past as would-be criminals turn to computer hacking and identity theft. Crime and criminals therefore adapt to new technology (Chapters 13 and 14).

Social and economic change can also affect how likely individuals are to participate in crime, and many theories which will be reviewed in subsequent chapters have explored this. In very general terms the massive changes which accompanied the growth of industrial or modern societies were related to crime. These saw the breakdown of small, pre-industrial communities characterized by strong bonds of religion, family and morality. They also saw the rise of materialism and increased economic opportunities. The growth of the consumer society not only increased opportunities for crime, it also led many people to expect more than they could achieve, thereby providing a motivation to commit crime. The latter decades of the twentieth century also saw major social and economic changes, including the decline of manufacturing industries and the growth of long-term unemployment. For many, family, economic, personal or consumer goals could no longer be achieved through legitimate employment leading to the emergence of new patterns of crime. These changes were also affected by the process of globalization, and some forms of crime now transcend national boundaries as 'hot money' can be passed around the world in milliseconds and there are now massive trades in smuggling or trafficking contraband goods, drugs and people. Culture has also been globalized and images via, for example, satellite television and Western cultural products can lead to feelings of relative deprivation on the part of populations in less affluent nations – these may lead to crime and even to terrorism (Young 2003; 2007a). As this book is being written, many fear that the economic downturn which commenced in 2008 will lead to a rise in some forms of crime, particularly theft and fraud.

Crime and social inequalities

Social inequalities have often been linked to crime and the majority of convicted offenders are young men from lower-class backgrounds. Accordingly, many theories related crime to aspects of lower-class life and culture and to poverty and deprivation. Later, the assumption that lower-class individuals were more likely to commit crime was criticized by those pointing to the largely undetected and unprosecuted crimes of upper-class offenders. Men and women have different conviction rates, raising the issue of how crime can be related to gender and conceptions of masculinity or femininity (Chapter 9). Young people are also convicted of crime in far greater numbers than older people and for different kinds of crime, raising questions about how age is related to crime and also to criminalization. Young people, being more likely to be 'hanging about' the streets, may be more likely to attract the attention of the public or police (Chapter 8). Attention has also been drawn to the different patterns of conviction of racial and ethnic groups (Chapter 10).

These dimensions of inequality also affect victimization, which is not evenly distributed throughout society (Chapter 6). Those who live in poorer inner city areas have a higher risk of being victimized by many forms of crime, and while the more affluent are not immune they can afford to protect themselves better. Women and men have very different experiences of victimization, with women being more likely to be injured and sexually assaulted at home and men more likely to be victimized in public places (Chapters 6 and 11). Children, young people and the elderly are also particularly vulnerable to family violence and members of racial and ethnic minorities are victimized by racially motivated offences (Chapter 10).

Social inequalities therefore affect crime in diverse ways and the criminalization process is also relevant. It cannot be assumed that because any group is more likely to be convicted of crime that they actually commit more crime. As we have seen, the social construction of crime, the creation of law and its enforcement are in themselves related to social inequality. Thus the crimes of lower-class youth, mainly street crime, property crime and public disorder, may be subject to greater amounts of public intolerance, media complaint, criminal law and policing than the offences, often not seen as crime, of older people who, if they wish to commit crime, are more likely to embezzle, defraud or evade taxes. These crimes are more likely to be committed in private, in comparison to the 'street crime' of young people.

Crime in Britain

This book focuses specifically on Britain and will emphasize British material and the relevance of criminological analyses in a British context. Crime in Britain must nonetheless be placed in a wider context. Many theories of crime have developed outside Britain but are nonetheless useful and relevant. Similar crimes occur across the world, albeit in slightly different forms and in different proportions. Crime itself is increasingly international, or global, and some forms transcend national boundaries.

The illegal drugs trade and many forms of organized crime are multinational criminal enterprises (Chapter 14). Britain is also part of an international community and a whole range of crimes such as war crimes, environmental crimes, the use of tax havens, human trafficking and illegal trades in arms or endangered species are matters of international concern and international laws (Chapters 14–17). A focus on Britain therefore should not imply parochialism.

There are also issues around what is meant by the term Britain, particularly since devolution. The United Kingdom of Great Britain and Northern Ireland encompasses three different legal systems – those of Northern Ireland, Scotland, and England and Wales – all of which have their own criminal justice systems and criminal laws. There are also very different 'national' and 'regional' identities, cultural traditions and different experiences of economic change and inequality, all of which may affect crime. While popular and academic work often talks about crime and criminal justice in Britain, it often refers, without acknowledgement, to 'England' or 'England and Wales' (Croall et al 2010). This masks many differences between crime trends and patterns. Discussions of, for example, issues surrounding race, ethnicity and crime should take into account the very different distribution of minority ethnic groups across Britain, and different experiences of crime, victimization and policing (Croall and Frondigoun 2010). Different cultural traditions may also affect the relevance of theoretical approaches – the study of violent criminal gangs, for example, may be less relevant in some cities than they are in Glasgow, Manchester or the East End of London. Northern Ireland has a particularly distinctive set of experiences in relation to political violence and so-called police deviance due to the Troubles (Chapters 11 and 17). This book is not intended to provide a comparative study of crime in Britain, but aims to be sensitive to local, regional and national variations and encompasses research and literature from these different areas.

Structure of the book

The book will explore how different kinds of crime are officially defined, socially constructed, researched and analysed. It will look at the relationships between crime and social inequality and apply these insights to specific patterns of crime. It aims to provide a comprehensive introduction to the study of crime and specific forms of crime and individual chapters will introduce relevant issues, theories and case studies. Detailed tables, charts, statistics and diagrams, widely available elsewhere, have been kept to the minimum necessary for illustration. The text should therefore be used along with supplementary texts, statistical material, now widely available on the Internet, and research reports covering topics in more depth. None of the chapters aims to be comprehensive, but to deal with key, if selective, issues and material. To help readers, a short list of key reading accompanies each chapter along with a series of questions and exercises for those who wish to reflect on the issues raised.

Crime has been explored by a variety of different academic disciplines, including biology, psychology, psychiatry, economics, geography and sociology. Criminology is centred around the study of crime and criminal justice and incorporates a variety of these perspectives (see, for example, Muncie et al 1996; Tierney 2006; Maguire et al 2007; Muncie et al 2010). The focus of this book on crime and society has two main implications. Firstly, it emphasizes the *social structural and cultural* aspects of crime, mainly, though not exclusively, using sociological perspectives. Psychological and biological theories, while important, will not be covered in detail. Secondly, the book's focus is on *crime* rather than criminal justice policy. The two areas cannot be separated entirely as crime is legally defined and the activities of law enforcement agencies affect which crimes are subject to prosecution and conviction. Studying the actions and attitudes of criminal justice agencies is crucial for an understanding of crime, as are processes of law-making and criminalization. Moreover, the study of crime is inextricably related to criminal justice policy and the significance of analyses of crime for policy will be discussed. Detailed discussions of specific policies lie beyond the scope of this text and are the subject of others.

The book is organized in three main parts as follows:

Issues in researching and analysing crime and victimization

Chapter 2 explores in more detail how crime is represented in the mass media and at other cultural representations, in order to further explore how crime is socially constructed and to pose crucial questions about how the 'reality' of crime differs from these perceptions. Chapter 3 looks at the problems and methods of researching crime and at sources of information about crime before giving a broad overview of aspects of crime in Britain. Chapters 4 and 5 are concerned with attempts to understand, explain and analyse crime. Chapter 4 deals with theoretical approaches which tried to explain crime by relating it to culture and social structure, while Chapter 5 looks at approaches which, having challenged many aspects of earlier theories, broadened the study of crime to include law enforcement, law-making and social control and at contemporary approaches. Chapter 6 turns to the previously neglected victim of crime, looking at the development of victimology, the impact of crime on victims and the fear of crime.

The relationship between crime and social inequality

Chapters 7 to 10 will examine the relationships between crime and social class, age, gender and race which were referred to earlier. Each chapter will start by looking at how these relationships have been defined, constructed and analysed before looking critically at what is known about offending and victimization. The way in which these relationships have been socially constructed will be explored along with how they have been viewed by criminological analyses and different dimensions will be outlined. Each chapter will conclude by discussing some of the major issues raised by these relationships, at areas worthy of further exploration and at the significance of the particular form of inequality in relation to other, interrelated, patterns.

Accordingly, Chapter 7 looks at the long-held association between crime and social class, which has also been related to economic factors, social deprivation, poverty and, most recently, to the rise of a so-called underclass and processes of social exclusion and inclusion. While the focus of this chapter is on the relationship between lower socio-economic status and crime, it must be recognized that those characterized as poor are very often unfairly blamed for crime and later chapters will deal with the crimes of the more affluent. Chapter 8 turns to the relationship between age, crime and victimization, where it will be seen that the activities of youth have been defined as a problem throughout history. It further explores the extent to which young people's structural position may make crime attractive along with increasing their vulnerability to victimization; it also looks at current concerns about young people's crime such as anti-social behaviour, gangs, so-called binge drinking and drug use. While young people have widely been identified as a major crime problem, older people and the study of ageing and crime have tended to be neglected, considerations which are important for a full exploration of the significance of age in relation to crime.

Chapter 9 focuses on gender and crime by exploring the 'gender gap' in crime and exploring the highly influential critique of criminological perspectives advanced by feminist criminology. While the main construction of the gender crime relationship focuses on men as offenders and women as victims, it will also be argued that male victimization and female offending need further exploration if the relationship between gender and crime is to be fully understood. Chapter 10 looks at the relationship between race, ethnicity, crime and victimization and issues raised by indications that some ethnic groups are over-represented in English courts and prisons. Criminological approaches to this topic will be outlined and issues of the racialization of urban unrest and racist violence, often described as 'hate crime', will be critically explored, before turning to the complex interrelationship between inequalities of class, race and gender.

Specific patterns of crime

Chapters 11 to 17 each focus on a specific form of crime. Each chapter starts with a critical examination of how each category is defined and constructed, followed by a brief account of its scope and the different patterns of crime which it encompasses. Subsequent sections focus on selected offences within categories and explores how they have been analysed. Each chapter will conclude with an exploration of how different forms of crime have been approached by theoretical perspectives – drawing on, extending and re-evaluating approaches discussed in earlier chapters. Finally, some brief points will be made about the implications of these analyses for relevant criminal justice and social policy.

The classification and contents of these chapters were guided by a number of considerations because for many the way in which different forms of crime, and their constituent categories, are constructed are subject to considerable debate. Is, for example, violent crime to be restricted to individual, interpersonal violence or should it encompass corporate and state violence? Is what has been described as 'sex crime' a distinct set of offences or is it part of a continuum of men's violence against women? Is organized crime a distinct category or merely a form of crime which involves organization? What *is* white-collar crime and is it *crime*? Should environmental or eco crime be the subjects of a 'green criminology'? Does it make any sense to talk about the crimes of the state? Should the threat of violence against innocent civilians be described as 'terrorism' and a distinction drawn between non state participants in an armed struggle and state terrorism such as carpet-bombing or torture? The different chapters largely reflect, but are also critical of, the way in which offences are classified both by law and in the bulk of criminological writing. Given the size and significance of these forms of crime, the approach is inevitably selective, and as with other parts of the book, guidance on appropriate reading is provided.

Chapter 11 looks at violent crime, including homicide, domestic violence and political violence and terrorism and Chapter 12 at sexual offences such as those against children, rape and sex work, although, as will be seen, these are difficult to separate from violent crime. Chapter 13 deals with offences which dominate the officially constructed area of property crime and fraud such as burglary, different forms of theft and largely non-white-collar frauds along with the growth of so-called cyber crime. Chapter 14 explores what is generally categorized as organized crime and at the fluid and changing organization of serious crimes by looking at the 'local' situation across Britain and at global dimensions such as drug-trafficking, human trafficking and smuggling. Chapter 15 introduces the study of white-collar and corporate crime, including serious frauds, corporate violence and crimes against consumers. This is followed by a consideration of environmental and 'eco crime' in Chapter 16, encompassing major issues such as pollution and toxic crimes, food crimes and bio piracy. Finally Chapter 17 looks at an area of growing criminological and political interest, that of state crime and at some of its forms such as genocide, torture, police deviance and at how states and corporations are jointly implicated in state corporate crime. Chapter 18 will attempt to draw out some of the major issues involved in the study of crime and will briefly discuss the significance of the study of crime and society for criminal justice policy.

Review questions

1 Locate a dictionary definition of crime. How would you evaluate this in the light of the discussion about defining crime in this chapter?

2 Discuss in a group what you mean when you use phrases such as '. . . *ought to be a crime*' or '. . . *that's criminal*' and . . . '*that's not really criminal*'. Consider how this reflects the social construction of crime.

3 Indentify activities recently subject to discussions about criminalization or decriminalization – for example, the criminalization of drugs or any specific drug, illegal downloads from the Internet or the use of tax havens. What considerations could or should be taken into account in redefining these activities? What and whose interests are involved?

Key reading

There are many discussions of the definition and construction of crime. A good start is to consult the introductory chapters of criminological texts such as:

Carrabine, F., Iganski, P., Lee, M., Plummer, K. and South, N. (2004) ***Criminology: A Sociological Introduction***, London: Routledge.

Hale, C., Hayward, K., Wahidin, A. and Wincup, E. (2009) ***Criminology***, Oxford: Oxford University Press 2nd edn.

Newburn, T. (2007) ***Criminology***, Cullompton: Willan Publishing.

Useful discussions can also be found in:

Lacey, N. (2007) **'Legal Constructions of Crime'** in M. Maguire, R. Morgan and R. Reiner (eds) *The Oxford Handbook of Criminology*, Oxford: Clarendon Press 4th edn.

Muncie, J. (2001) **'The Construction and Deconstruction of Crime'** in J. Muncie and E. McLaughlin (eds) *The Problem of Crime*, London: Sage.

Muncie, J., Talbot, D. and Walters, R. (2010) **'Interrogating Crime'** in J. Muncie, D. Talbot and R. Walters (eds) *Crime: Local and Global*, Cullompton: Willan Publishing pp 1–36.

Chapter 2
Crime and the media

This chapter will look at:

- ➜ Cultural representations of crime
- ➜ The effects of the mass media
- ➜ Moral panics
- ➜ Representing crime: contemporary cases

The majority of what we know about crime comes from what we read in the papers and novels and see on television, films or obtain through the Internet. We now live in a 'mediatised age' (Greer 2009: 177) and contemporary media include television, newspapers, magazines, radio, the Internet, mobile phones and Wireless Application Protocol (WAP) technology, with news being available on a 24-hour basis 'as it happens'. Entertainment media have also mushroomed, from live performances in theatres and clubs, through to films, television, DVDs, computers and game technology. Crimes can be filmed by witnesses on their mobile phones or caught on CCTV cameras and instantly made available on sites such as YouTube or Facebook. Crime features prominently in all of these media, and it sells. According to Reiner (2007a) around a fifth of news stories and a fifth of films are about crime, and around a quarter of prime television time in the UK is given to crime. A glance at station or airport bookshops will immediately confirm the dominance of crime fiction and 'real crime' books (Croall et al 2010). These different media reflect and reinforce the social construction of crime outlined in Chapter 1, making it crucial to critically evaluate how crime is presented.

The media is often criticized for exaggerating the least typical and under-reporting more typical crimes and for providing a simplified and distorted image of crime. It has been accused of glamorizing crime and leading to more, sometimes 'copycat', offences. It is blamed for demonizing some groups such as anti-social youth, who become 'folk devils' used to symbolize deeper social problems and to justify more repressive criminal justice policies.

As a means of introducing different ways of looking at crime, this chapter will explore some of these issues, looking at how crime is factually and fictionally represented, evaluating arguments about its effects and outlining the concept of moral panics. The final section will illustrate some of these themes by looking at how a few high-profile cases reflect these media representations.

Cultural representations of crime

Historical representations of crime

Crime has always been a staple of popular culture (Carrabine 2008; Marsh and Melville 2009) with popular legends and entertainments becoming classic literature and drama. It is a major theme in Shakespearean plays such as *Macbeth, Hamlet* and *Othello*, which in the sixteenth and seventeenth centuries were a form of popular entertainment. The legendary story of Robin Hood with its theme of a noble band of robbers stealing from the undeserving rich to give to the dispossessed poor was originally told, in various forms, through the oral ballad tradition, and it also highlights the malign presence of corrupt officialdom and an overfed, tyrannical clergy (Carrabine 2008: 23). It has been subject to many changes over the years and its enduring popularity can be seen in yet another film, released in May 2010, starring Russell Crowe and Cate Blanchett which contains a new take on the role of Maid Marian, not present in the earliest versions (Thorpe 2010). The pursuit of justice by bandits such as Robin Hood became a long-lasting narrative, despite the fact that they were generally far from 'noble'. Highwaymen such as the legendary Dick Turpin, hanged in York for horse-stealing in 1739, became epic heroes and, indeed, celebrities (Carrabine 2008).

Carrabine also recounts the sensational nature of crime reporting in Tudor and Stuart broadsides and pamphlets which highlighted murder and witchcraft and, in the seventeenth century, new printing technologies saw the emergence of gallows literature which recorded the last dying speeches of the condemned. Criminal trial reports detailed what he describes (2008: 88) as the 'transgressive underworlds and shadowy practices of deviant metropolitan subcultures' and criminal biographies focused on individuals. The blurred boundaries between information and entertainment were evident in the 'new journalism' of the nineteenth century (p. 100), which featured images of villains and aimed to democratize reporting by focusing on human interest stories involving crime, sexual violence and human oddities. The nineteenth century also saw the infamous Jack the Ripper murders of women in Whitechapel which were never solved but popularly attributed to a man of high status. In reporting these murders Whitechapel was depicted as an alien and dangerous place, and the word 'ripper' came to be used in later cases of serial killings of women such as the Ipswich murders, outlined in Box 2.7 (Marsh and Melville 2009). Changes in how crime has been represented in the twentieth century are outlined in Box 2.1.

Box 2.1 Changing representations of crime

Crime news

A study from 1945–1991 in two papers, *The Times* and the *Daily Mirror* revealed:

- A generally upward trend in the proportion of stories focused on crime (from under 10 per cent in the 1940s to over 20 per cent in the 1990s). The sharpest increase occurred in the late 1960s.

→

Box 2.1 continued

- Homicide is the most common type of crime reported, accounting for around one third of all crime stories.
- Other violent crimes are the next most common.
- Over the years there was:
  - a decline in stories about burglary without violence;
  - an increase in stories about drug offences.
- Reports about offenders tend to over-represent older and higher status individuals than officially recorded profiles of offenders.
- An over-representation of risks to higher status white people and disproportionate representations of women, children or older people as victims.

Film

- Crime is increasingly presented as an all-pervasive threat as opposed to a single 'one-off' intrusion into the established order.
- There is an increasing prevalence of police 'heroes'.
- Representations of violence have become more graphic since the Second World War: up to the early 1970s hardly any films showed more than a minor degree of pain or suffering.
- In TV shows, the police are more likely than in reality to 'get their man' although more recently a minority of offenders 'get away with their crimes'.
- The police are portrayed in a positive light, but there has been an increase in representations of corrupt, brutal and discriminatory police officers since the mid 1960s.
- There has been more graphic presentation of the suffering of victims which is more often the driving force of a story.

(Based on surveys carried out by Reiner and his colleagues (Reiner et al 2000; 2003) summarized in Reiner 2007a)

Crime news

It is generally agreed that crime features prominently in news and that specific kinds of crime are over-represented in comparison to the official crime figures; these will be explored in Chapter 3 (Jewkes 2004; Reiner 2007a; Marsh and Melville 2009). In general terms, crimes involving sex, violence and murder feature strongly, amounting to around 40 per cent of all crime-related stories on BBC Radio stations (Reiner 2007a). Murders and sexual offences involving strangers tend to be disproportionately represented in comparison to the more typical scenario of murders and assaults by someone known to the victim (see Chapters 3, 6, 11 and 12). This is more pronounced in tabloid than broadsheet newspapers and local compared to national television news bulletins. As illustrated in Box 2.1, this has become more evident since the Second World War, with more details of violence and a greater emphasis on aspects of victimization (Chapter 6). In general terms coverage focuses on criminal incidents rather than underlying factors, particularly in broadcast as opposed to print news. Coverage often presents a favourable image of the police as they more often detect crimes involving violence (Reiner 2007a).

Research has asked a number of questions about these representations. Why is crime such a major feature of news? Why do sexual and violent crimes feature so strongly? This has been associated with the range of factors outlined in Box 2.2. News inherently involves something 'new', and crime has a high novelty value which can be used to 'sell' stories and attract attention. News stories tend to be short, must 'fit' the space allotted by editors and be able to be expressed in instantly meaningful one-liner headlines. This leads to inevitable simplification, the use of dramatic language such as 'beasts' and to a narrative contrasting 'good' with 'evil'. Such simplification adds up, argues Jewkes (2004: 45), to a 'mediated vision of crime in which shades of grey are absent and a complex reality is substituted for a simple, incontestable and preferably bite-sized message'.

Journalists use a set of 'professional imperatives' in selecting stories which they know will attract attention (Chibnall 1977) and can be simplified, sexually titillated

Box 2.2 The construction of crime news

Crime news is affected by the following factors (Jewkes 2004):

- *Threshold*: News stories must cross a threshold of importance or drama. This may be lower for a local than for a national paper.
- *Predictability*: Planning news stories is made easier by relying on regular sources such as the police and courts.
- *Simplification*: Stories are fitted into easily recognizable categories (for example, the murder of a child); they focus on the act as opposed to explanations; binary oppositions such as 'good' and 'evil', guilty or innocent, normal and deviant are often used.
- *Individualism*: Crime is associated with individuals, diverting attention from any deeper social, political and economic issues.
- *Risk*: Risks are exaggerated by seeing 'all' as at risk; risks from strangers and 'others' are exaggerated.
- *Sex*: The sexual element in crimes is over-reported.
- *Celebrity*: Crimes involving celebrities have a lower threshold and more routine crimes will receive more attention. Criminals themselves may become celebrities.
- *Proximity*: News is more relevant if it can be related to either geographical or social proximity. Thus the greater emphasis on crime in local news and an over-reporting of crimes involving 'people like us' as opposed to 'others' – for example, the greater focus on middle-class children who go missing.
- *Violence*: The presence of violence permeates all media and the portrayal of violence has become more graphic.
- *Spectacle or graphic imagery*: Public incidents which can be caught on camera tend to be more represented than private violence and crime taking place at home or at work.
- *Children*: Crimes involving children whether as victims or offenders enhance the newsworthiness of a story.
- *Conservative ideology and political diversion*: Media coverage of crime tends to reflect the view that it is a threat to the 'British way of life' and needs to be dealt with by tough measures.

and dramatized. Today's celebrity culture also means that any crime involving a celebrity is more likely to be reported and, while white-collar or political crimes are often ignored, scandals involving celebrities or politicians are likely to attract high profile attention as indicated in the exposure given to MPs' expenses. Stories are also affected by the reliance of journalists on official sources, particularly in today's world where they have restricted budgets and are less able to undertake lengthy investigations. They are more likely to rely on the 'structured access' offered by police, press statements and court reports making official agencies 'primary definers' of crime and contributing to a largely positive view of the police (Reiner 2007a).

These factors also account for the relative neglect of some crimes. Frauds, for example, can be extremely complex, difficult for many people to understand, do not involve sex or violence, lack 'bleeding victims' and are more difficult to visually portray (see Chapters 13 and 15). When they do involve celebrities and fit other imperatives, they do receive more publicity (Levi 2008b; 2009). The reliance on official sources also lessens the likelihood that crimes of state agencies will be reported, and these are often only revealed by critical and investigative journalism (Chapter 17).

Fictional representations: film, television and literature

Fictional representations also reflect constructions of crime. Early novels very often featured crime, with one example being Defoe's heroine Moll Flanders who committed many crimes (Carrabine 2008: 9). Reiner (2007a) estimates that between a quarter and a third of total paperback output is a thriller of one kind or another and crime fiction dominates popular best-sellers. In April 2010, the top ten list of best-selling paperbacks included the three volumes of Stieg Larsson's Swedish trilogy, featuring Lisbeth Salander and filmed as *The Girl with the Dragon Tattoo*. These involve corporate corruption, murder and sexual violence. It also included Martina Cole's *Hard Girls* in which 'two female police officers pursue a killer targeting prostitutes', Jeffery Deaver's *Roadside Crosses* about a cyber stalker, James Patterson and Maxine Paetro's *The 8th Confession* in which 'killings of the rich raise suspicions in a women's murder club' and Karin Slaughter's *Genesis* in which 'Atlanta cops hunt a sadistic serial killer before he strikes again'. Only three out of the top ten novels were not clearly about crime (*Sunday Times* 2010).

Box 2.1 illustrates that crime is also a major feature of films, particularly the popular *film noir* genre. As well as films specifically about crime, Reiner (2007a) estimates that around half of all films contain significant crime content. Murder is a staple plot, from classic films such as those of Alfred Hitchcock (for example, *Psycho*) through to more contemporary heist movies which tend to over-represent elements of violence and planning in serious robberies. Films about sex crime have also become more common and play out a variety of complex themes, including the ever-present danger of the psychopathic stranger (Reiner 2007a).

The detectives

A major aspect of fictional representations, across film, television and novels is the detective story, which originated in the nineteenth century with fictional detectives such as Edgar Allen Poe's Auguste Dupin and Conan Doyle's ever popular Sherlock Holmes, first published in 1887. Like Robin Hood, Sherlock Holmes has featured in many films, the most recent being a 2009 release starring Robert Downey Jnr and Jude Law as Dr Watson. These novels emphasized, argues Carrabine (2008: 103), the eccentric brilliance of the urbane amateur sleuth, a narrative which continued into the twentieth century with the country-house murder novels of Agatha Christie, again still popular, featuring amateur detectives such as Hercule Poirot and Miss Marple. Very different were the American hard-boiled private eye detectives such as Raymond Chandler's Philip Marlowe, which also features the mean streets of Los Angeles. All of these were particularly popular, argues Carrabine, during a period in which the police were not seen as competent, particularly to deal with the crimes of the upper classes, whereas fictional amateur detectives had access to social circles closed to police officers.

While British 'country house' or 'heritage' (Carrabine 2008) detectives remain popular in series such as *Inspector Morse* and *Midsomer Murders*, the amateur sleuth gave way, with the professionalization of the police, to the police procedural featuring a number of popular detectives who reflected changes in policing styles. One of the earliest was the celebrated *Dixon of Dock Green*, which emphasized the community-based nature of policing in the 1950s and 1960s. This gave way to the harsher, more law-enforcement style of *The Professionals* or *The Sweeney*. Some, such as *Taggart*, also played on images of 'mean streets'. Another popular theme pits the fictional detective, who often sails close to breaking the rules in order to catch the criminal, against the bureaucracy of police departments and the law. While the police enjoyed considerable legitimacy during a large part of the twentieth century, this declined in the latter decades and corrupt police featured in series such as *Between the Lines*. More recently, suggests Carrabine, the popularity of medical dramas such as *ER* and *Casualty* has led to the development of forensic-science-based dramas such as *Waking the Dead, Silent Witness* and the hugely popular American *C.S.I.*

The fascination of crime

Other crime fiction, from Shakespeare plays and Dostoyevsky's classic *Crime and Punishment* onward, raise more complex moral and ethical issues and focus on the criminal psyche. The emphasis on drama, risk and victimization is also evident in the popularity of dramas about serial killers which makes violence more unpredictable and symbolically much more dangerous (Carrabine 2008: 112). Other films present the criminal as an anti-hero and yet others, such as those of the Coen brothers, can be seen as 'carnivalesque'. Films about sexual violence can, argues Rafter (2007), explore a variety of themes such as ever-present danger and some present a more nuanced view of offenders.

Fictional representations of crime illustrate its enduring fascination. To some, the detective novel's popularity lies in the ability of the often 'extraordinary' detective to solve a puzzle and to impose rationality on the uncertainty of crime. The detective, argues Carrabine (2008), is akin to a *flâneur*, an observer of society, who strips away the facade presented by different players revealing that all is not as it seems. This reassuring function may have changed in contemporary narratives. The celebrated crime novelist Ian Rankin (1999: 13) observes that 'good does not always triumph in today's crime fiction; evil cannot always be rationalised'. He further comments that crime fiction often says more about the world than mainstream or 'literary' fiction. Some locate crime in poverty and social problems while others recognize that it can also be associated with 'establishment' conspiracy and corruption. Very often the fictional detective is a maverick, a technique which enables a critical commentary on society; a feature of many narratives is the contrast between the moral code of the detective and the amoral corrupt world (Carrabine 2008). Rafter (2000: 9, cited in Carrabine 2008: 120/1) sums up the appeal of crime films which could be applied also to novels and TV series:

> they . . . provide escape from daily life, opportunities to solve mysteries, chances to identify with powerful and competent heroes and discussions of morality that are comfortingly unambiguous . . . they offer access to places most of us never get to in person such as drug factories, police interrogation rooms, glamorous nightclubs and prison cells . . . opening a window on exotica, crime films enable viewers to become voyeurs, secret observers of the personal and even intimate lives of characters very different from themselves. Crime films also offer us the pleasurable opportunity to pursue justice, often at the side of a charismatic and capable hero.

'Infotainment'

'Infotainment', identified as a feature of contemporary media, represents the blurring of boundaries between information and entertainment and can be seen in so-called docudramas, 'real crime' stories and programmes such as *Crimewatch* in which the 'facts' about a crime are presented in order to encourage witnesses to come forward. Infotainment shares the characteristics of other cultural representations. Programmes such as *Crimewatch*, for example, tend to dramatize crime in order to attract attention and over-represent serious sexual and violent crimes. In addition, argues Jewkes (2004), being based on police information they reflect crimes which are important to the police and, by presenting crimes which more often victimize women and girls, they reinforce women's 'at risk' status. They therefore (p. 166) represent 'a limited range of very serious crimes perpetrated against a restricted category of victims'. Recent docudramas on the BBC also indicate this tendency: *Canoe Man*, for example, dramatized the highly atypical case of John Darwin and his wife who faked his disappearance for insurance purposes, and a film about Joyti De-Laurey, the 'secretary who stole two million pounds' from her employers at Goldman Sachs is also scarcely typical. They, along with the *Five Daughters* series about the Ipswich murders detailed in Box 2.7, which immediately attracted over 5 million viewers (Deans 2010), were all screened early in 2010.

Is the media criminogenic?

The media has for long been said to have a direct impact on levels of crime and violence. Less liberal critics blame its focus on and indeed glamorization of violent crime for increasing levels of violence and for so-called 'coypcat' crimes (Greer 2009). Box 2.3

Box 2.3 Media made crimes?

- In Shakespeare's day, the Lord Mayor of London condemned plays, actors and audiences, and theatres were described as 'ordinary places for vagrant persons, masterless men, thieves, horse stealers, whoremongers, Coozeners, Coneycatchers, contrivers of treason and other idle and dangerous persons to meet together'.
- The famous author and magistrate Henry Fielding commented that 'too frequent and expensive Diversions among the lower kinds of People . . . hath almost totally changed the Manners, Customs and Habits of the People, more especially of the lower sort' (cited in Pearson 1983: 186–7).
- During the nineteenth century, music hall and lurid stories in 'penny dreadfuls' were blamed for inciting hooliganism (Pearson 1983).
- The 'horror' video *Child's Play* was popularly associated with the murder of 2-year-old James Bulger (see Box 2.6) when it was revealed it had been rented by the father of one of the boys accused of the murder and there were similarities between the killing and the video.
- The killings of 16 people in August 1987 in Hungerford by Michael Ryan, armed with a Kalashnikov rifle, were associated with his possession of violent films and magazines about survival kills and firearms. The killings bore similarities to the film *First Blood* – although it was never established that he had seen this movie.
- The film *The Basketball Diaries*, violent computer games and the music of Marilyn Manson were all popularly associated with the shooting of twelve school students and one teacher in Columbine High School in the US in 1999 (Greer 2009).
- Marilyn Manson's painting of the 'Black Dahlia' murder of 1940s actress Elizabeth Short was associated with the murder of Jodi Jones by her boyfriend Luke Mitchell in Dalkeith, Midlothian. In 2003, the trial judge commented that 'I do not feel able to ignore the fact that there was a degree of resemblance between the injuries inflicted on Jodi and those shown in . . . [the painting]'. Manson himself denied any such inspiration (Hurley 2005).

(Examples largely from Carrabine 2008; Marsh and Melville 2009)

lists some examples of these concerns, from Shakespearean England through to the twenty-first century. Others, more often from the left, associate exaggerated media representations and in particular moral panics with increasingly repressive policies. While it lies beyond the scope of this chapter to fully discuss the extensive research on media effects, this section outlines some main points and the next explores moral panics. The exaggerated representation of the risks of crime has also been associated with increasing fears of crime outlined in Chapter 6.

A considerable volume of research has now focused on the impact of media violence. While many studies claim to show a direct effect, particularly suggesting a relationship between childhood exposure to violence and violence later in life, most consider it to be inconclusive (Reiner 2007a; Carrabine 2008; Greer 2009; Marsh and Melville 2009). This is largely because many make a number of questionable assumptions. They often assume, for example, a 'hypodermic syringe' effect in which an 'injection' of violence leads to the recipient committing violence. A number of problems have been identified with these kinds of approaches (Reiner 2007a; Greer 2009; Marsh and Melville 2009).

- Many studies take place in what is effectively a laboratory situation, showing examples of violence and measuring reactions. This is very different to the 'real world' in which people consume the media in a variety of contexts and interpret its effects very differently.

- The subjective meaning of incidents of crime and violence depends less on the individual act than on the context in which it is portrayed. A slap or kick, for example, may be humorous in a 'slapstick' comedy, but is more sinister in a drama featuring domestic violence. Reactions may also depend on whether the character using violence is one who attracts sympathy or not.
- Rather than becoming violent as a result of watching films, people who are predisposed to be violent might *choose* to watch violent films.
- Even where there is an apparent correlation between watching violence and committing it, it cannot be assumed that the media 'cause' the violence as other factors, such as family, culture or socialization may be equally as important.
- People do not respond like zombies, and are not passive consumers of media.
- It is very often assumed that the effect of media consumption is restricted to largely lower-class consumers who form the bulk of those convicted of crime.

This is not to argue that the media has no effect, but that any effect is not immediate and direct. People interpret what they read or see in different ways and effects can be diffuse rather than direct. Greer (2009: 188) provides the chilling example of the young man who fatally shot eight people and then killed himself in Omaha in 2007, who left a note saying that 'now I'll be famous'.

Media effects on violence can be viewed in a different way. A major theme in sociological work on crime and deviance is that of anomie or strain theory in which Merton (1938) explores how media images of 'success' incorporate representations of desirable lifestyles and consumption patterns including 'must have' goods, style, fashion and other consumables (Reiner 2007a). This can generate dissatisfaction among those who cannot aspire to these goals and to feelings of relative deprivation where people feel that they have been denied something which they feel they deserve (Lea and Young 1993; Young 1999). These kinds of processes have been associated with a range of crime, social disorder and political protest (Chapters 4, 5 and 7).

Moral panics

A highly influential concept associated with crime and the media is that of the moral panic, defined by Murji (2006: 250) as a:

> disproportional and hostile social reaction to a condition, person or group defined as a threat to societal values involving stereotypical media representations and leading to demands for greater social control and creating a spiral of reaction.

Box 2.4 summarizes two classic studies of moral panics: Cohen's work on mods and rockers in 1964, and Hall and his colleagues' work on mugging in the early 1970s. The first highlights the exaggerated reaction to clashes between two youth groups in seaside towns which became associated with wider fears about social change and youth. The second deals with the emergence of the 'black mugger' as a folk devil which was associated with a perceived law and order crisis and the emergence of harsher, more punitive legislation. Moral panics are often said to amplify deviance

Box 2.4 Cases of moral panics

Mods and Rockers: 1964

Stanley Cohen's (1972) *Folk Devils and Moral Panics* is the classic work on moral panics in which he analyses the reaction to fights between rival groups in the South of England in the early 1960s. Over the wet bank holiday of Easter 1964, groups from London gathered in Clacton, Essex. What were in effect routine incidents and minor scuffles were interpreted as 'fights' between groups identified, according to their style of dress, as 'mods' and 'rockers'. Press reaction was intense and they became folk devils, whose activities were cast as symptomatic of the problems of the younger generation. The incidents were exaggerated and the numbers of arrests and reported incidents were typical for a bank holiday weekend. Subsequent reports of routine crimes described defendants as 'mods' or 'rockers', further associating them with criminal activity. Subsequent press speculation, fuelled by interviews with self-styled mods and rockers predicted repeat occurrences. On the next holiday weekend, the police, media and observers, who all arrived in strength, were expecting trouble and shops were closed. A small fracas broke out which rapidly escalated. Cohen's analysis suggests that the expectations of trouble played a part in creating the disturbance. Cohen identified three main processes: the exaggeration and distortion of the events; predicting subsequent events; using words such as 'Mod' to symbolize a whole form of youth style and status. This became associated with wider concerns: and to Cohen (1972/2002):

> mods and rockers symbolized something far more important than what they actually did. They touched the delicate and ambivalent nerves through which post-war social change in Britain was experienced . . . messages about never having it so good were ambivalent in that some people were having it too good and too quickly . . . resentment and jealousy were easily directed at the young, if only because of their increased spending power and sexual freedom. When this was combined with a too open flouting of the work and leisure ethic, with violence and vandalism . . . something more than the image of a peaceful Bank Holiday at the sea was being shattered.
>
> (Cohen 1972/2002 cited in Newburn 2009: 79)

Mugging

Stuart Hall and his colleagues studied the moral panic surrounding mugging in the 1970s (Hall et al 1978). This began when a case of robbery was described by a senior police officer as a 'mugging gone wrong'. Previously mugging was not seen as a crime common in Britain and the term was rarely used. This comment set in train a moral panic about the significance of an assumed rise in mugging. The researchers found no evidence that there was such an increase and accordingly asked how the reaction could be explained.

To them, mugging, associated with a growing problem in the inner cities and with black youth, assumed a symbolic significance. The moral panic reflected the orchestration of consensus through which dominant definitions and interpretations were disseminated. The media quoted the police, who in turn quoted the media – politicians used both and were in turn cited in the media. The media therefore acts as an 'ideological state apparatus' as it reflects, reinforces and disseminates ideas, values and beliefs. Mugging was perceived as a threat to key values associated with 'Englishness' – the family, the need for discipline, respectability and decency. The black mugger was subtly portrayed as an outsider, an alien, and thereby a folk devil – a scapegoat for economic and social decline. The moral panic was related to a crisis in hegemony, the maintenance of consent, brought about by declining economic conditions. The state needed to 'define away the crisis' – to see it in terms other than class relations. The black mugger was therefore a suitable folk devil.

(Young 1971a; 1971b) and were related to work which explored the social reaction to deviance (see Chapter 5). They are generally said to have the following characteristics (Critcher 2003; Jewkes 2004; Murji 2006; Garland 2008; Marsh and Melville 2009):

- The media adopt an exaggerated reaction to one or a series of incidents, involving saturation coverage and dramatic headlines.
- A group is identified with a style, subculture or set of activities which become associated with crime, deviance, disorder or conflict. Mods and rockers provide one example of this as do later moral panics such as 'hoodies', 'neds' or the 'booze and blade' culture.
- Some groups become 'folk devils'. These are very often groups who are already marginalized, can be portrayed as 'outsiders' and become scapegoats for a variety of problems.
- The subjects of the moral panic are seen as symbolic of a deeper social problem such as the effects of social change, the 'state of the country' or the condition of 'young people today'.
- The media predict future incidents – which may indeed occur and can be influenced by media reaction constituting a deviancy amplification spiral.
- Moral panics are typically accompanied by calls for, and in many instances, the introduction of, tougher policies.

Moral panics, often regarded as inevitable, also function to confirm consensual values by identifying in what ways incidents and groups are perceived to be deviant. Reactions to young people's deviance tend to be interpreted as signs of the decline

Source: Press Association Images

'The mods and rockers were the subject of Stanley Cohen's classic work on folk devils and moral panics.'

of the family and tougher discipline in families or schools is called for. They are likely to occur at times of social and economic change and uncertainty where moral values, social institutions and ways of life are seen to be under threat (Garland 2008). A major theme is that 'things aren't what they used to be' (Jewkes 2004: 70/1). Social divisions are often emphasized in contrasts between 'us' (decent, respectable and moral) and 'them' (deviant, undesirable outsiders). As well as being young, folk devils are most often drawn from lower-class groups and areas (see Chapter 7).

Moral panics also 'make things happen' (Garland 2008: 15), by leading to tougher and more repressive control strategies. Thus, argues Garland, the panic about mugging signalled a drift to a 'law and order society' and the panic about paedophiles has led to restrictive orders for sex offenders. The killing of Jamie Bulger (Box 2.6) was associated with harsher policies towards young people and moral panics surrounding drug trafficking, terrorism and organized crime have been associated with 'wars' involving repressive social control measures (Welch 2007 and see below). To critical criminologists, moral panics can be generated and used to support the interests of dominant groups (see Chapter 5). The moral panic concept has been extremely influential, so much so that it has become part of everyday language. It has nonetheless come under considerable criticism and prompted a number of questions summarized below:

- **What is an exaggerated response?** The concept implies an exaggerated media reaction – yet what response would be proportionate? While some moral panics can readily be interpreted as exaggerated, others, such as those surrounding mugging, may not be (Garland 2008). Waddington (1986), for example, criticized the implication in Hall et al's (1978) work that the reaction was disproportionate.
- **Is the concept too subjective?** Identifying a moral panic involves, therefore, a subjective judgement and moral panics are often associated with 'debunking' the media (Garland 2008).
- **Are moral panics temporary or recurring?** It is often assumed that moral panics are transitory and fade away. Yet some are long lasting and there have been recurrent panics about child sexual abuse and youth crime. This may signal a change from the 1960s which was arguably more consensual than today's world which is characterized by greater cultural diversity. More recently, argues Young (2007b: 63), 'images of the excluded, the immigrant, the drug user and the terrorist visit us daily, the intensity dropping and peaking like tremors, but never vanishing nor presenting temporary relief'.
- **Do moral panics provide only a superficial analysis?** Some have criticized work on moral panics for paying too much attention to reactions and not analysing the events themselves. This can be countered by pointing out that the reaction is the essence of the concept – other theories deal with the generation of the problems (see Chapter 5).
- **Are moral panics associated with consensus or conflict?** While to some, moral panics reflect a consensus over moral values, to others, this consensus is 'orchestrated'.
- **Can some kinds of crime be seen as 'merely' moral panics?** An important criticism of moral panics is that their focus on exaggerated responses appears to dismiss the 'reality' of crime and its associated harmful effects (see Chapter 5).

These are all important questions yet the concept remains influential and stresses the importance of questioning media representations. It directs attention, for example, to the way in which the media overreacts to some crimes, often those involving the most disadvantaged, and underreacts to others, particularly crimes of states or powerful corporations (Welch 2007 and see Chapter 17). As Cohen argues, it remains a way of 'conceptualizing the lines of power in society and the ways in which we are manipulated into taking some things too seriously and other things not seriously enough' (Cohen 1972/2002: xxxv, cited in Jewkes 2004: 85).

Representing crime: contemporary cases

While later chapters will include many more examples of moral panics, folk devils and misleading representations of crime issues, this section will look at some of the most prominent cases in recent decades and develop some of the themes outlined above. Typically, in line with the news imperatives outlined in Box 2.2, the media over-represent sexual and violent offences and those involving strangers and child victims. Simplified contrasts between villains and victims or 'good' and 'evil' are common. These reflect wider social relationships – the majority of folk devils are lower class, women are sexualized and children presented as 'innocent' or 'evil'. These are evident in recent examples of 'moral panics', and in what Innes (2004) describes as 'signal crimes', which become instantly recognizable and which signal wider societal concerns. The section will also look at the moral panic surrounding organized crime and will explore how white-collar offences, often neglected, are represented.

Focus on stranger danger

Reference has already been made to the way in which the media invoke the threat of 'stranger danger' in relation to, for example, serial killers, paedophiles lurking in school playgrounds or rapists targeting women in the street. Yet, as will be seen throughout subsequent chapters, many of these kinds of crime are committed by people known to victims, although this is not generally pointed out. As Box 2.5 illustrates, a school caretaker was eventually convicted of the murders of Holly Wells and Jessica Chapman. The stranger theme is also evident in relation to recent folk devils such as the cyber stalker, a 'shadowy paedophile lurking in the chatroom to seduce the unwary' (Marsh and Melville 2009: 65), or the identity thief lurking in people's back yards attempting to extract identity details from their rubbish (see Chapter 13).

Associated with stranger danger is the tendency to attribute crime to 'others' and to 'outsiders'. As illustrated in Box 2.9, organized crime is often misleadingly attributed to 'mafias' and 'alien conspiracies' (see Chapter 14). One of the dangers of such 'othering' and overemphasizing 'stranger danger' is the very false message it sends which can affect the discovery of offenders. The assumption that a stranger was involved in Holly Wells and Jessica Chapman's abduction, for example, diverted attention away from the killer and, as Wykes and Welsh (2009: 22) point

Box 2.5 The case of Holly Wells and Jessica Chapman

On 4 August 2002, in the small Cambridgeshire town of Soham, two 10-year-old schoolgirls, Holly Wells and Jessica Chapman (almost instantly reduced to 'Holly and Jessica') went missing. Their bodies were found two weeks later after a much-publicized search accompanied by an iconic image of the girls wearing Manchester United football tops.

- News reports focused on the spectre of an unknown and dangerous stranger, Internet 'grooming' and a sex offenders' hostel which had been opened nearby, a focus on 'stranger danger' which arguably distracted the police.
- It was eventually revealed that the killer was ***John Huntley***, the school caretaker, who was known and trusted by the girls. He was demonized in the press as a 'beast' and 'monster', and attention focused on an 'odd' relationship with his mother.
- Huntley's partner ***Maxine Carr*** was subsequently found guilty of perverting the course of justice by providing Huntley with a false alibi. She too was demonized, seen as a possible 'groomer', described in the *Sun* as a 'snivelling, selfish liar' and villified as if she shared equal responsibility with Huntley, although she was away at the time of the murder.
- Revelations of shortcomings in Huntley's vetting (he had been subject to previous allegations of sexual offences, although never convicted) led to the introduction of tighter vetting procedures.

(Based on Wykes and Welsh 2009)

Source: Getty Images

This image was widely circulated and immediately identified 'Holly and Jessica'.

out, 'what the media barely acknowledged was that he was a man living in a heterosexual relationship who was part of a close community and who was well known and trusted by local children'.

Age: villains and victims

Simplified contrasts are well illustrated in representations of children as 'angels' or 'evil monsters'. Children are often represented as quintessentially innocent and those who victimize them as 'beasts' or 'fiends', with paedophiles representing the 'folk devil par excellence' (Jewkes 2004: 97 and see Chapter 12). Not all child victims, however, are equally 'deserving', and Greer (2007) and Jewkes (2004) point to cases in which young victims from more obviously lower-class backgrounds and who have a history of running away or drug abuse receive far less sympathetic attention (see Chapter 6).

In contrast, children who kill challenge images of children as 'angels', which can lead to the extremely hostile reactions seen in relation to the killers of Jamie Bulger outlined in Box 2.6. They were generally depicted as 'evil', as freaks of nature, as

Box 2.6 The James Bulger case

- On 12 February 1993, 2-year-old James Bulger (nicknamed by the press as Jamie) was killed by two 10-year-old boys, Robert Thompson and John Venables. He was taken from the Strand shopping centre, Bootle, having wandered away from his mother. He sustained considerable injuries.
- A novel feature of the case was the visual evidence from CCTV cameras showing the two boys leading the toddler out of the shopping centre.
- Despite their age they were said to be old enough to understand the difference between right and wrong. Justice Moreland characterized their behaviour as 'an act of unparalleled evil and barbarity'.
- The case attracted extensive reaction with the then prime minister calling for people to 'condemn rather than understand' offenders, and the Home Secretary commenting that 'no excuses could be made for a section of the population who are essentially nasty pieces of work' (*The Times* 22 February 1993).
- The killers were represented as 'evil', as the 'spawn of the devil' and to Jewkes (2004: 91), citing a *Daily Mail* (25 November 1993) headline 'The evil and the innocent', the case illustrates how notions of childhood innocence and vulnerability coexist with images of mini-monsters.
- The case was seen as symptomatic of more generalized moral decline and rising youth crime.
- There was adverse reaction to the original custodial sentence of eight years, based on reasoning that this was a long time for a child. The then Home Secretary, responding to a tabloid petition signed by nearly three hundred thousand people, recommended increasing the sentence to fifteen years. This was rejected and the young men were released in 2001.
- By contrast a similar case in Norway was regarded as a tragic accident and the children concerned were regarded as victims.
- The arrest and subsequent imprisonment of one of the killers for a breach of his parole conditions in March 2010 received considerable attention, with James Bulger's mother commenting that he was 'back where he belonged' (*Telegraph* 3 March 2010) and the *Sun* proclaiming, 'Evil Venables back in Cell . . .' (20 March 2010).

(Based on Jewkes 2004 and D'Cruze et al 2006)

they had committed an evil act. Although many factors undoubtedly contributed to their offending, and similar cases elsewhere have seen child killers cast as victims, they were overwhelmingly demonized. To D'Cruze et al (2006: 78) this reaction indicates an inability to contemplate the defendants as ordinary little boys. The Bulger case also contributed to a rising tide of concern about and tougher policies towards young people, although these boys were younger than the norm and such murders are extremely rare (see Chapter 11). Young people have been subject to moral panics throughout the centuries (Pearson 1983; Muncie 2009 and see Chapter 8) and are very often cast as 'villains' rather than 'victims' with high levels of routine victimization receiving very little press attention (see Chapters 6 and 8).

Older people on the other hand, although dominating areas of white-collar crime and fraud, rarely feature as folk devils unless as 'drug barons' or 'Godfathers'. When they are convicted of more conventional crimes, these may be reported as almost humorous or as making a stance against the law, as in the case of a 73-year-old pensioner jailed for seven days in 2005 after refusing to pay her council tax. Media coverage led to a mystery donor paying her fine (Marsh and Melville 2009: 74).

Women: madonnas or whores?

Whether as victims or offenders, women's sexuality or lack of it is stressed and media treatment of the sexual elements in crime can be used as 'soft pornography' to increase sales (Soothill and Walby 1991, cited in Greer 2007: 40). Contrasting images include those of deserving and innocent, often virginal women and those who are tainted, fallen and have contributed to their own victimization. They are therefore 'virgins or vamps', 'madonnas or whores' (Jewkes 2004). When, as outlined in Box 2.7, five women were murdered in Ipswich, their status as sex workers

Box 2.7 The case of the Ipswich murders: women as victims

A major feature in reporting the murders of five women in Ipswich, Suffolk in 2006 by Steve Wright, the so-called 'Ipswich ripper' was the involvement of the victims in sex work. They were routinely described as the 'Ipswich Prostitute Murders' (for example, *Telegraph* 16 January 2008) and derogatory reference was made to the victims' work and drug abuse with terms such as 'vice girls', 'tarts', 'hooker' or 'pockmarked losers' being used (Bennet 2006). While some used the more politically correct term of 'working girls' and others publicly criticized this stigmatization, the overwhelming view was that these women were somehow less deserving victims and were in part responsible for their own victimization. A *Daily Mail* article of 18 December 2006 (cited in Marsh and Melville 2009: 108) commented that

> we do not share in the responsibility for either their grubby little existences or their murders. Society isn't to blame. It might not be fashionable, or even acceptable in some quarters, to say so, but in their chosen field of 'work', death by strangulation is an occupational hazard.

A recent television drama about these murders, *Five Daughters*, set out to provide a more accurate and non-stereotypical evaluation of the murdered women as daughters with families (Wark 2010).

dominated media coverage and persisted despite attempts to present them simply as women. This contrasts with the coverage of the murder of the *Crimewatch* presenter Jill Dando in 1999, who was presented as the attractive and innocent victim of a stalker.

Women who commit serious crimes are presented as 'doubly deviant' – as going against both the law and femininity (Eaton 1986; Wykes and Welsh 2009). Women who kill are often made out to be 'monsters' (Morrisey 2003) as the title of the film about the serial killer Aileen Wournos (see Box 2.8) demonstrates, and other female killers such as Rose West and Myra Hindley have also been seen to personify evil. Jewkes (2004: 113) lists a number of standard narratives used by the media in relation to women who commit serious crimes:

- *Sexuality and sexual deviance*: Women's sexuality is interrogated and 'constructions of deviant sexuality are almost a given'. Lesbianism, seen as 'dirty', is often imputed to deviant women and was alleged in a picture, taken in 1995, of Myra Hindley and Rose West holding hands in the high security wing of Durham prison.
- *(Absence of) physical attractiveness*: Women who offend are often portrayed as 'unfeminine' and Rose West's 'frumpy' appearance was not only commented upon but used to explain her crimes (Box 2.8).

Box 2.8 'Monsters' – women as killers

Myra Hindley: Along with Ian Brady, Myra Hindley was tried for five murders of children and teenagers in 1965, dubbed the Moors murders as two bodies were found in Saddleworth Moor near Manchester. The killings involved physical torture and sexual abuse. Hindley was repeatedly castigated as evil and assumed to have an equal share of responsibility. She has become, argue D'Cruze et al 2006, a 'prime exemplar of evil'.

Rosemary West was convicted, along with her husband, Fred, for the murders of ten young women and girls, including her 16-year-old daughter, during the 1970s. The killings attracted major publicity particularly as bodies were found in the Wests' garden and they involved sexual abuse. Fred West committed suicide in prison and escaped trial and conviction. Rosemary West was seen to have been complicit in the offences and was subject to 'just about every denigratory term applicable to women' (Wykes 2001 cited in Jewkes 2004: 114). The *Daily Mirror* likened her to a 'toad on a stone' (Jewkes 2004: 114), and she was variously described as lesbian, aggressive, violent, menacing, bisexual, liking black men, oral sex, kinky, seductive, a prostitute, oversexed, a child abuser, nymphomaniac, sordid, monster. Reports also focused on her 'frumpy' appearance and used this to explain her crime (Marsh and Melville 2009). She was said to have taken part in the killings as she was insecure about her looks and afraid of losing her husband. In contrast Fred West was represented as a good husband, hard worker and reliable provider, driven by a 'mad and terrible love' for his wife.

Aileen Wournos is one of the very few female serial killers and killed seven men in Florida between November 1989 and December 1990. She was executed by lethal injection in 2002. She has been the subject of many books and films including the film *'Monster'* (Rafter 2007). Media attention focused on her life as a prostitute and lesbian signaling that she had crossed the boundaries of an archetypal feminine woman and became an outsider. Her plea of self defence was widely ridiculed on the grounds of her prostitution, and her lesbianism was used to illustrate her 'man hating' behaviour. The film did explore her victimization from abuse as a child (Rafter 2007).

(Based on Wykes and Welsh 2009; Jewkes 2004; D'Cruze et al 2006)

- *Bad wives*: Whereas male criminals are rarely presented as 'bad husbands', deviant women, particularly those who kill a spouse or partner, are seen as the 'epitome of the bad wife'. Sara Thornton, who killed her violent, alcoholic husband was portrayed as sexually promiscuous and, in a notorious 'nagging wife' case, a judge, giving a two-year suspended sentence to a man who killed his wife, commented that the victim would have 'tried the patience of a saint'.
- *Bad mothers*: While male criminals are not often seen as 'bad fathers', women offenders are cast as 'bad mothers'. Women whose children have been abducted can also be portrayed as bad mothers – for example, James Bulger's mother was criticized for having turned her back on the child. Bad mothers are also seen as having colluded with fathers who abuse.
- *Mythical monsters*: Deviant women have been demonized throughout the centuries, from Greek legends such as that of Medea who murdered children and Medusa, the snake-haired monster who turned her victims to stone with a stare. Witches were persecuted and the 'wicked witch' imagery is often used. The picture of Myra Hindley is said to typify a 'brooding presence' and a symbolic representation of the 'horror of femininity perverted from its "natural" course' (Birch 1993, cited in Jewkes 2004: 124).
- *Mad cows*: Serious female offenders are often portrayed as 'mad', and 'normal' biological states, such as pregnancy, childbirth, menstruation or the menopause are pathologized and used to explain crime (see Chapter 9).
- *Evil manipulators*: When crimes are committed with male partners, the woman is often seen as manipulative or instrumental as happened with Myra Hindley, whose role was said to be less than Ian Brady's, and with Rosemary West and Maxine Carr – who was not even present at the time of the crime.
- *Non agents*: Depictions of women as mad, evil or controlled deny women any agency or power to make decisions. Neither academic work nor the public, argues Jewkes (2004: 129), are 'ready to confront the reality that women can be cruel, sadistic and violent' (and see Chapter 9).

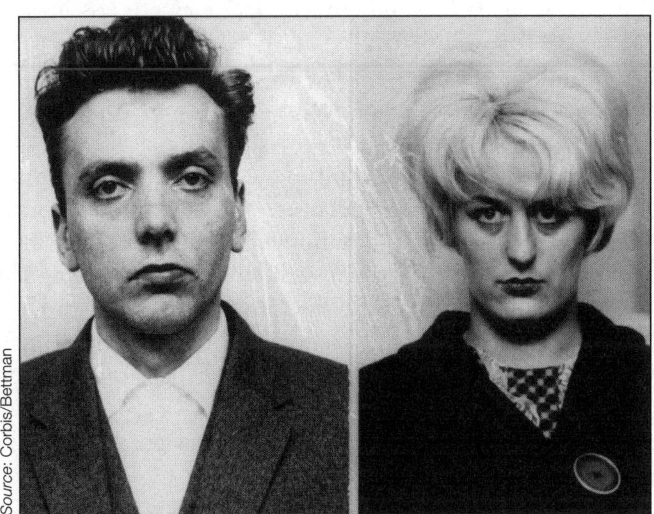

Source: Corbis/Bettman

These images of Ian Brady and Myra Hindley remain recognizable and for many years Myra Hindley's image came to represent the 'face' of 'evil'.

Ethnicity

Hall et al's (1978) work, outlined in Box 2.4, highlights the emergence of the 'black mugger' and, as will be seen in Chapter 10, ethnicity is an important feature of press representations, particularly those invoking 'aliens' and 'others'. Representations of urban unrest in Britain in the 1980s, such as those in Brixton, Bristol and Broadwater Farm, all featured black youth, and in the 1990s Jamaican 'Yardies' were associated with the drug trade (Keith 1993). Successive moral panics about minority ethnic groups have followed, including those about asylum seekers, often presented as 'criminal', and the threat of 'home-grown' Muslim fundamentalist terrorists, which has contributed to Asian youth experiencing racial harassment from the public and the police. Box 2.9 also illustrates this tendency in relation to organized crime mafias (see Chapter 14).

Socio-economic inequalities

Later chapters will provide many further examples of moral panics surrounding the 'underclass' and the 'socially excluded'; folk devils are typically 'dangerous people' from 'dangerous' places (Mooney 2008). It is lower-class children and youth who are perceived to be more adversely affected by violence on television and as will be seen in Chapter 6, lower-class victims may be seen as less deserving and as villains as much as victims. And, while the majority of moral panics and folk devils involve what might be seen as 'lower class' or street crime, the often more serious crimes of the more affluent and of corporations and state agencies (see Chapters 15, 16 and 17) are much less likely to be subject to moral panics or regarded as signal crimes.

White-collar and corporate crime

In general terms, white-collar and corporate crimes are less likely to be covered in the main sections of news broadcasts and papers, are often relegated to the end of news bulletins and do not attract large headlines (Tombs and Whyte 2001). Some are found in the business, financial, technology or environmental sections, but not as 'crime' stories. This is also the case with dramatic 'accidents' or 'disasters' which involve major harms, deaths and injuries such as oil spills, explosions in factories or transport incidents, many of which are subsequently attributed to managerial neglect. Initially these do attract sensational headlines but later investigations about their causes are less prominent and any criminal elements are underplayed. Cases of fraud and corruption are often described as 'wrongdoing' rather than crime, and what was arguably a major fraud on the part of high-street financial companies, who misled customers about the amount of their pensions, was described as 'mis-selling' (Croall 2001a).

The under-representation of white-collar and corporate crime is consistent with the 'news imperatives' as they lack key elements of sex, violence, immediacy or action and are less easy to simplify. They are also more difficult to represent dramatically and visually (Levi 2006; 2008b; 2009). Moreover, exposing major frauds often requires the kind of specialist journalism for which there are fewer resources.

Although there are fewer folk devils, some cases do receive considerable publicity and Levi identifies a number of themes including:

- Cases involving 'household names' or celebrities are more likely to be reported. After revelations of the involvement of senior executives in insider dealing in Guinness shares in the 1980s, the company changed its name to Diageo. In the United States the collapse of the energy giant Enron amidst allegations of fraud received considerable publicity and led to the introduction of more punitive sanctions (see Chapter 15).
- A spectacular 'fall from grace' or successful people 'going off the rails' is a popular theme.
- The fraudulent derivatives trading of the 'rogue trader', Nick Leeson, led to the collapse of Barings Bank in 1995. Part of the novelty of this story was that Leeson did not come from a prestigious background, being the son of a plasterer, and that the Royal Family had accounts at the well-established bank. He has now become a commentator on financial frauds, gives after-dinner speeches, has his own website and a film of his life starred Ewan McGregor.
- Some cases can involve elements of 'othering' such as the notorious Nigerian frauds inviting people to participate in bogus investment schemes (see Chapter 13).
- Cases involving 'deserving' victims such as 'widows and orphans' frauds are more likely to receive coverage.

Scandals, corruption in high places and in the police, corporate and state conspiracies, along with fraudulent sales practices and insider trading are also a staple feature of films about white-collar crime – albeit that they are less numerous than other crime movies and are classified as dramas not crime (Nichols 1999, cited in Friedrichs 2006a). They include many well-known and classic movies such as *Citizen Kane*, *All the President's Men*, *Erin Brokovich*, *Wall Street*, *Nixon* and *The Pelican Brief* (Friedrichs 2006a: 332–4). The tension between profitability and safety considerations features in 'disaster' movies such as *The Towering Inferno*, and the plot of the recent blockbuster *Avatar* deals with corporate and governmental conspiracies, eventually foiled, to destroy the way of life of the inhabitants of a different planet to extract natural resources.

The 'war' on organized crime

Recent moral panics have surrounded the threat, often presented as an 'alien conspiracy', of organized crime. This also illustrates, as indicated in Box 2.9, the use of exaggerated threats to support increasingly punitive policies. With organized crime, as with terrorism, the military language of 'wars' is often used. Primary amongst the folk devils of organized crime are the Mr Bigs of the drugs 'cartels', Mafia godfathers (where, asked Heidensohn (1996), were the Mrs Bigs or godmothers?) and gangsters such as the Kray twins. Famous gangsters have featured in Hollywood movies from the 1930s era of prohibition onwards, and serious criminals such as Jimmy Boyle (1977) and John McVicar, subject of the film *McVicar*, have written autobiographies. The fascination of organized crime is also seen in the popular TV series *The Sopranos*.

Box 2.9 The war on organized crime

Woodiwiss and Hobbs (2009) explore how American policies on organized crime have been based on the threat of an 'alien conspiracy' of foreign groups such as the Mafia.

- British fears about the threat of organized crime were influenced by the American 'war on drugs' in the middle of the twentieth century which was associated with the moral panic surrounding mugging and rising concerns about immigration and drugs. Britain obtained (Woodiwiss and Hobbs 2009: 119) 'its own drug barons, czars and Mr Bigs', crime organizations were described as 'armies' or corporations, and in 1987 the *Daily Mail* introduced the 'black mafia' and 'Yardies' as new folk devils.
- The 1990s saw a spate of Russian Mafia stories although the worst fears failed to materialize.
- Organized crime is still widely associated with foreign 'gangs' such as Albanians, Chinese triads and Turkish groups and it has been popularly associated with terrorists and asylum seekers.
- All of this, they argue, has amounted to the Americanization of drug and organized crime policy, associated with the strengthening of security and policing organizations such as the Serious and Organized Crime Agency (SOCA) and more punitive sentencing.
- It also contains racist elements as the organized crime 'folk devil' is presented as a global and external threat although it also includes many local and indigenous networks.

As with other media representations these can be misleading, by over-representing elements of action and violence and presenting an image of large, global criminal conspiracies, often consisting of immigrant groups such as the Chinese Triads, Japanese Yakuza or the Jamaican Yardies. Many forms of what is known as organized crime are, as will be seen in Chapter 14, far more accurately described as 'disorganized', consisting of small, indigenous enterprises forming transient and temporary networks.

Using the media to study crime

Given all its limitations, what can the media tell us about crime and can it be used to study it? In many ways the questions we ask about and our interest in particular kinds of crime are mediated in that they are affected by our existing knowledge – gained largely from the media. Moreover, the media is an invaluable source of information about specific cases and forms of crime, and is very often a starting point for further investigations. Its many uses will be seen in subsequent chapters. In general terms the media is useful to:

- **Explore how crime is socially constructed:** Many of the above analyses have been critical of the media, but at the same time have sought to reveal how it reflects and reinforces representations of offences, offenders, victims and patterns of crime.

- **Start research on crime:** The media often alert us to the existence of particular kinds of crime and search engines on the Internet and newspaper archives, many now online, can be used to direct the researcher to other sources of information.
- **Disseminate investigative journalism:** A major role of the media in democratic societies is its role as watchdog, exposing scandals and questioning government policies. Investigative journalism of, for example, human rights abuses, corporate frauds or political corruption are in themselves major sources of information.
- **Autobiographies:** Useful qualitative information about offenders' attitudes and motivations can be gained from offenders' autobiographies. While inevitably biased – they may, for example, be extended justifications – they can be used with caution.
- **Film and literature:** While fictional, these can, argues Rafter (2007), form the basis of a 'popular criminology', which, by exploring aspects of crime less amenable to objective, academic research such as offenders' psyches and moral and ethical issues, can add to other forms of inquiry (see also Rankin 1999).

Concluding comments

This chapter has explored many aspects of the relationship between crime and the media. Crime has always been a subject of great fascination featuring in tales and ballads such as that of the legendary Robin Hood which retain their resonance today. Dramatic images of crimes and criminals have long been a staple of the popular press. Crime dominates all contemporary media which tends to over-represent and exaggerate the least typical crimes and under-represent the most common and mundane crimes. Sex and violence are highlighted and moral panics create popular folk devils. While often associated with copy-cat crimes and increasing violence there is little evidence that the media directly 'cause' crime although by presenting idealized images of affluent lifestyles it can create feelings of failure which can lead to crime.

Many aspects of the issues raised in this chapter will be highlighted in later ones, which will also reveal many more folk devils, from anti-social youth, ladettes and gangs through to cyber stalkers, Internet groomers, terrorists, Internet pirates and human traffickers. Chapter 3 will contrast the over-dramatized images of crime presented in the media with the more seemingly factual picture presented by official figures on crime. The themes identified in media representation will be taken up in later chapters on the many explanations for crime, its complex relationships with social inequalities and specific forms of crime.

Review questions

1. Consult at least two newspapers and a television news bulletin. What proportion of items are related to crime? What kinds of crime? How is it represented? Which groups are most likely to be associated with crime?
2. How many films and television programmes have you watched in the last week? How many of these deal in some way with crime?

3 Taking a television series, crime film or novel as an example, consider how it represents crime, policing, offenders and/or victims. Why are fictional accounts of crime so popular?

4 List what you consider to be some contemporary moral panics. Consider the extent to which they 'fit' the main characteristics of a moral panic.

5 To what extent can it be said that media causes crime?

Key reading

There is now a considerable amount of literature on many aspects of the media and crime, the most accessible of which are:

Carrabine, E. (2008) ***Crime, Culture and the Media***, Cambridge: Polity Press. This provides a useful introduction, focusing on audiences and representations, including discussions of film and fiction as well as news and the organization of media industries.

Marsh, I. and Melville, G. (2009) ***Crime, Justice and the Media***, London: Routledge. This is particularly useful for those who are coming fresh to the subjects of criminology, sociology and the media and contains some very useful examples of historical and contemporary moral panics.

Greer, C. (ed.) (2010) ***Crime and Media: A Reader***, London: Routledge. This is an extremely useful collection, bringing together a broad selection of classic and contemporary work on the media and crime.

Jewkes, Y. (2004) ***Media and Crime***, London: Sage. This is an authoritative text covering areas of theory, the construction of crime news, and contains an extended discussion of moral panics along with discussions of media constructions of children, women and crime and surveillance culture.

Chapter 3
Finding out about crime

This chapter will look at:

- ➜ The creation of crime and offenders
- ➜ The role of victims and the public
- ➜ The role of police and law enforcers
- ➜ Researching crime
- ➜ Quantitative data on crime
  - – Official statistics and reports
  - – Victim surveys
  - – Self-report surveys
- ➜ Qualitative data
- ➜ Trends and patterns of crime
- ➜ National distribution of crime

An enormous amount of information about crime is now widely accessible through the Internet. The concerns reflected in moral panics, noted in Chapter 2, have led to official figures about crime being subject to scrutiny and politicized, with a particular focus on apparent rises and falls in violence and crime rates more generally. All information about crime, however, requires critical examination. How, for example, was information collected? Why was it collected and by whom? Which kinds of offences have been counted and which not? This chapter will start by looking at the processes which produce official 'crimes' and 'criminals' and will then explore different ways of carrying out research into crime. This will be followed by an introduction to the main sources of data about crime and a broad outline of what they reveal about offences, offenders and victims, overall patterns and variations across Britain. It will focus on broad issues, with more details being left to specific chapters.

Producing crime and criminals

The creation of official crime and offenders: the process of attrition

Events do not come clearly labelled as 'crime' or as theft, assault, robbery or murder, and officially defined crimes are produced by a process in which events are translated into crimes and offenders, illustrated in Figure 3.1. To be officially counted as crime, an event must be seen by a member of the public, a victim or law enforcer, who must interpret it as potentially a crime and decide to take further action. If a suspect is identified, the offence must be seen as serious enough and there must be enough evidence to justify prosecution. Only following conviction does a suspect become an official offender. The public, victims, police, other law enforcement agencies and prosecutors are therefore key definers of crime. Potential crimes and criminals disappear, in what has been described as a process of attrition, at many stages. In England and Wales for example, for 2008–9, out of over 10 million crimes reported to the British Crime Survey (BCS), just under 5 million were recorded by the police, and around 1⅓ million were 'detected'. Around half of these led to a charge or summons. At the end of the process, around 200,000 were found guilty at Magistrates Courts, and 61,500 at Crown Court (Ministry of Justice 2010). This section will explore these processes.

The role of the victim and the public

The role of victims and the public varies according to the offence. Some offences are relatively invisible and victims totally unaware of any harm or that some actions would be regarded as abnormal. The sexual abuse of children, for example, takes place in private and children are often not aware that anything is amiss. Other incidents, for example small acts of vandalism, may not be seen as important enough to bother with. Some activities are widely tolerated – how many people would report cannabis-smoking at a party? Public tolerance also varies – what is seen as serious in a quiet country village or suburb might be normal in a city centre. Even where further action is taken it might not involve criminal proceedings – theft at work, for example, might lead to dismissal or assaults to private reprisals.

This is confirmed in victim surveys, which reveal that many crimes are not reported. The 2006–7 BCS, for example, found that in England and Wales, while 93 per cent of thefts of motor vehicles and 81 per cent of burglaries were reported, only 32 per cent of cases of vandalism, 36 per cent of common assaults and 35 per cent of thefts from the person were reported (Nicholas et al 2007). Under half of all crimes reported to the Northern Ireland Crime Survey (NICS) 2007/08 were reported to the police, with burglary (77%) and vehicle-related theft (53%) having the highest reporting rates, reflecting the seriousness of the incidents and the associated likelihood of insurance claims (Freel et al 2009).

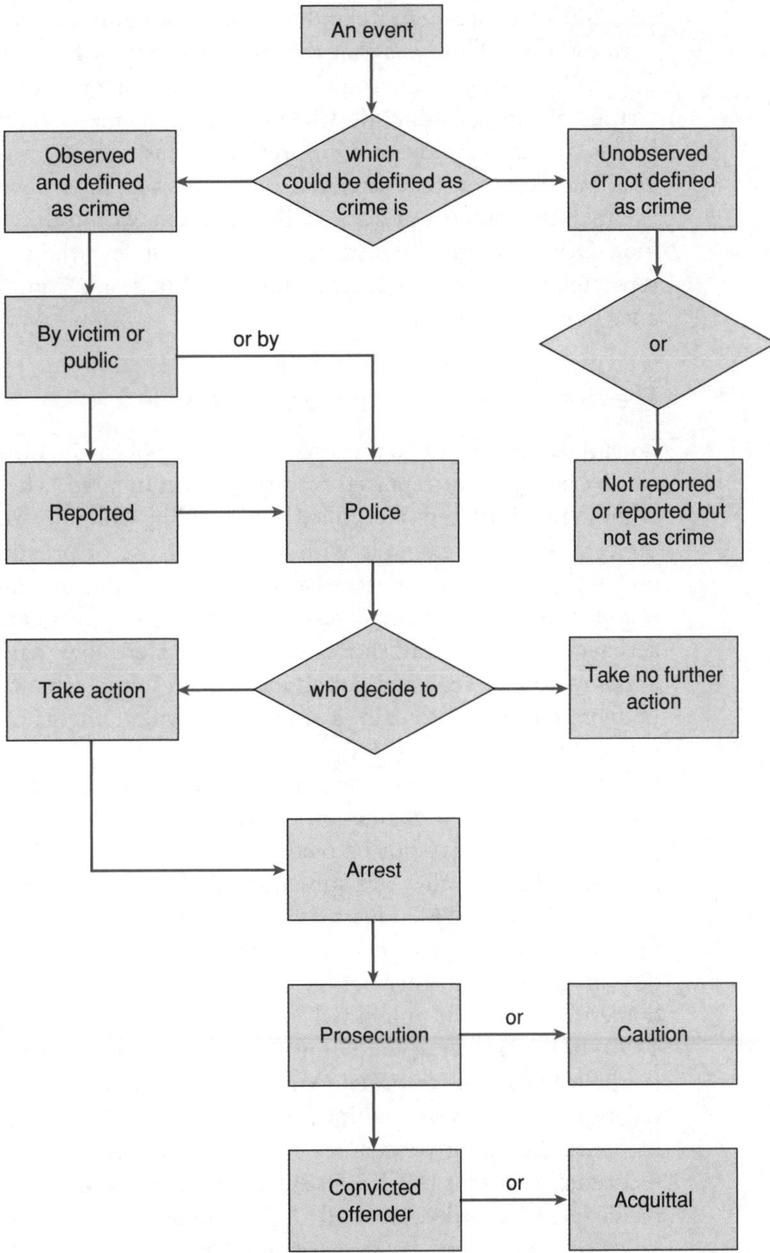

Figure 3.1 Creating crime and criminals

Why do victims not report offences? One of the main reasons is that the incident is too trivial and has not caused any major loss. Others feel that the police would not be able to do much about it. Around 72 per cent of those not reporting an offence to the BCS in 2006–7 gave these reasons. Others (16 per cent) considered that the matter was private and that they would deal with it themselves (Nicholas et al 2007). In Northern Ireland, the most common reason for not reporting a crime, cited by nearly half, was that the 'police could not have done anything' (Freel et al 2009). Embarrassment and a fear of subsequent court appearances may deter victims of rape or domestic violence, or companies who would rather conceal the frauds of their employees. On rarer occasions, victims may themselves be involved in crime – sex workers, irregular immigrants or those involved in illegal substance use might not report attacks or thefts as this would draw attention to their activities. Other victims distrust, are hostile to or fear the police. The higher rates of reporting property crimes, especially car theft, result from the requirements of insurance policies.

The role of the police and law enforcement

Potential crimes come to the attention of the police and other law enforcement agencies by being either reported or directly encountered. The majority of all recorded crimes are reported to the police by the public (Maguire 2007). Where there are no direct victims, for example with illegal drug use or prostitution, or where offences are difficult for victims to detect, such as pollution, the role of law enforcers becomes crucial. In other cases police officers on patrol encounter pub brawls, disturbances, public drunkenness or fighting. Here they have the discretion whether and how to intervene and not all incidents result in criminal proceedings. They may be more concerned to calm a situation down, acting as mediators or 'street politicians' (Brogden et al 1988).

Law enforcement decisions affect all subsequent stages. Not all complaints are recorded, creating a distinction between offences *reported* to and *recorded* by the police. Offences may not be recorded because they are not regarded as sufficiently serious or because they are subsequently defined as involving 'no crime' (Coleman and Moynihan 1996). This may happen when articles reported as stolen are subsequently found, when there is insufficient evidence to proceed or because victims do not press for further action or withdraw their complaint. Incidents involving domestic disputes or pub brawls may similarly be reported as 'no crime'. During the 1990s in England and Wales, for example, around 40 per cent of crimes reported to the police were not recorded (Maguire 2007), and there were also suggestions that recording figures were manipulated to improve clear-up rates. Changes were made in police recording procedures following the introduction of the national crime-recording standards (NCRS) in 2002 – with the assumption now being that reported incidents are recorded. Around 70 per cent are now recorded (Maguire 2007). These kinds of considerations have a major impact on the reliability of official statistics, especially as recording practices in different areas and jurisdictions may vary, complicating any comparisons. They also affect overall increases and decreases and changes can create apparent crime waves. For example, official rates of rape increased during the 1980s when the police, responding to complaints that they did not treat women's reports of rape seriously, recorded a higher proportion of incidents.

Still further decisions affect the production of an official 'offender' and Figure 3.2 indicates the very different proportions of crimes recorded and detected and those eventually resulting in offenders being found guilty or cautioned. Not all crimes are

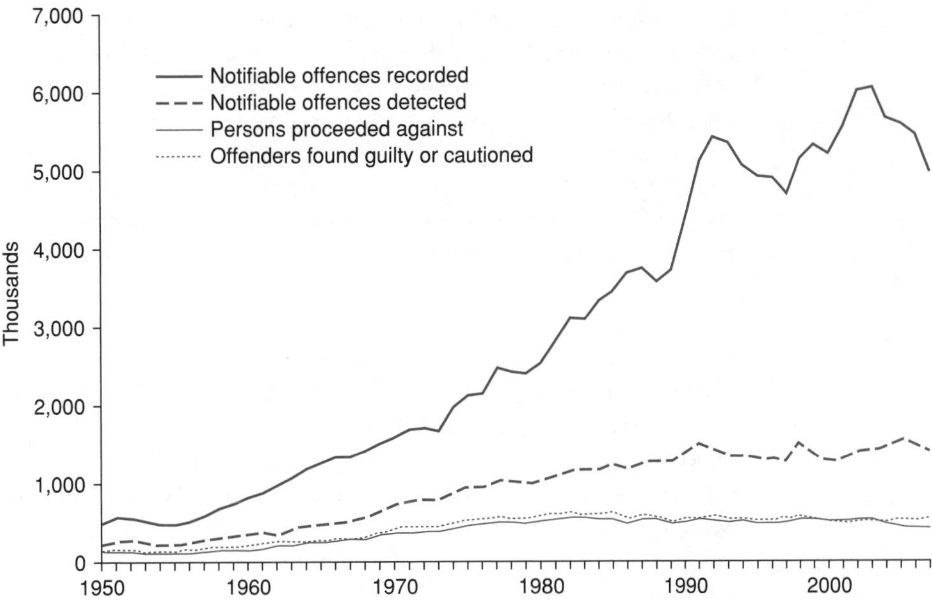

1. From 1998 the figures are for financial years. The recorded crime series was affected by new counting rules from 1998 onwards and by the NCRS from 2001/02 onwards.
2. Indictable offences with allowance for under-recording where appropriate.

Figure 3.2 Recorded crime, persons proceeded against and 'known offenders', 1950–2008

Figure 1.2 of Criminal Statistics: England and Wales p. 19 – Ministry of Justice (2010) *Criminal Statistics for England and Wales 2008*, London: Ministry of Justice, January 2010 available at *www.justice.gov.uk/publications/statistics*

'cleared up'. While popular images of the police centre around their detective role, in reality the vast majority of offences are solved because the informant can identify an offender, offenders are 'caught in the act', or an offender's identity is obvious when the crime is discovered. Only around 28 per cent of offences recorded by the police in England and Wales are subsequently cleared up, with homicide having the highest clear-up rate at around 88 per cent. Around 49 per cent of offences of violence against the person are cleared up and 30 per cent of sexual offences. Criminal damage and burglary have the lowest clear-up rates at 14 and 13 per cent respectively (Babb and Ogunbor 2008). The overall clear-up rate in Northern Ireland is currently 25.8 per cent (PSNI 2010). Variations between offences reflect their nature. When an assault is reported, the identity of the perpetrator is often obvious whereas burglars are less likely to be identified by victims. As is the case for recorded crime, comparisons between jurisdictions and different decades are complicated by changes in the way in which detection and clear-up rates are calculated.

Even if a perpetrator has been identified, they may not be prosecuted or convicted. A range of issues affects decisions by police and prosecution agencies to caution offenders, impose measures short of prosecution or to prosecute. Depending on the seriousness of the offence, prosecutors may decide not to proceed against physically or mentally ill offenders, or the very young or very old, feeling that the case is more appropriate for social services or victim–offender mediation. Some cases involve enforcement agencies other than the police, such as the Inland Revenue, Health and Safety Executive or Environmental Agencies who very often choose not to prosecute but to deal with the situation by negotiations, formal cautions and, in some cases, administrative penalties, all of which are seen to be more cost-effective (Croall 2001a; 2004; and see Chapters 15 and 16). Some of the factors affecting these discretionary decisions are:

Cost effectiveness

Like any other public organization, law enforcers are encouraged to be 'cost-effective'. There are not enough police officers to investigate all offences and, if all offenders were prosecuted, the costs of the criminal justice system would increase enormously. Successive governments have therefore introduced 'diversionary' schemes where offences are dealt with out of court, such as on-the-spot fines, special courts, or in Scotland, the Fiscal Fine.

The use of discretion

Law enforcers and prosecutors inevitably have high amounts of discretion and a range of factors, including local and national pressures and the attitudes of senior officers, all affect which cases are prioritized. Specific and often highly publicized campaigns may be launched against high-profile offences such as knife crimes or gang activity, subject to the kinds of moral panics seen in Chapter 2. Local partnership agreements between the police and other agencies mean that they are expected to consult over policing policies; national governments also set targets for specific forms of crime and anti-social behaviour.

Media sensitivity and public opinion

As seen in Chapter 2, the media can play a part in putting pressure on governments, local authorities and the police in respect, for example, of child sexual abuse, anti-social behaviour or knife crime.

Hidden crime

Recognizing and understanding these processes is vital as they warn against drawing any conclusions from official figures. They underline the existence of an unknowable dark or hidden figure of crime; indeed the first chapter of Coleman and Moynihan's classic text on crime figures is 'Haunted by the dark figure: criminologists as ghostbusters' (1996: 1). Incidents become 'classified' as offences of burglary, assault or criminal damage in a complex process of definition and redefinition (Kitsuse and Cicourel 1963). Officially recorded crimes and convicted offenders are in effect those who have survived the process of attrition and are not representative of all who break the criminal law. It is important to consider which crimes and offenders are more likely to be defined, recorded, detected and prosecuted before any generalizations are made about the extent of or trends in any particular form of crime. In general terms it can be suggested that crimes which are more visible and take place in public are more likely to be processed than those taking place in private. The so-called 'street' crimes of young people are more likely to be 'counted' than the 'suite' crimes of white-collar offenders which take place in offices and boardrooms or crimes which take place in the home. This further distorts relationships between age, gender or social class and offending.

Variations in the proportions of crime which are counted also mean that it can rarely be said with any certainty that any particular kind of crime is rising or falling, as any apparent increases or decreases could merely represent a change in the proportion of crimes reported to or recorded by agencies. Changes in police recording practices, as seen above, can create apparent crime waves, or alternatively reductions in crime. While it is often assumed that more police on the beat prevent more crime, they can also catch more and record more – thus more policing can increase crime rates.

Researching crime: social research

Social research, including surveys, interviews, questionnaires, observation, case studies and biographies is also used to study crime (Noaks and Wincup 2004; King and Wincup 2007). Research can be quantitative and qualitative, the former including statistics and large-scale surveys and the latter focusing on the quality rather the quantity of information, using more in-depth studies of offenders, victims or law enforcers. In deciding which methods to use, researchers must consider what resources are available, what questions to ask and how easily information can be gathered – particularly difficult for crime topics.

Different kinds of researchers are involved. Government departments have their own research units and government also sponsors research from outside agencies and universities. Universities can also obtain funding from a variety of independent research organizations, and there are a number of specialist research agencies, voluntary associations and special interest groups such as the Howard League for Penal Reform or Victim Support. Local councils, the police and other law enforcement agencies and industrial organizations also sponsor and carry out research. In Scotland, for example, the Scottish Institute for Policing Research (SIPR) involves the police and a number of universities, encouraging and carrying out research on a range of policing issues.

Accessing this research is now much easier thanks to the Internet, although great care must be taken in checking the authenticity, currency, reliability and validity of research accessed via the web. Tools such as Google and Google Scholar and the electronic and abstracting services of libraries can be used to identify appropriate research reports. Academic research is published in books, reports and academic journals such as the *British Journal of Criminology*, or *Criminology and Criminal Justice*, and many of these sources will be referred to throughout this text. This section will begin by looking at the problems encountered by researchers before outlining the main forms of quantitative and qualitative research and major sources of information about crime such as official statistics and victim surveys.

Research problems

Accessing information

The first hurdle faced by the researcher is accessing relevant material. The many statistics and research reports referred to above, which constitute *secondary* information (information collected by someone else) have many limitations. The researcher may therefore want to collect *primary* information, which means contacting public agencies who deal with crime, offenders or victims. This can be difficult as access to official agencies has to be negotiated and the researcher may encounter institutional barriers (Downes and Rock 2007). Agencies will want to know how the research results will be used, what the purpose of the research is and who is carrying it out. They may be defensive in case their activities will be subject to scrutiny and potential criticism.

Even more problems face the researcher who wants to focus on offenders. Firstly, where can they be located? The first avenue is to approach agencies dealing with offenders, but these offenders are inevitably unrepresentative. How can others be approached? Professional criminals, tax evaders, burglars and robbers do not advertise themselves and rarely practise their activities in public. Even if they are available, they too are likely to be highly suspicious. Researchers face other barriers. Their own backgrounds may limit access, and social class, age, ethnicity or gender all pose problems. It may be difficult, for example, for a middle-class, middle-aged researcher to carry out qualitative research with gangs or youth groups, or for a student or academic researcher to be admitted to the relatively closed world of the police or prison. Official agencies may view researchers as potential critics, whereas to offenders they might be seen as representatives of the criminal justice system. These difficulties also mean that a considerable amount of criminological research relies on official, government support, which limits the range of issues that can be investigated.

Moral and ethical issues

Research may be conducted for many reasons. It may aim to further knowledge about crime for its own sake or it may focus on a specific policy issue. It may be trying to understand and appreciate offenders and may explicitly or implicitly be critical of official agencies or government policies. Clearly, agencies are more likely to be sympathetic to researchers who appear to share their goals and whose research will be of use to them. This may compromise the objectivity of the researcher or the goals of the particular research. Similar considerations may affect research carried out with offenders or victims.

A good illustration of ethical difficulties is provided in classic studies in which researchers have posed as members of criminal groups. This avoids the suspicion which their presence might arouse and the possibility of the researcher affecting the group's behaviour. Such covert research, however, involves many ethical issues, not least of which is the dishonesty involved. In order to gain the respect of the group, researchers may be expected to participate in illegal activities and they inevitably gain information which could be of use to the police. This kind of research has become much rarer and researchers now have to seek permission from professional ethics committees and organizations such as the British Society of Criminology (BSC) who now issue guidelines for researchers. Other issues surround how far researchers can intrude into private matters. Interviewing the victims of serious crimes involves asking them to relive their experiences; of particular concern are those of sexual offences. Approaching offenders is also far from easy as they may be suspicious and, if in prison, may resent being treated as guinea pigs.

The safety of researchers

Researchers' safety also has to be considered, particularly if they want to work with groups outside formal institutions. Participants may have histories of unpredictable and violent behaviour, raising issues of where interviews should be carried out, how many researchers should be involved and how quickly assistance can be obtained. It is often preferable to hold interviews in institutional settings such as youth clubs or the premises of voluntary agencies rather than in the street or offenders' homes, but this limits the research to those who are involved with these agencies.

Research solutions

These difficulties have arguably led to an over-reliance on officially available information and work with offenders in institutions who provide captive populations. Some methods can partly overcome these problems, including:

Snowball samples

These aim to locate so-called 'hard to reach' groups not known to agencies, such as the homeless, illegal immigrants or drug-takers. A small number of initial contacts, possibly from agencies and the researcher's own personal or professional network are asked to provide, in confidence, other suitable contacts, who in turn lead to others. These have been used in studies of drug-taking and burglary (Parker et al 1988; Wright and Decker 1994). While this widens the scope of a sample, it may not be entirely representative and is also restricted to situations where groups of offenders know each other.

Public observation

Some crime is carried out in relatively public areas making it easier to observe and contact participants (Downes and Rock 2007). Many classic studies were carried out with youth gangs hanging about street corners, or sitting in pubs and clubs (see, for example, Whyte 1943; Downes 1966; Foster 1990). Other forms of crime are carried out in more public, organized settings – the researcher interested in football hooliganism may start by attending matches. Care has to be taken of course to avoid overtly dangerous situations. Observations in courtrooms can provide an insight into the kinds of offences and offenders which are characteristic of specific areas.

Information about crime

Quantitative data

Statistics and large-scale surveys, many from official sources, aim to estimate the extent of and trends in offences, offending or victimization. They also detail the personal and social characteristics of offenders. This quantitative data includes:

- Official crime statistics.
- Comparisons of crime statistics with other relevant figures – for example, correlations between crime and unemployment or economic deprivation.
- Victim surveys.
- Self-report surveys asking samples how much crime they have committed.
- Surveys measuring the personal characteristics of offenders.

Quantitative research produces extensive data, often, however, with few details. It may consist of a lengthy questionnaire issued to large samples asking respondents to tick boxes or pre-designed responses. This is generally used to generate statistically valid estimates and relationships. Many examples of this kind of data will be explored below and it is therefore important to outline briefly some of the general problems of this kind of research:

- It is often based only on officially defined crimes and convicted offenders.
- Statistics require interpretation. How, for example, could a statistical association between intelligence and criminal convictions be interpreted? Are offenders less intelligent, or are the least intelligent offenders more likely to be caught?
- A correlation, however strong, is not a cause. If, for example, an association is found between youth unemployment and crime it has to be asked *why* young unemployed people might commit offences. To answer this it might be better to talk at length to smaller numbers of this group.

Many of these problems are illustrated in some of the main forms of quantitative data such as official statistics, victim and self-report studies explored below.

Official statistics and reports

Official statistics and reports are often used as a starting point for investigating crime or particular offences. The Home Office and the Ministry of Justice, for England and Wales, the Scottish government and relevant agencies in Northern Ireland all collect a wide range of statistics which are published in bulletins and reports, as illustrated in Boxes 3.1, 3.2, and 3.3.

This information is now extremely voluminous, but great care has to be taken when using these sources. Questions which should be asked include:

- *What do the figures include?* A number of technical terms or broad categories (for example, notifiable offences, personal crime or acquisitive crime) are used and their meaning must be clarified (Davies et al 2007; Maguire 2007).
- *What do they leave out?* How might the kinds of crimes which are most and least likely to be observed, detected, prosecuted or convicted affect the figures?

Box 3.1 Official sources of information about crime in England and Wales

Ministry of Justice

Statistical bulletins (available from *www.justice.gov.uk/publications/statistics*) contain information about:

- **Criminal justice**: including
  - **The Criminal Statistics of England and Wales**; Motoring Offences; Arrests for Notifiable Offences; Women, Race and Ethnicity and the Criminal Justice System.
- **Courts and sentencing**: including
  - Judicial and Courts Statistics; Sentencing Statistics; Local Variations in Sentencing
- **Prison and Probation**: including
  - The Population in Custody; Probation Statistics; Statistics of Mentally Disordered Offenders
- **Reoffending**

Home Office statistics

(available from *www.homeoffice.gov.uk/rds/*) include:

- Statistical News Releases
- **Crime in England and Wales**: an annual publication with periodic updates containing a combination of Police Recorded Figures and the British Crime Survey (BCS).
- Occasional bulletins covering some areas in depth.
- Home Office Research Reports
- The **Offending, Crime and Justice Survey (OCJS)** asks young people about their attitudes towards and experiences of offending. Its aim is to examine the extent of offending, anti-social behaviour and drug use among the household population, particularly among young people aged from 10–25.

Statistical bulletins also cover English regions and **Crime in Wales** (Higgins et al 2009)

Websites of individual **police forces** also contain a variety of statistics and local breakdowns. Tables showing recorded crime figures for the **Crime and Disorder Reduction Partnerships** (CDPRs) in England and Wales can also be obtained along with **interactive maps** of local authority level police recorded crime data (both from Home Office website).

Reports of **other relevant government departments** who deal with aspects of crime include:

- The Health and Safety Executive
- The Environment Agency
- The Department for Business, Enterprise and Regulatory Reform
- The Inland Revenue

Box 3.2 Official sources of information about crime in Northern Ireland

- **The Northern Ireland Crime Survey (NICS)** closely mirrors the format and core questions of the British Crime Survey and contains information about levels of crime and public attitudes to crime.
- **Northern Ireland Police Service Recorded Crime Statistics** are recorded in accordance with the National Crime Recording Standard. This makes them comparable with those produced by the Home Office or by individual police forces in England and Wales. They are recorded on an annual basis.
- **The Northern Ireland Omnibus Survey** is conducted several times each year by the Central Survey Unit of the Northern Ireland Statistics and Research Agency and is designed to provide a snapshot of the behaviour, lifestyle and views of a representative sample of people in Northern Ireland.
- **The Ireland and Northern Ireland Drug Prevalence Survey** covers those aged 15 to 64 living in households in Northern Ireland and the Republic of Ireland. Responsibility for this survey lies with the Department of Health, Social Services and Public Safety, Northern Ireland.
- **The Young Person's Behaviour and Attitudes Survey (YPBAS)** in Northern Ireland uses self-completion questionnaires and covers young people aged 11 to 16. It was undertaken for the first time in 2000 and repeated in 2003 and 2007. The survey includes questions on drugs, policing, anti-social behaviour and personal safety.
- **The Belfast Youth Development Study** has been undertaken since 2001. The aim of the study is to investigate the risk and protective factors associated with adolescent drug use. The study comprises a core sample of approximately 4,500 young people who entered secondary school in 2000. The 2006 round includes on-line data collection.

Box 3.3 Official sources of information about crime in Scotland

An introduction (which can be found at *www.scotland.gov.uk/Topics/Statistics/browse/Crime-Justice*) includes:

- **Criminal Proceedings in Scottish Courts** (annual) includes information about: Police-recorded crime; Criminal Court proceedings; Persons proceeded against; Persons convicted by court and offence type; Persons convicted by age and gender; Sentencing.
- **Recorded Crime in Scotland** contains information about Police Recorded Crime broken down for individual areas.
- **The Scottish Crime and Justice Survey** (see, for example, MacLeod et al 2009)
- **High Level Summary of Equality Statistics** (with one chapter on crime)
- **High Level Summary of Statistics Trends** includes
  - Policing; Crime victimization; Perception of crime; Domestic abuse; Racist incidents; Drugs and alcohol; Violent crime; Crime recorded by and cleared up by the police; Criminal justice sentences; Prison population.
- **Annual Reports of agencies** such as:
  - The Children's Hearings Panel; Crown Office and Procurator Fiscal Service; Health and Safety Executive; HM Chief Inspector of Constabulary for Scotland; Prison Statistics; Scottish Household Survey; Scottish Courts; Risk Management Authority; Scottish Police Forces.

(For links to all these and other relevant websites see *www.cj.scotland.org.uk*)

Moreover, police records do not include criminal prosecutions made by other law enforcers. They give very little information about, for example, tax evasion, white-collar crime or the activities of the British Transport Police (Maguire 2007). Reports of other relevant government departments must therefore be sought.

- *What do they reveal about offences?* Statistical information rarely provides information about the seriousness or circumstances of offences.
- *How are offences categorized?*
- *How are they counted?* Many technical factors affect how offences and offenders are 'counted' (Maguire 2007). Several offences may be committed 'in one incident' in which case only the most serious is counted such as, for example, using a stolen credit card several times (Coleman and Moynihan 1996).
- *Have changes in reporting and recording methods or changes in the definition of offences affected rises and falls in the numbers of offences?* The introduction of the NCRS system and the reclassification of violent offences have affected crime figures. This is indicated in the small print accompanying tables (Maguire 2007).

Victim surveys

Since the 1980s, victim surveys – asking samples of the population how many crimes they, or members of their households, have experienced over a fixed period of time, along with aspects of people's attitudes to crime and policing – have expanded considerably (see Boxes 3.1, 3.2, 3.3). These include national surveys such as the British Crime Survey (BCS), inaptly named as it is restricted to England and Wales and whose main publication is now the annual volume *Crime in England and Wales*. The Scottish Crime and Justice Survey (SCJS) and the Northern Ireland Crime Survey (NCIS) provide information about these two jurisdictions. Victim surveys are also carried out by organizations such as local authorities and community safety organizations, as well as interest groups dealing with particular kinds of offences or victims such as child sexual abuse or women's victimization. National victim surveys are largely based on individual victimization and business organizations also conduct their own surveys of losses from crimes such as shoplifting. There is an International Crime Victim Survey (ICVS) although it is difficult to make meaningful cross-country comparisons. While victim surveys will be discussed more fully in Chapter 5, their main limitations are summarized below:

- Most surveys use standard classifications of crime – missing out, for example, many white-collar and financial crimes.
- The BCS is based on households – omitting organizations such as businesses, hospitals, schools or care homes.
- Early studies interviewed only those over 16 years – omitting younger teenagers and children.
- Their results reflect respondents' definitions of events which may not be the same as legal classifications.
- They are limited by respondents' memory.
- They are inevitably restricted to crimes which victims are aware of and miss out those which they cannot detect for themselves or have not defined as crime.
- They tend to capture single incidents and underestimate the full extent of repeat victimization.

Self-report surveys

Self-report surveys ask groups of the population how many times they have participated in criminal activity. They are often used with young people and aim to find out more about participation in crime than is revealed in official statistics. They can also provide more details about the class, age, sex or race of those who admit to offending. The BCS has included self-report studies about the use of illegal drugs and some studies combine questions about victimization, fears about and participation in crime. The Youth Lifestyles Surveys (YLS) provided invaluable information about young people's engagement in crime (Graham and Bowling 1995; Flood-Page et al 2000) and, since 2003, the Offending, Crime and Justice survey (OCJS) (see Box 3.1) has examined offending amongst 10–25 year olds and on occasion older age groups. The self-report method is also used in longitudinal cohort studies which follow a sample over many years to establish factors associated with both offending and desistance from offending. One such study currently underway is the Edinburgh Study of Youth Transitions and Crime (see, for example, McAra and McVie 2005; 2007; 2010).

The use of self-report studies has grown and they have provided extremely valuable information about people's participation in crime. They do, however, have many limitations including:

- *The accuracy of responses*. Even where anonymity is assured, respondents, especially schoolchildren, fear that their answers will be seen by parents or teachers and they may be reluctant to 'confess' to offences. Others may exaggerate.
- *Their scope*. They have been largely restricted to young people. It is less easy to gain access to groups of, for example, senior executives to ask questions about embezzlement or tax evasion.
- *They may reveal instances of less serious, trivial offences* which would not in any event have appeared in the criminal statistics.
- *They may use different time periods* – asking, for example, whether the activity has been engaged in within the last six months, the last year or indeed 'ever'.

Qualitative research

Qualitative research is more concerned with capturing the social meanings, constructions and definitions underpinning actions which cannot be 'captured' in quantitative research (Jupp 1989). It derives from interpretative sociology which argues that action cannot be understood without appreciating its meaning to those involved. Normally it involves lengthy interviewing or spending periods of time with a small number of people – usually offenders, victims or law enforcers. It explores how they perceive their experiences and actions and is often accompanied by illuminating examples. All material has to be interpreted as objectively as possible by the researcher.

The classic way of gathering qualitative data is to carry out extensive fieldwork with small groups, often described as participant observation or ethnography. This has a long tradition in the sociology of crime and deviance. It can be covert or overt – the latter being where the researcher openly observes and communicates with the group. In sociological studies carried out with young people, researchers lived with a group over a period of time, participated in their activities and attempted to appreciate their behaviour and lifestyle as fully as possible. During the 1950s and 1960s a number of studies were carried out in many parts of Britain with juvenile delinquents, school students, on street corners or in gangs, and they will be referred to in later chapters (see, for example, Downes 1966; Patrick 1973; Parker 1974). Control agencies have also been studied, illustrating how they view their role and what affects their decisions (see, for example, Cain 1973; Holdaway 1983; Hobbs 1991).

This kind of research has many limitations and problems of access and ethical dilemmas have already been pointed out. Fieldwork is also costly and time-consuming to conduct. Researchers must remain in the field long enough to gain acceptance and fully appreciate the group. Field notes must be rigorously maintained and dangers of overinvolvement avoided. Researchers must try to avoid contaminating the data with their own preconceptions and value judgements. While the covert researcher faces the ethical dilemmas of concealment, the overt researcher faces the problem that their very presence may change the group's behaviour. The material gathered can only be representative of one place and period of time and is restricted to accessible groups. There are, perhaps unsurprisingly, few ethnographic studies of crime in the stock exchange, tax evasion or political crime – as academics are generally not invited into positions to complete such studies (Punch 1996). Serial killers, drug 'barons' and sex offenders are similarly difficult to access. Delinquent youth, drug-takers and other groups whose activities are more public have been much more likely to be the subject of ethnographic research.

This kind of research is far less common than it once was. It is not, however, the only way of gathering qualitative data. Focus group research involves in-depth interviews with small, strategically chosen groups of offenders, victims or law enforcers and has become increasingly popular as a means of gaining qualitative information from larger numbers of participants. It is limited, however, by the nature of group interaction as groups can be swayed by more vocal and assertive individuals. As seen in Chapter 2, biographies and autobiographies can be used where few other sources of information exist – as might be the case with historical research or research on relatively inaccessible groups of offenders such as white-collar or professional criminals (Hobbs 1994). These share the limitations outlined above – they may not be representative and are inevitably based on respondents' interpretations of their behaviour. As Hobbs points out, autobiographies of notorious offenders may be written with the film in mind (Hobbs 1994)!

Crime trends and patterns

Despite the explosion of statistical sources about crime, it remains hazardous to make any but the broadest statements about trends and patterns, bearing in mind all the pitfalls of variations in the propensity of witnesses to report crime, police recording methods, definitions of what, for example, is counted as violent crime and how these might have changed over time or vary between different parts of the country or jurisdiction. There are now two distinct sources of figures, police recorded crime and victim surveys, the latter of which are generally regarded as more accurate. Since the BCS commenced in the early 1980s, the two have been compared, and the annual *Crime in England and Wales* now combines both. Nonetheless they provide different pictures of trends which can be confusing. Moreover, since the 1980s, crime figures, along with criminal justice, have been politicized (Reiner 2007d), with apparent rises and falls being regularly disputed and attributed, often falsely, to government action or inaction. Box 3.4 provides two examples of misrepresenting crime figures – one in which different newspapers reported the same set of statistics in completely different ways and the other where a politician was criticized for taking figures out of context. While subsequent chapters will look in more detail at specific issues, the following section provides a broad snapshot of some of the main patterns of crime.

Box 3.4 Misleading statistics?

1 An entry from the CJ Scotland website (*www.cjscotland.org.uk*) on 28/4/10 listed headlines following the publication of 'Racist Incidents Recorded by the Police 2004-05 to 2008-09' by the Scottish government:

'Racist incidents in Scotland increase by an eighth in five years' *Daily Record*

'Rise in number of race attack victims' *Herald*

'Aberdeen "is worst city for racism"' *Scotsman*

'Race-crime figures are shocking, say MSPs' *Press and Journal*

'Police record a fall in racist incidents in Scotland' *BBC*

The press release by the Scottish government: **'Racist Incidents 2004–05 to 2008–09'** highlights a 2 per cent decrease from 2007/8–2008/9. The overall number has increased from 2004–5 (see also Chapter 10).

2 In March 2010, an opposition spokesperson was criticized by the UK statistics authority for 'misrepresenting' data by suggesting increases in violent crime since 2002. This was inaccurate because the police have changed the way in which violent crime is recorded. The authority had in the past criticized the government (BBC News 2010a).

Is crime rising or falling?

In recent decades it has generally been assumed that crime is rising with the latest BCS reporting that around three-quarters of respondents think that it is increasing (Walker et al 2009: 10). Most indicators, however, suggest that it has fallen since a peak in the mid 1990s, although there was a massive rise from the early part of the century. Before the 1920s, fewer than 100,000 offences were recorded annually, whereas in 1994, 5 million notifiable offences were recorded (Barclay 1995). Rises and falls for specific offences in England and Wales are illustrated in Figure 3.3 and are broadly similar for other UK jurisdictions. A number of broad changes have been associated with this and not all of the rise can be attributed to a 'real' increase in crime. Reiner (2007d) identifies three broad periods:

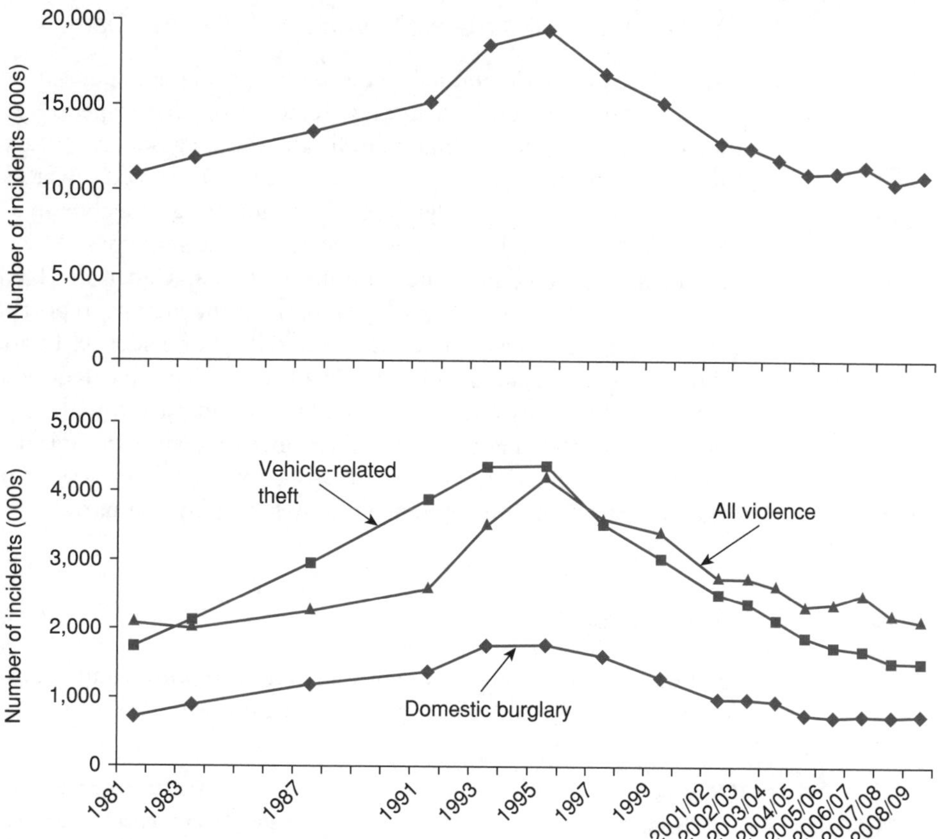

Figure 3.3 Trends in crime, 1981–2008/9

Source: Walker et al (2009), Vol. 1

The late 1950s–1980: A rapid rise in recorded crime

Overall crime rates are strongly influenced by so-called 'volume crimes' such as property crimes (as they make up so much of the total). Much of the increase in crime up to the 1980s was accounted for by rising levels of recorded burglary. This is generally attributed to a rise in recording, brought about by a variety of factors including rising numbers of police officers, the greater ease of reporting crime brought about by the growth in telephones and the rising value of consumer items in the home – in turn related to rising levels of insurance (Maguire 2007; Reiner 2007d). The growth of car ownership added to increased opportunities for crime.

The 1980s–1992: a crime explosion

While police recorded figures and the BCS indicated different patterns, most agree that crime, not only in Britain, increased dramatically during this period. This is generally attributed, argues Reiner, to a continuation of the above factors along with the impact of major economic and social changes brought about by de-industrialization and the decline of manufacturing industries and the high levels of unemployment and inequality which followed.

1992 onwards: ambiguously falling crime, rising fear

From 1992, the two 'counting' methods diverged. Police figures dropped from 1992–5 which could have resulted, argues Reiner, from fewer people reporting crime as they were accustomed to higher levels and, he suggests, from the police recording a lower proportion, as they were under pressure to record fewer crimes. From 1997 the divergence continued, with the BCS indicating a decline in victimization from 1995–2005/6 but police figures indicating some increases. Much of this could be accounted for by changes in counting methods. Under the NCRS, for example, police record a 'violent crime' on the basis of the victims' report rather than on the basis, as was previously the case, of some kind of evidence. In addition, in the late 1990s, common assaults and harassment were added to categories of violent 'crime' (Maguire 2007). Any increases up to 2004 would, therefore, be considerably smaller and there has been a consistent decline since then with victimization now said to be at its lowest level since 1981. The reasons for the fall are less clear although Reiner suggests that falling unemployment may have played a part.

Offence patterns

Figures 3.4a and b indicate the proportions of reported and recorded crimes, denoting, for England and Wales, the different proportions of offences suggested by BCS

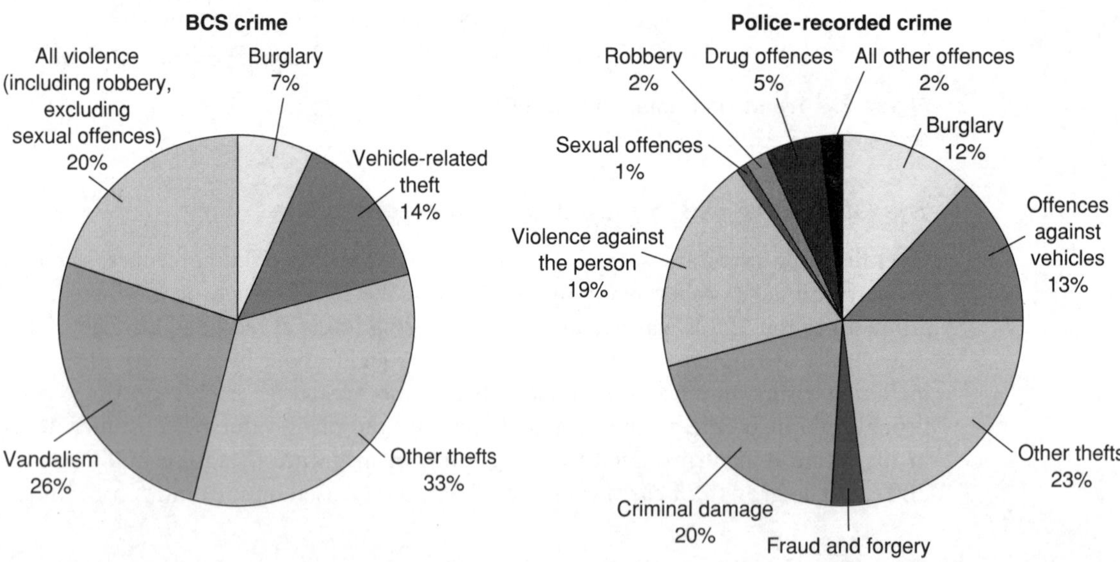

The 2008/09 BCS is a face-to-face survey of adults aged 16 or over resident in households who are asked about their experiences of crime in the year prior to interview. As such the survey provides estimates of crime against the **individual** and also **household property**.

Police-recorded crime statistics are an administrative data source based on crimes reported to and recorded by the police in 2008/09 and cover crimes against **individuals** and both **domestic** and **commercial property**.

(a)

Figure 3.4a BCS crime and police-recorded crime by type of crime 2008/9, England and Wales

Source: Walker et al (2009), Vol. 1, p. 16

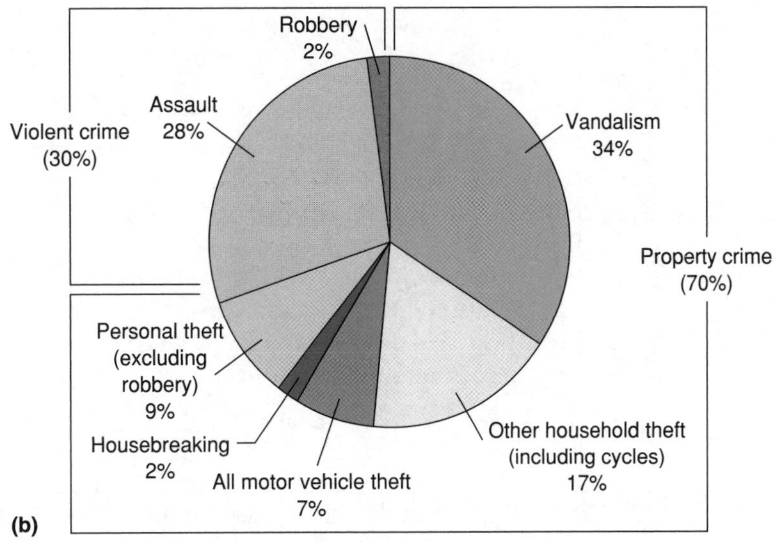

Figure 3.4b Proportion of SCJS crime in each aggregated crime group 2008/9

Source: MacLeod et al (2009)

and police-recorded crime, and, for Scotland, based on the SCJS, slightly different shares of property and violent crime respectively (see below). This confirms that, as outlined in Chapter 2, the media vastly over-represent the prevalence of violent and sexual crimes at the expense of more typical property crimes. Moreover, it will be seen in Chapter 11 that many violent crimes are relatively minor, and the figures are somewhat inflated by the inclusion, outlined above, of more trivial incidents. In 2007/8, for example, BCS figures indicate that half of violent crime reported by victims involved no injury and only 2 per cent recorded by the police were described as 'serious' – involving an actual or threatened life-threatening injury (Kershaw et al 2008). Knives were involved in only 6 per cent of cases, glasses and bottles in a further 4 per cent, and guns in only 1 per cent.

These figures have to be considered alongside reporting and recording variations – the discrepancies between BCS crime counts and police figures are in part attributable to the failure of victims to report less serious incidents to the police, and to the inclusion in police figures of offences which they themselves discover, such as drug offences. Offences against businesses such as commercial burglary and robbery are also not included in victim surveys.

Offenders

Criminal statistics which cover court proceedings provide some details of the characteristics of offenders, in particular sex and age, and Figure 3.5, based on Scottish figures, dramatically illustrates the so-called age 'curve', with crime peaking in the mid teens, along with the very different conviction rates of males and females. In England and Wales in 2007, the peak age for men being convicted for was 17, and for women, 15. Figures for race and ethnicity are provided in separate statistics on

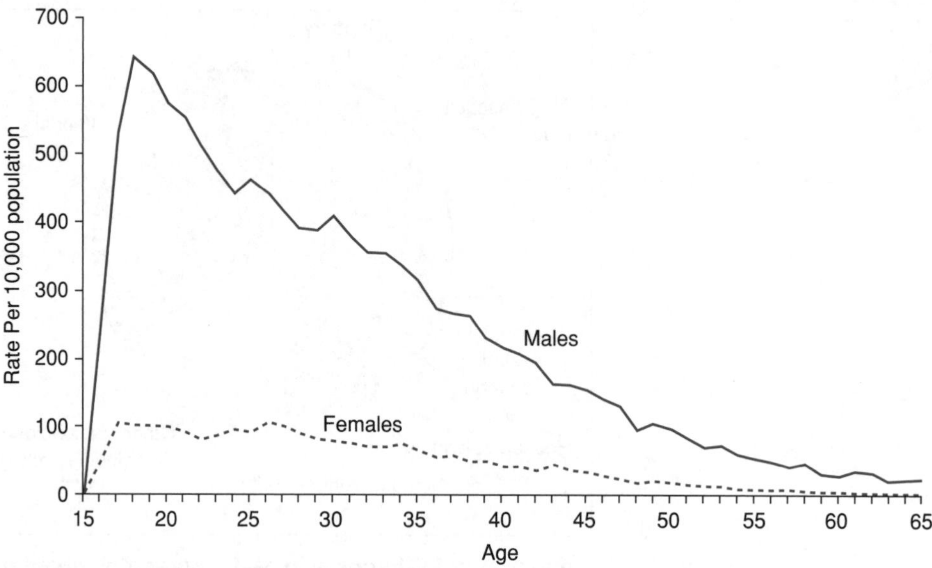

1. Mid-2008 population estimates for Scotland.
2. Common assault, breach of the peace, racially aggravated conduct or harassment, firearms offences and social security offences.

Figure 3.5 Individual offenders per 10,000 population with one or more charges provided in court in 2008–9 for a crime or relevant offence

Source: MacLeod et al (2009) p. 22

ethnicity and the criminal justice process, and prison statistics are also used to look at socio-economic status and race and ethnicity (see Chapters 6 and 10) although it is recognized that only a minority of atypical offenders are imprisoned. They indicate, however, that in comparison with the general population, the prison population contains

> many more males, young people, black people, poor people, poorly educated people and people with disturbed childhoods than one would find in a random sample.
> (Maguire 2007: 286)

It should, however, be pointed out that these figures do not necessarily represent any real differences in offending as some offences and offenders are, quite simply, more likely to be caught. The inclusion of more figures for white-collar or corporate crimes would alter the age distribution, as well as any attempt to look at social class, and the gender ratio would also be affected if full figures for family violence were available.

Victims

The growth of victim surveys has vastly increased knowledge about victims and victimization, discussed at length in Chapter 6. Some very general contrasts are illustrated in Figure 3.6, which challenge some of the popular images outlined in

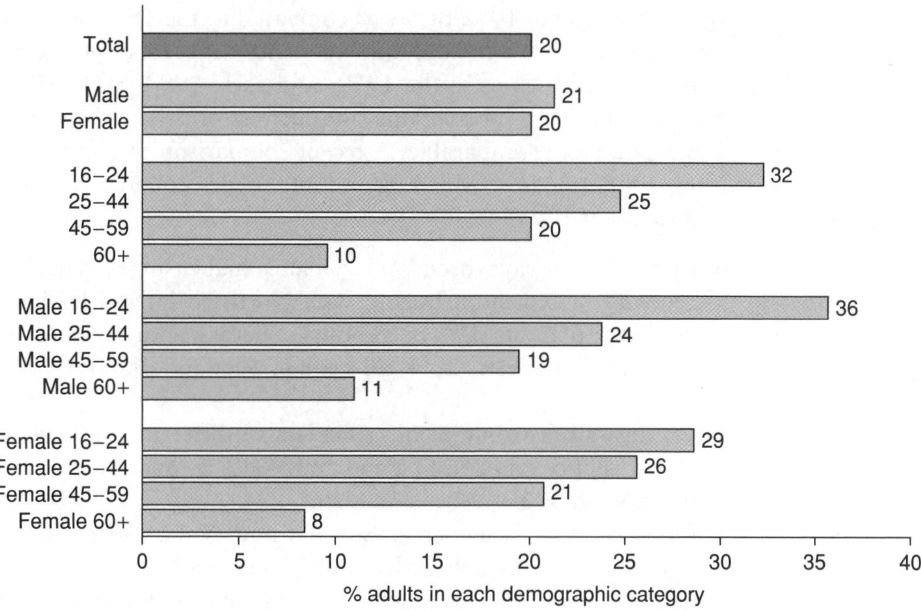

Figure 3.6 Varying risk of crime – proportion of adults who were victims of crime by age and gender

Source: MacLeod et al (2009) p. 35

Chapter 2. Older people have a lower risk of victimization, despite the publicity given to attacks on them, and young men aged between 16 and 24 are most at risk. Subsequent chapters will confirm some other now well-known features of victimization, for example that women are far more likely to be raped by acquaintances and murdered by spouses or lovers than by strangers. Young men are more vulnerable to assault and robbery. This is generally assumed to reflect their lifestyles as they are more likely to go to pubs and clubs where the majority of recorded assaults take place. These figures must also, of course, be interpreted in the light of crimes which are less likely to be counted (see Chapter 10). Older people and the very young are vulnerable to abuse in the home and members of racial and ethnic minorities are more at risk from racially motivated crimes (see Chapter 9).

National and regional distribution of crime

England and Wales, Scotland and Northern Ireland

Some international victim surveys indicated that England and Wales had a comparatively high rate of victimization, Scotland a medium rate, and Northern Ireland a low rate (Van Dijk and Mayhew 1993; Barclay 1995) and there continues to be variations between the three jurisdictions. During the 1980s, while both the BCS and recorded crime statistics charted rises, Scottish figures showed an increase in reporting crime but a fall in recorded crime (Kinsey and Anderson 1992). Differences widened when the 1992 BCS was compared to the 1993 SCS (Anderson and Leitch 1994) and Scottish cities did not experience the scale of public disorder experienced in many English cities in the 1980s and early 1990s (Fyfe 1997). It is not easy to compare different jurisdictions although efforts have been made to make some crime data more comparable. A recent comparison of crime surveys across the UK, using 2008/9 figures, with England and Wales counted as one jurisdiction, found that (Muir 2010):

- Crime has always been and remains higher in England and Wales than in Scotland or Northern Ireland with Northern Ireland having much lower levels of crime than its UK neighbours. Victimization rates are 23.4 per cent in England and Wales, 20.4 per cent in Scotland and 13.4 per cent in Northern Ireland.
- The overall distribution of crime is also different. Violent crimes make up just 20 per cent of crime in England and Wales compared to 29 per cent in Northern Ireland and 30 per cent in Scotland.
- Property crime is higher in England and Wales (80 per cent) than in Scotland (70 per cent) or Northern Ireland (71 per cent).
- Crime has not fallen as quickly in Scotland as in England and Wales or Northern Ireland since devolution in 1999.

These comparisons are illustrated in the national victim surveys. A comparison of the 2007/08 NICS and the 2007/08 BCS, for example, confirms the consistently lower risk of becoming a victim of crime in Northern Ireland than in England and Wales, figures for 2006/07 being 14.2 and 24.4 per cent respectively (Freel et al 2009). Figure 3.7 illustrates the differences between Scotland and England and Wales. These must be treated with some caution as some offences are differently classified. The

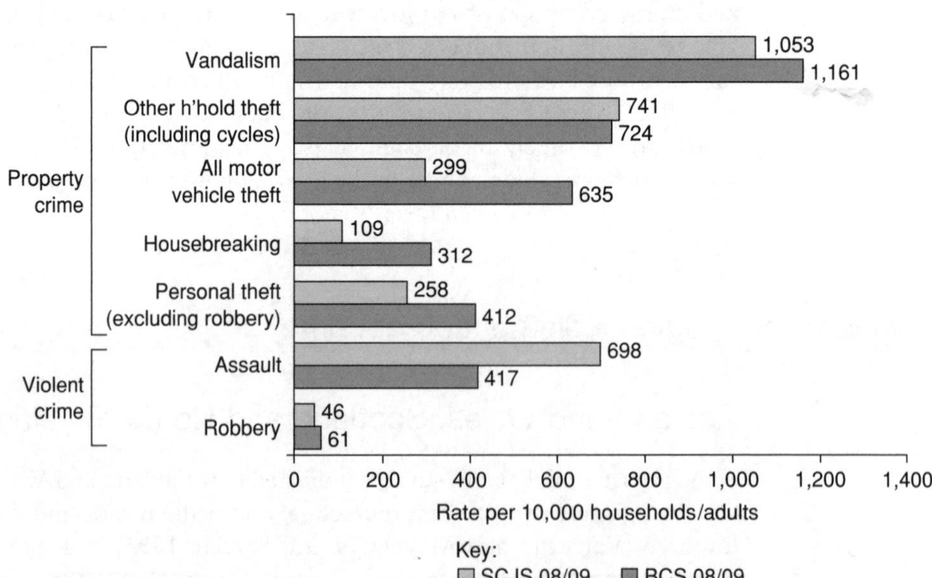

Figure 3.7 Comparison of incidence rates in Scotland with England and Wales

Source: MacLeod et al (2009) p. 29

Scottish offence of housebreaking, for example, is more narrowly defined than the English offence of burglary, but if the Scottish offence of 'other household offences' is taken into account, figures are still lower (Muir 2010).

While Wales is generally combined with England, as in 'England and Wales', a separate statistical bulletin for Wales indicates that it too has lower rates for most types of crime than England, illustrated in Figure 3.8 (Higgins and Millard 2009). It also reports that:

- In 2008/09 the total recorded crime rate in Wales (79 offences per 1,000 population) was below the rate for England and Wales as a whole (86 offences per 1,000 population).
- The recorded crime rates in Wales were the same or lower than the overall England and Wales rates in all the main offence groups with the exception of criminal damage.
- The total number of crimes recorded by the police in Wales fell by 3 per cent in 2008/09 compared with a reduction of 5 per cent across England and Wales as a whole.

These differences are not easy to account for, and are likely to be related to the many factors which underlie crime varying across different countries and regions. It is possible, for example, that cultural factors, such as greater levels of alcohol use and its association with violence may account for the higher proportion of violent crime in Scotland and more details of some of these variations will be explored in relevant chapters.

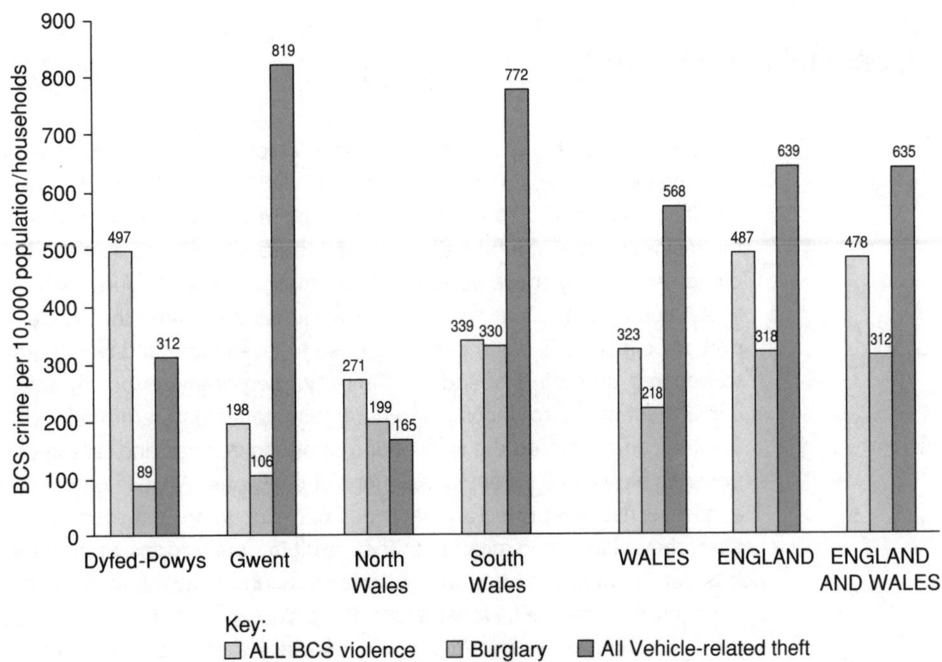

Figure 3.8 BCS incidence rate by type of crime for police force area in England and Wales 2008/9

Source: Higgins and Millard (2009)

Local variations

There are also regional and local variations in victimization and in general terms, risks of victimization are higher in urban than rural areas. In 2008/9, for England and Wales, the risk of being a victim of any household crime was 13 per cent in rural areas compared to 18 per cent for urban areas. Comparisons across English regions indicate that the risk of personal crime is significantly higher in London, which tends to have the highest victimization rates for all kinds of crime, and lower in the East of England and the South West region. Fifty-nine per cent of robberies were recorded in just three forces, the Metropolitan Police, Greater Manchester and the West Midlands (Higgins and Millard 2009). In Scotland, the number of crimes recorded per 10,000 population is higher in police forces which contain large cities, such as Strathclyde and Lothian and Borders, and lower in primarily rural police force areas such as Dumfries and Galloway and the Northern area (Scottish Government 2008). In Northern Ireland, the highest numbers of recorded crime were found in South Belfast, and the lowest in the rural region of Moyle (PSNI 2010).

Geographical differences are related to social differences, which will be discussed in more detail in subsequent chapters. Research has, for example, indicated the existence of crime 'hotspots', or high crime areas, micro areas in which residents are regularly victimized by a variety of crimes, and which are often linked to deprivation (Davies et al 2007). Review Question 2 below, asks readers to consult their own local crime maps.

Concluding comments

This chapter has looked at the processes which transform events into crimes and people into criminals. Appreciating this process is vital before any conclusions can be drawn from official crime figures. The chapter then explored the many ways of researching crime and the major sources of information about it, before turning to some of the broad patterns of crime revealed by these sources of information. Official figures were seen to have many limitations and tell us as much about what kinds of crime the police, often with the support of politicians and the public, choose to investigate and which groups are more likely to become convicted offenders. Similarly interpretations of any trends and patterns of crime must take into account the unrepresentative nature of many studies on crime. The latter section explored the distribution of offences, rises and falls in crime rates and comparisons between different jurisdictions and regions. While in general terms these indicate a massive rise in reported and recorded crime up to around the mid 1990s and a fall thereafter, they also have limitations. They exclude many forms of crime and many rises and falls can be attributed as much to changes and variations in 'counting' methods than to changes in crime itself. Nonetheless, there do appear to have been massive rises in some forms of crime up to the mid 1990s and falls thereafter. Some of the theories used to explain these trends will be explored in Chapters 4 and 5.

Subsequent chapters will take some of these broad indicators as a starting point for further analysis and critically evaluate how official information about crime affects our understanding of apparent relationships between crime and wider patterns of inequality such as age, gender, race and class. They also affect which crimes are more likely to be the subject of public and political concern. To the extent, for example, that sexual and violent crimes are over-represented and youth crime is the subject of moral panics, surveys and research focus more specifically on these kinds of crime. While, as seen above, a more balanced view may be gained from academic research, particularly qualitative, it too is affected by predominant assumptions about crime. Much research is funded by governments and universities who are themselves reliant on government funding and need to demonstrate their relevance to policy areas. Where crime is concerned this means researching the kinds of crime and asking the kinds of questions which governments prioritize. Obtaining funding to research crimes which damage the environment, financial crimes and crimes committed by state agencies is much more difficult as these are not considered to be part of the 'crime problem' to which governments seek an answer. To critical criminologists, as will be seen in Chapter 5, this underlines the association between official sources of crime, criminological research and what has been described as establishment or administrative criminology (Hillyard et al 2004).

Review questions

1. You (or your group) have been asked to carry out research on a particular form of crime. You should choose a form of crime which particularly interests you and consider what kinds of question you want to ask and what kinds of research you might carry out. You will also wish to consider:
   - **(a)** (i) What information would you like to gather?
     - (ii) Where would you locate it?
     - (iii) What problems might you encounter?
     - (iv) What kinds of research are most appropriate for this particular form of crime?
     - (v) What questions are you asking?
   - **(b)** (i) How is the particular form of crime defined?
     - (ii) How is it affected by the processes of defining and producing crime and offenders discussed in this chapter?
   - **(c)** (i) What kinds of information are widely available?
     - (ii) What can be learnt from official statistics and victim surveys? (This should involve locating relevant statistics.)
     - (iii) What other kinds of information are available?
     - (iv) What are the main limitations of these sources for the particular form of crime which you are investigating?
2. Locate a 'crime map' and other details of crime rates in your local area. How accurate do you think this is? Do any features surprise you and why? What offences might, for example, be over and under-represented?

Key reading

Few books are devoted solely to all the areas covered in this chapter, although most criminology texts contain a chapter on criminal statistics and refer to criminological research. Particularly useful are:

Coleman, C. and Moynihan, J. (1996) ***Understanding Crime Data: Haunted by the Dark Figure***, Buckingham: Open University Press. While somewhat out of date, particularly in terms of the figures it uses, this is an excellent account of the uses and limitations of the main sources of crime data and remains an entertainingly written and interesting introduction to the subject.

King, R. and Wincup, E. (eds) (2007) ***Doing Research on Crime and Justice***, 2nd edn, Oxford: Oxford University Press. This is a comprehensive collection of articles about researching different aspects of crime and criminal justice, looking at the problems encountered by researchers and at some solutions.

Maguire, M. (2007) **'Crime Data and Statistics'** in M. Maguire, R. Morgan and R. Reiner (eds) *The Oxford Handbook of Criminology*, 4th edn, Oxford: Clarendon Press. This is a comprehensive account of official crime data, containing a useful exposition of the major changes which have affected how crime is 'counted'.

Reiner, R. (2007d) ***Law and Order: An Honest Citizen's Guide to Crime and Control***, Cambridge: Polity Press. A readable account of aspects of crime and its control which contains interesting chapters on how crime statistics are constructed, how crime rates can be interpreted and some of the factors which can explain trends and patterns in crime.

Websites

Official statistics and surveys can be accessed through government websites as indicated in relevant Figures and below.

England and Wales:
www.justice.gov.uk/publications/statistics
http://www.homeoffice.gov.uk/rds/index.html

Northern Ireland:
http://www.psni.police.uk
www.nio.gov.uk/national-statistics

Scotland-links for all relevant statistics at:
www.scotland.gov.uk/Topics/Statistics/browse/Crime-Justice

An excellent source of links for Scottish crime statistics and research is CJ Scotland: **www.cj.scotland.org.uk**

Chapter 4
Understanding crime: crime, culture and social structure

This chapter will look at:

- ➜ The 'criminological project'
- ➜ Classical criminology
- ➜ Pathological offenders?
- ➜ Pathological crime?
- ➜ Pathological society?
  - Anomie
  - Social Disorganization and the Chicago School
- ➜ Pathological subcultures?

Scholars from many disciplines have attempted to understand the phenomenon of crime and the study now known as criminology developed from around the middle of the nineteenth century. Different disciplines such as law, psychology, sociology, economics and biology have all explored crime. No one perspective (a way of looking at crime) can fully explain or answer all the questions to be asked about crime, and there is no clear-cut history of which theories have predominated in different periods (Rock 2007a) although some have more resonance at particular historical moments (Valier 2002). In times of economic hardship, for example, explanations focusing on the relationship between social inequalities, economic factors and crime tend to assume greater importance.

Different disciplines look at crime in different ways, and ask different kinds of questions. Most commonly asked, perhaps unsurprisingly, is what makes people commit crime? This leads to other questions about what affects human behaviour in general. Are people free to choose actions or are their choices determined by their biological or psychological characteristics or social circumstances? Are those who commit crime somehow different and what form does any difference take? A major duality running through this kind of approach is whether criminals are 'born or made', that is, whether crime, like other physical characteristics, can be inherited, or whether aspects of the environment in which a person grows up is related to subsequent criminality. Research following the assumption that criminals are 'different' aims to identify these differences, often associated with deficits or pathologies and seen as abnormal. On the other hand, others see crime as normal in society, and indeed point out that it can perform a positive function for society as well as individuals.

Some theories reflect the popularized assumptions about crime and offenders prevalent throughout previous centuries and explored in Chapter 2. Descriptions such as 'evil', 'beasts' or 'fiends' imply individual biological or psychological deficits. Society itself can be seen as 'sick', and crime cast as a cancer attacking the fabric of society. Areas of cities, families and whole cultures can be seen as 'failing' or dysfunctional and as contributing to crime.

This chapter will broadly contrast sociological with other explanations, tracing the different ways in which crime has been associated with various pathologies, dealing largely, although not exclusively, with theories which developed up to the mid twentieth century. It will start by outlining individual theories which, while the focus of this text is on sociological approaches, are essential to our understanding of other approaches, which built on their perceived limitations. Subsequent sections will introduce sociological approaches. Durkheim's arguments about the normality of crime will be explored before a consideration of the anomie perspective, social disorganization and subcultural theories. Each section will outline a different approach and look at its strengths and weaknesses.

The criminological project

Early criminologists aimed to develop more rational and efficient ways of dealing with crime – often described as the 'criminological project'. The application of rational thought and scientific investigation reflected the optimism of an era in which scientific and industrial progress had fuelled the development of new, modern societies. It was felt that crime could be systematically measured, its causes scientifically established and a cure found. The criminal statistics, themselves produced by modern statistical methods, were assumed to measure crime. Crime had previously been seen as the product of 'demons', 'evil' or 'sinners' and punishments were often barbaric and unpredictable (Hopkins Burke 2005). Two major, contrasting, strands of criminology emerged out of this, described by Hopkins Burke as the 'rational actor' and 'predestined actor' models. What is now known as 'classical criminology' saw crime as the outcome of a rational decision-making process on the part of offenders and aimed to codify and apply rational thinking to criminal justice. Positivist criminologists started with the assumption that crime emerged out of biological, genetic or psychological factors which affected offenders' behaviour, meaning that crime was in a sense 'predestined'.

Classical criminology

The focus of classical criminology was primarily on devising rational means of punishing offenders, based on the underlying assumption that offenders chose to commit crime having weighed up its consequences. This was based on thinking which asserted that society was based on a 'social contract' into which people freely entered, giving up some of their liberties to protect the rest of society from threats to private property. In some versions of this, such as the work of Thomas Hobbes (Hobbes 1651/1968), life in a state of nature would be 'nasty, brutish and short' making the rule of law essential for the development of society. Thinkers in this tradition, such as Beccaria (1767/1963), Bentham (1970) and Mill (1963) assumed that people were naturally hedonistic and that crime arose from this trait. To Bentham, potential criminals made a rational calculation which balanced the pleasure to be gained from crime against the 'pain' of punishment. The aim of criminal justice and punishment was to deter people from choosing to commit crime by altering this calculation. Bentham, described as a 'hedonistic utilitarian' (Hopkins Burke 2005), further argued that criminal behaviour resulted from upbringing rather than being innate, that people are rational creatures who will seek pleasure while trying to avoid pain and that offenders lacked the self-discipline to control their passions. Punishment must outweigh any pleasure derived from crime, but law must not be so harsh as to reduce the greatest happiness of the greatest number.

The focus of classical criminology on rational punishment meant that it did not provide a full analysis of the causes of crime and, unlike postivism, it was not based on empirical research. It was nonetheless the first attempt to argue that crime could be studied in a neutral and objective way, and its view of the criminal as an actor freely choosing to commit crime re-emerged in the late twentieth century and is, as will be seen in Chapter 5, an important feature of many contemporary theories. At the same time there are serious problems with the notion of free will and rational choice. This cannot, for example, account for crimes committed by people who cannot be seen as responsible for their own choices, such as the very young or those suffering from mental illness, or for so-called 'crimes of passion', which may be spontaneous and not based on any form of rational calculus. The notion of 'free will' also fails to consider the extent to which offenders' decisions are constrained by their psychological, family or social circumstances such as poverty or social inequality. Therefore they neglect the social causes of crime along with the role of factors investigated by other criminologists, outlined below.

Pathological offenders?

In contrast to the 'rational actor model' are theories which assert that offenders' actions are predetermined. Criminals, it was argued, are different and a major thrust of research was to identify what factors distinguished between offenders and non-offenders. An enormous number of characteristics were investigated and this section will focus on biological and psychological approaches as these most clearly illustrate the research and thinking involved. Researchers used what were seen as experimental methods, based on quantitative research, which compared samples of convicted offenders with samples of the so-called normal, non-criminal population. In what Coleman and Norris (2000) describe as the 'spot the difference' method, they were, in effect, trying to develop a formula which could be hypothetically expressed as '*criminal parent + aggressive personality + broken home = crime*'.

Are criminals 'born' or 'made'?

Some of the earliest theories hypothesized that crime was biologically determined and could be inherited. Often quoted is the work of criminologists such as Lombroso

(1897), who, working in the late nineteenth century, claimed that criminals were biological throwbacks to an earlier stage of evolution and were distinguished by their body type. Others explored the extent to which criminality could be inherited and, like illness, has also been related to biochemical conditions. These main themes are summarized below.

Body types

From studies of offenders in custody, Lombroso concluded that they were distinguished by physical stigmata such as large hands, ears, feet and tattoos, receding chins and twisted noses (Lombroso 1897). He identified four categories of criminals:

- *born criminals* who could be distinguished by physical atavistic characteristics;
- *insane criminals*, described as idiots, imbeciles, paranoiacs, epileptics and alcoholics;
- *occasional criminals*, depicted as criminaloids who committed crimes in response to opportunities, but who had innate traits;
- *criminals of passion.*

Lombroso's work is cited in all criminology texts as he was one of the first to attempt to categorize offenders, although his work has been much discredited, particularly as his methods, based entirely on samples of prisoners, did not include a control group of non-offenders (Hopkins Burke 2005; Tierney 2006).

Source: Mary Evans Picture Library

His work echoed assumptions about the association of body types with other 'degenerates' such as gypsies, Jews and homosexuals and popular images of the time: Dracula, for example, was described as having massive eyebrows, sharp and protruding teeth, red lips, a cruel mouth, pointed ears, broad and squat fingers and long sharp nails, and as being deficient by not having 'a full man's brain' (Valier 2002: 18), and later writers returned to the topic. Some were linked to the eugenics movement, which associated criminality, along with alcoholism, feeble-mindedness and prostitution, to bad breeding and the criminal was said to be possessed of a hereditary deficiency of conscience and lack of self-control (Valier 2002). Goring's study of the English convict, based on 3,000 prisoners, found that while criminals did not differ in kind from law abiding persons, their characteristics suggested that there is a physical, mental and moral type of person who tends to be a criminal (Valier 2002; Hopkins Burke 2005). Other theories linked crime to athletic body types which were related to aggression and many studies up to the mid twentieth century measured physical characteristics such as height and weight (Sheldon 1949; Glueck and Glueck 1950).

It was always difficult to establish exactly how these characteristics could be related to criminality. While it might be assumed that some offences require physical strength and thereby be related to physical factors, many others, fraud for example, do not. In addition, physical features are related to social expectations and stereotypes – we might expect large or athletically built people to be aggressive. At the time Lombroso was writing tattoos were viewed negatively and easily associated with shady characters; nowadays, however, they are widely accepted.

Inherited criminality?

Others asked whether criminality could be inherited, like hair colour. One way of exploring this was to look at whether identical twins were both likely to be criminal, taking account of the possible effects of their similar environment. Identical twins brought up apart were investigated and while some association was found it was extremely difficult to separate biological inheritance from the environment as, even when adopted, twins are often raised in similar social and economic circumstances (Christiansen 1974). An apparently more promising way of looking at biological inheritance emerged with the discovery of the 'criminal gene'. Inmates from an institution for offenders considered to be 'insane' were discovered to have a different pattern of chromosomes – an extra 'Y' chromosome was subsequently linked to greater height and aggression. Later studies found, however, that this affected only a small proportion of the population and was found in non-criminals (Jacobs et al 1965; and see Williams 1994).

Biochemistry and crime?

Other biological approaches have investigated the possible role of biochemical processes in the brain – which may not be inborn, but a result of allergies, glandular problems, diet or even the consumption of junk food containing chemicals. Children affected by food allergies or glandular disorders do suffer from hyperactivity making them less likely to learn social skills and more difficult to discipline, and links with attention-deficit hyperactivity disorder (ADHD) have also been explored (Williams 1994; Newburn 2007).

There are many problems with these approaches and with the methods used, which almost always relied on samples of convicted offenders. Their main problems can broadly be summarized as follows:

Can they establish the causes of crime?

In order to argue that biological factors 'cause' crime, a very strong relationship would be necessary. Yet none of the characteristics found among samples of offenders is unique to criminals as they are also found among non-offenders and so-called 'normal' people. Moreover, many of these features are found in only a small number of offenders and affect only some kinds of offending.

Crime is socially constructed

A major problem with these theories is that, as seen in Chapter 1, crime is socially constructed. Its definition is dependent on cultural and social definitions and it encompasses a vast range of behaviour which is not consistently regarded as crime. How, therefore, can a tendency towards crime be biologically determined? Even if it could be assumed that a tendency to aggression could be inherited, whether or not aggression is interpreted as criminal depends on its social and cultural context. The boxer or soldier, for example, may be expected and indeed encouraged to display aggression, but this is tightly defined by rules.

Born or made?

Another major problem is illustrated in what is often referred to as the 'nature–nurture' debate – how much is inborn and how much affected by the environment? Body type, for example, can be related to diet, which is in turn related to social class and environmental factors. Children may not only inherit genetic characteristics but also learn a set of values from their parents. Thus if a child of criminal parents offends, it could be because they have learnt criminal values rather than being genetic.

The 'mad' and the 'bad'

Similar problems are encountered in exploring links between psychological traits and crime, which has been the subject of considerable research (see, for example, Hollin 1989; 2007). Crime has been linked to personality and to mental illness, in themselves difficult to define and measure. It is also debatable whether psychological dispositions can be inherited or are a product of the environment. This section will selectively focus on some major themes of this research while other psychological approaches will be encountered in later chapters.

The criminal personality?

It is often argued that some kinds of personality are related to crime – thus Eysenck (1977) related criminality to extremes of extraversion, associated with assertive, creative, dominant, active and sensation-seeking individuals; neuroticism, associated with anxious, depressed, moody, shy and emotional people with low self-esteem; and psychoticism, associated with people described as aggressive, anti-social, egocentric, impulsive and lacking empathy. Subsequent research has, however, not conclusively supported these theories which were linked also to body types. While some studies have found that young offenders in institutions scored highly on these scales, any associations could be a result of the traumas associated with being caught or a result of institutional life.

Crime and mental illness

Other forms of mental illness have been linked to crime. Schizophrenics may murder people when under the influence of delusions and depression has been linked to murder followed by suicide (West 1965 and see Chapter 11). There are, however, several problems with linking crime and mental illness and other psychological traits, summarized below.

- *The nature of the relationship*. As with biological theories, to see psychological characteristics as the 'cause' of crime would require a very strong relationship. Yet the mentally ill are no more likely to become criminal than anyone else.
- *Labelling the criminal mentally abnormal?* A circular argument may be involved as it could be assumed that because a person is criminal, they are abnormal and therefore must be mentally or psychologically disturbed. This may be part of a labelling process – if an individual's behaviour is deviant in one respect it must be in others (see Chapter 5).
- *The social construction of crime and mental illness*. Mental illness, like crime, is socially constructed and as indicated above there is no one yardstick against which mental 'normality' and 'abnormality' can be measured.

It can be seen from this very brief outline that many problems surround what are generally described as individual or pathological theories. This does not mean that they are irrelevant. Individuals turn to crime in specific circumstances and individual predispositions, such as mental illness, undoubtedly affect this choice. Nonetheless, these circumstances must also be placed in the context of an offenders' social environment, culture and socio-economic position and their behaviour is socially interpreted and defined. Another major problem with individual theories is their reliance on the so-called experimental method. Research is typically based on studies of convicted offenders, who form an unrepresentative sample of 'offenders', being compared with the so-called normal population, who cannot be assumed to be made up of 'non-offenders'. Any statistical associations may therefore reflect processes of detection and conviction as much as any intrinsic characteristics of offenders. Individual theories do, however, have a lasting appeal and some contemporary theories, as will be seen in Chapter 5, have returned to many of these themes and crime continues to be attributed to genetic or psychological predispositions.

Pathological crime?

Much early sociological work was informed by a functionalist approach which saw harmony and conformity as the norm for a healthy society. Society was likened to a physical organism with all parts playing a function in maintaining the whole, and law was seen as reflecting a consensus over right and wrong. Crime was therefore dysfunctional as it threatened the stability of society and indicated a social problem. Not all, however, shared the view that crime was pathological. The French sociologist, Emile Durkheim, writing in the turbulent decades at the end of the nineteenth century, linked crime to rapid social and economic change and argued that it could perform a social function.

Durkheim: the normal and the pathological

To Durkheim the argument that crime could be normal and healthy emerged from his concern to develop a functionalist approach and to establish sociology as a science. In one of his most famous works, *The Rules of Sociological Method*, he used concepts of 'health' and 'disease' to examine the functions of different phenomena. What was 'normal' and what was 'pathological' must, he argued, be scientifically established. If a phenomenon was present in all known societies, it could be assumed to be normal and its function determined. Following an extensive examination of official statistics he concluded that crime existed in all known societies, and was therefore normal. He then explored how it contributed to the health of society (Durkheim 1964).

To Durkheim, crime and immorality are yardsticks against which to measure conformity and moral standards. Crime is inevitable as, he argued, we cannot imagine a 'society of saints':

> Imagine a society of saints, a perfect cloister of exemplary individuals. Crimes, properly so called, will there be unknown; but faults which appear venial to the layman will create there the same scandal that the ordinary offence does in ordinary consciousness. If then, this society has the power to judge and punish, it will define these acts as criminal and will treat them as such.
>
> (Durkheim 1964, first published in 1895)

Furthermore crime integrates the community, as it serves to clarify and heighten what he called 'moral sentiments' and the 'collective conscience'. Crime brings people together and in talking about and condemning crime, rules are clarified and re-enforced. By identifying 'deviance', normality becomes clearer, and society unites in condemnation of the deviant. Durkheim likened crime to pain – while it is not desirable it is normal and useful.

Not all crime, however, is functional and he went on to argue that too much becomes pathological and can lead to disintegration. Too little crime, on the other hand, indicates that social control is too strong and can lead to stagnation. As Sumner (1994) points out, too much censure leads to inflexibility and some tolerance is needed to enable change. While those who flout or criticize the norms of society may be ostracized and branded as subversives or criminalized, social change and progress may emerge from challenges to normality.

While Durkheim's ideas appear to challenge common sense, they also appeal to it. The media often refers to horrific crimes uniting or bringing the community or nation together in the face of grief. As seen in Chapter 2, moral panics and 'signal crimes' are very often followed by analysis and calls for tougher laws to prevent such occurrences happening again, along with stronger policing and harsher punishment. It is also difficult, as Durkheim points out, to imagine a crime-free society. His recognition that deviance and crime can be a force for social change is also an important insight taken up in later work on criminalization (Sumner 1994). Nonetheless both his methods and arguments have been questioned. Consider the following points:

- Is his argument circular as he assumes that crime is functional because it is common?
- Durkheim, like many other theorists of the time, relied on official statistics, which have been seen to be unreliable.
- Seeing crime as functional to society may neglect its severe effects on individuals, families and communities (Downes and Rock 2007).
- Who is it functional to? The community sentiments which Durkheim discusses may be whipped up in support of establishment or dominant interests or used as a diversion from other problems as seen in Hall et al's (1978) argument that moral panics reflect an 'orchestration' of consensus (Chapters 2 and 5).
- At what point does crime cease to be normal and become pathological? Downes and Rock (2007) point out, for example, that instead of bringing people together crime may isolate them by making them stay in at night, lock their doors and avoid talking to strangers. It can therefore destroy rather than integrate communities.

Pathological society?

While Durkheim's ideas were influential, crime continued to be seen as pathological, with the society itself, the social structure, so-called social disorganization and deviant or delinquent subcultures all being identified.

Anomie

The search for unattainable goals

The notion of anomie also originated in the work of Emile Durkheim who, like many other sociologists of the time, was concerned with the effects of socio-economic change and its threat to social cohesion (Downes and Rock 2007). Then, as now, there were concerns about declining morals, the decline of religion, community and the family and their effect on crime. To Durkheim, social life in pre-industrial societies was based on small communities, and was 'mechanically' regulated by a common morality. This mechanical solidarity was a powerful form of social control, which received few challenges. The growth of industry saw what he described as a new division of labour, or organization of work. Small communities broke up as factories were located in towns. Durkheim envisaged that this would lead to a new form of organic solidarity – in which people's work and the contracts into which they freely entered would become the basis of a different kind of moral order and regulation. In the transitional period, however, the old ways of life and old moral standards were inappropriate.

This created what Durkheim described as 'anomie', a state of normlessness, in which people have few moral standards or constraints to guide them – they lack regulation (Durkheim 1970). Economic growth also heightened people's expectations – creating what he saw as boundless aspirations, which could rarely be fulfilled, leading to a situation in which they constantly searched for the unattainable. Downes and Rock argue that to Durkheim anomie is the 'peculiar disease of modern industrial man', and cite a passage which could equally well apply to current society – 'from top to bottom of the ladder', he argued,

> greed is aroused without knowing where to find ultimate foothold. Nothing can calm it, since its goal is far beyond all it can attain.
>
> (E. Durkheim, *Suicide*, cited in Downes and Rock 2007: 91)

In this situation the individual may be driven to crime or suicide. Again using official statistics, Durkheim claimed that anomic suicide was related to economic change. While, like his work on the functions of crime, his methods were criticized, the notion that crime and other forms of deviance can be related to the frustration and hopelessness of attempting to reach unattainable goals without moral regulation is a powerful one. It has contemporary echoes in the popularly held view that the individualistic self-seeking culture of the 1980s engendered greed and a lack of respect for others which, in turn, saw a variety of crimes flourish (Sumner 1994) and in current discussions of the economic crisis in which the individual 'greed' of, for example, bankers, was accompanied by an absence of either moral or financial regulation (Chapter 15).

Rebels, innovators, retreatists and ritualists

The concept was used and adapted by Merton, writing in the United States, where popular ideology emphasized the American 'dream' in which the United States was seen to provide equal opportunities and where status and rank were less important than achievement. This also created boundless aspirations. At the same time, the United States in the 1930s had many crime problems – many of which grew up around the prohibition of alcohol. As outlined in Chapter 2, gangster movies have a lasting appeal and originated in this era, and juvenile delinquency appeared commonplace in many cities. Merton drew on Durkheim's notion of anomie, arguing that there was a disjunction, or strain, between the culture which promised equal opportunities, and the social structure, which could not produce prosperity for all (Merton 1938). Mass production and consumption and advertising created wants and dissatisfactions. Materialism and wealth became universal goals whose pursuit

Adaptations	Goals	Means
Conformist	+	+
Innovator	+	−
Retreatist	−	−
Ritualist	−	+
Rebel	±	±

+ signifies acceptance; − signifies rejection

Figure 4.1 Adaptations to anomie

was constrained by social values and the law. Hard work, educational achievement and honest business were legitimate means of achieving the goals. Many found, however, that these did not lead to achievement, which created a strain experienced more acutely by those in the lower class – whose opportunities to achieve the goals were blocked. Individuals could adapt to this structurally induced strain in a variety of ways summarized in Figure 4.1.

Most people are not aware of any contradiction and continue to conform – aspiring to the goals and attempting to achieve them through work, promotion or education. Others adopt deviant adaptations. The innovator uses illegitimate means to achieve the goals. Thieves, robbers, fraudsters or organized criminals may turn to crime to obtain material goods and money. To many the innovator is the 'classic' criminal response characteristic of organized criminals who claim that they are merely 'doing business'. Others retreat from the struggle or 'drop out' by rejecting both the goals and the means. This may take the form of alcoholism, drug-taking or suicide or adopting an alternative lifestyle. Ritualists carry on with their day-to-day existence, having abandoned all hope of fulfilment or achievement – the means become the end and they become, in effect, stuck in a rut. Yet others reject the goals and the means and additionally attempt to substitute their own by taking a political or rebellious stance.

Evaluation

Anomie has become one of the most influential concepts in the sociology of crime. Its basic argument is very simple as it sees crime arising from a failure to achieve the goals which are seen as desirable in society. Before exploring its influence, however, some of the main questions raised in its evaluation must be considered (see, for example, Hopkins Burke 2005; Tierney 2006; Downes and Rock 2007). These include:

- *Are the adaptations clearly distinct?* Where, for example, does conformity end and ritualism begin? Many may simply fall into a rut of conformity but have abandoned any hope of success. Is this a deviant adaptation?
- *Why might people become innovators, retreatists, rebels or ritualists?*
- *Is anomie restricted to the lower social classes?* Might it not also be related to the crime of those higher up the social hierarchy who might similarly be frustrated at not reaching the height of their aspirations?
- *How can the theory be tested?* People do not always consciously plan or perceive their actions as motivated by frustrated ambitions.

- *It may become a circular argument* – anomie is inferred from high crime rates which in turn reinforce the theory.
- *Are there universally accepted goals?* Different groups may pursue different goals. Not all members of the lower class may expect to achieve, and women might have different goals from men – Merton's model assumes primarily male goals and it is 'gender blind' and says little about race (Valier 2002).
- *How relevant is it to societies in which, unlike the United States, there is no culture of equal opportunities?* In Britain, for example, when Merton was writing, not all would expect to succeed.
- *How does the situation come about in the first place?* Why can only some achieve? Laurie Taylor, for example, likens Merton's model to the analysis of a fruit machine whose payouts are rigged, but which most players wrongly perceive to be fair. According to Downes and Rock:

> The deviants are those who try to rig the machine to *their* advantage (innovators); who play it blindly and obsessively (ritualists); who ignore its existence (retreatists); or who smash it up and seek a better model (rebels). Nowhere however . . . does Merton tell us who is taking the profits, and who put the machine there in the first place. (Taylor 1971, cited in Downes and Rock 2007: 101)

Despite these powerful criticisms, anomie remains an influential concept and formed the basis of many subsequent theories. It is implied in popular explanations linking crime to consumerism and inequalities of income and wealth. It provides a persuasive explanation of relationships between crime and social disadvantage, and can also explain the apparent paradox of why crime rates appear to rise along with rising prosperity (Downes and Rock 2007, and see Chapters 5 and 7). Durkheim's ideas also recognize the search for ever greater fulfilment in a society in which there are fewer constraints on individualism and temptations are aroused by media and advertising images. To Sumner (1994) it recognizes the contradiction between the relentless search for profit and other forms of fulfilment and the need for moral regulation. Moreover, argue Downes and Rock, the many criticisms do not invalidate the model. While there may be few universal goals, different goals, if not achievable, also produce anomie. The deviant responses of school students who vandalize schools or truant could be related to their failure to achieve the school's official goals of high academic success. A similar strain between goals and legitimate means can exist in the workplace and be linked to thefts and fiddles among employees (Chapter 13). The rapid rise in crime in Russia following the development of capitalism has been taken to illustrate the significance of enhanced expectations without fulfilment. Moreover the gap between economically developed and third-world countries can lead to a form of globalized anomie which can be associated with crime and terrorism as film and television images of the affluent lifestyles of Europe and America are beamed across the world (Passas 2000; Young 2007a; and see Chapters 5, 7 and 15).

Social disorganization and the Chicago School

Popular theories also link crime to urban growth or decay, and this was echoed in the work of the Chicago School, the writings of a group of sociologists working in the University of Chicago, based on their extensive research into different aspects

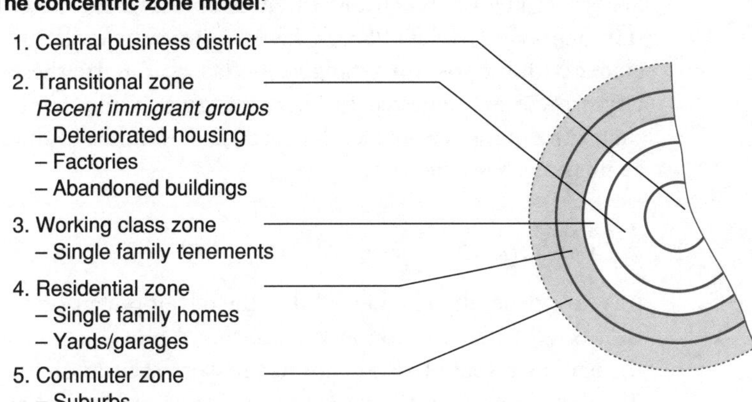

Figure 4.2 Map of Chicago indicating zone of transition

of life in that city in the 1920s and 1930s. Chicago was characterized by a colourful world of street gangs, speakeasies, hustlers, rackets, criminal gangs, prostitutes and drug-takers and was the home of Al Capone, the notorious gangster (see, for example, Sumner 1994; Valier 2002). The concentration of such a wide variety of deviant lifestyles in the inner city indicated what they saw as social disorganization which, to them, was brought about by a natural process of city growth.

To some writers in this school, cities grew according to a natural law, like a tree or plant, and some areas flourished while others decayed. As cities grow, different groups settle in different areas – a process repeated in patterns of resettlement (see, for example, Park and Burgess 1925). In many cities, early, wealthy, residents deserted the crowded and dirty inner cities for the more spacious suburbs. As cities grow, immigrants settle and develop their own communities. Each area is therefore subject to a process of invasion, dominance and succession as new groups move in and become dominant. As cities tend to grow outwards, the inner zone becomes the target of newly arrived immigrants and those at the margins of the legitimate economy who have to find the cheapest forms of housing. This creates a zone of transition which was seen as lacking stability and a dominant culture. Thus the *area* was seen as pathological – an inevitable result of the natural development of the city.

The Chicago School is also associated with fieldwork based on qualitative, observational research which produced a rich seam of studies of different cultures, of street life and the world of the delinquent gang (see, for example, Thrasher 1927; Shaw 1930; Shaw and McKay 1942; Whyte 1943). Many of these became classic examples of participant observation and remain fascinating insights into aspects of life in the inner city. By looking in detail at delinquent and adult gangs and a host of deviant lifestyles from the perspective of their participants, these studies challenged the perception that crime was the product of pathological individuals. Rather, they drew a picture of the normality, attraction and fun of crime and delinquency – delinquents were seen not as sad, pathological individuals but as individuals behaving normally within their own environment.

There is much appeal in the work of the Chicago School, particularly its focus on inner-city urban areas, long associated with crime. Many cities have 'dangerous areas' – signs of which are often dilapidated housing and other obvious neglect (Graham and Clarke 1996). Ghettos, slums, or twilight zones have long been associated with the so-called dangerous classes. But are these areas inevitably caused by city growth as suggested by the Chicago School? Are they disorganized? Why are their inhabitants viewed as dangerous? A number of questions must be asked when evaluating these theories.

Is there a natural law of city growth?

It is now generally recognized that the development of cities is far from 'natural' but is affected by socio-economic factors and housing policy. Housing policy in many British cities sought to destroy what were seen as slums and create new communities, often on the outskirts, or periphery of cities (Graham and Clarke 1996). It will be seen in Chapter 10 that complex socio-economic factors create demographic boundaries within cities which can be related to urban unrest and racial violence. City growth and the character of areas are therefore affected by a variety of factors which take a different form in different cities.

Disorganization, difference and diversity

To some observers, areas characterized by ethnic and cultural diversity, or associated with high crime, gangs, prostitution or drugs might appear to the outsider to be disorganized and to lack any sense of community. Yet in charting the world of the delinquent gang and many other deviant lifestyles, the Chicago School sociologists revealed many different forms of social organization. While the notion of disorganization implies disapproval and pathology, the words difference and diversity need not. Apparent disorganization could be interpreted as indicating a different form of organization rather than pathological disorganization. A circular argument can also be involved – because the area was characterized by high crime it was assumed to be disorganized, which in turn explained crime (Matza 1969; Sumner 1994; Downes and Rock 2007).

Scapegoating cultures?

The assumed pathological nature of disorganization gives rise to another problem. By describing different cultures as deviant, crime was in effect being blamed on the inhabitants' cultures, particularly immigrant cultures. Researchers were looking at these cultures from their own cultural viewpoint, using what some call a middle-class gaze. This could amount to scapegoating different cultures by seeing them as responsible for crime (Sumner 1994). It can also divert attention from the wider social, economic and political policies which may affect the processes described.

Despite these criticisms the Chicago School has proved influential. It provided rich, detailed descriptions of deviant lifestyles and its qualitative methods remain outstanding examples of sociological fieldwork. It drew attention to the geographical distribution of crime and to the importance of looking at crime in its local and cultural context.

Pathological subcultures?

The work of the Chicago sociologists emphasized the normality of delinquent, criminal and other deviant activities within groups. This indicated the existence of subcultures, a term which implies a departure, among a minority, from an assumed majority culture. Within subcultures an alternative value system is found in which deviant and delinquent activities are valued. Subcultures are also characterized by a distinctive language in which words, places, symbols or concepts take on a different meaning recognized and shared by participants. Dress, hairstyles, music, lifestyles, language or speech are all used to identify subcultures. Subcultural theories detail the activities and experiences of participants and interpret the meaning, to those participants, of the subculture along with exploring why they emerge. There have been many different versions of this approach, originating in the United States, and later developed in Britain. While based in different cultures and following a number of different theoretical traditions, a number of common themes can be identified:

- Crime and delinquency is associated with groups within which the activities are seen as normal and attractive – members' commitment is expressed in and inferred from their language and values.
- Their main focus has been on lower-class male subcultures.
- The subculture is seen as a collective response, or solution, to a shared problem, often construed as a failure to achieve cultural goals.

Theories differ in how they account for the emergence and persistence of subcultures and analyse the relationship between subcultures and so-called majority culture. To some, following the Mertonian tradition, subcultures are an adaptation to a strain between cultural goals and approved means; to others they signify opposition to or rebellion against the culture of dominant groups in society – young criminals are seen as rebels, albeit unconscious ones, against a system which denies them the opportunity to achieve. The following sections will look at a selection of the most influential subcultural approaches – starting with earlier American work. Contemporary examples, along with later work in cultural criminology, which follows the subcultural tradition, will be referred to in subsequent chapters. Finally, a number of questions will be raised in order to evaluate the perspective.

American subcultural theories

American subcultural theory was strongly influenced by the empirical work of the Chicago School and by Merton's model of anomie. It has been pointed out that this left open many questions. What, for example, is the mechanism through which anomie leads to crime? What adaptation might be adopted and why?

In an influential work, Cloward and Ohlin (1960) addressed the issue of how and why the potential delinquent should adopt one kind of response rather than another. They followed Edwin Sutherland (1947), who argued that those exposed to more criminal than non-criminal values learnt and were more likely to adopt criminal values in a process of differential association. Cloward and Ohlin argued that youth will be exposed to different kinds of criminal values depending on their local area and culture. They identified three main kinds of criminal and delinquent subculture:

- The *conflict* subculture was found in areas with a history and tradition of fighting, violence and 'gang warfare'.
- The *criminal* subculture was found in areas with a pre-existing criminal culture and adult organized crime. This also provides an illegitimate market to sell the proceeds of property crime.
- The *retreatist* subculture consisted of drop-outs such as drug-takers, winos, hobos, vagrants and bohemians.

The history and traditions of an area provide a pre-existing set of cultural values and what they describe as a structure of illegitimate opportunities. Delinquents engaging in property crime need a supportive economic structure to convert stolen goods into money, and must also learn how to steal cars or break into houses (see Chapter 13). Those wishing to consume illegal drugs require a source of supply. The cultural values of an area and its structure of illegitimate opportunities therefore affect the kinds of subcultures which develop. While the accuracy of Cloward and Ohlin's typology could be criticized, it will be seen in subsequent chapters that the notion of the illegitimate opportunity structure continues to affect analyses of crime.

A different argument was provided by Albert Cohen in *Delinquent Boys* (Cohen 1955). He disagreed with Merton that delinquency was necessarily directed towards achieving goals – vandalism or violence, he argued, were 'negativistic' rather than 'goal directed'. These responses could arise from a rejection of and opposition to mainstream goals. To Cohen, youth were subjected to a series of goals in the mass media and schools which provided a 'middle-class measuring rod' against which failure or success could be assessed. Feelings of failure experienced by lower-class youth led to a reaction out of which an oppositional value system rejecting middle-class values emerged.

These are only two out of many versions of classic subcultural theory which was enormously influential and has an immediate commonsense appeal. They appear to provide a convincing explanation of why lower-class youth might be attracted to crime as a means of achieving status or material goods or as a rejection of the value system under which they are seen as failures. Delinquency thus provides a solution. Nonetheless there were many problems with these theories, and many alternatives were offered, summarized below.

Were there delinquent subcultures?

Subcultural theories assume a male delinquent gang committed to and organized around delinquent activity. Later studies found, however, that these gangs were far from widespread and that their members showed a much lower commitment than suggested. In New York, for example, Yablonsky (1962) found that gangs were more typically made up of a few hard-core 'nutters', and a larger periphery of followers whose commitment was sporadic and who were less attached to delinquent values.

Culture and subculture

Many theories, like anomie, assumed the existence of a majority culture from which the subculture deviated. Others argued that there were many different cultures, in some of which forms of crime and delinquency were tolerated. An early critic of subcultural theory, Walter Miller (1958), argued that within what he called lower-class culture, 'focal concerns' centred on toughness, masculinity, and a tolerance of many forms of theft. Delinquent values were not therefore so much opposed to mainstream culture as a part of lower-class culture.

Too much delinquency?

In providing such a convincing account of why lower-class youth might become delinquent subcultural theory was accused of over-predicting delinquency by explaining too much. Accepting the official statistics, they looked mainly at lower-class life (Matza 1964). Furthermore, delinquent values were not necessarily oppositional. With Sykes, Matza found that delinquents regularly use what they called 'techniques of neutralization' to account for their actions, which echoed conventional values. Thus delinquents were likely to use one of the following strategies (Sykes and Matza 1957):

- A denial of the victim – '*They had it coming*'.
- A denial of injury – '*Didn't do any harm*'.
- A denial of responsibility – '*I was led into it*'.
- Condemning the condemners – '*Everyone's picking on me*'.
- An appeal to higher loyalties – '*I didn't do it for myself*'.

Rather than being committed to delinquency, Matza argued, delinquents drifted between conformity and deviance, directing attention to the attractions of delinquency and to its transitory nature (Matza 1964; 1969).

Application to Britain?

The subcultural approaches looked at so far were developed in America and did not always appear relevant to Britain where violent or criminal gangs were rarer and where there was no well-developed culture of equal opportunities. In Glasgow, where there was a tradition of violent gangs, who, although far less extensive and violent, modelled themselves on Chicago gangs (Davies 2007a; 2007b), Patrick (1973), like Yablonsky, found a group of hardcore leaders and less committed followers. The development of subcultural theory in Britain will be explored below.

British subcultural theories

Critiques of American subcultural theory influenced British work. In an influential study of delinquent youth in Stepney and Poplar in London, Downes found that youth did not conform to the image suggested by Cohen or Cloward and Ohlin. Delinquent activities were seen largely as 'fun' and the boys, primarily low-educational achievers, did not display any frustration at their lack of success, having never expected to succeed. Rather than being opposed to mainstream values they were 'dissociated' from middle-class and school values. Their delinquency could, however, be related to 'leisure goals' of youth culture. Compared to middle-class youth they could not afford to own cars or participate in expensive leisure pursuits but they did have more time for leisure, being less involved in educational pursuits. Searching for kicks and fun made delinquent activities an attractive solution to a leisure problem (Downes 1966).

Against the image of the rebellious, oppositional delinquent, there emerged a picture of the bored delinquent, drifting between conformity and delinquency. Delinquency was seen as no big deal, as something which simply happened in some circumstances. Arguably, however, Matza's model underpredicted delinquency (Downes and Rock 2007), and British work on subcultures developed further with the emergence of a host of youth and cultural styles in the 1960s and 1970s, including teddy boys, mods, rockers, hippies and the growth of illegal drug use. These alarmed the older generation and appeared to challenge conventional values. Many of these were studied by researchers based in the Birmingham Centre for Contemporary Cultural Studies, who approached subcultures from a different intellectual tradition, Marxism, which will be discussed more fully in Chapter 5 (Hall and Jefferson 1976; Muncie 1984; Brake 1985).

This approach was highly critical of earlier approaches based on the anomie tradition, with its emphasis on culturally shared, consensual goals. While they recognized the existence of dominant cultural goals, these were seen to be encouraged, disseminated and imposed by dominant groups through the mass media and school and did not reflect a real consensus. They also argue that there are many different cultures, including a working-class culture which is itself an adaptation to the dominant culture. Cultures are not static and are affected by local, national and international influences through films and television. Youth may ape the cultures they are exposed to in the media, such as 'celebrity culture', while at the same time being affected by their local culture. Thus cultures reflect a combination or pastiche of different cultural influences. Each new generation faces a new set of problems in the light of local economic conditions. Success goals may derive from the dominant culture or from the culture of their parents, often called their parent culture. In areas with declining industries youth faced the double whammy of being unable to achieve the goals of their parent culture *and* the dominant culture.

Subcultural styles were interpreted as representing a solution to these problems by expressing alternative status values and subcultures provided cultural 'space'. To Cohen (1972), for example, working-class youth subcultures in the 1960s developed out of changes in housing and employment which affected the working class as a whole. Communities became fragmented, and youth were faced by the contradictory ideologies of increasing affluence and traditional working-class ideology. Many of the traditional jobs which were valued were disappearing. Thus he argues: '[the] latent function of subculture is to express and resolve, albeit magically, the contradictions hidden or unresolved in the parent culture' (Cohen 1972). The skinhead style, for example, with its emphasis on hard, masculine forms of dress and behaviour, such as the Doc Marten boot, reflected images of parent culture but was adapted to modern conditions.

Source: Mirrorpix

Skinheads.

Evaluation: the delinquent rebel?

While these theories emerged from very different theoretical starting points, they are similar in some respects to anomie. Subcultures represent a form of resistance to mainstream or parent cultures whose goals are unachievable. These arguments also have considerable appeal. The social and economic changes of recent decades have meant that some young people are in effect excluded from mainstream society, and crime – as will be seen in particular in chapters on socio-economic status, youth, property and organized crime – can become an attractive way to obtain success symbols or provide a sense of achievement. In general, subcultural theories, by pointing to the attractions of crime and delinquency, provide an invaluable corrective to perspectives which view offenders as abnormal or disturbed individuals. As will be seen in Chapter 5, their insights have been further developed in the emergence of cultural criminology. Yet they too have many problems, summarized below.

Why the delinquent solution?

As outlined above, a major problem with early subcultural theory was that it could overpredict delinquency. While many theories recognized that not all lower-class youth adopted the 'delinquent solution', they could not sufficiently explain why the majority did not (Downes and Rock 2007).

Interpreting subcultures

Subcultural theory tries to explain why subcultures emerge and to analyse their content, or style, all of which is highly interpretative and cannot be directly tested (Cohen 1979). How can it be established that a particular subcultural style, such as the skinheads, do indeed reflect a desire to recreate the imagery of a long-forgotten industrial past? The interpreter is drawing on signs and symbols which appear to link the past to the present but may not always recognize the original style or the influence of contemporary consumerism. Thus Hobbs (1988: 131–2) points out that workers in East London would not have had their hair cropped or worn US army surplus flight jackets. Indeed, he argues, the perception of some youth that the community was under threat by immigrants would require a 'style of aggressive masculinity with a more visually intimidating image than the donkey-jacket, monkey boots (not Doc Martens) and sandwich box'.

The romantic rebel?

Subcultural theory can also present a somewhat idealized picture of the delinquent as a rebel – resisting and opposing an oppressive culture. This image may be far from accurate. Cohen's (1979) account, for example, stresses the 'imaginary' nature of such a response – the delinquent's resistance is not conscious, nor is it successful. Crime does not provide real jobs or real achievement and more rebellion may produce a harsher response. Interpreting delinquency in such a way may also neglect its other features. In an argument developed in Chapter 5, Young argues that these theories may romanticize the delinquent – portraying them as anti-heroes, when many of their activities have a devastating effect on victims and do not reflect any real resistance (Young 1986). Skinheads, for example, target youth from ethnic minorities and much property crime is directed not at the wealthy who might be seen to 'deserve it' but at the poor and powerless (Young 1975; Lea and Young 1993).

Delinquent boys?

A major problem with much subcultural theory is that it accepted the assumption that crime was overwhelmingly a problem of young male lower-class adolescents. This not only meant that it neglected to explore the potentially delinquent behaviour of middle- or upper-class youth, but it also neglected the maleness of the participants. Many theories assumed that the members of subcultures were boys without analysing why this was significant. Were girls absent from these subcultures? Or was their presence merely ignored by largely male researchers? Did girls have their own subcultures (McRobbie and Garber 1976)? Gender was recognized without being analysed. In many subcultural accounts what is effectively being argued is that young *men* need to find alternative ways of being a man. Feminist theories argue that subcultural theories have to recognize and analyse the development of *both* masculine and feminine forms of subcultural activity (see Chapter 9).

Concluding comments

This chapter has provided an introduction to different theoretical perspectives and readers are advised to look at some of the work cited, preferably in its original form, and consider for themselves many of the issues raised above. In general terms, classical criminology can be contrasted with the 'pathological' approaches focusing on the 'deficits' of individual offenders, be they biological, psychological or social. Many of these attempts to explain crime or to look for its causes were fundamentally flawed. They assumed that crime was pathological, they took its definition for granted, and based much of their research on convicted offenders. They assumed that crime was more prevalent in the lower classes and did not explore processes of criminalization and social control. They failed to identify the causes of crime which many now see as a fruitless task. Crime, as will be seen throughout this book, takes many different forms which may require different kinds of explanations, and cannot be reduced to simple cause–effect relationships; asking why offenders commit crime is only one of the many relevant questions.

Given all these failings, it could be asked whether these theories have any relevance to contemporary Britain. Some of this relevance has been referred to and, as will be seen, they have had an enormous influence on later theories to be discussed in Chapter 5, which have drawn on the strengths and attempted to address the weaknesses of these approaches. Many subsequent chapters will also illustrate that the concepts and arguments developed in these early theories remain important and influential. Durkheim's argument that crime can be functional has influenced later writing and challenges the commonsense view that crime is pathological. Anomie theory, with all its weaknesses, points to the possibility that crime is related to inequalities in the social structure and to the existence and significance of aspirations with insufficient regulation. It, along with subcultural theory, also indicates that crime can be seen as a normal, rational and attractive option for those who may be excluded from legitimate forms of achievement. These insights are as relevant today as they were then, as the discussion in Chapter 2, of the media's dissemination of consumer goals, unachievable for many, indicates.

Review questions

1 List points which could be used in a debate on the topic 'are criminals born or made?'.

2 Outline, in your own words, Durkheim's argument that crime is functional to society. Do you think that this has any contemporary relevance? Provide, for example, illustrations of reactions to crime which appear to perform an integrative and clarifying function.

3 Summarize the main points of anomie, subcultural, and social disorganization theories. What do they have in common? What kinds of criticisms can be made of their assumptions about crime?

4 Identify an example of a youth subculture associated with crime. Describe the main characteristics of this subculture – for example, its associated forms of speech, dress and 'style'. How might its emergence be explained by subcultural approaches?

Key reading

There are now many books, chapters of texts and handbooks on different criminological theories and students are advised to consult some original sources. The major texts are:

Downes, D. and Rock, P. (2007) ***Understanding Deviance: A Guide to the Sociology of Crime and Rule Breaking***, revised 5th edn, Oxford: Clarendon Press. This classic text covers the main sociological theories explored in this chapter and in Chapter 5.

Hopkins Burke, R. (2005) ***An Introduction to Criminological Theory***, Cullompton: Willan Publishing. This provides a comprehensive introduction to the context, strengths and weaknesses of the main criminological theories.

Tierney, J. (2006) ***Criminology: Theory and context***, 2nd edn, London: Pearson Education. This text is a thorough and engaging introduction to the main theories and their main criticisms.

Valier, C. (2002) ***Theories of Crime and Punishment***, London: Pearson/Longman. An interesting account of some of the main theories which seeks to place them in a historical context and to relate them to theories of punishment.

It is well worth reading some of the original works and good selections of original sources can be found in:

McLaughlin, E., Muncie, J. and Hughes, G. (eds) (2003) ***Criminological perspectives: Essential Readings***, London: Sage.

Newburn, T. (2009) (ed.) ***Key Readings in Criminology***, Cullompton: Willan Publishing.

Chapter 5
Understanding crime: from explaining to controlling crime in a global context

This chapter will look at:

- ➜ The labelling perspective
- ➜ Critical criminology
- ➜ Rational choice theories
- ➜ Conservative criminologies and right realism
- ➜ Left realism
- ➜ Cultural criminology
- ➜ The global context of crime

Criticisms of the theories outlined in Chapter 4 along with the apparently unstoppable rise in official crime rates outlined in Chapter 3, prompted governments to look for different kinds of solutions. Initially, 'correctional' or 'establishment' criminology came under criticism for accepting a primarily governmental agenda, pursuing the search for the 'causes' of crime and its solutions, often involving rehabilitative policies, which had failed to prevent recidivism. The 1950s and 60s was a period of rising affluence which, in theory, if crime was related to social deprivation, should have led to lower crime rates. This produced what Young (1997) described as an aetiological crisis – a crisis in how crime was explained. A variety of different and contrasting approaches, many building on earlier ones, emerged, some related to changing government agendas, and others criticizing these same agendas.

The 1960s saw a rising tide of criticism of established ways of thinking across many social sciences and, within criminology, the emergence of what came to be described as 'new', 'critical' or 'radical' criminology which challenged the methods and assumptions of earlier perspectives. It was particularly critical of the focus on 'official' crime and offenders, looking instead at how offences and offenders were 'created' by social control and aiming to understand the offender's perspective. Others explored how definitions of crime and the organization of social control reflected the interests of the powerful and effectively criminalized the powerless (Pearce 1976).

Later decades saw enormous social and economic change, deindustrialization and increasing socio-economic inequality. This, along with rising crime rates, prompted governments to look for new solutions – focusing less on what 'caused' crime, but on what could reduce it. Some asked why most people did not commit crime, shifting the emphasis to sources of conformity and control. Others returned to the notions of classical criminology, viewing crime as a 'rational' choice and focusing on the situations in which these choices were made. In what came to be called 'administrative' criminology, crime became a problem to be 'managed' rather than 'solved'.

From the 1970s crime became politicized with politicians vying with each other to be 'tough' on crime. The rising influence of neo-liberal economics and ideology also led to many politicians being critical of sociological approaches which appeared to 'excuse' crime by relating it to social inequality, and stressing the role of individuals and families. Rehabilitative policies were viewed as too 'soft' and more punitive approaches were advocated in what is generally described as 'popular punitivism' (Bottoms 1994). This was associated with the development of so-called 'conservative', 'neo-conservative' or 'right realist' approaches which developed arguments about the role of individual factors such as intelligence and socialization within the family. Critical criminologists challenged and sought to explore the impact of this punitive 'turn' on groups who became successively demonized and criminalized. So-called 'left realists' emphasized relative deprivation and later work developed some of the classic theories outlined in Chapter 4 in the context of contemporary society, culture and globalization which, it was argued, led to new forms of and opportunities for crime and to 'globalised anomie' (Young 2003).

This chapter will introduce these different ideas which developed simultaneously. It will start by exploring the labelling perspective and outlining the main ideas of critical criminology before turning to control theories and the growing emphasis on rational choice and crime prevention. It will then outline approaches associated with 'right realism' before turning to 'left realism', concerns with globalization and the rise of cultural criminology. Its emphasis is on the broad thrust of approaches which will be explored in more depth in subsequent chapters, as will the considerable contribution of feminist perspectives. It is also important to recognize that terms such as 'right' and 'left', 'conservative' or 'radical' are not necessarily associated with specific political parties but with general approaches. To critical criminologists, the 'new' Labour policies of the late 1990s and 2000s, while acknowledging the role of social inequalities, continued to place responsibility for crime on offenders and families (Chapter 7).

Constructing crime and offenders

The labelling perspective

The labelling perspective emerged from the well-established interactionist tradition in sociology, which stresses the importance of exploring the meanings involved in social interactions to make sense of behaviour. People behave according to how they define any given situation, a definition affected by everyday signs and symbols. A row of desks, for example, indicates a classroom, and those in that classroom behave according to well-established shared meanings. In everyday interaction we present ourselves to the world and express our identity by our speech, mannerisms, dress or body language and respond to others' cues. These everyday features of social interaction are often taken for granted and unconscious and are negotiated in new situations (Plummer 1979). The normality of everyday interaction can be

Box 5.1 Labelling

Howard Becker (1963: 8–9) argues that:

> Social groups create deviance by making the rules whose infraction constitutes deviance and by applying those rules to particular people and labelling them as outsiders. From this point of view, deviance is not a quality of the act the person commits, but rather a consequence of the application by others of rules and sanctions to an 'offender'. The deviant is one to whom that label has successfully been applied; deviant behaviour is behaviour that people so label.

revealed by any rule-breaking, which produces embarrassment, and we react to the deviant with a mixture of feelings such as suspicion, avoidance or disapproval. Exploring these complex meanings requires qualitative research methods, and research in this tradition studied offenders and law enforcers. Some of the main ideas associated with labelling perspectives are outlined below.

Creating outsiders

A key argument is that deviance is created by being labelled as such, as indicated in Becker's famous quotation in Box 5.1. A distinction can accordingly be made between acts which could be defined as deviant and those which have been labelled – between what Edwin Lemert (1951) called primary deviance, the initial act, and secondary deviance, which occurs after the deviant label has been applied. Being labelled as a deviant affects a person's subsequent behaviour, leading to further, secondary, deviance. A deviant label has a particularly profound effect as deviance is a 'master status' overshadowing other aspects of identity. People who are considered deviant in one respect are often assumed to be deviant in other respects. Physically impaired or blind people, for example, are often assumed to be hard of hearing and often complain that people shout at them or are protective and condescending. As seen in Chapters 2 and 4, offenders are often assumed to be physically or mentally 'abnormal'. Deviants experience stigma – people avoid and exclude them, are embarrassed, and behave differently towards them. Labelling people as deviant therefore creates 'outsiders' (Becker 1963).

The deviant identity

This impact on a person's identity can set in train a deviant 'career' in which the label leads to a changed lifestyle confirming their deviant status. The child labelled by a teacher as 'trouble' may join other troublesome children. These careers can also involve engaging in an established subculture, moving further outside 'normal' society. Subcultures resolve the problems of stigma and provide an alternative set of values in which negative evaluations are neutralized or resisted. The subculture of sex workers, for example, provides support and assistance, and justifications for the activity which neutralize the stigma (see Chapter 12). Some groups resist a deviant label, most notably homosexual groups, who successfully changed their description from 'queer' to 'gay'.

Official agencies create categories of deviance to make sense of behaviour which may be puzzling, confusing and threatening. If a person is behaving 'oddly', defining them as mentally ill explains their behaviour and creates expectations about future behaviour. Scheff (1966), for example, argues that those defined as mentally ill are expected to adapt their behaviour and non-conformity – which might include resisting the label – may be interpreted as a further sign of illness. Once in an institution, prisoners or the mentally ill go through a 'rite of passage' in which aspects of former identity are systematically removed. Clothes are often replaced by a uniform, and they become an inmate with a number. This may be experienced as a form of degradation as one's identity is being challenged. Institutions reward conformity – reassertions of individuality can be regarded as a further sign of deviance. Inmates of such institutions often form an inmate culture, attempting to re-establish choice and identity (Goffman 1968).

Deviancy amplification

As seen in the discussion of Cohen's (1972/2002) work on *Folk Devils and Moral Panics* in Chapter 2, strong reaction can lead to deviancy amplification and a self-fulfilling prophecy. A possible sequence is sketched out in Figure 5.1 adapted from Heidensohn (1989). This kind of amplification can occur in other situations where the police have to deal with, for example, demonstrators, football crowds or young people perceived to be drunk or 'anti-social'. In these kinds of situations, both groups 'expect' trouble and may well behave accordingly.

Evaluation

The emphasis in the labelling perspective on the ways in which social control creates further deviance suggests that intervention should be kept to a minimum.

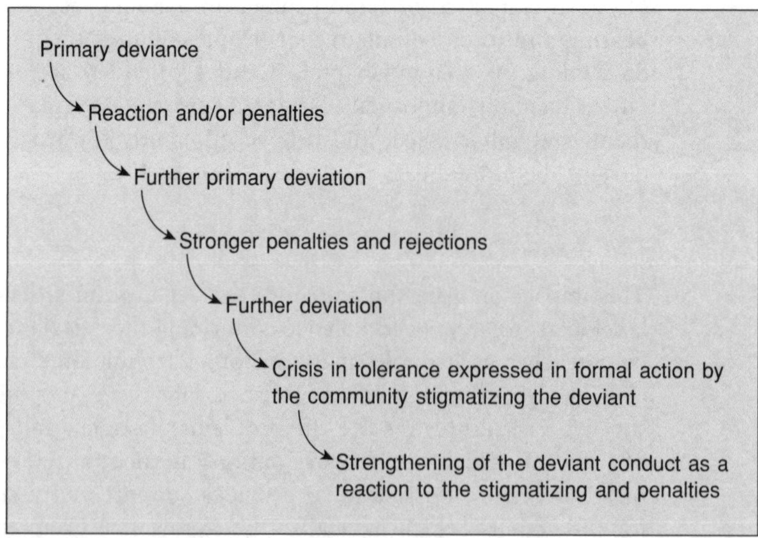

Figure 5.1 A deviancy amplification spiral
(Adapted from Heidensohn 1989)

These ideas have been extremely influential, not only in the analysis and treatment of crime but also in the fields of education, medicine and psychiatry. Braithwaite (1989a), for example, argues that any form of control or punishment must aim to avoid creating outsiders and oppositional cultures. Despite this, a number of questions have been asked, some of which do not invalidate the approach as they are based on a misconception of what labelling perspectives set out to achieve (Plummer 1979; Downes and Rock 2007). These are summarized below.

A perspective or a theory of crime?

Those primarily concerned with establishing the so-called 'causes' of crime were critical of the apparent neglect of the question of why primary deviance occurred in the first place. Plummer (1979) argues that this was never the intention – the primary focus was on the impact of labels. Many prefer nonetheless to describe labelling as a perspective rather than a theory, which does not aim to fully analyse crime but focuses on how crime and criminals are processed. It can also be combined with other theories (Plummer 1979; Heidensohn 1989; Downes and Rock 2007).

Is it too deterministic?

The apparent assumption that once labelled, the 'deviant' automatically responds with more deviance was criticized for being too determinist and assuming little choice. As pointed out above, however, labels can be resisted and, while many writers do imply a career, those labelled can withdraw from the process at any stage (Plummer 1979). This has been likened to proceeding down a long corridor with doors off to the side – some follow the corridor to deviance, others exit at different points.

The deviant's perspective

To others, the approach was too sympathetic to offenders, and many criticized Becker's (1963) call for a 'view from below'. Many studies looked at forms of crime such as drug-taking or delinquency where an appreciative stance was easier, and few looked at violent or sexual offenders. It was also overtly critical of official policy and was often linked with arguments for liberalizing laws. Offenders were portrayed as victims of harsh social control, presenting a somewhat romantic view of deviants and offenders (Young 1986).

Who has the power to define deviance?

To some critics, it neglected the power involved in defining crime and the political nature of deviant labels. While it was recognized that definitions of deviance could be resisted, labelling theorists did not explore the wider structure of political power. As will be seen below, these questions were taken up by critical and Marxist scholars.

Making sense of the phenomenon

The meaning of actions to participants and the categorization of behaviour was taken even further by the related work of phenomenologists who asked how meanings were established. To them, the meaning of any phenomenon cannot be taken for granted and researchers also attribute meaning to situations, a position which challenges how much we can 'know' about any phenomenon (Downes and Rock 2007). While it lies beyond the scope of this book to discuss fully the issues raised by phenomenologists, it is useful to outline briefly how some of their thinking has affected work on crime (see, for example, Hester and Eglin 1992). Phenomenologists advocate the use of ethnomethodology, which should not be confused with ethnography and which can be described as the 'study of members' methods of making sense, their methods of producing and recognizing "sensible" social actions and settings' (Hester and Eglin 1992: 14).

To phenomenologists, people 'produce' their own local social order and attribute meaning to everyday circumstances. The researcher must carefully unpack these unstated and taken for granted meanings. Short phrases may be used to encapsulate a wide range of related meanings which may not immediately be obvious. The police, for example, often use the phrase 'real police work' which implies dealing with 'serious' crime, detecting crimes and making sure that offenders are prosecuted and convicted (Holdaway 1983; Reiner 1992). Sudnow's (1965) work in American courts revealed official agencies' use of the phrase 'normal crimes' which incorporated assumptions about offenders, victims and the areas concerned. This was only evident when 'abnormal' crimes occurred, such as a middle-class youth committing a burglary, normally associated with lower-class youth. Normal crimes were routinely processed with police, prosecutor and defender working with shared assumptions of what would happen. Ethnomethodologists use the technique of conversational analysis to uncover these kinds of background assumptions.

The most influential phenomenological work of relevance to crime was Kitsuse and Cicourel's (1963) exploration of how the police categorize complex events into legal categories such as assault or burglary. Official reports are inevitably 'truncated' versions of what happened and are affected by the local context in which events and people are defined (Kitsuse and Cicourel 1963). While these kinds of studies revealed much about the often unstated assumptions underlying the processing of offenders and offences, phenomenology had limited influence. In one sense it appears to deny all advances of knowledge – if all research is contaminated by the observer, how can we trust the phenomenologist's interpretation? Many would prefer to believe that there is some 'reality' (Downes and Rock 2007). While their work was often meticulously detailed it was generally based on very small scale observations and led to few generalizations. Focusing on the minutiae of taken for granted assumptions, revealed, argues Sumner, a lot of trivia, which neglected the structural context – he likens it to:

> describing the flow of fluids in an engine . . . without telling us about the vehicle, its normal functions and the direction it travels in – or about the driver and what he or she has in mind for the passengers. (Sumner 1994: 241)

Critical criminology

Many criticisms of these and earlier theories originated from the perspective known as critical criminology, which developed from the 'radical' or 'new' criminology of the 1960s and 1970s, influenced by the work of Taylor et al (1973). In a critical and influential text they advanced an extensive critique of classical and positive criminologies and the criminological orthodoxies of the time. They critically reviewed the contribution of interactionism and Marxist theory arguing that a 'fully social theory of deviance' should look at

- the immediate and wider origins of the deviant act
- the immediate and wider origins of reaction
- the outcome of social reaction on further deviance

They also outlined the possibility of a 'crime-free' society based on socialist diversity and tolerance.

Critical criminology has challenged theoretical approaches and criminal justice policies along with exposing the ideological nature of dominant ideas about crime. Its main focus is on the structural, political and ideological factors underlying the definition of crime, the criminal law and its enforcement. While the labelling perspective drew attention to the power of social controllers, critical criminologists place this within a broader context – the former focuses on the daily routine of agency, while the latter aims to expose structural relations which involve the economy, the state and ideology (Scraton and Chadwick 1991). Critical criminology is constantly evolving and encompasses many different strands. This section will introduce some of its main ideas which will be further developed later in this and subsequent chapters. It will start by looking at the issue of conflict and consensus in relation to law-making, introduce Marxist perspectives and look at how it has broadened the questions asked about crime to incorporate the process of criminalization and at arguments that the study of crime should be refocused around social harm.

Law, crime and conflict

Critical criminologists' approach to how crime is defined can be starkly contrasted with the functionalist theories explored in Chapter 4, to whom criminal law reflects a consensus over values. To Durkheim (1964 (1895)), for example, it reflected the 'collective conscience'. Critical and conflict theorists stress the politically contested nature of criminal law and the role of conflict in, for example, creating law and policy. Social order, rather than being maintained by consensus, is maintained through a constant process of accommodation between different interest groups.

Different theoretical positions view this conflict in different ways. Pluralists stress the large number of different interest groups and see the eventual result as reflecting a balance of power. Interest groups must secure the support of others to be successful. Some groups have more power than others, but no one group holds a monopoly. The success of campaigns by gay people, minority ethnic groups, women's and victim groups to secure changes to criminal law and criminal justice policies indicates that law can be changed. This pluralist model is, however, rejected by Marxist-influenced theorists who argue that, despite the appearance of plurality, the interests of the ruling class tend to be consistently reflected. To appreciate this position some of the main ideas of Marxist theory must be briefly outlined.

Marxist perspectives

So-called Marxist or post-Marxist theories draw on the work of the nineteenth-century philosopher Karl Marx and encompass a range of different perspectives. Marx located law and the ruling ideas of any society to the economic structure in which two main classes, owners and labourers, were placed in fundamental opposition. Employment law, for example, reflects the subject position of employees. Marx's prediction that the ruling class would be overthrown failed to materialize in many countries which some interpret as reflecting the ability of the ruling classes to rule by obtaining the consent of other classes. This consent can, argue Marxists, be threatened in times of economic crisis when the inequalities of power and position of different classes become starkly evident. Marxist thinkers approached crime in different ways.

Crime and class consciousness

Some interpreted crime as an indication of class consciousness and a rebellion against class rule although, to Marx, criminals were part of the lumpenproletariat, a parasite class, and were not important in the class struggle (Hirst 1972). Marx's collaborator, Engels, did suggest a link between crime, poverty and the demoralizing effects of exploitation. Such a view, however, accepts that there are higher rates of crime among the lower class. How, under this approach, could white-collar crime be explained? Moreover, this notion invoked a false 'Robin Hood' image of the poor stealing from the rich whereas the poor largely steal from the poor and crime could hardly be seen as a successful revolt (Young 1975).

Crimes of the powerful and powerless

To other writers, the more interesting question was how ruling-class interests came to be reflected in legal and ideological conceptions of crime and social control, illustrated by the contrasting treatment of the crimes of the powerful and the powerless. The criminal law is used, they argue, largely to control the activities of lower-class offenders such as theft or burglary, which damage the interests of capitalism, whereas harmful business or commercial activities, which were not a threat to the interests of capitalism, were not defined as crime. Lower-class activities threatening social order, such as demonstrations, were also subject to public order legislation. Therefore the criminal law serves ruling-class interests by criminalizing the activities of the powerless (Pearce 1976). One problem is, however, that the activities of business *are* subject to the criminal law, which Marxists explained by arguing that these laws are largely symbolic and not well enforced (see Chapters 15–17).

The role of social control agencies

The police, courts and prisons also operate in the interests of the ruling class. In times of crisis, these agencies are more overtly used to control and contain perceived threats. While the formal ideology of the police emphasizes its service role in detecting and prosecuting criminals, their real function, argued critical criminologists, was to maintain law and order. Thus the police, along with courts and prisons, have long been used against working-class protests, illustrated in the rise of an increasingly tough 'control culture' in the 1970s in which industrial and political protests, such as the miners' strike of 1984, were policed with increasingly heavy and paramilitary tactics (Sim et al 1987).

Many of these ideas were in turn criticized as simplistic and circular. The assumption that all laws reflect ruling-class interests was difficult to refute, particularly as any examples of laws which appeared to contradict this were seen as merely symbolic. It was also difficult to establish *how* the ruling class secured such a situation, particularly given the plethora of interest groups involved in creating any particular criminal law. Who were the ruling class and how did they rule? Marxist thought was criticized for suggesting a rather mechanical conspiracy theory which could not be empirically substantiated.

Later versions were influenced by the ideas of the Italian writer Gramsci, who stressed the maintenance of consent through the operation of a hegemonic culture which legitimated the ruling class by accepting their 'right' to rule. Behind the 'velvet glove' of consensus, however, lay the 'iron fist' of class power, which becomes visible when law and social control become tougher. This formed the context for Hall and his colleagues' (Hall et al 1978) analysis of the moral panic surrounding mugging, outlined in Chapter 2, which they related to a crisis in hegemony brought about by a deterioration of economic conditions. The black mugger thus diverted attention from the economic roots of the crisis.

From crime to criminalization

This led to what has been described as the criminalization of black youth which will be discussed in Chapter 10. It also points to a process of criminalization involving the 'application of the criminal label to an identifiable social category' (Scraton and Chadwick 1991: 172). Imputing criminality to groups diverts attention from the economic or political roots of their activities, thus political protests are attributed to a disorderly 'rabble' and terrorists are depicted as 'common criminals', which neutralizes the political nature of their actions. This helps, argues Hillyard (1987), to attract popular support for anti-terrorist measures as it is easier to mobilize state intervention against criminal acts than to repress what might be perceived as a just political cause (see Chapter 11). Hillyard (1993) also pointed to the way in which, at the peak of the troubles, the Irish across Britain became a 'suspect community'. This kind of analysis can also be applied to contemporary issues such as the so-called 'wars' on drugs, organized crime or terror which are used to justify stronger police powers, and to the 'othering' of groups such as Muslims, particularly after the attacks on the World Trade Center in New York in September 2001 ('9/11'), in London in July 2005 ('7/7'), and the attack on Glasgow Airport in May 2007.

Criminalization, much as the creation of 'folk devils' identified in Chapter 2, tends to involve economically and politically marginal groups, who have few means to resist and can be cast as a threat. Throughout the centuries crime has been associated with so-called 'dangerous classes', and more recently with the 'underclass' (see Chapter 7). While some versions of critical criminology were criticized for focusing overmuch on class domination and neglecting issues of race or feminism, it has now extended its analysis to all structural relations of reproduction and dependency including patriarchies; the structural relations of neo-colonialism; the pervasiveness of institutional racism and imperialist legacy; slavery, colonization, immigration and migration (Chadwick and Scraton 2006: 99).

Beyond criminology – towards 'harm'

Given the seemingly inextricable association of criminology with 'statist' notions of crime, some contemporary critical criminologists argue for a 'zemiology', turning the focus from 'crime' to social harm. To Hillyard and Tombs (2004), crime is a 'myth' of everyday life, which criminology, by continuing to ask why people commit it, perpetuates. The social construction of crime excludes serious harms such as corporate crime and state crimes such as genocide and torture (Cohen 1996). Broadening the focus of inquiry to social harm would, they argue, enable these kinds of crime to be included along with all threats to people's welfare. Crime would thereby be placed in the context of other harms, many of which, such as pollution, poor diet or safety, are potentially more serious than the one-off events currently counted as crime. All of these harms are nonetheless avoidable and a harm approach would direct attention to who is responsible for these harms and how they should be dealt with. It would also direct attention to a broader range of options for dealing with all harms than the current narrow focus on criminal justice, including, for example, redress, negotiation and arbitration (Hopkins Burke 2005).

Which harms might be included? A list of harms is outlined in Box 5.2, many of which are related to economic processes such as globalization and economic restructuring. Their impact could be alleviated and they could be prevented by governments. Market dynamics produce both *direct* harms, where sections of the population are forced to live at or below subsistence level, and *indirect* harms such

Box 5.2 Avoidable harms

- **Physical harms**: including premature death or serious injury; so-called 'accidents' in the workplace; exposure to environmental pollutants; environmentally or industrially caused illness and disease; lack of adequate food or shelter; death, torture and brutality by state officials.
- **Financial economic harms**: incorporating poverty; property and economic losses occasioned by 'misselling'; misappropriation of funds by governments, private corporations and private individuals; increased prices for goods and services through cartelization and price-fixing; the widening income and wealth gaps between rich and poor.
- **Emotional and psychological harms**: occasioned by the above.
- **Cultural safety**: including access to cultural, intellectual and information resources, often denied to the poor.

Source: Hillyard and Tombs (2004) and see also Tombs and Hillyard (2004)

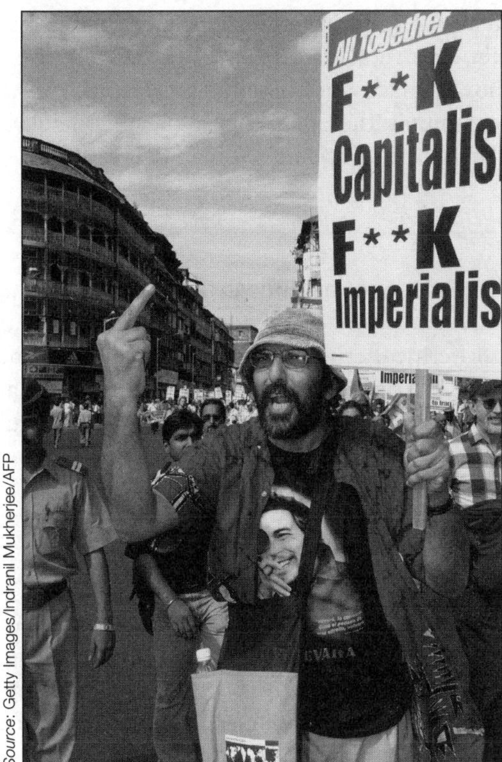

Source: Getty Images/Indranil Mukherjee/AFP

'To critical criminologists, capitalism itself can be regarded as criminogenic'.

as ill health, illiteracy, anti-social and criminal behaviour. Some of these effects were starkly illustrated in the financial crisis of 2008, in which the activities of those involved in financial markets across the globe were associated with job losses, public sector cuts, and reductions of income, pensions and financial security.

Harm can nonetheless be criticized as being too broad a concept and it could be argued that such ideas are unlikely to be accepted by criminology (Newburn 2007). There is also a danger that the criminal label could be extended by incorporating a wider range of harms. Muncie (2000), for example, points to the inclusion, within a purportedly broader conception of community safety, of harsh laws against anti-social behaviour which, as will be seen in Chapter 8, have exacerbated the criminalization of young people and have not included forms of corporate crime despite the theoretical potential to do so (Croall 2009b). Nonetheless the approach poses fundamental questions about *which* harms are selected for criminalization and why some serious harms, explored in Chapters 15–17, are not seen as part of the 'crime problem'. They also raise important questions about how and why societal tolerance of different harms changes.

Evaluation

Critical criminologists ask a number of important questions. They attempt to strip away or deconstruct dominant perceptions of crime and criminals, seeing crime not as a problem of individual offenders or strains in society but as a process related to wider economic and political structures of power. Their work is enormously useful in exploring why and how the activities of some groups are subjected to the criminal law and critically examining the operation of social control. Their ideas have, however, prompted a number of criticisms outlined below.

The ruling-class conspiracy?

Reference has already been made to the difficulty of directly relating law and social control to the direct intervention of the state or ruling class. Young (1986) has argued that some forms of critical criminology provide a mirror image of functionalism as all evidence can be interpreted as fitting the model. Their arguments can be perceived, like Durkheim's notion of the functions of crime, as circular. Similar criticisms can be made of the somewhat generalized attribution of crime and other social harms to 'neo-liberalism'.

Establishing the relationship

It is also difficult to empirically test many arguments. Downes and Rock (2007), criticizing Hall and his colleagues' work, argue that while they demonstrate how the moral panic develops they cannot establish its precise relationship to the assumed crisis. Analyses of political and media discourses are interpretative and can be selective as quotations may be taken out of context. The many research difficulties inherent in exploring the crimes, or the deliberations, of the powerful limit attempts to establish whose interests are, in practice, more influential (Tombs and Whyte 2003).

Attitude to criminal justice policy

Critical criminology has also been criticized for its apparent lack of interest in policy. Young (1997), for example, characterized it as left idealism. On the other hand, criticizing policies is in itself a contribution. If the crime problem is constructed on false premises, policies will inevitably be limited. Some strands of critical criminology have also been associated with an abolitionist stance which argues that the formal processes of police and prisons which criminalize some groups should be abolished or greatly reduced and more informal means of conflict resolution adopted. And as seen above, the social harm approach aims to encourage a different range of responses to criminal and other harms.

Focus on crimes of the powerful?

Critical criminologists have also been criticized for overemphasizing crimes of the powerful at the expense of crimes of the powerless. Many of their arguments, such as their analysis of social harm, are more relevant to discussions of corporate, white-collar or state crime than to street crime. This apparent neglect of the 'reality' of street crime formed the basis of Young's development of left realist criminology, discussed below.

Controlling crime: control and rational choice theories

At the same time as radical and critical criminology were developing, a new range of theories posed different questions to the 'dispositional' or pathological theories outlined in Chapter 4, and emerged in the context of a disillusionment with the rehabilitative policies with which they were associated. In an attempt to reduce crime, many of these approaches separated issues of control from the so-called causes of crime in offenders' motivations. This section will focus on some these approaches.

Crime and lack of control

Control theories, influential from around the 1970s, are based on the commonsense notion that crime is more likely to be committed when offenders have insufficient controls to constrain them (Downes and Rock 2007). Instead of asking '*why do people commit crime?*' they ask '*why do people not commit crime?*' Most people, it is argued, do not commit crime; they think it is wrong or they fear disapproval and punishment – thus attachment to conventional morality, family and conventional lifestyles are a form of control as illustrated in Box 5.3, which outlines Hirschi's influential arguments. In Britain, Wilson (1980) found in a deprived area that non-delinquents were distinguished by what she describes as 'chaperonage' which included fetching children from school, rules for coming in at night and restrictions

Box 5.3 Hirschi: control and the social bond

Attachment, argues Hirschi, is a key factor explaining why people do not commit crime. This derives from the process of socialization by informal agencies of social control such as the family, the community and the school. Thus:

> a common property of control theories at their simplest level is their assumption that delinquent acts result when an individual's bond to society is weak or broken.
>
> (Hirschi 1969, cited in Downes and Rock 2007: 202)

The social bond consists of four elements:

- **Attachment** to conventional values means that people care about other people's opinions, which constrains their behaviour.
- People become **committed to conventional behaviour** by investing time and energy in obtaining material goods and achieving a certain status.
- **Involvement in a conventional lifestyle** leaves them less time or motivation to deviate.
- Finally, they **believe** that this is right.

The delinquent is freer from these controls, has few attachments, is uncommitted to a conventional lifestyle and does not believe in the need to obey rules. In his research Hirschi found that delinquency was more common among boys who reported fewer bonds with their family based on measurements of, for example, parental supervision and intimacy of communication.

on their freedom to be in the street. Lax discipline was related to the stress of unemployment, disability or poverty.

Along with his collaborator Gottfredson, Hirschi later argued that all crime is related to an absence of self-control in the offender (Gottfredson and Hirschi 1990). Crime, along with other forms of behaviour such as smoking, drug abuse, or illicit sex, offers immediate gratification, thrills and excitement and provides short, as opposed to long-term gains. It generally requires little planning and harms others. Offenders lack the self-control to resist these short-term gains and gratifications by making long-term investments in, for example, work, home and family. They are described as 'impulsive, insensitive, physical, risk taking, shortsighted and non verbal' (Gottfredson and Hirschi 1990: 90, cited in Lilly et al 2002: 94). These characteristics are related to the quality of parenting, in particular to parents' monitoring of children. Arguing that this forms the basis of a 'general theory of crime', they reject any differences between white collar offenders and others.

Control theory, including variants such as control-balance theory developed in the 1990s, has been enormously influential. It has some empirical support and highlights factors which prevent many people engaging in crime. It can contribute to our understanding of, for example, differences between girls and boys as girls are subject to much greater levels of 'chaperonage' and control. It suggests policies based on increasing levels of commitment to conventional lifestyles and improving the quality of parenting and has been associated with 'early intervention' policies directed at preventing involvement in crime from an early age. This has contributed to its popularity among politicians and governments keen to attribute crime to individuals and families. Viewing offenders as lacking in self-control is also consistent with popularized negative portrayals of offenders. Nonetheless, it has many problems, summarized below.

- **Issues of motivation:** Control theories turned away from issues of motivation which cannot always be reduced to an absence of control (Hopkins Burke 2005). Is the assumption, for example, that we would all commit crime when the 'lid is off' (Downes and Rock 2007)? Why do individuals, albeit lacking self-control, turn to some forms of crime and not others?
- **Neglect of social factors:** While in many ways the appeal of control theory lies in its rejection of social factors, this also constitutes one of its major weaknesses. Social and economic circumstances affect the opportunities individuals have to become attached to a conventional lifestyle, through employment, for example, and the ability of parents to monitor their children can be reduced by the stresses of living with low incomes and sometimes multiple jobs (Currie 1996, and see Chapter 7).
- **Self-control:** While there has been some empirical support for an association between self-control and crime, it is a difficult concept for researchers to operationalize and measure, and it can involve a circular argument in that the very act of offending in itself can be interpreted as a sign of an absence of self-control. While this too rejects any social structural influence, failure to achieve educational or occupational success, associated with low self-control, is associated with lower-class backgrounds. Indeed, their argument that it applies to white-collar offenders is somewhat contradictory as in order to be in a situation to commit a

white-collar crime, individuals have shown some measure of commitment and success (Lilly et al 2002). As Hopkins Burke (2005: 214) puts it:

> Since low self control is also incompatible with the discipline and effort normally required to attain high office, it is difficult to see how corporate offenders managed to climb the corporate ladder in the first place!

Rationally choosing crime

In Britain, from the early 1980s, a succession of publications from the former Home Office Research Unit argued that much offending, rather than being predisposed, was opportunist, taking place in situations which provided the opportunity for committing crime without being observed or detected. Clarke argued that crime prevention was possible without understanding the causes of crime by reducing these opportunities and making offences more difficult to commit (Clarke 1980; Clarke and Mayhew 1980). Crime, he argued, resulted from a rational choice on the part of the offender who assessed the risks of any particular situation. This argument has an obvious appeal as reducing the opportunities for committing crime promised a much more cost-effective way of preventing it. An enormous amount of research focused on the immediate circumstances surrounding offences and reducing opportunities, strategies often described as situational crime prevention.

This included 'target hardening' by making the target of a crime harder to remove or vandalize. More effective security devices, better street lighting, identity marking and increased surveillance were all introduced and research focused on how criminals identify targets and which situations are most crime-prone (Bennett and Wright 1984, and see Chapter 13). Surveillance was particularly important as the chances of being observed, and therefore caught, were crucial. Some of this was based on the work of Oscar Newman, who argued that if space 'belonged' to someone it was defensible. If houses overlook a communal area, for example, vandals or thieves are more likely to be seen and identified. This suggested that crime could be 'designed out' of buildings and urban space by increasing informal surveillance (Newman 1972). While Newman's work had many criticisms, it does point to the significance of informal social control and raises important questions about 'features which enhance the social sense of belonging to a neighbourhood and make for a feeling of involvement rather than indifference' (Downes and Rock 2007: 214).

Later versions of rational choice theory addressed criticisms that it was somewhat simplistic by detailing the sequence of decisions which offenders make in relation to:

- The area in which to commit the crime
- How targets or victims are selected
- How offenders decide to take steps to avoid detection
- How offenders decide to recidivate.

A further objection was that not all decisions to commit crime can be perceived as 'rational' in that offenders may have miscalculated their chances of being caught, or may not have sufficient information to guide their choice. Offenders, argue Cornish and Clarke (1986), make the best choices they can, taking account of risks and uncertainties producing a limited or bounded rationality. Crime is therefore, they argue 'the outcome of the offender's choices or decisions, however hasty or ill considered these might be' (Hopkins Burke 2005: 44).

Research in the rational choice tradition suggested a variety of interventions, some of which have been apparently successful, although it is difficult to assess the extent to which crime has merely been displaced as offenders seek different opportunities. Further problems surround their neglect of the background factors affecting decisions about which crime to commit (Lilly et al 2002). Burglary, for example, may be motivated by a desire to make money, but that desire is rooted in a 'street culture' which values conspicuous consumption (see Chapter 13). Moreover, choices to commit crimes such as burglary or robbery take place within a wider cultural and structural context which makes these particular crimes a rational choice for residents in inner-city communities. Like other theories, therefore, they neglect the significance of social structural variables. Lilly et al further point to the difficulties of falsifying claims that decisions can be interpreted as rational. In what circumstances might a decision *not* be seen as rational?

Crimes of everyday life

From the 1990s attention turned to the relationship between crime and what Felson (1998), whose ideas are summarized in Box 5.4, describes as the structures and routines of everyday life which bring victims and offenders together. Predatory crime, argues Felson, is more likely to occur when offenders meet in time and space with a viable target in the absence of a capable guardian, a convergence which arises out of the routine practices of everyday life. A person who has to travel to work past places where they are likely to meet potential offenders, when alone, faces more risks. This is related to victims' lifestyles and changes in 'routine activities' can

Box 5.4 Felson: crimes of everyday life

Felson defines predatory crime as direct contact crimes in which one or more persons attack the person or property of another. He relates these to four main variables:

- The presence of motivated offenders (usually young males).
- The availability of suitable targets (persons or property). The word target rather than victim is because most crime is directed at property.
- The absence of capable guardians (such as family, colleagues, friends as opposed to police).
- The absence of an intimate handler (someone who can exert influence over the offender).

Suitability is determined by a formula, described as VIVA:

- **Value**: as calculated by offenders.
- **Inertia**: physical aspects of the person or property that hinder or interrupt its suitability as a target.
- **Visibility**: marks out people or property for attack.
- **Accessibility**: increases the risk of attack.

To which is added the **absence of capable guardians**.

reduce crime rates (Clarke and Felson 1993). In contrast with the past, in today's society, people, particularly women, are more likely to be out during the day, leaving many homes without 'capable guardians' and more at risk of burglary. People also carry more valuable goods, such as laptops or mobile phones, which become targets.

Evaluation

These approaches have proved enormously popular, offering the possibility of reducing crime simply and inexpensively. Individuals can play a major role in preventing their own victimization. These approaches are also politically neutral, with crime being seen as evenly distributed with everyone having the potential to commit it given a suitable opportunity (Lilly et al 2002). Like rational choice theories, however, they neglect the wider social context of offending and do little to address the question of how offenders come to be motivated in the first place, and why some are more motivated than others. Moreover, by including victims' lifestyles as a factor in crime, they can be interpreted as 'blaming the victim' (see Chapter 6). While many of the crime prevention measures they suggest are relatively straightforward, others involve increasing levels of surveillance, locks, bolts and bars. This can have an adverse effect on people's quality of life and can also produce oppositional responses in which offenders take pride in circumventing security measures.

Conservative criminologies and 'right realism'

While the theories reviewed in the previous section are compatible with a variety of political perspectives, others are more explicitly linked to 'new right' or 'neo-conservative' views (Tzannetakis 2006) and the populist punitivism (Bottoms 1994), referred to above. The term 'conservative criminology' is often used to describe a range of ideas deriving from the work of J. Q. Wilson, summarized in Box 5.5, a crime adviser to President Reagan, which have overtly conservative policy implications. They tend to reject any arguments that crime is linked to social inequality along with rehabilitationist or welfare-based policies (Lilly et al 2002). Responsibility for crime is placed firmly on individuals and families and welfare policies are seen to contribute to crime by encouraging dependency on the state (Murray 1990, and see Chapter 7). They return to the focus on biological and psychological 'deficits'.

These approaches have fundamental limitations. Like many other theories they fail to consider white-collar offenders, many of whose offences require high intelligence, and who are more difficult to associate with ineffective socialization (Lilly et al 2002). They reject any links between social structure and crime and show very little concern about issues of race and ethnicity or gender (Haines and White 2004; Hopkins Burke 2005). Some of their theories are implicitly racist and, like Murray's underclass theory, which will be discussed in Chapter 7, they 'blame the poor'. The harsh punishments which they advocate can arguably leave people further marginalized. To critical criminologists, these kinds of theories and policies exacerbate the demonization of entire groups.

Box 5.5 Arguments associated with 'conservative criminologies'

Right realism

- The term realist is associated with Wilson's argument that the 'reality' of crime must not be denied. In his book, *Thinking about Crime* (1975), he strongly criticized the decriminalization of crimes without victims such as drug-taking, abortion and homosexuality, arguing that crime is an evil requiring a concerted and rigorous response.
- Realism is also associated with his argument that attention should be focused on crimes which people worry most about: on street, rather than suite, crime.

Broken windows

- With Kelling (Wilson and Kelling 1982), Wilson developed the highly influential argument about 'broken windows', which signal the decline of an area and imply that 'no one cares'.
- If a street or area is seen as disorderly, a chain reaction will follow in which people will avoid the area and 'respectable' residents move out, leaving only weak and vulnerable residents and creating conditions for more serious forms of crime, drug-dealing and prostitution, to develop.
- Responses should be targeted at an early stage in this cycle and they recommended strategies including more benign community-based and more authoritarian 'zero tolerance' policing in high-crime areas in which community policing is a waste of time (McLaughlin 2006a).

Biosocial theories

Wilson links crime to an absence of self-control and attributes high levels of criminality and disorder to a weakening of sources of authority such as family, schools, religion and culture. With Herrnstein (Wilson and Herrnstein 1985), he developed a biosocial theory of crime which links crime to a combination of

- biological characteristics such as body types, aggression and low intelligence which affect an individual's ability to consider future and immediate rewards and
- socialization which affects the extent to which this biological predisposition will result in crime – thus 'bad families produce bad children'.
- aggressive and impulsive males with low intelligence; they are more likely to become criminal than young males with a 'bite of conscience' reflecting higher cognitive and intellectual development.

Low intelligence

Wilson and Herrnstein associated low intelligence with an inability to reason morally (Lilly et al 2002).

- In Herrnstein and Murray's *The Bell Curve* (1995), they argue that people's life chances in post-industrial America are determined by 'cognitive resources', and the 'cognitively disadvantaged' are more likely to fail at school, be unemployed, end up on welfare, produce illegitimate children and commit criminal acts.
- They have been criticized for being highly selective in choosing supporting data and in general intelligence has not been a good predictor of criminality (Lilly et al 2002).

Left realism

While 'right realism' influenced the policies of 'new right' governments, 'left realism', developed in Britain in the 1980s, was aimed at more social democratic, liberal policies, although it stressed the 'reality' of crime. It emerged out of critical criminology with one of its leading exponents, Jock Young, launching a major attack on the pathological theories of traditional criminology; the 'administrative' criminology based on rational choice and situational crime prevention approaches and on critical criminology. No single approach, he argued, had to date produced 'realistic' policies. Critical criminologists' and labelling theorists' focus on moral panics and criminalization effectively denied that crime was a 'real' problem and non-interventionist or abolitionist strategies were seen as idealistic and impracticable. He further criticized what he described as the 'left idealism' of critical criminologists for romanticizing lower-class crime and being overconcerned with the crimes of the powerful (Young 1986). Policies, he argued, should be based on what could be achieved, accepting that crime is a real problem. The basic ideas of this approach are outlined in Box 5.6 which illustrates left realism's rejection of

Box 5.6 Left realism

- **Crime *really* is a problem:** Left realists focused on the 'lived reality' of crime and on its 'real' and harmful effects. The 'romanticized' image of lower-class offenders committing crimes out of need was at odds with the reality that their crimes harmed those in an equally impoverished environment and indeed added to those disadvantages. Government victim surveys which tended to dismiss fears of crime as 'irrational' and as out of all proportion to risks neglected the more severe impact of crime on the poor as they were based on national, statistical averages.
- **The square of crime:** Outlined in Figure 5.2, the square of crime illustrates the dimensions of crime – offenders, victims, the public and the state and its agencies, all of which, and the interrelationships between them, are crucial to understanding and researching crime. Earlier theories focused on only one point of the square – on offenders, social control or the state and most neglected the victim. Research should investigate the causes of offending, factors which make victims vulnerable, social conditions which affect public levels of control and tolerance and social forces which propel formal agencies.
- **Multiple aetiology:** This phrase describes the need to look at multiple causes of crime in comparison with earlier approaches focusing on single causes.
- **Specificity:** These causes may be different for different offences, thus generalizations about 'crime' should be avoided. Any argument, for example, that unemployment leads to crime is inaccurate as it may lead to *some* kinds of crime in *some* circumstances.
- **Minimal intervention:** Following labelling approaches, realists argue for minimal intervention by the criminal justice system, but recognize the need for police and prisons to reduce crime. Intervention should be focused on each point of the square.
- **Rational democratic input and output:** Intervention should be based on democratic input and output. The impact of crime should be recognized and those affected should be consulted about policy. Radical victim surveys based on specific local areas would enable targeting resources on those whose need is greatest.

Source: Matthews and Young (1992); Young and Matthews (1992); Lea and Young (1993)

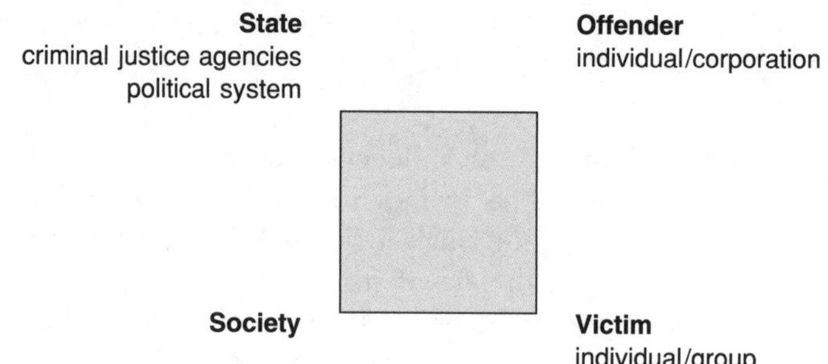

Figure 5.2 The square of crime
(After Young 1997)

approaches which look for a single cause of crime. It also indicates their stress on the social factors underlying crime and victimization.

Relative deprivation

A key part of left realist theory is the concept of relative deprivation. While crime has for long been linked with deprivation, successive studies failed to establish a clear association between income or unemployment and crime, and associating deprivation with crime also neglects white-collar crime (Lea and Young 1993, and see Chapter 7). One of the problems with anomie theory, identified in Chapter 4, is that not all have the same expectations. People's expectations are related to what they feel they deserve. They may compare their situation with others whom they would expect to equal – to a reference group. If these expectations are not met they can feel relatively, rather than absolutely, deprived. Thus unemployed youth may feel relatively deprived compared with employed youth and feel frustrated because their unemployment is not their fault. Young members of ethnic minorities may experience deprivation in comparison to white youth if they have experienced discrimination. Not all of these feelings will lead to crime – there are legitimate avenues to pursue many grievances. Crime is more likely when legitimate avenues are not open and the group is socially or politically marginalized – such as the young unemployed or members of minority ethnic groups. In later work Young (1999; 2007a) has extended this concept to explore global relative deprivation and, along with others he has also explored the complex relationships between relative deprivation, social exclusion and crime, to be discussed in Chapter 7.

Evaluation

The left realist approach proved popular for some time, particularly its re-assertion of the links between social inequalities and crime and its willingness, in comparison to critical criminologists, to engage with a policy agenda. By incorporating and attempting to synthesize the insights of anomie and subcultural theory with labelling approaches and recognizing issues such as gender, race and the plight of victims, it appeared to address many of the shortcomings of earlier theoretical approaches. Its impact on policy was somewhat limited although major cities did carry out victim surveys based on Young's methods (see Chapter 6), and left realists went on to study problems such as prostitution, street robbery and gangs (Lea and Young 1993; Matthews 1993; 1996). They came to be very critical of new Labour's policies on crime, which, they felt, were close to administrative criminology and favoured individual as opposed to structurally based theories (Young and Matthews 2003).

The strengths of the approach are related to serious weaknesses. Its attempt to blend earlier approaches led to criticisms that it was not a distinct approach (Downes and Rock 2007), selectively chose aspects of earlier theories to fit its model, and added little new. Its attempt to relate to policy was criticized as over-populist and as attempting to gain political acceptability. Many of its policies were very similar to those of so-called administrative criminologists and it was indeed dubbed 'left administrative' criminology (Downes and Rock 2007). Despite its claim to incorporate crimes of the streets and suites, it tended to focus largely on the former, prompting criticisms that it, too, neglected the crimes of powerful.

Its attack on critical criminology also provoked heated responses, including assertions that it had created the 'straw man' of left idealism only to knock it down. Their argument about the 'reality of crime' was seen as accepting the ideological construction of crime as a problem, accepting the establishment agenda, and failing to fully account for the class-based nature of law and structures of domination (Sim et al 1987).

Cultural criminology

Young, along with others, has also developed what are seen as the core concerns of sociological criminology in so-called 'cultural criminology', which, like left realism, is critical of administrative criminology and attempts to blend elements of sociological theories (see, for example, Hayward and Young 2004; 2007; Ferrell et al 2008). They take the notion of the inaccessibility of cultural goals for many from strain theory and notions of the excitement of crime and its positive function from the Chicago School and subcultural theory. From interactionism and phenomenology they take the significance of subjective meanings, a preference for ethnographic methods and for cultural analysis and deconstructing signs and symbols. While many in this tradition would not define themselves as Marxists, they also explore relationships between crime, culture, subculture and the wider economic environment, and contemporary analyses of subcultures build on the Gramscian Marxist tradition of critical criminology and the Birmingham School, outlined above. To all this they add elements of Katz' (1988) work on the seductions of crime which focuses on the moral and sensual attractions of 'doing evil'. Even extremely serious crimes such as serial killing, are, argues Katz, sensually attractive to perpetrators, and crime involves emotions such as humiliation, arrogance, ridicule, cynicism, pleasure and excitement. He refers to the 'sneaky thrills' of shoplifting, the hedonism and feelings of superiority in a robbery or 'stick-up' and the sensuality of homicide. Cultural criminology is also influenced by analyses of the late or post modern condition and the primacy of consumerism.

Box 5.7 **Cultural criminology: definitions and themes**

Hayward and Young (2004):

> [Cultural criminology] . . . is 'placing crime and its control in the context of culture: that is viewing both crime and the agencies of control as cultural products – as creative constructs . . .

Ferrell (2006: 104–5) cultural criminology:

> emphasizes the role of image, style, representation and meaning both within illicit subcultures and in the mediated construction of crime and crime control . . .
>
> conceptualizes crime as a subcultural phenomenon organized around symbolic communication, shared aesthetics and collective identity . . .
>
> focuses on dynamics of subcultural style as defining both the internal characteristics of illicit subcultures and external mediated constructions of them . . .

Young (2004: 13):

> Cultural criminology is of importance because it captures the phenomenology of crime – its adrenaline, its pleasure and panic, its excitement and its anger, rage and humiliation, its desperation and its edgework . . .

What is 'cultural criminology'?

There is no one, static definition as it represents an 'ongoing adventure' (Hayward and Young 2007: 103). Box 5.7 contains a series of quotations from some of its leading proponents indicating some of its key features. Contrary to rational choice approaches, it argues that crime may be far from rational and pursued for excitement and thrills. It is more than simply an economic response to deprivation, but responds to the emotional aspects of social inequality by stressing excitement (Hayward 2004). Both rational choice and structural approaches might, for example, attribute economic motivations to stealing a car, whereas to cultural criminologists this also represents a desire to possess a valued status symbol or to engage in the excitement and thrill of the kind of car chases featured in movies and television programmes featuring police pursuits. It therefore attempts to integrate structural analyses with emotions and to 'tell the story of crime' (Hayward and Young 2004). Katz' work was widely criticized for its neglect of social structural context, thus Young (2003) talks of 'Merton with energy, Katz with structure'. Its major themes include:

- **The pursuit of thrills and excitement:** These are illustrated in, for example, Lyng's (1990) concept of *edgework* which emphasizes the 'edgy' and risk-taking elements of crime, which challenges the 'limits'. To Presdee (2000; 2006), crime is likened to a '*carnival*', the traditional role of which is to provide a release from rationality but which was hitherto restricted to festivals. To Hayward (2004) teenage crimes such as vandalism, theft and the destruction of cars illustrate the pursuit of 'thrills' and crime is linked to risk-taking activity and challenging authority.

- **Style:** Ferrell (1995) identifies style as a crucial aspect of criminalization. It is embedded in visible aspects such as hairstyle, posture, clothing, cars and music. It links cultural meaning and criminal identity. In contemporary culture, ethnicity and social class are identified less with skin colour or money than with collective styles, which locate individuals and groups in society, carry the history of a group and can become a badge of resistance. They can also become stigmatic as legal authorities such as the police respond to these visible indicators, for example to particular styles or drivers of particular cars.
- **Consumerism:** The popular role of consumerism in modern culture is reflected in the popular phrases *'you are what you wear'* or *'you are what you consume'*. Our identity, argues Hayward (2004), is constructed through commodities. The move from a production to a consumer society creates perpetually unfulfilled desires as indicated in theories of anomie, along with an emphasis on hedonism and the pursuit of excitement. It can also, argues Hayward, lead to 'relative deprivation of identity' in which consumption is perceived as a 'right' which leads to frustration amongst those denied participation. The significance of consumerism is reflected in offenders targeting consumer goods such as I pods, the latest mobile phones or designer jewellery. Victims are often young people who carry goods of high value on their persons.

Cultural criminologists also point out that crime itself can become a commodity and a major feature of consumerism (Hayward 2004), referring to the way in which, as seen in Chapter 2, music, comics, computer games, films and the Internet reflect

Source: Reuters/Lucas Jackson

The popular game Grand Theft Auto illustrates what cultural criminologists describe as the commodification of crime.

the desirability of transgression as a consumer choice. This is not to suggest that there is a direct link between the consumption of such commodities and crime; rather, it points to the cultural significance of and popular imagery associated with crime.

Evaluation

Examples of cultural criminology will be explored in later chapters as its insights and methods can be applied to a wide range of offences and offenders – not only to youth crime but also to the cultural attractions of 'serious' crime and the 'seductions' of, for example, serial killing, genocide or torture. It is difficult to evaluate what is very much an evolving approach made up of many different strands. To some, such as Newburn (2007: 204) it represents a welcome return to sociological themes, and contrasts with the more narrow approach of rational choice theories and quantitative methods. Others, however, have criticized it as being an over-generalized and sweeping approach, particularly in relation to cultural analysis. Too much is made, argues O'Brien (2005), of limited ethnographic studies and, pointing to the argument that cultural inclusion and structural exclusion can lead to 'rampaging waves of "transgressive" and "expressive" criminal behaviour, it is unclear why it is only "relatively small numbers of mostly male individuals who are involved in these activities"' (O'Brien 2005: 609). Like left realism, some question the extent to which it is really new as work, for example, on style, and consumerism does little more than update earlier interactionist approaches. Like other cultural approaches, it has also been said to neglect economic and structural factors and, like subcultural theory, to romanticize crime (Tierney 2006).

The global context of crime

Globalization

The social changes of the late twentieth and early twenty-first century, referred to above, have taken place in the context of economic and cultural globalization which has also impacted upon crime (Aas 2007). Globalization, itself a contested concept, is generally associated with developments over the latter part of the twentieth century such as the growth of international trade, the rise of multinational corporations and increasing movements of capital and labour, goods and information. This has been enabled by the rise of global communications and modern technology, ease of travel and the ability to communicate worldwide unrestricted by previous limitations of time and space. It has been accompanied by what some describe as increasing convergence, or homogeneity, of economics, politics and culture. Cultural styles and consumer goods are similar across the world to a point where to some, social and cultural differences have disappeared. There has also been a convergence of economic, social and criminal justice policies with, for example, British concerns with 'anti-social' behaviour being echoed across Europe and elsewhere.

To its advocates globalization is essential for the prosperity of the planet and enables hitherto poorer countries to share the prosperity of the West. To its many critics, it is based on neo-liberal economics and free-market ideologies and global economic institutions such as the International Monetary Fund (IMF) or the World Bank; these tend to impose requirements that countries in receipt of loans adopt free-market policies. Many of the schemes which they finance benefit Western companies rather than the indigenous population – indeed some of the activities of the World Bank have been described as crimes of globalization (Friedrichs and Friedrichs 2002). Globalization has also been associated with widening income inequalities *within* and *between* nations, and the so-called global culture is criticized as reflecting the Americanization of culture illustrated in the notion of 'McDonaldization'. The extent to which cultures have changed or persist is also debated, although few dispute that local cultures must co-exist with and adapt to global conditions – with the phrase 'glocal' expressing the complex interrelationships between local and global culture.

Globalization and crime

How are these processes related to crime and to the criminological perspectives outlined above? To some, such as Bauman (1998), globalization divides as much as it unites and it has been related to spatial segregation, separation and exclusion, such as that which took place in areas of the West where the destruction and relocation of industries and employment destroyed entire communities. In place of the promised prosperity for all, there has been a polarization of wealth with, he cites, a mere 22 per cent of global wealth belonging to the 'developing' countries which account for approximately 85 per cent of the world population. The much-vaunted mobility is restricted to those who can afford it, leaving some communities trapped and unable to participate – indeed, he argues, the 'local' has become associated with social deprivation and degradation. Vast differences between the 'global elite' and the 'localized rest' have arguably contributed to new tribal and fundamentalist tendencies.

These processes have been associated with globalized anomie (Passas 2000) and, as seen above, to global 'relative deprivation' (Young 1999; 2003), as the enhanced aspirations of freedom, prosperity and happiness are not achievable for so many. Within many countries there is a growing gap between skilled and unskilled workers and the core of the labour force with permanent jobs, and the periphery, who can only gain casual employment. Inequalities have also grown between nations. This has produced, argues Passas, a set of global illegitimate opportunity structures and multiple motivations for crime amounting to global anomie. Crime can therefore represent the flip side of economic growth and is endemic to neo-liberal policies, a point also made by critical criminologists. To Young (1999; 2003; 2007a) cultural globalization involves portraying high Western standards of consumption, health care and material well-being which leads, in some populations, to 'righteous indignation' in which fundamentalism flourishes and terrorism takes roots.

Globalization can therefore have different effects on crime, many of which will be explored in later chapters. It can lead to crime among the most deprived and excluded in developed nations whose traditional employment has declined (see Chapter 7). It has been associated with crimes and political violence in Third World countries, among whom the promise of prosperity has failed to materialize. It has been linked with so-called transnational crimes in which people denied legitimate movement seek to enter the West illegally by being smuggled or becoming victim to traffickers (see Chapter 14). It enables companies to evade the laws of one jurisdiction to engage in activities in another which can exploit labour, avoid taxes or export hazardous production processes (see Chapters 15 and 16). In summary, as Barak (2001), argues, globalization produces:

- crimes of resistance among the dispossessed (*fundamentalism, terrorism*)
- acquisitive crimes (*in abandoned communities*)
- crimes of domination (*corporate crime*)

Concluding comments

This chapter has reviewed a very broad range of theories and, taken together with Chapter 4, readers might feel somewhat confused by the range of theories and the evident disagreement between them. How is crime to be analysed? Has all this theoretical work advanced our knowledge about crime? Which theories are more useful? Is crime itself a useful concept? There are no simple answers to these questions. Throughout later chapters the contrast between those which focus on individual characteristics and pathologies and those focusing on social structural and cultural factors will be highlighted. Some theories aim to contribute to governmental agendas, which have shifted from seeking to understand to controlling crime, while others criticize criminal justice policies for reflecting dominant ideologies and for their tendency to criminalize marginal groups. The theories looked at in this chapter have broadened the approaches of the classic theories outlined in Chapter 4 to stress the impact of wider social processes such as globalization and global cultures. It will be seen in subsequent chapters that all of these approaches assist our understanding of crime, often in combination. To them must be added the insights of feminist perspectives which will be explored in Chapter 8. More recent approaches have also included the victim of crime, and these concerns will be explored in subsequent chapters.

Review questions

1. Taking an example of deviance from your own experience, draw up a deviancy amplification chart to illustrate the ideas of the labelling perspective.

2. Which groups are currently subject to what you understand as a criminalization process? Outline the main features of this criminalization.

3. What are the strengths and weaknesses of rational choice and lifestyle based approaches?

4 Why is the phrase 'crime *really* is a problem' so significant for left and right realists?

5 Describe situations in which crime could be attributed to absolute deprivation and contrast these with situations in which it could be attributed to relative deprivation.

6 Consider the consumption patterns common among young people, and the most popular films, magazines, clothes and computer games. To what extent to they reflect the 'commodification' of crime and other themes of cultural criminology?

Key reading

As for Chapter 4, a number of texts cover the main theoretical approaches. Most of those recommended for Chapter 4 are also relevant such as:

Downes, D. and Rock, P. (2007) ***Understanding Deviance: A Guide to the Sociology of Crime and Rule Breaking***, revised 2nd edn, Oxford: Clarendon Press.

Hopkins Burke, R. (2005) ***An Introduction to Criminological Theory***, Cullompton: Willan Publishing.

Lilly, J. R., Cullen, F. and Ball, R. (2002) ***Criminological Theory: Context and consequences***, London: Sage 3rd edn is also particularly useful for American 'right' realist and other 'neo-conservative' approaches along with providing a good introduction to most theories.

Tierney, J. (2006) ***Criminology: Theory and context***, 2nd edn, London: Pearson Education.

Valier, C. (2002) ***Theories of Crime and Punishment***, London: Pearson/Longman.

Chapter 6
The victims of crime

This chapter will look at:

- ➜ The social construction of the crime victim
- ➜ The changing role of the victim
- ➜ Victimological perspectives
  - Conservative, radical, feminist and critical victimology
- ➜ Surveying victims
- ➜ The impact of crime
- ➜ The fear of crime
- ➜ The social distribution of victimization

The offender, rather than the victim, was the main focus of earlier theories of crime, although from around the 1970s the victim and victimization have featured more strongly (Chapter 5). To left realists, the 'reality' of victimization indicated the 'reality' of crime. To administrative criminologists, the victim plays a key role in the situations in which crime takes place and has a major role to play in crime prevention. To 'right' realists and conservative criminologists, the criminal justice process has been overly offender-centred and victims' interests in justice and punishment should be a major focus. Groups representing the interests of women and minority ethnic citizens drew attention to what some describe as the 'new victims' of sexual, domestic and racial violence and critical criminologists pointed to the many harms caused by corporate, state and environmental crime. As crime became politicized, so, too, did the victim. Victim's interests in having 'their' offender punished were emphasized in the popular punitivism of the late twentieth century, and the unrecognized needs of victims became subject to more welfare centred policies (Goodey 2005; Walklate 2007a). Concerns about the risks of victimization have also been associated with more general feelings of insecurity associated with globalization. The development of a 'risk society' and a 'culture of fear' (Furedi 2003), particularly in the wake of terrorist offences and natural disasters, also contributed to a general feeling that 'we are all victims now' (Mythen 2007; Walklate 2007a).

This chapter will start by exploring how victimization is socially constructed before outlining changing views of the victim. It will detail the main perspectives associated with victimology and discuss the role and significance of the victim survey introduced in Chapter 3. It will then look at the various ways in which crime affects individual victims and the general public. It is often said that the public have an exaggerated fear of crime and this assumption will be critically examined along with the general phrase 'fear of crime'. Further aspects of victimization, such as its social distribution, and fuller details of the findings of victim surveys as they relate to specific offences will form part of later chapters.

Constructing the victim

Like crime itself, victimization is socially constructed and the criminal law may not provide an adequate baseline for a definition. Box 6.1 details the UN definition, which, argues Goodey (2005), is not restricted to victimization from narrowly defined criminal offences, but embraces a wide variety of harms including emotional suffering and loss of rights. It includes abuses of state power along with harms inflicted in private as well as in public, which have often been neglected, and it includes the more indirect impact of crime on families and others affected by a crime.

Deserving victims?

Like the term criminal, the term victim is subject to social and cultural constructions. Often cited is Christie's (1986) notion of the 'ideal' victim assumed to be 'innocent' and to have done nothing to bring about victimization. These are generally described as 'deserving', in that they 'deserve' sympathy and support, and as seen in Chapter 2, some victims, most typically children and old people, attract more high-profile media attention. Walklate (2007a: 28) refers to a 'Little Red Riding Hood' imagery of the innocent child and the 'wicked wolf'. Deserving victims can be contrasted with less deserving ones such as the drunken victim of an assault resulting from a fight, the householder who leaves a window open or the woman who dresses in a way which men might interpret as provocative. These victims might be seen to have 'asked for it', although all of these representations reflect cultural assumptions and stereotypes (see Chapter 2).

Nonetheless, this contrast is deeply rooted in commonsense understandings of victimization and is reflected in law and policy. The techniques of neutralization

Box 6.1 Defining victims

The 1985 United Nations Declaration of Basic Principles of Justice for Victims of Crime and Abuse of Power definition:

> 'Victims' means persons who, individually or collectively have suffered harm, including physical or mental injury, emotional suffering, economic loss or substantial impairment of their fundamental rights, through acts or omissions that are in violation of criminal laws operative within Member States, including those laws proscribing criminal abuse of power . . . A person may be considered a victim, under this Declaration, regardless of whether the perpetrator is identified, apprehended, prosecuted or convicted and regardless of the familial relationship between the perpetrator and the victim. The term 'victim' also includes, where appropriate, the immediate family or dependants of the direct victim and persons who have suffered harm in intervening to assist victims in distress or to prevent victimization. (*www.unhcrhr.ch/html/menu3/b/h-comp49.htm*)

Source: Goodey (2005: 10)

described in Chapter 4 reflect the notion of the undeserving victim by suggesting that victims 'had it coming to them'. In a criminal trial, victims' credibility may become an issue as offenders attempt to justify their actions. Victim compensation schemes exclude victims who have contributed to their victimization and sentences vary according to the nature of victimization. Defrauding a 'vulnerable' pensioner, for example, may be seen as more serious than defrauding a company or the state (Levi 1989). This raises a number of questions. Is a burglary any less serious or the burglar less blameworthy because a window is left open? Is leaving a car radio or briefcase visible in a car inviting theft? Is rape less serious because a woman has invited a man into her home? Is an attack in a street the victim's fault for being in that street? The victim rather than the offender is, therefore, often blamed.

Equal victims?

Chapter 2 illustrated how notions of 'ideal' victims are reflected in the media. It also suggested, however, that not all such cases are treated equally and Box 6.2 outlines the contrasting way in which two missing girls were dealt with. Depictions of the ideal victim are related therefore to structural variables such as class, race or gender. In addition to the Millie Dowler case in Box 6.2, Greer points out that two similarly aged boys, Patrick Warren and David Spencer went missing at the same time as Holly Wells and Jessica Chapman (see Chapter 2). They were working-class boys from a West Midlands council estate, had been in trouble at school and one had been involved in shoplifting. While Holly and Jessica captured the hearts and minds of a nation, argues Greer (2007: 23), few knew about Patrick and David's disappearance. Similarly, the respective killings of black victims such as Damilola Taylor and Stephen Lawrence did not feature so strongly until more concerted appearances by their (also respectable) families – with the Lawrence murder initially being interpreted as victim-precipitated (see Chapter 10).

Box 6.2 Equally deserving victims?

In the summer of 2002, 13-year-old Milly Dowler went missing in Walton-on-Thames on her way home from school. Considerable press coverage featured family photos and videos, and her parents appeared in press conferences underlining their emotional trauma and asking for informants to come forward. The parents were clearly well-to-do and the home was depicted as stable and loving. Milly Dowler's body was found in September 2002, six months after her disappearance. The subsequent arrest of a man for the killing, in March 2010 (BBC News 2010b), led to more publicity and further use of the now iconic picture.

During the investigation, a body was found, subsequently identified as that of Hannah Williams, a working-class girl from a single-parent, low-income family. Yet there was little press coverage of her disappearance and murder. Greer (2007) found that there were a mere 60 articles about this, mostly after she was found, and Jewkes (2004: 53) argues that Hannah was forgotten as soon as she was found. According to a police spokeswoman her mother 'wasn't really press-conference material'.

Source: Greer (2007) and Jewkes (2004)

Other factors affect these variations, including cultural and geographic proximity and the assumed ability of the public to identify with victims. Mythen (2007) and Walklate (2007a) contrast the massive, saturation coverage of the exploding of the airliner over Lockerbie in Scotland in 1988 with a terrorist-inspired explosion around the same time in Niger which attracted little attention. Similarly, the major responses to the events of 9/11 and 7/7 can be contrasted with the often scant coverage of what, for many months, were almost daily attacks on civilians in Iraq. Thus the 'terrorist victim we are invited to imagine is an affluent white urban Christian Anglo-Saxon, not an impoverished Baghdadi Muslim' (Mythen 2007: 470).

Pariahs or saints?

The social construction of victims involves ambiguities summed up by Downes who talks of a 'hybrid of pariah and saint' (Downes, cited in Rock 2007b: 41). This is reflected in the dichotomy between the deserving (good) victim and the undeserving (bad) victim, and representations also tend to place victim and offender in a binary opposition. Yet offenders can also be victims, and drawn from the same social groups. Victimhood also carries some of the stigma of crime as people often avoid and are unsure how to behave towards victims. To Rock (2007b: 41), they have 'something of the "uncomfortable other" about them and are "riddled with taboos" '.

The image of the ideal victim also contains elements of weakness and passivity, and examples of archetypal victims reflect conceptions of vulnerability. The elderly and children are assumed to require protection and to be helpless in the face of an attacker and their status as ideal victims reflects their assumed dependency and powerlessness. Gender is also a major factor and some feminists reject the word victim preferring to describe women who have suffered from domestic violence as 'survivors' – implying a more 'active' role. It has also affected the way in which male victimization is portrayed – while men are more likely to be the victims of many forms of violent crime, they are cast as perpetrators rather than victims and the emotions associated with victims are seen as 'unmanly' (see Chapters 9 and 11).

The changing role of the victim

Victims were relatively invisible in historical portrayals of criminal justice, and Kearon and Godfrey (2007) trace their shifting role over time, from being an *essential actor*, through a *symbolic actor* to their current position as a *fragmented actor*. Although the state gradually assumed the right to publicly punish offenders over the centuries, it rarely prosecuted any but the most serious offences and, until the twentieth century, victims were 'central to the whole process of detecting and prosecuting crime' (Kearon and Godfrey 2007: 22). By the end of the First World War police forces had assumed their prosecution role which, along with the expanding regulatory agencies, led to the virtual disappearance of the victim from court.

From the nineteenth century onward the 'victim of crime' nonetheless became more prominent in popular and public discourse and images of the victimization of women and children played a symbolic role in law reform. The exploitation of female and child labour, for example, was a key factor in the nineteenth-century Factory Acts. Melodramatic images of victims were common in Victorian times which saw the emergence of deserving victims. Widows were seen as 'vulnerable' and 'little old ladies' featured as major victims of fraud in, for example, the railway boom (Robb 2006). This symbolic role, argue Kearon and Godfrey, persisted for most of the twentieth century and was related to the emerging concern for the victim in criminal justice policy. More recently the role of the victim has become more fragmented, with the symbolic role continuing along with images of 'vicarious' victimization in relation to the generalized 'culture of fear'. At the same time, 'new' victims emerged, as outlined above.

The rediscovery of the victim

From the mid twentieth century the victim was rediscovered in criminology and criminal justice policy, and emerged as a 'key player' (Goodey 2005). This has often been attributed to a victim 'movement', although concern with the victim of crime emanated from diverse sources and there was no single concerted campaign or coherent set of theories or policies (Newburn 2003; Davies et al 1996; Zedner 1997). Box 6.3 illustrates the factors associated with these developments many of which are related to the politicization of crime, the emergence of feminism and theoretical approaches such as left realism. On the other hand, the introduction of the Criminal Injuries Compensation Scheme in 1964 did not result from any campaigning by victims but represented an extension of state protection and insurance

Box 6.3 Factors associated with the rising prominence of the victim

- An increase in official crime rates.
- Revelations of extensive hidden crime by crime surveys.
- Heightened fear of crime.
- Public intolerance of increasing crime and social disorder.
- Failure of the rehabilitative or offender treatment model, and its replacement with retributive justice linked to victims.
- Revelations in research and the media of crime against vulnerable victims and victims' maltreatment by the criminal justice system.
- Recognition and politicization by feminists of the problem of violence against women and children.
- Recognition and politicization of the problem of racist violence.
- Politicization of rising crime rates by politicians focusing on 'law and order', 'crime reduction' and victims as 'vote winners'.
- Movement towards citizens' charters / patients' 'rights' that included victims.

Source: Goodey (2005: 13)

to crime victims (Rock 1990; Newburn 1995). This scheme, however, is highly selective and reflects the distinction between deserving and undeserving victims. It excludes anyone related to offenders or who might be seen as having contributed to the offence. The Home Office White Paper introducing the scheme illustrated the rationale for this:

> The Government does not accept that the State is liable for injuries caused to people by the acts of others. The public does, however, feel a sense of responsibility for and sympathy with the *innocent* victim and it is right that this feeling should find practical expression in the provision of compensation on behalf of the community.
>
> (Home Office White Paper 1964, cited in Newburn 1995: 150)

The voluntary sector was also concerned with victims, who had voiced a number of complaints about their treatment by the police and courts. They complained, for example, that:

- While they provided the police with essential information they were ignored after making an initial report.
- They were not informed adequately about the progress of investigations or whether they would be required in court.
- If called as a witness, they were ill-prepared for the often hostile cross-questioning from defence lawyers and faced reliving painful experiences and encountering offenders in court (Rock 1990; 1991).

A network of voluntary victim support schemes under the umbrella of the National Association of Victim Support Schemes (NAVSS) developed from 1974, aiming to provide emotional support and help for victims and witnesses (Rock 1991). A range of academic studies confirmed victims' need for support by exposing the impact of crime on individuals and revealing the extent of what came to be known as 'secondary' victimization by the criminal justice process (Davies et al 1996; 2003).

These developments were largely politically neutral (Goodey 2005; Walklate 2007a) although they enabled governments to appear to be doing something for victims. Other influences were more overtly political, in particular the rise of the 'new victims' referred to above, which challenged the conventional construction of crime and victimization. Women's groups argued that female victims were further victimized in the criminal justice process as the police often took little action against 'domestics' and failed to take complaints of rape seriously. In court, the rape trial could in effect become a trial of the victim. They also set up refuges for women in violent homes and support groups for the victims of rape (Dobash and Dobash 1992; Zedner 1997). Other campaigns involved racial harassment and hate crimes (see Chapter 10).

Risk and the culture of fear

Victims were further politicized towards the latter part of the twentieth century. Identifying the risks of crime was central to lifestyle-based approaches and featured strongly in the growth of national victim surveys – in themselves part of the increased focus on the victim. These were also related to responsibilization – the view that victims themselves were partly responsible for their victimization and should play a role in preventing it. The disillusionment with rehabilitation meant that doing something for victims became equated with doing something about crime. Some argue that victims' interests were hijacked as part of the rising tide of punitiveness. The popularity, for example, of retributive justice was said to reflect the interest of victims (Goodey 2005), so much so that the category of victim came to act as a 'key instrument of penal repression and policy formation around law and order' (Mythen 2007: 465). The ensuing 'victim-centred' policies and victim charters were, however, widely criticized as falling far short of a recognition of victims' 'rights' (Davies et al 2003; Walklate 2007a). They also involved the victim being seen as a consumer (Walklate 2007a) and as a commodity (Green 2007) in which the 'obsession' with insecurity led to development of new and expensive security devices.

These can be related to theories about risk and the more generalized 'fear' of crime and insecurity in contemporary society. As seen in Chapter 5, social theorists and criminologists have pointed to the insecurity brought about by globalization and late modern conditions, which some link to a 'culture of fear'. As Goodey (2005) explains, the concept of risk has shifted from a narrow, statistical calculation of the risk of victimization in victim surveys to the more generalized risk of crime and other insecurities brought about by a perceived loss of control over areas of life such as employment, financial security and crime. The rising crime rates of the last decades of the twentieth century also increased people's personal risk of victimization, heightened their fear of crime and questioned the ability of the state to control crime. To Furedi (2003), rising fears of crime and sporadic panics about extreme but rare acts of violence make concerns about risk a permanent condition and encourages victimhood in all of us. While very generalized (Mythen 2007), this nonetheless expresses the salience of victimization and the fear of crime which will be discussed below.

Victimological perspectives

The 'rediscovery' of the victim was associated with trends within criminology of which victimology is often regarded as a 'cousin' or 'sub discipline'. The victim was largely invisible in earlier criminology with, argues Rock (2007b), each set of theories having their own reason for neglecting the victim. Positivists were primarily concerned with the body and mind of the criminal leaving the victim outside their central field of inquiry. Early sociological theories such as functionalism were more concerned with the 'deep structures' of society and the functions of crime with 'no place for the pathos and pain of individual victimisation' (Rock 2007b: 39). While interactionists, with their focus on ethnographic methods, should have been more concerned with victims, they focused instead on crimes without victims, and indeed the offender was cast as the victim of the criminal justice process. And while critical criminologists were concerned with the harms caused by exploitation and corporate crime, they were less concerned with the more mundane victimization of everyday crime. Nonetheless, some victimological perspectives were linked to criminological ones. Some followed the methods and assumptions of positivism, and the victim was a central concern of administrative criminology, feminism and left realism. Critical victimology, which seeks to relate victimization to wider social structural factors, derived from critical criminology, and theories such as the culture of fear are related to what Mythen (2007) describes as 'cultural victimology'.

Conservative victimology

Early victimologists explored the extent to which the victim 'caused' crime by precipitating it and asked whether victims possessed any distinctive characteristics which made their victimization more likely (Walklate 1989; Davies et al 1996; Walklate 2007a). It was hypothesized that some people were more prone to victimization, that victims precipitated offences and that different lifestyles carried a higher risk of victimization. These arguments are summarized below.

Victim proneness

To von Hentig (1948), some groups were more prone to becoming victims. These included young people, women, the elderly, the 'mentally defective' and immigrants and he also referred to the wanton and the fighting victim. This was largely based on theoretical speculation rather than empirical study (Walklate 1989) and these notions clearly involve stereotypy. The idea of victim proneness also featured in the work of Mendelsohn (1947) who viewed some victims as culpable because they contributed to the crime. To him, victims ranged from the most innocent, such as children, to the most guilty, such as the person who attacks someone and is killed in retaliation.

Victim precipitation

Other studies attempted to establish the extent to which victims, especially of violence, directly precipitated an offence. In a study of police records, Wolfgang (1958) estimated that victims precipitated 26 per cent of homicides. Amir (1971) estimated that 19 per cent of rapes were victim precipitated, where women had agreed to sex but later retracted or had not resisted strongly enough. This attracted fierce criticism on the grounds that it implied that women were inviting rape, and some queried how strongly women should have to resist. Victim precipitation thereby became associated with victim blaming. Another difficulty was the reliance of these studies on official reports, which include the interpretations of investigators, and are not accurate and unbiased accounts of events (Walklate 1989; 2007a).

Lifestyles and victimization

As seen in Felson's work, detailed in Chapter 5, people's lifestyles are strongly associated with victimization as, quite simply, those who never go out are unlikely to be attacked in the street while many people live, work or spend their leisure time in places where crime is more likely. Earlier, Hindelang and his colleagues (1978) had argued that there was a strong link between routine daily activities and exposure to high-risk victim situations. Role expectations and structural characteristics such as class, age or gender were also important as they affected lifestyles and victimization could be related to the amount of time spent in public places. This can partly explain findings that victims and offenders tend to be of the same age group, live in the same area and are from the same social class. Both victims and perpetrators of assaults taking place in public, for example, tend to be young males who go out drinking.

These approaches are often described as conventional or conservative victimology, in that their view of the crime problem 'married well with conservative politics' (Walklate 2007a: 32). They focus largely on public and street crimes and were limited to crimes with identifiable victims, thereby neglecting corporate or white-collar crime (Davies et al 2003). The concepts of victim precipitation and victim proneness quite clearly involve victim blaming and writers uncritically accepted stereotypical assumptions about, for example, gender. Many assumed, as did Amir, that the woman who does not struggle enough has precipitated an assault (Zedner 1997). Lifestyle approaches can involve victim blaming by implying that those with more risky lifestyles can avoid victimization, which may not be possible for those who cannot avoid dangerous areas such as those who live or work in them. Therefore they neglect the structural dimensions of victimization and victim–offender relationships; while they describe groups and lifestyles with high risks, they do not explore the reasons *why* these groups face such high risks (Walklate 1989; 2007a). Despite these limitations, conventional victimology echoes widely held views about victims and affected criminal justice policy and subsequent research (Davies et al 2003).

Radical victimology

While later criticized for neglecting the victim, radical criminology was concerned to expose the 'human misery' created by the crimes of the powerful. Thus Box (1983), detailing deaths attributable to breaches of safety regulations, argued persuasively that corporate crime 'kills' and has real victims. A major part of left realism, outlined in Chapter 5, was the development of radical victimology (Young 1986). This was to focus on the structural basis of victimization and it was argued that large-scale victim surveys neglected the greater victimization of the poor and inhabitants of inner-city areas. Left realists argued for more qualitative, locally based victim surveys which would better reflect the 'lived reality' of crime and would attempt to tap hidden crimes of sexual violence and harassment (Jones et al 1986). The third Islington Crime Survey also included questions on experiences of corporate crimes such as consumer fraud, health and safety offences and offences committed by landlords (Pearce 1992). Radical victimologists also saw the victim survey as a form of democratic input into the framing of criminal justice policy (Davies et al 1996). While these surveys attempted to go further than national surveys, and, argues Goodey (2005), may have contributed to later sweeps of the BCS including questions on domestic violence, they were criticized for their reliance on 'positivist' survey methods, for not fully including elements of gender and race or exploring crimes of the powerful (Croall 2001a; Goodey 2005; Walklate 2007a).

Feminist victimology

Feminist approaches were highly critical of the stereotypical assumptions and victim blaming of conventional victimology, particularly in relation to rape, which re-enforced the construction of the passive and powerless female victim (Walklate 1996). They also criticized the focus on offences taking place in public which neglected violence in the home. As outlined above, they researched and campaigned to improve the treatment of female survivors. While victim surveys such as the BCS tended to ask questions which related to short time spans such as a year, feminists were concerned to expose the victimization of women over the life span. They were criticized, however, for using, in some studies, the 'positivist' survey technique and for emphasizing women's victimization at the expense of men's (see Chapters 9 and 11).

Critical victimology

Many of these criticisms came from an emerging critical victimological perspective. Mawby and Walklate (1994) called for a deeper understanding of the meaning of victimization and what is meant by words like 'lived reality'. They also argued for a critical analysis of the extent to which the 'rediscovery' of the victim served victims' interests or those of the state. It is also crucial, they argued, to relate the concept of victim to wider issues of state power and domination as is done for crime (Mawby and Walklate 1994). Such an approach, argues Walklate (2007a: 50), involves challenging the use of the term 'victim' and analysing the circumstances under which it might be applicable. It looks at the process through which victim status is assumed and at how a victim identity is developed. Rather than being concerned, as are positivists, with measuring the patterns and regularities of criminal victimization, or what she describes as the 'mere appearance' of things, it is concerned to capture 'underlying generative mechanisms'. It thus challenges the 'white male heterosexist view of criminal victimization implicit in "administrative" criminological concerns' and builds on the insights of radical victimologies. It relates the concept of 'victim' and the experience of victimization to broader questions of social structure and power, by exploring, in more depth than do positivist or radical victimologies, the interconnected links between social class, gender, race and crime (Davies et al 2007). It also recognizes and critically explores victimization which goes on 'behind our backs' – at the relatively hidden victimization in the home and workplace, the experiences of victimization on a global scale which are made less of in the West, and the more diffuse victimization associated with white-collar or corporate crime.

Surveying victims

What has come to be called the victim survey 'industry' played a major role in the development of victimology. Some of the main features of victim surveys were outlined in Chapter 3, and detailed findings in relation to specific issues will be given in later chapters, while this section focuses on the method itself and its main strengths and limitations. Following the growing use of victim surveys in the United States and some exploratory investigations in Britain (Sparks et al 1977), the first BCS was carried out in 1981, since when, in Britain and abroad, their frequency and scope has increased dramatically. They have been used by local councils, community planning and safety organizations, commercial and industrial groups, think-tanks and political parties and have fed into local and national policy forums and political debates. Internationally they are conducted in over seventy different countries (Hoyle and Zedner 2007). They have become more technologically sophisticated with the traditional interview being supplemented by telephone and computerized surveys and self-completion questionnaires for more sensitive topics. Their analysis has become more sophisticated, with crime being 'mapped' against socio-economic descriptions of neighbourhoods, and complex analyses calculating the 'risks' of crime and people's reported experiences of and worries about it.

As seen in Chapter 3, victim surveys aim to obtain a more accurate picture of crime than that provided by official criminal statistics and look at trends in and the risks of different crimes amongst different groups (Mayhew 1996). The aims of government surveys are inevitably policy-oriented and some, such as those carried out by local community safety partnerships or business groups, are framed around the issues considered most important by those commissioning the survey. This has placed many surveys firmly under the umbrella of administrative criminology (Walklate 2007a), although the method itself has been, as outlined above, adopted by more critical approaches.

The limitations of victim surveys

While victim surveys have produced an enormous amount of information they have many theoretical, methodological and practical problems. Many criticisms involve the method itself and their location within the positivist and administrative criminological traditions. This raises questions about what is asked, what is not asked and how answers can be interpreted. Some use different methods and definitions making their results difficult to compare and many offences are omitted. Respondents may not always remember incidents clearly. Some of the main issues are outlined below.

The victim survey method

Victim surveys typically involve quantitative research in which large samples of the population are asked about their experiences of different crimes over a fixed period of time, and respondents are asked, basically, to 'tick' boxes. Inevitably, complex experiences and emotions are reduced to very short answers to 'fit' predetermined categories. Events are labelled as 'offences' and how the offence has affected the victim is reduced to terms such as 'a lot' or 'not very much'. Complex feelings about safety and security are reduced to questions about being 'worried' 'a lot' or 'a little'. They cannot, therefore, fully capture the 'lived reality' of crime. Moreover, questions about specific crimes within specific time periods fail to reflect the impact of continuing states of affairs such as domestic violence, racial harassment or persistent disorder, vandalism and bullying which can, for some, become a 'normal' part of life (Genn 1988; Walklate 2007a).

Defining offences and victimization

Victim surveys inevitably omit many offences. Some may be unaware that activities which harm them are crimes, such as offences committed against young children, the mentally ill or elderly dementia sufferers. Early victim surveys were particularly weak in relation to domestic violence although there have been considerable improvements in recent years (see Chapter 11). Booster studies have also been used to explore experiences of racial harassment and the victimization of young people – major omissions from early studies. They are also limited to offences with direct effects on victims which omit many kinds of organized, environmental or corporate crime with more indirect and diffuse effects (Croall 2001a; Whyte 2007a).

Not all of these omissions are due to technical difficulties and, as will be argued in Chapters 15 and 16, questions could be asked about, for example, corporate crimes, some of which were included in the third Islington Crime Survey (Pearce 1992). They are not, however, widely regarded as 'crimes', nor are offences committed by state agencies. Ideological factors and the way in which crime and victimization is constructed therefore restrict the kinds of crime which are covered. The effects of some of the harms detailed by Tombs and Hillyard (2004), outlined in Chapter 5, could also be included enabling a comparison between crime and other harms.

Counting offences

Victims' accounts and experiences do not always fit readily into legal offence categories – particularly, as is the case with violent offences or assault, where these reflect degrees of severity. Victim surveys aim to compare victim reports with police records, and use legal criteria to determine how it can be classified. Other surveys use different criteria and often include incidents such as bullying or harassment which are not technically crimes. This makes surveys difficult to compare and produces different results.

Choosing samples

National victim surveys are typically samples taken from households which omit a range of 'hard to reach' groups, such as the homeless, those who live in hostels or temporary shelters, and those in prison or illegal immigrants. These groups, however, experience considerable amounts of victimization (Pain et al 2002; Goodey 2003; Croall 2007a).

The accuracy of victims' reports

To Walklate (2007a: 58) 'the main limitations of the criminal victimization survey can be summarized in two words: the respondent'. Victims may exaggerate incidents or fail to remember them at all. Some incidents will have been dramatic, arousing a range of mixed feelings and occasioning lengthy descriptions. Surveys cover a fixed time period which creates the problem of telescoping in which victims remember an incident but move it forwards or backwards in time. While these problems can cancel each other out, research indicates that more trivial incidents tend to be forgotten or telescoped backwards, whereas more serious ones are remembered and telescoped forwards. This may lead to an overestimation of serious incidents (Coleman and Moynihan 1996). In addition, victims may not wish to reveal particularly sensitive experiences, and despite attempts to overcome this, some surveys continue to underestimate the extent of violence and sexual abuse in the home (see Chapter 11). Moreover, as people's definition of 'crime' varies across subcultures, some victims may not report incidents which are, to them, part of life, but which to others would constitute something serious. This can of course work in a reverse fashion where respondents might report incidents of 'disorder' which may amount to little more than kids hanging around.

Interpreting victim surveys

All these limitations must be borne in mind when interpreting the findings of victim surveys. It is important to determine, for example, how the study was carried out, for what purpose, and exactly what questions were asked, and indeed, what questions were not asked. Surveys often deal with broad statistical aggregates which can be misleading. Considerable criticism, for example, surrounded the conclusions of the first BCS that the average person could expect a robbery once every five centuries; an assault resulting in an injury once every century; a car to be stolen once every sixty years and a burglary every forty years (Hough and Mayhew 1983). This gave a somewhat reassuring picture of people's risk of crime, leading to the conclusion that people's fear of crime was exaggerated. But, it could be asked, who is the average person? Local surveys, such as the Islington surveys produced far higher figures, suggesting that people's fears were far from unrealistic (Jones et al 1986).

Therefore, much as crime figures indicate which offences the police choose to act against, victim surveys indicate victimization from the crimes which surveys choose to ask about. If this is recognized and their results critically evaluated, victim surveys can provide a welter of information about people's experiences of crime and they do add enormously to our overall knowledge. Surveys such as the ICVS tell us, for example, that many forms of crime are experienced on a global scale even if they reflect primarily Western definitions (Goodey 2005). They have, moreover, despite an association with conservative and administrative criminology, proved themselves capable of being improved to incorporate other issues (Walklate 2007a). As will be seen in successive chapters, they are a useful source of information as a starting point for further research and indicate some ways in which crime impacts differentially on different groups.

The impact of crime

Victim surveys provide considerable information about the impact of crime, which involves more than the direct effect of individual offences on individual victims. Many offences lead not only to material loss or physical injury but have emotional effects. Secondary victimization, outlined above, must also be considered along with the indirect effects of offences on victims' families, bystanders, witnesses, offenders' families and the wider community. For some victims, crime is a recurring experience, and for others the threat of crime is important irrespective of any actual offence. This section will explore some of these different effects. As many of these will be looked at in more depth in subsequent chapters, it will focus on the general impact of victimization.

The objective and subjective impact of crime

A distinction is often made between the objective and subjective impact of offences (Walklate 1989). These different effects are illustrated in attempts to calculate the costs of crime, detailed in Box 6.4. The objective impact includes the immediate

Box 6.4 The economic costs of crime

A Home Office study (Brand and Price 2000) estimated the cost of selected notifiable offences including violence, sexual offences, robbery, burglary, thefts, fraud and forgery and criminal damage, with estimated costs based on information from the BCS and commercial victimization surveys. It found:

- The total cost of crime to England and Wales in 1999/2000 was around £60 billion, although this does not include the impact on the victim's or the public's quality of life.
- Twenty per cent of this is made up by the cost of the criminal justice response to crime, with around £19 million representing the cost of property stolen or damaged and nearly £18 billion representing the direct emotional and physical impact on victims.
- This is not a full figure as the study excluded a number of offences such as drug-trafficking, handling stolen goods, public order offences, fare evasion and many summary offences.

A later attempt provides estimated costs (at 2003 prices) for crimes covered by the BCS plus sexual offences and homicide. Estimated costs include costs to the criminal justice system and the victim including lost income, adverse health effects and stolen property. It also takes into account the more 'intangible' costs of the reduction in the victim's quality of life.

- On these calculations, homicide emerges as the crime with greatest costs – estimated as £1,310,000 to victims and £1,460,000 in total.
- Sexual and violent offences have higher costs than property offences with, for example, the total costs of sexual offences being estimated at £31,400 and serious wounding being estimated at £7,280 compared to the total cost of theft of a vehicle (the highest figure of all property offences) estimated at £4,410, domestic burglary at £3,270 and other thefts at £634 (Thorpe et al 2007).

financial or physical effect; however, as illustrated in Box 6.4, many offences have additional costs. Stolen items have to be replaced, damage to property must be repaired and, even if the victim is insured, claiming from insurance policies involves paperwork, time and trouble. This contributes to the 'nuisance value' of offences which also includes the time taken to report offences, give statements to the police and possibly attend court. Some offences can have far-reaching effects. Dixon et al (2006, cited in Walklate 2007a: 73) report, for example, that in 2002/3, 850,000 victims suffered loss of earnings, 180,000 moved home, and 32,000 changed jobs as a result of the crime.

These kinds of figures cannot fully encompass the subjective, psychological impact of offences on victims and their families, which inevitably varies according to the crime itself, the situation in which it takes place and the situation of the individual victim. For some, the offence can be little more than a nuisance or slightly annoying. In general, as illustrated in Figure 6.1, taken from the SCJS, victims report a mixture of emotions such as shock and anger and a smaller number of offences, often violent ones, have effects such as sleeplessness, panic attacks or depression (MacLeod et al 2009) and others have identified avoidance of particular places, recurrent memories of the event and, with serious crimes, post-traumatic stress syndrome and other psychological problems (Zedner 1997; Goodey 2005; Walklate 2007a). Burglary victims may report feelings that privacy has been invaded, and victims of economic crimes such as fraud also report feelings of violation of trust which

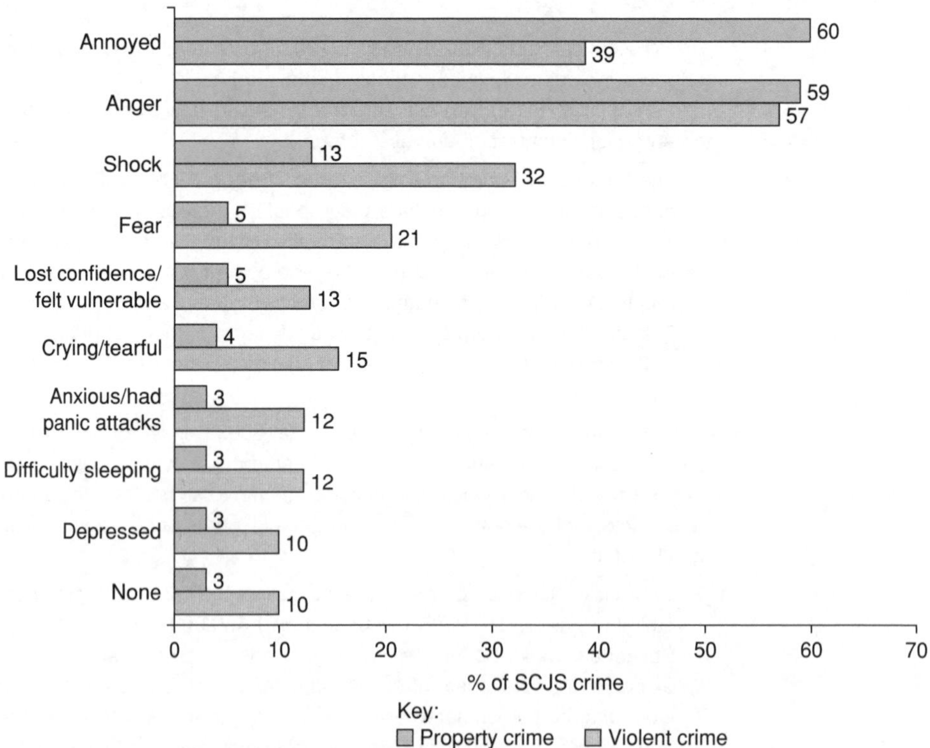

Figure 6.1 Emotional responses to crime

Source: MacLeod et al (2009)

are in some ways similar to the emotions experienced by rape victims (Levi and Pithouse 1992). All of these, however, shade into insignificance compared to the shattering effects of long-term abuse within families and intimate relationships, and serious crimes such as murder or rape.

The direct and indirect effects of victimization

Some crimes affect more people than those directly victimized, while others have no direct victim but have a diffuse effect on residents and communities, such as those outlined below.

Effects on families and relatives

Victims' relatives can also be adversely affected, seen most vividly in murder cases where relatives require counselling and support. In some cases, particularly those such as terrorist attacks or spree murders, when large numbers are killed in one incident, relatives have formed support groups to exert pressure on official agencies. The children of victims can also be affected – children of burglary victims may suffer from insomnia, nightmares and increased bed-wetting and children are also adversely affected by living in homes with violent parents (Morgan and Zedner 1992). Offenders' families are relatively 'hidden' victims. Drug addicts, for example, often steal from their families who may have to exclude offenders from their homes. Families of those suspected and convicted of murder also face problems such as possibly being under suspicion themselves and understanding and coming to terms with what has happened (Rock 1998).

Witnessing crime

Witnesses also suffer from shock, heightened fear and can feel threatened. In some offences they are directly threatened as, for example, in an armed robbery or other violent incident. They may fear intimidation if they give evidence to the police. They also suffer the nuisance and inconvenience of having to give statements and, like victims, can face hostile questioning in court as their evidence is challenged by defence or prosecution lawyers (Rock 1991). In some neighbourhoods witnessing crime forms part of an overall experience of crime which may affect young people's attitudes to crime and the police (Anderson et al 1994), and general feelings of safety.

The diffuse effect of crime

Some crimes have no direct victims and others have only a small effect on individual victims, but a larger, diffuse effect. Prostitution and illegal drug use, for example, can damage the reputation and quality of life in an area. Classic cases of fraud involve the employee or company charging a small amount extra for goods or taking a small amount from a bank account. Individual losses may be negligible but the net profits are considerable. Consumers may have to pay more to compensate losses from shoplifting and employee theft, and tax payers have to pay more to compensate for losses from tax evasion. If these kinds of offences are commonplace, trust and confidence in business or government declines (see Chapter 15). This indicates the narrow boundary between crime victimization and the wider range of avoidable harms identified by critical criminologists (Tombs and Hillyard 2004).

Secondary victimization

As outlined above, secondary victimization can occur when a victim comes into contact with the criminal justice process (Shapland et al 1985; Maguire and Pointing 1988; Davies et al 2003). Victims can feel let down by the police who are more concerned with the facts of the case at a time when they feel traumatized and in need of emotional support. Giving evidence in court can be traumatic and, outside the courtroom, victims can be brought face to face with the offender. Particularly problematic has been the plight of female victims of rape and child victims of physical and sexual abuse.

Repeat victimization

A crucial distinction within the study of victimization is the contrast between 'one off' victimization and what is often described as *repeat victimization* – victimization from the same crime on repeated occasions – or *multiple victimization* – victimization from not one, but several forms of crime. The BCS has reported, since the early nineties, that victimization in itself is a good predictor of subsequent victimization (Tseloni and Pease 2003, cited in Walklate 2007a: 77).

Box 6.5 Repeat victimization

In the **2007/8 BCS** (Jansson et al 2008):

- Around one third of all victims had experienced more than one crime, and just under a tenth had experienced both household and personal crimes. Just under a fifth had experienced multiple household crimes only.
- Victims of domestic violence were the most likely to experience repeat victimization with as many as 45 per cent having been victimized more than once and just over a quarter having been victimized three or more times.
- Vandalism and acquaintance violence also had high repeat victimization rates with theft from the person having the lowest level.

In the **2008/9 SCJS**:

- 6 per cent of adults were repeat victims of property crime and nearly 2 per cent of adults were repeat victims of violent crime.
- 36 per cent of victims of property crime were repeat victims;
- 38 per cent of victims of violent crime were repeat victims;
- The lowest repeat victimization rate was for personal theft (excluding robbery) – 13 per cent of victims.

It has also been suggested that the BCS underestimates repeat victimization due to its limited time period (Pease 1997). Later studies identified 'hot spots' of crime, areas in which more victims report successive victimization, often associated with so-called high crime areas. In part, repeat victimization can be explained by the kind of factors explored by administrative criminologists. Offenders may, for example, return to a target once they think that new goods have been purchased and they know how to break in. This is particularly likely in the absence of a capable guardian. People who are most at risk of repeated victimization are those who do not change their lifestyles.

These findings can, however, be criticized. While studies of 'hot spots' tend to focus on the characteristics of buildings or neighbourhoods, they fail to capture the 'lived reality' of such victimization. While a one-off crime may be experienced as a 'nuisance' and as something which can easily be dismissed, repeated experiences can have a more serious effect on victims' quality of life. This has previously been mentioned in relation to domestic violence, which has the highest rate of repeat victimization, and racial harassment. Furthermore, the reality of life in so-called 'hot spots' may involve many different incidents which become a part of normal life. In a rare and often quoted example of qualitative research carried out in such an area, Genn (1988) attempted to look in more depth at the experiences of crime in specific households, one described as 'Bleak House' in which offences such as violence and drug-taking were common and not perceived as anything out of the ordinary. The full extent of these experiences cannot be captured fully in a victim survey which, argues Walklate (2007a) focuses on the 'first' victim event. There is therefore a need for more qualitative work; as Foster (2002) puts it, the 'people pieces' which might reveal more about that lived reality.

The fear of crime

A major finding of early victim surveys was the seeming anomaly that people's fear of crime was, and continues to be, greater than their statistical 'risk' as measured by crime surveys. Indeed fear of crime became defined as a greater problem than crime itself (Walklate 2007a). Box 6.6 details some of the main findings from British victim surveys about fears and worries about crime. Many questions have been raised about this so-called fear of crime, and it has now, argues Goodey (2005: 66), become an 'unfashionable' term which has been more broadly related to discussions of the growing 'culture' of fear discussed above. Some of the main questions raised have been:

Irrational fears?

The disparity between people's stated fears of crime and their objective risks are well illustrated in Box 6.6 and Figure 6.2, and in recent BCS surveys (Lovbakke 2007; Moley 2008; Walker et al 2009). While less pronounced than previously, many respondents feel that crime is increasing despite the overall decreases outlined

Box 6.6 Fears and worries about crime

Some points from the Scottish (SCJS), Northern Irish (NCIS) and England and Wales (BCS) crime surveys:

- In 2008–9 people in Northern Ireland indicated higher levels of worry about crime than those in England and Wales. A greater proportion of respondents expressed high levels of worry across each crime type examined: violent crime (18% v 14%), burglary (15% v 11%) and car crime (14% v 12%).
- The 2008–9 BCS indicates a decrease in levels of worry about crime over the previous year and a fall of around one third since 1998.
- The proportion of NICS respondents reporting high levels of worry about crime have decreased consistently since 2003/04.
- The NCIS indicates that 10 per cent of adults feel 'very unsafe' when walking alone in their local area at night, a decrease of 2 per cent from 2008/09.
- Across Scotland, the majority of adults (66%) said that they felt safe (very 29%, fairly 37%) but 12% of adults said they felt very unsafe walking alone in their local area after dark and 21% said that they felt a bit unsafe.
- Females in Scotland were more likely than males to report feeling unsafe (44% of females compared with 20% males), as were the oldest adults, with the group most likely to report feeling unsafe being females aged 60 or over (55%).
- The 2008/09 BCS found that 16 per cent thought they were fairly or very likely to be a victim of burglary compared to an actual risk of 2 per cent.
- The NICS 2008/09 indicates that 15 per cent thought they were very or fairly likely to be a victim of burglary, compared with an actual risk of 1 per cent. A similar pattern emerged in terms of car crime (20% v 2%) and violent crime (11% v 3%).

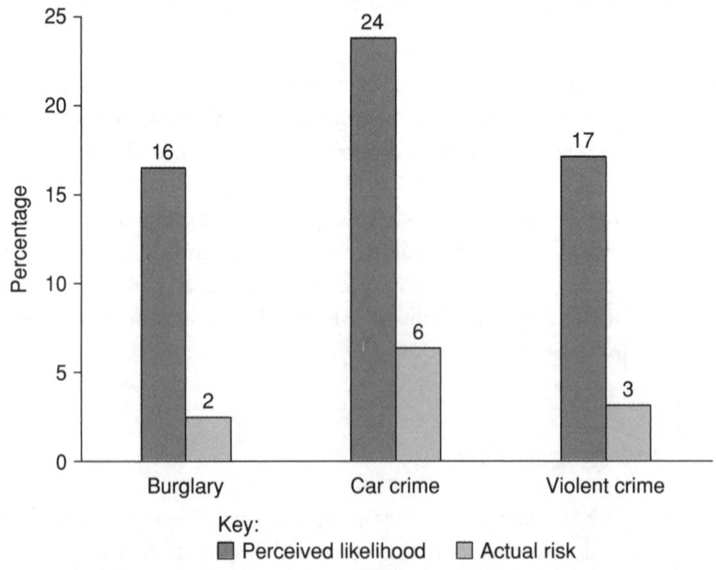

Figure 6.2 Perceptions of likelihood of victimization and actual risk by individual crime type, 2008/9 BCS

in Chapter 3. Fears and worries tend to be higher among those who read tabloid newspapers and fears about high-profile crimes such as knife and gun crime are higher than for other crime. Women worry more about violence despite their lower risk. It was previously found that those most at risk of assault, i.e. young men, express less worry about it, whereas those least at risk, i.e. the elderly, worry most (Zedner 1997).

How can these seemingly contradictory findings be interpreted? While governments used this anomaly to reassure the public, left realists, as seen above, pointed to the more rational fears of those inhabiting high crime areas. The higher fears of the elderly and the poor may also reflect the more severe impact which crime has on them. The elderly may worry more about violence because of their physical frailty and because they would take longer to recover from any attack. Those with low incomes are less likely to be insured and can least afford to replace stolen goods. They may also be most affected by the nuisance value, losing income and time in making repairs or going to court.

Others criticize the whole basis of the argument. What, for example, might a 'rational' fear of crime consist of (Sparks 1992, cited in Walklate 2007a)? People are urged to prevent victimization by, for example, taking care to lock doors and take security precautions. Do we expect worries to be related to risks? Kinsey and Anderson (1992) point out that while people worry about car accidents and take precautionary measures, this could be seen as sensible rather than irrational.

How is fear of crime measured?

A further set of criticisms relate to the difficulties of operationalizing fear for the purposes of victim surveys. What questions are asked, and are these the right questions? One of the standard questions asked, '*How safe do you feel being out alone in your neighbourhood after dark?*' does not actually mention crime (Goodey 2005). These are related to the way in which responses are 'codified into pre-existing "boxes" in order to satisfy the demands of positivist methodology' (Goodey 2005: 69). As such they cannot capture the dimensions of people's experiences which may change over time and vary according to emotional states. Earlier surveys found that some reporting not feeling safe and not going out at night, did not want to go out anyway. Old people may avoid walking on the streets at night, but this may be because they are afraid of falling in the dark. Others may not go out because they have childcare commitments, no car, nowhere they want to go or no money for leisure (Mirlees-Black et al 1996).

As mentioned above, surveys also often fail to put fears of crime in a wider context. The poor express higher fears of crime (Pantazis 2000), perhaps because its impact falls more heavily on them and they are also affected by worries about jobs and health which can be exacerbated by crime. People's answers to survey questions also prompt answers to issues which people may not have hitherto thought about, and Figure 6.3 illustrates, for England and Wales and Northern Ireland, that the vast majority of those reporting worries about crime also reported that it had a minimal effect on their quality of life. Worries about crime may also reflect the broader uncertainties and feelings of unsafety noted by the theories outlined above

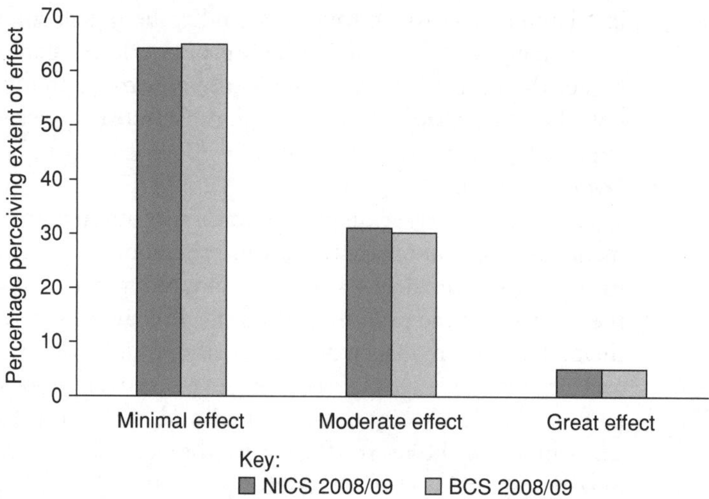

Figure 6.3 Perceptions of the effect of 'fear of crime' on quality of life (%) in Northern Ireland and England and Wales

relating to the culture of fear. Unpacking these complex relationships yet again underlines the need for qualitative rather than quantitative work. People's expressions of worry about crime and feelings of unsafety may also reflect the media focus on extreme but rare crimes which also fuels people's fears of 'outsiders' (Walklate 2007a).

Victimization and inequality

As seen above, radical and critical approaches to victimology lay great emphasis on the structural distribution of victimization, often not fully evident in standard victim surveys. This chapter has already indicated some of these relationships. It has been argued, for example, that the poor suffer more from victimization, particularly from repeat victimization. The higher risks for women from male violence have also been indicated along with the vulnerability of younger and older victims and members of minority ethnic communities, who, along with people from some faith communities, the disabled and homosexuals also face forms of 'hate crime'. These dimensions of inequality will be explored in more depth in the following four chapters.

To the kinds of victimization more evident in victim surveys must be added victimization from the crimes which are not included in these surveys which is considerable and, as will be seen in Chapters 14–17, unevenly distributed. Workers are killed and injured in unsafe factories, and residents in poorer communities are more likely to be harmed by chemical pollution and other forms of environmental crime. Poorer consumers are more likely to buy cheaper and dangerous goods, and women to be harmed by cosmetic products and surgery.

What has been referred to as 'occidentalism' has also meant that victimology has been relatively blind to victims who are among the poorest in the world (Hoyle and Zedner 2007; Walklate 2007a). Globally they are more vulnerable to human trafficking, exploitative labour practices and the damaging effects of toxic-waste dumping (Chapters 15 and 16). Moreover, citizens in less economically advanced countries also suffer a staggering range of human rights abuses, torture, hunger and poverty which would be intolerable in the West (see Chapter 17). Women across the globe are also major victims of sex trafficking, and countless women in less developed countries have suffered rape and other forms of abuse as a result of wars and genocide (see Chapters 14 and 17). Children's labour is also exploited and children can also be exploited as child soldiers (see Chapters 8 and 17).

Concluding comments

This chapter has explored many aspects of victimization and illustrated how it has emerged as a major element in analyses of crime. Indeed, as Zedner (1997: 607) points out, 'far from being simply a compartmentalized topic, victim research has impacted upon every aspect of criminological thinking and profoundly altered our picture of crime'. The victim survey is used not only to measure crime but to explore many different aspects of people's experiences of, attitudes towards and worries about crime although the limitations of its methodology have also been outlined. Research into victimization has also revealed much about the objective and subject impact of crime and concerns about the risks of crime have become politicized and linked to a culture of generalized fear and anxiety.

Despite all this, many aspects of victimization remain underexplored, and some commentators remain sceptical about the extent to which victims' interests have been fully recognized. Like crime, victimization is socially constructed, and this construction affects policy and research. Some victims are blamed and seen as less deserving. Victim surveys omit many forms of crime and, while violence in the home is now more widely recognized, its exposure required a political challenge, as was the case with racial victimization. Less attention has been paid to the victims of professional and organized, corporate, white-collar and state crime which, as will be seen in later chapters, are associated with considerable harms, albeit that they are often neglected. As Cohen (1996) famously argued, if the numbers of deaths associated with genocide, ethnic cleansing, torture and 'disappearances' are taken into account, it would be 'an insult to the intelligence' to compare them to victimization from the so-called conventional crimes featured in many victim surveys. Subsequent chapters will explore many of these themes as they relate to social inequalities and specific crimes.

Review questions

1 An exercise which can be done in groups. Locate a national or local victim survey and construct a short questionnaire based on questions about experiences of and worries about crime. Administer this to a range of respondents from across your network. Consider the following questions.

(a) How accurately do people respond?
(b) How are offences defined?

Do responses 'fit' the predetermined categories?

(c) Which offences are omitted?
(d) What do you think respondents mean when they say they are worried about crime and specific crimes?
(e) Are their fears out of proportion to their risk of victimization?

2 Consult national victim surveys and find information in relation to:

- The social distribution of victimization: which groups are more likely to be victimized by which crimes? How would you explain this? How might this distribution be affected by the crimes which are not counted?
- The extent of repeat victimization and who is most likely to be affected. Which groups worry about crime most? How would you account for this?

Key reading

There have been several recent texts and collections about aspects of victimization including:

Davies, P. Francis, P. and Greer, C. (2007) ***Victims, Crime and Society***, London, Sage. This explores several aspects of victimization in relation to social inequalities including chapters on age, gender, social exclusion and victimization, and victimization from corporate and white-collar crime.

Goodey, J. (2005) ***Victims and Victimology: Research, Policy and Practice***, London: Pearson, Longman. This is a comprehensive text which explores the main theoretical perspectives on victimization and applies these to victim policies.

Walklate, S. (2007) ***Imagining the Victim of Crime***, Maidenhead: McGraw Hill, Open University Press. This provides a thoughtful exploration of the social construction of the victim and different theoretical perspectives within victimology.

Walklate, S. (ed.) (2007) ***Handbook of Victims and Victimology***, Cullompton: Willan Publishing. This is an invaluable collection of chapters on many aspects of victimology, including explorations of its historical context, theoretical perspectives, gender issues and wider aspects of risk and victimization.

Chapter 7
Socio-economic inequalities and crime

This chapter will look at

- → Socio-economic status and offending
- → Socio-economic status and victimization
- → The dangerous class?
- → Criminology and the lower-class offender
- → Economic factors and crime: unemployment, recession and income differentials
- → The underclass
- → Social exclusion
- → Analysing class-crime relationships

The association of crime with lower-class people and areas has featured in previous chapters and has dominated criminological theories. Deficit theories sought to explain it by looking at individual pathologies and deviant subcultures. On the other hand, it formed the basis of the critiques of critical criminologists and labelling perspectives to whom it was a result of social control and criminalization processes. To conservative criminologists it was linked to a lack of self-control whereas contemporary sociological approaches focus on the widening gaps between rich and poor both within and between nations and the devastating impact of de-industrialization on lower-class communities and the growth of social exclusion.

Many questions can be asked about the relationships between socio-economic inequalities and crime. Do people from different socio-economic backgrounds commit different amounts or kinds of crime? Are they more at risk from crime? Do economic conditions and inequalities lead to crime? To what extent is the crime 'problem' constructed as one of lower-class crime? Is there a criminal underclass? Is crime related to social exclusion? This chapter will focus on these questions before turning to ways in which these relationships have been analysed, drawing on the theoretical perspectives outlined in previous chapters. It will largely focus on lower-class crime while recognizing the significance of white-collar, corporate and state crime, which will be dealt with more fully in Chapters 15, 16 and 17.

Socio-economic status and crime

Before exploring some of the relationships between socio-economic status, offending and victimization, a brief discussion of terms such as class and socio-economic status is necessary. It lies beyond the scope of this book to explore the many usages of the term 'class', let alone to look in detail at how the 'class structure' has changed in recent decades. The term socio-economic inequality has been used in preference as it encompasses many dimensions of economic inequalities along with aspects of employment, income and area of residence which are more amenable to measurement and used in, for example, crime surveys. Some statistical indicators combine different elements and talk about the 'most' and 'least' deprived and many writers use widely understood if often poorly defined terms such as 'rich' and 'poor', more and less 'affluent', lower class and upper class and these will be used although it is recognized that they are generalizations. Box 7.1 highlights some key features of economic inequalities in Britain which are most often related to crime and the different indicators often used in research are illustrated in the following sections.

Offending and socio-economic status

The socio-economic status of offenders is not, like age or sex, recorded although other sources, such as samples of known offenders, tend to confirm the assumption that

Box 7.1 Key features of inequality in Britain

- 'The United Kingdom is a deeply unequal society' (p. 26). In 2002, the wealthiest 1 per cent of the population owned a quarter of the UK's marketable wealth, while the wealthiest 50 per cent owned the vast majority (94 per cent) of it.
- Inequalities in Britain have widened between 1996 and 2006. The income of the poorest tenth of the British population increased by about a quarter compared to a rise of over 40 per cent for the richest tenth.
- In 2002, 11.4 million people (around one fifth of the population) in the UK were defined as living in poverty. While this number has fallen from 1997, it is still 60 per cent higher than in 1979.
- Poverty is associated with inadequate incomes and 'worklessness', a wider term than unemployment, related to the numbers dependent on benefits – many of which do not bring people over the official 'poverty line'. In 2006, there were nearly 3 million workless households accounting for over 4 million people.
- Unemployment falls particularly severely on young people, with, in 2006, those under the age of 25 accounting for over 40 per cent of unemployed people. They also suffer from lower incomes than older workers and lower benefit payments, with some young people being excluded from certain kinds of benefits. Young people therefore have a higher rate of poverty.

Source: Based on Grover (2008: 26–34)

the majority of convicted offenders come from lower-class backgrounds (Coleman and Moynihan 1996). One study of persistent young offenders found that only 8 per cent came from non-manual backgrounds (Hagell and Newburn 1994). As will be seen below, risks from all kinds of crime are highest in the most deprived areas which also indicates the lower-class status of offenders – unless, comment Coleman and Moynihan (1996: 108), it can be supposed that 'middle class burglars are travelling to poor areas hoping to find something worth stealing' which, they argue, is unlikely!

A stark illustration of the low socio-economic status of some convicted offenders is found in the prison population. In the 1990s, for example, 12 per cent of convicted and 17 per cent of remand prisoners in England and Wales were homeless at the time of their imprisonment and nearly half of unconvicted and a third of convicted prisoners were unemployed prior to their imprisonment (Grover 2008: 53). In Scotland, it has been found that many young offenders in prison had few educational qualifications, were unemployed and came from low income families (SCCCJ 2000). A study by Houchin (2005) of the population of Scottish prisons, summarized in Box 7.2, further illustrates the relationship between social deprivation and the prison population.

These kinds of figures cannot, however, be taken to indicate higher rates of offending, as all the processes of 'creating' official offenders, outlined in Chapter 3, must be considered. The prison population is a very small proportion of convicted offenders, who are a very small proportion of all offenders. Successive research on policing suggests that some areas, generally lower-class, are more intensively policed and lower-class youth, sometimes described as the 'usual suspects' or 'police property' are more likely to be arrested and taken to court (McAra and McVie 2005; Reiner 2007a). Decisions whether or not to caution or divert offenders are likely to be affected by parents' status, the nature of the home and where offenders live and, in court, those in employment are considered a better 'risk' than those who are unemployed – thus more unemployed people from deprived areas end up in prison.

Box 7.2 Social deprivation and the prison population

In a study for the Scottish Prison Service relating prisoner's postcodes to the socio-economic classifications of their areas, Houchin (2005) calculated that in Scotland:

- 28 per cent of prisoners, compared with 10 per cent of the general population, came from the 'poorest council estates'. For Glasgow the figure was 60 per cent.
- Half of the prisoner population came from 155 of 1,222 local government wards in Scotland; there was a high correlation between these 155 wards and social deprivation.
- The male imprisonment rate from the 27 most deprived wards amounted to 953 per 100,000 of the population compared to the national average of 237.
- The imprisonment rate for 23-year-old men from the 27 most deprived wards amounted to 3,427 per 100,000.
- 1 in 9 young men from the most deprived communities will spend time in prison at the age of 23.

In contrast, offences involving higher status offenders are less easy to detect and offenders, who are seen as more respectable, are more likely to be diverted and dealt with by administrative penalties or, if convicted, less likely to be sent to prison (Croall 2001a and see Chapter 15). Furthermore, not everyone has 'equal opportunities' to commit different kinds of crime. Those in work can avail themselves of opportunities to steal from clients or employers, where they are less likely to be caught, whereas those who are not in work, particularly those with fewer educational qualifications or technological knowledge, have fewer criminal options and may turn to crimes which require less skill and planning such as street robbery – often associated with poverty and deprivation (Hallsworth 2005). Critical criminologists also point out that the criminal law is less often used against the harms perpetrated by the more powerful, whereas the activities of the least powerful are more subject to criminalization. All of this suggests, therefore, a far more complex relationship between socio-economic status and offending than indicated by looking only at the characteristics of convicted offenders.

Victimization and socio-economic status

Relationships between socio-economic factors and victimization are complex. The higher levels of consumer goods, cars, jewellery and expensive items possessed by the more affluent make them attractive targets and levels of property crime can be expected to rise alongside a rise in available goods. At the same time, however, so-called 'hot spots' of crime are associated with areas characterized by high levels of deprivation. Moreover, while the rich have more goods to steal, they can also afford to protect them better. Thus, using data classifying areas according to demographic, employment and housing characteristics, the BCS has associated higher risks of crime with 'rising' *and* 'striving' areas (Aitchison and Hodgkinson 2003), with low income and 'affluent urban areas' (Ringham and Wood 2004; Upson et al 2004). Nonetheless, when a range of indicators are combined across Britain, as indicated in Figure 7.1 for Scotland and Figure 7.2 for England, the risks of most kinds of crime are greater for those living in the most deprived areas, and in England for those living in social housing and private rented accommodation (Walker et al 2009). Unemployed people were twice as likely to be victims of violence than employed people and those living in areas with high levels of physical disorder were also more at risk from violent offences (Walker et al 2009).

These inequalities are compounded when multiple and repeat victimization is considered. Closer analyses, for example of BCS data, indicate that 'hot spots' tend to be in areas with a mixture of poor, private rented housing and owner occupation and the poorest local authority estates, located either in inner city or overspill areas (Evans and Fraser 2003). Based on a more detailed analysis of BCS data, Hope (2001) found that:

- victims who are multiply or repeatedly victimized are more likely to live in high crime rate areas than those less frequently victimized;
- concentrations of crime risks coincide with concentrations of the 'poor'. Twenty per cent of communities with the highest crime rates have higher numbers of the 'poor' than the 'rich'.

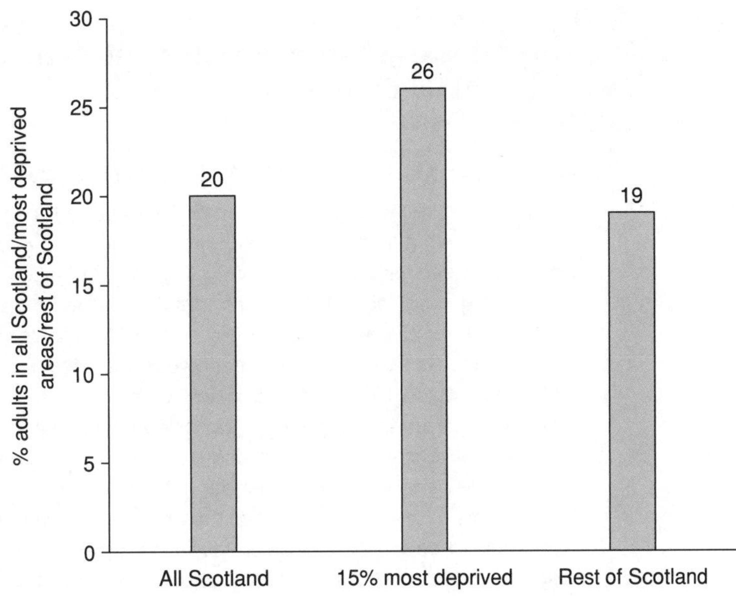

Figure 7.1 Varying risk of crime – proportion of adults who were victims of crime by area deprivation (Scotland)

Source: MacLeod et al (2009) p. 36

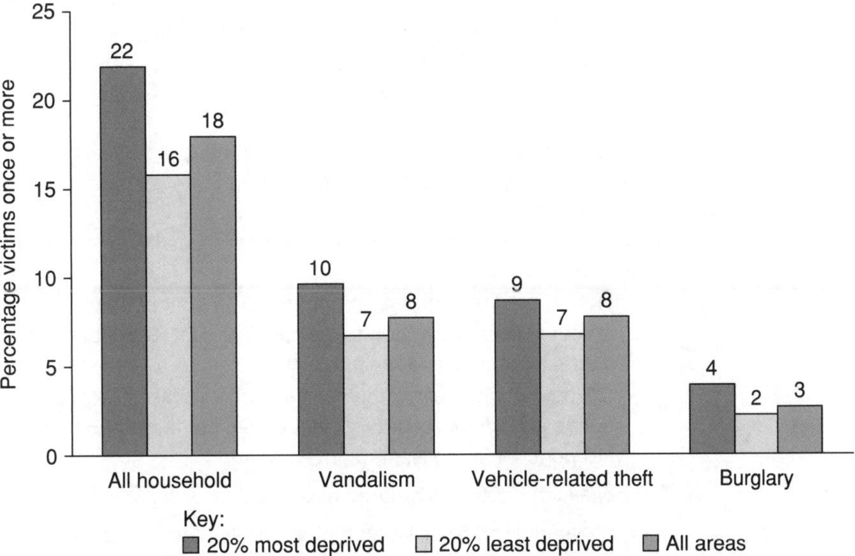

Figure 7.2 Risk of crime by level of deprivation in England, 2008/9 BCS

Source: Walker et al (2009) p. 146

Successive studies across the UK also reveal higher rates of worry about crime and safety amongst those in most deprived areas and those earning lower incomes, as illustrated in Box 7.3, with the exception of credit-card fraud and identity theft which are worried about most by the more affluent. Pantazis (2000), in a detailed

Box 7.3 Socio-economic status and fears and worries about crime

In *Northern Ireland*, the 2008–9 NCIS (Quigley and Freel 2010) found that:

- Worry about crime decreases as income increases: 26 per cent of respondents from households with a total income of under £10,000 were very worried about violent crime, compared with 9 per cent of those earning £50,000 or more.
- People living in social-rented accommodation worried more about crime and personal safety: 25 per cent in socially rented accommodation were worried about car crime compared to 12 per cent in owner-occupied accommodation with figures of 28 per cent and 16 per cent for violent crime.
- Respondents from the 20 per cent most deprived areas worried most about car crime; violent crime; burglary; walking alone after dark; personal safety; and crime overall; while people from the least deprived areas worried least.
- Respondents in the 20 per cent most deprived areas were more likely to consider themselves to be at risk of crime in the following twelve months: 27 per cent of people from the most deprived areas thought it likely they would experience car crime and 17 per cent violent crime, compared with NICS 2008/09 averages of 20 per cent and 11 per cent respectively.

In *England and Wales* in 2008–9 (Walker et al 2009):

- Perceived risks of and worries about burglary, car crime and violent crime were inversely related to income. Comparing the lowest income group (earning under £10,000) with the highest (earning over £50,000):
  - 18 per cent worried about burglary, 14 per cent about car crime and 21 per cent about violent crime, compared to 6 per cent, 8 per cent and 8 per cent respectively;
  - 22 per cent saw themselves at risk of burglary, 30 per cent of car crime;
  - 23 per cent of violent crime compared to 14 per cent, 21 per cent and 12 per cent respectively.
- These worries were also greater amongst those living in the most deprived areas where
  - 18 per cent worried about burglary, 19 per cent about car crime and 22 per cent about violent crime, compared to 7 per cent, 8 per cent and 8 per cent for those in the least deprived areas;
  - 23 per cent perceived themselves to be at risk of burglary, 32 per cent of car crime and 26 per cent of violent crime, compared to 12 per cent, 18 per cent and 10 per cent in the least deprived areas.

In *Scotland* in 2008–9 (MacLeod et al 2009):

- Compared to adults living in the rest of Scotland, those living in the 15 per cent most deprived areas of Scotland were more likely to:
  - feel unsafe: 46 per cent compared with 30 per cent;
  - see crime rates as increasing in their local area: 33 per cent compared with 27 per cent;
  - view crime as a big problem: 62 per cent compared with 51 per cent.
- In contrast, in Scotland, more of those in *higher* socio-economic groups and in the *least* deprived areas felt that they were likely to experience the fraudulent use of credit or bank details and identity theft.

examination of BCS data, also found higher levels of feeling unsafe in multiply deprived than in comfortable households. Moreover, crime has a much greater impact on the poor, who are less able to replace stolen goods and broken windows or doors and are less likely to be insured – which can lead to a vicious circle. Many insurance companies will not insure those who have been previously victimized, charge higher premiums in certain areas or insist on the installation of expensive security measures (Victim Support 2002; Goodey 2005). In this way, those who are more severely affected by property crime are less able to protect themselves from further victimization (Croall 2007a).

These figures relate to the kinds of crime measured by national victim surveys which, as seen in Chapter 6, exclude many crimes which can compound the greater impact of crime on the poor. While, for example, the rich present more attractive targets to fraudsters, and all citizens are endangered by environmental, safety or consumer crimes, the impact of these crimes also falls more severely on the least advantaged who live in the most polluted areas and are more likely to be employed in risky and dangerous workplaces (Croall 2001b; 2007b, and see Chapters 15 and 16). These kinds of victim surveys also tell us little about the 'lived reality' of repeat victimization and experiences of crime in so-called 'hot spots' (see also Chapter 6).

Constructing the class and crime relationship

Dangerous people in dangerous places

Crime has for long been popularly associated with perceptions of a dangerous class, often inhabiting particular parts of towns and cities from the 'rookeries' and 'underworld' depicted by Dickens and other nineteenth-century writers through to contemporary portrayals of the drugs, crime and violence characteristic of social housing areas. Discussions of crime and 'the city' inevitably conjure up images of these 'problem places' (Mooney 2008) rather than looking at 'the city' of bankers, brokers and financiers. A number of themes have been associated with these kinds of constructions.

The idle poor?

Worklessness has often been associated with indiscipline with assumptions that 'good work habits' encourage discipline and responsibility. The unemployed were often portrayed as 'idle' and their situation blamed on their 'workshy' nature. Increases in unemployment were perceived as a threat to law and order (Crow 1989), echoed in current fears about the impact of the recession on crime. The eighteenth-century economist Adam Smith argued that economic dependency could corrupt whereas the growth of commerce and manufacture increased independency and prevented crime (Pyle and Deadman 1994: 340). The unemployed are assumed to have more time and opportunity to commit crime – 'the devil makes mischief for idle hands'. On the other hand, economic booms can also produce higher rates of crime. One nineteenth-century commentator attributed an increase in convictions in the 1850s following the 'hungry 1840s', to the 'intemperance which high wages encourage among the ignorant and the sensual' (cited in Taylor 1997: 267). There are other problems with these notions. The employed also commit crime and worklessness is not in itself related to crime. No such negative imagery is applied, for example, to the retired, the 'idle rich' or redundant executives (Lea and Young 1993).

The undeserving poor?

Social and welfare policy has long reflected a distinction between the deserving poor, poor through no fault of their own, and the undeserving poor, seen as unwilling to work. This division was and is reflected in social policy with requirements that those applying for benefit should be actively seeking work. The undeserving poor were also associated with weak morals and a propensity to crime and drug abuse, and the labouring classes were often divided into 'rough' and 'respectable' elements. As will be seen below, this imagery was echoed in twentieth-century notions of the underclass and the dependency culture, said to be associated with crime.

Dangerous places?

The twentieth century saw major changes as cities grew, particularly from the 1950s onwards when older 'slums' gave way to new estates, often on the periphery of cities. Following the processes of de-industrialization outlined in Chapter 5, these became linked across the developed world with rising crime, incivilities and urban disorder. Popular images readily identify British 'problem estates', Scottish 'schemes', American 'projects' and 'ghettos' and French *banlieus* with crime and disorder and with what the President of France once described, following widespread rioting, as 'delinquent scum' (Mooney 2008). As Waquant (2008: 1, cited in Mooney 2008: 111) argues,

> the societies of north America, Western Europe and South America all have at their disposal in their topographic lexicon a special term for designating those stigmatized neighbourhoods situated at the very bottom of the hierarchical system of places that compose the metropolis . . . it is in these districts . . . that the urban outcasts of the turn of the century reside.

In the 1980s and early 1990s a series of disturbances erupted in many English cities, some drawing attention to peripheral estates (Campbell 1993; Graham and Clarke 1996). The rising concern with anti-social behaviour focused on so-called 'neighbourhoods from hell' and, as Mooney (2008) points out, these localities have come to symbolize all that is problematic about urban life and society more generally.

Criminology and the lower-class offender

So closely was crime identified with lower-class offenders that the majority of early criminological theories were effectively theories about lower-class crime. Even where individual characteristics such as low intelligence, socialization or educational achievement could in theory apply across social classes, the lower-class status of offenders led them to be cast as lower-class problems. While, as seen in Chapter 4, anomie theory could be applied to boundless aspirations or strains between goals and means at all levels of society, it was generally applied to lower-class crime patterns. Criminological analyses of the distribution of crime in cities echoed popular representations of dangerous areas characterized as disorganized, lacking stable communities and having high levels of cultural diversity. Little attention was paid to middle- or upper-class subcultures however 'deviant' they may have been. Control theories, while seemingly more neutral and of universal applicability, were also taken to indicate failures of parenting and control in lower-class areas. Many of these theories were, as seen in Chapter 4, criticized for 'overpredicting' lower-class crime and failing to recognize white-collar crime. Indeed, a key thrust of Sutherland's (1949) critique was that theories of crime which purported to be applicable to all were flawed as they could not account for white-collar crime.

A very different approach was signalled by the emergence of newer approaches from around the 1960s (see Chapter 5). Labelling theorists drew attention to the way in which agencies of social control selectively apprehended and processed particular groups of offenders, and to critical criminologists the 'problem' became not to explain lower-class crime, but the criminalization of lower-class activities which threatened law and order. They in turn, however, were criticized by left realists who accused them of denying the reality of lower-class crime, so often targeted at lower-class victims, and for focusing too much on the crimes of the powerful.

Contemporary approaches echo some of these ambiguities although the focus on the lower-class offender continues. While right realists and conservative criminologists reject any link between the social structure and crime, their focus on bio-social theories and lack of self-control associates crime with lower-class status and 'blames' the 'poor' for characteristics associated with both crime and poverty – itself seen as an individual weakness. Contrasted with these perspectives are those explored below which take a more sociological approach and develop structural and cultural analyses – looking, for example, at processes of social exclusion and at the impact of socio-economic change and neo-liberal economic policies and their accompanying ideology.

Dimensions of class, crime and the economy

Economic factors and crime

Crime has been variously linked to the impact of economic cycles, to unemployment and income differentials, although the evidence is often contradictory and difficult to interpret. Exploring these factors involves using largely quantitative methods and extremely complex econometric measures. Before looking at some of the findings of these kinds of investigations a few points should be borne in mind:

- *How reliable are statistical indicators?* The limitations of official crime statistics have repeatedly been outlined particularly when it comes to assessing apparent rises and falls in crime 'rates'. Economic statistics, such as unemployment statistics, are also constructed and unemployment has been subject to different and changing definitions. Trying to establish related trends is, therefore, hazardous.

- *What time lag should be allowed for?* Economic trends take time to have an impact on, for example, employment, which in turn takes time to affect crime.
- *The different effects of economic cycles on crime.* Economic cycles may have different and contradictory effects on crime. Economists refer to two alternative theories (Hale 2009):

    Opportunity theory suggests that crime will rise in a period of growth. Incomes rise and there are more goods in circulation creating more opportunities for crime. This is related to routine activity theories.

    Motivational theory suggests that during a recession the unemployed turn to crime as their legitimate income decreases leading to an increased motivation for property crime.

  If these theories are both correct economic cycles would have different effects on crime rates, making figures even more difficult to interpret (Pyle and Deadman 1994; Hale 2009).

Economic cycles

In very general terms, crime rose during the recession of 1989–1992 (Hale 2009), although not during the depression of the 1930s (Lea and Young 1993). Different crimes show different patterns. While some forms of property crime rise during recession, some forms of violent crime fall. This is because a large proportion of officially recorded violent crime consists of assaults involving young men drinking (see Chapters 3 and 11). During a recession, they have less money to spend and official rates of violent crime drop. In a study carried out for the Home Office during the recession of the 1980s, Field (1990) concluded that crime rates were more strongly related to personal consumption than unemployment. The more people have to spend, the lower the crime rate and, as personal consumption falls, crime rises.

This is related to both motivation and opportunity theories. In the short run recession affects a small group who move between criminal and legitimate economic activities. A sharp fall in consumption growth 'may trigger frustration as economic expectations are lowered' and undermine social controls (Field 1996: 117). When the economy recovers, this group moves back into legitimate employment producing an immediate fall in property crime rates. As the economy continues to recover, economic growth increases the opportunities for crime, producing higher rates (Field 1990; Pyle and Deadman 1994). Personal crime, on the other hand, increases more rapidly when consumption grows rapidly, as people have more money and go out more. These trends were particularly strong in England and Wales during the 1980s, where recorded property crime grew very rapidly at the beginning of the decade, whereas personal crime grew very little. Later years showed a reverse pattern with personal crime growing rapidly in 1987 and 1988, whereas property crime rose slowly. Field's conclusions were broadly accepted as confirming a relationship between property crime and the business cycle (Pyle and Deadman 1994).

Unemployment

The role of unemployment has been less clear (Pyle and Deadman 1994; Grover 2008). In a thorough review of research, Box (1987) found a slight but inconsistent relationship between rates of unemployment and recorded crime. A greater time lag is involved as employers take some time to increase or reduce labour (Pyle and Deadman 1994; Wells 1995). While Field argued that unemployment is not a major factor, Wells (1995) argued that police statistics confirmed a strong association between property crime and unemployment in areas of England and Wales such as Cleveland, Merseyside, Northumbria, Greater Manchester, South Yorkshire, West Midlands, Greater London and South Wales. Many argue, however, that the contrast between 'employment' and 'unemployment' is misleading. The rise in casual jobs which have little security and low income is also important. Unemployment also has a different impact on different groups – the key question in relation to crime may well be, for example, rates of youth unemployment. This directs attention to other indicators such as low income and income inequalities.

Income inequalities

While it has been difficult to establish clear links between unemployment and crime, there is more convincing evidence of an association between some forms of crime and income inequality particularly for young people. Box 7.1 indicates the widening income inequality which Hale's (1999; 2009) research suggested was positively related to a growth in burglary. The growth of a dual labour market in which a core of workers have more permanent jobs and a periphery are reliant on casual work has, he argues, produced a growing polarization between the work rich and the work poor. An economic model would suggest that given a choice between legal and illegal work, those who are either unemployed or working in insecure low-paid and low-skilled jobs, might well choose the greater rewards of illegal work. This has been found in American research and, in Britain, Machin and Meghir (2004) found a positive relationship between crime rates and widening male wage inequality along with a relationship between rising rates of property crime and falling wage levels between 1975 and 1996. Economic policies are also important. Hansen and Machin (2002) found that areas benefiting most from the introduction of the minimum wage saw decreases in crime whereas the later job seeker's allowance, which led to some people losing benefits, was associated with rising crime in the areas most affected (Machin and Marie 2004).

These econometric studies must be cautiously interpreted. While they can establish broad correlations they cannot explain them and any attempt to do so must take account of the different impact of economic change on individuals, groups and communities and how these might affect decisions to commit crime. They do, however, suggest some of the many interrelated factors involved. Unemployment in itself is not associated with crime, nor is it a watertight category. Its impact on younger people in low-paid and casual employment is the crucial factor. In reality, many move between low-paid casual jobs, sometimes balancing two or three jobs at the one time, in a struggle to feed families (Currie 1996). This group may well turn to illegitimate means of supplementing income. The devastating impact of de-industrialization, globalization and changing employment patterns which have reduced the number of jobs providing job satisfaction, pride in work or a stable and secure income will be further explored below. Statistical correlations miss out other crucial factors. They tend to be based on considerations of male unemployment or the impact of economic cycles on men and do not consider their impact on women (Grover 2008). They also reflect the primary concern with lower-class crime, and fail to consider how such factors might also affect different kinds of white-collar crime. During a recession, for example, some businesses, particularly smaller ones, may cut corners on safety or health regulations in a struggle to survive, whereas during boom times, financial frauds flourish in a rush to make large sums of money (Croall 2001a; 2010; and see Chapter 15).

The criminal underclass?

The impact of economic change coupled with rising crime rates in the latter part of the twentieth century gave rise to concerns about the emergence of a criminal underclass, echoing popular representations of 'dangerous people'. In the United States the term was used to describe areas in cities such as Los Angeles and the 'frostbelt' of de-industrialized northern cities characterized by high rates of gang warfare, drug offences, violent and property crime. Right realists such as Charles Murray linked this, in America and Britain, to permissive welfare policies and a culture of dependency passed on through generations (Murray 1990; 1996). It was typically represented as a class below the rest of society, consisting of those trapped by unemployment, low incomes or poor housing and who were socially and geographically isolated and excluded from the benefits of other citizens (Bagguley and Mann 1992; Taylor 1997; Grover 2008). Murray's arguments are outlined in Box 7.4. A number of major questions have been asked about this notion.

Is there an underclass?

The term 'underclass' was often used very loosely to, for example, characterize the situation of racial minorities, the situation of the very poor or the reserve army of labour (Bagguley and Mann 1992). There was little evidence that it formed a cohesive group or that its membership passes through generations, features essential to the sociological concept of social class (Bagguley and Mann 1992).

Empirical support?

There was little empirical support for Murray's arguments (1990; 1996), particularly those asserting links between illegitimacy, single-parent families, attitudes to work and crime, and the evidence he presented was highly selective. Bagguley and Mann (1992) ask if there is any evidence at all to show that women find social security benefits so attractive that they have children to obtain them? His account of Easterhouse, an estate on the outskirts of Glasgow, was challenged by those who pointed to the keenness for work shown by many residents along with their concerns about family and community life (Holman 1994).

Box 7.4

Charles Murray: the underclass?

On the basis of research in Britain, including Easterhouse in Glasgow, Murray (1996: 123) argued that

> Britain has a growing population of working-aged healthy people who live in a different world from other Britons, who are raising their children to live in it, and whose values are now contaminating the life of entire neighbourhoods.

He identified three key features of the underclass:

- *Illegitimacy*, while found across all classes, is most prevalent in lower-class communities. To Murray, 'communities need families' and 'fathers', as an absence of fathers provides young men with few role models and they become aggressive and run wild (Murray 1996: 124).
- *Increasing crime* devastates communities, fragmenting them and leading young men to look up to criminal role models.
- *Drop out from the labour force*: In Britain and America, many young, healthy, low-income males choose not to take jobs, and fail to see work as a source of respect. They do not obtain work habits and responsibilities. This affects whole communities as they cannot support families and find other ways to 'prove that they are men, which tend to take various destructive forms' (Murray 1996: 133).

The British 'underclass', like its American counterpart, is a result of liberal social welfare policies, which by providing public housing and social security enable young women to have children without the support of a father, and young men to choose not to work.

Othering the poor?

The 'underclass' notion in effect blames the poor and was used ideologically to divert attention from structural problems. It represented a form of 'othering' with descriptions often written as if describing foreign populations on excursions into unknown territory (Graham and Clarke 1996). To Campbell, it draws on a 'long tradition of class contempt for poor people' (Campbell 1994: 19). Bagguley and Mann illustrate the continuity of this, from the paupers of the 1830s who were described as 'feckless idlers who had been cushioned by the allowance systems', and the poor of fifty years later who were seen as a 'residuum whose behaviour was conditioned by their genes'. By the 1920s they had become a class of 'unemployables' who had lost the will to work (Bagguley and Mann 1992: 124). The notion of the 'underclass' is an ideology of the upper and middle classes. Rarely, they argue, do we hear of

> the Wall Street 'underclass' demoralized by their junk bond dependency culture! The divorces, white collar crime, drug taking, drinking, the phenomenal benefits of state welfare dependency (£7 billion in tax relief on mortgage interest alone in 1989), and the casual sex of the middle classes does not of course demoralise them.

In the United States, the 'underclass' was also associated with race, whereas in Britain class and area were more significant, with it being associated with traditional

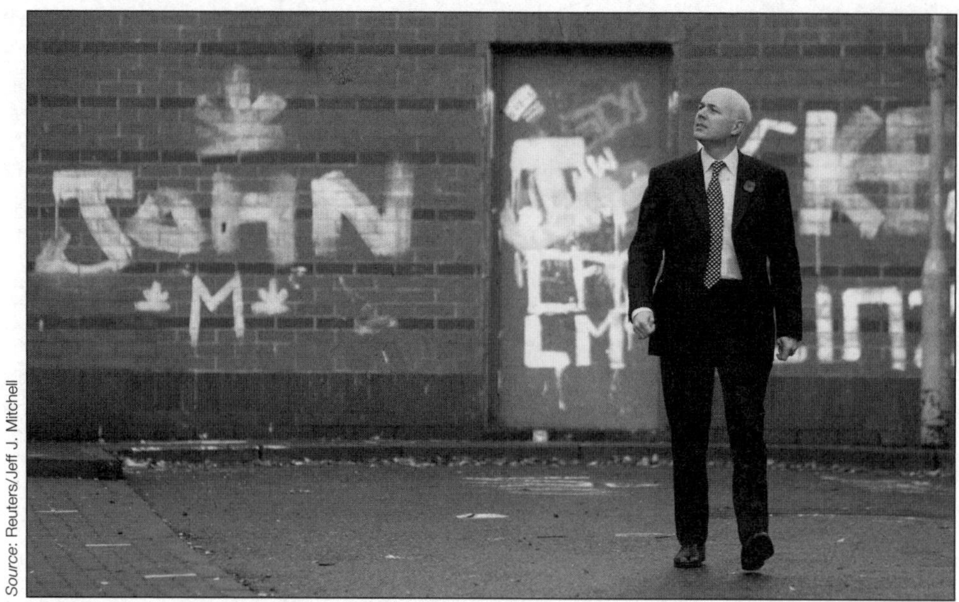

Source: Reuters/Jeff J. Mitchell

Easterhouse in Glasgow featured in Murray's depiction of the underclass and also in the Conservatives 'Broken Britain' theme, having been subject to research by Ian Duncan Smith's Centre for Social Justice.

lower-class areas such as the North East and North West of England and parts of Scotland – it may indeed have had a Celtic connotation (Bagguley and Mann 1992: 123; Taylor 1997).

As well as the criticisms above, stressing the role of the welfare state, the underclass theory, argues Currie (2007), is contradicted by cross-cultural evidence that those countries with more developed welfare states have less violence than the United States, which has the least developed welfare state. Nonetheless, few dispute that the processes of de-industrialization and globalization have had a fundamental impact and that there are areas of towns and cities characterized by a constellation of social problems including crime. To Taylor (1997; 1999), Murray and others correctly pointed to the real problems of the 'absolutely destructive effects' of structural unemployment magnified by the pursuit of free market economic policies with no real care for their human consequences. To him, older industrial cities of the north of England and lowlands of Scotland were

> plagued by what would previously have been quite unknown levels of theft and burglary, car stealing, interpersonal violence and also by a crippling sense of fear and insecurity, which cuts thousands of their residents off from the pleasures of the broader consumer society and the compensations of friendship and neighbourhood.
> (Taylor 1997: 285)

These problems, however, are caused by much wider processes than the development of a culture of crime or dependency. The structural aspects of these processes were more overtly recognized by those who argued that socio-economic change had led to the development of what came to be known as social exclusion.

Social exclusion

While the notion of the underclass was generally linked with the politics of the right, the concept of social exclusion was related to social democratic politics and, in Britain, to 'New Labour' policies. It was widely acknowledged to be a social rather than an individual issue, related to global processes and social change. The term came to virtually replace 'poverty' (Grover 2008) and incorporates interrelated economic, political and spatial dimensions. It is nonetheless a 'flexible and somewhat amorphous' term (Young 2007a: 102), difficult to define, and many refer to it as a discourse. Its use by Governments and policy-makers contains often unstated assumptions about its causes and it has been closely tied to policies aimed at achieving inclusion (Young 2007a; Grover 2008). These points are illustrated in a Cabinet Office statement of 2008 (cited in Clarke 2008: 52):

> Social exclusion is about more than income poverty. It is a short-hand term for what can happen when people or areas have a combination of linked problems such as unemployment, discrimination, poor skills, low incomes, poor housing, high crime and family breakdown. These problems are linked and mutually reinforcing. Social exclusion is an extreme consequence of what happens when people don't get a fair deal throughout their lives, often because of disadvantage they face and birth, and this disadvantage can be transmitted from one generation to the next.

While the social basis of exclusion is widely acknowledged, it is generally accepted that there are different versions (Young 2007a; Grover 2008). A 'weak' and a 'strong' version can be contrasted, with the weak version focusing on the individual characteristics and responsibility of the excluded compared to the strong version which stresses the structural and systemic causes of exclusion and incorporates issues of power. A number of writers have identified three broad approaches related to wider social policies (Young 2007a; Clarke 2008; Grover 2008; and see also Levitas 1998; Lister 2004).

- A *moral underclass discourse* (Grover 2008: 20) tends to individualize social exclusion and, as with the underclass, links state benefits to a 'dependency culture'. Policies focus on individuals 'improving' themselves through, for example, work.
- A *social integrationist discourse* (Grover 2008: 20) focuses on the role of work and economic inactivity, viewing the problem as a sort of 'hydraulic failure of the system to provide jobs' (Young 2007a: 103). This rules out 'direct' discrimination and focuses on work as the main route out of social exclusion through policies such as 'welfare-to-work'.
- *A redistributionist discourse* relates social exclusion to wider issues of social justice, rights and structural inequalities.

These reflect different sets of assumptions. In the first, closest to notions of the underclass, the excluded themselves are cast as the principal agency. This also, argues Young (2007a), signals a continuity from the new right to New Labour in the latter's somewhat nostalgic vision of the traditional family and community and stress on work as a way out. Crime is variously seen as a product of social exclusion but also, at the individual level, as a contributing factor to it and considerable emphasis is placed on individuals and families. Social exclusion is attributed to a lack of motivation and capability, and disorganized communities are perceived as producing and perpetuating inadequate families, particularly those with teenage single mothers who are seen as criminogenic (Young 2007a: 112).

Much of Young's critique is based on his work on the development of the exclusive society and its relationship to crime and responses to it, summarized in Box 7.5. This recognizes the way in which interrelated social, economic and geographical factors such as the growth of peripheral estates and mass private property have contributed to groups being excluded from participation in many aspects of society. But, Young argues, barriers are not fixed and the excluded are aware, through the media, and by working for and with the included, of their inability to achieve

Box 7.5 The exclusive society

Young identifies a series of factors contributing to a shift from an *inclusive* to an *exclusive* society including:

- declining employment in former industrial areas;
- a division between those in permanent and casual labour;
- the development of peripheral housing estates in which the 'poor' are spatially segregated;
- the growth of 'mass private property', such as shopping malls and leisure centres and private housing developments which exclude the poor.

An **inclusive society** is associated with:

- material and ontological security (a security of 'being'):
  - *for example, security of employment and feelings of safety*
- incorporating members
- attempts to assimilate deviance and disorder:
  - *'deviants' are dealt with in communities and families*

An **exclusive society** is associated with:

- material and ontological precariousness:
  - *for example, loss of secure employment and feelings of unsafety*
- the response to deviance involves more exclusion:
  - *for example, higher rates of imprisonment*

Relative deprivation accompanied by a **culture of individualism** leads to increasing crime which in turn leads to:

- **More exclusion** indicated by:
  - increasing *fear of crime* which leads to public avoidance of 'risky' situations;
  - rising *prison rates* involving penal exclusion;
  - *exclusion from public spaces* of groups suspected of 'crime';
  - the development of:
    - *'barriers' between areas in cities*
    - *a cordon sanitaire separating 'winners' from 'losers'*
    - *the 'outgroup' become scapegoated / defined as 'underclass'*
    - *processes of demonization.*
- **A 'bulimic society'** in which:
  - *cultural inclusion* (in which all are encouraged to aspire to the same material goals through mass media and culture) is accompanied by
  - *structural exclusion* which leads to emotions such as humiliation and degradation.
- **A culture of vindictiveness** in which the 'included' also suffer from insecurities of employment and the struggle to meet the goals of the consumer society. This leads to *relative deprivation downwards* in which the poor are seen to enjoy benefits and are 'othered' as the 'cause' of 'our' problems. This contributes to vindictiveness and punitivism which exacerbates processes of exclusion.

(Based on Young 1999; 2003; 2007a)

universally desired cultural and material goals. They are therefore culturally included but structurally excluded which can form a motivation for crime (see Chapter 13).

Life for the included is also far from secure, leading to perceptions of the poor as unfairly rewarded, and to a process of 'enemy creation' in which the poor become scapegoats. Simple, binary divisions between the included and excluded are misleading and Young also points to the way in which social policy and criminal justice policies can exacerbate process of exclusion. A cycle of exclusion can also be set in train by the actions of the included who use their economic and social capital to protect themselves by purchasing security (Hope 2000; 2001): for example, buying homes in safer neighbourhoods, sending their children to safer schools, insuring their homes (often, as seen above, not an option for the poor), replacing stolen goods, employing private security, avoiding dangerous places and using private as opposed to public transport (Goodey 2005: 138). The poor, on the other hand, are more likely to be trapped in poor neighbourhoods leading Hope (2001: 216) to argue that 'in a risk society . . . the threat of crime victimization is not just a consequence of social exclusion but also a contributory cause'.

The excluded are nonetheless cast primarily as offenders, whereas, as outlined in Chapter 6, there is a strong overlap between offenders and victims: 'dangerous places' are dangerous to their own inhabitants. Indeed victimization can in itself contribute to and be a factor in exclusion as illustrated in Box 7.6 which draws attention to the situation of the most excluded, generally assumed to be those who lack a stable home, are denied state benefits and who have no legal status as citizens. The homeless and immigrants without appropriate papers can be defined as particularly excluded (Goodey 2005) and they are subject to a 'spiral' of victimization and

Source: Alamy Images/HOBBS

The gated community represents an extreme example of how the 'included' protect themselves from the 'excluded'.

Box 7.6 Victimization and exclusion

- Victimization is often a direct cause of exclusion. Young people leave home to escape violence, 'chronic' victims may make themselves 'intentionally homeless' (Victim Support 2002), and political and state violence may force people to leave their home countries and seek refuge in other countries (Goodey 2003).
- This exclusion increases risks of victimization. The homeless lack shelter to provide minimal security, and report very high rates of victimization (Pain et al 2002) and irregular immigrants are vulnerable to exploitation by gangmasters, employers or landlords.
- These victims are less likely to report crime as they fear the police and other 'authorities'. They are also more likely to be seen as suspects rather than victims by the police, and as undeserving victims.
- They are less likely to be offered support or to know about support services.
- The most excluded are also victims of criminalization. Groups such as 'beggars', 'street people', 'bogus asylum seekers' or 'illegal immigrants' are often assumed to pose a 'threat'.

(Adapted from Croall 2007a: 65)

exclusion. Some are excluded due to previous victimization and, while subject to large amounts of crime, they are often unable to report this as they are likely to be seen as suspects rather than victims. Irregular immigrants and the young homeless (Grover 2008) can also be treated with resentment and disdain, echoing Young's arguments about vindictiveness.

Discussion

It can be seen from the above that there are many different ways of exploring the complex and contested relationships between socio-economic status, crime, victimization and criminalization. Some deny any relationship altogether whereas to others social exclusion and crime are interrelated consequences of economic policies, economic changes and political ideologies. Both popularly and academically the poor and the economy are blamed for crime in different ways. This tends to imply that crime is borne of necessity and constitutes a rational economic choice, a view contested by cultural approaches which point to the emotional aspects of deprivation and exclusion. Yet others point to the way in which crime has become associated with other aspects of social policy. Drawing on the above analyses and theoretical perspectives these issues are discussed below.

Blaming the poor?

As seen above the poor are blamed for crime by being assumed to commit more of it, for being responsible for the poverty which is assumed to motivate it and for not protecting themselves from victimization through risky lifestyles, and also for failing to take sufficient precautions and precipitating offences by, for example, being involved in fights. This is most evident in depictions of the underclass, with its contemporary echoes in the theme of 'Broken Britain'. The Centre for Social Justice (2008), associated with the new Welfare and Pensions Secretary, Ian Duncan Smith, stresses the role of families, individuals and the disease of worklessness highlighted in their campaign in the Glasgow East by-election of 2008 (Law et al 2010). It is also a theme running through many criminological theories in which the pathologies and deficits associated with crime were implicitly those of lower-class individuals. As seen in Chapter 5, these have re-emerged in right realist and conservative criminologies which, while rejecting any link with crime and structural factors, do associate it with low income and welfare dependency. This is individualized as the poor are seen to be responsible for their situation and for a decline in family and community values. As outlined in Chapter 4, sociological theories also cast lower-class subcultures negatively by associating crime with 'sub'cultures, 'dis'organization and urban decay, reflecting a view of the 'deviant poor' from the lens of the 'normal' middle classes. Moreover, the discourse of social exclusion, particularly its weaker version, while acknowledging the role played by economic change, echoes the view that the onus is on the socially excluded, for example, to obtain work.

There are many problems with this construction. It illustrates the stigmatization, demonization and criminalization of marginal groups highlighted by labelling and critical perspectives. The pervasive equation of crime with the poor or socially excluded neglects not only white-collar and corporate crime but also the often neglected crimes of the middle classes including tax evasion, defrauding insurance companies and not paying television licence fees (Karstedt and Farrell 2006). This is sometimes described as 'everyday' crime and is widely tolerated as opposed to the more condemnatory language used to describe the similar activities of social security 'cheats' and 'scroungers' (see Chapters 13 and 15). All of the crimes associated with the more affluent and powerful are also affected by socio-economic change. Blaming the poor for crime can also neglect their considerable victimization, some of it at the hands of the more affluent. They are vulnerable to, for example, loan sharking, the sale of cheap and substandard goods, exploitation at work by being paid less than the minimum wage and working in dangerous and poorly regulated sectors of the economy (Croall 2001b; 2009a; 2009b). Yet in this respect they can also be 'blamed' by working in risky jobs or taking on debts they cannot pay off.

'It's the economy, stupid'

Despite often contradictory research findings of studies, Reiner (2007a: 362) argues that the

> clear conclusion indicated by a review of the econometric evidence is that there is a plethora of material confirming that crime of all kinds is linked to inequality, relative deprivation, and unemployment.

The importance of relative as opposed to absolute deprivation is seen in the stronger relationships established between income inequalities and crime, than low income in itself. Absolute deprivation cannot nonetheless be ruled out as for some, particularly the most excluded, crime can be necessary for survival (Grover 2008). To Currie (2007), who relates crime to the growth of the market society in an argument outlined in Box 7.7, the adverse effects of extreme poverty on the home environment prevent parents from being able to raise their children effectively. An absence of long-term job prospects and economic marginality can have, he argues, corrosive effects on family stability.

The effect of the economy is also linked to control, routine activity and opportunity theories (Reiner 2007a; 2007b; 2007c) as the availability and desirability of goods creates opportunities to steal and to be able to sell them to people who otherwise could not afford them (see Chapter 13). As seen above it has also been suggested that groups of people move between work in the legitimate and illegitimate economies suggesting the application of rational choice models whereby crime becomes an alternative means of obtaining an income. Reiner (2007a: 357)

Box 7.7 Crime and market society

Elliot Currie (1996) summarizes the effects of market society on crime:

- *Market society promotes crime by increasing inequality and concentrated economic deprivation*. The polarization of work, which has led to an increase in unstable, part-time and low-paid jobs is, he argues, a result of deliberate economic and social policy. At the same time the real value of low wages has declined.
- *'Market society promotes crime by weakening the capacity of local communities for "informal" support, mutual provision and socialization and supervision of the young'* (Currie 1996: 345). As communities suffer from the long-term loss of stable incomes, they can no longer provide social support: 'If you're having tough times you can't lean on your neighbours . . . because they're having tough times too' (Currie 1996: 346).
- *'Market society promotes crime by stressing and fragmenting the family'* (Currie 1996: 346). The pool of 'marriageable men' who can support a family is reduced, leading to the proliferation of single-parent families. To survive economically some families must take on two or even three jobs – reducing their leisure time and time to spend with their children.
- *'Market society promotes crime by withdrawing public provision of basic services for those it has already stripped of livelihoods, economic security and "informal" communal support'* (Currie 1996: 347). In America welfare benefits have been reduced and many public services in Britain are short of resources.
- *'Market society promotes crime by magnifying a culture of Darwinian competition for status and dwindling resources and by urging a level of consumption that it cannot fulfil for everyone through legitimate channels'* (Currie 1996: 347). This echoes anomie theory. Currie paints a chilling picture of violent street crime, illustrating how it can be related to the pursuit of consumer goods or status. 'Some of our delinquents will cheerfully acknowledge that they blew someone away for their running shoes or because they made the mistake of looking at them disrespectfully on the street' (Currie 1996: 348).

points to the irony that rational choice theories, often associated with free market theories, must acknowledge this rationality. While, he argues, it is a 'straightforward inference of neo-classical economic theory that economic fluctuations affect the perceived costs and benefits of legitimate as compared to illegitimate actions', many following neo-liberal ideas reject any link between economic conditions and crime. Nonetheless, focusing on primarily economic motivations can, as seen in Chapter 5, neglect other aspects of the impact of economic inequality. Currie, for example, (Box 7.7) talks about the 'Darwinian' culture of competition and the consumer society thus drawing attention to cultural elements.

Cultural influences

Economic factors such as poverty or deprivation must be explored within the context of wider cultural influences as recognized in anomie and subcultural theory. Young (2007a) has, as seen in this and previous chapters, highlighted the emotional effects of economic deprivation including feelings of failure and humiliation. Downes (2004: 5) argues that the combination of a 'criminogenic concentration of people with multiple problems into residualised areas of social housing' and the dead end nature of service industry jobs, combined with a 'winner and loser culture, the cult of celebrity and the "in your face" exaltation of sudden wealth in the mass media' . . . translates 'readily into a commodity fetishism which fuels and justifies street crime'.

To Young (2007a: 204) an overemphasis on purely economic factors neglects the way in which subcultures in these kinds of areas can be vibrant and positive. Liberal othering, he argues, focuses on misery and seems incapable of detecting fun and resistance which can be provided by subcultures. Ghettoes are not always places of misery and participation in crime not only puts food on the table but can also provide elements of risk, excitement and thrills along with access to valued consumer goods and entertainment. As Hayward (2002: 86, cited in Grover 2008: 45) argues:

> The run-down estate or ghetto becomes the paradoxical space; on the one hand it symbolizes the systematic powerlessness so often felt by the individuals who live in such environments, and on the other the sink estate serves as a site of consumption that provides numerous illegal activities. The ghetto becomes a 'performance zone' in which displays of risk, excitement, masculinity and even 'carnivalesque pleasure' in the form of rioting are frequently perpetuated.

To explore these links fully, more qualitative research is clearly required.

The criminalization of social policy

A theme throughout the above discussions, particularly in relation to social exclusion, is the close, and to many growing, relationship between crime, criminal justice and wider areas of social and economic policy. Previous chapters have charted the punitive turn in criminal justice policy which signalled a departure from theories of crime which located its causes in individual pathologies or social inequalities. These were seen as 'soft', as 'excusing crime' and as denying the responsibility of individual offenders. This theme of responsibilization has affected other areas of social policy and is evident in the weaker versions of the social exclusion discourse in which blame is placed on parents; indeed, parenting orders specifically penalize parents for the activities of their children (see Chapter 8). It is also linked to Young's arguments about vindictiveness in which the precariousness of the included leads them to be more punitive towards the excluded.

What has been described as the 'criminalization of social policy' relates to the way in which depictions of the underclass and the discourse of social exclusion link crime to other 'social problems' such as sink estates, single-parent families, teenage pregnancies, unemployment, casual employment and general incivilities, issues previously regarded as largely welfare issues. Crime prevention policies have also become linked to welfare policies through, for example, 'partnerships' dealing with 'community' planning or safety which involve the police and other agencies. While words such as 'community' and 'partnership' imply consultation and inclusiveness, these also have exclusive elements. Consultations with the 'community' most often exclude those who are seen as 'problems' such as young people or the homeless. Gilling (2001), for example, argues that notions of inclusion involve excluding those who do not belong, and 'community safety' largely refers to the safety of the 'respectable classes' who fear the 'underclass'.

The significance of socio-economic inequalities

Discussions of social inequalities and crime have very often centred on social class and, as seen above, on elements of social deprivation. Later work has also drawn attention, as will be seen in the next three chapters, to age, gender and racial inequalities. Indeed, some might argue that these are, particularly in the contemporary world with its diversity of cultures and the break-up of traditional lower-class communities, equally as if not more important than socio-economic inequality. It will be seen nonetheless that these inequalities are closely interrelated. The impact of economic change has fallen particularly severely on the young and, as outlined above, youth unemployment and its effects are key factors in looking at crime. It is lower-class youth who constitute the focus of concern of those blaming the underclass or Broken Britain. It will also be seen that women have been adversely affected by the 'feminization of poverty' linking gender and socio-economic inequalities, and the socio-economic status of different racial and ethnic groups is also a key factor in relation to their experiences of crime and victimization. Disentangling all these interrelated factors is no easy task. Socio-economic inequalities do, however, underlie many other inequalities and this is also illustrated in many specific forms of crime, where the stresses and strains of living with worklessness or reduced incomes can be associated with domestic and sexual violence and homicide as well as property crimes. Moreover, even for the more advantaged, economic factors, often associated with 'greed', also play a part in the motivation for crime, and so-called power crimes, such as those involving the state, depend on asymmetries of power (Ruggiero 2007 and see Chapter 17).

Concluding comments

This chapter has explored many dimensions of the relationship between socio-economic inequalities and crime. While socio-economic inequalities are often cast as being a problem of lower-class crime, it has been argued that this neglects the crimes of the middle classes and the wealthy and powerful along with the victimization of the poor, at the hands both of lower-class and corporate and state offenders. Different kinds of crime can therefore be committed by different classes, and can be related to economic conditions and economic inequalities. The cultures of consumption and competition are also important in relation, for example, to crimes in the financial sector. Power inequalities lead to the criminalization of the crimes of the most marginal while others are tolerated and not constructed as 'crime'.

Many gaps remain in our knowledge about the links between economic factors and crime. There are, for example, as seen also in Chapter 6, very few ethnographic studies of the combined effects of poverty, deprivation and exclusion and the 'lived reality' of crime and victimization in estates characterized as 'problem places' which might also explore some of the ways in which crime not only represents a rational economic solution but also provides a sense of purpose, achievement and excitement. Some of these factors will be further explored in Chapters 13 and 14.

Socio-economic status is related to global inequalities as well as to the other dimensions of social inequality outlined above. The huge gap between nations in terms of income and standards of living have, as will be seen in later chapters, been associated with crimes such as human trafficking and the exploitation of workers and communities in Third-World countries. Further aspects of these relationships will also be explored in chapters looking at specific forms of crime, from those most often associated with lower-class offenders, such as violent, sexual, property and organized crime and those associated with higher status and powerful offenders such as white-collar, corporate, environmental and state crimes.

Review questions

1 Taking your own locality identify areas considered to be 'dangerous' and the 'dangerous people' with whom they are associated. What forms of crime and disorder are involved? To what extent might these areas be seen as 'excluded'?

2 Consult official statistics and victim surveys and explore the relationships between socio-economic factors and aspects of crime, risks of crime, and fears and worries about crime. How can these be explained?

3 What kinds of crime would you expect to rise in a recession and why? What economic indicators might help establish any relationships?

4 Write notes on:

(a) The criminal underclass.

(b) What is meant by the term social exclusion and how can it be related to crime?

Key reading

Few books have specifically addressed the relationship between crime, class and socio-economic inequalities. The following references are the most useful:

Grover, C. (2008) ***Crime and Inequality***, Cullompton: Willan Publishing. This covers many of the issues raised above and includes useful sections on socio-economic inequalities and social policy and the relationship between socio-economic inequalities and issues of gender, race and youth crime.

Reiner, R. (2007) 'Political Economy, Crime and Criminal Justice' in M. Maguire, R. Morgan and R. Reiner (eds) (2007) *The Oxford Handbook of Criminology*, Oxford: Clarendon Press 4th edn, pp 341–81. A clear and incisive account of the theories and ideologies associated with the relationship between economic factors and crime and their politicization.

See also **Reiner, R. (2007)** ***Law and Order: An Honest Citizen's Guide to Crime and Control***, Cambridge: Polity Press.

Young, J. (1999) ***The Exclusive Society: Social Exclusion, Crime and Difference in Late Modernity***, Sage and **Young, J.** (2007) ***The Vertigo of Late Modernity***, London: Sage. These set out in detail Young's influential and thought-provoking analyses of the major social and economic changes, their impact on society, crime and criminal justice policies, along with a critique of these and other policies relating to social exclusion and inclusion.

Chapter 8
Age and crime

This chapter will look at:

- ➜ Age and offending
- ➜ Age and victimization
- ➜ The social construction of age and youth
- ➜ The rise of the juvenile delinquent
- ➜ Criminology and the young offender
- ➜ Predicting crime
- ➜ Anti-social youth?
- ➜ Young people, drugs and crime
- ➜ Gangland Britain?
- ➜ Theorizing the age–crime relationship

Crime has been so strongly associated with young people's activities that many theories have dealt almost exclusively with youth crime. As seen in Chapter 2, youth are often subject to moral panics including the mods and rockers of the 1960s, the punks, skinheads, football hooligans, joyriders and muggers of the latter decades of the twentieth century, and the binge drinkers, gangs, 'hoodies' and anti-social youth of the 2000s. Crime can be represented as an 'age war' (Wahidin and Powell 2007: 235) between young offenders and older people, already identified as archetypal deserving victims. But young people are also victims and older people commit crime. Like crime itself, official rates of youth crime have fallen in the 2000s despite these moral panics (Muncie 2009). Nonetheless, young people do commit crime, some of it violent.

This chapter will start by critically exploring the relationship between age and recorded crime and victimization. It will look at how age is socially constructed and at how 'juvenile delinquency' emerged as a 'problem'. It will explore how criminology has dealt with the topic before, while recognizing that people of all ages commit crime, focusing on contemporary aspects of youth crime. The often more serious crimes of older offenders will feature in later chapters. It will explore the extent to which research can identify 'risk factors' associated with crime, and look at some contemporary aspects of youth crime, including anti-social behaviour, drug- and alcohol-related crime and involvement in gangs. Finally, the chapter will critically examine the state of our knowledge about the age and crime relationship, particularly its neglect of young people's victimization and older people's crime and victimization.

Age and crime

The law reflects how age is socially constructed by distinguishing between different age groups, although the age of criminal responsibility – the age at which individuals are said to be able to tell right from wrong – is disputed. Currently, this is lower across Britain than in other European countries, being 8 in Scotland and 10 in England, Wales and Northern Ireland although all jurisdictions are reviewing this (Davies et al 2009; BBC News 2010c). All jurisdictions also have separate proceedings for dealing with offenders under 16.

Age and offending

The high proportion of young people among convicted offenders was illustrated in Chapter 3 and is evident in most jurisdictions (Newburn 2007; Muncie 2009; Hopkins Burke 2008). Age curves such as those illustrated in Figure 8.1 for England and Wales, illustrate the 'peak' age of conviction for younger people and the declining rates for older people, although it should be borne in mind that children and those under 16 are often dealt with by diversionary measures. Despite a widespread perception that youth crime is rising, figures paint a 'controversial and contradictory picture' (Muncie 2009: 19), suggesting a 27 per cent drop from 1992–2004, followed by a 19 per cent rise from 2003–2006, although the OCJS records no increase in self-reported crime in these years (Roe and Ashe 2008). In Scotland, youth crime remained stable or has decreased from the mid 1990s with an increase from 2002/3–2005/6 for those under 16. Conviction rates for 16 and 17 year olds

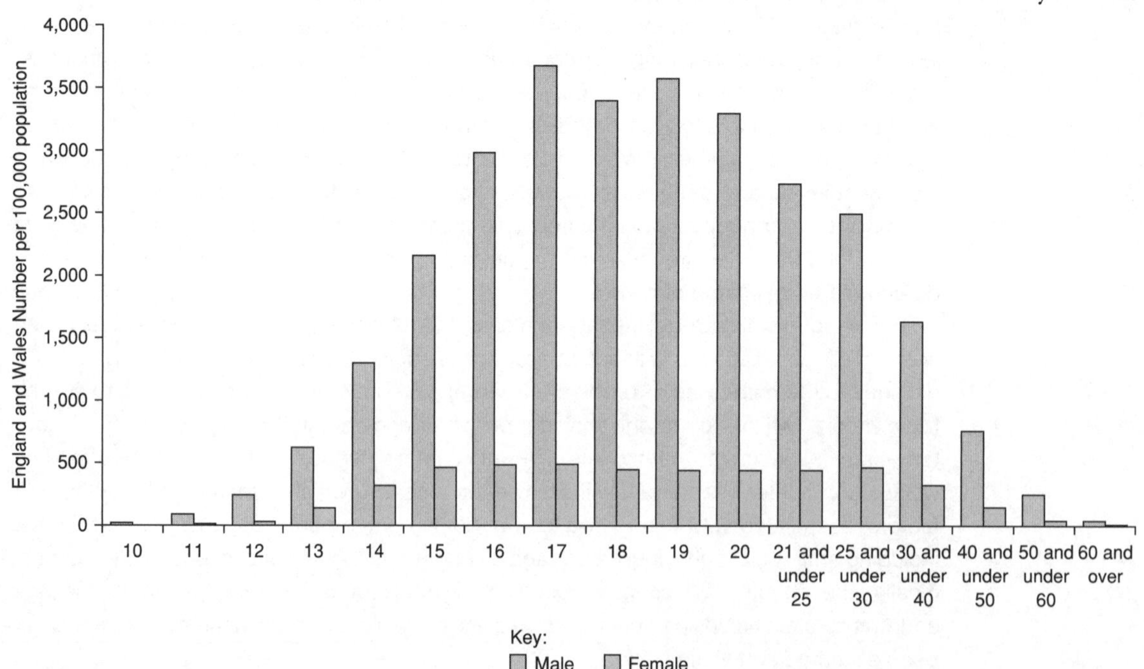

Figure 8.1 Persons found guilty for indictable offences per 100,000 population by age group, 2008

declined from the 1990s with a slight rise in 2006/7 – peaks coinciding with a more punitive stance towards youth crime by the then Scottish Executive (McAra and McVie 2010). This warns against reading too much into fluctuations in figures, all subject to the many factors which 'produce' offenders (see Chapter 3).

Self-report studies such as the Youth Lifestyle Surveys in England and Wales (Graham and Bowling 1995; Flood-Page et al 2000) and the later OCJS (Roe and Ashe 2008), summarized in Box 8.1, provide some indication of young people's involvement in crime. More people aged between 14 and 21 report larger amounts of offending and a much smaller proportion report 'serious' or 'persistent' offending, taken as committing three or more offences in the last year or one of a group of more serious offences such as violence, burglary, car theft or robbery. Persistence is also reflected by the estimate that 10 per cent of offenders were responsible for nearly a half of all crimes reported. In Scotland, a study in Edinburgh found that while half of 12 to 17 year olds reported committing at least one serious offence, only a quarter were persistent or serious offenders with serious offending peaking at 14 and declining to 17 (McAra and McVie 2010). These studies all suggest that most young people do not commit offences. For those that do, offending is often trivial and transitory – higher prevalence figures relate to minor acts of disorder or 'fighting' associated with hanging out on the streets, experiments in under-age drinking and status offences. This involves young people of all social classes. A much smaller minority of young people engage in more serious or persistent offending and

Box 8.1 Self-reported offending

4,554 young people aged between 10 and 25 were asked about 20 core offences in the last 12 months:

- The majority were law-abiding: over three-quarters (78%) had not committed any offences.
- Many broke the law only occasionally or committed relatively trivial offences.
- 6 per cent had committed an offence 6 or more times – they were classified as frequent offenders.
- 10 per cent of 10- to 25-year-olds had committed at least one serious offence.
- Serious and frequent offenders overlapped – 4 per cent of 10- to 25-year-olds were both frequent and serious offenders; 1 per cent had frequently committed serious offences.
- The most commonly reported offence was assault (committed by 12 per cent). Other thefts accounted for 10 per cent.
- Less common were criminal damage (4 per cent); drug-selling offences (3 per cent) and vehicle-related thefts (2 per cent). Only 1 per cent or less reported robbery or burglary.
- There was no change in levels of offending since 2003.
- 22 per cent had committed at least one act of anti-social behaviour in the last 12 months.
- Those who offended were also likely to engage in anti-social behaviour.
- Offenders were also more likely to be victims.

Source: Roe and Ashe (2008)

pursue criminal 'careers'. This group is more likely to come from deprived areas although this can reflect police activity (Muncie 2009; McAra and McVie 2010).

The apparent predominance of young people as offenders must, however, be critically examined. Statistics and self-report studies, as seen in Chapter 3, exclude many kinds of crime, and self-report studies are generally carried out only with those under 30. Old people do commit crime and predominate as offenders in crime categories which are less easy to detect. These include organized crime: so-called 'Godfathers', older fraudsters such as Bernie Madoff (Levi 2008b), business and corporate executives involved in financial and safety crimes and those responsible for state crimes, genocide and torture (Muncie 2009 and see Chapters 13–17). Adults are responsible for three times as many violent offences and five times as many sexual offences than young people (Muncie 2009). Indeed, it could be argued that these kinds of crime dwarf young people's crime in terms of seriousness and harm. A number of factors are widely assumed to contribute to the visibility of youth and the invisibility of older people's crime including:

- **Visibility:** Young people more often socialize in public places, which can in itself be perceived as threatening, and makes them an easier target for policing.
- **Illegitimate opportunities:** Young people have fewer opportunities to engage in crime in the workplace and are more likely to engage in more visible and detectable street crimes. Older people have more opportunities to avoid taxes, steal from their employers, defraud customers or make false insurance claims.
- **Age and experience:** Young people may lack the skills and experience required for some crimes such as financial or cyber crimes. They may also be less competent criminals and more likely to be caught than older, more experienced offenders (Pearson 1994a; Steffensmeier and Allan 1995).
- **Criminal careers:** Crime can be seen as a career. While most young offenders stop committing crime somewhere around their late teens, a minority 'graduate' from less serious, high-risk offences to more serious offences with a lower risk of being caught. Joyriders become car thieves, casual drug users become drug dealers, and thieves or burglars may turn to cyber crime, fraud or quasi criminal 'enterprises' (Chapter 14).

Age and victimization

Chapters 3 and 6 indicated strong relationships between age and victimization with the elderly emerging as less at risk from both violent and property crime, and young men emerging as most at risk from assault, which contradicts representations of the elderly as victims and the young as offenders. There is now much greater recognition of the victimization of children and young people and the often hidden victimization of the elderly has also to be acknowledged.

Young children's victimization

Young children are very often unaware of or unable to report harmful acts committed against them and are not included in victim surveys. Nonetheless they are subject to considerable victimization, often from those close to them. Over 10 per cent of homicides involve parents killing children with those under one being most at risk. The National Society for the Prevention of Cruelty to Children (2002) estimates that one in ten young adults suffer serious abuse or neglect during childhood. Recent decades have seen recurrent revelations of many forms of abuse in institutions for children including seminaries and orphanages – one of the most high profile cases being the systematic abuse and violence against 11–15-year-old boys and girls at Haut de la Garenne in Jersey (Muncie 2009). Children are also indirectly victimized by violence in the home and by the after-effects of crimes such as burglary (Morgan and Zedner 1992).

The victimization of young people

The victimization of young people was omitted from early victim surveys but is now more widely acknowledged with studies during the 1990s exposing considerable levels of crime against young people in the streets and in and around schools (Morgan and Zedner 1992; Hartless et al 1995). Half the respondents in an Edinburgh study had been victims of assault, threatening behaviour or theft from the person, and around a third had experienced bullying (Anderson et al 1994). Later studies, as outlined in Box 8.2, have confirmed this overall picture. Young people's victimization is related to their lifestyles and to their carrying desirable items such as phones, iPods or accessories. Much of this victimization is unreported (Francis 2007b). Box 8.2 also highlights the strong association between offenders and victims, particularly in relation to minor fights (Francis 2007b; Muncie 2009). These kinds of studies, however, as all victim surveys, should be treated with

Box 8.2 Young people's victimization from crime

4,554 young people aged between 10 and 25 were asked about victimization in the last 12 months.

- Half of those who had committed an offence had also been victims of a personal crime in the same period compared to about a fifth of those who had not committed any offence.
- Younger respondents aged from 10 to 15 were more likely than those aged 16 to 25 to report being a victim of a personal crime.
- Just over a quarter of young people had been a victim of either personal theft or assault in the last 12 months.
- 10- to 15-year-olds were more likely to have been a victim of a personal crime than 16- to 25-year-olds.
- The most common location for victimization amongst 10- to 15-year-olds was in school or college. For 16- to 25-year-olds incidents were most likely to take place at a pub, bar or nightclub or in the street.
- Victims of assault aged from 10 to 15 were more likely to know their perpetrators than those aged from 16 to 25.

Source: Roe and Ashe (2008)

caution. They often use different age groups, making comparison difficult, and checking off lists of offences does not capture the lived experiences of young people. They neglect victimization by corporate and white-collar crimes (Croall 2009a and see Chapter 15), and most do not ask about institutional or domestic violence (Francis 2007b; Muncie 2009). Nonetheless they do highlight young people's victimization, thus challenging views that they are the 'problem'.

The victimization of older people

There has been a growing recognition of the victimization of older people (Cain and Wahidin 2006; Powell and Wahidin 2006; Wahidin and Powell 2007; Williams 2010). As with younger children, older people are subject to physical and sexual violence at home and in institutions, and may not be able to report this victimization. Older people are also reliant on fixed incomes and need to make prudent investments which makes them targets of pensions frauds and misselling (Croall 2001b; Wahidin and Powell 2007). They have been subject to aggressive sales of burglar alarms, preying on their fear of crime (Croall 2009a), and of distraction burglaries (Lister and Wall 2006). They may also face negligence and deliberate harming by professional groups responsible for their care (Brogden and Nijhar 2006). Williams (2010: 419) reports a study by Mowlam et al (2007) on elder abuse within older people's homes across Britain in which 4 per cent of respondents over the age of 66 reported physical abuse and theft. Around a third of this was from partners, close family members, and neighbours and acquaintances respectively. Around three-quarters of abusers were men. The vulnerability of the elderly is reflected in higher levels of worry about crime (see Chapter 6) which may also be linked to fears about the greater impact of crime due to their relative poverty and fears of infirmity and disability, with those over 75 being most vulnerable (Wahidin and Powell 2007).

Constructing the age and crime relationship

Offending and victimization are therefore strongly related to age and its associated lifestyles. In turn, these are related to the social expectations surrounding age and to the structural position of different age groups, outlined below.

The social construction of age and youth

Perceptions of youth and childhood are not fixed by biological characteristics but have changed over time (Pearson 1994a). While childhood is now associated with innocence and children are assumed to need protection, children and youth were accorded a very different status in earlier eras (Muncie 1984; McLaughlin and Muncie 1993; Brown 2005; Muncie 2009). They were expected to assume adult responsibilities and work as soon as they were physically capable, without any protracted period of adolescence. Ariès (1962) suggests that conceptions of 'childhood' developed with the decline of child mortality whereby parents, who had placed little emotional investment in children, came to see them as needing nurture, affection and protection. Children then came to be seen as in need of discipline and an introduction to adulthood – creating the status of 'youth' (Muncie 1984; Anderson et al 1994). This was originally restricted to the middle and upper classes but spread to working-class children with the development of state education. By the twentieth century the concept of childhood was universalized and applied to all classes.

The rise of the juvenile delinquent

The activities of young people have long been the subject of public concern (see Chapter 2), linked to fears about social change, the break-up of the traditional family and community, the dwindling power of 'authority' and the pernicious effects of popular entertainment (Pearson 1983; 1994a). As early as 1603, a group known as the London apprentices were banned from playing football, playing music or drinking in taverns and were ordered not to 'weare their haire long nor locks at their eares like ruffians' (Pearson 1994a: 1116). During the nineteenth century and the industrial revolution youth crime was attributed to the decline of discipline and religion and the breakdown of the family, and young people were said to be imitating the popular dramas of theatres and music halls (Pearson 1983; 1994a). The early twentieth century saw the emergence of 'hooligans' with bell-bottom trousers, ornamental leather belts, neck scarves, peaked caps and short cropped hair.

The term juvenile delinquency became more widely used towards the end of the nineteenth century (McLaughlin and Muncie 1993; Muncie 2009). It was linked to lower-class homes and associated with parental irresponsibility, genetic factors and individual pathology. In what has been described as the 'child saving movement', largely middle-class reformers advocated policies which would 'save' delinquents. Juvenile justice was separated from adult justice, young offenders were sent to 'reformatories' or put in the charge of police court missionaries – the forerunners of the Probation Service (Muncie 1984; McLaughlin and Muncie 1993). Delinquency was thus firmly associated with working-class family life and delinquents were also subject to racialization and othering, being described as a 'class apart', as 'street Arabs' and 'savages' (Graham and Clarke 1996). Pearson notes that 'hooligans' were seen as an 'un-British' phenomenon – 'indeed we must allow that it was most ingenious of late Victorian England to disown the British Hooligan by giving him an "Irish" name' (Pearson 1983: 75). While cruelty to children was recognized, most concerns were about young people's offending (Morgan and Zedner 1992).

To Muncie (2009) constructions of the young offender reflect recurrent concerns about social control – concern about the delinquent reflected concerns about unemployment and lack of discipline, and in the early twentieth century concerns about street leisure were accompanied by the emergence of the troublesome adolescent. The view that young offenders required welfare-based approaches gave rise to notions of the 'troubled offender' with delinquency being linked to psychological problems or a neglect or lack of moral education.

Fears of young people's lawlessness and disorder are not therefore new. Indeed, argues Muncie (2009: 79), they tell us more about adult concerns for 'morality, national security, unemployment, leisure, independence, and imperialism' than they do about young people's offending and they also reflect deep-seated fears about the rapid progress of social change – of modernity (Pearson 1994a). Older generations experience loss and regret in the face of massive social change, may feel that their world is falling apart and recall former times with nostalgia. These memories may not be accurate and they may interpret 'folk memory' by recalling an altogether more peaceful time. Young people, on the other hand, welcome the new and unfamiliar, and become a symbol of social change and breakdown. This may account for the hysteria which young people's activities attract and for their 'demonization' (Pearson 1994a).

Older people, on the other hand, are less likely to be cast as criminals and more as victims and when older people do offend it may be regarded as somewhat abnormal. Indeed, Brogden and Nijhar (2006) suggest that the murders of several old people by Harold Shipman (see Chapter 11), himself an older man, were not treated with as great an uproar as would have been expected by other 'mass murders'. Old people are often represented in 'ageist' terms as being dependent and vulnerable and when they do commit crimes, their age is not seen as a major factor. Groups of bankers suspected of fraud, for example, would not be generally described as 'gangs' or 'feral', and older people are rarely seen as going on the rampage.

Criminology and the young offender

The youth of offenders was so taken for granted that the term delinquency became virtually synonymous with crime. Brown (2005) comments, for example, that Britain's first criminology journal was the *British Journal of Delinquency*, changed in 1960

Source: Reuters

Harold Shipman was associated with the murders of largely elderly victims – his age and appearance contradict stereotypes of violent and young offenders.

to the *British Journal of Criminology*. From individual theories to sociological criminology 'the offender' was assumed to be young, generally male and from an 'other' group, be it defined by social class, place or ethnicity.

Pathological theories sampled the 'hapless population' (Brown 2005: 29) of young people, often those in custodial institutions for young offenders, based on the assumption that delinquency could be 'nipped in the bud'. Factors such as intelligence, personality, the size and constitution of families, maternal deprivation and parental supervision were studied; these would be less appropriate for older offenders whose offending could not, as Sutherland (1949) pointed out in relation to the hypothetical criminality of the Vice President of a major corporation, be attributed to maternal deprivation. These assumptions continue in the current focus on 'risk factors' outlined below.

Sociological criminology also focused on the young delinquent, on the 'corner boys' and delinquent 'lads' whose street-based leisure made them more visible to the police and to criminological researchers. Following the Chicago School, much work focused on the delinquent gang and the subcultures within which delinquency flourished. As outlined in Chapter 4, this work was criticized for overpredicting delinquency and exaggerating young people's involvement in gangs (Matza 1964), a criticism borne out by the often temporary nature of young people's involvement in crime outlined above, although as outlined below there are contemporary concerns about youth gangs. Although critical of official statistics, much work associated with labelling perspectives involved young people and they were in turn criticized for neglecting 'serious' white-collar, organized or violent crime. Nonetheless, interactionist work played a major role in illustrating the extent to which police activity and the media targeted young people who were more likely to become the 'usual suspects' and 'folk devils' (Cohen 1972 and see Chapters 2 and 5).

To critical criminologists, fears of the law and order threat posed by the unemployed in times of economic crises, outlined in Chapter 7, involved the criminalization of lower-class young people and the introduction of increasingly stringent controls on young people. Throughout the 1980s policies such as the withdrawal of benefits to young people who did not work or live with their families led to crime or begging becoming a means of survival for homeless young people, many of whom had left their families following violence (Carlen 1996; Carlen et al 1997; Pain et al 2002). New age travelling and squatting, which could be seen as creative responses to this exclusion (Carlen 1996) were in turn controlled in the 1994 Criminal Justice and Public Order Act, with young people's protests being dismissed as further signs of their lawlessness. Particular styles of music and rave and acid house parties were also controlled, with the 1994 Act criminalizing a style of music. As Brown (2005: 63) comments:

> No account of criminalization could be complete without reiterating the gloriously funny and also 'chilling' section 63(1) (b) defining rave music as 'sounds wholly or predominantly characterized by the emission of a succession of repetitive beats'.

As will be seen below, this has continued into the 2000s with the emergence of increasingly punitive controls directed at anti-social behaviour (Burney 2009) and young people's drinking (Measham and Moore 2008).

Dimensions of age and crime

Predicting youth crime

The search for factors to predict crime has been a recurrent theme and has focused on the young. During the 1990s this was associated with concerns about persistent offenders, said to be responsible for a large proportion of offences. Hagell and Newburn (1994) identified a very small number of offenders whose backgrounds indicated general disadvantage along with indications that they had led more chaotic lives than other adolescents, having experienced a high frequency of dramatic events such as accidents, crashes and stabbings along with 'disruption and loss' and truancy. In general they reported good relationships with parents, although a quarter had no relationship with their fathers and reported family discord. They also reported higher use of drugs and half had been referred for counselling or psychological help for drugs, fighting, anger, depression, offending and school exclusions. They were therefore 'far from typical of adolescents as a whole' (ibid: 93).

The Edinburgh Youth Transitions study also found that serious offenders were more likely to be male; to come from poor or deprived homes; to live in single-parent homes and to report lower levels of parental supervision; to drink and use drugs more often; to hang around the streets more often and to consider themselves to be members of a gang. They had higher scores on scales of impulsivity and risk-taking behaviour. They also reported more serious levels of victimization from violence and bullying and a quarter reported self-harm (McAra and McVie 2010).

The search for what are now called 'risk factors' is often linked to the developmental criminology associated with the work of Farrington (2007), who has identified a range of individual, family and environmental factors associated with 'chronic' offenders, outlined in Box 8.3. The Youth Lifestyles Survey identified factors such as the use of drugs, disaffection from school and persistent truancy, low parental supervision, hanging around in public places or having friends who had been in trouble with the police (Flood-Page et al 2000). Others have identified a lack of education and skills which is in turn related to truancy, mental health problems and poor relationships with parents (Hopkins Burke 2008).

Box 8.3 Factors associated with 'serious' offending

Individual factors
- Low intelligence
- Impulsivity
- Attention problems
- Low school attainment

Family
- Poor parental supervision
- Parental conflict
- An anti-social parent
- A young mother
- Large family size
- Coming from a 'broken' family
- Low family income

Environmental
- Peer association
- Living in an area of social deprivation
- High delinquency rate schools

(Adapted from Farrington 2007; Muncie 2009: 27)

Useful as these surveys are, many can be criticized. Like other quantitative studies they report correlations rather than establishing underlying processes. As Muncie (2009: 28) argues, they identify *what* factors may be involved but not *how* or *why*. They also neglect the impact of labelling and indeed being apprehended by the police can in itself be regarded as a 'risk factor' (McAra and McVie 2007; Muncie 2009) and risk factors have been associated with early intervention policies which, by bringing the young person into early contact with official agencies risks triggering off a criminal career. Focusing on individual and family factors can also downplay the material and structural context of offending. Hopkins Burke (2008: 227) argues that the emphasis in Farrington's original work on a combination of individual, family *and* environmental factors has been lost in later work which prioritizes family factors – reflecting, he suggests, governmental priorities. He cites the influential government policy document *No More Excuses* of 1997 which reduced risk factors to 'being male', poor parental discipline, criminal parents and poor school performance. These studies are also restricted to conventional crimes – there has been little equivalent work on the 'risk factors' associated with organized or white-collar crime (Muncie 2009).

Anti-social youth?

The late 1990s and early 2000s saw the emergence of anti-social behaviour, aptly described by Burney (2009: 17) as a 'hydra-headed monster that represented a spectrum of bad behaviour, from serious to merely irritating, afflicting neighbourhoods'. The scourge of anti-social behaviour became a key element of politicians' rhetoric and a raft of legislation was passed including provisions for the Anti-Social Behaviour Order (ASBO), dispersal zones, exclusion orders, curfews, Acceptable Behaviour Contracts and parenting orders. Similar laws were passed in Scotland and Northern Ireland despite the more welfarist Scottish approach to children who offend (Croall 2006; McAra and McVie 2007). There was also an expansion of research and academic work (Squires 2008a; Burney 2009; Millie 2009). To critics, the 'creation' of anti-social behaviour is a prime example of the criminalization of young people's activities – why, in the face of declining rates of youth crime, did this become such a concern? Are claims about anti-social behaviour exaggerated? This section will outline the emergence of anti-social behaviour and will explore the extent to which it can be seen as a real problem.

As for youth crime in general, concerns about disorderly behaviour, particularly that of the lower classes, are not new. Historically, public disorder, concerns about nasty neighbours, vagrants and beggars were reflected in the broad term 'breach of the peace' (Burney 2009). When the 'new police' emerged in the early nineteenth century, action was taken against vagrants, prostitutes and public drunkenness. Lower-class leisure pursuits, such as drinking, playing pitch and toss, dog and cock fighting were also subject to local by-laws. Contemporary concerns about anti-social behaviour, previously linked to a behavioural disorder, surfaced around the 1980s and was linked, as outlined in Chapter 2, with the killing of James Bulger and with populist concerns about a perceived rising tide of disorder and incivilities in areas of social housing, involving '*neighbours from hell*'. Policies stressing the

Box 8.4 Anti-social behaviour

The 1998 Crime and Disorder Act introduced Anti-Social Behaviour orders to be used when a person acted:

> *In a manner that caused or was likely to cause harassment, alarm or distress to one or more persons not of the same household as . . . [the perpetrator]* (cited in Millie 2009: 8).

The government was keen to encourage ASBOs and emphasized the 'scourge' of anti-social behaviour. Introducing the Anti-Social Behaviour bill in 2003, David Blunkett, then Home Secretary, said that the bill would:

> *Empower people across the country once and for all to get a grip on the scourge that bedevils their communities: the anti-social behaviour that makes other people's lives a misery* (cited in Burney 2009: 37).

On the introduction of similar legislation in Scotland in October 2004, the Justice Minister, Cathy Jamieson, stated that the measures were:

> *designed to help communities across Scotland stand up to the scourge of antisocial behaviour . . . and that . . . consultations indicated . . . we had struck a chord with the ordinary, hard-working people of Scotland who . . . had had enough of . . . behaviour which . . . brings misery to lives and which knocks the stuffing out of a community's confidence* (Scottish Executive 2004).

need to act against incivilities were based on Wilson and Kelling's (1982) *Broken Windows* thesis (see Chapter 5), which despite its many criticisms was accepted somewhat uncritically (Hancock 2006; Burney 2009) and anti-social behaviour became a key part of New Labour policy (Burney 2009). Box 8.4 illustrates some of the political rhetoric and legislation.

What is anti-social behaviour?

Most commentators agree that the term is flexibly used, difficult to define and not clearly articulated in legislation. In 2003, the Home Office issued a list of behaviours deemed to be anti-social based on a one-day count on 10 September 2003, outlined in Box 8.5 along with the percentage of reports in each category.

This raises some questions – how, for example, are 'nuisance', 'rowdy behaviour' or 'noise' defined and at what point do they become 'anti-social'? How serious or trivial were these incidents? More or less any behaviour may be anti-social in different contexts and levels of tolerance vary. Anti-social behaviour is therefore related to people's *perceptions* of behaviour which they don't like (Burney 2009) or is 'really' annoying (Millie 2009). It tends to be applied to behaviour falling short of serious crime (Millie 2009), often being described as 'sub criminal' or 'low level' crime or disorder. The term tends to be restricted to public as opposed to private behaviour and implies elements of persistence – like racial harassment, one instance may not be significant whereas repeated incidents can seriously affect someone's quality of life. The term has nonetheless become well established. *The Times* used the words 'anti-social' or 'antisocial' 74 times in 1993, but 292 times

Box 8.5 Anti-social behaviour: listed in a one-day count on 10 September 2003

	Percentage of 66,107 reports
Litter and rubbish	16
Criminal damage/vandalism	12
Vehicle-related nuisance	12
Nuisance behaviour	12
Intimidation/harassment	8
Noise	8
Rowdy behaviour	8
Abandoned vehicles	8
Street drinking and begging	5
Drug/substance misuse and drug dealing	4
Animal-related problems	4
Hoax calls	2
Prostitution, kerb crawling and sexual acts	2

Source: Home Office (2003), cited in Millie (2009: 11)

in 2003, and in 2002 the BCS 'rebranded' the general list of 'disorders' which it asked respondents about as 'anti social behaviour' (Burney 2009). The word ASBO is now widely used and popularly understood.

Is it a real problem?

It has been argued that anti-social behaviour is 'talked up'. Looking at BCS evidence along with a survey in England, Wales and Scotland, Millie (2009) argues that only around 20 per cent of the public perceive high levels of ASB in their area, and reported that it had very little effect on their quality of life. Nonetheless, stronger concerns were voiced in urban areas, and in areas with high levels of social deprivation and social housing. Millie concludes that while the problem is nowhere near as widespread as often alleged, there are areas where it does cause concern. Others agree that the problem is 'real' (Burney 2009), and that it reflects concerns in the 'poorest communities which have been "left behind" by marketization and the consumerist onslaught of the late twentieth century' (Hughes and Follett 2006: 161).

This is important when considering popular explanations of anti-social behaviour – which, like the 'risk factors' discussed earlier, appeal to bad parenting and low school achievement. Yet while few dispute the importance of parental supervision it is dangerous to engage in 'parent blaming' as it is not clear what constitutes 'good' or 'bad' parenting and there are many examples of 'good' parents having 'anti-social' children and 'bad' parents with 'good' children (Millie 2009). To Burney (2009), 'blaming the parents' can distract attention from the real problems faced by parents in the most deprived communities such as those outlined in Chapter 7.

Criminalizing young people's behaviour?

While there may be a 'real' problem, most also agree that ASBOs represent a further example of criminalization and of 'defining deviancy up' (Hughes and Follett 2006). To Burney (2009), the phrase 'anti-social behaviour', as opposed to the more general term 'incivilities', singles out individuals for blame and exclusion. While originally used to refer to neighbourhoods characterized by social housing and associated with issues like rubbish and litter, not exclusively the fault of young people, young people have been the target of public and political concerns (Hughes and Follett 2006; Squires 2008a; Burney 2009). In Millie's survey, three-quarters of respondents associated anti-social behaviour with young people and considered young people and poor parenting as major causes (Millie 2009). To Burney (2009: 71) the level of anti-youth rhetoric amounts to 'paedophobia'.

It is also argued that ASBOs have become increasingly punitive and can exacerbate exclusion (Burney 2008; McIntosh 2008). The small amount of research on the subjective impact of ASBOs suggests that some young people's lives are severely affected. Exclusion orders can, for example, mean that young people have to leave home and lose contact with their families – leading in some cases to homelessness. In other situations, what is effectively house arrest can become oppressive and can lead to increased consumption of drink or drugs (Burney 2009: 147).

The targeting of young people's activities must also be placed in the context of the de-industrialization and changing use of urban space outlined in Chapters 5 and 7, and the consequent fracturing of social relationships in traditional working-class communities (Hancock 2006). Housing policy is important. The introduction of the right to buy council housing reduced available stock and created a situation in which the most desirable properties became owner-occupied, leaving 'hard to let' properties to those who could not afford to buy or move out – largely the elderly, young families, single-parent families and the homeless (Hancock 2006; Burney 2009). Drug dealing spread in these areas and care in the community policies led to mentally ill people also being housed in them. This mixture contributed to the fears of older residents, themselves feeling insecure and vulnerable, of the activities of young people, themselves adversely affected by the relative deprivation and cultural inclusion and exclusion (Young 2007a) outlined in Chapter 7.

These kinds of analyses underline the marginalization and powerlessness of young people. Critics of ASB and community safety policies point to the contradiction that while words such as 'empowerment' are often used, young people are seen as the problem and are rarely 'listened to' (Brown 2005). Little research has focused on the 'lived realities' of anti-social behaviour and particularly the impact of ASBOs on young people. Burney (2009: 192) also contrasts the vehement opposition to proposals to subject suspected terrorists to stronger laws and house arrest with the acceptance and lack of criticism of the exclusion zones and effective house arrests applied to young children.

Young people, drugs and alcohol

Another major concern of the 2000s has been young people's consumption of drugs and the rise, in towns and cities across Britain, of a 'booze and binge drinking culture'.

This raises a number of questions, some similar to those raised by anti-social behaviour. How is young people's drug-taking constructed as a problem? Has drug-taking amongst the young been normalized? Does taking drugs lead to participation in crime? Do recent concerns about 'binge drinking' reflect a real change in young people's behaviour or are they yet a further example of criminalization?

The social construction of drug use

It is important to examine briefly how drug use has been socially constructed and subject to prohibitions. Technically a drug is any substance which modifies the functions of an organism (Whittaker 1987) and many are used to relieve or cure illness while others are consumed on an everyday basis – many readers will 'need' a dose of caffeine before starting the day! Drugs have different effects – in general, alcohol, barbiturates, tranquillizers and heroin are depressants, caffeine, amphetamines, cocaine and tobacco are stimulants, whereas others such as cannabis, LSD and MDMA distort perceptions (South 2007a). The line between normal and deviant drug use is very narrow and culturally specific. While the use of heroin or morphine for *medical* purposes is approved, its use for *pleasure* is not, and it is often *young* people's *recreational* use of drugs which attracts concern compared with widespread acceptance of going to the pub or drinking at home for people of all ages or classes. Deviant drug use is popularly associated with addiction, although most people who drink do not become alcoholics and heroin can be combined with a so-called 'normal' lifestyle (South 2007a). Many famous artists, poets and politicians such as Charles Dickens, Byron and Disraeli were all reported to have been regular opium users (Whittaker 1987) and cultural expectations and norms surround their use.

Drugs are controlled in different ways. Some are prescribed and others, such as alcohol or cigarettes, are licensed. Controls address perceived problems – restrictions on alcohol, for example, aimed to stop factory workers drinking when they should be at work (Ruggiero and South 1995; South 2007a). From the 1960s further phases of criminalization were directed at young people's drug-taking. Currently, illegal drugs are graded in relation to their assumed effects and the severity of sentences (South 2007a). Class A drugs include heroin, cocaine, LSD and MDMA, popularly known as Ecstasy; Class B covers amphetamines and barbiturates; and Class C, tranquillizers and some mild stimulants (South 2007a).

Young people's consumption of drugs

The increase in recreational drug use in the 1960s was followed by the so-called 'heroin epidemic' of the 1970s and 1980s, linked to the increasing availability of cheaper forms from Iran, Pakistan and Afghanistan. The 1990s saw the emergence of a 'poly drug' culture involving LSD, amphetamine, Ecstasy and Ketamine used in a 'pick and mix' culture (South 2007a). The rave and dance culture brought a wider range of young people into contact with drugs and the early twentieth century has seen changing patterns of alcohol consumption related to so-called 'binge drinking' (Measham and Brain 2005; Hayward and Hobbs 2007).

Young people's consumption of drugs is now so widespread that some have argued that it has become 'normalized'. In the 1990s, research among 14–15 year

Box 8.6 Young people and drugs

- While many young people experiment with drugs, these are often 'softer' drugs and most do not become regular users.
- A much smaller minority move on to 'harder' drugs and an even smaller minority become addicted (South 2007a).
- Drug consumption tends to peak around 20–24.
- Patterns vary across the UK, with higher rates being noted in England and Scotland in comparison to Northern Ireland and Wales (Newcombe 2007).
- Some towns and cities, such as the 'old' heroin cities from the 1980s – Manchester, Liverpool and Carlisle – came to act as 'depots' supplying smaller satellite towns during the expansion of the 1990s (Seddon 2006).

olds in the metropolitan North-West of England argued that the prevalence of drug use had risen so substantially, involved such a wide range of drugs and involved so many young people across class boundaries that recreational drug use had become 'normal' (Measham et al 1994). Critics argued that this was an exaggeration and did not acknowledge the differences between occasional and persistent use (South 2007a), although it did draw attention to the broad acceptance of drug use among a wider range of young people. While estimates vary and it is important not to confuse lifetime prevalence with incidence figures over a period of time, the former being higher, a few broad generalizations can be made about young people's consumption of drugs outlined in Box 8.6.

It has also been suggested that girls and women are 'catching up' with young men, particularly in relation to cannabis, ecstasy, participation in the dance drug culture and in more regular sessions of alcohol consumption (Measham et al 1994; Measham and Brain 2005). In the 1980s drug use was primarily associated with white youth, although it is now associated with Caribbean communities and although young Asians are noted for lower rates of drug use (South 2007a), some suggest that they too are 'catching up' (Seddon 2006). While young people from all social classes experiment with drugs and become addicts, heroin addiction and drug trafficking have been associated with areas of highest deprivation (Seddon 2006; South 2007a). This may be related to the need for poorer addicts to commit crime to support a habit and participation in the drugs economy can provide alternative employment for people in deprived areas (Pearson 1987b and see Chapter 14). On the other hand, the current 'binge drinking' phenomenon cuts across traditional class associations as its participants can afford sessional weekend drinking (Hayward and Hobbs 2007).

Drugs and crime

It is often assumed that drug-taking leads to crime. This relationship can take several forms. Selling, producing or using some drugs is in itself criminal as is consuming alcohol under the age of 18. Alternatively, drug consumption can directly lead to crime – either through the pharmacological effects of a drug on, for example, violent crime, or by necessitating property crime to support a drug habit. Alternatively, involvement in crime and criminal subcultures can lead to drug use (Burr 1987).

The evidence to support these relationships is mixed. The very transitory nature of many young people's drug use led one Home Office review to conclude that 'most recreational drug use lacks obvious links with crime' (Hough 1996: 4). On the other hand, the minority who are involved in *both* drugs and crime do turn to crime to support a heroin or crack/cocaine habit. McSweeney et al (2006: 107) conclude that 'a small proportion of problem users – unlikely to exceed 100,000 in number – finance their use through crime'. This group, they suggest, spend around £400 per week on drugs, funded through shoplifting, burglary and selling drugs. The majority, however, were involved with crime *before* drugs thus lending support to the argument that crime can precede drug use. Clearly more than a simple cause and effect relationship is involved (South 2007a). Drinking, crime and drug-taking may all be part of offenders' lifestyles (Parker 1996).

The effects of alcohol on crime are also contested. Official figures suggest that alcohol-related crime costs around £7.3 billion per annum (South 2007a) and alcohol is the main drug present in many violent crimes. While this will be discussed more fully in Chapter 11, in general there is little evidence to support a pharmacological link operating independently of cultural and other factors. As will be seen in Chapter 10, while racial attacks are often accompanied by heavy drinking, alcohol does not lead to racism and alcohol use *and* aggressiveness feature in male, lower-class subcultures. Moreover, while many offenders have consumed alcohol at the time of an offence, it cannot be said to lead to crime in general – there are few suggested links, for example, between alcohol and fraud or white-collar crime and not all who drink turn to crime (South 2007a).

Booze, binge drinking and the night-time economy

Alcohol use and anti-social behaviour are linked in images of disorderly and drunken young men and women in town centres at the weekend and the punitive reaction to this phenomenon could well be interpreted as the demonization of young people's leisure (Measham and Moore 2008). Analyses suggest a more complex situation, and it is important to place the phenomenon of binge drinking in its wider socio-economic context.

Measham and Brain (2005) provide an interesting analysis of so-called 'binge and brawl' behaviour arguing that there have been real changes in patterns of drinking brought about by a number of factors including:

- The rise of a '*culture of intoxication*' manifested in increasing sessional consumption of alcohol. This is related to the normalization of soft drugs from the 1990s and the emergence of a culture of hedonistic consumption in which deliberate intoxification became part of weekend leisure.
- The *recommodification of alcohol* in which the drinks industry produced and marketed a range of products such as alcopops and stronger alcoholic drinks in an attempt to compete with drugs. This was accompanied by an overhaul of traditional drinking establishments, including the rise of café and dance bars, to attract a younger age range – a move from 'spit and sawdust' to 'chrome and cocktails'.

Source: Reuters/Yiorgos Harahalis

- Young people engaged in '*determined drunkenness*', encouraged by the widespread marketing of 'shots'.
- This is related to the *transition to a consumer society* in which consumption becomes a major source of identity and which exploits hedonism.

'Binge drinking' is, therefore, more than a moral panic and reflects a real change which Measham and Brain relate to contradictory government policies. At the same time as condemning anti-social behaviour, the government, in 2003, liberalized restrictions on alcohol consumption – justified by appeals to a 'continental café style culture'. This was consistent with the interests of alcohol manufacturers although at the same time the marketing of alcopops and the use of 'happy hours' were criticized. This also took place within the context of urban regeneration and the contribution made by the night-time economy which filled the void left by de-industrialization (Hayward and Hobbs 2007). This produced, argue Measham and Brain, a combination of seduction and repression – a 'carnival of consumption' was encouraged alongside increasingly repressive controls on 'deviant' drinkers and those who could not afford to participate, such as the homeless or street beggars.

Gangland Britain?

Despite apparently falling rates of both youth and violent crime, from the mid 2000s onwards, considerable attention by governments, academics and the police has surrounded an apparent rise in violent gangs, often linked to weapons, in English cities

Box 8.7 'Gangland Britain'?

The rise in gangs?

- In 2007, the Metropolitan Police identified 172 youth gangs in London, many armed, estimated to be responsible for 20 per cent of youth crime, and 28 gang-related murders (cited in Pitts 2008: 4).
- Glasgow's gangs have been subject to recurrent concerns and the Centre for Social Justice (2008) estimated more than 170 gangs in Glasgow, which, were a similar ratio of gangs to population to apply, would produce over 1,000 gangs in London.
- Glasgow's youth gangs have also been subject to publicity. In February 2006, Glasgow's *Evening Times* launched a special investigation into:
  - **'The gangs that shame Glasgow'** *Evening Times*
  - **'No place for gang culture in today's Glasgow '** *Evening Times*
  - A later, 2008 headline: **'Gangs 448 crimes in just 11 months: top cop reveals spree as purge on yobs begin'** (Access via *www.dailyrecord.co.uk*, *Daily Record* 29 February 2008)

Hallsworth and Young (2008) argue that these kinds of representations overstate the position citing the following cases:

- The murder of 7-year-old Toni-Ann Byfield and her father in 2003 was reported as gang related because Mr Byfield was a known drug dealer suspected by the police to be 'closely affiliated' to a ruthless cartel of Jamaican crack dealers. It transpired from evidence in court that the Byfields were shot dead by a lone gunman who made his living robbing drug dealers.
- 10-year-old Damilola Taylor bled to death on a stairwell on a housing estate in Peckham in 2006. His murder was reported as gang related and the two brothers subsequently convicted were said to be members of two gangs – the Young Peckham Boys and the Out to Bomb Crew. Yet little reliable evidence linked them to either group, nor was it clear how they might be related to Damilola's murder. What is known about the two boys is that they lived very chaotic and disturbed lives.

such as Birmingham, Manchester and London (Hallsworth and Young 2008; Pitts 2008), and the continued activities of Scottish gangs, notably in Glasgow but also Edinburgh and Dundee (Mooney et al 2010). Box 8.7 illustrates some of the more dramatic representations of this phenomenon, along with some cases which appear to question them. A major question is whether this 'gang talk' (Hallsworth and Young 2008) is yet another moral panic about youth crime or whether, as Pitts (2008) suggests, there has been a real change.

As outlined in Chapter 3 and above, while American subcultural theory was very much based on the existence of the 'delinquent' gang, these were extremely rare in Britain (Downes 1966), and English work on youth crime has tended to focus on youth subcultures and on moral panics. Glasgow has stood out from other cities with a longer established gang culture (Patrick 1973; Davies 2007b; Mooney et al 2010). There has therefore been relatively little research on which to base any estimates of changes.

A major difficulty underlying any such attempt is that there is no clear definition of a 'gang' and the word is used in many different ways. Some people would talk generally of going out with the 'gang', meaning a closely knit group of friends. Nor need a gang be associated with crime. Attempts at definitions (Pitts 2008) often involve elements of criminality, durability, territoriality and conflict, often the basis for gang 'wars', and some kind of organized structure. Many now recognize that the term is used for very different kinds of groups, and Pitts (2008: 18) cites Hallsworth and Young's (2008) typology which can be taken to represent a continuum, consisting of:

- *The peer group*: a small, unorganized, transient grouping occupying the same space with a common history. Crime is not integral to their self-definition.
- *The gang*: a relatively durable, predominantly street-based group of young people who see themselves (and are seen by others) as a discernible group for whom crime and violence is integral to the group's identity.
- *The organized criminal group*: members are professionally involved in crime for personal gain, operating almost exclusively in the 'grey' or illegal marketplace.

Hallsworth and Young (2008) criticize exaggerated accounts of a rise in gang violence. Firstly, they query the empirical evidence. Much violent crime, they argue, is committed by individuals and pairs, not groups, and recorded decreases in violent crime question an increase in gang violence. While not disputing the existence of gang-related violence they argue that some cases attract publicity but are, in fact, relatively rare. Furthermore, other accounts of young people's violence, such as those dealing with the night-time economy, do not refer to gangs. They also argue that, as Box 8.7 indicates, the media and official agencies overstate the problem and the word gang has been used pejoratively with, in England, racist overtones by stressing the involvement of black youth. Other depictions, such as those of the conservative Centre for Social Justice (2008) have used gangs as a means of highlighting 'Broken Britain' (Mooney 2009; Law et al 2010; and see Chapter 7).

On the other hand, Pitts (2008) argues that there has been a change, associating gangs which he studied in three London boroughs with increasing concentrations of family poverty, structural youth unemployment and growing numbers of 'young, black and estranged' youth. The rise of the drugs market is also, he argues, crucial as street crime and drug dealing is a core activity. Hallsworth and Young (2008) would not dispute this; however, they argue, the focus on gangs serves to distort understanding and divert attention away from these underlying factors.

As with anti-social behaviour and binge drinking, gang violence would seem to be more than 'just' a moral panic, although it has arguably been 'talked up'. What is needed, argue Hallsworth and Young (2008), as with so many areas of youth crime, is more qualitative research aiming to understand participants' perspectives and placing the phenomenon in a broader context of local, national and global cultures. Much gang research has been more concerned to map and measure the extent of gang activity. It is also important to recognize important variations across the UK – while some of the gangs Pitts (2008) studied had Afro-Caribbean members and were visibly influenced by that culture, Glasgow gangs are more locally based and their culture transmitted through generations. As respondents in a study in Glasgow's East End indicate (Frondigoun et al 2008) '*grandparents, parents, brothers have all been in the gang*' and so '*they pass on a lot of stuff*'. There were even reports of parents encouraging their children when a gang fight broke out.

Discussion

A major theme emerging from the study of age and crime is that young people's involvement in crime is very often exaggerated and their behaviour is often subject to demonization and criminalization. Nonetheless they are involved in crime and it has been argued that there have been changes and these require some explanation. At the same time, however, children and young people's victimization is often overlooked and some have called for a youth victimology. This chapter has also, reflecting criminology itself, arguably focused overmuch on the young, and many are extremely critical of the neglect of older people as offenders and victims. This section will explore these issues before exploring the significance of age in relation to other inequalities.

Young people and crime: individuals, families, culture and structure

As the majority of criminological approaches have equated crime with young people, the analyses of youth crime outlined above echo the approaches outlined in previous chapters. Contemporary approaches continue to reflect the tension between the role of individuals and families and the role of structural and cultural factors. The search for 'risk factors' to provide an 'evidence base' for policy and the rhetoric surrounding anti-social behaviour follow the long traditions of positivist, administrative and also conservative criminologies. Their appeal lies in placing responsibility for youth crime on offenders and their families who can be subject to intervention. Yet the problems of these approaches have also been seen. Identification of factors such as 'being male', 'poor parental supervision' and having criminal friends says very little about the social or cultural context within which these are constructed as problems. Like the 'poor blaming' theories explored in Chapter 7, they implicitly blame lower-class youth, parents and communities.

Other analyses, particularly those of anti-social behaviour, binge drinking and gangs, point to the continuing and real effects of social and economic change drawing on, for example, the impact of structural youth unemployment, social exclusion, the withdrawal of benefits to young people and the impact of housing policy which has had profound effects on some areas. Efforts at regeneration have also led to changes in the traditional leisure pursuits of different social classes. The move to a consumer-based society has potentially exacerbated the relative deprivation experienced by the young, who form a major market for a wide range of cultural products such as music, technology, fashion or cars. This means that they are strongly affected by the cultural inclusion coupled with structural exclusion outlined by Young (2003; 2007a; and see Chapters 5 and 7).

Yet as was also seen in Chapter 7, crime is not only an economic response, although for some young people it may be necessary for survival. It also must be seen in a cultural context although the diversity of contemporary youth cultures challenges traditional subcultural theory. Contemporary youth engage in an extremely wide range of subcultures such as poly drug and dance cultures such as 'gangsta rap', Bhangra, and rave which cut across traditional lines of class, ethnicity or gender. Not all can be characterized as 'resistance', with consumerism leading to a 'form of incorporation into the logical requirements of consumer capitalism' (Winlow and Hall 2006, cited in Muncie 2009: 213). It has become increasingly difficult to differentiate elements of 'authenticity' in subcultures from commercialization. Yet, as cultural criminologists argue, culture, albeit in more fluid forms, remains enormously significant for understanding young people's activities. New cultures of intoxication and elements of gang culture stress the excitement, the edge work and the attractiveness of crime which is an escape from boredom.

Young people's expressive leisure, from simply hanging about street corners to brawling outside bars nonetheless attracts harsh responses and young people's vulnerability to demonization, outlined in previous chapters, has been confirmed in this one. This may be related to the almost universal tendency of the young to challenge convention and to prompt nostalgia on the part of older generations who feel threatened by the change as Pearson (1994a) suggests and it can also reflect the vindictiveness which Young (2007a) links to the insecurity of the included.

Towards a youth victimology?

It was argued earlier in this chapter that the victimization of children and young people is often overlooked and there have been arguments for the development of a youth victimology (Muncie 2003; Francis 2007b; Muncie 2009), which would, argues Muncie (2009: 164) reverse the 'conventional criminological logic' by revealing the extent of offences against (rather than committed by) young people, the extent of familial and institutional abuse and violence and 'the range of social harms to which young people are routinely exposed through state negligence or indifference'. Following the social harm approach (Hillyard and Tombs 2004) discussed in Chapter 5, it would encompass a range of global and local harms not currently seen as criminal, such as the continuance of child poverty in rich nations and the indiscriminate targeting of groups of children through curfews and dispersal zones which itself amounts to victimization. Box 8.8 illustrates some examples of victimization which would be included. Such an approach would, argues Muncie (2009), reveal a hierarchy of victimization whereby some abusive and violent events which involve children are high profile, while others, such as the harms outlined above, receive very little attention.

Ageing and Criminology

Criminology, argue Cain and Wahidin (2006: 1), has undertheorized age, the last bastion in explorations of crime and inequality. Indeed, older people, or the 'un-young', are often accorded deviant, outsider status, being depicted as frail, dependent and not fully contributing to society. The word 'abuse', so often used in conjunction with 'elder', often associates this issue with social welfare rather than crime and can downplay the harm perpetrated against older people (Brogden and Nijhar 2006; Williams 2010). Moreover, the casting of older people as vulnerable has led to their

Box 8.8 Harms against children

A youth victimology would include (Muncie 2009):

- The victimization of young people in custody by techniques such as physical restraint, solitary confinement and strip-searching. Muncie points to the deaths of 29 children in penal institutions in England and Wales between 1990 and 2005 – children most likely to be drawn from the most disadvantaged, damaged and distressed neighbourhoods.
- The global dimensions of children's victimization such as organized sexual exploitation and trafficking; the exploitation of child labour; the impact of war on children; the use of child soldiers and child slavery. Around 218 million children aged between 5 and 17 worldwide are estimated to work as child labourers.
- In the UK Muncie identifies:
  - 5,000 child prostitutes, 75% of which are girls;
  - 5,000 children who, according to a Joseph Rowntree Foundation report, are forced to work as 'sex slaves';
  - the use of the UK as a transit point for the movement of child slaves;
  - reports that 14–17-year-old girls from China and Africa have been forced to work as domestic servants in the UK or in the sex industry.
- The reliance, by global and British-based companies, on young people working in slavery to produce goods.
- The use of child soldiers, some as young as 7 or 8 years old, in armed conflict. While the United Nations Optional Protocol to the Convention of the Rights of the Child prohibits the forced recruitment of children under 18 and their use in hostilities, many countries continue to recruit people as young as 16 and, despite having ratified this protocol the UK reserves the right to deploy under-18s in 'exceptional circumstances' – with one report revealing the 'inadvertent deployment' of under 18s to Iraq between 2003 and 2005.

real fears being dismissed as irrational, as with children. A critical gerontological approach would challenge the infantilism involved in stereotypes of ageing and a tendency to homogenize older people (Wahidin and Powell 2007).

The neglect of age permeates feminist and critical criminologies who have tended to prioritize issues of gender, race and class. Feminism, while exposing the widespread victimization of women and children in the home, has not explored the feminization of later life. Women live longer yet the greater vulnerability of older women, particularly those aged over 75, to domestic and institutional abuse, often perpetrated by male relatives and female carers, has often been neglected (Powell and Wahidin 2006). Older people are also regularly subject to harassment including name-calling and stone-throwing (Pain 2003). To Powell and Wahidin criminological neglect of these issues is in itself a form of ageism.

Older people's victimization, although often overlooked, is interrelated with other inequalities. Archetypical victims of fraud are, for example, 'little old ladies' or Aunt Agathas (Levi and Pithouse 1992; Croall 2001b) which invoke both 'sexist' and 'ageist' stereotypes. These can lead to targeting older women on the grounds of their *assumed* financial incompetence. At the same time, it is important not to homogenize older people – some are *more* knowledgeable and experienced than the young which can protect them from some forms of fraud (Croall 2009a; Titus 2001), and the casting of older people as especially vulnerable masks the increasingly affluent, active and positive lifestyles enjoyed by elders (Pain 2003). Older people, like children, are also adversely affected by a wide range of global and corporate harms, some of which play on ageing. Old people are also consumers and some products claim, often falsely, to mitigate the effects of ageing such as 'anti-wrinkle' creams, drugs to alleviate impotence, and baldness cures (Croall 2009a and see Chapter 15).

Harms against older people, like younger, often lie at the bottom of Muncie's (2009) hierarchy of victimization. Brogden and Nijhar (2006), for example, point to how neglect of the 'early deaths' of older people in institutions receives far less high profile media coverage than would be the case with other avoidable deaths. A political economy of ageing would involve exploring the extent to which this can be related to older people's lack of economic contribution to society and the reliance of younger people on inheriting older people's wealth. Other socio-economic factors are also important. Wahidin and Cain (2006) draw attention to care homes in which staff are often underpaid and undertrained. While not wishing to 'demonize' these staff they point to findings that higher levels of abuse have been related to untrained staff (Gorgen 2006).

While often cast as victims, older people also commit crime and explorations of the impact of ageing on crime is particularly underdeveloped. As argued above, older people are involved in more serious crimes such as frauds, domestic violence, sexual offences and state and corporate crime – yet age is rarely theorized as a factor. Aspects of age as it is socially constructed may be of relevance. The economic pressures placed on those in their middle years who have to pay mortgages and bring up families could be seen as criminogenic and associated with anomic 'strains' in relation, for example, to avoiding taxes or thefts and fraud at work. Some crimes require age and experience for their commission and the widely used concept of the criminal 'career' implies progression from one stage to another. There is, however, far less knowledge about the 'top' of criminal careers than the 'bottom', assumed to involve young people. To what extent, for example, do fraudsters move to more serious frauds (Levi 2008a) or safe breakers to computer crime (Hobbs 1995), and to what extent is this determined by considerations of expediency or age? Alternatively, as Levi (2008b) comments, older people might shy away from the technicalities of some forms of cyber crime. Moreover, while there is a growing volume of work on the problems of older people in prison (Wahidin 2009), very little is known about older people's experiences with the police or the criminal justice process.

The significance of age

Age is clearly related to class and gender as well as to racial inequalities, prompting the question of whether age can be seen as a separate factor. Its importance can be seen in a number of ways referred to above. Albeit subject to criminalization, young people's lifestyles and culture make them more likely to inhabit public spaces and attract critical attention from the police and the older generation who may be fearful and critical. On the other hand, the greater expertise and experience of older people can enhance their criminal opportunities and help avoid detection. Victimization can also be age specific (Pain 2003), and some offences are inherently 'ageist'. Children and young people are particularly powerless to resist both sexual and physical abuse and, in the former, their youth enhances their attractiveness. As was also seen above, older people's assumed infirmity and incompetence can also make them targets. A crucial, but often underexplored, aspect of age relates to power asymmetries – children, for example, are often victimized by parents, and older people by their children. Young and old people are physically vulnerable and, more particularly, their economic dependency and social marginality can make them less able to resist both victimization and, for young people, the demonization of their activities.

Concluding comments

An exploration of the complex relationships between age and crime reveals therefore that despite the almost universal association of youth with crime, people of all age groups commit crime and cause serious harms. Children and the elderly in particular can be victimized on the basis of their age. Different age groups, however, experience different levels of criminalization which is related to wider social constructions of age and its associated lifestyles and responsibilities. The focus on visible street crime along with the tendency of young people to engage in expressive street-based behaviour has for long attracted criticism and challenges from older people, exacerbated by the after-effects of de-industrialization and the increasing focus on anti-social behaviour. Social change is manifest also in the explosion of new cultures such as the culture of intoxication. At the same time, however, it has been argued that to fully explore the relationship between age and crime more attention should be paid to age rather than youth as a factor in both offending and victimization and to the general political economy of ageing. Furthermore, age is closely interrelated with other forms of social inequality which will be the subject of successive chapters.

Review questions

1. Outline and account for the overestimation of young people's crime and the underestimation of older people's crime.
2. What is meant by anti-social behaviour? Look at crime surveys and identify who is most likely to consider it to be a problem and how much it affects them. How would you interpret these findings?
3. Explore how and why young people's activities are 'demonized'. You might wish to consider:

(a) Any recent examples in recent press coverage of crime and criminal justice policy?
(b) Was youth crime an issue in the moral panic you identified in Chapter 2?

Focus on your local area and experiences:

(c) Is youth crime an issue in your local area?
(d) What kinds of youth are associated with 'trouble' or anti-social behaviour?
(e) How are they perceived in school and by local schoolchildren?
(f) Where do they live?
(g) Are the young residents of any particular area near you identified with 'trouble' or anti-social behaviour and/or 'crime'? Are there any obvious gangs?
(h) How are they described?
(i) Do you 'know' if they are really involved in crime?
(j) Are specific places perceived as 'dangerous'?

4 Look at some self-report studies of young people's drug-taking and consider:

(a) How many young people report taking different drugs once in their life?
(b) How many report persistent drug use?
(c) What are the most common drugs?
(d) How does drug consumption vary according to gender, age, class and ethnicity?
(e) Do you think that drug use is 'normal' for young people?
(f) Do you consider these levels of drug use to be a problem?

Key reading

There are now a number of very good texts on youth crime in general and specific aspects of it. Particularly useful are:

Brown, S. (2005) ***Understanding Youth and Crime: Listening to Youth?***, Maidenhead: Open University Press 2nd edn. A critical and engaging analysis of youth crime placing much emphasis on the perspective of young people.

Burney, E. (2009) ***Making People Behave: Anti-social Behaviour, Politics and Policy***, Cullompton: Willan Publishing. An excellent and critical review of the emergence of the 'anti-social behaviour agenda' with useful chapters on how policies against it have been implemented.

Muncie, J. (2009) ***Youth Crime***, London: Sage 3rd edn. A now classic text on the topic covering the history of youth crime and justice, issues of offending and victimization, explanations and subcultures from a critical criminological perspective.

Wahidin, A. and Cain, M. (2006) (eds) ***Age, Crime and Society***, Cullompton: Willan Publishing. An invaluable collection of articles challenging the criminological neglect and providing examples of older people's offending and victimization.

Chapter 9
Gender and crime

This chapter will look at:

- ➜ The gender gap
- ➜ Men, women and offending
- ➜ Men, women and victimization
- ➜ The feminist critique of criminology
- ➜ Feminist perspectives
- ➜ Rational economic women?
- ➜ Men, masculinity and crime
- ➜ Gendered victimization

A noted criminologist once commented that 'if men behaved like women, the courts would be idle and the prisons empty' (Wooton 1959: 32, cited in Walklate 1995: 20), reflecting women's lower conviction rates. While early theoretical approaches took for granted that offenders were male, this 'maleness' was not discussed and girls were absent from studies of delinquent boys. Previous chapters have reiterated, however, that questions must be asked about official statistics. Is there really such a large gender gap? How much of women's crime is relatively invisible? Are men more likely to be seen as the usual suspects and to be criminalized? It was also seen in Chapter 6 that a major thrust behind the so-called rediscovery of the victim was the substantial hidden victimization of women in the private sphere.

Since the emergence of the feminist critique, from the 1960s, the 'problem' of gender and crime has been constructed in different ways. Why, for example, did women commit less crime than men and how could their offending be explained when they did? Did they commit crime for similar, or different, reasons to men? Feminist criminologists challenged the assumptions and perspectives of 'malestream' criminology (Cain 1990) and sought to apply a gendered 'lens' to crime and victimization (Walklate 1995). Later attention turned to why men committed more crime and to their often neglected victimization (see Chapter 6). This chapter will explore many of these issues, starting by critically examining what is known about the gender gap, before looking at how criminology has dealt with the issue of gender and crime, at the feminist critique and the contribution of feminist perspectives. It will then explore some key dimensions of the gendered nature of crime and victimization and at explanations for both women's and men's crime and at their experiences as victims. Finally, it will critically explore some key issues in the study of gender and crime, and will examine the significance of gender for our overall understanding of crime.

The gender gap: male and female involvement in crime

The words sex and gender are used in official publications and academic discussions and need to be briefly explained. The word gender is often preferred to sex, which relates primarily to biological differences. Gender, on the other hand, reflects the social construction of biological differences between the sexes. To sociologists, differences in the social roles, expectations and identities encapsulated in constructions of 'masculinity' and 'femininity' transcend biologically determined characteristics. These are learnt during socialization when cultural norms of what it means, for example, to be a 'man' or a 'woman', 'husband', 'father', 'wife' or 'mother' are transmitted. While often assumed to be 'natural', closer exploration reveals that these roles are socially constructed and constructions of both 'femininity' and 'masculinity', likened by some to 'scripts' for behaviour, vary across cultures and subcultures. Gender roles are also relational in that, for example, the role of 'mother' is related to that of 'father' or 'child'. Gendered relationships also reflect power through the operation of patriarchy, outlined in Box 9.5. Talking about crime and victimization as 'gendered' therefore involves more than detailing the different patterns of offending and victimization of men and women, but points to the assumptions which form the context for, for example, men assuming that women are 'asking for' rape by their behaviour and dress.

Men, women and offending

The consistent and almost universal finding that men are more likely to be convicted of crime, highlighted in Chapter 3 and illustrated in Box 9.1, requires little reiteration. In 2007, in England and Wales, three-quarters of offenders found guilty or cautioned were male (Ministry of Justice 2008), in 2008, in Scotland, 84 per cent were male (Scottish Government 2010) and in Northern Ireland, in 2006, males constituted 87 per cent of those found guilty at all courts (Northern Ireland Office 2010). Often cited is the finding that of the population in England born in 1953, 34 per cent of men, compared to only 9 per cent of women, had been convicted for a serious offence by the age of 46 (Heidensohn and Gelsthorpe 2007). It has therefore been argued that criminal convictions are relatively 'normal' for males but unusual for females (Heidensohn 1996). A further source of information on differing rates of crime and victimization for men and women are the Justice Department annual publications on Women in the Criminal Justice System provided under Section 95 of the Criminal Justice Act – often known as 'Section 95 reports'. Some of the main characteristics of male and female offending, replicated across Britain are detailed in Box 9.1.

This illustrates some of the now well-known differences between male and female offending rates. Women tend to commit less serious crimes and are more likely to be first offenders, reflected in lower rates of custodial sentences. They have a lower 'peak age' of offending than men, and desist from offending at an earlier age. Men, on the other hand, tend to have longer criminal careers and to commit more serious offences. Men and women are convicted for different kinds of offences, although it

Box 9.1 Men, women and offending

Based on various sources including Northern Ireland Office (2010); Ministry of Justice (2009); Scottish Government (2010)

- Women are less likely to be convicted than men across most offence categories.
- Women's criminal careers are shorter and tend to peak in the mid- rather than late-teens.
- Women are less likely than men to be sent to prison for equivalent offences and when they do go to prison, they tend to serve shorter sentences.

Variations in offences

- Men are more likely to be convicted of murder or manslaughter. In England and Wales in 2007, 213 suspects were male and 21 female (Kershaw et al 2008).
- Men predominate as offenders in sexual and violent offences.
- Women's share is greater for property offences.
- Women's share is more than men's only for prostitution-related offences and failing to pay a television licence.
- Women's offending is most often related to shoplifting, public order offences and petty assault.

Self-report studies

According to the OCJS for *England and Wales* (Roe and Ashe 2009):

- Women constitute 40 per cent of those admitting any sort of offending.
- Males were more likely than females to have offended and to have engaged in anti-social behaviour (ASB) in the previous 12 months.
- Males aged between 10 and 25 (12 per cent) were more likely than females (8 per cent) to say they had committed a serious offence and were also more likely to be classed as frequent offenders (8 compared with 3 per cent) and as serious and frequent offenders (5 compared with 3 per cent).
- Within the 10–25 age group males were also more likely to have carried a knife, committed a violent offence, handled stolen goods and engaged in anti-social behaviour.

Scotland:

- The 2008/9 SCJS indicates that 74 per cent of offenders, where the offender was identified by victims, were male.
- One Scottish study found that the majority of both boys and girls aged 14 and 15 reported offending, with similarities in rates of, for example, shoplifting and damage to property (Jamieson et al 1999, cited in Burman 2004).

is important to point out that both feature in all offence categories – women are convicted of violent and sexual offences although they have lower rates for murder, serious violence and professional crime. Prostitution is primarily defined as a female offence whereas sexual offences, including sexual assaults, are primarily perpetrated by men (see Chapter 12). When women are convicted it is more likely to be for offences involving theft and handling stolen goods and fraud and forgery (Walklate 1995; Burman 2004). Men also dominate serious crimes which are not included in the statistics such as terrorism, organized crime, corporate and state crime (Silvestri and Crowther-Dowey 2008 and see Chapters 14–17).

Conviction rates do not, as reiterated in previous chapters, provide an accurate indicator. It has been argued, for example, that considerable amounts of female crime are 'masked' (Pollak 1961), or that the police and courts are chivalrous towards women while criminalizing men. The general conclusion has, however, been that hidden female crime is unlikely to exceed hidden male crime, particularly in view of male dominance of domestic violence, white-collar, corporate, state and organized crime. Discussion of these issues can also be assisted by self-report studies, which, despite their limitations, do suggest a narrower gap for some kinds of offences. As seen in Box 9.1, as many as 40 per cent of young women in England and Wales report offending, and one Scottish study reported similar rates of offending for boys and girls. While this does narrow the gap boys continue to report higher rates of more serious and persistent forms of offending.

While these kinds of figures have been remarkably consistent (Heidensohn and Gelsthorpe 2007), the last few decades have seen a gradual narrowing of the gap in relation to some kinds of crime, and recurrent concerns about women's, and particularly young women's, involvement in violence and anti-social behaviour. In general terms the gender gap has decreased from around 7:1 in the 1950s to just over 5.1 in the 1990s (Walklate 2004). Recent S 95 figures (Ministry of Justice 2009) report that in 2007 in England and Wales, men were 11 times more likely than women to go to prison compared with a figure of 21 times more likely in 1994.

The 'new' female offender?

There have been recurrent arguments that women are becoming more involved in crime as a result of their changing status vis-à-vis men. The much criticized 'liberation hypothesis' of the 1970s, outlined in Box 9.2, claimed that a 'new female criminal' was emerging. This notion has re-emerged in the twenty-first century with evidence, in many countries, of a narrower gender gap in self-report studies, the reduction in gender ratios for some kinds of crime, and an increase in the numbers of women sent to prison. There have also been suggestions that women are more heavily involved in violence against their intimate partners than often assumed (Chapter 11). This has been accompanied by the emergence of new female criminal characters such as the 'girl gang', the 'mean girl' and the 'ladette' who are able and willing to participate in a culture of violence and drinking (Silvestri and Crowther-Dowey 2008: 25). According to some press reports, British girls are said to be among the most violent in the world with one report (*Guardian*, 24 January 2006, cited in Silvestri and Crowther-Dowey 2008: 28) claiming that nearly one in three Scottish and English adolescents admitted being involved in fighting. A recent article claims to expose 'the shocking rise of UK's girl gangsters' citing women's involvement in cocaine and armed gangs in the UK as well as the US (Thompson 2010).

There is, however, little hard and fast evidence to support these often dramatized assertions and atypical cases tend to receive more publicity. Research among young girls in Scotland found little evidence of either an increase in violence or gang

Box 9.2 Liberation and the 'new female criminal'?

Adler argued that:

> Women are no longer indentured to the kitchens, baby carriages or bedrooms of America . . . in the same way that women are demanding equal opportunity in fields of legitimate endeavour, a similar number of determined women are forcing their way into the world of major crimes. (Adler 1975, cited in Heidensohn 1996: 155)

There were many criticisms of this link between 'emancipation' and crime (Smart 1979) including:

- There was no evidence that any increase in women's crime was associated with measures of emancipation (Box and Hale 1983).
- Any apparent increase in women's share of property offences was more likely to be due to economic marginality than to 'liberation'.
- Like convicted male offenders, female offenders are overwhelmingly drawn from the lower classes whereas liberation and equality most affected middle-class women.

This could mean that any increase in female participation in crime is due, not to emancipation, but to greater poverty.

membership and that only a very small minority engaged in violent acts. Girls tended to perceive violence not only in physical terms but also in terms of threats, name-calling and taunting (Batchelor et al 2001; Batchelor 2002). While self-report studies do indicate girls' participation in drinking, taking illegal drugs and petty offending, boys are still more likely to be involved in more serious and persistent offending. Heidensohn and Gelsthorpe (2007: 393) conclude that there is 'greater gender parity in some kinds of delinquent behaviour but that the traditional divides persist in others' citing work on the night-time economy in which most of the 'weekend warriors' are young, working-class and male (Hobbs et al 2003). The greater involvement of women in domestic violence is also less certain and it is widely accepted that men's violence against women is more persistent and serious (Silvestri and Crowther-Dowey 2008 and see Chapter 11).

Any increase of women and girls in the criminal justice process could also result from higher levels of punitiveness towards girls' offending (Heidensohn and Gelsthorpe 2007). Worrall (2004), for example, found that many convictions of young girls were for minor acts of violence against care workers and the police. This resistance to discipline would formerly have been treated as a welfare issue but is now being criminalized. Higher rates of arrests of girls in relation to so-called binge drinking and violence may also reflect the greater tendency to police young people intensively and the criminalization of anti-social behaviour seen in Chapter 8 (Heidensohn and Gelsthorpe 2007). A 'backlash' against feminist arguments for equity and 'equivalence' might also have led to higher rates of intervention and incarceration. Snider (2003), for example, argues that the 'mean girl phenomenon' is contributing to new forms of regulation, surveillance and discipline.

Men, women and victimization

Chapters 3 and 6 have already outlined the different experiences of men and women of victimization. Box 9.3 provides an overview of these and Figure 9.1 graphically illustrates the different relationships between victims and offenders. Gendered victimization is most often explored in relation to violent crime, as property crime such

Box 9.3 Male and female victimization

Based on Walker et al (2009), Northern Ireland Office (2010) and MacLeod et al 2009.

- Men aged 16–24 have the highest rates of victimization – in the 2008/9 SCJS, for example, 36 per cent of men reported victimization compared to 29 per cent of females of the same age. Rates are more similar for all other ages.
- Men are much more likely than women to be the victim of violent crime with the BCS, SCJS and NICS all indicating that twice as many men as women experience violence in the previous year.
- Women are more likely to be victims of sexual offences and 'domestic' violence. In Northern Ireland 86 per cent of victims of sexual offences were women, and twice as many women reported domestic violence than men.
- BCS figures for 2007/8 indicate that women were three times more likely to have suffered domestic violence than men (0.6 per cent and 0.2 per cent respectively) and 85 per cent of victims of domestic violence were women.
- In England and Wales men are over three times more likely to be victims of stranger violence than women: 2.1 per cent of men were victims, compared with 0.6 per cent of women, whereas women are much more likely to experience violence from someone they know well.
- In 2007/08 in England and Wales, police recorded 11,648 offences of female rape compared to 1,006 offences of male rape.
- Women comprise the minority of homicide victims. In England and Wales, for 2006/07, around a quarter of victims of the 734 offences recorded as homicides by the police were women.

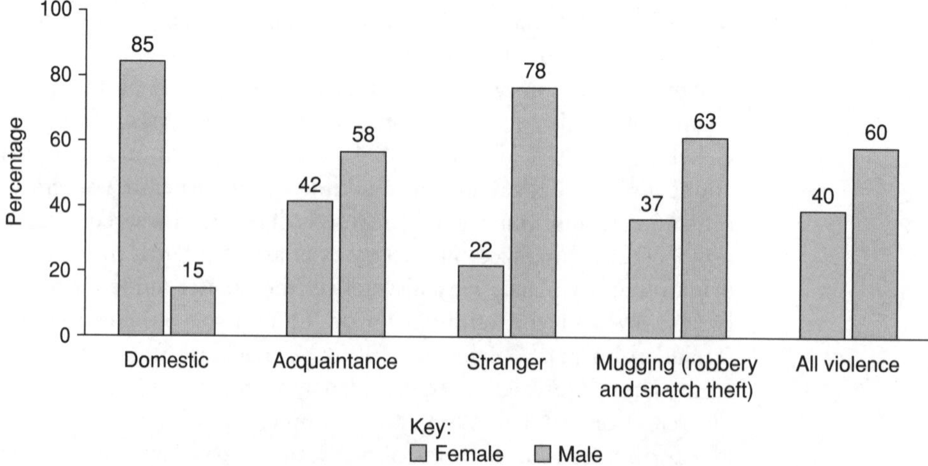

Figure 9.1 Percentage of violent incidents by sex and type of violence, 2007/8 BCS

as housebreaking victimizes 'households'. Lifestyle factors also play a role accounting, for example, for the higher victimization of men in public spaces, by people they do not know, and women's greater victimization in the home. Box 9.3 also illustrates the much higher victimization of women by sexual assaults (see Chapter 13), and Figure 9.1 illustrates the tendency for women to be victimized by someone they know (see Chapter 11).

Some crimes specifically target women, and can be described as gendered. Sexual offences, ranging from harassment and unwanted attentions to assault are obvious examples but, as will be seen below, they can also involve state and corporate crime. Men's victimization can also be gendered – they too can be victims of sexual assaults.

Constructing 'gender and crime'

From the 1960s onwards criminology was accused by feminists of being 'gender blind' by taking for granted that offenders were male and that women rarely committed crime. Some theories had argued that crime was 'unfeminine' and that women were 'naturally' less criminal than men. When they did commit crime, it was seen as 'unnatural' and very often medicalized or pathologized. Violence in the home was regarded as a social welfare rather than a crime issue, often dismissed by the police as 'domestics'. The early focus was very much on *women*, with 'the problem' to be explained being their lower crime rate and hidden victimization. Later approaches moved towards a more fully gendered analysis taking account not only of women's offending but also of the *gendered* nature of men's. 'Crime', tacitly accepted as 'male crime', had been related to subcultures, age, class, social deprivation and race – but not to gender. 'The problem' therefore became how to account for the maleness of crime whether offenders were working class, black, young or indeed 'sex beasts' (Wykes and Welsh 2009). This focus on men also raised issues about victimization.

The feminist critique

The feminist critique of criminology emerged from the second wave feminism of the latter part of the twentieth century. Particularly important were Heidensohn's (1968) initial 'critique and inquiry' of the deviance of women and Carol Smart's (1976) *Women, Crime and Criminology*. This signalled what can be described (Gelsthorpe 2002) as the 'pioneering' phase of feminist criminology, which challenged elements of biological determinism and the gendered stereotypes and assumptions which characterized early criminology, along with what can be described as an amnesia in relation to female offenders.

The weaker sex: biological and psychological approaches

Feminists were particularly critical of the kind of pathological approaches outlined in Chapter 4. Women were assumed to be 'naturally' less criminal than men, an assumption linked to biological differences and hormones, and their reproductive functions were related to weakness and lack of aggression. These factors were also brought into play in explaining female crime which indicated some abnormality and indeed delinquent girls could be seen as more 'masculine'. Female offenders were 'medicalized' by linking offending to mental illness and 'women's problems' such as pre-menstrual tension and the menopause. This was reflected in the greater numbers of women referred for medical and psychiatric reports in court (Edwards 1981).

The arguments against biological and other pathological theories rehearsed in earlier chapters are relevant (see Box 9.4). A more sociological perspective questions the reduction of gender differences to biological factors, and women cannot be said to be innately less disposed to crime as many women do commit crime. Nor can men be assumed to be 'naturally' criminal as the majority of men do not commit crime. Moreover, as will be seen below, women's involvement in crime cannot be attributed to pathological factors. Despite these criticisms these kinds of explanations have had a lasting impact on popular representations of female criminals which, as seen in Chapter 2, depict 'deviant' women as 'unwomanly' and 'sexless creatures' (Wykes and Welsh 2009).

Box 9.4 Pathological constructions of the female offender

- Wykes and Welsh (2009: 58):

  > there is in positivist criminology a double bind for women, who at their most female are characterized by their biology as frail, dependent, emotional and illogical and therefore vulnerable to corruption or loss of control and in need of protection; whilst those appearing as neither frail nor emotional are necessarily therefore not natural women but rather masculinised. Either way women are biologically blamed.

- Lombroso and Ferrero saw women as being less evolved than men and closer to primitive types and argued that natural selection had bred out their criminal tendencies. The female criminal was therefore more abnormal, and more 'evil'.

  'Women are big children . . . their moral sense is deficient', and the female criminal was masculine and virile, showing 'an inversion of all the qualities which specially distinguish the normal woman; namely reserve, docility and sexual apathy' (Lombroso and Ferrero 1895: 153, cited in Heidensohn 1996: 114).

- W. I. Thomas saw delinquency among 'unadjusted' girls as a sign of sexual delinquency. They were unadjusted to social change and, for the deprived, crime was related to a desire for 'costly and luxurious articles of women's wear' which disorganized the lives of many 'who crave these pretty things' (Thomas 1923: 71, cited in Heidensohn 1996: 117).
- Cowie and colleagues argued that women's chromosome pattern was different to men's and related female delinquency to biological and masculine traits. Delinquent girls were described as 'oversized, lumpish, uncouth and graceless' (Cowie et al 1968: 167, cited in Heidensohn 1996: 123).

The invisible sex

Other approaches looked at the different social roles of men and women with sex role theory suggesting that crime is more consistent with male roles. Boys are brought up to be tough, to look after themselves, to be protective of women and to be 'breadwinners' and a certain amount of violence is tolerated and indeed encouraged. Girls, on the other hand, are socialized into the more caring roles of wives and mothers, and fighting and non-conformity are viewed as unfeminine. Sex role theory, however, based on functionalist approaches, rarely questioned the 'naturalness' of these role distinctions or the gender relationships which they reflected. They too, therefore, saw criminal women as 'abnormal' (Heidensohn 1996).

To other sociological approaches, including most of those outlined in Chapter 4, issues of class, social deprivation and age were more significant than gender. Delinquent 'boys' were discussed in a gender-neutral way and women, whether as offenders, victims or conformists, were largely invisible. The anomie paradigm discussed goals as if they were universal. Acknowledging that men and women might have different goals would have raised different kinds of questions. If, for example, women's goals were different and centred round the home and family rather than material success, could this explain their lesser criminality? Alternatively, it could be asked whether failure on the part of women to achieve their goals could be related to women's deviance.

Subcultural theory similarly neglected gender and, as outlined in Chapter 4, major questions surrounded girls' invisibility. Were the strains of adolescence different for girls, suggesting a different 'solution'? McRobbie and Garber (1976), for example, argued that girls' culture was centred around the private space of the 'bedroom', and that girls experienced a strain between preparing for their future role by being available to boys without at the same time being seen as 'sluts'. Teenybopper and fan culture could resolve this problem by idolizing the male 'star' with little risk to a girl's reputation. Yet girls were and are involved in delinquency and do get involved in gangs, although this could be 'sexualized'. One study, for example, found that girls were assumed to be involved in gangs through sexual involvement with boys in the gang. Interventions were justified on the grounds of moral danger, rather than crime (Shacklady-Smith 1978).

New, radical and critical criminology fared little better, with feminists pointing out that Taylor, Walton and Young's *The New Criminology* made no reference to gender (Heidensohn 1996). While labelling theory looked at how stereotypes affected the production of deviants, gender did not feature significantly. Critical and radical approaches, with their focus on class, control, criminalization and the crimes of the powerful were also criticized as gender blind. While power featured in work on criminal law, the relationship between gender and power involved in, for example, laws on rape, prostitution, family and sexual violence were not systematically explored, although these have now, as a result of feminist work, been incorporated into many critical approaches.

Control theories did have the potential to explore gender, as girls and women are subject to greater control. Girls are more likely to be 'chaperoned' by parents and discouraged from hanging about on the streets. As adults, family roles and expectations centre around childcare and the home. Indeed, the family itself can become a means of controlling women. While this appears a convincing argument, it is difficult to substantiate empirically and it also rather unquestioningly accepts stereotypical notions about gender (Heidensohn 1996) and confirms the passive stereotype of women. Women and girls may resist gendered stereotypes and resent the different treatment they receive.

Feminist perspectives

The feminist critique was related to similar challenges across a range of disciplines which also rendered women invisible and used biological arguments and stereotypical assumptions to analyse gender differences. Feminists challenged what they saw as the subordination of women throughout society, seen most clearly in education, employment and the family. While it lies beyond the scope of this book to discuss these developments fully, some of the central ideas of feminism will be outlined to illustrate the broader context within which feminist approaches to crime developed. Box 9.5 outlines one of the central notions of feminism, that of patriarchy.

Box 9.5 Patriarchy

Patriarchy can broadly be defined as 'a system of social structures and practices in which men dominate, oppress and exploit women' (Walby 1989: 214). It is made up of six structures which involve social relationships and practices (Walby 1989; 1990).

- A patriarchal *mode of production* in which women's labour is expropriated by husbands within marriage and the household. While many individual women choose to be 'housewives', the domestic division of labour disadvantages women as a whole.
- Patriarchal relations in *work* where women are excluded from paid work or segregated within the labour market.
- A patriarchal *state* which excludes women who have less representation in government or branches of the executive such as the judiciary, police and legal system. While there have been struggles over women's right to vote and for equal rights at work, other laws affecting gender relationships are determined by men – for example, divorce, prostitution, marriage, sexuality, pornography and fertility.
- The maintenance of patriarchy through *male violence* over women. Women are subject to the threat of violence at home, in public, or at work, from sexual harassment, flashing, sexual assault and abuse.
- Patriarchal relations are also seen in the *regulation of sexuality*. Laws promote the norm of the nuclear family and heterosexual relations by criminalizing homosexuality and prostitution.
- Patriarchal *culture* is reflected in institutionally rooted notions of masculinity and femininity and disseminated through institutions of cultural production such as the media and education.

Contrasting feminist approaches

Feminism encompasses many different strands, derived from contrasting theoretical traditions which approach the question of crime and criminology in different ways. Discussions of feminist criminology (Gelsthorpe 2002; Walklate 2004; Heidensohn and Gelsthorpe 2007) often refer to broad distinctions between liberal, standpoint, radical, socialist, and postmodern feminism, which ask different questions about crime and criminal justice.

- *Liberal feminism* has largely been associated with the assumption that women are treated differently to men in a largely male-dominated criminal justice system. It seeks to expose inequalities of opportunity and discrimination with the aim of securing equal opportunities. The kinds of research carried out reflect this focus and it is linked to what some describe as feminist empiricism by arguing for more research on women's issues involving more female researchers and participants (Walklate 2004). It has also been associated with research on women offenders thus 'adding women in' to criminological inquiry (Gelsthorpe 2002). Walklate (2004) argues that there is much to be gained by such an approach but that it does not seek to alter or challenge what other perspectives perceive as the fundamentally masculinist nature of criminal justice whose institutions are patriarchal and assume the male criminal. They accept men as the norm and believe that 'equality' can be achieved.
- *Feminist standpointism* refers to both radical and socialist feminism, and stresses the importance of understanding the world through women's eyes. Most 'knowledge', they argue, is male knowledge and should be challenged. It involves developing knowledge which 'allows women to speak for themselves, rather than knowledge about men's worlds which so often presumes to be about women's worlds too' (Heidensohn and Gelsthorpe 2007: 385). Standpointism has been associated with a call for researchers to carry out research done 'by women, with women and for women' (Walklate 2004: 45). It has been criticized for prioritizing women's knowledge and a consequent neglect of men.
- *Radical feminism* stresses the role of the patriarchal state and sees patriarchal domination as the most significant element of power. To radical feminists, sexual violence and the threat of it is a major part of men's control over women. Radical feminists played a major role in the women's movement and an active role in drawing attention to women's physical and sexual victimization, campaigning for policies such as shelters for female survivors. They are often associated with the general argument that 'all men are potential rapists'. While seeing women's interests as paramount, in casting men as the source of women's victimization, they, along with other versions of 'standpointism', can be seen as 'essentialist' and as neglecting other forms of inequality, such as economic or racial inequalities as they affect women.
- *Socialist feminism*, as its title implies, is linked to socialist and Marxist ideas and it relates gender inequalities to those of class. It emerged as a reaction to what was seen as the neglect, by Marxists, of the way in which women are oppressed by both men and capitalism (Walklate 2004).
- *Postmodern feminism* argues against essentialism and stresses the role of difference (Walklate 2004). It sees women as being 'othered' and cast as inferior, with

positive features of difference being 'excluded or marginalized by phallocentric thinking' (Walklate 2004: 46). It seeks to deconstruct ideas and language and problematizes the category of 'woman' which denies differences along lines of sexuality or race. It completely rejects the scientific basis of the 'modernist' Lombrosian project which characterizes criminology and argues that it is futile to attempt to challenge this and that feminists should abandon criminology (Smart 1990).

Feminism and crime

As with feminism, no single approach can be described as 'feminist criminology', and there have been many debates amongst writers associated with it (Gelsthorpe and Morris 1988; 1990; Heidensohn 1995; Walklate 1995). Despite this, a number of core elements of feminist thinking were identified which are broadly summarized below (Gelsthorpe and Morris 1988; Heidensohn 1995; Valier 2002).

- To feminists, the question of women is central.
- Feminist approaches are critical of the stereotypical images of women which dominated earlier theories.
- To advance a feminist argument means accepting that women experience subordination on the basis of their sex and working towards the elimination of that subordination.
- Criticizing earlier theories or simply 'adding on' studies of women to studies of men is not sufficient. Gender must become a central feature of analysis. This can only be achieved by rethinking the sociology of crime and criminology and 'engendering' it and exploring it with a gendered 'lens' (Rafter and Heidensohn 1995; Walklate 1995).
- Theories of crime should take account of both men's and women's criminal behaviour and victimization. If, for example, crime is related to unemployment, its different effect on men and women and its relationship to their different patterns of crime should be explored.

Many aspects of feminist approaches will be developed in later chapters on specific patterns of crime, while others, such as their work on the criminal justice process, lie beyond the scope of this text. The following sections will draw on these ideas, exploring how crime has been approached from a more specifically gendered lens, and looking at aspects of women's and men's offending and gendered victimization. An evaluation and critique of the contribution of feminist work will form part of the concluding section.

Dimensions of gender and crime

Rational economic women?

The primacy accorded to pathological and medicalized versions of female criminality meant that questions about whether women's as well as men's crime could be related to economic factors were not asked, and the economic models of crime outlined in Chapter 7 have been criticized for neglecting women and for perpetuating gendered assumptions of men as breadwinners. It can be argued, however, that economic factors do play a major part in women's crime.

The social and economic changes outlined in Chapters 5 and 7 have severely affected women. The growth of young male unemployment reduced young men's ability to provide for a family, there was a growth in female-headed single-parent families which led, during the 1980s, to the feminization of poverty (Carlen 1988; Grover 2008). As many as 50 per cent of one-parent households lived in poverty, with twice as many households headed by women falling below the poverty line than those headed by men (Pantazis and Gordon 1997). Grover (2008) argues that women continue to earn less than men, are more likely to work part-time and, despite successive equal opportunities policies, remain in jobs coded as 'feminine' such as health and social work, education and childcare. Moreover, women are concentrated in the lowest paid work in these sectors. They are also more likely than men to live in workless and single-parent households with, in 2001/2, as many as 53 per cent of lone-mother households being counted as living in poverty. Employment and social policies continue to be affected by assumptions that the male is the primary 'breadwinner' and that women's, or 'mother's' role is to be at home.

Women's involvement in crimes such as benefit fraud or shoplifting have often been associated with hardship and a need to put food on the table (Walklate 1995), as the burden of childcare so often falls on women. Studies of women in prison have found that many offences are motivated by need rather than greed, to supplement meagre state benefits, and to provide children with clothes, toys or food and trying to get more from the 'social'. Not paying television licences or heating bills may in effect become crimes of necessity for poor women (Carlen 1988). The impact of poverty on women is also reflected in the numbers of women imprisoned for failing to pay their television licences and the subsequent fine which has a lower priority than paying for basic necessities such as food, rent and heating (Pantazis and Gordon 1997). Working in the sex industry has also been associated with largely economic factors (McLeod 1982; McKeganey and Barnard 1996; Phoenix 2007; and see Chapter 12). Phoenix (2007: 25) outlines how it can be a 'strategy for survival':

> Entrance to prostitution is shaped by everyday political and economic structures that . . . maintain women's economic dependency on men and on families; shape their poverty relative to men; limit their access to full-time, secure employment; place on women the burden of childcare and domestic responsibilities; ensure that welfare security is mediated through and by women's relationships in families and with men; and maintain welfare benefits at near destitution levels.
>
> (Phoenix 2007: 25)

Linking crime to poverty among women can nonetheless reinforce notions of women as victims by depicting them as trapped in their dependency to men, as 'gendered economic victims' rather than as perpetrators of economic or of violent interpersonal crimes (Davies 2007a: 177) and it is important to recognize other features of their involvement in crime. The women in Carlen's (1988) study also revealed a search for excitement. It could be a response to the boredom of being unable to afford to engage in the consumerism highlighted by cultural criminologists and could also represent a form of resistance to dependency on, for example, 'crap jobs' and financial dependence on men. It can therefore represent a reaction to what Carlen describes as the 'class' and 'gender' deals implied by societal norms. In a study of shoplifters, Davies (2005) also found a more complex set of motivations with some women 'stealing' to order: while their motivations were economic, they also obtained excitement and fulfilment from what to them was a means of obtaining an income (Davies 2005).

The tendency to cast women offenders as victims and thereby deny their agency, extends across areas of offending, and forms a major issue in discussing whether sex workers and the victims of human trafficking should be regarded as victims or as women who, in many cases, have chosen a particular path in preference to other means of obtaining money and pursuing a better life (see Chapters 12 and 14). The small amount of research on female white-collar offenders, often from lower levels of the occupational hierarchy, has also led to them being cast as committing crimes largely from 'need' rather than 'greed' (Daly 1989; Croall 2003) but they too can be seen as 'greedy'. While very few studies of professional and organized crime have included women, there are female traffickers and drug dealers (see Chapter 14). Women can also be involved in torture and, while possibly atypical, the iconic image of the torture in the Abu Ghraib prison in Iraq was of a female soldier. The 'shock factor' in this was also that she appeared to be deriving pleasure from her situation. All of these instances challenge the predominant view of women as victims rather than as victimizers (Davies 2007a) and it is also important to question what rational choice might mean applied to women (Davies 2003; 2005).

Source: Press Association Images (PA Photos)

The images of torture in Abu Ghraib prison in Iraq were regarded as particularly shocking as they involved a female solider Lynndie England.

Box 9.6 Hegemonic masculinity

Connell provides a normative model of masculinity with a set of cultural expectations emphasizing toughness, aggression, power and control (Walklate 1995; 2004). Jefferson (2001, cited in Walklate (2007c: 152) defines it as the

> set of ideas, values, representations and practices associated with being male which is commonly accepted as the dominant position in gender relations in a society at a particular historical moment.

- Moving beyond essentialism, Connell recognizes that gender involves social relationships and *not all men either commit crime or subordinate all women*.
- He identifies *multiple masculinities*, all related to a hegemonic masculinity which, similar to the hegemonic culture outlined by Gramscian Marxists (see Chapter 5), legitimates the social domination of masculinity and serves as a benchmark of 'manhood'.
- This also reflects the *dominance of middle-class, white heterosexual men* and masculinities can be part of coercive apparatuses – seen, for example, in the masculinities displayed by corporate, military and political elites (Silvestri and Crowther-Dowey 2008).

Men, masculinity and crime

While generally neglected, the maleness of crime did feature in some theories. In Miller's (1958) analysis of lower-class subcultures, toughness and holding one's own in a fight emerged as 'focal concerns'. Willis' (1977) research on the 'lads' also stressed sexist elements in their subculture. Analyses of masculinity have expanded considerably in recent decades and of particular importance has been the work of Connell (1987; 1995; Connell and Messerschmidt 2005) and his concept of hegemonic masculinity outlined in Box 9.6.

Along with the work of Messerschmidt (1995; 2005), to whom crime among young men is described as 'doing masculinity', Connell's work can be related to crime. From around the 1990s crime was characterized as symptomatic of a 'crisis' in masculinity resulting from the inability of young men to live up to expectations of providing for a family, and joyriding, theft and burglary have been interpreted as alternative means of expressing masculinity, of taking risks and of providing for families (Campbell 1993). This, however, argues Grover (2008), assumes a single form of masculinity, and relationships with class are problematic. Messerschmidt, following the insights of strain, left realist and structural theories, sees crime as a means of accomplishing masculinity when other resources, such as work, are withdrawn. In later work, answering criticisms about the relationship between masculinity and other factors, Messerschmidt focuses on the relationships between class, ethnicity and masculinity – men, he argues, can 'do' class and ethnicity as well as gender.

Alternative masculinities have been identified and associated with different forms of crime. Being involved in 'business', for example, whether of a legitimate or illegitimate nature, can be seen as a quintessentially masculine concern and organized crime reflects elements of lower-class violent male cultures and subcultures (Hobbs 1995, and see Chapter 14). In the business world, male aggression can be related to white-collar crime – in takeovers the predator company is often depicted as male and the target as female and the language of war and competition are used (Punch 1996). While financial frauds do not involve violence, they may nonetheless reflect the value placed on aggressive and 'risky' business tactics (Levi 1994).

To Jefferson (1997), references to masculinities are overdeterministic and pay insufficient attention to emotions and the psyche. What makes, for example, some, but not all, men turn to crime? For Jefferson, the key issue is 'how in reality men deal with their own life histories and psychic formations with regard to masculinities' (Silvestri and Crowther-Dowey 2008: 65). This draws attention to the subjective way in which individual men negotiate their experiences in relation to dominant ideals of masculinity. Gadd (2002, cited in Silvestri and Crowther-Dowey 2008), for example, points out that violent men, rather than simply 'doing masculinity' experience guilt and shame and distance themselves from 'violent, dangerous men'. Focusing on the psyche has in turn been criticized on the grounds that all offenders have psyches and biographies and that these are not unique to masculinities (Hood-Williams 2001).

The exploration of masculinities can therefore provide interesting insights although it has also attracted considerable criticism, much of it directed at a tendency to essentialism, to generalizing across different areas of 'crime' and to neglecting other factors which may be more important that masculinity (Walklate 2004; Heidensohn and Gelsthorpe 2007; Silvestri and Crowther-Dowey 2008). Critics also point to the tautology of associating crime with masculinity in which 'the maleness of crime becomes the source of its explanation' (Walklate 2004: 80). To Walklate, this reflects a failure to address issues of the multiple relationships between femininity and masculinity and differences between them. Yet others question the way in which a focus on masculinity overemphasizes the negative aspects of masculinity and fails to fully explore the dominance of heterosexual as compared to homosexual masculinities (Collier 1998).

A major question is how significant masculinity is in comparison to other factors. To some writers, following Katz, the 'seductions' of crime such as risk-taking, desire- or pleasure-seeking are seen as quintessentially masculine, whereas to others, masculinity may not be the key element in such motivations – women can, as seen above, be attracted by the thrill or buzz of crime and, as seen in Chapter 8, these attractions are also related to age. To critics such as Hall (2002), masculinity may not be the most useful concept for understanding the nature of male violence, particularly that which is associated with the desperate situation of economically marginal and powerless men. Some of these questions will be addressed in the final section after an exploration of gendered victimization.

Gendered victimization

Gendered victimization occurs when people are victimized on the grounds of their gender. Feminists' focus on sexual and domestic violence outlined previously was crucial in exposing gendered violence but may neglect other aspects of women's victimization. It also neglected men's victimization which, as outlined earlier, is greater than women's. Yet it is only recently that feminists have asked, '*Can men be victims?*' (Walklate 2004; 2007c; Davies 2007a; 2007b). This section will focus on what is known about gendered aspects of victimization as they apply to both men and women, revealing some relatively underexplored areas.

Women as victims

The significance of women's victimization in the home at the hands of men needs little reiteration (and see Chapter 11), and outside the home, women are also subject to what feminists have identified as a continuum of male violence on the basis of gender (Kelly 1988). To feminists this reflects assumptions related to patriarchy, for example that men have a right to touch and fondle women or that women are men's property, and they have been depicted as living in a climate of 'unsafety' (Stanko 1990a; 1994).

This focus has arguably neglected many other forms of gendered victimization of women including, for example:

- Women's experiences of violence in institutions, at work or in other settings. Welfare workers and nurses are three times more likely than average to be victimized (Davies 2007b).
- As workers, women are more likely to suffer miscarriages and respiratory ailments from poor working conditions and to be exploited in sweatshops in the UK and across the globe (Croall 2007b).
- Women are trafficked for the purposes of sexual exploitation (see Chapter 14).
- Women are raped during wars (see Chapter 17).
- Women, in some communities, can be subject to 'honour killings' or 'forced' marriages.
- Female consumers, as outlined in Chapter 6 and above, can be the target of sales and marketing frauds for goods and services which play on idealized images of femininity (and see Chapter 15).
- They can be the target of frauds such as 'widows and orphans' frauds (Levi 2008b).

This indicates that the gendered lens should also turn to places such as the workplace, war, the school, the playground and to institutions such as care homes, hospitals and prisons (Davies 2007a).

To feminists, this gendered victimization reflects the operation of the patriarchal state and patriarchal culture with violence against women being one of the structures of patriarchy described by Walby (1990). Male domination and their proprietoral rights over women's bodies are reflected in law with rape in marriage only relatively recently having been criminalized across the UK, and many men who kill their wives explain their actions by appealing to the sentiment '*if I can't have her no one can*' (Chapter 11). The treatment of female victims in the criminal justice process amounts to the effective condoning of these practices by the patriarchal state. This includes police reluctance to intervene in so-called 'domestics', their denial of credibility to rape victims and the treatment of rape victims in court along with the medicalizing of female offenders. The additional aspects of women's victimization identified above can also be related to patriarchal practices. They reflect, for example, a gendered division of labour in which women's work is often associated with low pay and exploitative conditions. The harms associated with pharmaceutical products such as contraceptive devices or cosmetic surgery can be associated with patriarchal assumptions, on the part of a male-dominated industry, about the 'need' to alter women's bodies to conform to images of 'femininity' (Finley 1996; Simpson and Elis 1996; Croall 2007b).

A major problem with these accounts is, however, that they can perpetuate the 'woman as victim' stereotype, referred to above (Davies 2007a; Walklate 2007c). Women who are trafficked are often denied agency by being cast as victims as are women who choose to work in the sex trade (Brooks-Gordon 2010 and see Chapter 13). They also neglect the victimization of men. As Davies (2007b: 181) points out, women should not be allowed to 'hijack harm and suffering for themselves'. Men are more victimized by violence, much of it at the hands of other men. Men are also trafficked and their labour exploited. In the areas of state and corporate violence, pointing to the gendered victimization of women should not be taken to imply that women are *more* victimized than men who are also subject to harms as a result of work and consumption (Davies 2007a; Croall 2007b).

Men's victimization

There are also many instances of men being victimized in a gendered way. Sexual offences, as well as victimizing women, also involve boys being sexually assaulted by older men, often parents or other known and trusted men such as teachers or clergymen. Male rape has been seen as the 'last taboo', with rape laws being very much based on women. Male rape is gendered in that it is often related, particularly in the prison setting, to male dominance. Men perceived to be deviant or 'abnormal' men can also be vicitimized, with homosexuals being victims of homophobic attacks. Violent crime can also be gendered. Many so-called male on male assaults involve contests of honour and reputation where fights involve assumed insults to 'manhood' (Polk 1994 and see Chapter 11). Boys and adult men are victims of domestic violence in both hetero- and homosexual households. Prisons reflect and reinforce subcultures of male on male violence (Sim 1994). Men can be victimized by working in 'men's jobs' associated with a macho culture of risk in which taking safety precautions is avoided (Tombs and Whyte 2007 and see Chapter 15). Male consumers can, like women, be targeted by products and services reflecting perceptions of 'maleness' and masculinity. Their preference for 'risky investments' can also make them the target of fraudsters.

Gender is also an important factor in the relative invisibility of male victimization. Men, as suggested in Chapter 6, may find it less easy to accept and report victimization as being a victim can be associated with being 'weak and helpless' (Stanko and Hobdell 1993). As Goodey (2005), in a much quoted comment, points out, 'big boys don't cry'. Men may not, therefore, report crimes to the police, feel they can 'handle it' themselves, and do not want to admit offences to victim survey interviewers. They may also have ambiguous attitudes to violence – Hall and Winlow (2003, cited in Davies 2007a) suggest that being 'beaten up' may be indicative of manhood to young men, and, in Glasgow, scars from knife attacks may be seen as a sign of respect (Ferris 2002). Male rape involves considerable stigma and men fear that admitting to having been raped may be taken as an indication of homosexuality. Admitting vulnerability of any sort may also be a deterrent (Davies 2007a).

Nonetheless, male victimization can be considerable and sexual offences in particular have a serious impact. Men may be more reluctant to seek help or express their feelings and yet are emotionally affected by crime which can have long-lasting effects (Stanko and Hobdell 1993). While in general men are more likely to report anger when victimized, they also report feelings of vulnerability and powerlessness particularly when they are sexually assaulted (Walklate 2004; 2007c). In their responses and coping strategies, they tend to seek explanations for their victimization, for example that they were overpowered or entrapped, which reflect stereotypes of masculinity. As Walklate (2007c: 158) points out, they need to keep a sense of themselves as men – a challenge that women do not have to face. Many of these points suggest areas worthy of more research and theorizing.

Discussion

It is evident that the study of gender and crime is complex and that many questions remain. What, for example, has been the impact of feminist perspectives? How can they be evaluated? What questions remain underexplored? And finally, what is the significance of *gender* as opposed to other social inequalities in relation to crime and victimization?

Has anyone been listening?

Two of the leading writers in feminist criminology have questioned its impact by asking '*has anyone been listening?*' (Heidensohn and Gelsthorpe 2007: 407). Heidensohn has repeatedly criticized criminologists for not taking the feminist critique seriously by, for example, 'tacking on' women as an afterthought and not taking up the challenge of *integrating* the subject of gender (Heidensohn 1996). Clearly there has been some change – criminology texts and journals look very different today than they did in the 1960s, and all address gender issues and gendered violence. Issues such as domestic or child 'abuse' were regarded as largely social welfare issues but have now been subject to considerable research, addressing victimization, policing and criminal justice, and substantial policy changes have ensued. The sections above have incorporated a considerable volume of research on gender issues. Teaching syllabi include issues of gender, many criminology and social science courses have modules in 'Gender Crime and Justice', and the study of gender (along with other social inequalities) is one of the 'benchmarks' for criminology degrees. In other respects, however, the concerns of criminology remain very much focused on male crime, and gender is often a neglected variable.

Heidensohn and Gelsthorpe (2007) note these changes in teaching, research and policy while at the same time referring to a 'selective deafness'. Some issues remain unresolved and there is, they argue, 'still work to do to ensure that issues identified by feminists working within criminology do not remain unheard' (p. 411). In addition, as the rising numbers of women in prison indicate, in the area of social control there are signs of increasing punitiveness and the discourses of risk and popular punitivism remain largely gender blind (Silvestri and Crowther-Dowey 2008).

Questions for feminism?

Along with others (see, for example, Walklate 2004), Gelsthorpe and Heidensohn also acknowledge and address the many criticisms of feminist approaches. Most often cited are those advanced by Downes and Rock (2007) in their key text, earlier versions of which were criticized by feminists for neglecting gender. They have argued that the feminist critique of earlier theoretical approaches is misplaced. To them, sociology and criminology have been 'crime led', focusing on male crime because it is statistically most prevalent. Gender is not the only neglected variable, as race and white-collar crime, along with crimes of the middle-aged, the elderly and those in rural communities, have been similarly underexplored. Moreover, theories developed for male criminals can be and have been applied to women. The labelling perspective is not intrinsically difficult to apply to women and both anomie and subcultural theories are relevant. Later subcultural writers did discuss sexism and racism within subcultures and the approach can also be applied to female subcultures (Downes and Rock 2007).

Within feminism, writers took a different stance towards the centrality of patriarchy and the focus of feminist criminology. Chesney-Lind (2006, cited in Silvestri and Crowther-Dowey 2008: 27) has, for example, commented that the focus on 'liberation' and crime was a 'costly intellectual detour'. Other writers have disputed the extent to which the feminist approach is distinct from or superior to other approaches. Carlen (1992), for example, argued that apart from patriarchy there is little to distinguish feminist approaches from others, although she does not deny their contribution. She also criticizes the central role of gender which, she argues, diverts attention from inequalities such as class or race which are important for women. Her work, outlined above, associated women's crime with poverty, and she argued that a left realist approach, combined with feminist insights, could better analyse these problems. Feminist approaches were also criticized for neglecting the experiences of black women and the dimension of race (Mama 1989), a criticism which was generally accepted.

Nonetheless there remain some awkward questions for feminist perspectives. Echoing the question 'can men be victims?', it can be asked if women can be serious offenders? While statistically rare, women do feature as serial killers, sexual abusers, terrorists, torturers, traffickers and fraudsters – as Davies (2007a) points out, these are very popular topics for student dissertations. Part of the attraction may lie in their atypicality, yet a serious and extended study of these topics would address serious gaps in our knowledge and present a further challenge to essentialism. Women who choose crime and who derive pleasure, thrills, status and economic independence from it challenge the predominant view of women as propelled into crime either through poverty or victimization. The association of women's crime with 'risk factors', such as a history of victimization from familial abuse and poverty, tends to perpetuate the 'pathologizing' of women's crime and may, however much based on a concern for women, perpetuate the myth of women's passivity. At the same time, however, the possibility that 'equivalence' in terms of perceiving women's crime as motivated very much in the same way as men's can contribute to a punitive backlash should be recognized (Silvestri and Crowther-Dowey 2008). Neglecting women's serious offending reinforces the essentialism of seeing men as 'the' criminal problem, an issue which also affects theories exploring masculinity. The brief exploration of men's victimization illustrates that it constitutes a further awkward question aptly illustrated in the way in which 'can men be victims' has become a question, when, statistically, men have always predominated as crime victims.

These considerations indicate some of the ways in which a fully gendered approach might develop. It would have to take on board men as victims as well as women as serious offenders (Davies 2007a). It would also have to move away from the duality of masculinity and femininity recognizing a variety of feminities and masculinities. In contrast to the work on masculinities and crime, there has been little equivalent work on femininities (Walklate 2004). As Davies (2007a: 96) argues:

> attention has inevitably focused upon the 'woman question' and how in turn this has had implications for our understanding of the 'man question'; femininities and masculinities; and ultimately the complete 'gender matrix' where women are victims and offenders and men are offenders and victims, where women victimize other women and (male and female) children and where men experience victimization from women and other men.

Black, Asian, homosexual and classed masculinities and femininities would also need to be explored along with different sexualities (Walklate 2004). It could also be argued that across Britain specific forms of masculinity may be associated with Scottish, English, Irish, Welsh or other regional or religious identities, which may be of importance to cultural conceptions of violence and specific practices, particularly given different levels of violence across different regions and jurisdictions.

The significance of gender?

This raises the question of how gender relates to other dimensions of inequality such as class, ethnicity, race or age, and the significance of gender has been questioned. Walklate (2004: 83), for example, asks to what extent, and in what circumstances, masculinity is the key variable in committing crime or experiencing victimization and how and under what circumstances class, age or ethnicity might also be key variables? As seen above, sexual violence is quintessentially gendered and involves assumptions about sexuality and sexual relationships. While these may also be related to class, race or age, gender can be argued to be the most significant variable. It is widely recognized as being far less significant to victimization from property crime where socio-economic or geographic factors may be more important. 'Hate crimes' (see Chapter 10) often involve racial or religious divisions and although women do suffer from 'hate crimes' gender is not always central (Davies 2007a). As Davies argues in the same passage cited above, 'gender matters but sometimes it might matter on a par with class-race-age. Alternatively while gender matters it might not matter quite so much as class-race-age'.

Concluding comments

This chapter has outlined many elements of the relationship between gender and crime, which will be further developed in later chapters on specific crimes. Gender inequalities and relationships are deeply rooted although their exact relationship to crime is as yet unclear and distorted by false stereotypes of men as aggressive criminals and women as passive victims. Most now recognize that both men and women commit very similar kinds of crimes for similar reasons. Poverty and socio-economic inequalities may be a major factor in male and female crime, although in a different way for different crimes. Women may more readily turn to sex work, for example. Both men and women can seek thrills and excitement from crime yet we know relatively little about women's involvement in serious or violent crime. Both men's and women's victimization can be gendered, not only from sexual and domestic violence but from institutional, corporate and state crime. Gender clearly operates alongside the other forms of social inequality discussed in this section and should not be taken in isolation. As Walklate (1995: 192) argues:

> Gender may hold some of the clues to the 'crime problem', but it would be misguided to think that it holds all of the answers. A gendered lens certainly helps us see some features of the crime problem more clearly perhaps; but how and under what circumstances is that clarity made brighter by gender or distorted by it?

Review questions

1 Using a 'gendered lens':

(a) Look at popular representations of crime in televised crime dramas and/or the press. How do these reflect gendered images of victimization and offending?

(b) Look at an example of the work of early anomie, subcultural, or critical criminologists, possibly one studied for Chapter 3. How does it reflect what feminists describe as 'gender blindness'?

2 Is there any evidence to suggest that women and girls are becoming more involved in crime? Identify and locate some relevant material including, for example, self-report studies.

3 Locate and summarize some official figures and research on

(a) Male and female involvement in different kinds of crime

(b) Male and female risks of victimization from different kinds of crime

Critically evaluate what they tell us about differential offending and victimization.

4 Do women and men commit for similar or different reasons?

5 How would you assess the argument that forms of crime and victimization are related to masculinity? Provide an illustration focusing on one particular form of crime or victimization.

6 Outline the main arguments associated with feminist perspectives and list their main strengths, contributions and possible weaknesses.

Key reading

There have now been a large number of books devoted to gender and crime. The best recent sources include:

Heidensohn, F. and Gelsthorpe, L. (2007) 'Gender and crime' in M. Maguire, R. Morgan and R. Reiner (eds) *The Oxford Handbook of Criminology*, 4th edn, Oxford: Clarendon Press. Written by two of the most influential feminist criminologists, this chapter outlines the main issues in looking at gender and crime along with a critical evaluation of feminist perspectives and their influence.

Silvestri, M. and Crowther-Dowey, C. (2008) ***Gender and Crime***, London: Sage. A good and comprehensive survey of the main topics covering issues of offending and victimization with a good account of masculinity approaches.

Walklate, S. (2004) ***Gender, Crime and Criminal Justice***, Cullompton: Willan Publishing. An updated version of an influential text, this covers a range of issues including the main theories, feminist perspectives and issues involving criminal justice.

Wykes, M. and Welsh, K. (2009) ***Violence, Gender and Justice***, London: Sage. An interesting and critical introduction to gender issues, focusing on issues of violent and sexual crime with some interesting examples of media representations and the law.

Chapter 10
Race, ethnicity and crime

This chapter will look at:

→ Race, ethnicity and offending

→ Race, ethnicity and victimization

→ Constructing race and ethnicity and its links to crime

→ Criminology, race, ethnicity and crime

→ Urban unrest

→ Violent racism and 'hate crime'

Race and ethnicity form a major part of the tendency, seen in earlier chapters, to attribute crime to 'others'. In nineteenth-century Britain, the Irish were depicted as part of the 'dangerous classes' whereas recurrent urban disturbances in England in the 1980s, 1990s and early 2000s were attributed to different minority ethnic groups. Exploring any relationship between race, ethnicity and crime involves asking similar questions to those asked in relation to gender, class or age. To what extent are offending and victimization affected by race and ethnicity? Do some groups experience greater criminalization? How significant are race and ethnicity in comparison to gender, age or socio-economic status? It is also important, as it was with these other inequalities, to avoid generalizations and essentializing differences between 'minority' and 'majority' patterns of crime or victimization. Specific historical, spatial, cultural and local experiences need to be recognized as different areas of Britain have experienced very different patterns of minority ethnic settlement.

This chapter will begin by critically exploring what can be learnt from official statistics and surveys about both crime and victimization. It will then examine how race and ethnicity, and their links with crime, have been popularly constructed and subjected to criminological analysis, including a discussion of the so-called 'race and crime debate'. It will then look more closely at analyses of specific issues of urban unrest and racist violence, sometimes referred to as 'hate crime'. The concluding section will outline contemporary critiques of and developing approaches to this topic, explore what questions remain to be investigated and discuss the significance of race as compared to other inequalities. In line with many other texts, the main focus of the chapter is on race and ethnicity, although it is recognized that these are closely interrelated with aspects of religion or nationality.

Race, ethnicity, crime and victimization

Before exploring patterns of offending and victimization it is important to look at how the terms race and ethnicity are defined. These terms are highly contested and there is no simple way of categorizing people into racial or ethnic groups. The widely used term BME (black and minority ethnic) has little specificity and masks differences between Asian, African, Caribbean, Chinese and many other groups. Often-used phrases such as 'minority' and 'majority' are also misleading. Many so-called immigrant communities now contain third and fourth generations who were born in Britain and who identify themselves, as the census now asks, in a variety of ways such as 'black British', British Pakistani, Black Scottish or Black Welsh. The term 'white' also contains people who define themselves as Irish, Scottish, Welsh, English, Australian or other European nationalities, whereas 'white' groups such as Jews or Eastern Europeans are often seen as 'ethnic' minorities. In practice, different sets of statistics and research projects often use different terminologies making comparisons hazardous. This chapter will follow the terms used in cited material, will use BME as a shorthand term when referring to overall comparisons, but will be more specific when appropriate.

A number of factors need to be taken into account when looking at any figures. Box 10.1 indicates considerable variations in proportions of the population across Britain and within regions and cities. They are also not evenly distributed between socio-economic or age groups. These differences can be relevant to crime figures – if, for example, members of a particular group are more likely to be

Box 10.1 Proportions of racial and ethnic groups in Britain

The **2001 Census** indicates that:

- Minority ethnic groups formed 13 per cent of the population in England, 4 per cent in Wales, 2 per cent in Scotland and 0.85 per cent in Northern Ireland.
- 2 per cent of the population of England and Wales are Indian, with Leicester having the highest proportion (25.7 per cent). Indians make up 0.3 per cent of the Scottish population.
- In England and Wales, 1.1 per cent of people are Black Caribbean, 0.9 per cent are Black African. Black Caribbeans form over 10 per cent of the population of the London boroughs of Lewisham, Lambeth, Brent and Hackney. In Scotland, Caribbeans formed 0.04 per cent of the population and 0.2 per cent defined themselves as Black Scottish.
- Bangladeshis formed 0.5 per cent of the population of England and Wales, with the highest proportion in the London borough of Tower Hamlets (33.4 per cent). They formed 0.04 per cent of the population in Scotland.
- Chinese people form more than 2 per cent of the population in Westminster, Cambridge, City of London and Barnet and are also the largest group in Northern Ireland, concentrated in Belfast.

Box 10.2 Socio-economic inequalities and ethnicity

- **Unemployment**: In 2002, 12 per cent of young white males were unemployed, compared to 31 per cent Black African, 27 per cent Black Caribbean, 28 per cent Pakistani and 41 per cent Bangladeshi.
- **Employment:** BME people tend to be concentrated in sectors associated with low pay. In 2001, nearly half of Bangladeshi men worked in the lowest paid jobs in the catering trade. Black Caribbean men tended to be concentrated in low-grade service sector occupations.

  In Scotland, minority ethnic groups are twice as likely to be unemployed as White Scots, and Indian, Pakistani and Chinese employees work longer hours.
- **Income**: In general, BME people have lower incomes. In 2004, the median hourly wage for white males was £9.31, and the lowest for Pakistani and Bangladeshi men at around £6.25 per hour.
- **Poverty**: In 2005/6 18 per cent of white people lived in households in the bottom fifth of incomes compared to 61 per cent Pakistani and Bangladeshi, 34 per cent Black non-Caribbean and 43 per cent Black Caribbean people. In Scotland the most deprived tenth of the population contained 9 per cent Pakistani, 10 per cent Bangladeshi and 11 per cent White Scottish (Scottish Executive 2006).

Sources: Grover (2008: 126–28) and Scottish Executive (2006)

younger and unemployed, they might be expected to feature more strongly as offenders and victims, reflecting the strong association between age and official crime rates (Fitzgerald 1995; Coleman and Moynihan 1996; Phillips and Bowling 2007; Grover 2008). As indicated in Box 10.2, some, but not all, minority ethnic groups are found amongst the most socially disadvantaged which can also affect experiences of relative deprivation, crime, policing and victimization.

Official statistics do not record the race or ethnicity of convicted offenders. Some countries do not collect any information about racial or ethnic differences due to political sensitivity and in case it is used against groups, or because, as in France, it goes against the universality of citizenship (Goodey 2007). In Britain, as is the case with gender, Section 95 of the Criminal Justice Act 1991 brought in more systematic information in the annual *Statistics on Race and the Criminal Justice System*, and there are Scottish and Northern Irish figures which do not contain so many breakdowns due to the smaller numbers involved. The OCJS contains figures on self-report (Sharp and Budd 2005), and the BCS now looks at racial and ethnic variations in victimization, at offences which victims consider to be racially motivated and at fear and worry about crime (Francis 2007a; Goodey 2007). In Northern Ireland, the police have published figures since 1997 (Jarman and Monaghan 2003) including statistics on 'hate crimes and incidents' (Police Service of Northern Ireland Statistics 2008b), which includes religion-based and sectarian crimes. Other jurisdictions also produce figures on Racist Incidents and Racially Aggravated Offences defined in Box 10.4.

Race, ethnicity and offending

Given all these problems, figures must be interpreted with great care. As no details of offenders' ethnicity are routinely provided the main sources of information are numbers proceeding through the criminal justice system and in prison. Box 10.3 details some headline figures about the involvement of racial and ethnic groups with police activity and prisons. There are strong indications that in England and Wales black people are over-represented throughout the process, with proportionately more being stopped and arrested by the police and being awarded custodial sentences. Asians, previously considered to be under-represented, are over-represented in terms of stops and searches and arrests. These kinds of breakdowns are less easily available for Scotland and Northern Ireland. In Scotland, for example, the police do not routinely collect details of stops and arrests although research indicates that Asian youth feel that they are disproportionately stopped (Reid Howie 2002; Frondigoun et al 2007). Prison figures for England and Wales indicate that the proportions of black people far exceed their proportion in the population, which has been less evident in Scotland although recent figures do show an increase. These figures cannot be taken to indicate higher levels of offending, as they may result from the differential exercise of discretion in the criminal justice process and the demographic characteristics of different populations.

This is highlighted by the different picture provided by self-report studies which indicate that in England and Wales, Asians report lower rates of involvement in crime than either white or black youth, and the OCJS found that white people and

Box 10.3 Race, ethnicity and criminal justice: some selected figures

Police activity

England and Wales:

- Of the 955,000 searches under section 1 of the Police and Criminal Evidence Act 1984 carried out in 2006/7, 15.9 per cent were of black people, 8.1 per cent of Asian people and 1.5 per cent of 'other' people.
- Relative to the general population, black people were 7 times more likely and Asian people 2 times more likely to be stopped and searched as white people.
- Relative to the general population, black people were 3.6 times more likely to be arrested than white people.
- Black people formed 6 per cent, and Asian people 4 per cent, of those cautioned for notifiable offences in 2006.

Prisons

- In June 2007, members of BME groups accounted for 26 per cent of the total prison population in England and Wales.
- In Scotland, the 2008 Prison Statistics indicated that 4.3 per cent of the prison population were from minority ethnic groups.

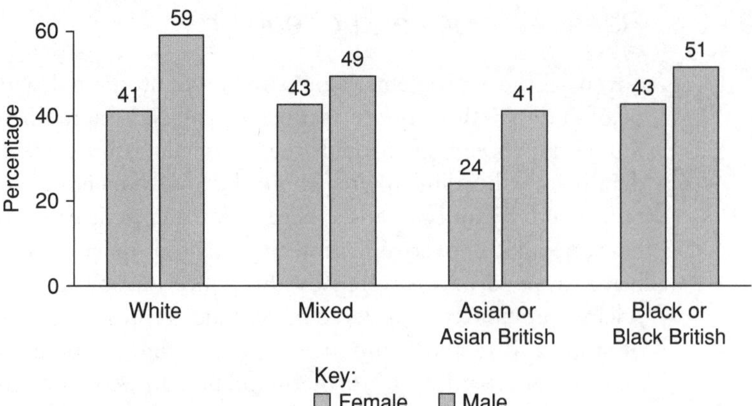

Figure 10.1 Percentage of males and females who reported ever offending, by ethnicity, ages 10–25, 2003

Source: Ministry of Justice (2009)

those of 'mixed' ethnic origin were most likely to report having committed a crime, as illustrated in Figure 10.1, compared to black and Asian groups (Sharp and Budd 2005: 8, cited in Phillips and Bowling 2007).

Race, ethnicity and victimization

The BCS indicates that BME groups, taken as a whole, have higher rates of victimization overall (Salisbury and Upson 2004). These differences can, however, be attributed to socio-economic factors and area of residence. BME groups also show higher levels of worry about crime, particularly burglary, car and violent crime (Francis 2007a). As will be seen below, however, the racial element of a crime may not be recorded.

Racist crime involves incidents in which members, or assumed members, of specific groups are victimized on the grounds of that membership and will often involve the use of racist language, or in the case of vandalism, racist slogans or symbols (see Box 10.4). There had been consistent complaints that the police failed to take reports of racist crime seriously and high-profile racist murders such as those of Stephen Lawrence in England and Surjit Singh Chhokar in Scotland, outlined in Box 9.6, confirmed these concerns about the way in which cases were dealt with by police and prosecutors. In the Lawrence case, the assumption that Stephen and his friend were victims hampered the investigation and both cases revealed serious failings and led to changed policies in their respective jurisdictions. Offences were redefined as outlined in Box 9.4 and changing recording procedures introduced (Webster 2007; Francis 2007a; Goodey 2007; Phillips and Bowling 2007; Iganski 2008). Some figures on racial victimization are summarized in Box 10.5.

These indicate varying rates across the UK. The highest numbers of racist incidents are recorded in London, followed by Greater Manchester and the West Mid-lands. In England and Wales, the lowest numbers outside the City of London were reported in North Yorkshire, Dyfed Powys, North Yorkshire and Cumbria, all below 300 (Francis 2007a), although these do not take account of population numbers.

Box 10.4 Racially motivated offences: some definitions

- **Racist incidents**: England and Wales and Scotland have adopted a 'victim-centred' definition of racist incidents as those 'perceived to be racist by the victim or any other person'.
- **Racially aggravated offences**: These were introduced in England, Wales and Scotland, in 1998. An offence is considered to be racially aggravated if, either at the time of committing the offence or immediately before or after it, the offender demonstrates hostility based on the victim's membership (including association with members of a group) or presumed membership (as seen by the offender) of a racial group; if the offence is motivated (wholly or partly) by hostility towards members of a racial group based on their membership of that group. The definition was widened in 2001 to include religiously aggravated offences, and the Powers of Criminal Courts (sentencing) Act 2000 also imposes a duty on sentencers to treat evidence of racist and religious motivation as an aggravating factor.
- In Northern Ireland **'hate incidents'** are defined as any incident perceived by the victim or any other person as being motivated by prejudice or hate (PSNI 2010).

Box 10.5 Aspects of racial victimization in the UK

Racial incidents

- *England and Wales*: The numbers of racist incidents recorded by the police rose from 13,936 in 1997/8 to 57,902 in 2004/5. In large part this may reflect changing definitions and confidence in reporting.
- *London*: The 'capital of hate crime' (Iganski 2008: 47) has the highest total number of racial incidents although there are indications of a decrease 2000–2005. Asians reported 10 times more incidents of victimization (10.64 incidents per 1,000 population), than did whites. The highest rate was found in Havering (27.75 per 1,000). The mean rate for black groups was 9.23 incidents per 1,000 of the population.
- In *Scotland*, The total number of racist incidents fell from 2006/07 to 2007/08, following a steady increase since 1999 (Scottish Government 2009c). The highest rates are found in urban areas (Aberdeen, Dundee, Edinburgh and Glasgow). Around 50 per cent of victims were of Asian origin, the majority Pakistani.
- In *Northern Ireland*, PSNI statistics for hate incidents detail 976 racial incidents, of which 757 were crimes, between 1 April 2007 and 31 March 2008, a 6.8 percent decrease over the previous year. Of these, violent racial crimes accounted for 37.4 per cent, of which 204 were woundings and assaults (PSNI 2008a; 2008b).

In Scotland, the highest numbers taking account of the population, were recorded in Glasgow and Edinburgh (22.1 and 21.3 per 10,000 population respectively), followed by Dundee, Aberdeen, Falkirk and Stirling (all exceeding 10 per 10,000). The lowest rates were found in Orkney, Shetland, Argyll and Bute and the Scottish

Borders. These suggest an urban rural variation, although racist violence does happen in rural areas. Overall Scottish rates are lower than in England and Wales, with the highest rates, for Glasgow and Edinburgh, well below those cited by Iganski (2008) for London, outlined in Box 10.6 (Croall and Frondigoun 2010).

The introduction of new policies and recording procedures are widely held to have contributed to the rising numbers of these offences since the 1990s. Despite increasing reporting and recorded levels, however, it has been argued that the extent

Box 10.6 Cases of racist murders

Stephen Lawrence

On 22 April 1993 the black teenager Stephen Lawrence was stabbed to death in Eltham, south-east London, by what was widely accepted to be a group of hostile and abusive white youths (Bowling and Phillips 2002; Newburn 2003). No one was ever charged or convicted of murder. The conduct of the investigation was widely criticized by the victim's family, interest groups and the media. The police initially assumed that Lawrence and his friend Duwayne Brooks had initiated the violence and failed to follow up leads. In 1997 the government set up the MacPherson Inquiry, 'to inquire into the matters arising from the death of Stephen Lawrence . . . and to identify the lessons to be learned for the investigation and prosecution of racially motivated crimes' (cited in Newburn 2003: 90). The Inquiry reported in 1999 (MacPherson 1999) and:

- Confirmed the police denial of any racial motive for the murder, along with the racist stereotyping of Duwayne Brooks;
- Stated that there was, 'no doubt whatsoever but that the first MPS investigation was palpably flawed and deserves severe criticism' (para. 2.10);
- Criticized the use of inappropriate and offensive language along with insensitive and patronizing handling of Mr and Mrs Lawrence;
- Found that the 'investigation was marred by a combination of professional incompetence, institutional racism and a failure of leadership by senior officers' (para. 46.1). This included a 'lack of direction and organization in the hours after the murder, little or no pursuit of the suspects, inadequate processing of intelligence, ill thought out surveillance and inadequate searches';
- Concluded that the black community was 'over policed . . . and underprotected' (MacPherson 1999: 312).
- Made 70 recommendations for policy.

Surjit Singh Chhokar

Surjit Singh Chhokar was stabbed to death outside his home in Overtown, Lanarkshire, on 4 November 1998. In March 1999 Ronnie Coulter was tried for his murder. He lodged a special defence naming his nephew Andrew Coulter and David Montgomery as the killers; both had originally been arrested and charged with the crime along with Ronnie Coulter. He was found not guilty of murder but guilty of assault, with the trial judge, Lord McCluskey, criticizing the then Lord Advocate: 'For reasons I cannot begin to understand, only one of those persons was put in the dock.' In November 2000 Andrew Coulter and David Montgomery were tried for the murder but were found not guilty although Andrew Coulter was convicted of breaking into Mr Chhokar's flat, stealing a giro and cooker, and cashing the benefit cheque fraudulently.

The outcome led to claims of institutionalized racism in the Scottish police and criminal justice system, and the Lord Advocate ordered two inquiries into the case:

- One investigated Crown Office decision-making in the case, found evidence of racism and recommended greater monitoring of ethnicity in the criminal justice process (Campbell and McKay 2001).
- The other report reviewed how prosecutors liaised with the Chhokar family and found that the family's needs had not been met (Jandoo 2001).

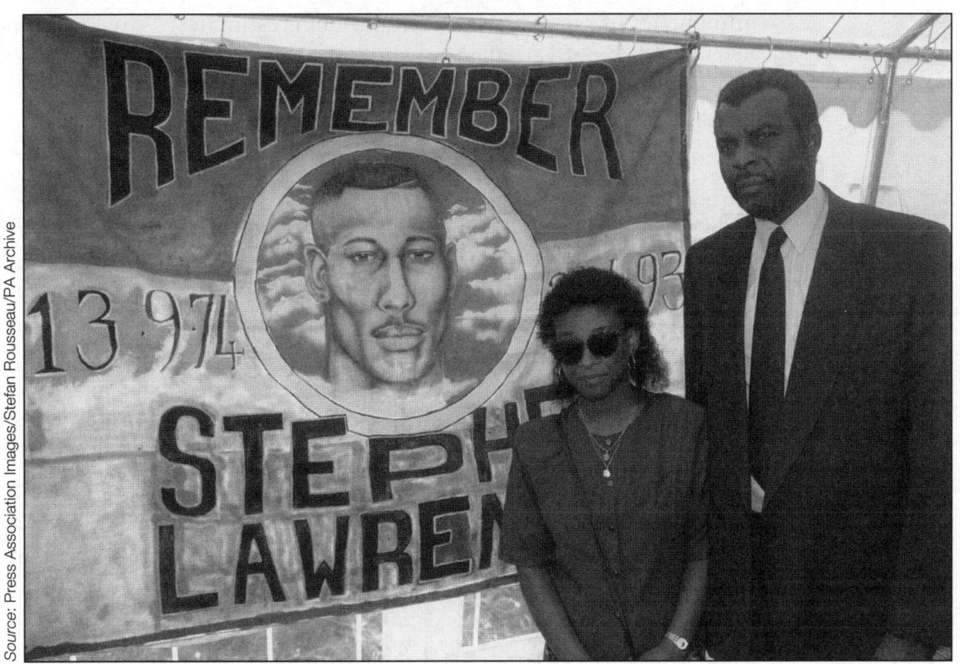

Source: Press Association Images/Stefan Rousseau/PA Archive

Stephen Lawrence's parents alongside a poster of their son.

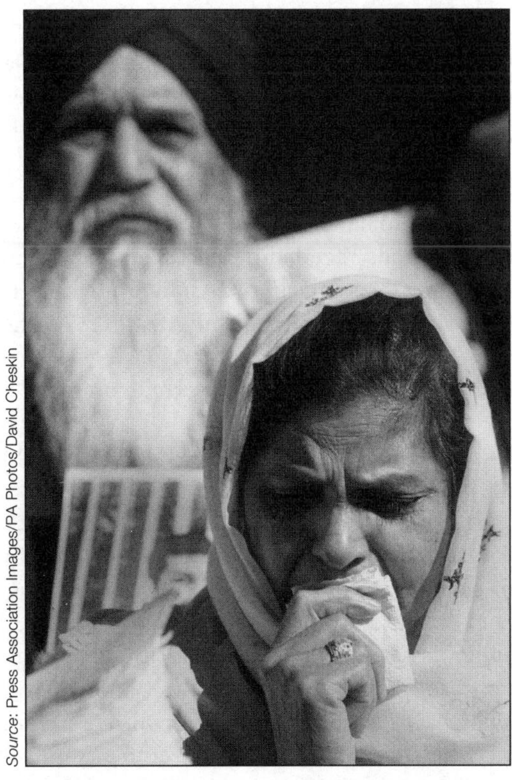

Source: Press Association Images/PA Photos/David Cheskin

Surjit Chhokar's parents.

and impact of racist offences remain underestimates. While many appear to be 'low level' incidents of verbal abuse and harassment, they can be, like sexual harassment, so persistent that they can have a more serious impact.

Constructions of race, ethnicity and crime

The complex issues outlined above reflect the construction of race and ethnicity around assumed differences. Most typically, minority groups are cast as 'other' making them targets for criminalization and crime is often, in many countries, attributed to 'aliens' or foreigners. Aspects of race were implicit in some criminological perspectives whereas others associated racialization with criminalization. This section will start by looking at constructions of race, ethnicity and racism and their association with crime. It will go on to explore how criminologists have approached these issues, including biological and social structural approaches, to the so-called 'race and crime' debate, and successive phases of criminalization.

Constructing race and ethnicity

Definitions of race and ethnicity have been strongly contested and their meanings have shifted over time. While once assumed to be biologically determined, research failed to establish any biological differences between so-called races, and it is now recognized that race is a socially constructed category generally associated with relationships of inferiority and superiority (Miles 1989; Holdaway 1997; Webster 2007; Smith 2009a). During colonial expansion indigenous or 'native' populations, often distinguished by their 'darker' skin and described as 'savages' or 'barbarians', were deemed inferior to 'civilized' white Europeans (Miles 1989). Slavery was the most extreme form of racial domination.

Defining race is therefore a social process of differentiation reflected in racialized speech and assumptions that racial differences are significant (Miles 1989). Describing an individual or group as 'black' or 'Asian' implies a racialized relationship if this is seen as 'the' significant distinguishing feature. As the term race is so often linked to difference, domination and oppression, some have argued that it should be abandoned. Some place the term in inverted commas, 'race', to indicate its problematic nature.

Ethnicity is a broader term which does not carry the 'biological baggage' of race (Smith 2009a: 24), and is more often associated with interrelated characteristics such as culture, religion, country of origin or language. While race is often seen as a fixed category, ethnicity is associated with perceptions of identity. It often, however, carries notions of superiority or inferiority, being used, for example, along with the word minority. The word ethnic in descriptions of ethnic food or crafts is often used to imply 'foreignness'. Rarely is the 'majority' described as 'ethnic', thus the preference for the phrase 'minority ethnic group', and for the term 'diversity' rather than difference which also implies an inferior difference/deviation *from* the 'majority' (Mason 1995; Hudson 2007). Like race, ethnicity can become the basis for atrocities, seen most vividly in the 'ethnic cleansing' in the former Yugoslavia in the latter part of the twentieth century. Both race and ethnicity have been associated with other concepts:

Discrimination

Discrimination should be distinguished from prejudice which involves a *belief* that a category of people are inferior. Discrimination, on the other hand, occurs where *actions* treat people differently on the grounds of race or any other ascribed characteristic. If a black person is stopped by the police for no other reason than their blackness, this constitutes discrimination. This is an example of *direct* discrimination where the actor is conscious of making a discriminatory decision. Discrimination can also be *indirect*, resulting from policies and practices which produce unequal outcomes – described as *institutional discrimination* where there may be no deliberate or conscious discrimination. The police, for example, by perceiving black people as suspects rather than victims, as was the case with Stephen Lawrence, have been held to practise institutional discrimination, confirmed by the MacPherson Report (1999).

Racism

The term racism was previously used in relation to a belief that a racially defined group was different and inferior, but is now more widely used to describe actions which produce unequal effects on racially defined groups, thereby incorporating prejudice, direct and institutional discrimination. Some argue, for example, that the disproportionate numbers of black people in prison in itself indicates a racist criminal justice process. Racism implies relationships of power and domination, and some argue that it can only be applied to racism against 'black' minority groups, using the term black to refer to *all* minority groups. This can be criticized for using the term so widely that it prevents a full understanding of the social processes involved (Miles 1989), and apparent racism against white groups such as the Irish, travellers or Romanies renders the concept inadequate to reflect the more complex picture of racial and ethnic relationships in the twenty-first century (Webster 2007; Smith 2009a).

While biological notions of racial inferiority have been discredited, a 'new racism' based on cultural conceptions was said to have emerged in Britain from the 1960s onwards, drawing on the legacy of colonialism and fuelled by the wave of immigration in the post-war period and fears that the country would be 'swamped' by coloured immigrants (Gilroy 1987a). 'Multicultural communities' were equated with 'problem communities' and it was argued that discourses of patriotism, nationalism, 'Englishness' and 'Britishness' make no mention of and exclude minority ethnic groups, thus 'there ain't no black in the Union Jack' (Gilroy 1987a). Whether born in Britain or not black youth were seen as 'immigrants', as outsiders whose lawlessness posed a threat to 'British culture' and the 'British way of life'. Similar fears were associated with a shift in the construction of racism with the arrival of economic migrants from Eastern European countries (Smith 2009a) and, as will be seen below, with the perceived terrorist threat from Muslims – illustrating the close relationship between racism and religion. Racism, argues Smith (2009a: 22), has shifted from being associated with essentialist categories such as white or black, and with 'monolithic, all-pervasive and institutionalized practices'.

Criminalizing race

Race has often been associated with popular constructions of the 'dangerous places' and 'dangerous people' referred to in Chapter 7 – the word 'ghetto' derives from concentrations of racial, ethnic or religious groups. The association of the word 'hooligan' with the Irish has already been referred to, and in the nineteenth and early twentieth centuries the Irish were associated with crime and disorder in Liverpool and Glasgow. Jews were associated with the underworld and American depictions of the 'underclass' had strong racial connotations (Webster 2007).

Black people became associated with crime following the post war period of immigration when they were linked to drugs, which was followed by the moral panic about the 'unBritish' crime of mugging (Hall et al 1978 and see Chapter 5). As will be seen below the urban disturbances in England in the 1980s were associated with primarily black communities and phrases such as policing a 'multicultural' society were constructed around the 'problems' of racial and ethnic communities (Keith 1993).

Black youth are now associated with gun crime, homicide and gangs. As Hallsworth and Young (2008) argue,

> the gang problem is always a problem of Jamaican 'Yardies', the African Caribbean Ghetto boys, the Muslim Boys, the Chinese Triads, the Turkish/Kurdish Baybasin Clan, the Asian Fiat Bravo Boys and so on.

References are also made to 'black on black' crime – yet the phrase 'white on white' crime is rarely used (Phillips and Bowling 2007). While the 'fear' of 'black crime' has not disappeared, it will be seen below that new racialized folk devils have emerged.

Criminology, race, ethnicity and crime

While not intrinsically racist, biological approaches involved racial assumptions. Lombroso (1897), for example, concluded that 'many of the characteristics found in savages, and in the coloured races, are also to be found in habitual delinquents' (cited in Phillips and Bowling 2007: 422). The focus on physical appearance and references to the 'atavistic' throwback echoed notions that criminals were a 'race apart' (Webster 2007). Biological arguments re-emerged with Herrnstein and Murray's (1995) work on crime and intelligence, discussed in Chapter 6, as to them, intelligence varies across racial groups. While widely criticized, the popularity of their work demonstrates the continuing appeal of concepts of racial difference (Smith 2009b).

Other criminological theories implied racial differences. A major criticism of the Chicago School's focus on urban decay and social disorganization is that it scapegoated immigrants whose 'sub'cultures were seen to contribute to disorganization, and the identification of organized crime with the Mafia, and thereby to Italians, represents a further tendency to attribute crime in America to 'unAmerican' activities (Pearce 1976). Anomie, while focusing on universal cultural goals, applied well to those, such as black and immigrant groups, who faced greater blocked opportunities for achievement, and a major feature of left realism's focus on relative deprivation was their argument that minority ethnic groups faced greater levels of relative deprivation.

The race and crime debate

In Britain, criminological analyses were dominated by the so-called 'race and crime' debate triggered by discussions of the role played by the police in producing the disproportionate involvement of black youth in the criminal justice process. This involved administrative criminologists, left realists and critical criminologists (Hudson 1993).

- *Administrative criminologists* used largely quantitative statistical techniques and empirical research to look for a 'race factor' which could be disentangled from the impact of demographic factors such as age, class and area of residence which in themselves would produce different levels of minority groups in the criminal justice process in different areas. Their search was for direct rather than indirect discrimination (Hudson 1993), and there was little qualitative work looking at decision-makers themselves or at the subjective experiences of groups throughout the process (Holdaway 1997; Smith 1997). This produced rather inconclusive findings, particularly as any racial element co-exists with others – it may, for example, be only one amongst many factors in a decision to stop an offender (Holdaway 1996; 1997).
- *Left realists* argued that the higher involvement of black people in the criminal justice process reflected both racism on the part of criminal justice agencies and the structural position of minority ethnic groups (Lea and Young 1993). If socio-economic deprivation was a factor in crime, higher rates among minority ethnic groups, who are also among those most deprived, would be *expected*. Arguments that all disproportions were the result of police racism implied, they suggested, that all groups should be convicted in equal proportions. During the 1970s and 1980s Asians were under-represented among those who came into contact with the police – did this imply, they asked, that the police were partial to Asians?

  A crucial aspect of their argument was the assertion of links between relative deprivation and crime and the structural position of minority ethnic groups. Whereas first-generation immigrants are largely economically motivated, those in the second generation internalize social expectations for equal opportunities only to be denied – producing relative deprivation.

  Police racism was not denied and relationships between the police and the black community were seen as constituting a deviancy amplification spiral in which the strong police reaction to crime in black areas produced hostility to the police and a withdrawal of co-operation from older residents who perceived the police to be hostile to black people as a whole. This led to the police having to resort to 'harder' policing tactics and eventually to 'flashpoints' such as the urban disturbances of the 1980s (Lea and Young 1993).

- *Critical race theorists* such as Gilroy (1987b) fiercely contested these ideas as they underplayed structural processes of racism and criminalization and accepted the 'new racist' 'myth' that black crime is a problem (Gilroy 1987b). To such theorists, the conflict between police and black youth is about race and not crime, and accepting the 'reality' of black crime played into conservative and new right racist views about the pathological nature of black culture. Against this they argued that popular imagery, including the moral panic about mugging, amounted to a racialization of crime, in which black youth are scapegoated for rising rates of crime and lawlessness.

The 'race and crime' debate is now perceived as rather narrowly constructed and most would accept that many factors underlie the disproportionate levels of black people in the criminal justice process (Phillips and Bowling 2003; 2007), although the MacPherson Report acknowledged the widespread nature of institutionalized racism.

'New Criminalizations'

Analyses of the criminalization of minority ethnic groups are also related to the social and economic restructuring described in earlier chapters which strongly affect patterns of migration. Immigrants in the post-war period were needed to fill vacant positions in the labour market. Immigrants, however, form a major part of the 'reserve labour army' needed in some economic periods but which can be surplus in later ones – and some minority ethnic groups suffered considerably following economic restructuring. To critical criminologists, they therefore became convenient scapegoats for the apparent increase in lawlessness and crime. Economic change also led to the economic and residential segregation of some Asian communities who became associated with increasing fears of crime and disorder (Ray et al 2004; Webster 2003; 2007).

Whereas Asians had been associated with a lack of involvement in crime, the late 1990s saw emerging concerns about 'gangs' of second-generation Asian youth, who, as will be seen below, came to be associated with crime and disorder in the North of England (Webster 1997). In the wake of 9/11, suggests Hudson (2007), factors previously held to mitigate against crime amongst Asians, such as religion and close-knit families and communities, were recast, through revelations of forced marriages and honour killings, as features enabling criminalizing and 'othering' aspects of Asian culture. The greater criminalization of Asians is illustrated in higher rates of stops and searches and imprisonment – leading to a situation, argues Hudson (2007: 163), in which the Muslim Asian is now well established as the 'enemy within'.

Criminalization has involved other groups, identified on a variety of ethnic, racial, national and religious grounds. The end of the cold war, the decline of the Soviet Union and the admission, into the European Union (EU), of the so-called Accession countries saw renewed fears of 'swamping', along with fears of the emergence of 'new Mafias' involved in professional and organized crime. In this process, argues

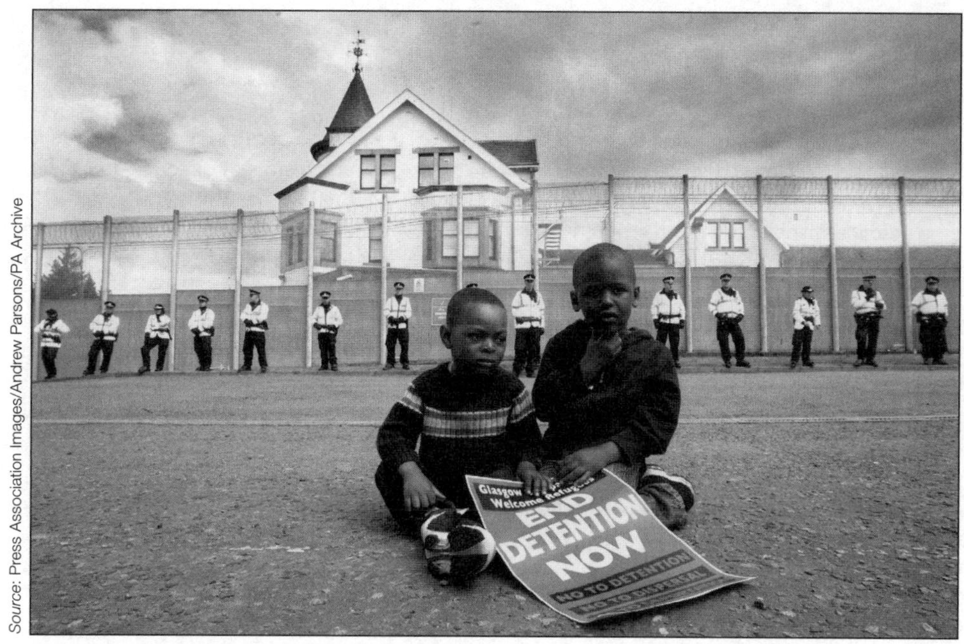

Source: Press Association Images/Andrew Parsons/PA Archive

Asylum seekers became criminalized by being associated with detention and control.

Hudson (2007), the criminalizing discourse of migration has melded with that of religion and ethnicity, directing attention to Muslims and Arabs. It has also extended to those not perceived as 'genuine' migrants. Asylum seekers were subject to criminalization despite there being an almost complete lack of information about their actual involvement in crime (Cooper 2009). This involved a blurring of the boundaries between crime and refugee or asylum status – illustrated in the commonly used but factually incorrect term 'bogus' asylum seekers (it is impossible to be a 'bogus' seeker). Asylum seekers, however, have high risks of being victims of crime, such as abuse, harassment, forced involvement in the sex trade and exploitation by gangmasters. They often fear reporting crime for fear of reprisals or deportation. Their criminalization is compounded, argues Cooper, by the much publicized involvement of the police and prison service, by increasingly punitive measures, dawn raids, and by the use of words such as 'detention' and 'offenders'.

Dimensions of crime, race and ethnicity

Urban unrest: racialization, criminalization and socio-economic disadvantage

The interrelationship between all these factors is well illustrated in analyses of outbursts of urban unrest, mainly in England. While rare, these become signal events and lead to official inquiries, popular, political and academic discussion and debates

Box 10.7 The Brixton disturbances

- The unrest in Brixton was triggered by a policy aiming to clamp down on street crime, known as SWAMP 81. It involved intensive stop and search tactics which had a more severe impact on black youth. One such encounter triggered widespread 'rioting' and looting.
- While regarded as 'race' riots, the significance of race is disputed as not all participants were black and they did not involve black people fighting white people (Scarman 1981; Keith 1993; Holdaway 1996).
- They were also attributed to the spiral of mutual hostility and resentment exacerbated by SWAMP 81.
- Some popular and political reactions denied any elements of social deprivation or race – the then Prime Minister, Margaret Thatcher, saw them as examples of mindless hooliganism and a 'spree of naked greed' (Solomos and Rackett 1991).
- The official Scarman Inquiry (Scarman 1981) blamed a combination of material and social disadvantage and police activity and described SWAMP 81 as ill advised.
- His argument that social disadvantage played a role was criticized by Margaret Thatcher on the grounds that it constituted an effort to 'excuse' them (Grover 2008).

about multiculturalism and diversity (Webster 2007; Smith 2009b). The respective roles played by race, policing, social deprivation and residential concentration have been widely discussed, and they also reflect the shifting focus of concern to Asian groups outlined above.

While some contest the term 'race' riot as overdramatic and containing elements of racialization, many urban disturbances have been associated with racial factors. So-called 'white race riots' in 1958, in which West Indians in Nottingham and Notting Hill were attacked, were linked to the 'colour problem' (Webster 2007: 91). Particularly significant was the spate of incidents across England in 1980 and 1981 in, for example, Bristol, Brixton, Toxteth in Liverpool, Mossside in Manchester and Handsworth in Birmingham. Box 10.7 outlines some of the features of and responses to this event. Later disturbances in the 1980s took place in London and the association between race, crime and disorder, argues Keith (1993: 247) became a symbol of the 1980s:

> At a simple symbolic level British Black communities are, for white society, associated with racist stereotypical notions of law and disorder, powerfully connoted by the images of burning buildings and angry crowds so frequently seen on the screens of British television sets in the 1980s.

The Scarman Report following Brixton led to the introduction of many reforms in relation to community policing, police training and establishing better links between the police and minority ethnic communities. A crucial feature of these was their association with 'multiculturalism' (Webster 2007; Grover 2008; Smith 2009b) – the view that different cultures should be enabled to flourish. Concerns about police racism nonetheless continued as seen in the discussion of the MacPherson Report above, and multiculturalism itself came under attack and was challenged by, amongst other things, the punitive policies towards asylum seekers and the increasing criminalization of Asian groups referred to above (Grover 2008).

Source: Press Association Images/PA Archive

The Brixton disturbances were described as 'race riots' and associated with black people.

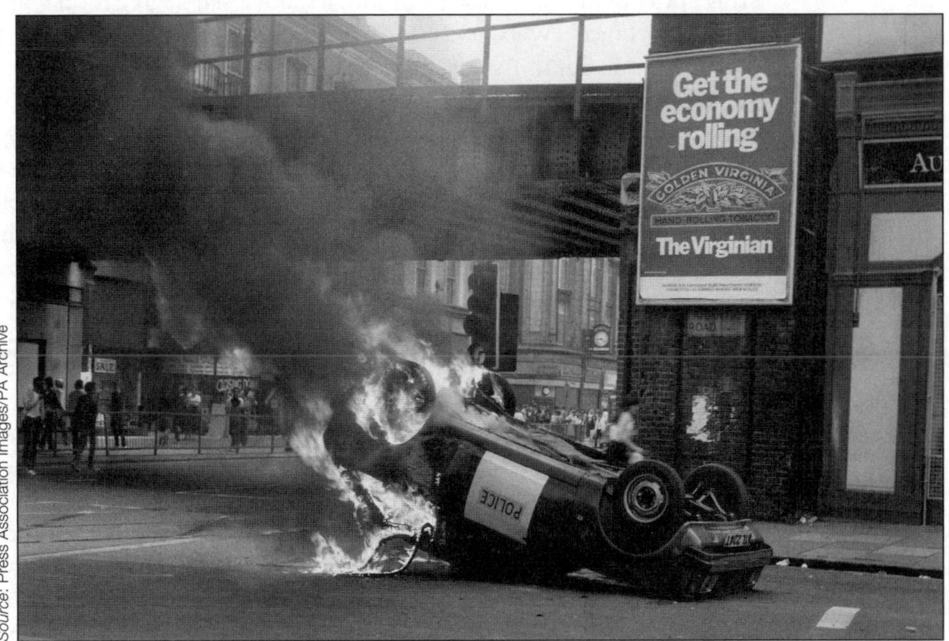

Source: Press Association Images/PA Archive

The riots in Bradford in July 2001 were associated with Asian youths.

This was also linked to a number of disturbances involving Asian youth. Asians had been involved in disturbances, often linked to protecting their communities from racism and resisting far right political activity (Webster 2007). From the mid 1980s to early 1990s racist violence against Asians increased alongside allegations that Asian young men were involved in street rebellion, gang violence, crime and drugs (Webster 1997; 2007). Disorders in 1995 were associated with Asian young men wishing to protect young Asian women in their areas from public prostitution, drunkenness, rowdiness and intimidation, all of which they felt the police were failing to do (Webster 2007). In 2001, separate incidents took place in the Northern English towns of Bradford, Burnley and Oldham involving largely Pakistani and Bangladeshi youth. A variety of factors were associated with these incidents including (Webster 2007; Grover 2008):

- Self-defence against perceived threats of right-wing political activity;
- Poor relationships between Asian and white groups particularly in Bradford;
- Poverty and social exclusion were stressed in reports in Burnley and Oldham;
- Cultural differences and the self-segregation of Asian people involving parallel lives (Cantle 2001, cited in Grover 2008: 135).

The Home Office-commissioned Cantle Report of 2001 focused largely on what was perceived to be the self-segregation of the Asian community who were very distinct in terms of language, religion and employment and had separate community bodies and social and cultural networks. Some saw this as a result of multicultural policies.

These notions were contested. While few dispute that there are, particularly in the North of England, high levels of residential concentration amongst Asian groups, this does not amount to segregation, let alone self-segregation which implies an element of 'choice' (Webster 2003). Segregation can be attributed to a combination of other factors. South Asians, argues Webster (2003; 2007), share the housing aspirations of all groups and want to move to more affluent areas. There has been some dispersal but 'out' movements have not exceeded the expanding, often younger, population in traditional areas of settlement. In a process often described, misleadingly, as 'white flight', more affluent white residents who are more able to obtain social housing move out. Moreover, in many Northern English towns, the decline of the textile industry and the overall effects of de-industrialization impacted most severely on Pakistani and Bangladeshi communities. This, coupled with discrimination in housing policy, trapped some groups in the most deprived areas, a concentration more visible in smaller towns than larger ones, producing what Webster (2003) describes as 'colour coded' areas.

Webster (2003) relates these processes to relative deprivation and to Young's (1999; 2007a) analysis of social exclusion outlined in previous chapters. As Young stresses, borders are not fixed and boundaries between adjacent areas become symbolic. Disturbances often occur at the borders between colour-coded areas and are strongly affected by often 'mythical' perceptions of inequality and relative deprivation and local histories of Asian resistance to racism. The police are often seen as unable or unwilling to protect Asian communities. In Oldham, for example, there were so-called 'no go' areas. The disturbances could, therefore, only be explained by understanding the specific local historical, cultural and economic context of the locality within which there were 'local geographies of fear'. Official views which stressed notions of self-segregation, Asian cultural separateness and the failure of multiculturalism thereby downplayed the role of racial, social and economic disadvantage. To Grover (2008), culture was seen as both the cause and the solution, through calls for more integration and assimilation, and emphasizing the role of 'Britishness'.

Violent racism and 'hate crime'

Many of these themes are also relevant to analyses of violent racism, which, argues Bowling (1999: 307, cited in Francis 2007a: 111), should be regarded 'as a form of racism rather than a form of violence'. As outlined above, one problem with this term is the extent to which it can involve white as well as black victims, particularly as there have been more widespread reports of crimes involving white victims. The definitions outlined in Box 10.4 reflect some of these issues, and defining offences according to victims' definitions includes white victims. The term 'hate crime' is also used although it is viewed as a difficult (Hall 2005) and indeed 'slippery' (Iganski 2008: 1) term. Hate is difficult to define, and many so-called 'hate' crimes are not associated with strong feelings of hatred. Its use reflects an assumption that hate crimes 'hurt more' (Iganski 2008: 6), reflected in the heavier sentences attracted by racially aggravated offences, although these can be criticized as unequal (Hall 2005; Iganski 2008). Hate crime is a wider term than violent racism as it can encompass crimes based on elements of sexuality, religion, disability or nationality. For reasons of space and consistent with the focus of this chapter, this section will focus primarily on crimes involving race and ethnicity although their interrelationship with other factors is recognized.

The nature of violent racism

Some features of these offences were discussed above and are summarized in Box 10.5, although it was argued that these figures cannot fully reflect the nature, extent and particularly the impact of violent racism. As is the case for other forms of violence, violent racism ranges along a continuum. At the most extreme end lie the genocides and ethnic cleansing which will be discussed in Chapter 17, followed by the racist murders such as those outlined in Box 10.6. While racist killings are relatively rare in Britain, at least 62 murders between 1970 and 1982 were attributed to race hate (Iganski 2008: 14) and Iganski details a number of murders in the 1990s and 2000s with black, Asian and asylum-seeking victims which have involved allegations of racial motivation.

At the other end of the continuum lie a plethora of more everyday incidents involving name-calling, verbal abuse and pushing and shoving. Iganski (2008) points out that many incidents take place in the context of everyday encounters, and few incidents lead to physical harm. Webster (2007: 87) reports that many interviewees described racial conflict as 'just fighting between individuals and groups of young people'. In Scotland most recorded incidents take place in the street, shops and houses and involve minor assaults, fire-raising and vandalism (Scottish Government 2009c).

This should not, however, be taken to downplay the distressing effects of these incidents which can be regular features of the experiences of minority ethnic individuals (Bowling 1999). A study by Chahal and Julienne (1999) in Glasgow, Belfast, Cardiff and London reports that incidents were too numerous for respondents to remember and accurately count. The potential impact of these persistent incidents was starkly illustrated in an East London survey which found that in six months thirty Bengali families experienced on average four and a half attacks. One family reported a sequence of stone-throwing, chasing, being threatened and prevented from entering their flat, being punched and verbally abused and armed robbery. The continual threat of harassment and violence meant that most of the women were afraid to go out and many children were not allowed to play outside (Sampson and Phillips 1992). Chahal and Julienne (1999) found similar instances and that the fear of being a victim of racist harassment shaped the quality of people's lives. Children became isolated and family and friends were reluctant to visit areas with a high risk of victimization. In one Scottish study respondents perceived an increase in incidents following 9/11 and 7/7, which permeated their general feelings of safety (Frondigoun et al 2007). Many blamed media coverage of terrorist incidents and stereotypes – they were called 'Bin Laden' or told to go 'back to Afghanistan'.

Gender is also a factor. Images of black women's sexuality are racialized and expressed in verbal abuse and Pakistani women, for example, are taunted with being Paki 'whores'. In one study, young women wearing headscarves noted more 'looks' which made them feel uncomfortable (Frondigoun et al 2007). Perceived racism against Asian women can contribute to the development of informal, vigilante-style groups, giving the impression of interracial violence (Webster 1997). Chahal and Julienne (1999) point out that the impact of racial harassment is often more severe on women who are at home than on men who are out at work. Spalek et al (2009) found that female victims of domestic violence in some Muslim communities are more reluctant to report violence fearing that their religious beliefs and their reluctance to break marriage vows will not be taken into account.

Who commits violent racist offences?

While information is sparse, there are strong indications that perpetrators of racist violence are rarely stereotypical racist bigots allied to right-wing extremist groups (Iganski 2008). Studies indicate a preponderance of youthful offenders, including those as young as 12. Webster (2001) identified a group of 'violent racists' aged between 12 and 21 from a socially disadvantaged housing estate, who displayed aggressive racism whenever they encountered Asians. Chahal and Julienne (1999), on the basis of victim reports, also identify children, with the approval of their parents, as being perpetrators. Ray et al (2004) in Manchester found that most offenders knew their victims, were very rarely 'specialists' in racial violence and came from disadvantaged backgrounds (see Box 10.8). Many came from disrupted backgrounds, lacked educational qualification, most were unemployed and none had a well-paid or highly skilled job.

Explaining racist violence

A number of interrelated explanations have been advanced for racist violence and hate crime (Bowling 1999; Bowling and Phillips 2002; Francis 2007a; Iganski 2008) including:

- *Socio-economic deprivation and marginalization* have been related to perceived competition over scarce resources, in which 'they' are perceived to have advantages which 'we' don't have. Empirically, however, links with social deprivation are not conclusive. While some forms of racist violence are concentrated in areas

Box 10.8 Racially violent offenders

In a study of racially violent offenders Ray et al (2004) found that:

- Many were from disadvantaged backgrounds and had been adversely affected by the decline of local industries which meant that few could aspire to former masculine role models.
- Their main encounters with South Asians were with those who ran businesses and who were therefore perceived to be more successful and as having unfair advantages in relation to social security and housing.
- Racism was denied as a main motive for offending, even when racist abuse was used, although offenders spoke 'uninhibitedly' about their violence which was clearly a 'routine strategy of domination or survival' to many (p. 354).
- Their attitudes reflected deeply embedded and taken for granted local and cultural racism, feelings of defensive territoriality and fears of being swamped.
- Their actions can be explained in terms of emotions, including shame at their own failure to achieve and feelings of grievance, unfairness and powerlessness when comparing their situation to Asians.
- Asians were seen as taking over businesses, as making money while not being 'hard grafters' whereas blacks seen as more macho and 'like us' (p. 356).
- Violence represented an attempt to re-establish control and to take revenge. To the authors, the contrast between community decline and economic exclusion in their area and the consumer-centred city life in central Manchester provides a context in which

  > real deprivation and the collapse of traditional local employment have thrown traditional ways of making sense of experience into confusion. Communities once defined by the shared experience of the manufacturing industry lose coherence and stability along with affluence; long cherished cultural expectations of working class masculinity become unrealizable with the erosion of their material basis; and the inherited meanings of territory and neighbourhood become fractured and uncertain'. (p. 364)

of high social deprivation, it also occurs in rural, suburban and relatively prosperous areas. Iganski (2008) did not find a significantly higher number of incidents in London boroughs with high levels of socio-economic disadvantage. Moreover, argue Bowling and Phillips (2002) violence itself is not always linked to periods of economic recession. Nonetheless, as will be seen below, social deprivation and exclusion are major factors linked to others.

- *The size of, and perceived increases in, minority ethnic groups in specific areas* have been associated with assumptions that violence is related to perceptions of 'too many' immigrants in a locality. This is, however, argue Bowling and Phillips (2002), a flawed argument. Historically, even very small minority groups have faced racist violence, and it also fails to explain violence against Jewish people. It is possible, they argue, that in some areas violence may increase along with increasing numbers of minority groups and that it constitutes a form of white territorialism. In London, Iganski (2008) found some relationship between 'race-hate victimization' and traditionally white strongholds which had experienced a sudden growth of residents from minority ethnic communities.

- *The activities of extreme right-wing organizations*, particularly those who are now able to organize themselves globally on the Internet have also been seen as a factor. While evident in some high-profile cases, it is not a major factor in the majority of everyday incidents (Iganski 2008).
- *The role of national cultures* might explain variations across countries – the Holocaust, for example, could have been seen as a peculiarly German phenomenon. It is also possible, suggest Bowling and Phillips (2002: 117), that colonialism, slavery and support for South African apartheid might indicate a 'specifically English cultural variant' of violent racism.
- *Alcohol* and drunkenness feature in many incidents, but this is the case for violent crime in general and it is unlikely to affect levels of racism (Bowling and Phillips 2002).

It is likely, therefore, that a combination of factors is involved. Iganski (2008) argues that some offenders may be linked to extreme right-wing groups and ideologies, whereas others are more affected by social disadvantage. Webster (2007) identified a 'continuum' of 'normal' 'aggressive' and 'violent' racists and some were involved in other forms of criminality. Many also stress that racist views are normal and that perceptions of advantage and disadvantage are deeply embedded in the cultures into which young people are socialized. To Webster, widespread racist hostility legitimizes violence. Iganski (2008: 31) argues that anti-Jewish incidents reflect a 'commonsense' 'anti-Semitism' which can be triggered by some assumed grievance or irritation and he further argues that many forms of 'hate crime' derive from 'stocks of knowledge which constitute a structural edifice of bigotry' (p. 39). Indeed, he argues, the ordinariness of many incidents in this cultural context is more uncomfortable than attributing violent racism to a smaller group of identifiably bigoted individuals. Some of these complexities are well illustrated in Ray et al's (2004) discussion of research carried out in Manchester, summarized in Box 10.8, which resonates with many of the themes above and of earlier chapters. It also underlines the importance of looking at the local historical and economic context.

Discussion

Relationships between race, ethnicity, crime and victimization are, therefore, especially complex. Previous research was somewhat narrow and has left some areas relatively underexplored, and there has been a tendency to use very generalized terms such as 'black', BME, 'white' or 'british' which neglects many variations and can perpetuate false dichotomies and essentialism. A final point to be considered is the significance of race in comparison to other important factors such as socio-economic status, gender and age.

A minority perspective?

Phillips and Bowling (2003) express a number of these criticisms in a call for a 'minority' perspective in criminology. There is a need, they argue, to move away from the 'polemical and now sterile' race and crime debate towards a more multi-dimensional approach to understanding minorities' experiences of victimization, offending and criminal justice (p. 270). This would involve more qualitative research focusing on the 'lived experiences' of minority communities and a reorientation of theory and methodology. In arguing for a minority as opposed to a 'black' perspective, they want to move away from essentialist categories and recognize that hate crime can incorporate non-racial minorities. Minorities should themselves be involved in collaborative research which would involve a historical understanding and a recognition that

> 'processes of social and economic marginalization not only have consequences for involvement in deviant behaviour among minority groups, but these are compounded by policing and criminal justice processes'. Phillips and Bowling (2003: 278)

Along with others (Hudson 2007), Phillips and Bowling argue that criminologists have been reluctant to explore 'taboo' questions. There has, for example, been little work focusing on BME offending. In much the same way that female offenders have been cast as victims of gendered violence and feminized poverty, BME offenders are cast as victims of discrimination and violent racism. It is also the case that, even allowing for moral panics and criminalization, some patterns of criminality are associated with racial and ethnic groups. Already mentioned has been the more prominent involvement of black people in gun crime, and immigrant groups such as Chinese Triads, the Italian and later the Russian 'mafia' and the Jamaican Yardies along with others are involved in organized crime, trafficking and the drugs industry; this in turn is related to global economic and social factors and the disadvantaged situation of immigrant groups (see Chapter 14). The differential involvement of different groups in different kinds of crime could also become an invaluable means of exploring the role of identities and culture in relation to crime patterns. Cultural criminologists, for example, focus on a variety of youth cultures, and the role of ethnic cultures is also worthy of exploration. To avoid essentialism, Phillips and Bowling argue that any such research should be comparative and ensure that there is no reification of race or ethnicity. A study, for example, of robbery, identified with an over-representation of black offenders, should compare black and white offenders.

The diversity of ethnic groups

It is also crucial to explore the heterogeneity of minority groups and to move away from broad categorizations of black or Asian. There are many other groups and Phillips and Bowling also call for more research on diverse issues such as anti-Semitic violence, violence against refugees, asylum seekers, travelling communities, and groups from the New Accession countries – who may also be subject to racism from older established minority groups. In addition, the experiences and identities of third and fourth generation members of minority groups may be very different from other generations. Young Asians in Scotland, for example, argued that they would be less likely to 'put up with' racism than their elders, and reacted strongly against verbal harassment such as exhortations to 'go home' – to them, Scotland is 'home' (Frondigoun et al 2007). They are also more likely to adopt 'hybrid' identities, such as Scottish Muslim or Scottish Pakistani – visibly illustrated by Scottish entertainers wearing tartan turbans and young Asian and black men wearing kilts (Croall and Frondigoun 2010).

This raises a less often discussed feature of British work on race, ethnicity and crime, which is that it is almost entirely about England and makes few references to the different situations in Scotland or Northern Ireland, which have had fewer instances of urban disturbances involving racist elements but where sectarianism may be more relevant. Yet as seen above, racist incidents in both these jurisdictions have risen since the 1990s although they remain lower than England – perceptions echoed by Asian youth in one study, on the basis of their family networks, that things were 'worse' in the north of England (Frondigoun et al 2007). There is, therefore, considerable scope for comparisons across Britain exploring the interrelated effects of historical, demographic, cultural and socio-economic factors. To references to 'Englishness' or 'Britishness', should be added discussions of 'Scottishness', 'Irishness' or 'Welshness'. These can in themselves become the basis of 'racist' or hate crime which, in Scotland and Wales, emerges as 'Anglophobia' and of course the Irish, as seen above, have long been subject to criminalization.

While not discussed at length in this chapter, religion can also be significant. In Northern Ireland and the West of Scotland areas can be 'colour coded' as 'blue' and 'green', reflecting Protestants and Catholics, and be associated with hate crime. Some verbal abuse against young Asians is based on the assumption that they are Muslim and may be worse for men with beards and women wearing hijabs. The anti-Semitic incidents described by Iganski (2008) could be triggered by the wearing of a yarmulke. Phillips and Bowling's minority perspective would also extend to such issues.

The significance of race?

A final question relates to the significance of race in comparison to other forms of inequality. It can be seen that in many areas the stereotypical offender is the young black male from a low socio-economic background. Which is the most important factor? Youth, maleness, socio-economic status or race? Some instances of apparently racist violence may be little different to low-level fighting, defence of urban territory or other forms of incivility. These kinds of incidents are more likely to involve young men and to occur in socially deprived areas, and the impact of de-industrialization and changes in local economies has been stressed throughout other chapters. Like any other offenders, individuals in minority ethnic groups may commit crime for economic reasons and to achieve some form of desired status, thrills and excitement. Nonetheless, the impact of de-industrialization and changes in cities have impacted more severely on some minority ethnic groups, and perceptions that 'they' are gaining an unfair advantage draw on deeply rooted cultural racism. It can also be argued that race and racism provide an additional dimension in shaping young people's identities and the different cultures and subcultures to which they belong, which may in turn affect motivations to commit crime and the kind of illegitimate opportunities open to them. Race and ethnicity are therefore interrelated with other characteristics but can be seen as an added dimension.

Concluding comments

This chapter has explored many aspects of the often-contested relationship between race, ethnicity and crime. Exploring this issue is particularly complex due to the problems of clearly defining race and ethnicity, obtaining useful information about its relationship with crime and establishing to what extent a 'race factor' can explain any variations in offending or victimization. Very much as victimization is gendered, it can also be racist and, as with other forms of violence, seemingly trivial incidents can have considerable effects. Race has formed a major part in popular constructions of crime and particularly vulnerable, marginal, minority groups have been subject to criminalization. The chapter also explored areas of urban unrest and hate crime, finding that these are related to many similar factors to other crimes, notably the impact in recent decades of the decline in many industries and the growth of social deprivation – which, when combined with the effects of relative deprivation can produce both urban unrest and hate crime. Despite the considerable volume of work on the topic, however, many areas remain relatively unexplored with less attention having been paid to minority ethnic offenders and the factors which might lead to crime, and there has been a tendency to ignore variations between minority ethnic groups and between different parts of the UK. Exploring these variations could in itself vastly increase our understanding of this complex topic. Finally, it was seen that race is intricately interrelated with other aspects of social inequality, and this will be seen in later chapters dealing with specific patterns of crime.

Review questions

1. Using local newspaper reports along with your own perceptions and those of your friends and neighbours, consider the extent to which crime has been racialized in your own local area.
   - (a) Are some kinds of crime attributed to particular racial or minority ethnic groups?
   - (b) Are particular areas associated with racial or ethnic 'problems'?
   - (c) How are these constructed?
   - (d) How can experiences in your local area be related to discussions of the significance of race as a factor in crime and victimization?
   - (e) How do they relate to other dimensions of inequality such as age, class or gender? (This may be related to your answers to the questions in Chapter 7.)

   If you cannot identify any such areas or experiences, why do you think that this is the case?
2. Locate and critically evaluate data on experiences of racial victimization and fears and worries about crime among different racial and ethnic groups. How do they illustrate some of the points made in sections on this topic?
3. Outline the main points of the 'race and crime' debate. Why has it been criticized as being too narrow?
4. List some of the factors used to explain racist violence. How can they be combined and how are other criminogical perspectives relevant?

Key reading

The best contemporary sources for this topic are:

Bhui, H. S. (ed.) (2009) ***Race and Criminal Justice,*** London: Sage. This very useful collection contains a series of articles on defining and constructing race with analyses of the move away from multiculturalism, along with work covering policing, the criminalization of asylum seekers and many other policy issues.

Iganski, P. (2008) ***'Hate' Crime and the City,*** Bristol: Policy Press. An interesting and thought-provoking book on the concept of hate crime and a discussion of empirical research looking at aspects of it in London.

Phillips, C. and Bowling, B. (2007) 'Ethnicities, Racism, Crime and Criminal Justice' in M. Maguire, R. Morgan, and R. Reiner (eds), *The Oxford Handbook of Criminology* 4th edn, Oxford: Clarendon Press. A thorough and comprehensive introduction to the main issues involved in this topic with an analysis of available information and an account of the main theoretical approaches.

Webster, C. (2007) ***Understanding Race and Crime,*** Maidenhead, Berkshire: McGraw Hill, Open University Press. A good and comprehensive text containing useful analyses, in particular of the association of Asian young people and crime based on the author's own research.

Chapter 11
Violent crime

This chapter will look at

- ➜ Definitions and constructions of violence
- ➜ The scope of violent crime
- ➜ Homicide
- ➜ Domestic violence and abuse
- ➜ Political violence and terrorism
- ➜ Understanding violent crime

Violent crime is the most threatening form of crime and arouses the strongest emotional reactions. Official figures, however, suggest that serious violent offences form a relatively small proportion of reported and recorded crime, although as with other forms of crime they do not necessarily provide an accurate picture. Violent crime ranges from relatively minor assaults to mass murder and takes place in many settings: in public, at home, at work, on the football pitch and in pubs, clubs, schools and hospitals. While, as outlined in Chapter 2, offenders are often represented as 'crazed' or as 'psychos', many forms of violence are a regular feature of everyday life and previous chapters have already suggested that it can be linked to interrelated features of gender, age, class and race.

This chapter will largely focus on those forms of violent crime included in official categories, omitting sexual violence which is the subject of Chapter 12. It is recognized that these categorizations omit serious forms of violence such as state and corporate violence, explored in later chapters. It will start by looking at how violent crime is socially constructed and at the extent of officially recorded violent crime. It will then explore three selective and contrasting aspects of violent crime in more depth including murder, arguably the most serious form of violent crime, violence in the home along with political violence and the perceived threat of 'new terrorism'. Finally it will explore the ways in which criminological perspectives have been applied to violent crime.

What is violent crime?

Violent crime is categorized in different ways. Statistics and police-recorded crime figures currently divide it into three main categories: violence against the person, sexual offences and robbery. Violence against the person is further divided into 'more serious' offences such as homicide and more serious wounding and it includes 'other offences' such as common assault, harassment and assaults on a constable. Broadly speaking, these official categories deal with interpersonal violence and Jones (2000: 4) describes violence generally as the 'infliction of physical injury by force'. Many questions can, however, be asked about constructions of violence, and which forms of violence are regarded as 'crime'.

Constructions of violence

Instrumental or expressive violence?

Violence can be instrumental, used to further financial gain, or expressive, in which violence is the main feature of the offence (Brookman 2003). It is difficult in practice to separate these elements. Individuals engaging in serious organized crime, for example, might choose to use violence because they experience an 'added' thrill, whereas others deliberately avoid violent confrontations (Stanko 1994; Hobbs 1995; and see Chapters 13 and 14).

Must violence be physical?

While violence is most often associated with physical harm, it is increasingly recognized that it also involves psychological and emotional harm forming a continuum ranging from name-calling, abuse or harassment through to actual injury (Kelly 1988) and the *threat* of violence can be equally as distressing as physical harm.

Violence or abuse?

Many forms of violence in the home were formerly regarded as 'abuse' rather than 'crime' which to some implied that they were less serious. More recently, some prefer the term 'abuse' as it acknowledges the emotional and psychological impact of violence and its threat (see below).

What do official categories leave out?

It has widely been argued that official constructions of violence, which focus on interpersonal violence perpetrated by individuals, leave out many forms including:

- *Institutional and corporate violence*: Deaths and other harms result from institutional policies and practices such as, for example, the neglect of quality, safety or environmental regulations (Wells 1993; Levi et al 2007; and see Chapter 15). These do not fit the social construction of violence as there is no specific intent to harm individual victims (Tombs 2007).

- *State violence*: Wars, which contain the most extreme forms of violence, involve 'war crimes' such as genocide, 'ethnic cleansing', mass rape and torture (see Chapter 17). A very fine line also divides *legitimate 'force'* from *illegitimate violence*, particularly in relation to the activities of, for example, police and army officers (McLaughlin 1996; and see Chapter 17).
- *Political violence*: A very narrow line also divides the political violence of state agencies used against dissidents from the 'terrorism' perpetrated by those who seek to overthrow governments. It will be seen below that the term 'terrorist' is highly contested.
- *Violence against non-human animals*: Conceptions of violence focus on human, as opposed to non-human animals and different definitions of 'cruelty' are used (Beirne 1999; 2007).
- *Violence against nature*: To criminologists advocating a 'green criminology', activities which contribute to the destruction of the planet, such as environmental degradation, can also be constructed as violence (White 2008; Walters 2010a; and see Chapter 16).

Official categories of violent crime refer, therefore, only to some forms of violence. They overemphasize public violence and underemphasize violence in the home, the violence of official agencies and the dangerous practices of institutions (Stanko 1994; Kelly and Radford 1996; Tombs 2007). In so doing they misrepresent the 'real' amount and impact of violent crime. Violence carries many different meanings depending on its context and to Stanko (2003: 3), 'what violence means is and will always be fluid, not fixed'.

The scope of violent crime

Research issues

Many of the problems of researching and assessing the extent of violent crime have already been referred to. It could be assumed that, because violence threatens or causes injury, it is more likely to be reported to the police, but this is not the case. Many incidents involving injuries are not reported and even where medical attention is required may be treated as accidents due to, for example, embarrassment, fear of reprisal or feelings that the incident is too trivial. Victims may also feel that they themselves provoked an attack. It was also outlined in Chapter 6 that the BCS under-represents violence in the home and different survey methodologies use different definitions and time periods making comparison difficult. Official measurements also reveal little about the nature and context of violence. Assaults, for example, can be sexually or racially motivated and take place at home, at work, in the pub, at a football match or in the street – all of which have very different meanings.

Officially recorded violent crime

Some of the main features of official statistics on violent crime have already been noted (Chapters 3 and 6) and they and others are outlined in Box 11.1. In general violent crime accounts for about a fifth of all reported crime with slightly higher rates in Scotland. Men, particularly lower-class young men, dominate violent crime, as both victims and perpetrators. Women are more likely to be victimized in the home and men by strangers. Stranger violence between men, which can end up as homicide, is likely to take place in urban areas and in pubs and clubs (Levi et al 2007). Some occupational groups have higher rates of violent victimization with the police topping the list followed by health and social welfare professions (Levi et al 2007). Around half of violent crimes in England and Wales do not involve injuries and a minority in all jurisdictions are counted as 'serious' and involve serious injuries.

Box 11.1 Features of violent crime

England and Wales, 2007/8

- Violent crime accounts for 21 per cent of BCS crime, and 19 per cent of police-recorded crime.
- Half of violent crime involves no injury.
- Most serious violence against the person (involving intended or inflicted injuries) represents 2 per cent.
- Between 2006/2007 and 2007/8 BCS reported violent crime fell by 12 per cent as did Police Recorded 'most serious violence'.
- The number of violent incidents has fallen by half since 1995 and violent crime is now at a similar level to 1981.
- The risk of being a victim of violent crime in the 2007/08 BCS was 3.2 per cent; men were almost twice as likely as women to have experienced violent crime and 87 per cent of violent incidents involved male offenders.

(Home Office Statistical Bulletin: *Crime in England and Wales* (2007/08). Available at: *http://www.homeoffice.gov.uk/rds/pdfs08/hosb0708.pdf*)

Scotland: the SCJS (Walker et al 2009) 2008–9 indicates risk rates of:

- 4 per cent for violent crime for all adults;
- Less than one half of one per cent for being a victim of serious assault;
- Less than one half of one per cent for being a victim of robbery;
- 40 per cent of victims of violent crime were not injured, with younger victims and those in the most deprived areas being more likely to suffer an injury;
- Only 7 per cent of victims suffered head injuries, broken bones or internal injuries.

Northern Ireland (PSNI 2010):

- In 2008–9, a total of 29,468 offences against the person were recorded of which 12,696 were assault occasioning actual bodily harm and 791 involved grievous bodily harm;
- Most categories of violent crime indicated a decrease.

As seen in Chapter 3, the processes underlying reporting and recording offences along with variations in classifications, most notably the inclusion from 1998 of more minor assaults within the figures, make interpreting trends particularly difficult (Levi et al 2007). Taking a long-term view, rates of violent crime in the twentieth century were far lower than previous centuries, although there were strong indications of a rise from the mid 1950s to the mid 1990s, followed by an overall decline with some fluctuations for different kinds of violent crime. These fluctuations may, suggest Levi et al (2007), reflect changes in forms of violence such as the rise of public violence associated with the night-time economy outlined in Chapter 8.

There has recently been public concern about apparent increases in the use of firearms and knives, although these affect a very small proportion of offences and more often involve the use of airguns rather than more lethal weapons (Levi 2007). Some figures in relation to the use of knives are outlined in Box 11.2. While they are used in a number of homicides it is important to bear in mind that figures relate to the relatively small proportion of serious violent offences. Nonetheless, carrying knives for protection does give some grounds for concern, particularly in Scotland,

Box 11.2 Knife crime?

'Knife crime' is difficult to define and measure and claims of increases are hard to justify as few systematic statistics were gathered before it was defined as a particular problem. It can be used to describe a variety of offences, varying in severity from carrying a knife for protection in a public place to producing a knife as a weapon during the course of a robbery or sexual assault (Royal Armouries Museum December 2007).

England and Wales: the **2007–8 BCS** indicates that:

- For selected serious violence categories, 19 per cent involved knives.
- Knives were involved in 37 per cent of all cases of wounding with intent to do grievous bodily harm and attempted murder.
- Sharp instruments (which need not be knives) were involved in 35 per cent of recorded homicides in 2006/07.
- The proportion of violent incidents where a knife was used has remained at or below 8 per cent since 1995.
- Surveys suggest that around 3 per cent of young people aged 10 to 25 had carried a knife in the last 12 months for their own protection (the most common reason), for use in crimes, or in case they got into a fight. The most commonly carried knife was a penknife (46 per cent).

(*Crime in England and Wales* 2007/08. Available at: *http://www.homeoffice.gov.uk/rds/pdfs08/hosb0708.pdf*)

- In *Scotland* 'knife crime' is also perceived to be a major problem, with figures suggesting that knives were used in almost half of homicides between 1981 and 2003 (Leyland 2006).
- In *Northern Ireland* (Northern Ireland Office 2006), violent crime involving knives was said to have increased in 2005/2006 with knives being used in 44 murders in the period 2001/02 to 2005/06 and in 27 attempted murders. While violent knife crime increased between 2004 and 2005, there has been a decrease since 2002.

although again it is important to note that only a minority of young people are involved.

Varieties of violent crime

Homicide

Homicide is perhaps the most fascinating of all crimes and its prominence in classical and popular literature and drama was discussed in Chapter 2. The different social meanings of murder are reflected in terms such as matricide, infanticide, patricide or fratricide which imply family relationships, femicide a gendered relationship, assassination a political motive, and manslaughter a less deliberate killing. Contrary to popular perceptions, few involve violent gangs or sexual motivations and most occur in more mundane settings (D'Cruze et al 2006).

Defining and counting homicide

Legal classifications of homicide include murder, manslaughter and, in England and Wales, infanticide (Brookman 2005; 2010; D'Cruze et al 2006), although a very fine line divides 'murder' from 'accidents', 'licensed killings' by law enforcers or euthanasia. Contrary to what might be assumed, not all murders are reported. Some deaths, particularly of the terminally ill, may be cases of euthanasia (Levi 1997) and, more gruesomely, not all bodies are discovered and some 'missing persons' are murder victims (Brookman 2005). As for violence in general, homicide rates declined in the twentieth century, although there has been a steady increase in England and Wales since the mid 1960s.

Homicide rates vary across Britain. Scotland and Northern Ireland have a higher rate than England and Wales, and Glasgow and Belfast have high rates for individual cities. Northern Ireland's rate is affected by the Troubles without which it becomes more similar to the rest of the UK (Soothill et al 1999, cited in Brookman 2005). Deaths due to the Troubles have fallen and five deaths were associated with the security situation in 2008–9 (Northern Ireland Office 2010). Scotland's, and particularly Glasgow's, high rate has been associated with larger numbers of male confrontational homicide and more use of lethal weapons, with more violent incidents being likely to end in murder (Brookman 2005). Latest Scottish figures suggest a recent decrease, with Glasgow's rate falling from a peak of 39 in 2003–4 to 24 in 2008–9 (BBC News 2010d). Although high in relation to other UK and many European cities, UK rates are relatively low compared with other countries. The world average homicide rate was, for example, 7.6 per 100,000 of the population in 2004–6, with England and Wales at 1.5, Northern Ireland at 1.8 and Scotland at 2.3, well below the average. Highest homicide rates are concentrated in Africa, with a rate of 69 per 100,000 in South Africa, the Caribbean, with a rate of 55.2 in Jamaica, and South America (Brookman 2010).

Despite popular mythology, most are now aware that the majority of homicides involve people known to each other, and members of families are often 'prime

Box 11.3 Types of homicide

Brookman (2005) constructed the following typology based on Home Office data from 1997–2001 indicating the percentages associated with each type as follows:

- **Domestic homicide** (31%) consisting of
  - male offender/female victim (76%)
  - female offender/male victim (19%)
  - sexual intimacy (where there was or had been an intimate sexual relationship between the victim and the offender) (17%)
  - family intimacy (14%).
- **Confrontational homicide** (male on male killings unrelated to one another) (22%);
- **Homicide in the course of another crime** (7%);
- **Gang homicide** (1%);
- **Context unknown** (23%);
- **Unusual cases** (serial killing/recklessness/others) (16%).

suspects'. Box 11.3, based on the Homicide Index, illustrates some of these points, also indicating the small proportions of gang homicides and serial killings. The main forms of homicide are briefly summarized below.

Confrontational homicide

Confrontational homicide involves men killing men, often in seemingly routine or trivial incidents. They have been described as 'contests of honour and lethal violence' (Daly and Wilson 1988), as 'quintessential masculine matters' Polk (1994: 183) and typically involve maintaining 'face'. Based on a study in England and Wales, Brookman (2003) distinguishes between:

- *Confrontational homicides* resulted from face-to-face encounters and arguments, could be seen as 'accidental' and involved no intent to kill. Participants had often been drinking and they took place in front of an audience. They can be characterized as an 'assault gone wrong'.
- *Revenge homicides* were associated with a perceived grievance or grudge, were premeditated and often took place in or near the victims' home. They involved situations in which formal avenues for redress were unavailable and offenders need to sustain an image (Brookman 2003; 2005).

In both types, each of which accounted for half of the total, the majority of offenders had previous convictions for violence and tended to be white and unemployed.

Femicide

Femicide involves men killing women and consists of intimate femicides in domestic settings (the majority) and stranger femicides, which account for less than 8 per cent of all homicides. Femicide accounts for under a third of homicides across Britain and over half involve women being killed by a current or former partner or boyfriend. Around two-thirds of stranger femicides occurred in the course of another crime such as robbery or involved reckless drivers, leading Brookman (2005: 147) to conclude that the majority 'bear no relation to the commonly held notion of a stranger lurking in an alleyway ready to pounce upon an unsuspecting victim'.

Intimate partner femicide is often related to separation and attributed to jealousy with accounts in court reflecting the theme, '*if I can't have her, no one can*' (Lees 1992). Brookman (2005) further suggests a distinction between long-term partnerships and more spontaneous 'sudden rage' homicides involving less well-established couples. Feminists have linked these kinds of killings to men's assumption of ownership over women.

Women who kill

Brookman (2005) summarizes the characteristics of homicides committed by women which constitute around 11 per cent of homicides across the UK. Those with intimate partner (32 per cent) or child victims form the majority. Women who kill are typically aged between 25 and 40 and are from lower-class backgrounds, are unemployed and have low educational levels. A knife or sharp weapon is often used and alcohol is often present. Killings of intimate partners most often follow persistent physical and sexual violence. Compared to domestic femicide, argues Brookman, women are not attempting to gain control over partners but to gain control from partners. A very small number are for sexual or financial motives.

Women who kill are generally portrayed as either 'mad' or 'bad' in responses structured by gender which, as seen in Chapter 2, portray them as more deviant than men (D'Cruze et al 2006) and despite the most common cases being domestic, atypical cases attract most attention. Female killers are often, argues Morrissey (2003), presented in courts and the media in ways which deny women any agency. They tend to be 'monsterized', portrayed as evil and inhuman, subject to mythification, or portrayed as powerless victims of oppression.

Murders of children

Child murders, as also outlined in Chapter 2, also attract considerable attention, particularly the least typical cases involving male strangers. As is often stressed, the majority of children who are killed are killed by parents, often at home. Overall, the murder of children under 16 constituted 14 per cent of homicides in England and Wales in 1995–2000, with 36 per cent involving children under one. Distinctions can be drawn between (Brookman 2005):

- *Female-perpetrated neonaticide* (killing within the first 24 hours of life): Almost all of these involve mothers killing babies. Mothers were often young, unprepared for an unplanned pregnancy and babies were passively killed by suffocation.
- *Female-perpetrated infanticide*: This is considered as a separate offence in England and Wales and has been strongly linked with post-partum depression.
- *Female-perpetrated fatal child abuse*: Around 1–2 child deaths per week result from persistent child abuse. Some also die in single incidents in which frustration

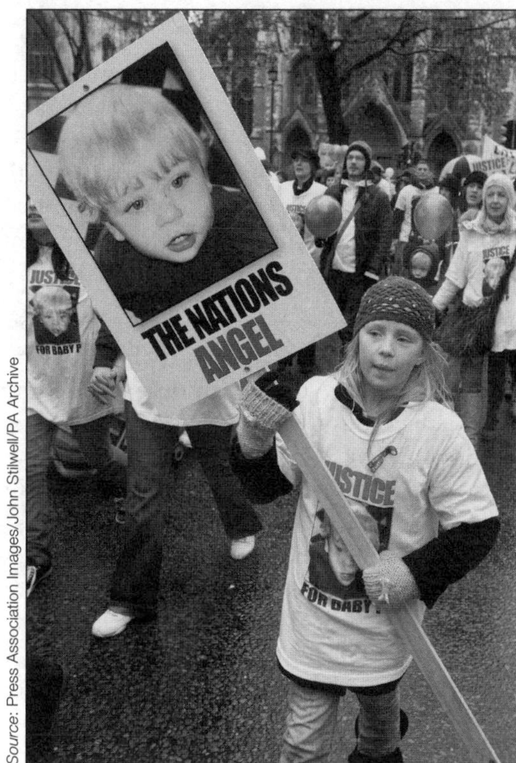

Source: Press Association Images/John Stilwell/PA Archive

Baby P's death following abuse by his parents attracted criticism of Haringey Social Services Department.

or aggression boils up, often linked to inadequate parenting skills. Some of these receive high-profile publicity which often highlights failings on the part of social services such as the case of Baby P, who died in 2007 after long-term abuse from his mother and her boyfriend.

- *Male-perpetrated paternal child homicide*: This takes two forms. Around half involve fatal assaults resulting from physical discipline. Filicide followed by suicide occurs when fathers kill children and then commit suicide. This has been linked to depression and to feelings of hopelessness, powerlessness and uselessness which can result from financial or employment difficulties and feelings of failure to live up to the expectations of fatherhood (Adler and Polk 2001, cited in Brookman 2005).
- *Male-perpetrated killing outside the family*: These form a minority of child killings. In 1995–2001 there were 32 cases involving 24 male and 8 female children (Brookman 2005). A quarter of these resulted from reckless driving or arson, and a further quarter involved teenagers and were broadly similar to confrontational homicides outlined above. A further quarter had no clear motive with five cases involving sexual motives. Thus, concludes Brookman (2005: 198), they amount on average to one child per year compared to 'around 40 sons, daughters or stepchildren killed by men'.
- *Children who kill children*: These are extremely rare despite the considerable attention given to cases such as the killing of James Bulger (see Chapter 2). Many 'children' who kill are in fact teenagers and again these are similar to the confrontational homicides outlined above.

Multiple murder

Multiple murder, involving three or more victims, is also rare. This section will focus on 'serial killing' although it can also involve corporate homicide (see Chapter 15) and deaths associated with terrorism (see below) (Brookman 2005). Almost 90 per cent of offenders are male, along with over half of victims. As with other murders, many victims are family members, acquaintances or friends and a high proportion of perpetrators kill themselves. Three main forms have been identified (Gresswell and Hollin 1994; Holmes and Holmes 1998; Brookman 2005):

- *Mass murder*: Killing three or more people at one time and in one place (Holmes and Holmes 1998), most typically a lone assassin killing several people. Typical offenders are 'pseudo commandos', young men obsessed with firearms, 'set and run' killers who plan a lethal episode and escape, 'psychotic killers', including leaders of cults who initiate mass suicides of 'disciples', and men who kill their family before committing suicide (Gresswell and Hollin 1994; Brookman 2005). They are often described as loners and almost always kill themselves afterwards.
- *Spree murder*: Killing three or more people over a period of less than 30 days. This takes place in different locations and perpetrators are most often male, described as impulsive and frenzied. They make little effort to evade detection and often kill themselves or are killed by the police.
- *Serial murder*: Killing three or more people over a period of more than 30 days, with a significant cooling-off period between killings (Holmes and Holmes 1998). It most typically involves repeated killing over a long time with no direct connection between killers and victims. Victims may come from an identifiable group such as prostitutes. Killers are often motivated by fantasies, seeing themselves as visionaries or missionaries.

There is little evidence to support popular perceptions that these forms of murder are increasing, and they are relatively rare in the UK, which has not seen the high-school shooting phenomenon associated with the US and elsewhere. Offenders tend to be pathologized as they are seen as so abnormal. In some cases, however, such as that of Dr Harold Shipman, outlined in Box 11.4, multiple murderers are indistinguishable from other members of the population.

Box 11.4 The case of Harold Shipman

Dr Shipman, a family doctor, is regarded as Britain's most prolific serial killer – convicted of only 15 murders but believed to have killed over 200. He does not fit into traditional criminological stereotypes, he was not poor, was well respected, held a well-respected job and was liked by his patients. Holmes & Holmes (1998) would categorize Shipman as a *power and control* serial killer who likes to have the power over life and death. He killed himself in prison, and as neither he nor his wife agreed to be interviewed, little is known about his likely motives (D'Cruze et al 2006). Coleman & Norris (2000) point out that Shipman was a highly regarded medical doctor in a society that reveres such a profession. Medical professions walk a thin line between being in control and taking control – perhaps they ask, Shipman fell off this line?

As so many murders result from fights, many domestic, they are very similar to other forms of violent crime. Some features do nonetheless stand out. Brookman (2010: 231) draws attention to the 'micro environment' of homicide which often involves alcohol, 'rage' and arguments which get out of hand. Alcohol is not an independent factor, as most people who drink do not kill, but, argues Brookman (2005: 156),

> young men, from similar backgrounds, coming together and consuming significant quantities of alcohol make for a potentially volatile mix as they mingle together with a shared emphasis on protecting and projecting a tough macho identity.

Murderers are particularly subject to pathologizing and being perceived as 'evil' (D'Cruze et al 2006), particularly where they challenge stereotypes of passive women or innocent children. Yet many murderers, along with perpetrators of extreme violence such as torture or genocide (see Chapter 17) appear rather ordinary. Indeed, Harold Shipman's 'evil' was in many ways linked to his ordinariness (D'Cruze et al 2006: 28). Describing killers, particularly mass killers, as psychopathic can be a circular argument with offenders assumed to be abnormal because their acts are so bizarre. It may be, argues Brookman (2010: 229), that some people simply like killing others. Levi et al (2007: 709) comment on one study (Dobash et al 2001) of convicted male killers, which found that although some had alcohol, drug or mental health problems they were very similar to the general prison population and a 'surprisingly large percentage did *not* appear to be mentally disturbed or to come from a severely dysfunctional family or personal background'. While mental illness does feature, particularly when, as seen above, parents kill children, these murders are also associated with failures to live up to idealized images of 'motherhood' or 'fatherhood' against which, particularly for lower-class parents, actual experiences fall short and lead to feelings of powerlessness and failure.

Structural factors such as gender and class are therefore important. The links between femicide and patriarchal ideas is evident as is the importance of 'honour'. The vast majority of homicides involve offenders and victims from primarily lower-class backgrounds and, more broadly, high homicide rates tend to be found in societies with higher levels of social inequality (Brookman 2010). It could therefore be suggested that men are more likely to use violence as a resource when other avenues to redress grievances are unavailable (Polk 1994; Brookman 2003; 2005) and Katz (1988) argues that affluent men are in a better position to escape humiliation. Other forms of homicide are also related to the stresses and strains of poverty and unemployment.

Domestic violence and abuse

It has been recognized for some time that the home, conventionally regarded as a refuge, is a major site of violence (Saraga 1996), and that 'the single most significant risk to women's safety. . . . is entering into a heterosexual partnership arrangement' (Wykes and Welsh 2009: 43). It was recognized in the nineteenth century when cruelty to children and wife battering were perceived as largely lower-class problems (Saraga 1996). Yet the home was seen as a private domain and indeed judges considered that men could legally chastise their wives for adultery or not fulfilling their role (Dobash and Dobash 1992). As seen in Chapter 8, concerns about children focused on delinquency, and child abuse was largely seen as a social welfare problem (Morgan and Zedner 1992; Parton 1985). This continued until after the Second World War, a period which idealized the nuclear family and parent and motherhood (Saraga 1996), although few dispute that there was violence in the home throughout this period. From the 1960s onwards it became far more widely recognized and feminist and other criminologists conducted what Hoyle (2007) describes as pioneering work, exposing and analysing different forms of family violence (see Chapter 6).

Assessing the extent of domestic violence

The terms used to refer to violence in the home have been considerably contested and have changed over time as illustrated in Box 11.5, and definitional issues affect what is counted in surveys. The limitations of victim surveys in relation to domestic violence were outlined in Chapter 6 and include their inability, due to the survey methodology, to capture its full impact as it represents a continuous state of affairs. Moreover, respondents may be unwilling or too embarrassed to divulge their experiences. Hoyle (2007) distinguishes between quantitative studies and feminist qualitative research, which focuses on the 'lived experiences' of victims. The BCS did adapt by using self-administered questionnaires and broadening questions to include aspects of emotional, sexual and 'partner abuse' and repeat victimization (Wykes and Welsh 2009). The different definitions do nonetheless mean that survey

Box 11.5 Domestic violence or abuse?

- Before the 1970s much violence in the home was described as 'abuse', a term criticized for downplaying elements of violence. Yet violence is most often associated with physical injury, which neglects the considerable emotional, psychological and economic harms which may not be regarded as 'criminal' or 'violent'.
- This has been recognized in victim surveys and official definition in England and Wales of domestic violence is now:

> Any incident of threatening behaviour, violence or abuse (psychological, physical, sexual, financial or emotional) between adults, aged 18 or over, who are or have been intimate partners or family members, regardless of gender or sexuality'.
>
> (cited by Robinson 2010: 245)

- Some Welsh publications (Robinson 2010) and the Scottish government now use the term 'domestic abuse' more widely, recognizing the need for a broader definition encompassing psychological, emotional, financial and social features (McMillan 2010).
- The term 'domestic' has also been criticized for restricting the definition to violence between partners in the home.
- Research has more recently focused mainly on 'intimate partners' and heterosexual couples although the term can also include violence involving children and parents, as in the Baby P case, same sex couples and those with disabilities.

Box 11.6 Selected aspects of domestic violence in the UK

England and Wales: the **2006–7 BCS** found that

- 7 per cent experienced domestic violence within the past year of which
- 59 per cent suffered abuse on more than one occasion and
- 9 per cent had been victimized more than 20 times in the last year.
- Lifetime prevalence studies indicate that 33 per cent of women and 22 per cent of men have been victims of domestic violence.

(Hoare and Jansson 2008, cited in Robinson 2010: 246)

Scotland: the police recorded a total of 53,861 incidents of domestic abuse in 2008/9 amounting to an incidence of 1,039 per 100,000 population (Scottish Government 2009a, cited in McMillan 2010).

- 84 per cent of victims were female, and perpetrators male.
- 61 per cent of victims had previously experienced domestic abuse
- 44 per cent on four or more occasions.

The SCJS (Scottish Government 2009b, cited in McMillan 2010) found:

- less than a fifth of all domestic abuse incidents were reported to the police
- an incidence rate of 5 per cent for all survey respondents and
- a prevalence rate, from age 16, of 18 per cent.

figures, such as those outlined in Box 11.6. must be interpreted extremely carefully and that comparisons over time and between countries are very difficult to make (Hoyle 2007; Wykes and Welsh 2009; Robinson 2010). This illustrates different ways of representing the extent of domestic violence with up to a third of women in England and Wales reporting having suffered from it during their lifetime.

Different methodologies, however, produce very different pictures. Considerable controversy has surrounded the findings of 'family violence studies' which suggest, contrary to feminist-inspired studies focusing on violence against women, a gender symmetry in which women's share of domestic violence equals that of men. This has attracted heavy criticism, in particular from Dobash and Dobash (2004), who make the following points:

- *Family violence studies* adopt an 'act based' approach which counts single instances of acts such as slaps, kicks or threats to leave as 'violent' without considering the context of these acts.
- *Violence against women* approaches look at a constellation of factors which, when combined, amount to violence.
- Following interviews with couples in which the male partner had been convicted of violence they concluded that while women did commit violent acts they were not as persistent or likely to involve injury. The men did not experience these acts as particularly violent.

Family violence studies therefore establish that violent acts take place in many homes but say little about the use of violence as a means of control. Men's violence is more likely to involve serious injury, whereas women's is more often in self-defence. Thus, argues Hoyle (2007: 151), women's violence differs from that of men in terms of its 'nature, frequency, intention, intensity, physical injury and emotional impact'.

Varieties of domestic violence

Domestic violence therefore takes many different forms and Hoyle (2007) cites work by Johnson (2000) which distinguishes between:

- *Common couple violence*, which is low in severity and takes the form of mutual violence arising out of specific arguments. There is no desire to control.
- *Intimate terrorism* is more serious and escalates over time. It normally involves a desire to control a partner and is almost exclusively male.
- *Violent resistance* primarily involves women fighting back or defending themselves and seeking to escape the relationship.
- *Mutual violent control* is relatively rare but underresearched and involves situations in which both partners are controlling and violent.

Family violence studies refer to what Dempsey (2006) describes as 'weak' forms of domestic violence such as common couple violence which do not involve the attempt to control which 'strong' forms do.

The controlling nature of male violence against women is well illustrated in qualitative studies such as the work of Liz Kelly (1988), in which women revealed the effects of threatened and actual violence often accompanied by forced sexual activity which undermined their self-confidence. Very often violence erupted in situations where men asserted control by criticizing women's performance of domestic duties or participating in work or education outside the home. Women experiencing such violence suffered a severe loss of confidence, autonomy and sense of self. Some experience mental breakdowns and many writers stress the serious consequences for women in terms of missing work and long-term health, mental and emotional problems (Robinson 2010). The combined nature of different kinds of abuse is illustrated in Robinson's (2010) Cardiff study in which women reported combinations of violence as follows:

- physical abuse, including being hit, kicked, choked or strangled (93 per cent);
- emotional abuse such as threats to family or friends or to take children away, along with repeated questions about women's activities and attempts to control what they wore or ate (98 per cent);
- financial abuse which extended beyond arguments over bills to tactics of control in which partners refused to work, generated shared debts and stole from women (64 per cent);
- sexual abuse including rape and pressure to have unwanted sex (25 per cent).

Women themselves can be blamed for seeming to tolerate violence as seen in the commonly asked question: '*Why does she stay?*' (Kelly 1988; Walklate 1989). To Walklate (1995: 1), rephrasing this question as '*Why doesn't she leave?*' reveals aspects of gendered power relationships and women's lives. Women may have no financial resources and may be afraid of losing their children. They may have nowhere else to go. They are often socially isolated by their partner's activities, and believe they can change him.

Gender and domestic violence

Many analyses of domestic violence draw on similar themes to those exploring both homicide and violence in general and will be discussed later. It has in particular been related to the role of alcohol, to family dysfunction and to the characterization of women as suffering from a 'battered woman' syndrome, which now has little credibility. Domestic violence is often pathologized. The feminist approach linking male violence to patriarchy has been particularly influential in shaping perspectives on domestic violence and interventions against it – many point out that the refuges, exposees of domestic violence and criticisms of police reactions have played a major role in shaping policy (Hoyle 2007). The tendency to stress the role of masculinity has nonetheless formed part of the criticisms of feminism identified in Chapter 9. It has been said to be overdeterministic, to lack objectivity and to be unable to explain all aspects of domestic violence, particularly that involving lesbian couples (Hoyle 2007).

In prioritizing gender it has also arguably underplayed the role of class. For some time the feminist 'orthodoxy' cast domestic violence as a problem for all women irrespective of class. Surveys repeatedly indicate, however, higher rates in lower-class, low-income households and in social rental housing (Robinson 2010), indicating an interrelationship between gender and class. While there has been far less attention given to the experiences of minority ethnic groups, in some of which patriarchal authority can take the form of honour killings, once socio-economic status is taken into account, variations by ethnicity are also reduced (Hoyle 2007). While it is clear therefore that power and control are central to many forms of domestic violence, it is necessary to move beyond patriarchy and explore other relationships – as outlined in Chapter 8, for example, older people are also victimized as are the disabled.

Political violence and terrorism

In the late twentieth and twenty-first century so-called 'new terrorism' has become a major political and security issue. There has been relatively little specifically criminological attention paid to the topic (Mythen and Walklate 2006; Ruggiero 2006), although between 11 September 2001 (9/11) and 2006, Furedi (2007) identified nearly 8,000 books and 1,413 monographs with terrorism in the title. The term terrorism and the extent to which it is new have, however, been questioned. Those who participate in political violence are often portrayed as 'evil' and 'fanatics' and it attracts extremely strong reactions to the extent that it can be argued that analysis of terrorism is inseparable from the 'war on terror'. This section will address some of these points, recognizing that space dictates a selective approach.

Defining Terrorism

Political violence, including revolutions, uprisings and assassinations has a long history going back to Greek and Roman times (Ruggiero 2009; Weston and Innes 2010). Governments also justify the use of excessive 'force', often of questionable legitimacy, to suppress movements using political violence and deny their legitimacy by describing them as 'criminal'. Political violence therefore includes what Ruggiero (2006: 1) describes as *institutional violence from above* and *anti-institutional violence from below* involving both 'state' and 'non state actors' (Weston and Innes 2010). What is described as 'criminal' political violence depends therefore on who is doing the defining. When governments are cast as oppressive, uprisings or revolutions are regarded as legitimate and a very fine line divides freedom fighters from terrorists, guerrillas from soldiers, or martyrs from crazed suicide bombers. An often repeated observation is that today's terrorists can become tomorrow's government as happened in, for example, Northern Ireland and South Africa.

The word terrorism is therefore a form of censure. Some definitional issues are summarized in Box 11.7 and there have been at least a hundred attempts to define it (Furedi 2007). The majority stress its random and unpredictable targeting of civilians to put pressure on governments. But this is also a feature of violence from above (Ruggiero 2006: 6), and targeting civilians is a tactic in war as evidenced in the Second World War which saw the blitz on UK cities, the carpet bombing of

Box 11.7 Defining terrorism

McLaughlin (2006b: 432–5) summarizes some issues involved in defining terrorism:

A general definition:

- 'Terrorism is defined as an essentially pre-meditated political act. The intention is to inflict serious injury on the civilian population and to influence government policy by creating an atmosphere of fear and threat, generally for a political, religious or ideological cause'.

Perceptions of terrorism:

- 'Terrorism is often associated with violence that is intended to spread fear and insecurity by deliberately targeting civilians who have no chance of defending themselves . . .'
- 'It is conducted by substate groups and is revolutionary in nature . . .'
- 'Terrorists are routinely portrayed as psychologically deranged, fanatical individuals who operate in a clandestine manner . . .'

Against this characterization it can be argued that:

- 'The targeting of unsuspecting civilian populations is not the sole preserve of officially defined terrorist campaigns . . . the totalizing nature of contemporary wars, in conjunction with the lethal nature of the weaponry available means that there is the distinct possibility that "collateral damage" . . . [and] mass civilian casualties will continue to be excessive . . .'
- 'Are those who are officially labeled "terrorists" any more psychopathological than soldiers in conventional armies? . . .'
- 'Only nation states can be truly terrorist as only they have the wholesale capacity to deploy "terror" as a mode of domination and institutional governance . . .'
- 'Critics argue that Western governments are cynically using a "politics of fear" and the "war on terrorism" to justify the move to a "national security" or a "surveillance state" . . .'

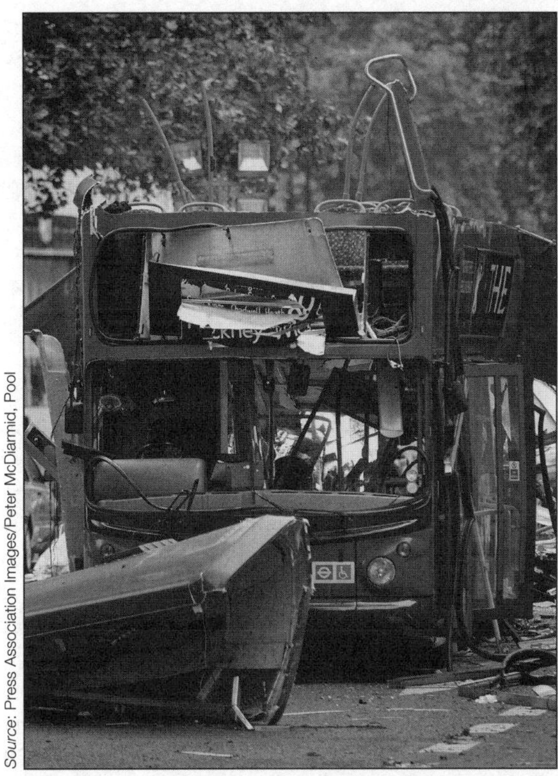

Source: Press Association Images/Peter McDiarmid, Pool

Terrorism, as in 7/7, is associated with mass deaths and destruction but may be difficult to distinguish from what can be described as state terrorism.

Source: Reuters/Goran Tomasevic

German cities and most dramatically the use of nuclear bombs in Hiroshima and Nagasaki. More recently the 'shock and awe' tactics used in the war on Iraq were also directed at civilians (Furedi 2007; 2009). The label terrorism is most often applied, argues McLaughlin (2006b: 434), to the powerless as opposed to the powerful and many argue that it should not be used. On the other hand, while few dispute that state terrorism exists, it cannot, argues Furedi (2009), be characterized in the same way as, for example, the bombings in the London underground on 7 July 2005 (7/7), which do involve distinct practices (Furedi 2009).

New terrorism?

What, therefore, distinguishes the so-called 'new terrorism'? A distinction can, for example, be made between groups earlier in the twentieth century such as the Red Brigades in Italy (Ruggiero 2009), or the IRA in Northern Ireland who believed they were fighting a 'just war' or an 'armed struggle' against injustice, had clear goals and were based in one country. Violence, while extreme, was relatively limited, was directed at specific targets and was constrained by the need to gain popular support. Funding came from supporters and for some, such as the IRA or UVF, by acquisitive crimes (Turk 2004; McLaughlin 2006b; Ruggiero 2006). Later groups such as Al-Qaida operate across continents, are not directed against specific regimes, do not have specific goals and often base themselves in training camps in failed states (Mythen and Walklate 2006; McLaughlin 2006b). They do not need to obtain local community support in the same way as earlier groups (Furedi 2009). In Northern Ireland terrorist groups aimed to strengthen their support through legitimate political activity and providing 'social services' such as the attempts by the IRA to control disorder where the police lacked legitimacy (Weston and Inness 2010). Social distance can lead to more extreme violence. When, for example, adversaries are closer, targets are more often specific government departments or individuals (Ruggiero 2006).

'New terrorism' is also associated with fears of 'new technology' and weapons of mass destruction. So far these have not emerged, as so-called 'new' terrorists have, like their predecessors, converted everyday technologies and situations into weapons and targets as happened in 9/11, although suicide bombers use innovatively designed vests (Weston and Innes 2010). Terrorists adapt to new situations and now operate in an era of global communications and 24-hour news aiming, as with 9/11, for worldwide coverage and maximum impact. To some, Al-Qaida represents the 'McDonalds' of terrorism, approximating a global brand with local franchises (Aas 2007). Also distinctive is the asymmetry between such groups and global superpowers making victory impossible (Ruggiero 2006).

Criminology and terrorism

However defined, criminologists have tended to focus on reactions to terrorism rather than attempting to apply criminological perspectives to participants, and the broad range of groups make generalizations difficult (Furedi 2009). Many perspectives are, however, relevant and most are critical of popular portrayals of terrorists as mindless 'fanatics' brainwashed into their 'evil' acts. Thus:

- *Individual factors?* Positivists such as Lombroso questioned the 'delinquent' nature of political offenders and failed to find degenerative characteristics among martyrs (Ruggiero 2006). They also looked at economic and political causes and discussed political violence in the context of tyranny. It can also be argued that viewing terrorists as crazed individuals is illogical. Their activities require careful planning, and for some, scientific and technological expertise (Furedi 2009; Weston and Innes 2010). Although some who want to commit violence are attracted to terrorism, and there are undoubtedly some charismatic individuals such as Osama Bin Laden, individual factors are generally considered to be less appropriate (Turk 2004).
- *Becoming a 'soldier'?* Studies of terrorists, while, perhaps for obvious reasons, rare, confirm their difference from popular stereotypes. Participants tend to reject the 'terrorist' label, defining themselves as, for example, participants in 'collective action', a 'just war' or an 'armed struggle' (Ruggiero 2009: 3). Convicted members of paramilitary groups in Northern Ireland stressed their status as soldiers and 'political prisoners'. Turk (2004) argues that members of politically violent groups are socialized, typically going through a process from active, often radical, political commitment to a willingness to engage in violence, although few take that eventual route. To Hamm (2005), terrorist subcultures are very similar to other forms of subculture and socialization takes place in everyday locales such as streets, prisons and paramilitary training camps.
- *Structural and geopolitical factors*: Political violence develops out of perceptions of inequality and injustice whether religious, ethnic, tribal or regional. It has been linked to regimes with a history of colonialism and, more recently, post-colonial economic and cultural penetration, and severe, almost polarizing inequality (Ruggiero 2006). Globally, argues Turk (2004: 274)

  > these facts have facilitated the identification of the West as the source of global economic and political disadvantage, military weakness and cultural malaise, which provides a credible focus for resentment and moral outrage in the recruitment of terrorists and the mobilization of supporters as sympathisers.

- *Anomie?* The significance of inequality suggests the relevance of anomie and strain theory. To Durkheim, political violence could form an integrating function and his analysis of suicide included altruistic suicides for a specific cause (Ruggiero 2006). Merton's anomie paradigm, outlined in Chapter 2, identifies political rebellion as a rejection of goals and means and an attempt to replace them. Chapter 5 referred to contemporary work on relative deprivation and social exclusion and a globalized version of Merton in which representations of the advantaged West can fuel political violence, drawing on combinations of poverty and indignity (Mooney and Young 2005; Young 2003; 2007a). While linked to inequality and injustice in this broad sense, it is not necessarily the poorest who participate. Indeed, many participants come from educated, professional middle-class backgrounds (Turk 2004; Ruggiero 2006). Some are extremely skilled and commitment is often associated with an appreciation of political ideas and ideologies. Those presumed to have been involved in the 9/11 attacks were, for example, not from poor backgrounds, had frequent contact with the West, and were highly skilled. The individuals convicted for the failed attempt on Glasgow Airport in July 2007 were doctors – which exacerbated the reaction to their activities.

- *Interactionist and critical theories*: Points about the close relationship between political violence from above and below derive from critical perspectives. Weston and Innes (2010: 857) point out that while actions harming civilians can lead to a decline in popular support, perceived overreactions, such as occurred in Northern Ireland, by the Army or the Royal Ulster Constabulary (RUC) (see Chapter 17), can increase support in a form of 'legitimacy contest'. To Ruggiero (2006), violence from above and below become clones of each other through a dynamic escalation, in which each side answers random violence with random violence, to 'pure' violence which occurs when, overtly or covertly, mass violence on civilians takes place. Mooney and Young (2005) point to a spiral of demonization as each side exposes clear evidence of the inhumanity of the other. Terrorists are subject to an extreme form of criminalization (McLaughlin 2006b) and their legitimacy is denied. Defining terrorists as 'criminal' or 'fanatics' questions any suggestion that they have rationally chosen such a path (Ruggiero 2006). Casting participants as the 'enemy' further conceals the fundamental asymmetry between oppositional groups and the state.

  This kind of escalation can lead not only to further acts of violence from below but to more repressive measures and the abuse of legitimate force from above. Fear of terrorism is often said to be out of proportion to objective risks (Furedi 2009) and Aas (2007) points out that fewer than 1,000 have been killed by international terrorism per annum for the last 30 years, although this has arguably increased in recent years. Nonetheless, the threat of terrorism has been used to justify the harsher and more punitive measures associated with the so-called 'war on terror' and to its 'collateral damage' in bombing campaigns targeting civilians, the use and effective condoning of torture, and a host of other state and state corporate crimes (see Chapter 17).

Understanding violent crime

The kinds of violence outlined above are so varied and take place in so many different settings that it is not easy to identify the factors underlying it. Some violent incidents can be described as everyday and occur within families, friendship networks workplaces and male gatherings, whereas others, such as mass murder and political violence can be described as extreme or 'pure' violence (Ruggiero 2006; Levi et al 2007). Some murders are little different to everyday forms of violence whereas extreme violence is often pathologized. Yet, as seen above, a combination of factors are likely to be involved along with the interrelated effects of structural inequalities. This section will focus on these approaches, drawing on some of the material outlined above.

Violence as pathology

While a range of 'abnormalities' are often assumed to characterize violent offenders, there has been little evidence supporting biological, particularly essentialist theories linking men's violence to excess levels of testosterone, their inability to control their 'natural aggression' or to chromosomes (Stanko 1994). Like other biological theories they can only account for a small minority of cases and neglect social factors (Jones 2000). Links between violence and mental illness are similarly limited. While mental illness and other psychiatric and psychological problems undoubtedly play a part in some homicides and other extreme forms of violence, these are a minority. Considerable concern has been aroused by high-profile murders and attacks by schizophrenics released from institutions although these are rare and, argues Jones (2000), schizophrenics form only 1 per cent of the population and only around 0.05 per cent of these engage in violence. Linking serious violence to psychopathy, now described as anti-social personality disorder, can also be a circular argument as the label is typically applied after the killing. Indeed 'psychopath' is a metaphor for 'those who are not like us' (Jones 2000: 41, citing Rafter (1997: 250). Psychiatric theories also focus on the most serious and extreme cases and say little about social and cultural influences (Levi et al 2007). It has been seen that even extreme forms of violence can be related to excitement and buzz or, with political violence, to rational and considered choices. It can also be a means of seeking gratification, as the seemingly irrational and bizarre accounts of serial killers demonstrate (Katz 1988; Stanko 1994). To Katz, violence can be valued for itself and be a chosen option: it gives a 'high', and offenders can claim a 'righteous rage'. Focusing on these aspects alone, however, can exclude the social situation and gendered nature of much violence (Polk 1994).

Alcohol features in many violent incidents, particularly domestic violence and confrontational homicide. Levi et al (2007: 704) cite BSC findings that offenders were perceived to have been under the influence of alcohol in 44 per cent of all violent incidents, and the growth of the night-time economy, associated with 'staggering' amounts of violence, is also important (Winlow et al 2003: 178 and see Chapter 8). This does not, however, indicate a pharmacological effect, as not all who drink become aggressive, and its effects depend on the context. It can, for example, affect a person's ability to interpret behavioural cues – which can make the seemingly inappropriate response of violence more understandable where a simple comment is interpreted as an insult, particularly in the context of lower-class male subcultures (Levi et al 2007).

Cycles of violence?

The domestic setting of much violence has drawn attention to what have been described as 'dysfunctional' families, the 'battered wife syndrome' and so-called cycles of violence. The battered wife syndrome was associated with an addiction to violence and 'learned helplessness' with 'battered wives' cast as unable to cope, withdrawn, dowdy and either nagging or submissive (Dobash and Dobash 1992; Saraga 1993). The phrase was originally used to underline women's suffering but was later rejected by feminists on the grounds that medicalizing the problem involved victim blaming and diverted attention from the abuser (Dobash and Dobash 1992; Brookman 2005). Attributing violence in the home to dysfunctional families is somewhat circuitous as it is the violence which is said to indicate the abnormality (Saraga 1996).

More support is attracted by the argument that some families are characterized by cycles of abuse, based on findings that many violent offenders have suffered violence in childhood and women who have been abused are more likely to abuse their children (Jones 2000). There are also some indications that women who kill have suffered from longer lasting and more severe violence and sexual assault (Brookman 2005). On the other hand, these arguments cannot explain why not all who have been abused subsequently abuse, not all who are violent have been child victims, and why women, while suffering from child and domestic abuse, are less likely to abuse (Levi 1997; Jones 2000). Cycles of abuse arguments do little more than confirm that women who resort to violence are themselves victims of violence (Brookman 2005).

Masculinity, class and violence

The neglect of structural and cultural factors by pathological theories forms one of their main criticisms and many links between structural inequalities have been seen in this as in previous chapters. Men dominate violence to the extent that some, particularly radical feminists, see the 'problem' of violence as violent men seeking to control women and asserting proprietorial rights (see Chapter 9). A common mitigation for men who kill their partners is their adultery or their failure to carry out domestic chores, and confrontational violence is, as outlined above, associated with insults about manhood or women (Polk 1994). Work by both Kelly (1988) and Mama (1989) also identified women's efforts to gain independence by education, work or participation in activities outside the home as important. Women can be blamed for their victimization which effectively denies their agency.

The many criticisms of these views were seen above and in Chapter 9. Is it being suggested, for example, that all men are potentially violent? There is no biological basis for this view and these arguments can overpredict male violence in the same way that subcultural theories were said to overpredict lower-class crime (Levi 1997). Others have argued that the continuum of violence, by including trivial incidents, exaggerates the problem of violence against women and children (Wykes and Welsh 2009), although Kelly (1996) argues that it does not see all forms of violence as the same. Nonetheless, women's violence remains a problem for feminism which tends to see it as defensive and thereby related to male power (Kelly 1996). This is less applicable, however, to women's violence towards their children or to violence in lesbian couples, identified in Chapter 9 as requiring more attention. Furthermore violence among men is not universal and is related to socio-economic and cultural factors. As seen in previous chapters, age and race can also be important factors.

A 'subculture of violence' (Wolfgang and Ferracuti 1967) has been identified and many of the studies above relate violence to men's honour and perceived respect. The subcultural theories of the early twentieth century all indicated the importance of 'being a man' in lower-class subcultures (see Chapter 3) and the toughness and aggression of male lower-class subcultures have been related to organized crime (Hobbs 1995), football violence (Williams 1994) and violence in prisons where both officers and male prisoners share the lower-class hegemonic culture of masculinity

(Sim 1994). It has more recently been illustrated in studies of bouncers in the night-time economy who are employed specifically to use the threat of violence and their knowledge of violence derived from their working-class status becomes a saleable commodity. Thus, argue Winlow et al (2003: 171), 'hardness' is part of bouncers' cultural capital and central to their 'male self'. Mental and physical toughness is accentuated in the way in which they present themselves, and in aspects of their body size and shape, clothing, facial expressions and general demeanour.

It is generally lower-class subcultures that are characterized as violent, and the links between domestic violence and homicide and lower-class offenders has been outlined. This, suggests Levi (1997), could be linked to the low esteem identified by pathological approaches and to the effects of poverty and unemployment which place increased strain on personal relationships and, taken together with poor housing, can mean that poorer families have to spend more time together in restricted space (Jones 2000). As seen in relation to confrontational homicide, violence can be a means of protecting masculine status and may be the only resource open to men with few other economic resources, and one which is culturally condoned. More affluent men can express masculinity and settle disputes without resorting to violence. Business tactics or 'macho management' might, for example, suggest a different form of aggressive masculinity (see Chapter 15 and Levi 1997). Class and gender are therefore closely related and socio-economic factors further contribute to the failure of parents to live up to cultural ideals of motherhood and fatherhood. Inequalities and a sense of injustice can fuel political violence. Other inequalities are also important – violence within families is also intergenerational and older people, as seen in Chapter 8, can be its victims. Some forms of violence, particularly expressive violence, are associated with youth and, as seen in Chapter 10, race forms an additional dimension of the violence associated with lower-class masculinity.

Concluding comments

This chapter has explored some of the issues of defining violence and critically evaluated official constructions of violence and the statistics which are based on it. It has pointed to the range of settings in which violence takes place and explored three selected forms of violence, which illustrated some of the problems of constructing violence and the different contexts in which it takes place. The many different kinds of violence makes drawing any conclusions about its roots hazardous, although it was argued that a combination of theoretical perspectives are needed to understand it. While some violent people do have mental health problems, depicting them as 'crazed' is inaccurate and serves to draw attention away from the way in which violence can be subculturally tolerated and be a response to social and economic inequalities and perceived injustices – be they local or global. Violence can be a rational choice and can be thrilling and exciting. Feminism has been very influential in understanding violence, much of which is male, but it has limitations when exploring aspects such as women's violence, particularly to children, and it is also more limited in relation to violence with racial or age dimensions. Indeed, the study of violence illustrates the interrelationship between different dimensions of inequality including disparities of power.

These observations are important when considering policies in relation to violent crime, many of which, such as individual counselling or therapy focus on individual offenders. Helpful as these undoubtedly are, tackling violence effectively requires an understanding of the cultural sources of violence which, for example, feminist campaigns against domestic violence aim to do. Tackling the social inequalities which produce individual feelings of failure or political movements against injustice is more difficult but it is nonetheless important to recognize their effects on different forms of violence. The interrelationship between forms of control and forms of violence is also important as the case of political violence indicates where overreaction can trigger an increase in the violence itself.

This chapter has inevitably focused on a selective range of violent offences. Space has prohibited a full exploration of, for example, robbery, stalking or violence in the workplace, all of which involve similar themes. In following recent work on domestic violence which focuses on intimate partners, it has not fully explored child physical abuse as suffered by Baby P, or other forms of violence within the home. The approaches to understanding violence outlined above are also less easy to apply to corporate and state violence which will be looked at in more depth in Chapters 14–17.

Review questions

1 Select one specific form of violent crime and consult official figures and other research.
   (a) What does this tell you about how the offences are defined, who is most likely to commit them and which groups are most at risk from them?
   (b) What are the main gaps in the information?

2 Find some details of murders, for example look at recent cases reported in the press. How do these 'fit' the typologies and explanations outlined above?

3 Identify the main points in arguments that the words terrorism and terrorists should not be used.

4 List the main factors which have been associated with violent behaviour, and outline what role they might play.

5 Outline what you understand by a feminist approach to violent crime. List its strengths and weaknesses.

Key reading

This chapter has been based on a wide range of sources and books that have covered different aspects of violence and violent crime. Sources which provide particularly good introductions include:

Brookman, F. (2005) *Understanding Homicide*, London: Sage. A comprehensive text on murder, using the author's own research, and covering studies of homicide in Britain along with detailed accounts of different forms of murder.

Jones, S. (2000) ***Understanding Violent Crime***, Milton Keynes: Open Press. One of the few texts to deal with violent crime as a whole, this provides a useful introduction to the main theories of violent crime along with an extensive critique.

Levi, M., Maguire, M. and Brookman, F. (2007) 'Violent Crime' in M. Maguire, R. Morgan and R. Reiner (eds) (2007) *The Oxford Handbook of Criminology*, Oxford: Clarendon Press 4th edn pp 687–732. This article provides an excellent introduction to the extent and scope of violent crime in Britain and the main theories which have been applied in attempts to explain it.

Ruggiero, V. (2006) ***Understanding Political Violence: A Criminological Analysis***, Maidenhead: Open University Press. This is a comprehensive and critical exploration of the definitions and nature of political violence from 'above' and 'below' along with an introduction to and an extensive critical evaluation of criminological approaches. It concludes with a detailed argument about the criminogenic nature of war.

Chapter 12
Sex crime

This chapter will look at

- ➜ Constructions of 'sex crime'
- ➜ The scope of sexual offences
- ➜ Rape
- ➜ Sexual offences against children
- ➜ Selling sex
- ➜ Understanding sex crime

Sexual offences share many of the characteristics of violent crime and, as seen in Chapter 2, attract lurid headlines and moral panics about sex 'fiends', 'perverts' or 'beasts'. Like violent crime, it is seen as abnormal but is also related to cultural norms of sexual relationships and socio-economic factors. It can involve elements of 'victim blaming', with women and even children being said to have provoked offences, and is surrounded by a pervasive mythology. Many different approaches can be used in its analysis. The first part of this chapter will look at how sexual offences are officially categorized and socially constructed, followed by an exploration of the nature and extent of sexual offending and victimization. Aspects of rape and child sexual abuse, considered to be at the extreme end of the continuum of sexual violence, will be outlined before turning to the sale of sex. Finally, the main theoretical perspectives used to understand sexual offending will be outlined, drawing on the discussion of violent crime in Chapter 11.

Constructing sex crime

What is considered to be 'sex crime' reflects changing constructions of 'normal' or 'deviant' sexual activity (Greer 2006). Sexual relationships with children are generally prohibited although the 'age of consent' is contested. Legislation in the 1960s legalized some forms of homosexuality, and rape within marriage was made a crime at the end of the twentieth century. 'Paedophiles' were subject to moral panics in the 1990s and 2000s (see Box 12.7), and their typical representation changed from men in 'grubby' raincoats to being manipulative and intelligent (Thomas 2005: 1). The development of the Internet has given rise to new offences of 'grooming' and expanded the distribution and consumption of pornography, and globalization has enabled the rise of 'sex tourism' which exploits more relaxed laws about sexual activity with young people, often related to poverty (Aas 2007). These constructions are illustrated in debates over descriptions of, for example, homosexuals as 'gay' or 'queer' or those who sell sex as 'prostitutes' or 'sex workers' (see Box 12.9). The construction of sexual offences, generally defined as the 'inducement or coercion of adults and children into sexual activities to which they have not consented' (Thomas 2005: 3), raises a number of interesting questions which go far beyond simple issues of definition or description.

Consent

Issues of consent are crucial in defining sexual offences but are problematic. Consider for example:

- **The age of consent:** this varies across countries and changes over time. For heterosexual activity it was reduced to 16 in England and Wales but is 17 in Northern Ireland and elsewhere. It was previously older for homosexual activities but was also reduced to 16 in 2000. Children under this age are deemed not to be able to give informed consent.
- **Interpreting consent?** Difficulties of establishing consent are most starkly illustrated in discussions of rape which raise the issue of when '*no means no*'. Women who dress in a certain way or indicate by body language or by accepting invitations are often taken to be inviting sexual activity. Before rape within marriage was criminalized, it was assumed that marriage implied consent.
- **Gender bias** is implicit in notions of consent as it is most often women or children whose consent is deemed important (Thomas 2005; 2009).

The continuum of sexual offending

Not all sexual offences involve physical harm and most accept that sexual violence ranges along a similar continuum to other forms of violence (Kelly 1988), from uninvited sexual innuendos through unwanted sexual advances to more serious instances of stalking, grooming or attempted and actual forced sex. Offences which do not involve physical activity produce considerable psychological and emotional harms and women can experience men's advances, verbal statements and body language as invasive, particularly, as with racial or other forms of violence, when they take place regularly in, for example, workplaces or public spaces.

The social construction of 'normal sex'

Changing definitions reflect constructions of 'normal' and 'natural' sexual activity, generally based on the norm of heterosexual activity between adults, previously restricted to that within marriage. For much of the twentieth century, sex outside marriage was seen as deviant for women and homosexual activities were criminalized. Trading sex is also seen as abnormal although it tends to be women who *sell* sex who are pathologized rather than the men who *buy* it, although this is now changing.

Public and private dimensions

The control of sexual activity varies according to where it takes place and reflects conceptions of privacy and the sanctity of the home and family, reflected in the long-standing exclusion of rape within marriage. During the 1970s and 1980s social workers were subject to criticism for intervening in families where child sexual abuse was suspected (Morgan and Zedner 1992). Publicly seeking sex is more likely to be criminalized with, for example, laws in the 1960s on homosexuality and the sex trade reflecting a distinction between private and public acts of 'indecency'.

Occupational sex crime

Sexual offences also take place in occupational settings. Women may be sexually harassed or worse by colleagues and those above them in the occupational hierarchy, using the threat of job loss to stop them complaining. In other circumstances the law recognizes special relationships of trust and sexual activity between teachers and pupils, doctors and patients are subject to prohibition irrespective of consent. Rape and sexual violence are also associated with wars and genocides (Letherby et al 2008; Marchbank 2008).

The scope of sexual offending

Research problems

Estimating the extent of sexual offences is particularly difficult and, as outlined in earlier chapters, many, particularly those involving children, are under-reported to victim surveys and the police. Many are subject to what is known as a process of attrition in which, as will be seen below, only a very small proportion of offences are prosecuted or convicted. There are often no visible injuries and no witnesses, and in trials the victim's version of events is pitted against the defendant's. This can be a disincentive to report offences. As is the case for violence, these difficulties affect what is 'counted' and comparisons are often difficult due to the different methodologies used. Moreover, such studies as there are of offenders tend to be of convicted offenders, not the most typical.

Estimating the extent of sexual offending

For all these reasons, official figures and victim surveys are often taken to be underestimates. As for violence, figures distinguish between less and more serious assaults as outlined in the Scottish definitions outlined in Box 12.1, and it is important to distinguish between *incidence rates* – experiences over the period of a survey – and *prevalence rates* – experiences over a longer period, normally lifetime. Far fewer figures relate to child sexual abuse, even more difficult to 'count'. Box 12.2 provides some figures for the main categories of offences across Britain although comparisons are hazardous and, due to small numbers, in Scotland and Northern Ireland there are too few individual cases to enable detailed breakdowns.

Box 12.1 Sexual offences

The SCJS defines Sexual Offences (MacLeod et al 2009) as:

- *Stalking and harassment*: receiving obscene or threatening correspondence; receiving obscene, threatening, nuisance or silent telephone calls; someone waiting outside the home or workplace; being followed around or watched;
- *Less serious sexual assault*: indecent exposure; sexually threatening behaviour; touching sexually when not wanted;
- *Serious sexual assault*: forcing/attempting to force someone to have sexual intercourse or forcing/attempting to force someone to take part in other sexual activity when they do not want to.

Box 12.2 Sexual offences as reported to victimization surveys

Incidence rates (*for last year*)

In *England and Wales* in 2001:

- *More serious sexual offences*: 0.5 per cent of women; 0.3 per cent rape.
- *Less serious sexual offences*: 2 per cent of women.
- *Any form of sexual assault*: 0.2 per cent of men.

In *Scotland*:

- *Serious sexual assault*: less than 0.5 per cent of adults.

→

Box 12.2 continued

In *England and Wales*:

- *Stalking and harassment*: 8 per cent of women and 6 per cent of men.

In *Scotland*:

- *Stalking and harassment*: 6 per cent of adults; equal numbers for men and women.

Prevalence rates (*during course of lifetime*)

England and Wales:

- *Some form of sexual assault*: 24 per cent women and 5 per cent men.
- *Serious sexual assault*: 7 per cent women (5 per cent rape); 1.5 per cent men (0.9 per cent rape).
- *Stalking and harassment*: 19 per cent women; 12 per cent men.

Scotland:

- *Serious sexual assault*: 5 per cent women and 1 per cent men.

Relationships between offenders and victims

Scotland: The SCJS found that victims knew offenders in:

- 65 per cent of cases of stalking and harassment;
- 27 per cent indecent exposure;
- 77 per cent of sexual threats (45 per cent were partners);
- 34 per cent of unwanted sexual touching (18 per cent were partners);
- 96 per cent of women victims reported male offenders;
- 48 per cent of men reported male offenders; 40 per cent female offenders;
- For *serious sexual assaults* experienced since the age of 16:
  - 56 per cent involved partners;
  - 90 per cent involved male offenders;
  - 8 per cent female.

England and Wales:

- *Rape*:
  - 54 per cent offenders were intimates in the worst cases suffered since the age of 16;
  - 29 per cent were known to victims;
  - 17 per cent were strangers;
  - 4 per cent were 'date rape'.
- For *aggravated stalking* involving *female* victims:
  - 37 per cent offenders were intimates;
  - 59 per cent were other known persons;
  - 7 per cent were strangers.
- For *male* victims:
  - 8 per cent were intimates;
  - 70 per cent were other known persons;
  - 30 per cent were strangers.

Northern Ireland (NOTA 2006):

- The offender was known to the victim in more than two fifths of cases.
- Over 90 per cent of abusers were male; one third teenagers.

Source: Walby and Allen (2004); MacLeod et al (2009)

Nonetheless, some general points can be made. The vast majority of sexual offences are those considered to be less serious (see Smith et al 2010), with only a minority reporting serious sexual offences. Nonetheless, nearly a quarter of women report some form of sexual assault over their lifetime. As for violent crime, intimates are more likely perpetrators than strangers, with the exception of indecent assaults on women ('flashing') and stalking men. A large proportion involves female victims and male perpetrators. In Northern Ireland, for example, 86 per cent of victims in 2008–9 were women (Quigley and Freel 2010), although men do report serious sexual assaults, and some female offenders are identified. Students can be particularly vulnerable: a study carried out on behalf of the National Union of Students found that one in four students had been subjected to an unwanted sexual experience with 5 per cent reporting rape. Only 4 per cent reported these incidents to the university and only one in ten to the police, largely due to shame and embarrassment, fearing that they would be blamed (BBC News 2010e).

Varieties of sexual crime

Rape

Many features of rape have already been outlined and are summarized in Box 12.2. While newspaper reports focus on sensational cases involving sex 'fiends' (Soothill and Walby 1991), stranger and so-called 'date' rapes are less common. Rapes most commonly take place in public places, followed by victims' and perpetrators' homes (Kelly et al 2005). Legal and social constructions of rape, and its surrounding mythology, reflect notions of 'real rape' which permeate the way in which it is dealt with throughout the legal process. Rape has a particularly severe impact. In Kelly's (1988: 171) classic study, women, immediately after rape, experienced feelings of guilt, shame and worthlessness and felt 'upset, numb, dirty, ashamed, angry, wanting to forget, abused, guilty and fearful'. Its long-term effects include post-traumatic stress conditions, women's attitudes to men and sex, recurrent flashbacks, dreams and nightmares. Walby and Allen (2004) found that over half of women who had been subject to serious sexual assault reported depression or other emotional problems with 5 per cent reporting suicide attempts.

Constructing rape: real rape?

Some of the ways in which the law defines rape are outlined in Box 12.3, and it also illustrates that until recently, it was defined relatively narrowly as men raping women, through penetration, outside marriage. Only gradually was the serious impact of other kinds of rapes recognized, including rape in marriage, often more persistent than 'one-off' stranger rape, and the 'last taboo' – male rape (Gillespie 1996; Lees 1996). New laws have attempted to deal with these issues although in England and Wales at any rate, the law remains gender specific (Cook and Jones 2007).

Constructions of rape are strongly affected by the notion of 'real rape' described as an 'attack at night, in a public place, by a stranger who uses force' (Kelly and

Box 12.3 Legal constructions of rape

- Until the late twentieth century, the offence of rape required proof that the vagina had been penetrated by a penis, reflecting a 'male heterosexual obsession with one object and one opening' (Walklate 1995: 81–2).
- Absence of consent also had to be proved.
- It excluded forced sexual activity falling short of penetration or which involved oral or anal sex and male rape.
- Rape within marriage was also excluded. Sir Matthew Hale CJ laid down that:

  > the husband cannot be guilty of a rape committed by himself upon his lawful wife, for by their mutual matrimonial consent and contract the wife hath given up herself in this kind unto her husband, which she cannot retract.
  >
  > (*Source*: Sir Matthew Hale CJ 1736, cited in Zedner 1992: 272)

- Marital rape was made an offence in Scotland in 1985 and in England and Wales in 1994.
- The 2003 Sexual Offences Act in England and Wales moved towards a more gender neutral definition, extending the definition of rape to include the mouth as an orifice and codifying the concept of reasonableness in relation to consent.
- A man is now said to commit rape if he 'intentionally penetrates the vagina, anus or mouth of a non-consenting person with his penis' (Hollin et al 2010a: 507).
- In Scotland, the new Sexual Offences (Scotland) Act of 2010 will widen the definition of rape to include anal and oral penetration and that by the use of an object and will include male and transgendered women as victims (McMillan 2010).

Radford 1996: 21). This is strongly related to the rape 'myths' outlined in Box 12.4. These are often heard in everyday conversation, in the accounts of rapists and in court. They amount to victim blaming, casting women as really wanting or provoking sexual activity and as able to resist. They absolve the rapist of responsibility as women have provoked his so-called uncontrollable urges. Women's insistence that they did not consent is denied credibility in the often-heard phrase: '*no really means yes*'. They also reveal commonsense understandings of what Walklate (1995: 83) describes as the 'cultural activity of seduction'. A woman's agreement to go to a man's home, for example, is taken to imply a willingness to engage in sexual activity. These notions are so pervasive that wherever victims are known to offenders, consent becomes an issue (Kelly and Radford 1996). Some American research suggests that male rapists often assume that 'no really meant yes' and experience little guilt (Scully 1990).

The 'mythological' nature of these assumptions (Walklate 1995) is revealed by asking, for example: Why should no *not* mean no? Why should a woman be assumed to 'want it' when she says that she doesn't? How can a woman fight back when this might provoke further violence and injury? Why should women not be free to go anywhere they choose or dress as they choose without seeming to 'ask for' sexual advances? Why would women exaggerate or lie about rape? To feminists these 'commonsense' notions assume men's right to sexual activity, even where consent is denied, thereby illustrating the pervasiveness of men's sexual domination. To Kelly (2008) they deny the legitimacy of women (and children's) accusations.

Box 12.4 Rape myths

Women really want and enjoy rape.

'They enjoy it.' 'They want it.' 'Women say no when they mean yes.' 'It wasn't rape, only rough sex.'

Women provoke rape.

'They ask for it.' 'They deserve it.' 'Women lead men on.'

It only happens to certain kinds of women.

'Nice girls don't get raped.' (Zedner 1992)

Women lie about it.

'They tell lies.' 'They exaggerate.' 'Women cry rape.' (Walklate 1995)

Rape can be prevented.

'They didn't fight hard enough.'

Rapists are sex fiends.

'Men who rape are sick.'

Source: Kelly (1988)

The process of attrition

Despite considerable policy changes in processing rape cases the proportion which result in a successful conviction remains small and recent studies (Kelly et al 2005; Burman et al 2009), in Britain and elsewhere, have focused on this 'justice gap' (Kelly 2008) and on the process of attrition charted in Box 12.5. Across the UK, the highest proportion is lost in the early stages, with between half and two thirds dropping out at the investigative stage. Kelly et al's comprehensive (2005) study identifies these stages:

- *Reporting rape*: many rapes are not reported to the police and cases involving known perpetrators are least likely to be reported (Box 12.5). The majority of reports are made within 24 hours. Reasons for not reporting included the time which had expired and women's fears of not being believed and of the criminal justice process. Women who did report rape expressed a desire to sanction the perpetrator and to protect others.
- *False allegations*: were believed to have led to the loss of around 8 per cent of cases. More of those involved younger victims and known offenders. The police also cited mental health problems, drug and alcohol use and inconsistencies in victims' accounts. Many of these reflected 'cultural scepticism' on the part of the police.
- *Lack of evidence*: accounted for over one-third of discontinued cases, in which victims were unable to give the police a clear account. In some cases the decision not to proceed was linked to perceptions of a lack of victim credibility.

Box 12.5 Attrition in rape cases

England and Wales

- Three quarters of rapes were reported to the police;
- One quarter of those were 'no crimed';
- The vast majority did not proceed beyond the investigative stage;
- Only 14 per cent reached trial stage;
- The conviction rate was 8 per cent.

(*Source*: Kelly et al 2005)

Scotland

- Fewer than one in ten recorded rapes were prosecuted;
- 3.7 per cent led to a conviction;
- 40 per cent of all rape and attempted rape cases coming to court led to guilty verdicts (compared to 90 per cent of cases overall);
- 30 per cent of rape and attempted rape cases led to not guilty verdicts and 24 per cent were 'not proven' (accounting for 45% of all not proven verdicts).

Source: Scottish Government (2009a)

- *Victim withdrawals*: accounted for one-third of cases lost at the police stage. This was related to a variety of factors including the availability of women police officers, crisis workers and forensic examiners and, while 70 per cent of respondents were satisfied with the initial police response, some cited a fear of court processes and not being believed or discouraged from carrying on.
- *Discontinuation by CPS*: this involved only a small proportion. Reasons included CPS assessments of victims' credibility taking account, for example, of 'inappropriate material' on complainants' sexual history.
- *Court and trial*: some did not proceed to trial due to late withdrawal or the case being discontinued at court.

A prominent feature throughout the criminal justice process is the pervasiveness and persistence of notions of 'real rape' and the stereotypical myths surrounding it. These may affect women's initial definitions of what has happened as 'rape'; Cook and Jones (2007: 128) argue that a woman measures her experience against 'every rape she has ever heard about'. Less than half of women experiencing an assault meeting the legal definition of rape define it as such, a figure dropping to around a third when the perpetrator is a current or ex-partner (Kelly et al 2005). On the other hand, when additional physical injury occurred, nearly two-thirds defined it as 'rape' (Walby and Allen 2004). Notions of real rape also affect later processes. A culture of scepticism on the part of police includes assumptions that women frequently lie about rape which outweighs signs of visible injuries or lies on the part of the defendant (Jordan 2001: 72, cited in Kelly et al 2005). Institutional rules, previous and predicted experience and gendered expectations are all therefore involved in attrition and, to Kelly et al, the police, CPS and the judiciary all work with 'gender schemes' which determine what is considered appropriate and inappropriate behaviour for men and women.

Despite the broader legal definition of rape, therefore, the concept of real rape continues to affect the criminal justice process and the popular media (Kelly 2008; Walklate 2008). It creates the paradox that while assumed to be traumatizing, in reality rape often takes place within the 'messiness of everyday lives and can be far more mundane' (Kelly 2008: 274), which can discourage women from defining forced sex as rape. The pervasiveness of these constructions are also illustrated in a 2005 ICM Poll cited by Walklate (2008: 46) in which

> 26 per cent of those asked thought that a woman was partially or totally responsible for being raped if she was wearing sexy or revealing clothing and more than one in five held the same view if a woman had had many sexual partners, with 30 per cent 'blaming the woman' if she was drunk.

To Walklate the law reflects 'white man's law' and 'male knowledge' and real reform depends on changing these cultural stereotypes (Kelly 2008).

Sexual offences against children

Until the latter decades of the twentieth century, child sexual abuse was associated with incest, which became a criminal offence in 1908 in England and Wales and was seen as primarily a lower-class problem associated with overcrowded slums (Morgan and Zedner 1992). It was 'rediscovered' after a series of high-profile cases including the 1987 'Cleveland crisis', in which more than a hundred cases of sexual abuse were diagnosed in three months, leading to considerable criticism of doctors' diagnoses and of social workers removing children from home (Walklate 1989; Morgan and Zedner 1992). Feminist research exposed and raised issues about child victimization as it did for sexual and domestic violence against women. As outlined in Box 12.8, the 1990s saw rising concerns about and the demonization of paedophiles (Thomas 2005; Kitzinger 2008). The 2000s have seen the emergence of the 'new' phenomenon of Internet sexual offences and 'grooming'. As with other sexual and violent offences, sexual offences against children are surrounded by myths and are more likely to be perpetrated by family and other trusted adults. This section will briefly explore some of these themes.

Defining and counting sexual offences against children

The age of consent is crucial in defining this group of offences, and reflects the notions of childhood outlined in Chapter 8. While the age of consent in England and Wales is 16, some offences now distinguish between 13 and 13–16 year olds (Hollin et al 2010b). As Thomas (2009) points out, while both are offences, a sexual relationship between a 17-year-old boy and a 15-year-old girl is considered very differently to that between a 17-year-old boy and an 8-year-old girl (Thomas 2009). As for other sexual offences a continuum can be identified ranging from seemingly trivial touching, nudging and kissing, often justified as 'normal' father–daughter petting, to forced oral and anal sex (Kelly 1988). Offences include rape, sexual assault, causing or inciting a child to engage in sexual activity, the abuse of a position of trust involving children and taking and distributing indecent images of children.

The difficulties of estimating the incidence or prevalence of offences have been referred to in previous chapters and victim surveys are less useful. From police figures of recorded crime, Hollin et al (2010b) note that the most prevalent offence is sexual assault on a female aged between 13 and 16 and that female children are more likely to be victims than male, particularly from rape of a child between 13 and 16 years of age. Police figures underestimate offences and lifetime prevalence studies have suggested that around a quarter of girls and a tenth of boys are likely to experience some form of child sexual abuse before the age of 16 (Walklate 1989). Perpetrators are mainly men, with a figure of 95 per cent being most commonly advanced (McLeod and Saraga 1988; Walklate 1989; Kelly 1996). Offenders are typically known whether within the family or in a professional capacity (Thomas 2005; Hollin et al 2010b).

The mythology of sexual offences against children

Sexual offences against children are surrounded by a similar mythology to that identified for rape, illustrated in Box 12.6 (Kelly 1988). Children are said to fantasize or seduce, it is said that little harm is done and mothers can be blamed (Walklate 1989). As for rape, these are pervasive, affect how allegations of abuse are dealt with and can be accepted by survivors. One of Kelly's interviewees was told by a psychiatrist that 'you must realize that you can't blame other people, you must have been a very sexual child' (Kelly 1988: 177).

As for rape myths, close examination prompts several questions. How can children, who have no sexual experience, want or provoke abuse? Walklate (1989) points out that it would be difficult for children to make up stories and that while young teenagers may be seen as provocative this is not intentional. The notion that

Box 12.6 The mythology of child sexual abuse

Children like it.

'They want it.' 'Girls get pleasure.' 'They don't object so they must like it.'

Children provoke it.

'They ask for it.' 'Girls are provocative.'

It only happens in some kinds of families.

'. . . girls who come from problem families; large families; rural families.'

Children can't be believed.

'They tell lies.' 'They exaggerate.' 'Girls fantasize about incest.' 'Girls accuse men to gain attention.'

They could have prevented it.

'If they had resisted, they could have prevented it.' 'They should have told someone.'

Source: Kelly (1988: 36)

victims are not 'harmed' contradicts studies which show long-term effects such as neurotic disorders, anxiety, sleep problems, depression, self-destructive behaviour, feelings of isolation, stigma and poor self-esteem (Kelly 1988; Morgan and Zedner 1992; Walklate 1989). The view that it only happens in abnormal families may reassure that 'it can't happen in my family', yet 'it' happens in families across the social spectrum. It can also take many different forms including those outlined below.

Occupational sexual offending against children

A major group of sexual offences are perpetrated by those in occupations dealing with children which, like many white-collar crimes (see Chapter 15), involve an abuse of the trust located in an occupational role. Box 12.7 outlines some cases and Thomas (2005: 134) points to suggestions that workplaces dealing with children can become 'honey pots' attracting offenders. Some have involved teachers and, indeed, the British private boarding school has been stereotypically associated with sadism and sexual abuse (Thomas 2005). Following the kinds of cases highlighted in Box 12.7, all sexual activity between school staff and young people under 18 was criminalized in 2000. Sports clubs and voluntary organizations have also been subject to greater protective legislation. Continuing publicity surrounds the worldwide issue of sexual abuse in the Catholic Church and its cover-up, culminating in a letter from the Pope to Irish Catholics. Children's homes have also been accused of providing a haven for child abuse, with many cases revealed during the 1980s (Thomas 2005: 138), many after a long period of time has elapsed.

Box 12.7 Cases of workplace sexual offending against children

- In 1990, a headmaster, a mathematics teacher and an English teacher were imprisoned for sexually assaulting pupils at Crookham Court School in Berkshire. The preceding investigation was said to have led to tightening Inspection regimes for private boarding schools in 1989.
- The Waterhouse Report in 2000 investigated the widespread sexual abuse of boys in Gwynedd and Clwyd in North Wales, going back to 1974, and occurring across residential childcare and fostering in the public and private sectors. Two institutions were particularly prominent: the local authority community home Bryn Estyn near Wrexham, whose deputy principal and two senior members of staff were convicted, and Bryn Alyn Community, also in Wrexham. The offending took many years to come to light, and other members of staff did not report the abuse due to a 'cult of silence' (Thomas 2005: 140–1).
- The revelations, in many countries, about child sexual abuse and its cover-up have led to much criticism of the Catholic Church. These are illustrated by the Irish case involving Fr Brendan Smyth, believed to have abused at least 20 children over a 40-year period and who was convicted of more than 90 offences before his death. The current head of Ireland's Catholic Church, Cardinal Brady, admitted being present when two teenagers complaining of abuse signed an oath of silence and reported this to his then superior. He was criticized for not reporting it to the police and has also acknowledged suspending another priest in Armagh, said to have paid £45,000 compensation to a woman alleging sexual abuse. In March 2010, the Pope apologized for 'serious mistakes' among Bishops and openly expressed 'the shame and remorse that we all feel'. (BBC 2010f; 2010g; 2010h)

Sex crime and the Internet

The Internet has become an accessible vehicle through which sexual offenders can immediately satisfy their fantasies with presumed anonymity (Quayle and Taylor 2003, cited in Davidson and Martellozzo 2008). Internet sexual offences against children involve two main categories – those who use the Internet to target and groom children for the purposes of sexual abuse and those who produce and/or download and distribute indecent illegal images of children (Davidson and Martellozzo 2008; Hollin et al 2010b). They include:

- Internet grooming, criminalized by the Sexual Offences Act of 2003 and the Sexual Offences (Scotland) Act of 2005, in which an offender interacts with a child or young person aiming to gain trust to prepare them for sexual abuse. Scottish legislation also includes meeting a child, following preliminary contact, with the intention of performing sexual activity;
- The construction of sites to exchange information and indecent images of children;
- The organization of criminal activities using children for prostitution and to produce indecent images of children;
- The organization of criminal activities promoting sexual tourism;
- The dissemination of indecent images shared by sex offenders which has become a large and lucrative industry.

Different types of offenders have been identified ranging from opportunistic browsers to online groomers, physical abusers and distributors of indecent images, and some Internet offenders ‘cross over’ into physical abuse in the ‘real world’ (Hollin et al 2010b). Many attempts are targeted at 12–13 year olds, particularly active on the Internet, and it is important to recognize that males as well as females are targeted (Davidson and Martellozzo 2008). Davidson and Martellozzo suggest that there is evidence that these offences are increasing and that they involve increasingly younger children. As this has only been recently criminalized, care has to be taken not to overdramatize offences. Considerable publicity, for example, surrounded the conviction of a man in March 2010 for the rape and murder of Ashleigh Hall in Sedgefield in October 2009, after he had contacted her via Facebook, and attracted her with a picture of a young, bare-chested man (BBC News 2010i).

Protecting the public from paedophiles?

Box 12.8 charts the moral panic about paedophiles, popularly described as ‘twisted’, ‘weirdo’, ‘depraved’, ‘pervert’, ‘sexual predator’ or ‘sex beast’ (Kitzinger 2008: 370). The public protests and campaigns in the 1990s and 2000s were linked to the so-called community protection approach to sexual offences which prioritizes protecting the public from the risk of child sexual offenders over their rehabilitation or interests of justice (Hebenton 2008). While the moral panic arguably exaggerated the risks, to dismiss these protests as moral panics could detract from their wider significance. To Kitzinger (2008), the media cannot summon up protests from nowhere and the lower-class estates in which they took place were those suffering from the worst effects of de-industrialization and perceived government neglect. The housing of high-profile sex offenders on such estates could be taken to constitute yet another disadvantage. Public feelings can also be related to the ‘primal feelings’

Box 12.8 The case of paedophiles

- The term paedophilia was rarely used before the 1990s (Critcher 2003, cited in Marsh and Melville 2009: 61).
- During the 1990s a paedophile panic built up, fuelled by revelations of sexual offences in residential childcare homes and those involving Catholic priests.
- In 1996, 'Megan's Law', requiring the notification of sex offenders in the community, was passed in the US, and the theme of 'paedophiles in the community' swept across the UK.
- In 1997, the Sex Offenders Act created a national UK register of convicted or cautioned sex offenders.
- The panic continued in 2000, with the murder in July of 8-year-old Sarah Payne by a known paedophile, accompanied by massive publicity and regular appearances of the family on television. Sarah's mother, Sara Payne, has continued to campaign and was appointed Victims' Champion in January 2009.
- An example of media representation is a *Daily Mirror* front page asserting that 'Hanging these bastards is really too good for them' (cited in Marsh and Melville 2009: 62).
- In July 2000, the *News of the World* led a 'media-orchestrated' outcry and a 'naming and shaming campaign' publishing the names, photographs and location of 200 individuals on the Sex Offenders Register and calling for the government to introduce stricter sentences.
- This led to protests and brutal attacks on suspected paedophiles. Prolonged rioting in 2001 on the Paulsgrove Housing estate in Portsmouth led to innocent families being forced out of their homes and into hiding.
- The representation of paedophiles overemphasizes stranger danger, whereas child sexual abusers are more likely to be someone known and trusted. Thus, argues Critcher (2003, cited in Marsh and Melville 2009: 65) the paedophile label contributes little to our understanding of the frequency or nature of sexual abuse.

Source: Jewkes (2004) and Marsh and Melville (2009)

(Hebenton 2008: 323) aroused by the despoliation of childhood innocence – seen also in extreme reactions to child homicides.

Nonetheless, such demonization can have an adverse impact, and the introduction of sex offenders' registers and extreme reactions arguably drove sexual offenders 'underground' thereby escaping supervision and treatment; many practitioners argued against more stringent legislation. Kitzinger (2008: 361), referring to a tragic case in 1997 in which a girl died in a house burnt down in a protest, also points to the irony that considerable resources have had to be spent protecting sex offenders from the public rather than the other way round. Thomas (2009: 297) also suggests that 'othering' sex offenders can create a 'jurisprudence of difference' in which they have fewer rights than other offenders. Efforts to understand offenders have also been adversely affected. It will be seen below that the assumptions underlying community protection may overemphasize the pathological nature and persistence of offending. To feminists, 'othering' paedophiles and viewing them as abnormal individuals detracts from the normality of male sexualility and the pervasiveness of the myths outlined above (Kitzinger 2008).

Selling sex

The sale of sex is associated with prostitution which has existed throughout history – thus its description as the 'oldest profession'. It has often had an ambiguous legal status. During the nineteenth century, it was subject to Contagious Diseases Acts following concerns about the health of soldiers who consorted with prostitutes and the spread of AIDS again drew attention to the assumed public health risks of prostitution (McKeganey and Barnard 1996; Phoenix 2008). Public prostitution has also been a major concern with so-called 'red light' areas and their associated kerb-crawling and street trade arousing resentment and fears among residents (Matthews 1993; Williams 2008). More recently prostitution has been associated with problems such as sex trafficking, illegal immigration, the exploitation of women and children, the drugs market and organized crime more generally. This has led to a shift towards more punitive, zero-tolerance policies and tightening control (Phoenix 2008; Brooks-Gordon 2010).

It is important, nonetheless, to recognize the very fine line between an illegal exchange of sex for, as the law defines it, 'any financial advantage or provision of goods and services', and the more widespread use of sexualized images from legal and illegal pornography through to advertising campaigns using sexualized images to sell perfumes or cars (McKeganey and Barnard 1996; Brooks-Gordon 2006; O'Neill 2008). The law is strongly contested, reflected in the often-heated discussions of whether those who sell sex should be described as 'sex workers' or 'prostitutes' (outlined in Box 12.9), which permeates all discussions of this topic. This section will explore many of these issues.

Box 12.9 Prostitutes or sex workers?

Contrasting descriptions of those, mainly women, who sell sex as 'prostitutes' or 'sex workers' permeate discussions of definition, analysis and policy. The different terms are highlighted in media coverage of the murders of those who sell sex, such as the Ipswich murders outlined in Chapter 2. Some major points:

- The term prostitute is seen as degrading and associated with negative stereotopy of women as 'whores', 'hookers' and 'tarts'. The legal term, 'common prostitute' confers a stigmatized status.
- The term sex worker, on the other hand, preferred by many who work in the trade, highlights that selling sex is an occupation, often freely chosen, and that participants should have equal rights to protection and health care as those in legitimate occupations.
- The term 'sex worker' has, however, been criticized as implying the 'normalization' of selling sex and underplaying the situation of participants as victims of male violence. This can occur as part of their work and, for some, physical or sexual violence precedes their participation in sex work.
- The debate involves issues of agency – to what extent are women who sell sex to be cast as victims or as free agents.
- The debate affects considerations of policy:
  - *Abolitionist approaches* (linked to some forms of feminism) argue that 'the problem' is men who consume sex, and that they, particularly kerb crawlers, should be criminalized. Women should be encouraged to move away from participation in prostitution.
  - *Legalization approaches* (linked to other forms of feminism) argue that selling sex should be recognized as something which men and women choose to do and that forms of legalization or licensing would better protect sex workers from exploitation.

Offences related to prostitution

In Britain, prostitution itself is not a crime, although many activities associated with it, outlined in Box 12.10, are. The influential Wolfenden Report of 1957 distinguished between the sale of sex in public and in private, with soliciting in public being regarded as a relatively low-level offence (Brooks-Gordon 2010). Since then, as outlined above, laws have strengthened and have shifted from attempting to 'manage' prostitution to trying to abolish it (Phoenix 2008). Clients have been criminalized and it has become increasingly difficult for women who wish to operate, alone or with others in private, to do so. Some cities, such as Edinburgh, set up 'tolerance zones' in which the street trade was managed, and co-operation was established with licensed businesses such as massage parlours, arrangements which had been threatened by new laws. As outlined in Box 12.9 and below, who should be criminalized is a contested issue.

Given its nature, the extent of the prostitution is difficult to estimate and numbers of arrests and convictions are highly dependent on discretionary police policy.

Box 12.10 Prostitution offences (England and Wales)

- **Public offences**
  - Soliciting
  - Kerb crawling
  - Sex in a public lavatory
  - Disorderly behaviour
  - Anti-social behaviour
- **'Controlling offences'**
  - Causing or inciting prostitution for gain
  - Controlling prostitution for gain
  - Keeping a brothel
- **Indoor offences**
  - Breach of planning regulations
  - Keeping a disorderly house
  - Allowing children in brothels
  - Landlord knowingly allowing use of premises as brothel
  - Tenant knowingly allowing use of premises as a brothel or for prostitution by a single person
  - Breach of tenancy agreement
  - Breach of licensing requirements
- **Advertising offences**
  - Graphic advertising likely to 'deprave or corrupt'
  - Placing adverts for prostitution in public telephone box
  - Criminal damage

A *common prostitute* is a man or woman who 'on at least one occasion and whether or not compelled to do so, offers or provides sexual services to another person in return for payment or a promise of payment to them or a third person'.

Source: adapted from Brooks-Gordon (2010: 542–3)

Brooks-Gordon (2010) reports a total of 1,258 soliciting offences in England and Wales in 2007/8 and, following the more stringent laws in 2003 against brothels, an increase in these offences were followed by a decrease. Trafficking offences, used to justify stricter laws, are less prevalent than often assumed and 'impressions that the sex industry is rife with trafficked people or traffickers are highly misleading' (Brooks-Gordon 2010: 549) (and see Chapter 14). Brooks-Gordon further cites estimates of somewhere between 35,870 and 48,393 sex workers in the UK, and in Scotland it is estimated that around 1,400 women are involved in street prostitution, the majority in Glasgow (McMillan 2010).

Participants in the sex trade

It is difficult to generalize about women who engage in the sex trade, although they have generally been found to have a history of poverty, social insecurity, violence and sexual abuse within the family and drug or alcohol problems (McLeod 1982; O'Neill 2008; Phoenix 2008). Phoenix also points to the withdrawal of benefits from young people and the growing number of school exclusions as factors behind young women falling into a spiral of drug or alcohol abuse and sex work. The majority of research has, however, been carried out with female street workers and different characteristics may be associated with indoor workers and male sex workers (Wilcox and Christmann 2008).

It is also important to look at clients, with suggestions that over 4 per cent of the male population paid for commercial sex in the last five years (Brooks-Gordon 2010). They were most likely to be aged between 25–34, resident in London and unmarried or separated. They encompassed all sexualities, and while men form the majority, women and couples are clients of male prostitutes (Wilcox and Christmann 2008). Despite stereotypical representations, many men aim to replicate normal sexual relationships and carry on seeing one woman for long periods of time (Earl and Sharpe 2008). Disabled clients are a core group for the indoor trade (Sanders and Campbell 2008). Many are introduced to prostitution and 'tricks of the trade' by friends and supportive networks have been identified (O'Neill 1996), although in some places this has eroded due to the influx of drug-using women.

Street and indoor trades

Research also indicates contrasts between street and indoor trades:

- *The street trade*: Working on the street carries higher risks of being arrested and more street prostitutes are likely to suffer from drug or alcohol abuse (Sanders and Campbell 2008). The murders of street workers draw attention to the dangers which they face and they are more at risk from violence. Kinnell (2006) reports, for example, that 90 sex workers were murdered in the last decade and street sex workers in the UK are twelve times more likely to die from violence at work than women of a similar age. Research suggests that physical attacks, sexual assaults, rapes, broken bones, bruises and burns, kidnapping, harassment from neighbours and community groups, having money taken by boyfriends, partners, pimps and other men occur on a regular basis (Phoenix 2008). Street workers have to go to isolated locations to avoid the police.

- *Off street and indoor markets* include massage parlours, saunas, brothels, clubs, escort agencies or individual premises with one or more workers (Sanders and Campbell 2008). In contrast to the street, many premises ensure hygiene, prohibit drugs, screen clients for risks of violence and some operate rotas to enable flexibility and also employ receptionists. Some see themselves as providing a much needed service particularly to disabled clients and there is a distinct occupational culture. They are also safer being less visible and there is safety in numbers (Sanders and Campbell 2008).

Male sex workers

A small study in West Yorkshire (Wilcox and Christmann 2008) looked at men who worked independently from home as 'sole traders', advertising their services as escorts or masseurs. They differed from descriptions of women sex workers and those of 'rent boys' often seen as exploited and coerced. All the men, a mixture of homosexual and heterosexual, had freely chosen their work, only a small number had experienced either physical or sexual abuse, some reported high sex drives, and most lived in private rented accommodation or owned their houses. They emerge as a largely satisfied group, as 'businessmen' engaging in a career like any other, involving non-problematic commercial activity and providing enjoyment and flexibility. They had few experiences of violence and, the authors suggest, involvement in sex work for these men was unlikely to be seen as a 'problem' requiring a 'solution' (p. 132).

Regulating sex work

A variety of motivations have been associated with engagement in the sex industry. Economic necessity is a major factor for women and, particularly for those with few educational qualifications or skills, it provides a higher income than many alternatives (Matthews 1993). For others it is necessary to support a drug habit. Phoenix (2008), while confirming the role of economic factors, also argues that for some, prostitution is a route to a better life. It can be a rational choice although few would choose it were they in better circumstances. Considerable controversy, however, as outlined in Box 12.9, surrounds the extent to which these choices can be seen as coerced.

To some feminists, politicians and policy-makers, prostitutes are victims of poverty and male violence. Women are coerced into sex work with the real 'villains' being men who purchase their services and commodify women's bodies. To them, selling sex is wrong and undermines feminist campaigns. Men who buy sex should be criminalized and laws should seek to abolish the sale of sex. Women should be protected, not criminalized, and intervention should aim to support women and encourage them to leave the sex trade (see, for example, Brooks-Gordon 2010; O'Neill 2008; Phoenix 2008). Some politicians and policy-makers further link prostitution to organized crime, trafficking and the drugs trade (see Chapter 14) which has contributed to the more punitive policies outlined above.

To other feminists and academics, this argument denies women's agency and their choice to engage in sex work. To writers such as Brooks-Gordon (2006; 2010), there is nothing wrong with selling sex, which involves a consensual, commercial arrangement. It need not involve exploitation, and the sex trade, if legalized, could contribute considerably to the economy (O'Neill 2008). While violence and exploitation are recognized and condemned, legalization would reduce violence by enabling better regulation. Against arguments that this would sanction the sale of sex and assist trafficking, they argue that trafficking has been exaggerated (see Chapter 14) and that centuries of prohibition have not so far limited the sale of sex.

Zero tolerance and abolitionist policies have also been associated with adverse effects, particularly where restrictions are placed on providing support and advice to women who are not actively seeking a way out. It may have the somewhat ironic result that protective legislation might lead to greater exclusion for the most vulnerable street workers (Phoenix 2008). Furthermore, criminalizing kerb crawlers has not had the desired effect of making the streets safer. McMillan (2010), for example, reports that the criminalization of kerb crawlers in Scotland ended the de facto tolerance zones operating in Edinburgh and Aberdeen and put women at greater risk of violence. Increasing intervention in the indoor trade, justified by looking for illegal immigrants and victims of traffickers – often cast in any event as offenders (Chapter 14) – also makes it more difficult for women who wish to work together for their own safety. To some this amounts to moral authoritarianism and women can be deprived of citizenship rights by refusing to accept their victim status, and contributes to economic, cultural and emotional exclusion (Scoular and O'Neill 2007). Abolitionist policies also fail to recognize or tackle the economic deprivation underlying entry into sex work. Not all are victims; rather, they are 'just poor women struggling to survive' (Phoenix 2008: 41).

Understanding sexual offending

The perspectives used to analyse sexual offending are broadly similar to those outlined for violent crime. Sex offenders are often pathologized whereas to feminists sexual offending has its roots in patriarchy although, as seen above, this has been contested and economic factors also play a major role. The extreme reactions to sexual offending and the adverse impact of laws also indicate the importance of labelling and criminalization. This section will draw on the above sections and the arguments outlined in Chapter 11.

The pathological sex offender

Sex offenders have been associated with a variety of pathologies. Biological approaches are often considered to be particularly relevant, although suggestions that offenders have excessive sex drives or high levels of testosterone have had little explanatory value (Sampson 1994). Sexual offending has also been related to men's desire to reproduce, contradicted by offences involving children and the elderly (Sampson 1994). There is therefore little evidence to support notions that offending is related to men's uncontrollable urges (Stanko 1994). Personality and psychiatric theories have fared little better. While some sex offenders do suffer from a mental illness the relationship is not strong and there is a growing consensus that 'sexual offending is unconnected to mental health' (Thomas 2005: 29).

'Social-cognitive' theories have attracted more support particularly those relating sexual offences to cognitive distortions. In these, offenders, many of whom share the views outlined in the 'myths' surrounding sexual abuse, are said to misinterpret cues, have attracted more support (Thomas 2005; Lacombe 2008; Hollin et al 2010a; 2010b). Thus they believe that they have 'done no wrong', that the victim 'led them on', or they are 'in total denial about the crimes' (Thomas 2005: 33). These are related to cognitive behavioural approaches which assume that offenders have consciously chosen to commit sexual offences, albeit based on distorted thinking, 'hardened' into fantasies. Other deficits associated with sexual offending include 'empathy deficits' and intimacy deficits, related to difficulties of establishing and maintaining intimate relationships. Empirical links are not strong although some offenders do indicate higher levels of emotional loneliness and isolation (Hollin et al 2010a; 2010b). Hollin et al (2010b) conclude that 'while complex models of sexual offending have been advanced, this complexity is not always matched by a strong evidence base'.

Lacombe (2008), on the basis of research in what he describes as a 'sex offender school' using cognitive behaviour therapy, suggests some limitations. Offenders were encouraged to acknowledge their crimes as part of a crime cycle, to explore their deviant sexual fantasies and how their offences related to overt and covert planning. The role of cognitive distortions was stressed and they were likened to sex addicts. Yet not all offenders had engineered offences, some simply taking advantage of situations, and not all reported fantasies. Offenders' accounts were, however, rejected by therapists and some went so far as to manufacture fantasies to keep therapists at bay (p. 70).

These therapies underline the often-made assertion: '*once a sex offender, always a sex offender*' and stressed offenders' risk of re-offending. Their identity as sexual offenders became 'a "pivot" around which all other aspects of their personality revolved' (p. 72), to labelling perspectives, a master status. The community protection 'trope' (Hebenton 2008: 324) also rests on assumptions of uncontrolled sexual compulsion, specialization and persistence, which may be far from the empirical reality. Against this, many so-called paedophiles live in the community and are in many respects 'normal'.

'Cycles of abuse' theories have also been applied to sexual offending, drawing on research findings that many offenders have suffered abuse. These may be appropriate for individual offenders as the long-term effects of abuse include low self-esteem and a reduced ability to enjoy sex; abusive behaviour can also be learnt. Many who engage in the sex trade report having been abused as children (Matthews 1993; O'Neill 1996). But, as with violence, previous abuse cannot explain offending behaviour fully, as not all who abuse were abused and not all who were abused subsequently abuse (Sampson 1994). Moreover, it cannot account for the gendered distribution of offending. Men outnumber women as abusers but women outnumber men as victims. Therefore it is unlikely that all abusive men could have been abused as boys and it cannot explain why most women who have been abused do not subsequently abuse (Thomas 2005).

As for other forms of crime, therefore, pathological approaches are useful for understanding and treating some individual offenders but they cannot explain sexual offending in general. Moreover, they are often based on the rather atypical sample of serious offenders in prisons or institutions in which individual pathologies are emphasized (Sampson 1994).

Men controlling women?

Feminist criticisms of these approaches have been well rehearsed and need little reiteration. Sexual violence is a further assertion of the male propriety over women seen in Chapters 9 and 11 and is reflected in the mythology surrounding sexual violence and in everyday encounters in which women report sexual language and unwelcome touching and fondling. To radical feminists men use sexual violence as a means of controlling and dominating women and often cited is Brownmiller's argument that rape 'is nothing more or less than a conscious process of intimidation by which *all* men keep *all* women in a state of fear' (Brownmiller 1975, cited in Sampson 1994: 9). To some men rape is a 'conquest' (Scully 1990; Scully and Marolla 1993) and in war it is a means of emphasizing victory (see Chapter 17). Conceptions of 'real rape' and the powerlessness of children who are abused reflect the exercise of male patriarchal power. To some, but not all, feminists, women who sell sex are cast as victims of male violence.

Some major problems for the feminist approach have also been outlined in previous chapters and centre around the focus on *male* violence against *women*. Far less well explored is men's victimization from sex crime and women's participation in it. It could be argued that some male rapes are related to the exercise of masculine power and domination (Lees 1992; Gillespie 1996). In prison, for example, heterosexual men rape other men as a means of humiliation and domination (Sampson 1994; Sim 1994). This does not, however, apply to homosexual experiences of rape or sexual assault. Women who sexually abuse also constitute a problem for feminists and, as seen in relation to sex work, complex issues surround the extent to which women freely consent to sell sex and whether this can exist outside a framework of violence against women. It is also significant that male sex workers are not 'problematized' in the same way as women. Also underexplored are women clients of the sex industry and consumers of pornography.

Inequalities other than gender are also important. Children are particularly vulnerable both within and without the patriarchal family. Boys are victims from the sexual abuse of adults such as teachers, carers or clergymen. Racial inequalities are also relevant with black or Asian women being particularly vulnerable to harassment and violence based on racialized images of sexuality and taunts such as 'black whores'. As will be seen in Chapter 14, the sex trafficking industry and the growth of sex tourism have been associated with the desirability of women of specific racial and ethnic backgrounds, often from poorer countries where lower living standards can be exploited (Aas 2007).

Class and socio-economic factors are also therefore related and a further less explored feature of sexual violence is its apparently greater incidence in lower-class households, although this could reflect greater involvement with official agencies.

It is also possible, however, that the stress and low self-esteem associated with poverty and unemployment can heighten tensions and facilitate sexual as well as physical violence. Gender is therefore likely to be related to other factors which deserve further exploration.

Wider cultural and structural factors are also significant. It has been pointed out, for example, that sexual offending takes place in the context of a growing, globalized commercial sex industry in which sexual aids and pornography are widely sold, to women as well as men, and it is difficult to distinguish between the illegal exchange of sex and perfectly 'normal', legal and consensual legal exchanges (Brooks-Gordon 2006). While these developments and, for example, the sexualization of young children may well be criticized, they challenge the view of sexual violence as related either to pathological sexual proclivities or male power over women. Anomie theory could also be applied as sex is so highly promoted that it creates, in the Durkheimian sense, boundless aspirations which cannot be satisfied and which can lead to deviant responses (Sumner 1994).

The dangers of labelling and othering sexual offenders and sex workers have also been outlined along with the adverse effects of criminalization. These can play a role in excluding offenders and sex workers, exacerbating their situation and discouraging them from seeking support. Pathological assumptions can confirm, as Lacombe's (2008) analysis suggests, the sex offender's deviant identity and underplay aspects of normality which might better assist their rehabilitation. As with many other aspects of crime, criminalization affects the most vulnerable such as isolated and unemployed sex offenders and the most vulnerable street sex workers.

Concluding comments

This chapter has explored how sex crime is constructed around issues of consent and normal sexual activity. It has revealed something of its scope although official figures are inevitably underestimates. It went on to examine different aspects of sexual offending, critically exploring rape myths and revealing how notions of real rape continue to affect the process of attrition in which so few cases produce convicted offenders. Child sexual abuse is also surrounded by mythologies, and despite popular conceptions of children being preyed on by shadowy strangers it is more likely to be perpetrated in the home or by people the child knows and trusts. Demonizing sex offenders may not only exaggerate their manipulativeness but may discourage them from seeking help. Prostitution involves a different set of issues, raising complex questions about the extent to which female sex workers can be viewed as victims of male sexual violence or as individuals freely choosing to sell sex in the context of a growing sex industry. A variety of approaches were outlined which, taken together, can assist our understanding of sexual offences. Pathological theories were contrasted with feminist perspectives, for many of whom sexual violence is yet a further example of male patriarchal domination. Some feminists, however, have taken issue with the portrayal of women sex workers as victims and the desire to abolish prostitution, arguing this denies women agency. The significance of gender can also be questioned as class, age and race inequalities are also important, as are global inequalities related to the global sex industry.

As with other chapters, this one has had to be selective and many other sexual offences could have been included. Stalking, for example, has been criminalized which recognizes the emotional aspects of sex crime, and it was argued that the line between 'illegitimate' and 'legitimate' sexual activity is a very fine one, also illustrated in the many issues surrounding the criminalization of pornography.

The contrasting approaches to sexual offending also indicate different policy directions and the insights of labelling perspectives and critical criminologists are also relevant in relation to demonization, criminalization and the impact of tougher and more punitive measures. While concerns about the prospect of convicted offenders being released back into the community may be understandable, the publication of information raises important questions about offenders' rights (Hebenton and Thomas 1996) and dangers of excluding them. Policy in relation to prostitution also illustrates the paradox of legislation seeking to protect women further by punishing them and excluding them from help and support, while failing to eliminate the problem. Overpunitive reactions, therefore, fail to reduce the problem and can indeed exacerbate it. Some form of legalization, including for example, licensing premises to be used for sex work, could enable more attention to hygiene and health and prevent some violent victimization.

Review questions

1. How and why are victims of sexual violence so often blamed for their own victimization?
2. Locate some figures about the extent of rape, how many women report it, and the process of attrition. How would you explain the continuing failure to convict more rapists?
3. To what extent has the Internet enabled new sexual offences to develop? Outline some examples.
4. Locate some examples of the way in which women who sell sex are described. Should they be described as 'sex workers' or 'prostitutes'? Give reasons for your answers.
5. Outline the feminist argument that sexual violence reflects male power over women. How would you evaluate this argument? This should further develop your answer prepared for Chapter 11.

Key reading

A number of books deal with different aspects of sex crime, and the most useful for understanding the issues outlined in this chapter are:

Brooks-Gordon, B. (2006) ***The Price of Sex: Prostitution, policy and society***, Cullompton: Willan Publishing. This provides a critical and engaging account of the legal issues and contemporary debates over work in the sex industry and its legal control.

Letherby, G., Williams, K., Birch, P. and Cain, M. (eds) (2008) ***Sex As Crime***, Cullompton: Willan Publishing. An invaluable collection of articles on a number of issues in relation to sex crime, including studies of sex workers, male and female, and different perspectives on rape and the demonization of paedophiles.

Thomas, T. (2005) ***Sex Crime: Sex offending and society***, Cullompton: Willan Publishing, 2nd edn. This text provides a comprehensive introduction to the main forms of sexual offending and a critical account of policies, particularly in relation to child sexual abuse.

Walby, S. and Allen, J. (2004) ***Domestic violence, sexual assault and stalking: Findings from the British Crime Survey***, Home Office Research Study 276, London: Home Office. This research-based publication provides a thorough and comprehensive survey of sexual offences and many of the issues surrounding research.

Chapter 13
Property crime

This chapter will look at:

- ➜ Defining and constructing property and volume crimes
- ➜ The scope of property crime
- ➜ Volume crime: burglary
  - Theft: theft at work; shoplifting
  - The stolen goods market
- ➜ Fraud
- ➜ Cyber crime

Property crime dominates officially recorded crime and victim surveys and encompasses an enormous range of offences, from minor acts of vandalism and theft to fraud and cyber crime. It involves very different kinds of offenders, from largely amateur teenage burglars and shoplifters to older and more skilled offenders whose activities lie on the fringes of organized crime. Often assumed to be economically motivated it can also provide emotional rewards and be widely tolerated within subcultures. While many of its forms are unambiguously criminal, a very fine line divides some forms of theft and fraud from widely tolerated 'fiddles'.

This chapter will focus on the main forms of officially classified 'property crime' which inevitably overlap with organized and white-collar crime. This chapter will deal primarily with what can broadly be described as 'blue collar' and non-occupational frauds, leaving more serious financial and corporate frauds to Chapter 15. It will start by looking at how property crime is officially and socially constructed and at some of its main characteristics. It will then look at some of its major forms starting with so-called 'volume' crimes such as burglary and different forms of theft before turning to a range of frauds. A further section will explore offences popularly associated with cyber crime, asking what is 'new' about this area and which offences can properly be so described. Finally some points will be made about how property crime can be analysed and understood.

What is property crime?

Official categories of property crime include burglary (in Scotland, housebreaking), theft, fraud and forgery and criminal damage. Broadly speaking, it involves stealing and dishonestly obtaining or damaging another's property, with property including tangible items and money along with intellectual 'property' such as copyright. The BCS define property crime as 'the various ways that individuals, households or corporate bodies have their property damaged or are deprived of it by illegal means (or where there is intent to do so)' (Walker et al 2009: 74). Like other crimes it tends to be associated with strangers and popular representations emphasize its more serious forms, conjuring up images of burglars trashing houses and shadowy internet villains and fraudsters preying on innocent investors. As with other forms of crime, these images downplay its more mundane and everyday nature. It is also important to recognize that it does not only relate to single events such as burglary or theft but 'concerns all the dimensions involved in the taking, distributing and buying of stolen goods' (Presdee 2009: 201), and is intricately related to the desirability of property and the public's willingness to buy 'knocked-off' or fake goods. Constructions of property crime involve, therefore, the following issues:

Volume crime?

The phrase 'volume crime' refers to the large proportions of property crime in reported and recorded crime. It is a major target of the crime-prevention policies based on the rational choice and lifestyle approaches outlined in Chapter 5. To Presdee (2009), it is a managerial term.

What is 'criminal' theft and fraud?

The borderline between theft, fraud and other activities is very narrow. In the workplace, for example, the words 'fiddles' or 'perks' describe a number of activities which are legally theft or fraud but which are widely tolerated (Ditton 1977; Mars 1982). Few who pay for goods or services in cash perceive themselves as defrauding the Inland Revenue, and few who buy suspiciously cheap goods in market stalls, car boot sales or pubs regard themselves as 'handlers of stolen goods' (Henry 1978; Presdee 2009). Like many other crimes, therefore, property crime is socially constructed.

What is dishonesty?

Fraud involves the concept of 'dishonesty'. Yet can criminal dishonesty be separated from many everyday commercial exchanges? Sellers aim to persuade buyers that their product or service is better than others through advertising or verbal persuasion. Are all these claims 'true'? When 'conned' by an overzealous salesperson, at what point do victims see themselves as the victim of a fraud?

Property crime and 'stranger danger'

As with sexual and violent crime, fears of property crime feature 'stranger danger' – the intruder or the pickpocket. Yet much property crime involves those closer to us, at home, at school or at work. Fraud is often perpetrated by someone known and trusted, some within the family (Levi and Pithouse 1992) and very large amounts of unreported thefts take place at home or at work.

Who are the offenders?

Property crime is often identified with lower-class offenders although a far wider range of people are involved, albeit that their activities are often not seen as crime. Official statistics do not always distinguish between offences with very different social meanings. Managers and workers steal from work and defrauding the Inland Revenue involves tax evasion and benefit fraud.

The scope of property crime

Problems of measurement

Property crime has a large hidden figure which varies according to the crime. Victim surveys, as already indicated, show that many victims do not report property offences, particularly where losses are trivial. Victim surveys such as the BCS or the SCJS focus on households and omit institutional victims such as shops, companies, warehouses, banks and building societies although there are now a number of commercial victim surveys and estimates of the costs of theft and fraud. This makes comparisons between victim surveys and police figures difficult. Official statistics, as outlined above, also say little about the context of offences and the large hidden figure includes the 'everyday' crimes of those across the social spectrum who routinely commit minor forms of theft and fraud – some of it captured in the OCJS. All of this should be born in mind when looking at official measurements of property crimes.

Official measurements of property crime

Some figures on property crime were outlined in Chapter 3, and, as it dominates official figures on crime, trends are very similar to those for crime as a whole. Box 13.1 provides some broad figures and illustrates the distribution of property crimes with thefts, including those in the workplace, shoplifting and theft of bicycles having the largest proportions, followed by vehicle-related thefts and burglary – although with burglary there is a disparity between reported and recorded crime due to victim surveys' exclusion of commercial burglary. Fraud and forgery, less easy to capture in victim surveys and often undetected, accounts for a much smaller proportion.

Property crime reflects the general trends of crime showing rising rates up to the mid 1990s, falling rates, including dramatic falls, to the early 2000s, since when they

Box 13.1 Forms of property crime

Theft

- In 2008/9 vehicle-related theft crime formed 14 per cent of BCS crimes and 13 per cent of police-recorded crime in England and Wales in 2008/9 (CEW). 33 per cent of BCS crimes and 23 per cent of police-recorded crime were described as 'other thefts' which incorporate thefts from the person, other theft of personal property, other household thefts and bicycle theft (Walker et al 2009).
- In the 2008/9 SCJS, all motor vehicle theft constituted 7 per cent of reported crime, with 'other' household theft, including bicycles, forming 17 per cent. Personal theft, excluding robbery, accounted for 9 per cent. The incidence rate for motor vehicle theft, housebreaking and personal theft excluding robbery were lower in Scotland than in England and Wales (MacLeod et al 2009).

In *Northern Ireland* theft formed 24 per cent of all recorded crime, with vehicle-related theft constituting 7 per cent and 30 per cent of all thefts (NOI 2010).

Burglary

- Burglary constituted 12 per cent of police recorded crime in England and Wales in 2008/9 and 7 per cent BCS crimes. Housebreaking constituted 2 per cent of offences reported to the SCJS in 2008/9 (MacLeod et al 2009) – but note counting differences. In Northern Ireland it constituted 12 per cent of recorded crime (NOI 2010).
- Households with younger residents, students and the unemployed had higher risks of burglary as did both social and privately rented accommodation than owner occupiers and those with lower levels of home security (Walker et al 2009).

Fraud and forgery

- Fraud and forgery accounted for 3 per cent of crimes recorded by the police in 2008/9 in England and Wales. This category is dominated by cheque and credit card frauds which are undercounted as continuous offending – for example, the frequent use of one credit card is only counted once (Maguire 2007; Coleman and Moynihan 1996). Many forms of fraud are dealt with by regulatory agencies and not by the police, and are therefore not included in the criminal statistics (Maguire 2007). The SCJS reports that in 2008/9, 3.6 per cent of adults reported card fraud and 0.8 per cent identity theft (MacLeod et al 2009). Fraud and forgery constituted 3 per cent of recorded crimes in Northern Ireland (NOI 2010).

Damage to property

- Criminal damage, which includes vandalism, amounted to 26 per cent BCS crimes and 20 per cent police-recorded crime in England and Wales 2008/9. It formed 34 per cent of crimes reported to the SCJS in 2008/9 (MacLeod et al 2009) and 26 per cent of recorded crimes in Northern Ireland (NOI 2010).

have been relatively stable with the exception of some small rises in the last two years – popularly attributed to the recession. As will be seen below, however, these trends reflect a variety of factors, not least of which are changing opportunity structures and technologies which have led, for example, to falling rates of car theft and reductions in some forms of credit card fraud – although there have been rises in other forms of fraud. More details will be provided in the specific examples outlined below.

Varieties of property crime

Volume crime: burglary and theft

This section will focus on so-called volume crimes providing a series of snapshots of the key features of the main crimes, illustrating their diversity.

Burglary

Burglary encompasses commercial and household burglary, distraction burglary, and a growing number specifically targeting car keys (Copes and Cherbonneau 2006; Moley 2009; Maguire et al 2010). Forced entry distinguishes burglary from other thefts, thus the Scottish offence of housebreaking, and this feature accounts for victims feeling insecure and that their home has been invaded (Mawby 2001).

Most research has focused on household burglary which constitutes nearly half of all burglaries. Burglary rates fell until around 2008, although it is too early to attribute small rises to the recession (Maguire et al 2010). Aspects of the risk and impact of burglary were outlined in Chapters 3 and 6. It is more prevalent in urban and socially deprived areas and therefore impacts most severely on the most vulnerable (Mawby 2001), and those least able to afford insurance are often targets of repeat burglaries (Croall 2007a). The effects of burglary extend from financial losses to its 'nuisance value' and severe emotional and psychological effects. Mawby also found that victims feared that burglars would come back, questioned why 'my' house has been targeted and some reported long-term health effects.

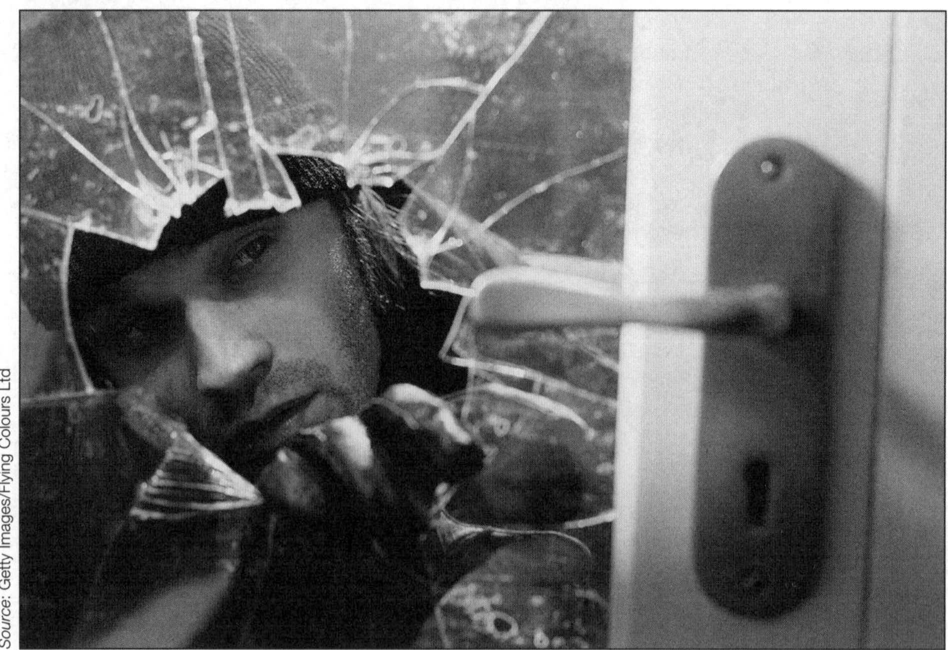

Source: Getty Images/Flying Colours Ltd

Burglary is often feared because it is experienced as a stranger invading the home.

It is difficult to generalize about the characteristics of burglars as so few are caught and those who are tend to be atypical (Mawby 2001). Most agree that they tend to be largely young, lower-class men and mainly white (Maguire et al 2010). Many work alone and, while having networks in the hidden economy, they are not strongly linked to professional or organized crime.

Being directed towards crime prevention, much work on burglars has focused on the way in which they choose their targets, gain entry and search properties, and what kinds of goods they are likely to steal. It has been argued, for example, that they use a range of 'cognitive skills' which help them to evaluate potential targets, enter a dwelling, search targets quickly and efficiently and convert stolen goods into money (Bennett 1989; Wright and Decker 1994; Nee and Meenaghan 2006). Cues include the level of surveillance, how likely they are to be observed, the general upkeep of the property, visible expensive items, the type of car parked outside, get-away routes and signs of occupancy. In searching a property they develop a sense of where desirable items are likely to be found and work speedily to avoid detection. They therefore possess 'expert' skills (Nee and Meenaghan 2006). Burglars can also be differentiated by level of planning and how far they travel to commit offences. Maguire et al (2010) distinguish between planners, searchers and opportunists, and Mawby (2001) distinguishes between 'amateurs' and professionals, the latter being older, more likely to plan their offences and likely to travel further.

Why do burglars burgle?

Most agree that burglars' motivations are largely economic and that burglary is a relatively quick and easy way of getting money to meet economic necessities, to feed a drug habit or to support a hedonistic lifestyle (Bennett and Wright 1984; Wright and Decker 1994; Mawby 2001). It can be, in effect, an 'occupation' providing a regular source of income (Maguire et al 2010). It is particularly appropriate for young men with few occupational or educational skills whose criminal options are also limited and some offenders prefer it to robbery which involves a higher risk of violence and face to face interaction (Wright and Decker 1994).

While the primary motivation is economic, not all steal to obtain necessities, and a recurrent theme has been the use of proceeds to finance a lifestyle based on stylish clothes, alcohol and drugs and conspicuous consumption (Bennett and Wright 1984; Shover and Honaker 1992; Wright and Decker 1994; Mawby 2001; Presdee 2009). Some, though by no means all, report obtaining thrills and excitement from burglary although this is secondary to the economic motivation. While drugs are a factor in many burglaries, as seen in Chapter 8, the relationships between drug-taking and property crime are complex and it is not necessarily a causal factor (Mawby 2001).

Theft

Theft involves a very wide range of offences ranging from minor thefts of purses or wallets, through to major thefts involving thousands of pounds. Statistics provide a very limited amount of information about the location of thefts, the amounts involved or its social organization and this section will look briefly at some of its main forms.

Car theft

Cars have always been attractive targets for thieves. Many features which we now take for granted like registration numbers, log books and keys, all originated from the need to prevent theft although owners were at one time advised not to lock their cars as they frequently had to be moved (Webb and Laycock 1992). The key-operated starter was introduced in 1949, by 1969 all new cars had to be fitted with steering locks, and more recently the introduction of the electronic immobilizer which requires a chip in the key to start the car has had a major effect on car theft and burglary. Although this section will focus on vehicle-related theft, cars have also been associated with a wide range of 'car crimes' including speeding, careless or drunken driving (Corbett 2003).

Property offences against vehicles involve stealing from a car, taking a car without the owner's consent for temporary use, as in so-called 'joyriding', or TWOCing, and stealing a car for permanent use, often to re-use it or its parts by car 'ringing' – effectively changing its identity. Thefts from a vehicle accounted for around two-thirds of vehicle crime in England and Wales in 2007/8. Car thefts 'peaked' around 1992 and have fallen quite dramatically since then, now being around the same level as the 1960s, in part due to improved security (Brown 2010). As with other property crimes, vehicle thefts are more common in urban, deprived areas and car thieves tend to be lower-class young men. Many offenders have previous convictions suggesting that they have been committing the crime for some time (Brown 2010).

Joyriding, a term associated with using cars for pleasure, has been a recurring phenomenon from the 1970s (Parker 1974) through to the urban disturbances of the early 1990s which saw dramatic displays of joyriding and clashes with the police (Campbell 1993). Many studies of joyriders stress the excitement and 'buzz' involved (Light et al 1993) and expressions of pride in driving skills (Webb and Laycock 1992: Campbell 1993). Part of the attraction for some is the police chase; others develop a career in car crime, moving from stealing from cars, through joyriding and then to stealing for profit which may also involve organized crime (Spencer 1992; Webb and Laycock 1992; Light et al 1993).

A major feature of contemporary car crime is that keys are needed to steal a car and many are now stolen with the keys left inside. Following interviews with car thieves, Copes and Cherbonneau (2006) identified a number of strategies:

- *Alert opportunism*: involved being alert to opportunities provided by cars being left with keys inside. These were related to street life and could materialize in the course of carrying out other crimes.
- *Active search*: this involved more motivation and some thieves waited outside shops and petrol stations. In some cases, they committed burglaries for the sole purpose of stealing car keys.
- *Use of force*: a small number resorted to carjacking which many avoided, fearing violence and face to face confrontation.
- *Manipulation*: situations for stealing keys would be sought by, for example, making test drives with car dealerships and swapping or making moulds from keys.
- *Master keys* could be stolen from manufacturers.

Why steal cars?

A range of motivations are involved in vehicle theft and the above examples suggest a difference between joyriders, for whom excitement and thrill are more important,

Box 13.2 CRAVED items

C	**concealable**
R	**removable**
A	**available**
V	**valuable**
E	**enjoyable**
D	**disposable**

Sources: Clarke (1999), cited in Tilley (2010), and for cars, Brown (2010)

and more professional car thieves for whom economic factors are more important (Brown 2010). Cars present attractive targets, and the CRAVED criteria, outlined in Box 13.2, operate – the identity of a car can be changed, they are removable, readily available, have an established value, are enjoyable for many and can be disposed of (Brown 2010). Some professional car thieves steal highly desirable cars to order and offenders can adapt to a changing opportunity structure (Copes and Cherbonneau 2006). The demand for stolen cars and the desire to steal for pleasure are also strongly related to 'car culture' (Corbett 2003; Brown 2010). Cars can come to symbolize identities and the desirability of some models is reflected in joyriders choosing sportier models. This is also gendered, being largely a male preserve and some link car theft to anomie, whereby the failure of less affluent young men to achieve cultural goals surrounding car ownership may lead to theft (Corbett 2003; Brown 2010).

Shoplifting

Shoplifting, also known as shop or customer theft, rose dramatically, more than other forms of property crime, from the Second World War (Tilley 2010). This is often accounted for by changes in shopping, with modern retailing having removed face to face contact between the seller and the consumer. Supermarkets have more goods and fewer employees, thus reducing levels of surveillance (Tilley 2010). Official figures most probably underestimate shoplifting and many shops do not calculate how much 'shrinkage' is attributable to customers or to staff. The Commercial Victimisation Survey estimates around 25 incidents per year for all shops, far in excess of police recorded figures, leading Tilley (2010: 51) to talk of an 'eye-watering' volume of shop theft in England and Wales. He also outlines some of its major characteristics. Items targeted by shoplifters are reflected in the CRAVED criteria outlined in Box 13.2 and tend to be expensive, small and high-demand items such as CDs, jewellery, medicines and cigarettes. More males than females are convicted, although women are more likely to be involved in shoplifting than other crimes (Chapter 9). In a 2004/5 study of convicted offenders (Speed and Burrows 2006), three-quarters were male, one half were aged between 18 and 29, 90 per cent were white European (in line with the local population), and 10 per cent were unemployed.

Why shoplift?

As for other forms of property crime, economic motivations predominate. Shoplifting is relatively easy, requires few skills and can be morally justified on the grounds that shops, not individuals, are victims and can 'afford it'. Shoplifting is often chosen to obtain money for drugs although again there is no direct causal link and it can be part of a 'career' providing a sense of achievement as well as an income (Davies 2005 and see Chapter 9).

Theft at work

Much theft at work is hidden as many employers do not count or report it and deal with it by dismissal. The British Retail Consortium estimate that it accounts for 8 per cent of losses from crime, compared to 64 per cent from theft by customers (Gill and Goldstraw-White 2010). Employee theft can be perpetrated by employees at all levels as the often used terms 'white-collar' and 'blue-collar' crime indicate. In general white-collar crime involves more serious crimes perpetrated by professional and senior employees (see Chapter 15). Employee theft is widely practised and built into workplace subcultures supporting a range of 'fiddles' or 'perks'. It involves not only tangible items, from stationery to large amounts of money, but also the theft of 'time', as in unauthorized breaks or 'sickies', or indeed computer time, as when employees run their own businesses using employers' computers (Mars 1982).

Studies of employee theft have generally been carried out with lower level employees 'fiddling' and stealing from both employers and customers (Ditton 1977; Henry 1978; Mars 1982). These are related to the opportunities provided by the job – quite simply, if employees do not handle cash, they cannot steal it (Croall 2001a). A range of other features are also important and Mars (1982; 2008) argues that these, illustrated in Box 13.3, are more important than employee status.

The primary motivation for theft at work is economic with subcultures tolerating fiddling, justifying it as part of a 'total reward' system to make up for low wages. Indeed, management can be complicit by turning a blind eye fearing that stricter control may lead to more formal industrial unrest. Mars (2008) argues that the widening gaps in rewards within organizations and the rise in casual employment may be criminogenic by providing grounds for resentment and moral justifications for 'fiddles'.

The stolen goods market

Property crime is closely associated with the market in stolen goods, which have to be converted into cash by selling them in street markets, pubs, car boot sales or in shops where their origins will not be questioned (Henry 1978; Foster 1990). Others are sold by 'hawkers' and an increasing role is now played by e-sales (Sutton 2010). Some use a professional 'fence', a middle person between the thief and the consumer, who may also be associated with organized crime groups. Some goods, such as cars or car parts, have to be disguised and re-created (Sutton 2010).

Choices about which goods to steal are related, as illustrated in the CRAVED criteria, to their marketability with items such as DVDs, mobile phones or laptops

Box 13.3 Criminogenic occupations

Mars (1982; 2008) relates theft at work to the nature of jobs, identifying:

- '*Hawk*' jobs, such as those of sales personnel, which provide autonomy and opportunities for fiddling.
- '*Donkey*' jobs such as the supermarket cashier or call-centre work, which involve little autonomy and close supervision. These leave few opportunities for theft, but may encourage sabotage.
- '*Wolfpack*' jobs involve teams and can produce highly organized fiddles.
- Jobs involving '*passing trade*' such as those in hotels and restaurants also provide opportunities which are likely to increase given high levels of mobility in the globalized economy.
- '*Gatekeepers*' introduce providers of services to purchasers thereby providing opportunities for theft and corruption, but this may decline with the Internet having become a 'virtual' gatekeeper.
- Asymmetric relationships between employers or clients and employees in terms of expertise are also '*fiddle prone*'. Where customers or employers lack technological expertise, they cannot judge the need for, or value of, a service. This includes professional occupations such as lawyers and accountants along with plumbers or computer technicians. The proliferation of 'experts' leads to an increase in these opportunities.

being relatively easy to steal and sell (Sutton 1995; 2010). Manufacturers regularly update these, thereby creating a market for second-hand items as wealthier consumers buy new models and sell old ones, often bought by poorer consumers. The legitimate trade in second-hand goods provides 'cover' for stolen goods.

The market also involves consumers who are willing to buy, and indeed to order, goods which they know or suspect are 'knocked off'. The extent of what Sutton (2010: 71) describes as 'crimemongers' is illustrated in findings by the OCJS of 2003 that as many as 7.2 per cent of respondents admitted buying goods which they knew or believed to be stolen in the last twelve months. Just over 1 per cent of children had bought a stolen mobile phone. Involvement in buying and selling stolen goods most often involves young single males living in the most deprived areas although it is not only the poorest who buy them. Indeed, argues Sutton, people's willingness to buy stolen goods makes acquisitive offending a rational choice and sellers can be viewed as entrepreneurs providing a valuable local service.

Fraud

The difficulties of defining fraud have already been referred to with words such as 'cons' or 'scams' expressing less serious condemnation. It is committed by employees at all levels and non-occupational frauds are perpetrated by 'outsiders' against businesses, organizations and government departments. As clients, consumers or householders, individuals are victimized by fraud and indeed many commit frauds when making insurance or expenses claims and filling in tax forms. Some frauds form part of serious and organized crime, the subject of Chapter 14, whereas corporate and white-collar frauds are discussed in Chapter 15. This section will briefly describe a variety of frauds which illustrate its ubiquity and diversity.

Estimating the extent of fraud is particularly hazardous as so much of it is undetected and unreported and there is no single source of figures (Doig 2006; Levi and Burrows 2008). Organizations do not always detect offences and are often reluctant to report them to the police. Governments have recently taken a stronger approach to fraud prevention which has included attempts to estimate the costs of fraud, although figures are difficult to compare, often being based on different years. There have also been attempts to bring together figures from commercial victim surveys, business organizations such as the Retail Consortium and the Association of Payment Clearing Services (APACS); BCS figures for frauds which victims can report; and OCJS figures for people who report participation (Allen et al 2005; Wilson et al 2006). Some of these are summarized in Box 13.4 although they should be treated with caution (Levi and Burrows 2008). Brief summaries of selected features of some of the main categories of fraud are provided below.

Box 13.4 Estimating the costs of fraud

Figures for England and Wales, taken from Wilson et al (2006) except where indicated.

- HM Customs and Excise 2003/4 estimates revenue losses at between £.4.8 and £5.4 billion.
- The Association of British Insurers (ABI), estimated the level of fraud in a 1999 survey as £645 million, with 3.9 per cent of 11.1 million claims being suspect (cited in Allen et al 2005).
- The Association of Payment Clearing Services (APACS) estimated the annual cost of plastic card losses in 2004 as £504.8 bn. The introduction of chip and PIN has been associated with a fall in total card losses.
- The NHS counter fraud service estimated the cost of patient fraud in 2003/4 as £87.2 million, a reduction from 1998–9. This consisted of
  - pharmaceutical patient fraud £47 million
  - dental patient fraud £30 million
  - optical patient fraud £10.2 million
- The Department of Work and Pensions estimates overall loses to fraud at £910 million broken down into:
  - £380 million from frauds involving income support, jobseeker's allowance, pension credit, minimum income guarantee;
  - £270 million from frauds involving housing and council tax benefit;
  - £40 million from Disability Living Allowance;
  - £30 million from retirement pensions (1995 figures);
  - £40 million from Carers Allowance (1996 figures);
  - £10 million from Incapacity Benefit;
  - £40 million from instrument of payment frauds – theft and forgery of girocheques and benefit order books.

Frauds against public money

Revenue fraud

Tax frauds have been noted throughout the ages. Wealthy Romans buried jewellery and homeowners in eighteenth-century England bricked up fireplaces to avoid the hearth tax collector (Minkes and Minkes 2010). Tax frauds involve individuals not declaring earnings fully to the Inland Revenue or placing funds out of their reach, although it is difficult to draw a line between illegal tax evasion and legal tax avoidance, such as using complex financial schemes or placing money offshore in tax havens (Chapter 15). An OCJS study found that 2 per cent of 18–65 year olds eligible to pay tax admitted income tax fraud with higher rates among men, those with higher educational qualifications and the self-employed. The latter can be explained by greater opportunities (Allen et al 2005). Another form of tax evasion is 'mooonlighting' or 'ghosting', doing work which is not declared, admitted by around 2 per cent in the OCJS sample (Allen et al 2005). Many people are complicit in this form of fraud by paying less cash for work which will not go through the books.

Benefit fraud

Tax fraud is often compared to benefit fraud (Cook 1989; Minkes and Minkes 2010), and similar numbers, around 1.8 per cent of those eligible, report engaging in it. As might be expected, higher rates were reported in low income areas (Allen et al 2005). Estimated losses from different kinds of benefits are outlined in Box 13.4. While little researched, this has been strongly associated with economic hardship and feelings of frustration (Cook 1989; Doig 2006; Minkes and Minkes 2010). Participants contrast their activities with serious fraud, believing that 'everyone is on the fiddle' and some choose benefit fraud in preference to other forms of crime, with some taking any opportunity to work without declaring it. There are also examples of organized benefit frauds. It often attracts greater condemnation than tax fraud reflecting contrasting constructions. It can be cast as trying to gain more from the taxpayer, whereas fiddling the 'tax man' is often morally justified as taxation is widely seen as too high (Cook 1989).

Frauds on the NHS

The extent and nature of patient frauds in the NHS, largely through falsely claiming exemption from prescription charges, is also outlined in Box 13.4. It should be noted that this does not include the considerable volume of 'white-collar fraud' perpetrated by doctors, pharmacists and dentists, which have been associated with high costs in England and Wales and more recently in Scotland (Croall 2001a; Mooney et al 2010). In England and Wales, estimated losses have decreased since the NHS Counter Fraud Service became operational.

Frauds on businesses

Expenses frauds

Employers are the main victims of expenses frauds, although they are also prevalent in government departments and indeed, as recent revelations indicate, in Parliament.

These frauds are often subculturally tolerated and, like employee theft, seen as part of a total reward system, also present in the House of Commons (Doig 2006). The OCJS found that, of those with the opportunity, 6.7 per cent had made false claims in the preceding year. Younger men and those in middle income groups were more likely to report these frauds (Allen et al 2005).

Insurance fraud

Box 13.4 also indicates the costs of insurance fraud which 5.1 per cent of those eligible reported to the OCJS with higher numbers amongst males, younger age groups, and households with relatively low incomes. A survey by the Association of British Insurers (cited in Doig 2006: 84) found that 7 per cent admitted fraudulent claims and nearly half had been tempted, but they paint a different picture of offenders suggesting that people who make false claims are more likely to be university-educated home-owners, male, aged over 35 and 'not the type of people you might perceive to be dishonest'. Perpetrators often justify insurance fraud by expressing resentment against insurance companies (Doig 2006; Karstedt and Farrell 2006) and businesses threatened with bankruptcy can set fire to premises to claim on insurance (Clarke 1989).

Frauds against individuals

Advance fee frauds

Advance fee frauds involve promises of high rewards if money is provided 'up front', rewards which do not materialize. Classic examples are the so-called Nigerian frauds in which opportunities to release funds which the investor will then share are offered on receipt of bank details or money. One such offer received by the author is reproduced in Box 13.5. Offers of attractive investments target risk-takers confident they can spot a fraud and other examples include paying to set up a 'homeworking' business, to work as models, sending money to a partner in an internet 'romance' to travel to the UK, premium-rate telephone prize scams and pyramid selling (Doig 2006; Mackenzie 2010b). The recent cessation of flights due to volcanic ash produced a new version with e-mails claiming to be from the Civil Aviation Authority claiming that travellers affected could receive £2000 on receipt of an administration fee (BBC News 2010n). Advance fee frauds have a long history although e-mail has made it much easier and cheaper to reach large numbers of people.

Bank and mortgage frauds

The keenness of banks and building societies to lend money, which featured in the recent financial crisis, was also associated with an increase in bank and mortgage frauds in the early 2000s (Doig 2006). These basically involve making false representations about income, employment records and other personal details to open up an account in order to perpetrate a further fraud or to obtain a loan or mortgage.

Cheque and credit card frauds

Box 13.4 also illustrates the considerable losses associated with cheque and credit card fraud. While these have declined, particularly since the introduction of chip and PIN technology, there has been an increase of card not present (CNP) frauds,

Box 13.5 Advance fee fraud: an example

Dear Friend,
My name is Mr.XX. I work with the Bank of Africa in Abidjan Cote d'Ivoire. I have been mandated by the director of allocation board committee to seek for a reliable and trust worthy firm or individual from your country who can assist them to receive the total sum of US$7M. The fund have been approved for payment by the Government under the ministry of works.

SOURCE OF THE FUND: The fund originated from various contracts awarded to foreign (FIRMS) for the reconstruction of network pipeline and renovation of the International Airport. The original contracts value was purposely over invoice by the Allocation Board Committee to the tune of US$3.5Million on each contract. Before they could use the umbrella of the original contractors to claim this fund, The political crises started where lives and properties was lost and destroyed in the year 2002. Now the new prime Minster headed former rebel leader Mr. SOLO GUILLAUME decided to pay off all the outstanding contract debts to redeem back the image of the country.

RIGHT NOW: The outstanding over invoiced $7M have been approved for payment and for this fund to be claimed now. It has to be with the help of a foreign firm or an individual, who will act as the beneficiary. The Director of the Board knows everything about the contract details. However, due to his position, he don't want to be notice now hence my goal is to find a reliable and trust-worthy firm or individual to receive this fund in a foreign account.

TO TRANSFER THIS FUND: All modalities have been worked out, as i am the person incharge for this payment as the Bank of Africa foreign operation manager. All you have to do is to send me a reply indicating your interest and details will be sent to you for you to send your bank details to receive the $7Million.

in which false details are provided in Internet and telephone sales (Levi 2010). Around a fifth of card fraud results from stolen or lost cards and 1 per cent of respondents in the OCJS reported using someone else's card or details without the owner's permission, with highest rates amongst those with no qualifications living in more deprived areas (Allen et al 2005; Wilson et al 2006). Similar numbers of males and females report committing this kind of fraud. Levi (2010) lists the main credit card frauds as:

- counterfeit card fraud in which cards are printed, embossed or encoded without permission from the issuer;
- fraudulent possession of card details which are used in CNP frauds, in phone, mail order, fax or Internet transactions;
- fraud using lost and stolen cards;
- mail non receipt frauds in which new cards are intercepted;
- identify theft fraud in which stolen or false details from cards are used to open or takeover an account.

While credit card fraud is seen to be a major problem, Levi (2010) points out that fraudulent transactions make up a mere 0.12 per cent of all transactions.

Long firm fraud

Long firm fraud has been known for centuries, and basically involves setting up one or more businesses and obtaining goods on credit with no real intention of ever paying. Levi's (1981; 2008a; 2010) research on these 'phantom capitalists' identifies a number of skills. The 'front man' has to be able to obtain goods on credit and needs to be able to tell a good story when negotiating credit. Skills are also involved in avoiding conviction and imprisonment. Top-class fraudsters adjust their public persona to the environment, can quickly decide how to deal with people and judge whether people are trying to con them. Face to face skills may now be less relevant as the Internet enables the creation of fraudulent corporate identities. These skills and knowledge limit participation – so-called 'hard men', argues Levi, do not have the 'savvy' to operate a business. While cast as 'villains', many offenders believed that their activities were not wrong and provided them with opportunities to live a good life. They were excited when carrying out a successful fraud although a career in long firm fraud could also be stressful with the constant risk of detection and imprisonment. Long firm fraudsters straddle boundaries between white-collar, organized and so-called conventional criminals and they do not fit the stereotypical tropes of the poorly educated lower-class offender. At the same time they are not wealthy or powerful elite members, although they see themselves as 'businessmen' rather than 'villains'.

The diversity of offences and offenders means that few generalizations can be made about offenders about many of whom little is known. They are clearly from more diverse backgrounds than other property offenders. While some frauds typically involve lower-class young men, women feature in tax, insurance, expenses and benefit frauds and tax and insurance frauds also involve well-educated, higher paid individuals. Doctors and lawyers can moonlight as well as plumbers and builders. Moreover, as is the case with the stolen goods market, a wide range of people are complicit in revenue frauds, even if they do not regard their activities as in any way deviant.

Victims are also heterogeneous and all taxpayers are indirectly affected by all revenue frauds. Those who fall victim to advance fee frauds are not among the poorest as they have to have the money to advance. To Mackenzie (2010b: 144) they are 'normal individuals whose greed has got the better of them'. Commercial institutions are also major victims although often seen as less deserving and able to absorb the costs. As Levi points out (2010: 155), frauds against card issuers and industrial companies almost never generate the moral panic seen in the more spectacular 'widows and orphans' investment and savings frauds (and see Chapter 2). The doctrine of *caveat emptor*, let the buyer beware, leads to some victim blaming and victimization also has an emotional impact with many victims reporting embarrassment and shame (Mackenzie 2010b). Different kinds of frauds affect different groups with women being more likely to be victims of homeworking scams and men being more likely to take risks on purportedly rewarding investments (MacKenzie 2010b). While older people are often seen as more vulnerable, younger people may be more prone to take risks (see Chapter 8).

The diversity of frauds and fraudsters also makes looking for motives difficult. Some are highly planned, others are opportunistic and offenders display different levels of skill. In relation to long firm fraud Levi (1981; 2008a) has developed a typology which has broader application. He distinguishes between 'villains' and 'honest businessmen' and identifies:

- Preplanned frauds in which the business is set up with the intention of defrauding suppliers;
- Slippery slope frauds which occur when businessmen continue to trade and obtain goods on credit although there is a high risk that unless their business situation improves, they will be unable to pay for the goods;
- Intermediate frauds, in which a formerly legitimate business turns into a fraudulent one.

Fraudsters are clearly economically motivated although this is not always linked to hardship and need, as is the case with benefit fraudsters. White-collar offenders have been said to be motivated by greed as well as need (Croall 2001a; Doig 2006) and many fraudsters are typically depicted as enjoying a 'lavish lifestyle'. Some pride themselves on their skills and Mackenzie (2010b: 142) talks of the 'highs' and competitive kicks involved in successful sales – mirroring legitimate sales personnel. As for other property offenders structural theories can also be applied and cultural tolerance is also a factor in revenue, benefit, expenses and insurance fraud.

Cyber crime

Many of these crimes use the Internet and there have been fears about the activities of hackers, cyber stalkers, cyber terrorists and identity thieves – amounting to a cyber crime 'tsunami' (Yar 2006; Wall 2007). A number of questions can, however, be asked. To what extent does cyber crime represent anything distinctively new? Many of the frauds described in the previous section existed long before the Internet. What forms does it take and how prevalent is it? Who are cyber criminals and cyber victims? Can it be analysed in the same way as other crimes?

Cyber crime has no clear definition but refers to a 'diverse range of illegal and illicit activities that share in common the unique electronic environment in which they take place' (Yar 2006: 5). Existing legal categories are more used to dealing with theft, fraud or vandalism involving tangible as opposed to 'virtual' goods and services. While some forms of cyber crime are widely recognizable as fraud or theft but *use* the Internet, others are in effect *created by* the Internet (Wall 2007 and see Box 13.6). To Wall, the acid test of whether an activity is a 'true' cyber crime is whether it could exist without the Internet. Advance fee frauds have existed for centuries but are facilitated by electronic communications, whereas if the Internet were taken away tomorrow, computer 'attacks' would disappear.

How therefore has the Internet affected crime? In general, it has altered time and space relationships enabling people to communicate with thousands of others on a global basis in milliseconds, without the need for letters, phone calls or travel (Yar 2006; Wall 2007; Williams 2010). Fraudsters can target thousands of potential victims quickly and cheaply and with far fewer risks of detection. There is now less need for 'hard' copies of films, DVDs or CDs which can be downloaded. It has reduced the need for face to face interaction and people can easily create multiple identities. Fraudsters can, for example, attempt to sell goods or services and pose as

Box 13.6 What is cyber crime?

Yar (2006: 10): cyber crimes are 'computer mediated activities that are illegal'. Wall (2007) identifies categories of cyber crime related to a shift from first, second and third generation:

- Crimes using computers to facilitate an 'ordinary' crime: illegally gathering information or selling items.
- Cyber crime which utilizes new opportunities for committing traditional crimes across a global span of networks: hacking, fraudulent sales and trading in sexually explicit materials.
- 'True' cyber crimes, wholly mediated by technology: 'virtual violence', computer 'attacks' and botnets.

Activities can be grouped as follows:

- Computer integrity crimes which involve breaching computer security mechanisms, including hacking, virtual vandalism, planting viruses, taking over computer systems and Denial of Service (DoS) offences.
- Computer-assisted crimes in which networked computers are used to acquire money, goods or services.
- Computer content crimes such as the dissemination of pornography or racist and hate literature.

satisfied customers to enhance their marketing. The growing dependency of businesses, individuals and governments on electronic communications makes them vulnerable to attack – thus the fear of cyber terrorism.

Mercifully, these potential threats have not so far materialized although some viruses have had considerable effects. Estimating the extent of cyber crime is extremely difficult. Like fraud, many cyber crimes are not detected and companies may not want to reveal their vulnerability. Individual victims may feel that there is little to be gained by reporting incidents, and would not know who to report them to (Yar 2006). Most agree, therefore, that there is a massive hidden figure of cyber crime. On the other hand, as will be seen below, commercial organizations have a vested interest in 'talking up' the problem (Yar 2006; Wall 2007). UK-wide business surveys provide vastly different estimates (Williams 2010). In general over 20 per cent of businesses report virus attacks and sabotage, between 10 and 20 per cent report fraud and data theft, and smaller numbers report DoS attacks (see below). Larger companies were more likely report fraud, viruses and other attacks and the public sector may be more prone to fraud and data theft and less to virus attacks and hacking. Around 18 per cent of individual households report viruses, 12 per cent e-mail harassment and 21 per cent receiving offensive or upsetting material. A brief outline of some of the major forms of cyber crime follows.

Cyber 'attacks'

'Attacks' on computers and networks take a variety of forms. They involve the use of *malware* which includes viruses, worms and Trojans all of which adversely affect

Box 13.7 'Botnet smashed'

A BBC News (2010j) report covers the arrest, in Spain, of three men responsible for what is described as one of the world's biggest networks of virus-infected computers.

- The so-called Mariposa botnet was made up of nearly 13 million computers in 190 countries including PCs inside over one half of Fortune 1000 companies and over 40 major banks.
- This network was designed to steal sensitive information, including usernames, passwords, banking credentials and credit card data from social media sites and other online e-mail services.
- The 'gang' made money by renting out parts of the botnet to other cyber-criminals, selling stolen credentials and using banking and credit card information to make transactions via so-called money mules.
- Defence Intelligence, an Internet security firm which was part of the investigation, suffered a DoS attack as apparent retaliation.
- All those arrested were Spanish with no criminal records and limited hacking skills and were identified only by their Internet names: netkairo, aged 31, johnyloleante, aged 30 and ostiator, aged 25.
- The network had been monitored by a major investigation involving, among others, the FBI and the Spanish Guardia Civil.

computer operation. Trojans and spy ware can be used to extract details of users and communications and to create so-called 'botnets' in which entire networks are taken over and spam e-mails sent out across the entire network. Offenders can create and control 'zombie' computers and hold companies to ransom by threatening a Denial of Service (DoS) attack in which companies' websites, particularly those used for commercial sales, are rendered inoperative through viruses or barraging the site with so many e-mails that the system collapses. Box 13.7 outlines a case illustrating the potential impact of botnets. Attacks can cause considerable losses with one 2003 estimate suggesting an annual average cost of £120,000 to clean up after virus attacks (Williams 2010). The 2002/3 BCS found that just under a fifth of households in England and Wales using the Internet were affected by a virus in the last year and 1 per cent of an OCJS sample (10–65 year olds) had knowingly sent a virus in the last year, with males and 10–15 year olds being more likely to do so (Allen et al 2005). While computer attacks used to require technical knowledge and skill, they have now been made more routine by the manufacture of software (Wall 2007; Williams 2010).

Hacking

So-called 'hacking' can be likened to criminal damage or vandalism (Yar 2006). Again, this used to involve highly technical skills but is facilitated by readily available software packages. Hackers gain access to sites and some alter information. 'Hacktivists' are politically motivated and aim to damage the reputation of targeted sites. Hacking raises fears about cyber espionage, changing or stealing information, and cyber terrorism (Williams 2010), although Yar (2006) points out that terrorists have been more likely to use the Internet for research and communication with other groups and there is little evidence that they are likely to destroy it. Around 2.2 per cent of Internet users in the 2002/3 BCS had experienced hacking and around 2 per cent of under 25s, mostly male, reported hacking to the OCJS (Allen et al 2005). To Wall (2007), these numbers are not very high. To Yar (2006), hacking is a form of youth crime and can be part of male subcultures. A quarter of those under 19 in a recent survey reported accessing their friends' Facebook accounts by 'cracking' their passwords. This was largely for fun, although a fifth of those involved thought that they might make money out of it (BBC News 2010l).

Internet frauds

Internet frauds also include Internet auctions which can be linked to the stolen goods market, and in which prices can be manipulated by 'shill bidding', where the fraudster makes false bids, artificially pushing up the price. Many internet frauds on banks and commercial organizations are facilitated by attempting to obtain personal identification data, account details and passwords through 'phishing' (based on 'fishing'). This typically involves 'spoof' e-mails purporting to be from ISPs, banks or other organizations falsely claiming that the service will be terminated if personal data is not confirmed. Some provide links to fake websites to enhance authenticity. Many predict that, given the increase in Internet banking and the spread of social networking sites such as Facebook, on which users place identification data, these may well increase (Wall 2007; Williams 2010). The UK Cards Association has reported rises in phishing attacks between 2008 and 2009 and an increase in total online banking losses attributable to phishing to £59.7 million. It also identified 'spear phishing', the targeted phishing of a small group of people using fake social networking websites to gather personal information (BBC News 2010l). Williams (2010) however, cautions that all such estimates be critically evaluated.

Identity theft

Phishing plays a major role in identity theft which, while not new, or dependent on the Internet, is often seen as part of cyber crime. Identity theft is an umbrella concept involving 'the criminal acquisition of an individual's personal data to gain an advantage' (Semmens 2010: 172). It incorporates offences such as passport theft, credit card fraud and election fraud, and can be implicated in illegal immigration, benefit fraud and terrorism, all of which involve the use of another person's data. It involves stealing the 'portfolio' of personal data necessary for identification from wallets, computers, intercepting mail or using social networking sites for which personal data is provided. It can be stolen from government departments or banks as high-profile cases have revealed. Identify theft can be partial, as when cards are stolen, used for fraud and then disposed of, or permanent, as in 'identity hijack' where a person adopts someone else's identity. Estimates of its costs tend to be rather unreliable due to the variety of offences and very little is known about offenders. Some are street-level thieves and any involvement of more skilled and professional offenders is as yet unclear. Individual victims may lose very little financially but it has an enormous nuisance value as all details have to be changed and identity re-established. It can also be emotionally stressful (Wall 2007; Semmens 2010). There are also suggestions that it is increasing with the credit agency Experian suggesting a 20 per cent rise from 2008–9 (BBC 2010m).

'Piracy'

There have recently been attempts to toughen the law against and to terminate Internet access for those involved in illegally downloading music, films and other intellectual copyright. It has been estimated that the audio–visual industry loses £800 million through copyright theft, and that the music industry lost £1.1 billion between 2003 and 2006 (Williams 2010). Intellectual property theft raises complex legal difficulties as, unlike the theft of tangible items, no one can be said to be 'permanently deprived' of anything, but are prevented from profiting from the labour which has gone into creating music, film or written word. 'Piracy' has increased enormously since the Internet has made it so easy to download and distribute music or films, and many young people, who form the largest group of offenders, see very little wrong with these activities (Yar 2006). Allen et al (2005) found that 15 per cent of Internet users admitted such theft, more often men, those under 25, and in full-time education. Tools assisting downloads are now readily available and pirate distributors hold lists of subscribers. Illegal downloads can also be distributed electronically, thereby avoiding the costs of producing and distributing 'hard copy' (Yar 2006).

There is, argues Yar, a need to question the way in which 'piracy' – a somewhat loaded word – is subject to criminalization, and its costs are often exaggerated. These are based, for example, on calculations of the costs of purchasing a cinema ticket or a CD, yet it is by no means certain that all who download would ever pay the full price. He also questions whether artists lose as much as is assumed as they very often assign copyright to commercial companies. Indeed, widespread downloading can broaden a musician's fan base, producing higher attendance at concerts.

This brief outline of so-called cyber crime illustrates its diversity and the difficulties of reaching any clear conclusions about what might motivate offenders. Those participating in more serious frauds can be broadly contrasted with young hackers seeking an exciting challenge, whereas very little is known about those involved in botnets and large-scale virus attacks. While fraudsters' motivations are economic, skills are also involved and cyber crime is not so clearly related to poverty and deprivation as other property crimes. As Yar (2006) points out, the poorest do not have equal access to computer networks; those in full-time education emerge as offenders in some frauds and even though hacking has been substantially 'deskilled' it still requires a modicum of computer knowledge. Downloading music and other copyright items is widely tolerated particularly among young people and hacking can reflect elements of masculinity along with cultural criminology's emphasis on escapism and risk-taking (Wall 2007). The tendency to criminalize young people's activities, seen throughout earlier chapters, is a feature in relation to piracy, and fears about cyber crime can be related to wider social tensions and anxieties about technological change (Yar 2006).

Understanding property crime

The diversity of property crime means that a range of approaches are necessary to understand it. Its primarily economic motivation suggests that pathological approaches are of less relevance and volume crimes have been dominated by rational choice and lifestyle perspectives. It is evident from above, however, that it cannot simply be attributed to rational choices and that cultural and social structural factors are also important; the fine line between legal and illegal cons, scams, fiddles and theft and fraud also raises issues of criminalization.

Patterns of offending

Before exploring these perspectives, it is important to outline the variety of offenders involved and four main types of offending can be suggested:

- **The 'everyday' offender**: The phrase everyday crime is used to describe the activities of large numbers of people who do not regard their behaviour or themselves as 'criminal'. Examples include downloading music or films, inflating expenses and insurance claims, 'borrowing' from employers and willingly buying 'knocked-off' goods or 'paying in cash'. Typically this is justified on the grounds that 'everybody does it' or that 'they' can afford it.
- **Young people having fun**: Large numbers of young people, from 10 upwards, engage in property crime, much of it expressive rather than instrumental. Vandalism has long been recognized as a form of youthful expressiveness, and joyriding and computer-hacking appear very similar. A minority of young people engaging in these forms of crime go on to criminal careers (see Chapter 8).
- **The unskilled opportunist**: Some offenders do not deliberately plan specific offences but are open to the possibility of committing crime given the opportunity and do not envisage embarking on a serious criminal career. They might steal CRAVED goods, fiddle expenses, steal goods at work, a credit card or even a car, given an opportunity. They may also graduate to involvement in more serious crimes.
- **The skilled and motivated property offender**: For a minority of offenders 'thieving' becomes a way of life, involving a distinct set of skills, but falling short of involvement in the kind of criminal groups associated with organized crime, dealt with in Chapter 14. The skilled property offender is more likely to be older, from a predominantly lower-class background, and engage in more careful planning of car theft, burglary and possibly some forms of fraud and cyber crime, although so little is known about these kinds of offenders that it is difficult to generalize. Hobbs (1995) has argued, for example, that former robbers and thieves may have turned to the Internet as targets have become better protected.

The rational property offender?

Property offences have been a major focus of crime-prevention research aiming to apply rational choice and lifestyle approaches, outlined in Chapter 5. These have undoubtedly produced interesting insights, highlighting the many choices which offenders make and the importance of opportunity factors. These are not evenly distributed – the employed, for example, have more opportunities for theft and fraud at work, with different occupations providing different illegitimate opportunity

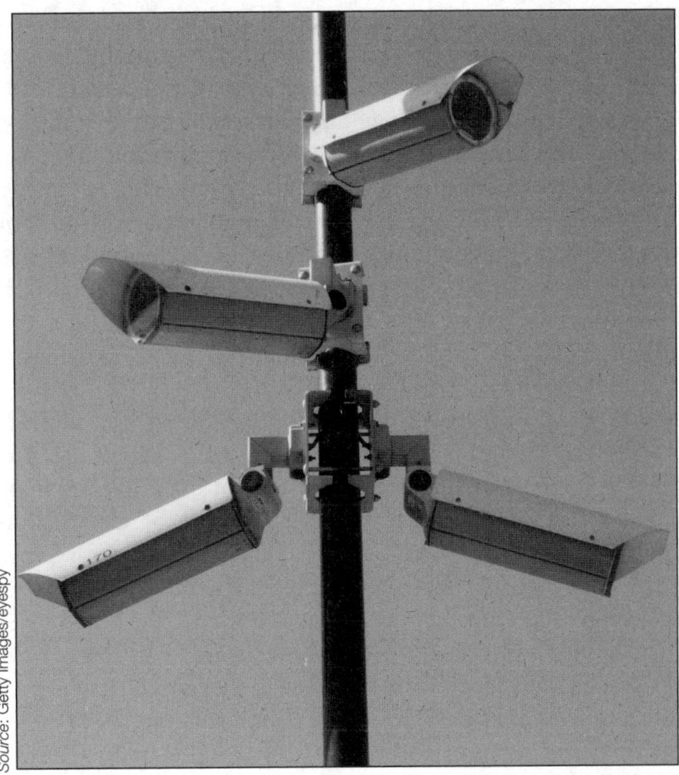
Source: Getty Images/eyespy

structures. Technological skills and access to computers are also important for many forms of fraud. Technological changes have also affected targets and reduced and changed the skills required for car theft and credit card fraud. The introduction of the 'capable guardian' of CCTV has also affected many forms of property crime as have the many security precautions taken by individual householders.

It is nonetheless difficult to gauge the impact of these policies on the total volume of property crime as any decrease could be due to other factors: potential offenders might have turned to other forms of crime – attracted, for example, by the greater ease, anonymity and lower chance of detection associated with Internet-based offending, widely assumed to be rising, although estimates must be treated with caution. Moreover, many forms of property crime provide rewards which are not strictly economic. Joyriders, young computer hackers and some fraudsters are attracted by the fun and thrills of offending, suggesting the operation of other factors.

The attractions of property crime

As outlined above, many offenders are from lower-class backgrounds and lack educational qualifications or occupational skills. Property crimes are often cast as crimes of 'need', compared to the crimes of 'greed' associated with white-collar offences (see Chapters 7 and 15). Many burglaries, thefts and benefit frauds are related to economic necessity. It was also seen in Chapter 7 that these are affected by economic factors and widening income differentials. Property crime is central to the anomie paradigm as it represents the 'classic' innovative response to failure to achieve economic goals. Its significance can also be seen in the primacy given to stealing, and selling to a largely willing market, highly desirable consumer goods.

Simple contrasts between need and greed are, however, inappropriate. Some steal or cheat to maintain a consumer-based lifestyle involving designer clothes and 'must have' items such as the latest versions of mobile phones or sports cars. As seen in Chapters 5 and 7, a combination of cultural inclusion and structural exclusion constitutes a toxic mix in which the most deprived experience frustration and indeed humiliation (Young 2007a). Property crime is a means of possessing desirable items and also, as cultural criminologists suggest, provides thrills, risk and a sense of achievement.

Participation in property crime is also facilitated by cultural and subcultural justifications and neutralization techniques (see Chapter 4). Fiddling taxes, for example, can be morally justified in the face of excessive levels of taxation (Cook 1989), and resentment against the excess profits of large corporations or their failure to pay a 'fair day's wage' can provide justifications for expenses fiddles, theft and fraud. Young people downloading from the Internet or cracking into websites see very little wrong with their activities.

Socio-economic status is also closely interrelated with other inequalities, particularly age and gender. Hacking and piracy, for example, are associated with young men, and can be seen as part of 'oppositional' subcultures (Yar 2006). They, along with joyriding and other offences, can further be related to masculinity, seen most starkly in 'car culture'. Campbell (1993), discussing joyriding in the 1990s, talked of how representations of aggressive masculinity in the media and advertising were reflected in the preference of joyriders for high-performance cars, speeding and car chases with the police in which both joyriders and the police play out fantasies. Women, on the other hand, are more likely to be involved in shoplifting or benefit fraud, often linked to economic necessity, although for them too, excitement and a sense of achievement can be important (Carlen 1988; Davies 2007a). As outlined in Chapter 10, more research is needed on the involvement of minority ethnic groups and links between different cultures and particular forms of property crime.

The role of labelling, moral panics and differential criminalization is also significant. Joyriders were 'folk devils' for many years and current fears focus on cyber terrorism, identity theft and Internet 'piracy' which has been talked up by the largely commercial interests to which it poses a threat. As with other moral panics these can be related to fears of the 'new' and the risks posed by technology. While some property offences and offenders are feared and 'othered', closer analysis reveals that a very fine line divides their activities from everyday forms of crime which are widely tolerated.

Concluding comments

This chapter has dealt with a wide variety of offences and offenders, which, taken together, dominate officially recorded crime and reported victimization. It has raised questions about how concepts such as theft, fraud, cyber crime and volume crime are constructed and about the narrow line between offences widely regarded as criminal and those widely tolerated within cultures and subcultures. It revealed a wide range of motivations for offending ranging through economic need, a desire to enjoy consumer-based lifestyles to the greed of those pursuing lavish lifestyles. Offenders range from those engaging in one-off opportunistic offences to those for whom property crime in effect becomes a 'full-time' occupation and who might move on to a 'career' in the more serious crimes to be dealt with in Chapter 14.

No one approach could hope to encompass such a wide range of crimes, some of which involve rational choices and careful planning, while others are more closely related to culture, to youth subcultures and indeed to cultures of masculinity. It is also related to economic inequalities, anomie and social exclusion. As with so many forms of crime it illustrates the interrelationship between inequalities highlighted in earlier chapters – women and men engage in different property crimes for similar and different reasons, and people of different ages and employment backgrounds have a different set of opportunities for different kinds of crime.

As for other chapters, only a selected range of crimes and issues could be explored. Vandalism also raises issues about youthfulness and expressivity, and potential differences between ethnic groups in relation to different forms of property crime could be further related to cultural factors. The study of crime in virtual worlds involves asking interesting questions about constructing and controlling 'virtual' violence and harassment (Williams 2006). A further underdeveloped area is the involvement of 'middle-class' offenders in so-called 'everyday' crimes. This raises important questions about the extent of, motivations and justifications for these crimes and about why they should be regarded as 'everyday' while the 'piracy', thefts and frauds of largely lower-class offenders are regarded as unambiguously criminal. Labelling and criminalization perspectives are, therefore, highly relevant.

The kinds of analyses outlined above also have some messages for policy. They illustrate, for example, some of the strengths of crime-prevention policies indicating the impact of simple changes, such as electronic immobilizers or PIN numbers. At the same time, the possible displacement of activities to, for example, Internet crime has also been suggested and it is not at all clear exactly what effect such policies have had. Also suggested are the dangers of overreaction to, for example, youthful hackers or 'pirates' who are far from the stereotype of 'cyber terrorists'.

Review questions

1. Compile a list of property crimes and consider how many 'offences' you and those you know have committed. Which ones do you, and your group, consider as 'criminal'?
2. To what extent has the Internet affected patterns of property crime? Which crimes can be said to constitute 'real' cyber crime?
3. To what extent can different forms of property crime be related to
   - (a) consumer culture?
   - (b) rational choice?
   - (c) social deprivation?

Key reading

A large number of books and articles deal with different aspects of property crime. A particularly good source of recent articles covering a broad range of offences is:

Brookman, F., Maguire, M., Pierpoint, H. and Bennett, T. (eds) (2010) *Handbook of Crime*, Cullompton: Willan Publishing.

Levi, M. (2008a) ***The Phantom Capitalists: The organization and control of long-firm fraud***, revised edn, Aldershot: Ashgate. The re-edition of this research on one group of fraudsters contains a comprehensive analysis of fraud in general and long-firm fraud in particular, covering social and legal constructions, the law and its enforcement and a full analysis of offenders' motivations based on extensive interviews. The introduction reflects on changes in fraud since the original research was carried out.

Mawby, R. (2001) ***Burglary***, Cullompton: Willan Publishing. A comprehensive text, including original research, on forms of burglary and experiences of victimization along with crime prevention policies.

Wall, D. (2007) *Cybercrime: The Transformation of Crime in the Information Age*, Cambridge: Polity Press. This is an engaging and comprehensive text dealing with the definition, construction and rise of cyber crime. It includes a number of case studies and looks at its legal status and the difficulties of policing and prosecuting it.

Chapter 14
Organized crime

This chapter will look at:

- Defining and constructing 'organized crime'
- The scope of organized crime
- The organization of serious crime in Britain
- Trafficking in illegal drugs
- Human trafficking and smuggling
- Understanding the organization of serious crime and its prohibition

Many myths surround organized crime which has, as seen in Chapter 2, been both romanticized by association with Mafia-style 'Godfathers' and demonized by images of monolithic criminal cartels subject to the 'war' on organized crime. It is associated with global illegal trades in drugs, arms, endangered species, art and human beings and, locally, with gangs and 'local firms'. Informed accounts, however, suggest a more complex picture and point to the wide variety of individuals and groups involved and to the close relationship between the legitimate and illegitimate economies. This chapter will start by looking critically at constructions and definitions of organized crime before exploring its scope. Selected aspects will then be outlined, looking at what is known about British organized crime before turning to what is often seen as its global reach, involving the production and supply of illegal drugs, and at human smuggling and trafficking. Finally, it will explore how organized crime can be understood.

What is organized crime?

The definition of organized crime is particularly contentious, and many dispute the usefulness of the concept itself (Wright 2006; Levi 2007; Edwards and Levi 2008). It has been associated with 'professional' crime, likened by Sutherland (1987) to a legitimate profession with its own distinctive system, language, laws, history, traditions, customs, methods and techniques. Mack (1972) distinguished between 'part-time' and 'full-time' criminals, the latter being associated with specific crafts and skills and with occupational identities such as 'thief', the 'cheque forger' or 'safe breaker'. It was also linked to an 'underworld', related to the stolen goods market (Chapter 13) and which also functions as a labour market and an informal means

Box 14.1 Definitions of organized crime

European Commission and Europol (2001):
Organized crime must contain at least six of the following characteristics and all four of those in *italics*:

- *Collaboration of more than two people*
- Each with own appointed tasks
- *For a prolonged period of time*
- Using some form of discipline or control
- *Suspected of the commission of serious criminal offences*
- Operating at an international level
- Using violence or other means suitable for intimidation
- Using commercial or businesslike structures
- Engaged in money-laundering
- Exerting influence on politics, the media, public administration, judicial authorities or the economy
- *Determined by the pursuit of profit and/or power*

Article 2 of the United Nations Convention against Transnational Organized Crime:

(a) 'Organized criminal' group shall mean a structured group of three or more persons, existing for a period of time and acting in concert with the aim of committing one or more serious crimes or offences established in accordance with this Convention, in order to obtain, directly or indirectly, a financial or other material benefit;
(b) 'Serious crime' shall mean conduct constituting an offence punishable by a maximum deprivation of liberty of at least four years or more serious penalty;
(c) 'Structured group' shall mean a group that is not randomly formed for the immediate commission of an offence and that does not need to have formally defined roles for its members, continuity of its membership or a developed structure.

(*Source*: Wright 2006: 9)

Sage Dictionary of Criminology (Gill 2006: 280):
Organized crime refers to the 'ongoing activities of those collectively engaged in the production, supply and financing for illegal markets in goods and services'.

of socialization into the values and norms of the crime business, such as 'honour among thieves'.

Many of these images are, however, somewhat dated (Hobbs 1995; 2010a). Organized crime is now more widely used to refer to the activities of criminal organizations such as the Mafia or the Chinese Triads and more recently with the 'new' mafias associated with Eastern European countries and other migrant groups. It is also associated with the perceived threat of transnational organized crime (TOC) (Ruggiero 2000; Woodiwiss 2003; Edwards 2005; Woodiwiss and Hobbs 2009). The so-called 'war' on organized crime involved the expansion of domestic and international law-enforcement organizations after the break-up the former Soviet Union which in turn led to attempts to define it. Some official definitions are outlined in Box 14.1. They have been subject to considerable criticism with questions including:

How organized is organized crime?

Organized crime is popularly associated with a structured, hierarchical organization, a command structure and division of labour and strong loyalty among participants – often based on images of the Mafia. Yet the Mafia is primarily organized around the family, and is not a typical example of organized crime which in reality is less tightly organized and, indeed, disorganized (Fijnaut 1990; Ruggiero 1996a).

Is organized crime transnational?

The 'war' on organized crime focused on the threat of transnational organized crime (TOC) although this too can be contested. The term transnational implies groups located in several jurisdictions (Wright 2006: 23), yet while many illegal trades do move goods from one country to another, they are 'cross border' rather than transnational as perpetrators are based in one country (Van Duyne 2003).

To what extent is organized crime local?

Organized crime is also strongly related to local neighbourhoods, cultures, histories and traditions. Illegal goods or services may be imported from abroad but are sold in local neighbourhoods – thus the term 'glocal' is often used (Hobbs 1998).

To what extent can organized crime be seen as a 'business'?

Many analysts of organized crime view it as a business, involving the manufacture, distribution and sale of officially illegal goods and services, filling gaps left by legal businesses (Ruggiero 1996a). Like legitimate business it must secure finance, recruit personnel and adapt to the market but it must also find ways of avoiding law enforcement (Levi 2007).

How can the crime industry be distinguished from legitimate industry?

Sutherland (1949) distinguished between white-collar crime, involving a primarily legitimate business, and organized crime, which involved primarily illegitimate businesses (see Chapter 15), although in reality it is not easy to separate these two categories. Organized crime needs a base for customers to access its services which often involves setting up a legitimate business 'front' which can also 'launder' the proceeds of crime. Illegal businesses, like legal ones, expand, and diversifying into legal businesses carries a lower risk of detection, conviction and imprisonment. To Ruggiero (1996a), corporate and organized crime involve similar activities and, as will be seen below, they are also interdependent. The distinction also reflects assumptions about the respectability of businesses as the term is more often used solely to describe the business activities of 'underworld type' figures (Levi 2007: 777).

These considerations have led many to question the very use of the term organized crime. The definitions developed by the EU or the UN could, for example, be applied to anything from a four-person low-level racketeering outfit to highly complex, international networks engaged in human smuggling or money laundering (Rawlinson 2009). Nonetheless, it could also be argued that serious crimes, involving the same people, acting in concert over a period of time are distinct. Most academic commentators, however, argue for a move away from definitional disputes. To Levi (2007: 779), it is less interesting to ask what 'it' is, than to look at how some crimes are organized and who gets involved. Hobbs (1994) prefers the phrase 'serious crime community' which implies a looser form of organization, and the term 'enterprise crime' has also been used. Some now use the phrase 'the organization of serious crimes' (Edwards and Levi 2008).

The scope of organized crime

Research issues

Estimating the nature and extent of professional and organized crime is difficult and official statistics or victim surveys are less appropriate. Even where relevant, statistics provide few clues as to whether organized crime is involved and the most successful serious criminals are less likely to be caught and delegate more risky and visible activities to lower-level employees (Ruggiero 1996a), making studies of convicted offenders unrepresentative. Victimization is often indirect and as trades involve willing suppliers and consumers, there is no clear victim. Other forms of research are also difficult – professional criminals are even more unlikely than most offenders to welcome sociological or criminological investigation and a host of practical and ethical difficulties, such as becoming involved in criminal activity or fears for personal safety, surround any form of covert research. There are, therefore, fewer ethnographies or in-depth studies of offenders although they do exist (Hobbs 1994; 1995). There are, therefore, as will be seen below, many gaps in our knowledge and, as Van Duyne and Levi (2005: 74) point out in relation to drug traffickers, 'we have to proceed like an archaeologist describing a Neanderthal community on the basis of a few bones, a tooth and an arrow point'.

Estimating the extent of organized crime

Some indication of the vast scope of organized crime is illustrated in Box 14.2 which lists the wide variety of activities and the range of illegal goods and services associated with it. It produces, distributes and sells a host of illegal products such as drugs, trades in products which, like cigarettes or tobacco, are legal in themselves but are contraband where tax has not been paid, and it launders illicit profits through other trades such as those in counterfeit goods.

Box 14.2 Criminal enterprises

- The drugs market – the manufacture, distribution and sale of prohibited drugs
- The illegal arms market – obtaining and distributing prohibited arms
- 'Human smuggling' – providing transport for illegal immigrants – and 'trafficking', which involves employing irregular immigrants as servants or labourers, includes 'sex trafficking' when women are employed in the sex industry
- Illegal trade in stolen art works and antiquities
- The distribution and sale of goods subject to excise – for example, contraband cigarettes and 'bootleg' alcohol
- The manufacture, distribution and sale of counterfeit goods
- Money laundering
- Organizing robberies, car thefts or shoplifting where items are stolen to order
- Selling stolen goods
- Protection rackets – in which businesses are asked to pay to 'protect' themselves from violence, arson or other forms of damage
- Organized frauds – for example, social security or excise frauds
- Long firm frauds
- Involvement in the sex industry – including prostitution and pornography
- Illegal drinking clubs – selling alcohol outside normal licensing arrangements
- Providing and arranging venues for banned or controlled leisure pursuits – for example, rave parties; boxing and wrestling bouts
- Organizing illegal gambling
- Arranging for the illegal disposal of industrial waste
- The distribution and sale of goods banned in one country to another country
- Dealing in goods subject to import controls or health and safety regulations – for example, trading in meat unfit for human consumption; frauds on the European Union
- Corruption – paying law enforcers and other state agencies and politicians to avoid investigation
- The transmission of pornography via the Internet
- PIN frauds

A considerable volume of information about organized crime, including estimates of its extent and costs are provided by Law Enforcement agencies such as the National Criminal Intelligence Service (NCS), the Serious and Organized Crime Agency (SOCA) and the Scottish Crime and Drugs Enforcement Agency (SCDEA), and in July 2009 the Home Office announced a new 'Al Capone-style' strategy for tackling serious and organized crime (Home Office 2009; Travis 2009; and see Box 14.3). This estimates that around 25,000–30,000 people are involved in organized crime in Britain including lifetime criminals, the durable core, through to 'clusters of subordinates', specialists and others at the lower end. The estimated annual cost of organized crime is between £20 billion and £40 billion, which includes:

- *Societal harms* such as the impact of fear and distrust; losses to taxpayers from smuggling and fraud and the costs of dealing with organized crime and its effects.
- *Harms to individuals* such as losses from organized frauds; victimization by drug-related crimes, including gun crime; harm caused by drug abuse and the exploitation of trafficked persons.
- *Losses to businesses* including losses through fraud and the costs of preventing it; victimization by drug-related thefts and loss of revenue from counterfeiting or piracy.

Broken down by different categories of crime estimated costs are:

- £17.6 billion from drug-related crime
- £7.8 billion from financial fraud
- £4.1 billion from the smuggling of spirits, tobacco and diesel
- £2.4 billion from organized immigration crime.

Geographically organized crime is centred in Britain's major cities including London, Liverpool, Birmingham, Manchester and Glasgow – with networks to other cities. In Northern Ireland, there have been links between organized crime and former terrorist groups, who used crime as a means of obtaining money for arms.

Varieties of organized crime

The organization of serious crime in Britain

The literature on organized crime has been dominated by ideas originating in the United States where it soared during the period when the sale and consumption of alcohol was prohibited, creating an illegal market. This prohibitionist tendency was extended to drugs and the development of the 'war' on organized crime. The British, and indeed the European, experience of organized crime has, however, been very different. There was no prohibition of alcohol and up to the 1960s the so-called 'British system' of prescribing rather than criminalizing drugs was associated with a relative lack of highly organized crime groups. From around the 1980s, however, British concerns became 'Americanized' with the emerging fears of new mafias, Jamaican Yardies and other crime groups (Wright 2006; Woodiwiss and Hobbs 2009). As illustrated in Box 14.3, the global threat of organized crime continues to

Box 14.3 **The threat of organized crime**

In the forward to the government's Serious and Organized Crime Strategy (Home Office 2009) Gordon Brown, then Prime Minister, stated:

> Our National Security Strategy, updated in June, identified serious organized crime as one of the major threats we face – and one that is growing across the world. Where once they were confined to a single neighbourhood, today's criminal networks span the globe – from Asia, Africa or South America, to the streets of our towns and cities. Their activities – drugs, weapons, people trafficking, fraud, counterfeiting and financial crime – ruin lives and damage communities, cost taxpayers and legitimate businesses billions in lost revenue, and cause misery across the world, undermining fragile states and perpetuating poverty and conflict.

The introduction to the document states:

> Organized crime is increasingly a multi-billion pound global business: trafficking in drugs and people, fraud and financial crime cost the UK Exchequer alone in the region of £30 billion a year. As laid out in our National Security Strategy, the global reach of serious organized crime can undermine and corrupt economies, societies and governments and can cause or exacerbate state failure, in some cases leading to civil war and violent conflict. Compared with the 'family businesses' of days gone by, today's organized crime networks are more agile and inventive, quick to embrace new technologies and seek out new markets and supply routes. They are run like sophisticated and modern multi-national businesses.

In a forward to the SCDEA Annual Report (2009), the Director General stated:

> Scotland may be a small country on the northwest edge of Europe. But the drugs that end up in our backstreets have made it here from routes that straddle the continents – from Afghanistan in the case of heroin and South America in the case of cocaine. Those commodities bring with them a trail of economic, social and political destruction – a continuum of harm – that scars our planet and its people.

dominate official concerns. Yet many argue that in the UK and Europe, crime organizations, albeit affected by global changes, remain locally based (Hobbs 1998; 2002). They are related to local cultures and traditions which vary across Britain, with a somewhat unique situation in Northern Ireland.

Changing patterns of organization

Organized crime in Britain has a long history. Pickpocketing is one of the earliest and most enduring criminal 'crafts' (McIntosh 1975) and eighteenth- and nineteenth-century travellers faced the threat of highwaymen, armed robbers and travelling gangs of pickpockets (Emsley 1996; Hallsworth 2005; Wright 2006). In the early twentieth century local 'firms' in London, Manchester, Birmingham, Bristol and Glasgow were involved in racecourses, and 'gang wars' in Sheffield involved competition over the control of gambling (Hobbs 1994; Wright 2006). Glasgow was characterized as Britain's 'Chicago' although its protection rackets were nowhere near the scale found in Chicago (Davies 2007a; 2007b). During the Second World War a black market in rationed goods emerged and local firms created monopolies in relation to protection rackets, illegal gambling and prostitution. Up until the 1980s, firms dominated by 'elder statesmen' in different cities co-existed with little competition and exploited new opportunities to produce cheap copies of audio, then video, cassettes through to DVDs and new ways of transmitting pornography (Hobbs 1994).

According to Hobbs (1994; 1995; 1998; 2002; 2010a), the social and economic changes which eroded traditional skills and crafts also affected serious crime. If, he argues (1995: 28), 'the unwritten code of the underworld ever existed, it is now as outdated as an Ealing comedy'. The growth of the drugs market led to diversification into drug-trafficking which produced more competition and increasing violence. The growth of the enterprise culture eroded traditional loyalties and encouraged the development of a variety of legitimate, semi-legitimate and illegitimate 'entrepreneurial' activities. Professional crime fragmented as old crafts, such as the safebreaker, were deskilled and new opportunities emerged. The local 'firm' is still important but has increasingly mutated and adapted to global markets. In Hobbs' (1995) study of 'serious criminals', he found few 'Mr Bigs' and the 'thieves', formerly central to organized crime mythology, were described as 'dinosaurs'. More typical were offenders involved in a variety of legal and illegal enterprises.

Criminal organizations in Britain

Contemporary forms of serious crime in Britain illustrate how it has adapted to changing circumstances along with variations across the UK. Box 14.4, for example, outlines the growth of trading in contraband cigarettes and alcohol, often associated with individual 'entrepreneurs', typically from areas with high unemployment, and not strongly linked to traditional organized crime groups. Other forms of organized crime use extortion and protection rackets, described as doing 'business with gloves off' (Hobbs 2010b: 734). Glasgow's so-called crime 'lords' have long been associated with protection rackets, and extortion was a tactic

Box 14.4 Organizing crime: cigarette smuggling

The trade in cigarette smuggling, along with that in 'bootleg' luxury goods and alcohol, has its roots in different rates of taxation in European countries (Van Duyne 2003; Hornsby and Hobbs 2007). Most contraband tobacco moves from the low price Baltic to the UK passing through transit countries such as Germany, the Netherlands and Belgium which also have illegal markets (Van Duyne and Antonopolous 2009).

- Trades often start with unemployed individuals importing cheap cigarettes sold in car boot sales or local markets.
- High demand and an initially low risk of capture lead to expansion, often by employing friends and family and linking with networks in the underground market, not always linked to organized crime, although in the Netherlands there were contacts with 'intermediate' and 'higher' trade levels (Van Duyne 2003).
- Hornsby and Hobbs (2007) describe the growth of a British entrepreneurial firm which expanded from 'pensioner days out', through employing friends and acquaintances to a well-organized, efficient and highly profitable smuggling and distribution network.
- The business ceased as it became threatened by competition, including the use of violence, from more 'serious' members of the criminal fraternity seeking to diversify.

associated with the notorious London gangs involving the Krays, who moved their activities from the East End to arranging security for illegal gambling clubs in the West End. It has, argues Hobbs (2010b), now mutated and is associated with the need for security in the night-time economy where bouncers act as 'gatekeepers' between legitimate and illegitimate industries. Extortion, argues Hobbs, is an entry level crime for career criminals who often start by providing security.

Local 'firms' are involved in a range of other activities and businesses. Glasgow's organized crime groups, for example, are involved in the drugs trade, protection rackets and in legitimate saunas, security businesses and taxi firms. In a study of small businesses in three different areas, Tilley and Hopkins (2008) found that while few reported extortion, far more had been invited to participate in trades in counterfeit and stolen goods and smuggled tobacco and alcohol, although they did not always perceive this to be associated with organized crime. They relate these experiences to the 'crime chemistries' of local areas. In one high-crime area in the East Midlands, where residents were mainly white and lower class, they found a long established network of local crime families whose businesses centred around pubs which were effectively an 'office'. Arcades were used to launder money from illegal trades and garages were used to cover the sale of stolen cars.

Organized crime in Northern Ireland differs from the rest of the UK due to its history of paramilitary involvement and the land border with the Republic of Ireland. Although many of the paramilitary groups have now decommissioned their weapons, they are still said to be involved in serious crime: the Provisional IRA were widely believed to have been behind the massive bank robbery (£26.5 million) at the Northern Bank in December 2004 (BBC News, 2005; Levi 2007). Furthermore, in its Annual Report and Threat Assessment, the Organized Crime Task Force and Independent Monitoring Commission (IMC) (2007) linked major paramilitary organizations on both sides of the political and religious divide to organized crime activity. The Ulster Defence Association (UDA), Ulster Volunteer Force (UVF), and the Provisional Irish Republican Army (PIRA) were singled out as active in counterfeiting, extortion, drug-dealing and other financial crimes. It is thought that the major players in drugs were loyalist, whereas republicans were more heavily involved in smuggling and fuel laundering (IMC, 2006a). In its 2006 report this commission reported that:

> Paramilitaries have roots in some parts of the community which enable them to profit more readily from major crime. For example, they control outlets for illicit alcohol, fuel and tobacco and sell goods within those communities. There is thus often what is described as a symbiotic relationship between the paramilitary criminal and the community, the former supplying goods for which there is a public demand and the latter tending to view the illicit trade as both beneficial because of the lower prices it offers and as victimless. (IMC 2006a paras 4.2 and 4.3)

Serious crime and violence

Violence is a major element in Britain's organized crime, being used to control competitors and enforce protection rackets. It is also rooted in the male working-class cultures explored in Chapters 9 and 11. To Hobbs (1994), part of the informal order of the illegitimate marketplace is that men doing business also do violence – seen in the example of bouncers in the night-time economy. It is also linked to the patriarchal family. Glasgow's gang culture is extremely violent, reflected in phrases such as the notorious 'Glesca kiss', locally described as a 'heeder to the nose' (Campbell 2001: 59) and the 'Glesca kiss-off' or 'Glasgow goodbye' being translated as 'a bullet up the arse' (Jeffrey 2002: 164). One of Glasgow's former serious criminals describes violence as acceptable, a sign of 'manhood', a means of settling grievances, a form of economic control and meting out rough justice, and a source of excitement and pride (Ferris 2002; Croall 2003). Scars are seen as a mark of respect, and masculinity is reflected in disapproval of sexual violence and violence against 'civilians' and non-combatants, including women.

The attractions of serious crime

Involvement in serious crime is strongly associated with lower socio-economic status. To Hobbs (1995), working-class criminal entrepreneurs draw on a male working-class culture which has always adapted to formal and informal economies and which values entrepreneurship and 'sharp practice'. The cigarette-smuggling trade thrived among the unemployed for whom it provided an alternative, and more interesting, way of securing an income. Glasgow's gangs have always been associated with inner-city lower-class areas and later with peripheral schemes.

Involvement in serious crime is not only related to economic motivation. To Ferris (2002), a criminal career enabled money to be made more speedily and with more excitement than the legitimate alternatives. This echoes Hobbs' (1995) argument that the straight world cannot offer the same financial rewards or excitement. A drug dealer in Hobbs' study is described as part of an urban elite at play and conspicuous consumption rather than pure economic necessity forms an important part of offenders' motivations.

Serious though these activities are, most commentators agree that organized crime in Britain is very different to the United States and also differs from the somewhat exaggerated descriptions of official statements. The SOCA website, for example, contains cases of criminal 'gangs' which, while referring to serious activities, fall far short of the imagery of highly organized 'cartels'. A so-called 'organized crime gang', convicted in February 2010 for running a prostitution ring using trafficked

Source: Alamy Images/ilian studio

Money laundering is a means of converting "dirty" money from criminal activities into "clean" money and is a crucial part of organized crime.

women and girls from Nigeria, consisted of one family based in Castlemartin, Wales who provided instructions to brothels in Northern Ireland. A report of the seizure of assets including over £870,000 cash and 12 residential properties in July 2009, following cross-border fuel-smuggling in County Armagh, involved three brothers. Family 'firms' and loosely organized networks of friends and acquaintances appear more common and are indeed often more efficient (Levi 2007; Van Duyne 2003). Also evident are close links between legitimate and illegitimate business, and the ready market for and cultural tolerance of many activities. The trade in contraband cigarettes, for example, is rarely seen as 'criminal' (Van Duyne 2003; Tilley and Hopkins 2008). These points will be taken up below.

The illegal traffic in drugs

The market in illegal drugs is the largest criminal market and the one most often associated with criminal 'cartels' and transnational organized crime. It is an international trade and drugs are produced in countries of origin, transported through transit countries before being imported and distributed for retailing to clients at a local level. It involves a wide variety of organizations and, due to its nature and the constant need to avoid law enforcement, it is subject to considerable fluctuation and change. This section will cover some of its main features.

What is the illegal traffic in drugs?

In Chapter 8, it was seen that the legal or illegal status of particular drugs shifts over time and reflects political and social processes. The illegal 'drugs market' is associated with drugs whose production, trade and consumption are subject to worldwide prohibition as defined in Box 14.5. Box 14.6 summarizes the main features of

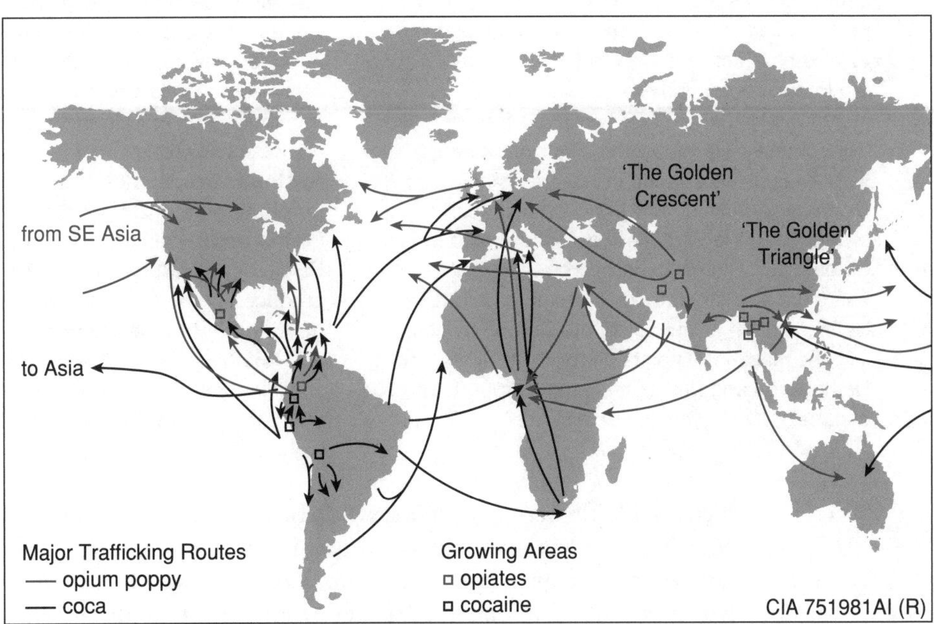

Box 14.5 Illegal trafficking in drugs

Definition: The United Nations Convention against Illicit Traffic in Narcotic Drugs and Psychotropic Substances of 1988: Article 3 prohibits:

> The production, manufacture, extraction, preparation, offering, offering for sale, distribution, sale, delivery on any terms whatsoever, brokerage, dispatch, dispatch in transit, transport, importation or exportation of any narcotic drug or any psychotropic substance contrary to the provisions of the 1961 Convention, the 1961 Conventions amended or the 1971 Convention. (Cited in Paoli et al 2010: 626)

The UK illicit drugs market was estimated to be worth £5.3bn in 2003/4 broken down as:

- 28% crack
- 23% heroin
- 20% cannabis
- 18% powder cocaine
- 6% amphetamines
- 5% ecstasy (Pudney et al 2006, cited in McSweeney et al 2010)

Box 14.6 Drugs: production and supply routes

- **Heroin** is derived from morphine, a derivative of the opium poppy. By 2007, Afghanistan, whose economy is dependent on the drugs industry, accounted for about 92 per cent of the world's supply. Myanmar accounted for 5 per cent and Mexico, a major supplier to the US, for 1.5 per cent. Turkey is the main gateway for Afghan heroin which is typically transported by road to Western Europe using what is known as the Balkan route, and Albania also plays an increasing role. From 1991 onwards the so-called 'silk route' emerged to serve Russia and other Eastern European countries via Tajikistan.
- **Cocaine** is derived from the coca plant and production, in laboratories, is concentrated in Colombia (the largest share), Peru and Bolivia. There are also laboratories in Spain and the Netherlands. It is smuggled into Europe by sea, and the main entry points are ports in Spain, the Netherlands and Belgium – some in imports of bananas. Private yachts are also used.
- **Cannabis** comes in two main forms, herbal (marijuana) and resin (hashish). It is produced all over the world and marijuana can be grown domestically. It is now estimated that over half of the herbal cannabis consumed in England and Wales is home-grown. Hashish is made in Morocco (the largest), Afghanistan and Pakistan. Cannabis is rarely smuggled over long distances and the most important smuggling route runs from Morocco via Spain to the north. It is mainly transported by road in trucks or by ship from Pakistan to Europe.
- **Synthetic drugs**: Most common are **amphetamine**, mainly produced in Europe (Netherlands, Poland, Baltic states and Belgium); **MDMA** (ecstasy or XTX), mainly produced in the Netherlands and Belgium, and **methamphetamine**, produced mainly in China and South East Asia. It is produced in large or small laboratories. There is less long-distance smuggling except from Europe to Australia.

illegal trades in heroin, cocaine, synthetic drugs such as ecstasy and cannabis, which constitute the main groups of illegal drugs. This indicates that much heroin originates in Afghanistan, cocaine from Colombia and South America, hashish from Morocco, and manufactured drugs from a host of illegal laboratories, many in

Holland, and that a growing proportion of cannabis is now 'home grown'. Box 14.6 also outlines the variety of methods used to transport drugs and they are concealed in, for example, containers of bananas, car or truck engine parts, or by 'body packing', concealing drugs in parts of the body. Drugs often arrive in UK ports and are then distributed via 'hubs' in major cities to be sold in streets, multi-storey car parks, houses, pubs or clubs.

Who is involved?

The drugs market is often conceptualized as a pyramid, with an upper level involving production and wholesaling, a middle level for distribution, and a lower level involving retail sales (Wright 2006; Levi 2007; McSweeney et al 2010). This may not, however, be accurate (Pearson and Hobbs 2001) and many of the complex flow charts provided by law enforcers (Wright 2006) reflect a tendency to look for clear-cut organizational characteristics (Van Duyne and Levi 2005). Research suggests a range of one-person businesses, groups of family and friends, along with a small number of hierarchal organized networks (Pearson and Hobbs 2001; Pearson 2007). Businesses are ever-changing. Small businesses grow into larger ones; on the other hand, there have been suggestions that drug-smuggling groups have become smaller due to increasing international mobility, the ease of electronic communications and increasingly diverse migration flows (Paoli et al 2010). One study in the 1990s identified groups – including friendship networks, largely eliminated by policing, legitimate businesses for whom drugs were a sideline, professional criminals who had diversified into drugs, opportunist property offenders and retail specialists, as stable organizations rarer in Britain than the US (Dorn and South 1990; Dorn et al 1992; see also Ruggiero and South 1995).

The upper level

Relatively little is known about the so-called upper level although it is clear that there are a variety of organizational forms (Van Duyne and Levi 2005; Dorn et al 2005) including (Levi 2007: 790):

- *Politico-military groups* who operate from a specific niche. They are hierarchical and prone to use violence against competitors and the state.
- *Business criminals* seeking personal enrichment. Vertical integration is evident and they are involved in source and transit zones, sometimes in distribution, but rarely in retail. Core groups are relatively permanent, violence is a last resort and there is some involvement in other criminal markets.
- *Adventurers* who enjoy taking risks. They are often individuals and groups of friends, are largely opportunistic and operate at different levels of the market. They are very fluid and mutate rapidly.

It is now generally agreed that transporting, warehousing and importing heroin into the UK is increasingly dominated by Turkish and Albanian groups, with cocaine being dominated by Colombians (Pearson and Hobbs 2001; Pearson 2007; Paoli and Reuter 2008). There are also a number of independent dealers (Paoli and Reuter 2008). Amphetamines and cannabis, on the other hand, involve more heterogeneous and indigenous groups, often originating in small-scale supplies among friends.

The middle level

More research has dealt with the middle level (Pearson and Hobbs 2001; Van Duyne and Levi 2005; Pearson 2007). Pearson (2007: 82) looks at how this has developed. In the mid 1980s, heroin was largely supplied by dealers and user-dealers operating from flats in socially deprived housing estates. Following high numbers of arrests they re-emerged in inner-city neighbourhoods and in multi-storey car parks, where they faced competition and threats of violence. They then adopted a 'drive-by' service, but users snatched the drugs and ran away. They readjusted to a 'pizza-style' delivery in which purchasers ordered drugs via public pay phones and later mobile phones. The emerging rave club scene saw individual dealers, previously only supplying friends, move into middle market positions. They constitute a more educated and affluent group who wanted high quality drugs, sought little profit, and got involved to avoid contact with organized criminals. Thus, argues Pearson (2007: 83) neat typologies are confounded by the 'messy actualities' of the drug market. Pearson and Hobbs (2001) found that London was regarded as the centre of the middle market with Liverpool and Manchester vying for 'second city' status. In the North of England, South Asians were involved in a heroin distribution system buying in bulk from Turks.

The lower level

Retail sales are located in open-air, street-level settings or closed settings such as pubs and clubs (Pearson 2007; McSweeney et al 2010). The higher risks of detection faced by lower-level dealers means that selling is often delegated to more marginal groups, particularly those from deprived areas. Many, particularly in the indoor market (Paoli et al 2010), are indigenous, and many are users. Across Europe, the outdoor street market, the least comfortable and highest risk, also involves foreign dealers, particularly recent immigrants, who are culturally marginalised (Paoli and Reuter 2008; Paoli et al 2010).

A very wide range of individuals and organizations are, therefore, found in the drugs market, with many departing from the stereotype of transnational crime cartels. It includes families and groups of friends, reflecting the greater security associated with working with people who can be trusted (Paoli et al 2010). Many participants have no ties with the underworld, rather there are networks or partnerships of independent traders or brokers (Hobbs and Pearson 2001: Paoli et al 2010). Strong law enforcement can make smaller enterprises less visible whereas larger organizations can more easily flourish in countries with weak law enforcement such as that in producer countries (Paoli et al 2010).

Characteristics of participants

Although women are found at all levels, the drug trade is dominated by men (McSweeney et al 2010), and participants at higher levels tend to be over 30. Minority ethnic groups are heavily involved as illustrated by the prevalence of Turkish, Albanian and Colombian groups. Paoli and Reuter (2008) associate this with a variety of factors:

- Groups from countries of origin or transit speak the language and know about production and transport networks.
- Geographical proximity – seen in the case of Turkey.

- The cultural strength of the family, particularly where there are strong extended family links as with Albanians, or where the head of the family is accorded status and authority (Van Duyne and Levi 2005).
- Within immigrant communities there is less likelihood of being reported to what might be regarded as hostile law enforcement agencies.

It is important, however, that immigrant involvement is not taken to confirm the 'alien conspiracy' model of organized crime and does not divert attention from the involvement of domestic organized crime groups, particularly in relation to cannabis and synthetic drugs, and there are also cross ethnic network linkages (Pearson and Hobbs 2001).

The vast majority of known participants in the drugs market are from lower-class and deprived backgrounds although this may reflect more intensive policing in lower-class areas and the greater vulnerability of street-level dealers. The increase in home-grown cannabis and the manufacture of synthetic drugs, which requires expertise, have involved different kinds of participants. Some cannabis dealers, particularly in the Netherlands where cannabis is more widely tolerated, can indeed be described as 'petit bourgeois' (Van Duyne and Levi 2005). Nonetheless, high profits make involvement in the drugs trade, as with other forms of organized crime, an attractive prospect for those in the most deprived sections of the community. Profits are not the only motivation or attraction. Involvement in the drugs market can provide some regularity and a purpose to the day (Pearson 1987b), a chance to participate in the conspicuous consumption associated with consumer culture (McSweeney et al 2010) and a release from the everyday boredom of low-paid regular employment or unemployment.

Violence

While people do get killed in the drugs market, particularly in source countries (McSweeney et al 2010) and in shootings associated with 'turf wars' (Wright 2006) the role of violence can be overplayed. Van Duyne and Levi (2005: 86), for example, argue that drugs are not necessarily associated with violence: some 'underworld violence' has little to do with drugs and violence runs the risk of attracting unwanted attention from the police.

The impact of law enforcement

The prohibition and criminalization of drugs has been said to escalate the harms associated with drugs and the so-called war on drugs arguably creates 'collateral damage' (McSweeney et al 2010: 609). Current strategies have not substantially reduced the trade in illegal drugs and closing off one supply chain often leads to the emergence of another (Van Duyne and Levi 2005; Paoli et al 2010). The 'costs' of illegal drugs can also be exaggerated – as seen in Chapter 8, for example, some crime associated with drugs could be assumed to occur in any event, and the drugs trade can boost the economies of deprived neighbourhoods (Pearson 1987b). Moreover, Van Duyne and Levi (2005: 179) point out that most crime money is eventually processed through the 'big national laundering machine'. As in other areas of organized crime, therefore, there are strong arguments for alternative forms of control.

Box 14.7 Defining human trafficking and smuggling

From the **United Nations Convention Against Transnational Organized Crime Trafficking Protocol (2000):**

> Trafficking in persons shall mean the recruitment, transportation, harbouring or receipt of persons, by means of the threat or use of force or other forms of coercion, of abduction, of fraud, of deception, of the abuse of power or of a position of vulnerability or the giving or receiving of payments or benefits to achieve the consent of a person having control over another person, for the purpose of exploitation. Exploitation shall include, at a minimum, the exploitation of the prostitution of others or other forms of sexual exploitation, forced labour or services, slavery or practices similar to slavery, servitude or the removal of organs.

People Smuggling: UN protocol (as above)

> The procurement, in order to obtain, directly or indirectly a financial or other material benefit, of illegal entry of a person into a State Party of which the person is not a national or permanent resident.

Source: from SOCA website *www.soca.gov.uk/threats*

Human smuggling and trafficking

Human trafficking and smuggling, sometimes likened to slavery, is related to flows of migration. It is primarily associated with sexual exploitation although it also includes trafficking for labour and the illegal trade in human organs. It is not easy to define and Box 14.7 contains United Nations definitions of trafficking and smuggling. These distinguish *trafficking* from *smuggling* by the use of force and deceptive

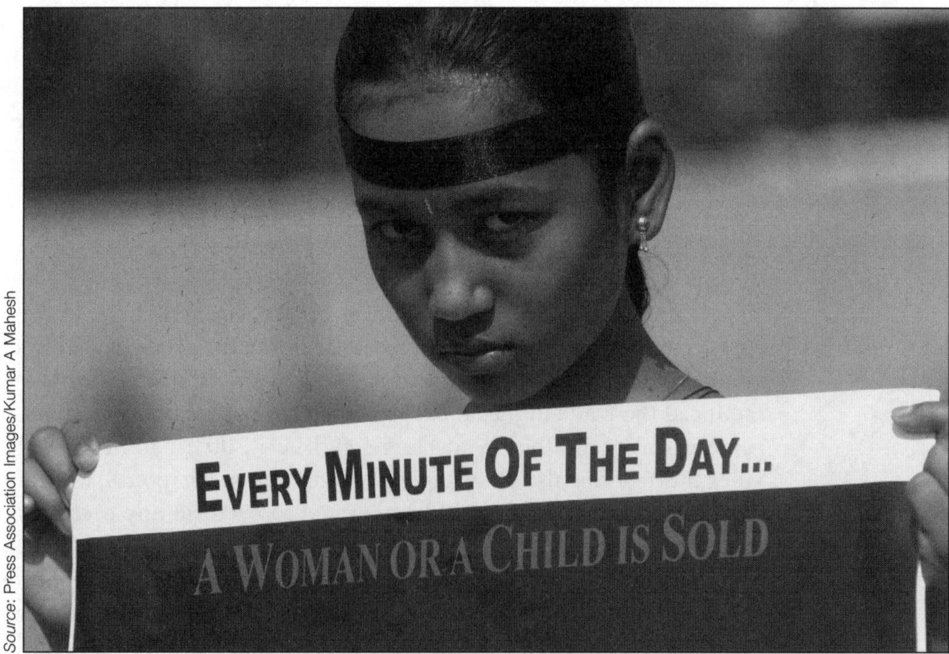

Source: Press Association Images/Kumar A Mahesh

promises of employment. Those who pay to be smuggled are generally aware of what employment they are going to and are free on arrival in the destination country. In practice, however, these distinctions are hard to maintain. How, for example, is 'force' to be defined and at what point is the victim deceived (Kelly 2007)? Participants may willingly pay for a passage, only to have passports and money taken away on arrival and be told that they must work off the debt. There is, therefore, as for violence and sexual violence, a continuum ranging from irregular migration, through smuggling to trafficking (Kelly 2007: 88).

Definitional difficulties contribute to the difficulties of assessing the extent of smuggling and trafficking and there is a dearth of reliable information. This is largely due to the difficulties of gaining information from either traffickers or those who have been trafficked. Many estimates and 'guesstimates' are inaccurate (Di Nicola 2007; Goodey 2008). Information tends to be based on detections by enforcement agencies and information from voluntary victim support groups, but many of those trafficked do not speak the language and do not seek help, being frightened by the risk of detention and deportation (Goodey 2003; 2010). Calculations typically indicate an estimated range, illustrated in Box 14.8.

Most of those who contact agencies are women trafficked for sexual exploitation. Far less is known about trafficking for labour, although it is reported that considerable numbers of smuggled or trafficked individuals are employed in agriculture, domestic labour, hotel and catering, construction and care homes, in 'dirty, dangerous and degrading' industries characterized by low pay and casual work (Lee 2007: 4).

Box 14.8 The nature and scope of human trafficking and smuggling

- A 'well-grounded' study published by the International Labour Office (ILO) in 2005 estimates the minimum number of persons in forced labour at any given time as between 2 and 4 million. Forced labour for sexual exploitation accounts for 43 per cent of this total, economic exploitation for 32 per cent with 25 per cent mixed or undetermined (cited in Di Nicola 2007: 64).
- In the UK, Kelly and Regan (2000) identified a total of 271 trafficked women over a five-year period based on police figures. The 'real scale' is estimated to be anywhere between 142 and 1,420 annually.
- The UK Government's Joint Committee for Human Rights Report on Human Trafficking 2005–6 reports government estimates of 4,000 victims of trafficking for prostitution in the UK at any one time (Amnesty International 2008).
- A 2006 UNICEF UK report suggested at that there are at any one time 5,000 child sex workers in the UK, most of them trafficked (cited in Amnesty International 2008).
- In Scotland, Lebov (2010), on the basis of interviews with agencies, identified 79 victims of trafficking from April 2008 to March 2009. Fifty-two were women although the gender of a further 21 was unknown. Around two-thirds had experienced sexual exploitation. Where country of origin was known most originated from Asia (the majority from China) and Africa.
- SOCA indicates that work is obtained in agriculture, horticulture, marine farming, textiles, catering, construction, nail bars, care homes and car washes and in criminal ventures such as cannabis cultivation and pirate DVD selling.

Particularly invisible are those recruited for domestic labour, who may experience abuse as well as exploitation (Lebov 2010).

The organization of human trafficking

As is the case with drug-trafficking there are countries of origin, transit and destination (Turner and Kelly 2009). Movements have most often been from poorer countries in Southern and Eastern Europe, Africa and Asia, to the more affluent West. The UK is a destination country with people arriving through Channel ports or Ireland, before moving on to other cities (Lebov 2010). Eastern Europe has been a major source of trafficked women (Morawska 2007), although this may be declining as freer and easier movement across Europe has made the trade less profitable and more women are now said to be coming from Africa and Asia, particularly China (Lebov 2010). Recruitment, transport and arrival at a destination form the main elements of human smuggling and trafficking (Goodey 2010).

Recruitment

Travel agencies, word of mouth and advertisements are the main forms of recruitment which takes place in the country of origin. Ideal recruiters are someone the person knows and older women are more credible (Morawska 2007), some being previously trafficked persons (Kelly 2007). Some women are 'seduced' by 'love affairs' and promises of marriage, and others are recruited through advertisements for employment or marriage prospects. Marriages, some arranged through Internet marriage agency sites can also end up with sexual exploitation and degrading and inhuman treatment (Amnesty International 2008: 9).

Transport and arrival

Long uncomfortable journeys are common. 'Thousands' are said to die (Aas 2007: 30), dramatically illustrated in the cases of the 58 Chinese migrants who suffocated in a lorry on their way from Holland to Dover, having travelled 8,000 miles from Fujian, China after paying Chinese Snakehead gangs for their passage (BBC News 2001), and the deaths of some of the 30,000 African migrants in 'rickety boats' who attempted to reach the shores of the Spanish Canary Islands (Aas 2007: 30). With trafficking, passports are taken away on arrival, and individuals can be placed in debt bondage to pay back the passage, often being housed in overcrowded accommodation and having rent extracted from their earnings (Goodey 2003; 2010; Morawska 2007). A recent *Guardian* report (Laville 2009) highlights the plight of 'hundreds' of Chinese workers being kept in virtual slavery, living 11 to a room in East London working in a factory producing pirate DVDs. Migrants in these kinds of situations are watched very closely and threatened with violence if they try to leave.

Who is involved?

As for drug traffickers, a very diverse range of individuals and groups are involved (Lee 2007). Major crime organizations such as the Russian mafia and the Chinese Triads or Snakeheads (Lebov 2010) have reportedly been involved along with Albanians. Some organizations are responsible for 'end to end' packages including recruitment, transit and arrangements in the destination country (SOCA 2010), whereas other groups are responsible for only one part of the chain. While it would appear that the majority of traffickers are men, women are involved: there have been some cases of women playing a major role and, indeed, Shelley (2007) argues that this is one area of organized crime where women can play a leading role.

Minority ethnic communities

As for drug-trafficking, minority ethnic communities are involved and ideally placed to arrange for trafficking (Kelly 2007). They have often developed commercial routes from countries of origin, know about transport and speak the language and local dialects. There may also be established communities in countries of transit – the Chinese, for example, rapidly set up communities in the former Yugoslavia to assist smuggling. Communities in destination countries can provide a network for employment. Alongside Albanian groups, Chinese Snakehead groups are said to have been involved in Scotland (Lebov 2010). As is also the case with drug-trafficking it is important to avoid the dangers of falling into the 'alien conspiracy' theory (Turner and Kelly 2009).

Global inequalities

The trade in illegal migration can be placed in the broader context of widening global inequality, wars such as those in the former Yugoslavia, the transition in former communist regimes in Eastern Europe (Kelly 2007), persecution, poverty and economic deprivation in the developing world along with the growth of the sex industry and the desire for cheaper goods and services in the West (Aas 2007; Lee 2007). Exploring the 'conducive' context for trafficking and smuggling, Kelly (2007: 81) identifies impoverishment and the lack of a sustainable income, weak governance and economic infrastructure, corruption and the declining status of women in source countries. This is linked to what Aas (2007: 41) describes as the feminization of migration indicated in the higher numbers of women migrating from the South to the North to carry out 'women's work that affluent women are no longer willing or able to do'. She also points to the contradiction that globalization promotes free flows of people but restricts them to those who can afford to travel. The poor face restricted entry to the fortress continents of Europe, North America and Australia. Aspects of globalization are also seen in the portrayal, by largely Western culture, of images of material comfort. Along with escaping poverty, some women are motivated by the possibility of potential marriage, employment and status (Morawska 2007). Aas (2007) points to the *Pretty Woman* scenario referring to the film where a sex worker ended up marrying a rich client.

This raises the critical issue of whether those paying for illegal migration should be cast as victims or offenders – related to the issues of agency outlined in relation to sex work in Chapter 12. To what extent are those involved in smuggling or trafficking aware of and willing to work the sex industry? Some know that they will be sex workers but are unprepared for the extent of abuse from traffickers, hotel owners and clients. Gendered and moral assumptions therefore surround women who migrate (Westmarland 2010). They may be used as informers against traffickers only to be detained themselves, being in a 'no man's land' and being seen neither as victims nor offenders (Goodey 2003: 166).

The focus of research and public concern has largely been women trafficked for sexual exploitation which has tended to neglect male victims and the exploitation of boys (Morawska 2007). Also relatively neglected is the involvement of women as traffickers. Human trafficking and smuggling also illustrate close links between the legitimate and illegitimate economies. Employers, clients and hotels in the legitimate economy are, argues Kelly (2007), complicit, thus providing an example of the legitimate economy benefiting from the services of organized crime (Ruggiero 1996a; Aas 2007).

Understanding organized crime

The majority of the criminological perspectives outlined in previous chapters can be applied to serious crime although pathological approaches appear less appropriate, given the higher levels of skills and knowledge associated with offending. To Lombroso, the Mafioso lacked the stigma of criminality (Ruggiero 1996a). To Hobbs (1995) professional criminals want to earn money, live in the same world as anyone else, have families, worry about the future and have to cope with a rapidly changing world. For many, the interesting features of organized crime lie in its different patterns of organization, its relationship to broader structural and cultural factors, its similarity to and relationship with the legitimate economy and with processes of prohibition, law enforcement and criminalization. This section will outline some of these issues.

The crime business

Small is beautiful

Analyses of organized crime have tended to view it as a business, albeit one not subject to competition, corporate or business law, which, like any other business, identifies market niches, organizes production, distribution and selling, employs staff and adapts to changing markets. This is reflected in the emphasis, in official definitions, on stability and hierarchical organization. Yet in reality it encompasses an enormous variety of organizations. There are 'cartels' although some high-level traffickers see themselves primarily as 'businessmen' (Van Duyne and Levi 2005). There are smaller 'family firms' based in indigenous and migrant communities. Other enterprises are based on networks of friends and there are, as seen in relation to the drugs market, one-person businesses which can develop into larger organizations. Many form loose networks to help with purchasing and transporting goods, and many have few links with so-called organized crime. At the lower end of the employment hierarchy are found those who carry the highest risks, who possess fewer skills and have little knowledge of the levels above them. They are very often drawn from among the most deprived, in both indigenous and migrant communities. Crime organizations, therefore, differ considerably from popular and government stereotypes.

A number of factors account for this. To be successful, serious offenders need to adapt to new circumstances, particularly changes in law enforcement. Larger organizations are more visible and easier to detect and the less that those at the lower levels, who are more likely to be caught, know about the organization the safer those at the top will be. Offenders need to be able to trust those that they work with or employ, thus the significance of family, friendship and ethnic ties. Improved transport and communication have also changed the nature of serious crime as it is easier for the individual entrepreneur or small firm to travel to obtain supplies, as with cigarette smugglers. At the same time, businesses grow and can be taken over, while new ones develop around new niches, such as those involved in the supply of drugs in the night-time economy. In short, as Levi (2007) argues, where some forms of organized crime are concerned, 'small is beautiful'.

Boys' business?

Serious crime is generally seen as a 'boys' game' (Hobbs 1995), and Turner and Kelly (2009) are critical of the 'gender blindness' of the literature on organized crime which fails to explore its 'maleness' and neglects women's involvement. Yet it has been seen that women are involved, play a significant role in human smuggling and trafficking, and their involvement in drug-trafficking is in similar proportions to those found for other crimes (Van Duyne and Levi 2005). At the same time, many forms of organized crime draw on elements of traditional masculinity which might mitigate against women's involvement. Hobbs (1995) points to the declining employment opportunities for working-class males, as in many local areas the crafts, skills, traditional trades and unskilled work, crucial in defining and shaping images of masculinity, have now disappeared. Crime exploits local opportunities and draws on a male working-class culture which has always adapted to formal and informal economies. A 'residue' of traditional masculine working-class culture with a potential for violence and instrumental physicality provides a cultural inheritance ideally suited for engagement with serious crime which represents an intersection of old neighbourhood values and new global markets (Hobbs 1995). These have also been associated with the night-time economy and the commodification of violence by, for example, bouncers as outlined in Chapter 11.

An innovative response?

The discussion of masculinity is closely related to class and British local gangs and firms have long been identified with lower-class communities. Anomie and social disorganization theory emerged during the rise of organized crime in the prohibition era in the United States and organized criminals are a classic example of Mertonian 'innovators'. Indeed, one noted sociologist saw this kind of crime as a 'queer ladder of social mobility' (Bell 1953). The notion of the 'entrepreneur' is associated with being 'maverick' and innovative (Ruggiero 1996a). The Chicago School described and mapped the many different forms of crime organization in the zone of transition (Chapter 4). A crucial part of the 'illegitimate opportunity structures' described by Cloward and Ohlin (1960) is the existence of a pre-existing criminal economy and subculture. These are also related to specific local areas, cultures and traditions.

To those in deprived areas, participation in crime has considerable attractions. It can offer an alternative to the daily drudgery of low-paid jobs or from unemployment and boredom, as seen with the cigarette smugglers (Van Duyne 2003). The risks, excitements and highs of involvement in wheeling and dealing echo the themes of cultural criminology and indeed Van Duyne and Levi (2005) found that some high-level criminals who could afford to retire carried on, because they enjoyed the challenge of outsmarting law enforcement. It enables participation in the consumer society and the generation of wealth, with some enjoying extravagant lifestyles. Globally, the attraction of life in the West is a strong factor for irregular migrants whose motivations may be more than economic. It is also important to note that the class base of serious crime may be changing with the emergence of more highly skilled drug traffickers particularly in relation to synthetic drugs.

Migrant business

The role of ethnicity is peculiarly complex and sensitive (Paoli and Reuter 2008), as it is important, while recognizing the involvement of minority ethnic communities in smuggling and trafficking, to avoid any association with the so-called 'alien conspiracy' theory which diverts blame for organized crime from indigenous offenders to 'others' and thereby from social structural factors. Rather it draws attention to the role of immigrants in organized crime in a broader context of social and economic inequality and exclusion both globally and within Western countries (Aas 2007). It is also related to the unique situation of migrant communities in terms of familiarity with and networks within countries of origin which assist the development of illegal trades. Global cultural, political and economic factors are also important. Wars, rapid social change and weak governments are all important factors underlying the trades in illegal drugs and human trafficking.

Links between legitimate and illegitimate businesses

It was also seen above that the line between legitimate and criminal businesses is hard to draw and some criticize false dichotomies. Ruggiero (1996a) points to the different relationships between legitimate and illegitimate industries. Thus:

- *Organized crime provides a service to legitimate enterprises*: This happens, for example, in the trade in stolen art works, where private individuals, art traders and auction firms use organized crime groups as 'go betweens'. It also occurs in the illegal trade in arms (Chapter 17), and the disposal of toxic waste (Chapter 16). Smuggled and trafficked people are also employed across a range of legitimate industries, including care homes, hotels, farms and the sex trade, making them complicit (Kelly 2007). To Ruggiero, organized crime performs an ancillary role for the official economy, providing a clandestine 'tertiary' sector.
- *Legitimate enterprises provide services to organized crime*: Legitimate business may knowingly or unknowingly assist organized crime by, for example, laundering money through banks and legitimate businesses (Van Duyne and Levi 2005). Organized criminals also use the services of otherwise legitimate professional groups such as accountants or lawyers.

- *Joint enterprises*: In some cases organized crime and legitimate industry work together as seen in examples of frauds on the European Union whose agricultural subsidies and complex regulations make partnerships useful as illegitimate entrepreneurs require access to officials and to legitimate business activities (Ruggiero 1996a).

Criminalizing business?

Analyses of organized crime also suggest that prohibitions, law enforcement and broader economic policies contribute to the spread of serious crime. The 'war on drugs' and organized crime in general runs the risk of causing collateral damage (Paoli et al 2010) by creating illegal markets and all the costs in terms of violence, law enforcement and harm which comes with them. Quite simply, if goods and services which people desire are banned, criminal entrepreneurs will provide them to a willing market. Controls on immigration and global inequality form the basis of human trafficking, and organized crime adapts to law enforcement tactics. The exaggeration of the 'threat' of organized crime forms part of the culture of fear outlined in Chapter 6, and can also fuel fears of 'others' more generally (Woodiwiss and Hobbs 2009).

Moreover, the success of prohibitionist policies can be questioned across the spectrum of serious crime which continues to flourish. Some, including Van Duyne and Levi (2005: 182) also point out that the perceived threat to public health posed by, for example, drugs, is relative. Legal drugs such as alcohol and cigarettes also carry health risks and there is no 'war' on calories or on the 'merchants of death' who produce unhealthy and fattening food and contribute to the so-called obesity epidemic. As with other areas of crime, pointing to an apparent 'moral panic' does not deny that serious crime groups exist, exert violence and make considerable profits (Levi 2007). It does, however, draw attention to the politicization of organized crime (Hobbs 2002), to the Americanization of policy towards it (Woodiwiss and Hobbs 2009), and to the criminalization of only some forms of business.

Concluding comments

This chapter has explored selected aspects of the vast range of activities generally associated with organized crime. It has suggested that, rather than consisting primarily of large, monolithic, hierarchical organizations, it encompasses individual 'entrepreneurs', small, local and family 'firms' and loosely connected networks. The term 'organization of serious crimes' is therefore more appropriate (Edwards and Levi 2008). Organizing serious crime involves, like any other business, seeking out market opportunities and organizing production, distribution and supply. Criminal entrepreneurs must adapt to law enforcement and seek out new opportunities often created by social and economic changes, such as globalization, the growth of the market in drugs and demands for new forms of illegal leisure. Involvement in organized crime is strongly related to economic disadvantage whether in local working-class communities affected by the decline in traditional skills and employment opportunities or by global inequalities and patterns of migration. As for other forms of crime, the close interrelationship of gender, age, class, racial and global inequalities are significant and a combination of approaches are required to fully understand it.

It has also been seen that criminalization, labelling, moral panics and the creation of 'folk devils' such as 'Mr Bigs' or Godfathers, combine to provide a misleading picture of organized crime. Criminalization in itself can be questioned as punitive policies towards drugs, the sex industry and other forms of forbidden leisure have generally failed to substantially reduce these trades raising important questions about why some forms of leisure and some goods and services are criminalized. This is further related to the close relationships between so-called legitimate and illegitimate businesses which will become evident in Chapters 15 and 16. Organized crime can also perform services for governments, as will be seen in Chapter 17.

Review questions

1. Outline the difficulties of defining and researching organized crime. To what extent is it victimless and how might a victim survey be designed? Which groups might be described as its victims?
2. Are you aware of the involvement of what might be called 'organized' or serious crime in your local area? What form does it take?
3. Why might the term 'serious organized crime' be preferable to 'organized crime'?
4. Looking at one specific form of organized crime outline arguments for and against criminalization.

Key reading

A variety of studies and texts deal with different aspects of serious and organized crime, many focusing on the specific areas outlined above. These include:

Edwards, A. and Levi, M. (eds) (2008) ***The Organization of Serious Crimes: Developments in Research and Theory***, Special issue of *Criminology and Criminal Justice* Vol. 8 (4). An invaluable collection of articles on many aspects of the organization of serious crimes including an account of research, discussions of frauds, human trafficking and local businesses and issues of policing and control.

Lee, M. (ed.) (2007) ***Human Trafficking***, Cullompton: Willan Publishing. An interesting and comprehensive collection of articles by noted researchers and academics on the issues surrounding, organization of and policies towards human smuggling and trafficking.

Van Duyne, P. C. and Levi, M. (2005) ***Drugs and Money: Managing the drug trade and crime-money in Europe***, London: Routledge. A thorough exploration of the drugs market across Europe, including incisive analyses of the organization of the market, insights gained from interviews with offenders, and an account of the 'money trail'.

Wright, A. (2006) ***Organized Crime***, Cullompton: Willan Publishing. This is one of the few British texts to address different forms of organized crime, along with issues of analysis and control.

Chapter 15
White-collar and corporate crime

This chapter will look at:

- ➔ Defining and constructing white-collar crime
- ➔ The scope of white-collar crime
- ➔ Corporate and serious frauds
- ➔ Corporate violence
- ➔ Crimes against consumers
- ➔ Understanding white-collar and corporate crime

The next three chapters turn to the 'crimes of the powerful', to white-collar, corporate, environmental and state crime (Pearce 1976; Whyte 2009), which are less likely to be popularly, politically or academically regarded as 'crime' despite the major harms which they cause. They do, however, attract considerable concern, particularly in the wake of the financial crisis of 2008 and the frauds which were associated with it, along with high-profile cases where deaths from so-called 'accidents' have been subsequently attributed to corporate neglect. These have led to calls for tougher regulation and involve aspects of white-collar and corporate crime.

This chapter will start by considering the contested definitions and criminal status of white-collar and corporate crime and how they differ from other crimes, before briefly outlining their nature and scope. It will then explore selected aspects in more detail, looking at serious corporate frauds, offences associated with corporate violence (Chapter 11), and at the many ways in which consumers are defrauded and physically harmed. It will then examine how criminological perspectives have approached white-collar and corporate crime and will also ask to what extent organizations can be criminogenic. Corporate crimes with a primarily environmental impact will be the subject of Chapter 16 and state-corporate crime will be explored in Chapter 17.

What is white-collar and corporate crime?

The definition of white-collar crime has always been contentious (Croall 2001a; Friedrichs 2006a; Nelken 2007). It was first defined by Edwin Sutherland (1949: 9) as 'crime committed by persons of high social status and respectability in the course of their occupations'. This challenged the prevailing criminological focus on lower-class offenders and sparked off many debates about aspects of white-collar crime. Some of these issues are briefly summarized below.

Is white-collar crime 'crime'?

In his research, Sutherland included activities such as false advertising or food adulteration, which were not at the time subject to criminal law but which to him were as harmful as other crimes. This was strongly criticized by assertions that criminologists should not include non-criminal activities and should not imply that some acts *should* be crime (Tappan 1977). This led to extensive debates over whether white-collar crime was 'really' crime and *why* the harmful activities of the 'powerful' were not subject to the same kind of criminalization.

Is it 'real' crime?

Some business activities are prohibited by criminal law but have an ambiguous status, often being seen as 'not really crime' (Aubert 1952; Croall 2001a; Nelken 2007). Offences involving health, safety or environmental law, for example, are more likely to be regarded as 'quasi' or 'technical' crimes, and are often described as 'not really criminal' (Croall 1988). Laws and regulations are typically described as 'protective' rather than criminal and criminal prosecution is seen as only one amongst many tools, such as persuasion and education, to secure compliance, and indeed as a last resort. A different language surrounds these 'regulatory' offences which are often seen as 'wrongdoing', 'violations' or 'breaches' rather than 'crime' or 'offences' (Croall 2001a). Events in which death, injury or disease result from inattention to regulations are generally described as 'incidents', 'accidents' or 'disasters' rather than as 'crimes' (Wells 2001).

Who are offenders?

Sutherland's identification of high status and respectable offenders also creates difficulties (Shapiro 1990; Ruggiero 1996a; Croall 2001a). How can the rather vague terms 'high status' and 'respectable' be defined? Employees at all levels steal from their employers, defraud consumers and neglect or circumvent regulations (Levi 1987; Croall 1989; and see Chapter 13). Are only some to be counted as white-collar offenders? If so, where is the line to be drawn?

Crimes for or against organizations?

In some cases the corporation, rather than the individual, is responsible and most now distinguish between:

- *Crimes against organizations* where offences are carried out individually or in groups by employees or service providers for their own personal gain. This is sometimes referred to as individual white-collar or occupational crime and is closely related to the thefts and frauds in the workplace explored in Chapter 13.
- *Crimes for organizations* in which the motive is not personal gain but the profitability or survival of the organization. This is referred to as corporate or organizational crime, the latter term being applicable also to crimes involving state agencies and non-corporate organizations.

While widely used, the distinction is not watertight and some crimes, such as corruption or tax evasion, can be corporate or individual.

Crimes of the powerful?

To critical criminologists white-collar and corporate crime along with state crime are 'crimes of the powerful' (Pearce 1976; Whyte 2009). Debates over whether or not they are 'really' crime reflect, they argue, the power of business groups to exert their influence over the criminal law and its enforcement. It will be seen below, however, that this may be too simplistic and fails to account for the crimes of many small businesses which form a substantial proportion of offenders in relevant categories (Croall 1989; 2010). Nonetheless, elements of power are important and the term 'power crimes' (Ruggiero and Welch 2009) has been suggested to reflect the asymmetric power of offenders over victims such as employees or consumers.

What should be included?

These issues have led to debates over what activities should be included within the category. Some argue that *only* those against the *criminal* law should be included, while at the other extreme it can be argued that the concept of harm be used to avoid tortuous debates over definition (Tombs and Hillyard 2004). It can be argued that the first option is too restrictive and the second is too wide and many accept that not only criminal but also international, administrative or other laws can become benchmarks as they reflect a censure of activities and impose a penalty, albeit not a criminal one (Green and Ward 2000). This would incorporate regulatory criminal offences along with competition laws, professional regulation and offences which breach Human Rights and other international laws and conventions.

Also included are the many harmful activities lying in the 'spaces between laws' (Gilbert and Russell 2002) or those which breach the 'spirit' but not the letter of the law, such as tax avoidance (McBarnet 1988). These typically involve deliberately avoiding laws by using practices which are 'legal' but clearly against the spirit of the law. These include moving money to, or locating production in, countries with laxer regulations. Other practices are legal in these countries but illegal at home such as bribery or the exploitation of child labour. Passas (2005) uses the telling phrase 'lawful but awful' to describe a variety of corporate activities which, while lawful, are widely regarded as immoral or anti-social such as the production of tobacco or weapons. Calling many of these crimes would, however, be a 'bit of a stretch' (Passas 2005: 773). These discussions also raise issues about changing views about business activities. In future centuries, for example, the production and sale of tobacco, the use of asbestos, or the exorbitant rewards and bonuses awarded to chief executive officers of corporations could well be seen as major crimes of the twentieth and twenty-first centuries (Friedrichs 2006a; 2009).

What distinguishes white-collar and corporate from other crimes?

Given its contested nature, can white-collar and corporate crime be clearly distinguished from so-called 'conventional' (non white-collar) crime? A number of characteristics have generally been taken to differentiate it from many other forms of crime (Clarke 1990; Langan 1996; Croall 2001a).

- Offences tend to be *invisible*. Their location in workplaces makes them easier to conceal – as Clarke (1990) points out, offenders are legitimately present at the crime scene and concealment is assisted by offenders' 'inside knowledge' of organizational procedures (Croall 2001a).
- They are often extremely *complex* as they rely on technical or scientific knowledge. Many participants may be involved and months and even years of investigation may be needed to unravel who is responsible for what.
- Within organizations a '*diffusion of responsibility*', in which functions and responsibilities are delegated, makes it difficult to legally or morally identify a 'guilty' person. One person may break a rule, but others are responsible for issuing instructions and monitoring compliance. Individuals 'pass the buck' up or down the chain of responsibility with employees 'blaming' employers for not preventing offences and employers blaming employees for failing to comply with instructions (Fisse and Braithwaite 1993; Croall 2001a; Wells 2001).
- *Victimization* is also *diffuse* as outlined in Chapter 5. Many offences have a 'rippling effect', affecting individuals very little but yielding considerable profits (Sutherland 1949). There may be no direct relationship between the offender and victim, for example where an employee's failure to check a safety device causes an injury.
- The invisibility and complexity of offences makes them difficult to *detect*.
- They are also difficult to *prosecute* due to the difficulties of obtaining sufficient evidence and establishing who is 'guilty'.
- These factors contribute to *lenient treatment*, with few offenders being prosecuted and even fewer ending up in prison.
- This is further related to the *ambiguous criminal status* of offences, outlined above.

The scope of white-collar and corporate crime

Research issues

Many of the difficulties of researching this area of crime have been outlined above and in previous chapters. Difficulties of detection and prosecution and the unawareness of victims, who, even when harmed, may not regard offences as 'crime', mean that official statistics are particularly unreliable. Many offences are dealt with by enforcement agencies other than the police who do not record them as 'crimes' but as 'fatal accidents', 'incidents' or 'complaints'. Victim surveys exclude most offences, although there have been some surveys of institutional victims, as seen in Chapter 13. These are inevitably limited to offences of which victims are aware. Other forms of research are also difficult. Offenders are not generally accessible, especially in financial and commercial enterprises. The complexity of offences also means that considerable financial, scientific or legal expertise, not always possessed by criminologists, is required to analyse them fully (Levi 1987).

Added to this are ideological issues deriving from the ambiguous criminal status of these offences. While some could be included in victim surveys and more accurate estimates could be obtained, many activities are not seen as sufficiently important to investigate. As Levi and Burrows (2008) point out, what governments choose to count is in itself interesting. It is particularly notable that only recently have the estimates of government losses from tax evasion been undertaken (outlined below and in Chapter 13), in comparison to the much more detailed information about other crimes in victim surveys and numerous statistical bulletins. As outlined in Chapter 3, it is also more difficult to obtain funding for research into these kinds of crime than for others, again reflecting assumptions of which crimes are more worthy of attention (Tombs and Whyte 2003).

Nonetheless, there is a considerable volume of research. Sources include enforcement agencies which are more approachable and can assist understanding of how offences and offenders are processed (Carson 1971; Hawkins 1984; Hutter 1988; Cook 1989). A small number of studies have explored offenders' accounts and motivations. As is the case for professional and organized crime, case studies, investigative journalism, court observation and reports, biographies, media reports, interviews with enforcers and reports and investigations by a range of interested organizations are all useful. Many of these lie outside the scope of criminological research but can be readily accessed through the Internet (Tombs and Whyte 2010) and, while many activities are not seen as 'crimes', they are nonetheless perceived as issues worthy of research and investigation (Croall 2009b).

The nature and extent of offences

Given all these difficulties it is extremely difficult to estimate the extent of any particular form of white-collar and corporate crime let alone its 'total' cost. A number of estimates and guesstimates, many of dubious validity, have been advanced, although few would argue with the conclusion that both economically and in terms of physical harms, its cost and impact far exceeds that of conventional crime. Box 15.1 lists some of the major forms of white-collar and corporate crime and, while no estimates are provided, indicates their potential cost and the difficulties of having no central source of information. Even 'conservative' estimates of the total costs of white-collar and corporate frauds are enormous (Levi and Burrows 2008), the toll of death, injury and occupationally induced disease far outstrips the total of

Box 15.1 Forms of white-collar and corporate crime

Corporate/organizational crime

Crimes against consumers include:

- 'Food frauds': adulterating or falsely describing the contents of food by major food manufacturers or supermarkets (see also Chapter 16)
- Manufacturing or selling food 'unfit for human consumption'
- Selling goods with short weight
- Offences under the Trade Descriptions Act, including car 'clocking' (turning back odometers), counterfeiting and otherwise misdescribing the quality or contents of goods
- Manufacturing or selling dangerous goods

Health and safety offences

- Failure to comply with health and safety regulations covering all industrial or commercial premises and transport. These include considerations of:
  - passenger safety
  - the safety of workers
  - the safety of consumers
- Economic crimes against employees
- Breaches of wages legislation; paying below minimum wage
- Breaches of anti-discrimination legislation
- Employment of illegal immigrants; use of gang masters

Financial frauds

Including:

- The sale of financial services such as pensions or savings plans.
- Insurance frauds

Other offences

Including:

- Corruption
- Breaches of competition laws
- Crimes of professional groups: lawyers defrauding clients; doctors' prescription frauds; accountants involved in corporate frauds and book-keeping offences
- Academic crime: e.g. plagiarism
- Global white-collar and corporate crime
- Corporate tax evasion
- Crimes of world financial institutions
- Crimes against workers in third-world countries (e.g. exploitation of child labour, paying low wages)
- State corporate crime

homicides (Tombs 1998; 2000), and consumers lose and commercial enterprises gain vast sums from a host of essentially fraudulent sales practices.

Varieties of white-collar and corporate crime

Corporate and serious frauds

This section will focus on some of the most serious frauds, many of which involve corporations. Some major cases are outlined in Box 15.2 and Box 15.3 summarizes

Box 15.2 Cases of corporate and serious frauds

BCCI

The Bank of Credit and Commerce International (BCCI) closed in 1991 amidst revelations of widespread fraud and corruption with an estimated $10 billion owed to 800,000 depositors in over 70 countries (Passas 1995). One indictment spoke of a $20 billion swindle, UK local authorities were said to have lost up to £100 million, and the Western Isles council lost around £24 million (Croall 1992).

The governor of the Bank of England identified a 'criminal culture' within the bank and illegal activities included nepotism, money laundering, mismanagement, bribery, corruption of politicians, evasion of foreign exchange regulations, false accounting, misappropriation of depositors' money, blackmail, massive fraud and the provision of finance for illegal arms deals (Punch 1996; Passas 1995; Minkes 2010). The bank made losses in stock-market trading, using clients' money to cover a series of fictitious loans, and money was shifted around from one account to another, from country to country, thereby evading regulators.

Enron

The collapse of the giant energy company, Enron, in 2001, revealed frauds and illicit accounting practices and several of the participants, including Kenneth Lay and Jeff Skilling received lengthy periods of imprisonment. Top executives had sold stock while knowing that the company was in danger of collapse, debts had been transferred to affiliate companies and shell companies were created (Rosoff et al 2003). Enron was associated with a 'culture of arrogance', with the board of directors, many of whom had potential conflicts of interest, being unable and unwilling to take any action. Crucial issues surrounded the complicity of auditors, with the major accountancy firm Arthur Anderson being described as neither vigilant nor scrupulous (McBarnet 2006). The case led to tens of thousands of lost jobs; lost pensions; higher prices; higher rates of interest; less money for investment, charities and government resources; physical and mental distress; erosion of trust in major institutions (Friedrichs 2004: 115).

The financial crisis of 2008

The full extent of fraud involved in this crisis has yet to be calculated but to date (Hutton 2010):

- Bernard Madoff was imprisoned in 2009 for operating the largest Ponzi scheme in history, said to involve $50 billion (BBC 2009b).
- The former chairman of Anglo Irish Bank was arrested in March 2010 after failing to disclose details of loans worth millions from the bank.
- Two former directors of Northern Rock were fined large sums for deliberately misleading analysts prior to nationalization.
- Goldman Sachs has been accused by the US Securities and Exchange Commission of 'defrauding investors by misstating and omitting key facts'.
- A court-appointed examiner in the United States has established that the collapsed investment bank Lehman knowingly manipulated its balance sheet, hiding around $50bn loans and investments. Its accounts were audited by the British firm Ernst and Young.

cases of what is often described as 'misselling' rather than fraud. It can be immediately seen that these all involve major sums of money, have a catastrophic impact, including the loss of jobs and pensions and investments, and indirectly affect tax payers through lost revenue or where the government has to 'bail out' failing institutions. To these could be added the massive figures associated with tax evasion, some of which were outlined in Chapter 13. The use of tax havens alone, for example, has been said to cost as much as £8.5 billion from high net worth individuals resident in the UK, £3 billion from large UK companies and £7 billion as a result of illegal tax evasion. This amounts to a total of £18.5 billion per annum which would take 4.5 pence off the basic rate of UK income tax (Murphy 2005). Also illustrated are the ambiguities associated with white-collar crime, with some offences being unquestionably criminal, others being subject to civil and administrative penalties and others arising from what were seen at the time as 'normal' activities.

Serious frauds have been known throughout the ages with hoarding food to push up its price, fixing prices and profiting from misleading rumours dating as far back as the 4th century BC (Geis and Edelhertz 1973; Geis 1988; 2007). The growth of modern business prompted questions about moral and ethical business behaviour and the noted commentator Daniel Defoe could, in 1720, find little difference between lawful industry and business and unlawful desires for exorbitant wealth (Ruggiero 1997b). The development of the joint-stock company was associated with frauds, company promoters were described as vampires, bloodsuckers, wolves and vultures, and the Stock Exchange was known as the 'thieves' kitchen'. The 'railway mania' of the nineteenth century saw the dishonest promotion of railway companies which involved market rigging. Whole families were 'ruined' and women were prominent victims (Robb 1992; 2006).

More recent decades have seen major cases of high profile frauds, some outlined in Box 15.2. These accompanied what was described as 'casino capitalism' involving 'cowboy capitalists' 'fiddling with money' using currency trades, corporate takeovers or futures trading which exploited the deregulation of financial markets. The 1980s and 1990s saw the junk bond and financial scandals in Wall Street and the collapse of Barings Bank following the derivatives trading of the 'rogue trader' Nick Leeson (Punch 1996), the notorious Guinness insider-dealing case in Britain (Levi 1995), and the collapse of the Bank of Credit and Commerce International (BCCI), outlined in Box 15.2. In the United States, the Savings and Loan debacle revealed the massive extent of thrift operators' risky investments in junk bonds, stocks and commercial real estate, the costs of which, including bailing out insolvent thrift companies (like building societies) were estimated in 1989 at around $200 billion and could amount, by 2021, to as much as $473 billion (Calavita and Pontell 1993; Calavita et al 1997).

A further series of major cases took place in the early twentieth century with the collapse of the major energy supplier Enron, also outlined in Box 15.2 (Rosoff et al 2003). It is seen as 'paradigmatic' of other cases (Friedrichs 2004) and to Tillman (2009b) contains the worst elements of frauds in which 'rank and file' investors lose out and the company's losses are hidden in a maze of partnerships within partnerships. It also illustrates the increasing involvement of 'collusive networks' of insiders, executive officers, accounting firms and other professional groups in perpetrating

Source: Reuters/Keith Bedford

The financial crisis of 2008 has revealed many frauds and has also led to heightened concerns about the prosecution of bankers.

accounting and balance statement frauds – to the creation of 'smoke and mirrors' (Friedrichs 2004). While based in the United States the impact of these frauds is global, seen most vividly in the major financial crisis of 2008/9. At the time of writing, the full extent of fraud involved in this is only beginning to be evident although as outlined in Box 15.2, a number of senior individuals in major companies have been prosecuted and investigations have revealed major frauds.

Fraud and the 'new economy'

A variety of factors have been associated with these recent developments, many of them relating to changes in finance and regulation such as:

- *The financialization of the 'new' economy.* An economic shift from the production of goods to the production of financial services such as 'derivatives' or 'hedge funds' has been associated with an emergent business knowledge elite (Tillman 2009a: 378). These are complex and difficult to understand, even by insiders, and were most prevalent in the United States in the dot com and energy trading sectors which transformed gas and electricity into commodities to be traded on financial markets (Tillman and Indergaard 2006: 477; Tillman 2009a). This distance from 'real' products or profits created a situation in which profits and accounts could be falsified to the extent, argues Friedrichs (2006b), that it approximated a postmodern state of hyper-reality in which short-term gain was prioritized with an almost complete indifference to the 'real' demonstrable value of a product or service. Indeed, so complex were the processes that key players could no longer fully grasp the scope and character of the financial edifice they had constructed.

- *Normal business practice.* These activities were widely tolerated and seen as 'normal business', a theme characteristic of fraud through the ages in which perpetrators perceive themselves to be 'business' persons and not 'criminals' (Levi 2009). This 'normalization' features strongly in many other forms of organizational crime.
- *Payment systems and the bonus culture.* How people are paid is crucial. The payment of commission encourages a 'hard sell' and was linked in particular to the misselling of pensions outlined in Box 15.3. The high salaries paid to chief executives can be seen as 'criminogenic' in that they may well encourage them to falsify profits to justify their large payment (Friedrichs 2009). They, along with the now notorious bonus culture, said to encourage risky investments and reckless loans, have become a political issue in the wake of the 2008 financial crisis.
- *Financial deregulation.* It is also widely acknowledged that many of these practices flourished in a period of financial deregulation based on the ideas of neo-liberal economics in which any interference with the market and financial services through regulation was seen to be hampering enterprise. The pensions misselling cases arose out of the government's desire to privatize the pensions market. Regulatory failure is seen as a contributory factor to the financial crisis of 2008/9 (Braithwaite 2009) where regulators failed to act and, even in wake of the crisis, have been said to be reluctant to pursue prosecutions, particularly in Britain (Hutton 2010).

Box 15.3 Cases of misselling financial products

- **Pensions misselling**: During the 1990s cases of pensions misselling in Britain were described as the 'worst financial scandal this century'. These followed government policies to encourage employees to purchase private pensions. In the ensuing 'hard sell' it was estimated that as few as 9 per cent of companies complied with legal requirements. Lloyds bank failed to warn employees that the policies could produce a much smaller pension than the company scheme they were leaving and failed to explain the value of the benefits or their links with inflation. By 1998 the cost of these frauds amounted to an estimated £11 billion and 49 companies, many 'household names', had been fined (Croall 2001a; Slapper and Tombs 1999).
- The 1990s also saw a series of **mortgage frauds** with risky mortgages being sold to high-risk customers. Around 5 million cases led to estimates that financial losses could amount to as much as £130 billion (Fooks 2003; Tombs and Whyte 2010).
- A number of British banks have also been fined by the Financial Services Authority (FSA) for **misselling payment protection insurance** – by October 2008, 19 firms had been fined with a record fine of £7 million being imposed on Alliance and Leicester, who were said to have trained staff to put pressure on customers who questioned the inclusion of supposedly optional policies in their quotes (Minkes 2010).

Corporate violence

The term corporate violence (see Chapter 11) challenges the predominant concept of violence as involving immediate, direct confrontation between individuals (Tombs 2007; 2010). It refers to instances in which corporate activity results in deaths, injuries, disease or emotional trauma. These are often described as 'accidents' or 'disasters' yet these words imply chance and inevitability whereas it will be seen that they are very often avoidable, being attributable to breaking or neglecting regulations. Corporate violence also raises serious issues about the extent to which corporations can be said to be responsible for offences. This section will explore key aspects of what is sometimes described as safety crime (Tombs and Whyte 2007).

During the industrial revolution, new technologies and industrial processes involved serious threats to the safety of workers and the public and there were many attempts, during the nineteenth century, to control some of the worst cases, including the exploitation of female and child labour in factories and mines (Carson 1971). The twentieth century saw new processes causing deaths and disease (see Box 15.4), many of which, such as the use of asbestos, whose risks were known, were not dealt with as crime. Cases such as that of the Ford Pinto car, introduced in the 1970s, highlighted important questions about corporate responsibility. It was known that a design fault meant that the petrol tank would explode in a collision, yet the car was not recalled after the costs of recall were balanced against the predicted costs of claims from deaths and injuries (Dowie 1977; Punch 1996). Around 500 deaths were eventually associated with the car although the Ford Motor Company was acquitted of reckless homicide (Cullen et al 1984). While major, high-profile cases attract most attention there is also a regular toll of individual workplace deaths such as the two Scottish coal workers crushed by a dumper truck (*Herald* 26/08/08); the electrician killed working on a fitness centre in Dundee for Mitie (*Herald* 15/10/08); the employee crushed to death in a sweet factory in Bournemouth in 2008 (BBC News 2010o) and the 55-year-old man being crushed by a crane in Larne (BBC News 2010p).

'Counting safety crime'

Safety crime typifies the problems of 'counting' white-collar and corporate crime. Many offences are not discovered or reported and not counted as 'offences' and there is no central source of information. Tombs (2000; 2010) has made a series of attempts to calculate some estimates and to compare them with other crimes:

- *Deaths*. Tombs (2000) collated separate statistics for fatal injuries at work in the course of sea fishing, transport and communications work, and driving in the course of employment. To this he added deaths from occupationally caused lung diseases such as asbestosis. He concluded that these deaths far exceeded that from homicide. While not all could be regarded as crime, reliable estimates by the Health Safety Executive attributed around 70 per cent to managerial responsibility. In 2006–7, across Britain, the HSE recorded 241 fatalities in the workplace.

Box 15.4 British cases of corporate violence

- 192 passengers died when the *Herald of Free Enterprise* sank near Zeebrugge in 1987. A statutory investigation found that '[f]rom top to bottom the body corporate was infected with the disease of sloppiness' (Sheen Report 1987 para. 14). The subsequent prosecution of directors and managers and the company for manslaughter resulted in acquittals. It was said that the company could only have been found guilty if its 'controlling minds' had been guilty (R v P & O European Ferries (Dover) Ltd (1990) 93 Cr App Rep 72). The speed at which the ferry had to turn around to maximize trips, the long shifts which the assistant bosun had to work, repeated warnings about previous occasions when ferries had sailed with open doors and the inherent design weaknesses of roll on–roll off ferries have all been associated with the disaster.
- In 1987, 31 people died in a fire in King's Cross Station, London. No prosecutions followed although a subsequent report criticized management safety policies (Wells 2001).
- In 1988, 34 people died in a rail crash in Clapham, London, subsequently found to have been due to faulty signal wiring. British Rail was convicted for failing to ensure the safety of employees and passengers (Wells 2001).
- In 1988 the world's worst off-shore disaster occurred when the *Piper Alpha* oil production platform operated by Occidental Petroleum was destroyed after a series of explosions, killing 167 workers. A subsequent inquiry criticized the company, finding shortcomings in preparations for a major emergency (Cullen 1990). The Report was also critical of the Department of Energy's enforcement, finding that its inspections were superficial and it was understaffed by 50 per cent. Occidental were not subsequently prosecuted for any offence (Ross and Croall 2010).
- In 1994, four teenagers drowned in Lyme Regis Bay while staying at an adventure centre. The two directors of the company were convicted of manslaughter – the company had used unqualified staff and ignored safety warnings (*Independent* 9/12/94, cited in Croall 1997).
- In December 1999 a family of four were killed in Larkhall, Scotland, when their house was destroyed by a gas explosion, caused by leakage from severely corroded pipes. After a six-month trial, a jury found Transco plc guilty of an offence under s.3 of the Health and Safety at Work Act, for failing to replace the corroded pipes when they had known since at least 1986 of the need to replace them (Tombs and Whyte 2007; Ross and Croall 2010). The judge imposed a £15 million fine, the highest UK fine for a health and safety offence, stating that throughout the trial 'the corporate mind of Transco had little or no remorse' (Carloway 2005).
- In October 2000, 4 people were killed and a further 102 injured when a GNER train derailed at Hatfield. The crash was subsequently attributed to a broken rail and the construction firm Balfour Beatty and five rail executives were unsuccessfully tried for corporate manslaughter but were fined £13.5 million for offences under health and safety regulations (Tombs and Whyte 2007).
- In May 2002, 7 people died and 76 were injured when a WAGN train crashed in Potters Bar, Hertfordshire, subsequently attributed to a faulty set of points. While not prosecuted, Network Rail and Jarvis accepted legal responsibility for claims arising from the crash (Tombs and Whyte 2007).
- In May 2004 an explosion destroyed a factory in Maryhill, Glasgow owned by ICL Plastics, killing 9 workers and injuring 33. The explosion was caused by liquid petroleum gas (LPG) escaping from corroded pipes (Ross and Croall 2010). A subsequent report found that the explosion was the fault of the company and that there had been non-cooperation with the HSE along with a failure by the HSE itself who had shown 'an inadequate appreciation of the risks associated with buried pipework and unventilated voids; and by a failure to properly carry out check visits' (Gill 2009: 94). A report carried out by academics, based on the testimony of seven ICL workers and former workers, suggested a lengthy history of inadequate safety measures and lack of consultation with workers about safety (Beck et al 2007).

In Scotland, in 2007/8, there were 32 fatal and 2,721 major injuries to workers, along with 5 fatal and 1,267 non-fatal injuries to members of the public (see www.hse.gov.uk/statistics/regions/scotland/index.htm).

- *Non-fatal injuries*. Many non-fatal injuries are not reported or investigated by anyone. Labour Force surveys, which can be likened to BCS data, suggest 274,000 non-fatal but reportable injuries in 2006–7, approximating to 1,000 per 100,000 workers. While precise comparisons with injuries occasioned from assaults are impossible, Tombs (2010: 10) concludes that 'work is much more likely to be a source of violence in Britain than those "real crimes" recorded by the Home Office'.
- *Occupationally caused disease and illness*. Work can also make people ill – in Scotland, for example, HSE figures indicate that 113,000 people in 2007/08 suffered from an illness which they believe was caused or made worse by work and across Britain, the 2006/7a Labour Force survey suggests that 2.2 million suffered from such an illness. Tombs (2010) cites figures collated by the Greater Manchester Hazards Centre which estimate an annual total of up to 50,000 deaths from occupational illnesses including 18,000 cancers, 6,000 deaths from 'work-related obstructive lung disease', and 20,000 heart disease deaths. A major killer in Britain and across the globe is asbestos, deaths from which amount to around 4,000 per annum in Britain and are estimated to peak between 2011 and 2015 (Tombs 2010).

Source: Press Association Images/Stefan Rousseau/PA Archive

The Hatfield rail crash which killed 4 raised issues about the difficulties of finding companies guilty of manslaughter.

Corporate responsibility?

A major issue in relation to corporate violence is the extent to which *companies*, as opposed to individuals, can be said to be 'guilty' and, as illustrated in Box 15.4, many companies associated with major incidents have not been successfully prosecuted or convicted under 'real' criminal law, but under criminal regulatory law such as Health and Safety legislation. This is due to the difficulties of finding a company guilty under criminal law, a key part of which is the concept of individual guilt and *mens rea* – the guilty mind. Individual employees and managers typically argue that they did not intend to kill or injure, and were 'only following orders'. In the *Herald of Free Enterprise* case, for example (see Box 15.4), the immediate cause was the failure by the assistant bosun to close the bow doors of the ferry as he had fallen asleep. The chief officer and the captain had not checked that the doors were closed, nor was there any system of checking, and a proposal to install alarm bells had been rejected. Despite this, the company could not be convicted as no one individual who could be considered to be the 'controlling hands' or 'minds' of the company, could be held individually responsible.

This doctrine of identification has hampered convictions as it is difficult, particularly in a large company, to identify who is in control and it is argued that management cannot be everywhere. These issues were important in other cases outlined in Box 15.4 such as the rail crashes in England (Tombs and Whyte 2007), and the TRANSCO case in Scotland which has a separate homicide law (Ross and Croall 2010). The recent Corporate Manslaughter and Corporate Homicide Act of 2007 which applies across the UK, has attempted to move away from the doctrine of identification enabling an organization to be found guilty if the way in which its activities are managed or organized by its senior management is a substantial element and it also refers to a gross breach of a duty of care which falls far below what can reasonably be expected of the organization in the circumstances.

Are organizations crime prone?

The organization is a key site of offending and, as the Ford Pinto case so dramatically illustrates, group decisions can have catastrophic consequences. Punch (1996; 2000) identifies a large number of factors which can affect these decisions – some managers 'knowingly' break the law and deliberately take risks, whereas others are incompetent. Yet other offences arise from tacit or overt managerial pressures, deriving from external market pressures. He further identifies a wide range of factors including the nature of the market, design features, business strategy, ideologies, safety considerations, organizational pressure, working practices, warnings, procedures, and scheduling.

These factors will be discussed further below, but they suggest that organizations can be crime prone, or criminogenic, and raise the possibility that some organizations are more so than others. Highest rates of fatalities, for example, are found in industries such as construction characterized by casual employment and lack of unionization and the need for small firms to cut corners to compete with large contractors (Tombs and Whyte 2007). Other organizational features include the extent to which safety is prioritized. Other cases outlined in Box 15.4 and above indicate the importance of the organizational or corporate culture in which safety regulations are routinely broken and checks are not carried out. In some jobs, particularly those surrounded by a culture of machismo, safety precautions can be seen as a hindrance and neglect can become 'normalized' where, for example, workers routinely don't wear safety helmets or work without full safety guards.

Profit and safety

Corporate violence is often attributed to conflict between profit and safety. As seen in relation to the Ford Pinto, Zeebrugge and other cases, production pressures or speed targets can lead to safety being neglected and improvements rejected on the grounds of cost. These can also be related to broader political and economic factors. Carson (1981), for example, attributed the high toll of individual deaths and injuries on North Sea oil rigs to a 'political economy of speed' resulting from government's economic pressure to extract the oil as quickly as possible. This led to a failure to introduce effective regulatory arrangements, leaving a void in which neglect of safety became a norm. The subsequent Piper Alpha case, outlined in Box 15.4, provided some support for this argument. To Slapper and Tombs (1999), it was also a factor in railway companies' decisions not to install devices to alert drivers to signals.

Regulation

This in turn draws attention to issues of regulation, the failure of which is a factor in many cases including the ICL explosion. Sporadic inspections and a lack of prosecutions encourage perceptions that offences can be committed with few risks or severe penalties. The £15 million fine levied in the TRANSCO case signalled the seriousness of the case and a feeling that the law should be reformed. Deregulation has also characterized the enforcement of safety legislation, and recent years have seen a reduction in the number of Health and Safety officers along with a reduction in investigations, inspections and prosecutions to the extent that Tombs and Whyte (2009) talk of the 'collapse' or degradation of regulation.

Crimes against consumers

As they rarely involve high-profile cases involving mass deaths or millions of pounds, crimes against consumers have received less attention than other offences and they are often described by 'softer' words (Mars 1982) such as 'misselling', 'cons', 'marketing malpractice' or 'consumer detriment' (Croall 2009a). Nonetheless, they are associated with physical, emotional and economic harm and, while often having, as Sutherland (1949) pointed out, a more 'rippling effect', can produce large profits for offenders. They are generally taken to encompass offences involving consumer protection law, including those relating to the quality, safety, content and description of goods and services (DTI 2004). The DTI exclude food offences, which will be explored in Chapter 16. Box 15.5 outlines some selected examples.

Box 15.5 Crimes against consumers

Consumer safety

- The recent Consumer Law Review (2009) contains estimates that unsafe goods coming through only one port, Felixstowe, particularly toys and fireworks, cause or contribute to 95,000 injuries, 100 fires and 3 deaths per annum.
- *Unsafe products*: A DTI (2005) investigation of 11,998 home accidents found that 1.6 per cent of fatalities, 0.4 per cent of serious injuries and 0.6 per cent of minor injuries were attributable to 'product fault' mostly due to poor servicing or maintenance of gas and electrical heating equipment. A *Which?* (2004c) report claimed that seven people each year are killed by unrecalled unsafe products.
- High street chains, including Argos and Homebase, were ordered to pay up to £20 million in compensation in April 2010 to 2,000 people who received chemical burns from sofas (BBC News 2010q).
- *Cars*: The DTI has estimated that consumers lose up to £4 billion per annum for unsatisfactory car repairs and services. In 2002, a 'mystery shopping exercise' carried out by Trading Standards Officers rated over half of garages as poor or very poor – 17 per cent carried out unnecessary work. One third of fast-fit centres unjustifiably recommended brake components or tyre replacements (DTI 2002).

Economic harms against consumers

- *Dairy product price fixing*: In 2007 the OFT fined several leading supermarket chains including Sainsbury's, Asda and Safeway. In addition several major dairy processors, Dairy Crest, Wiseman and the Cheese Company admitted colluding to increase the retail prices of milk, butter and cheese. While this involved a small cost to individuals, the total gain was substantial, reflected in the agreed penalties of around £116 million (OFT 2008, cited in Minkes 2010).
- *'Fixing competitions'*: In 2008 the BBC were fined £400,000 by Ofcom for encouraging viewers and listeners to phone in and enter competitions which they had no chance of winning (Minkes 2010).

The extent of consumer crime

Estimating the extent of crimes against consumers raises similar issues to safety crime. A very large number are not reported, and even if they are, rarely lead to investigation and prosecution. Nonetheless, their physical and economic costs, some examples of which are outlined in Box 15.5, are considerable. In 2008, the Office of Fair Trading (OFT) published the results of a survey attempting to assess the extent of what they describe as consumer 'detriment', defined as 'any instance where a customer suffers as a result of their dealings with an organization, partly or wholly as a result of the organization accidentally or deliberately treating the customer unfairly' (Office of Fair Trading 2008). The survey estimated total annual costs of £6.6 billion and also found that:

- Around a third of respondents reported one problem or more in 12 months.
- Over half of the problems involved sums of below £5, with 4 per cent involving over £1,000.

- The highest proportion of problems involved telecommunications, domestic fuel and personal banking.
- The highest costs were associated with insurance, followed by home maintenance and personal banking.
- Personal time spent rectifying the problem, welfare and psychological effects proportionally increase with financial detriment levels.
- Respondents in lower social grades and income bands are more likely to have experienced psychological and welfare effects as a result of the problem.

As with the workplace harms outlined above, not all of these reports involve dishonesty, let alone crime, yet even a substantial proportion would add a significant amount to the costs and impact of crime.

Like any other 'crime survey' this is inevitably restricted to incidents of which respondents are aware and cannot uncover elements of deception in widely tolerated and 'normal' marketing practices. These, subject to labelling or advertising laws, include practices such as packaging cosmetics in elaborate and luxurious-looking containers which actually contain very little. A very narrow line also distinguishes what would be seen as acceptable 'puffery' from deceptive descriptions. The Advertising Standards Authority, for example, ruled against Estée Lauder's claims that products reduce the appearance of cellulite (Lister 2005). Holiday companies have also been criticized for misleading descriptions, and for the well-known 'bait and switch' technique: this offers very low price holidays subsequently found to involve flights at unpopular times, thereby encouraging customers to pay more for times which are more convenient (Croall 2009a). As seen in Box 15.5, the car industry is also a major offender with high proportions of garages recommending unnecessary work or charging for work which has not been done.

The impact of consumer crime

Box 15.5 also illustrates that unsafe consumer products can kill or injure. Pharmaceutical products have particularly been associated with physical harms such as the notorious Dalkon Shield contraceptive which was associated with infections, septic abortions and infertility, and was responsible for the deaths of at least eighteen women in the United States alone. It was marketed following questionable tests and continued to be distributed in the Third World after it was banned in the West (Finley 1996). Cosmetic products contain chemical 'cocktails' of up to 9,000 chemicals, many of whose effects, some carcinogenic, have yet to be fully tested (Croall 2009b). It has been estimated that most women in Britain absorb around 2kg of chemicals through cosmetic products every year (Woods 2005). Cosmetic surgery has been associated with deaths and long-term health problems and the chemicals in household cleaning products have also been associated with a range of allergies and potential long-term effects – indeed, their growing use has been associated with higher rates of cancer among women who work at home (Thomas 2001). The frauds associated with the car industry also involve the practice of selling 'cut and shuts' which have been associated with deaths and injuries (Croall 2009b).

Conning consumers

Many consumer offences are built into 'normal' commercial business practices in which conning or swindling consumers are routine. Consumer crime well illustrates the very narrow line between activities such as

- Those unambiguously regarded as crime such as turning back car odometers or selling unsafe products;
- Those regarded as 'not really crime' but subject to a host of regulatory and administrative penalties such as advertising and labelling;
- The 'lawful but awful' practices of manufacturers who produce consumer goods in countries abroad with less stringent regulations, export products whose dangers are known, or routinely produce goods whose contents, many of which, like chemical perfumes and additives are unnecessary, are potentially dangerous but untested and unregulated.

Crime prone industries

Some industries have been characterized as criminogenic. In the pharmaceutical industry, for example, intense competition, the enormous profits which a successful drug will produce and high development costs have been associated with practices such as falsifying test results, bribing medical professionals, continuing to sell products after their dangers are known or exaggerating the effects of a drug (Braithwaite 1984). The car industry, dominated as it is by large manufacturers, is similarly competitive and only low profit margins can be obtained from selling new cars, leaving sales and servicing as the main profitable areas. This encourages what Leonard and Weber (1970) described as 'coerced' economic crime. Similar factors could well be involved in the travel or entertainment industries, both highly competitive. Moreover, the quality and contents of some products are particularly difficult for consumers to judge and they must rely on the advice of experts. This particularly applies to pharmaceutical products and car sales and services and makes these trades particularly 'fiddle prone' (Mars 1982).

Caveat emptor?

Consumer crime can also be related to the prioritization of profit at the expense of consumer safety or the quality of goods. Controlling competition for the benefit of companies at the expense of consumers also features in price fixing. Many areas of consumer law are premised on the assumption of *caveat emptor*, let the buyer beware, and the rhetoric of consumer legislation stresses the importance of the consumer being informed and warned of potential abuses. This can involve 'victim blaming'. Yet many consumers cannot judge the hidden dangers of goods. Furthermore, the most affluent are more likely to be armed with information and knowledge leaving poorer consumers more 'vulnerable' – a concern acknowledged in consumer protection publications. The stress on the informed consumer also reflects the anti-regulatory ideology referred to in relation to safety crime and it has also seen deregulation and attempts at decriminalization. The recent Regulatory

Enforcement and Sanctions Act (2008) assumes, for example, that the criminal law is 'overused' and that many issues should be dealt with administratively.

Understanding white-collar and corporate crime

It is often assumed that traditional theories of crime are difficult to apply to white-collar and corporate crime although it will be seen that many are appropriate and also that its organizational location provides a further dimension. This section will explore some of the main theoretical approaches and issues.

Rotten apples?

Individual and pathological theories have generally been seen as less applicable. As Sutherland (1949: 257–8) famously commented, criminologists

> would suggest in only a jocular sense that the crimes of the Ford Motor Company are due to the Oedipus complex, those of the Aluminum Company of America to an inferiority complex, or those of the US Steel Corporation to frustration and aggression, or those of du Pont to traumatic experience.

There have been attempts to explore whether personality traits such as a propensity to take risks, aggressiveness, ambitiousness, drive and egocentricity could be associated with offending but as Box (1983) suggested, these are equally as likely to be associated with business success. The role of agency cannot, however, be ruled out, particularly in relation to serous financial frauds. Senior personnel in the Enron case were universally described as greedy, lacking basic moral integrity and keen to be accepted by political and social elites. The money taken from the company was used to fund multi-million-dollar mansions, extravagant vacations, yachts, private jets and helicopters (Friedrichs 2004: 121).

Individual factors may also be important as dominant senior managers can determine the 'tone' or 'culture' of an organization, and some managerial 'types' have been associated with offending. Clinard (1983), for example, found that financially oriented and more mobile managers were more likely to prioritize profits and act illegally than more professionally or technically oriented ones. In general, however, attempts to attribute corporate crime to individual factors have been criticized on the grounds that blaming 'rotten apples' takes attention away from the 'barrel' (Doig 1984).

These criticisms apply to other approaches. To Gottfredson and Hirschi (1990), white-collar crime is little different to other crimes and is related to the self-interested pursuit of pleasure and lack of self-control (Chapter 6). Rational choice theory focuses on the extent to which risks of detection, prosecution and level of sanction affect managers' decisions to commit crime (Paternoster and Simpson 1993) on the assumption that those involved in business are 'amoral calculators'. It will be seen below, however, that a much more complex range of factors affect corporate decisions, which are not made in isolation but are heavily influenced by organizational structures and cultures.

Decollaring white-collar crime?

As outlined in previous chapters, white-collar crime has often been taken to represent the reverse of the common criminal stereotype, with the crimes of wealthy and powerful offenders exploiting, injuring and stealing from the poor. Yet as outlined above, these stereotypes are far from accurate and there is a much more complex relationship between inequalities, offending and victimization.

A highly influential study from the United States, carried out by researchers from Yale University, found such a predominance of offenders from lower levels of the occupational hierarchy that they refer to 'middle-class' as opposed to white-collar crime (Weisburd et al 1991). Levi (1987) found that prosecutions for fraud more often involved 'mavericks' than 'elite insiders' and his 'phantom capitalists' are not drawn from elite backgrounds (Levi 1981; 2009). Across a range of offences including safety crimes and those against consumers, small businesses, whether 'respectable' members of the 'petit bourgeousie' or 'rogues' and 'cowboys', predominate (Croall 2010). These kind of findings have been associated with what some have described as a 'decollaring' of white-collar crime (Levi 2008b: lxxviii), focusing largely on the occupational thefts and frauds outlined in Chapter 13 and departing considerably from Sutherland's and other criminologists' association of white-collar crime with power and high status (Friedrichs 2002b).

The relative absence of wealthy and powerful offenders amongst those convicted can moreover be related to the activities and assumptions of law enforcers and the nature of offences. Smaller establishments, like, for example, smaller shops or street traders, are more visible than larger companies (Hutter 1988; Croall 1989). Discussions of regulatory law often make the assumption that the criminal law is directed at the minority of 'rogues' whereas the majority of 'respectable' businesses are willing to comply (Croall 2004; 2010), and smaller businesses are more likely to be cast as 'rogues' or 'cowboys' more deserving of prosecution. Small businesses may also be vulnerable as the proprietor is more readily identifiable as the responsible person (Tombs and Whyte 2007; Croall 2010). In contrast, wealthy offenders or large corporations can avoid breaking the law by employing expert advice on 'creative compliance' and staying within its 'letter' while flouting its 'spirit' (McBarnet 1988; 2006). They can afford expensive legal advisers to negotiate with enforcers and contest cases in court – producing more lenient outcomes (Croall 1989). Corporate activities such as the misselling cases or marketing malpractices are also less likely to be fully criminalized, often as a result of business influence over law. Power therefore remains important.

Similar issues are raised by victimization where, as with other forms of crime, the more affluent, particularly investors, are prime targets and, as outlined in earlier chapters, have more cultural capital and can take more steps to avoid offending (Chapters 6 and 7). They do not need to buy cheaper second-hand cars, use cowboy builders or buy cheap unsafe or counterfeit goods (Croall 2009a; 2009b). They are also more likely to be aware of their rights. Moreover, while everyone is endangered by unsafe industrial practices, it tends to be lower-level workers who are killed in industrial 'disasters', a vulnerability often related to the relative powerlessness of workers in 'risky' jobs (Tombs and Whyte 2007). Moreover, as also seen in Chapters 6 and 7 global inequalities underlie the ability of corporations to locate themselves in less developed countries and exploit cheap labour and/or produce cheap and less safe goods. These considerations confirm the association between white-collar and corporate crime and socio-economic status and power.

Gendering white-collar and corporate crime?

Studies of this topic have been characterized as 'gender blind' (Snider 1996) although the maleness of offenders has long been commented upon (Croall 2003). While women's share of recorded fraud is higher than for other crimes, this is attributable to non-white collar, sometimes known as 'pink-collar' forms of cheque and credit card fraud (Levi 1994; Dodge 2006). There have been few high-profile female white-collar offenders and Snider (2008) observes that in the post-Enron era corporate cultures consist largely of aggressive, ambitious, driven Type A personalities, primarily male, white and privileged. As outlined in Chapter 9, some have also related aggressiveness in the City to an alternative form of masculinity.

In contrast there have been some suggestions that women in business may be more ethical although it has also been popularly argued that as women become more equal a desire to be 'one of the boys' might lead to greater participation in crime. There is little evidence to date to support or reject these contentions. In the United States, the so-called 'domestic diva' (Dodge 2006: 387) Martha Stewart was convicted and imprisoned for obstructing justice and making false statements to the FBI, and one married couple were involved in the Enron debacle. While women have been involved in serious financial crimes, they form a very small proportion. Why this is the case remains largely underresearched.

Where victimization is concerned, feminists have echoed their arguments in relation to other crimes by associating corporate power with patriarchy. As seen above, many products and services are targeted specifically at men or women and reflect idealized images of masculinity and femininity. Some of the most notorious examples of corporate crime have involved products designed to alter women's bodies either through cultural representations of 'beauty' or controlling their reproductive capacities (Szockyj and Fox 1996). The Dalkon Shield case provides one example as do the sale of cosmetic products, cosmetic surgery and the use of silicone breast implants (Croall 1995; Szockyj and Fox 1996; Croall 2009a). The risks of household products also adversely affect women (Croall 2009a). It was also seen in Chapter 9 that women's assumed financial or technical incompetence may make them vulnerable to, for example, car repair and service and financial frauds (Croall 2001b; 2009a). Gender interacts with class and does not only involve women as victims. As outlined above, many workplace fatalities and injuries are associated with traditionally male-based industries. Women, on the other hand, are particularly vulnerable to low pay, harassment and illegal discrimination (Croall 1995; 2001b; Szockyj and Fox 1996).

Criminogenic organizations?

Unlike other forms of crime the organization is a major focus and many have sought to identify criminogenic factors. These include the diffusion of responsibility which makes attributing 'guilt' difficult (Punch 1996; Croall 2001a) and the 'illegitimate opportunity structures' associated with 'fiddle-prone' occupations outlined in Chapter 13 (Mars 1982; 2008). This includes occupations requiring specialist technical or professional knowledge and it was seen above that consumers' assumed ignorance of the inner workings of cars or the technicalities of financial products makes them vulnerable as are those, including employers, who do not understand the technical aspects of information technology.

The economic environment of a business also has a differential impact. Some forms of white-collar crime increase during recessions where the need to prioritize profits can create severe pressures to cut corners on safety. Intense competition was also seen to be a factor. In these kinds of situations, anomie theory can be used as blocked opportunities for 'success' produce innovative responses (Box 1987; Passas 1990). Economic booms are associated with other financial offences such as insider dealing and aggressive takeovers and the questionable practices associated with the 'new economy'.

Corporate cultures and subcultures are also important and deviance can become normalized in specific organizational contexts. This was the case, argues Vaughan (1998), in the Challenger Space Shuttle disaster, in which the shuttle was launched despite knowledge that launching in cold weather was dangerous. The decision was sanctioned by a 'normalization of deviance' in which risk-taking was acceptable and there was a strong belief in the technical excellence of the Apollo missions. To Punch (1996; 2000), this illustrates situations in which 'good' managers unconsciously come to accept risks. This is also associated with the pressure to make profits, which, while not a daily obsession, underpins crucial decisions. The manager becomes '*homo economicus*', an 'organization man', individual thinking becomes absorbed by group thinking and individual ethical values are suspended. Evidence of riskiness is filtered out in a form of tunnel vision and cognitive dissonance. Managers become what he calls 'amoral chameleons', learning to live with a conflict between personal morality and corporate 'group think'.

Criminogenic cultures?

Cultures within organizations reflect wider cultural values which tolerate and indeed encourage many of these 'normal' business practices (Braithwaite 1989b; Punch 2000). The ambivalent moral and criminal status of these crimes has been related to a broader 'culture of competition' (Coleman 1987), or 'culture of callousness' (Currie 1996), particularly in a market society in which 'everyone is on the take' (Taylor 1999), epitomized in the celebrated slogan 'greed is good' (Punch 1996; Ruggiero 2000). Sykes and Matza's (1957) techniques of neutralization, outlined in Chapter 4, are also relevant. Victimization can be denied by notions such as *caveat emptor* or assumptions that workers choose to work in risky jobs (although in practice they have little choice), blame can be routinely denied through the diffusion of responsibility, and offences justified by appeal to the higher goals of 'business' or profits (Punch 2000). Rationalizations are assisted by the use of euphemistic expressions such as 'risk assessment' or the 'cost benefit analysis' leading to the Pinto decision.

The insights of cultural criminology can also be relevant in relation to the 'thrill' or 'machismo' of working in dangerous environments, or, as was the case in oil rigs in the North Sea, at the 'frontiers of technology' (Carson 1981) along with 'making a killing' on the stock exchange and deceiving gullible consumers into parting with large sums of money. This, along with the elements of greed and the 'lavish lifestyles' enjoyed by fraudsters provide the lure of white-collar crime (Shover and Hochstetler 2005).

Criminogenic capitalism?

These factors are in turn related to the ideologies associated with capitalism, neo-liberalism and globalization and, as outlined in Chapter 5, capitalism's prioritization of profit can be seen as criminogenic (Slapper and Tombs 1999). Deregulation and regulatory failure have been identified as factors in many of the offences outlined above and is related to the neo-liberal view that business regulation is a 'bad' thing and involves too much red tape. Proponents of the free market argue that the market will regulate itself as workers will choose not to work in risky environments, consumers will not purchase dangerous or substandard goods and investors will avoid placing their money in institutions which might fail. Yet it has also been seen that this is not always possible and that deregulation is associated with the low rates of prosecution and lenient sentences which lessen any deterrent value of law and reinforce the cultural tolerance of the harmful practices outlined above. Globalization also provides an important context for the kinds of 'lawful but awful' practices which continue to operate in the spaces between laws.

Concluding comments

This chapter has explored many aspects of the vast area of white-collar and corporate crime and has illustrated the many ambiguities which, to Nelken (2007), pervade defining, researching and understanding the subject. It has argued that while it is difficult to estimate the extent of this vast area of crime, it most probably far exceeds that of other crimes involving violent offences which kill and injure and make people ill and frauds on a grand scale which affect people's livelihoods, their investments and financial security, particularly for old age. Serious frauds were linked to the financialization of the 'new economy' and a conflict between profits and safety underlies other offences, particularly those relating to health and safety in the workplace and consumer crimes. While often seen as less amenable to criminological explanation, it has been argued that many criminological approaches can be applied to its understanding but that the organization and subcultures within it are also crucial factors. As Punch (1996: 84) points out, 'the organization is the offender, the means, the setting, the rationale, the opportunity, and also the victim of corporate deviance'.

This chapter, like others, has necessarily been selective. Many questions, for example, surround strategies such as price-fixing and breaches of competition laws, and the crimes of those in professional occupations, often particularly invisible because they are dealt with by private rather than public law, also raise very interesting questions, not least about how they are regulated and sanctioned. Other aspects, such as crimes against the environment and state corporate crime will be the subject of Chapters 16 and 17 respectively.

A key question in relation to the so-called crimes of the powerful is how and why they are not subject to the same kind of criminalization as other crimes. This, taken together with the shortcomings in regulation, raises important questions about the exercise of corporate and financial power and the ideology of neo-liberalism.

Review questions

1 As for professional and organized crime, consider how you might design a 'victim' or 'crime' survey of white-collar and corporate crime.

(a) What activities would you include and why?

(b) What difficulties would you encounter?

Taking account of all the forms of white-collar, corporate and organizational crime described in this chapter, consider how many times, and in what ways, you have been victimized by it in the last three months.

(a) How does this compare with victimization from other forms of crime?

(b) Which forms of corporate and white-collar crime cannot be looked at in this way?

2 Take one form of white-collar or corporate crime and consider how you might go about researching it. What would be your main sources of information?

3 Consider whether white-collar and corporate crime can and should be dealt with as crime. What are the difficulties of holding companies legally liable?

Key reading

There are now a range of texts available on this subject although fewer with a specifically British focus. Some of the best sources include:

Croall, H. (2001a) ***Understanding White Collar Crime***, Buckingham: Open University Press. This covers most of the topics considered in this chapter including issues of definition and construction, offending and victimization, the scope of white-collar crime and theories attempting to understand it, along with analyses of policing and sentencing.

Friedrichs, D. (2006a) ***Trusted Criminals: White collar crime in contemporary society***, Wadsworth 3rd edn. Regularly updated, this is one of the most comprehensive texts on the subject covering many different forms of white-collar and corporate crime, providing useful case studies and analyses of policy.

Nelken, D. (2007) 'White Collar Crime', in M. Maguire, R. Morgan and R. Reiner (eds), *The Oxford Handbook of Criminology*, 4th edn. Oxford: Clarendon Press. A critical account of the ambiguities surrounding white-collar crime, theoretical perspectives used to approach it and major policy issues.

Tombs, S. and Whyte, D. (2007) ***Safety Crime***, Cullompton, Willan Publishing. A good introduction to the issues involved in safety crime, with case studies, an account of recent legislative developments, a critical evaluation of how safety crime is subject to the law and an exposition and analysis of critical criminological perspectives.

Chapter 16
Crime and the environment

This chapter will look at:

- ➔ Defining and constructing environmental crime
- ➔ The scope of environmental crime
- ➔ Pollution and toxic waste dumping
- ➔ Food crime
- ➔ Bio-piracy
- ➔ Analysing environmental crime

Crimes and harms adversely affecting the environment have assumed greater significance in the light of global warming and there have been successive calls for the development of a 'green' criminology (South 1998a; 1998b). They do not, however, feature in major texts such as the *Oxford Handbook of Criminology* (Walters 2010a), and are often subsumed under white-collar and corporate crimes, with which they share many similarities. Boundaries are blurred between criminal, illegal and 'lawful but awful' activities (see Chapter 15), and gaps in regulations and enforcement allow many crimes to flourish. They also raise important issues about harms to animals and to nature (White 2008). While often relatively invisible, they have an enormous impact, ranging from the mass deaths associated with pollution and toxic waste to the accumulated effects of thousands of individual pollution incidents and seemingly trivial cases of fly-tipping, littering and misleading descriptions of food. This impact very often falls most severely on the least advantaged and their analysis raises crucial questions about the tension between economic development and the environment.

This chapter will start by exploring the conceptual and definitional issues surrounding environmental or green crime. It will investigate the nature and scope of these crimes and look in more detail at specific forms such as the production and disposal of hazardous substances, sometimes known as toxic crimes, crimes involving food and issues of bio-piracy, before exploring how criminological analyses can assist our understanding of these offences and at the issues which they pose for criminology.

What is environmental crime?

There is a 'politics of definition' in relation to crimes against the environment (White 2008: 88). Generally speaking, 'the environment' encompasses land, air and water and a starting point for looking at crime is environmental protection law. As for white-collar and corporate crime, this raises questions about the focus of criminal law, the nature of environmental harm and what should be included. Many distinguish between three broad perspectives on environmental crime outlined in Box 16.1 which affect issues of definition and construction outlined below.

Defining environmental 'crime'?

Activities damaging the environment are largely subject to the kind of criminal regulatory laws seen in Chapter 15 and are widely regarded as 'not really criminal', often being described as 'violations' or 'exceedence' (Walters 2010c). Other activities are widely tolerated and considered to be normal practice and many fall into the 'lawful but awful' category (Passas 2005). As for corporate crime, there have been suggestions that the harm approach outlined in previous chapters is more appropriate although this can be viewed as too wide. In an attempt to resolve this, Green et al (2007) suggest including actions identified as harmful by widely respected environmental groups. This would include, for example, intensive logging, some of which is legal and some illegal, which threatens biodiversity and entire species and contributes to global warming. Lynch et al (2001), discussing toxic crimes, argue that it is also justifiable to include avoidable harms, such as the use of

Box 16.1 Approaches to environmental or eco crime

- **Environmental justice** explores equity of access to and the use of environmental resources across social and cultural divides along with the impact of state and corporate actions which damage the environment and impact on the poor and powerless.
- **Ecological justice** focuses on the relationship and interaction between humans and the natural environment. When humans develop technology to meet their material needs, such as housing, agriculture, business and consumption, these actions may damage or harm other living things as well as inanimate and non-living objects such as soil, rock, water or air.
- **Species justice** emphasizes the importance of non-human rights and rejects any hierarchy of existence with human beings at its pinnacle. Arguments for animal rights stress that 'rights' are about ensuring health and well-being while minimizing pain and suffering, emotions not restricted to humans.

Source: Walters (2010a; 2010c); White (2008)

dangerous pesticides, when there are non-harmful alternatives. More disagreement surrounds the inclusion of activities which harm the environment but which are not currently subject to widespread condemnation such as having large numbers of children, driving 'gas guzzlers' or furnishing homes with timber products (White 2008; Walters 2010a).

Which activities damage the environment?

White (2008: 88) argues that the 'conundrum of definition is made worse' when it is recognized that some of the most serious forms of environmental harm constitute 'normal social practice' and the harmfulness of some activities is disputed. Building motorways and extracting mineral resources pose long-term environmental threats yet are generally acceptable and the damaging effect of industrial practices is often contested.

Environmental, green or eco crime?

Dispute also surrounds how the category should be described. As calls for a 'green' criminology increased (South 1998a; 1998b) some feared confusion with the area generally known as environmental criminology which focuses on how an individual's environment, including family and socialization, affect the likliehood of their becoming criminal. The term 'green crime' could be misleading, implying a link with the 'green' movement (White 2008). Official categories of 'environmental crime' are often regarded as narrow, encompassing, as they do in the UK, activities such as fly-tipping, littering and vandalism. These are largely individual, anti-social activities as opposed to systematic corporate activities which harm the environment (Walters 2010a). Some advocate the term 'eco crime' as it is broader and moves away from state defined categories. Eco crimes, explains Walters (2010a: 2010c), transcend national borders and include crimes against natural resources. Others argue that the term environmental crime, which is broadly understood, should be 'reclaimed' (White 2008: 7).

The role of non-human animals?

Also criticized are 'anthropocentric' approaches which focus on human beings and their economic interests while neglecting harms to what are sometimes described as 'non-human animals' and the environment itself. The term 'non-human animals' is used to stress the prioritization of humans, but many simply use the term animals. The criminal offence of 'cruelty' to animals is often relatively neglected (Pierpoint and Maher 2010), and the definition of what constitutes 'cruelty' is higher for humans than for animals with some practices being acceptable for animals which, if applied to humans, would be unacceptable (Beirne 1999; 2007). This includes testing products on animals and factory farming.

How does environmental crime relate to other crime categories?

It has been seen throughout previous chapters that tight boxes cannot be drawn around offence categories and environmental crime clearly overlaps with other categories. Much of it is corporate, some involves organized crime and some involves state agencies. Individuals commit environmental offences although the broad thrust of work in the area focuses on its institutional nature. Lynch et al (2001), for example, define toxic crimes as corporate crimes and exclude individual behaviours such as illegally dumping oil, paints or household solvents in domestic rubbish or pouring them down the drain, as these pale in comparison to the organized production and disposal of hazardous waste by legitimate business.

As is the case for corporate and other crimes, therefore, a broader inclusive approach can be justified and will be taken in this chapter, which will use the broadly accepted term 'environmental crime' while recognizing its potential limitations.

The scope of environmental crime

Box 16.2, which lists the main forms of environmental crime, illustrates its vast scope. It includes activities lying on the borderline between criminal and illegal, those which are widely regarded as harmful and the 'ecocide' (White 2008) associated with the use, in wars, of chemical agents. It also includes incidents occasioning mass deaths, pollution causing major diseases such as those outlined in Box 16.3 and a host of 'local' issues such as chemical leaks, the pollution of rivers with farm effluent, water pollution, noise and traffic pollution and the illegal destruction of trees or illegal dog fights. Some have a more obvious and direct impact than others which affects how they are reacted to (White 2008). Major chemical leaks or oil spills, such as the leak in the BP oil well in May and June 2010, posing an enormous threat to wildlife and the economic infrastructure of the Mexican Gulf, are more likely to occasion media and political concern than, for example, the less immediately visible inclusion of chemical additives in food products.

Research issues

As for corporate crime, there is no centralized source of information about environmental crime, and a wide range of sources, most from outside criminology, have to be used. Offences rarely appear in victim surveys, not being considered as 'criminal', and often being invisible. Like corporate or state crime, research is further hampered by difficulties of access and obtaining information, much of it regarded as confidential, and, as it is not widely regarded as part of the criminological agenda, funding tends to be scarce (Tombs and Whyte 2003).

Nonetheless, very much as for other crimes, a wide variety of sources can be used. Despite limitations, records of enforcement agencies, such as the Environment Agency for England and Wales and the Scottish Environmental Protection Agency (SEPA), can be a useful starting point and provide details of prosecutions and fines. Investigative journalism and news sources can also be used, and a number of

Box 16.2 Main forms of environmental crime

- **Pollution: air, land and water:**
  - factory emissions
  - chemical pollution
  - farm waste (slurry)
  - sewage and landfill
  - nuclear waste and contamination
  - illegal dumping of oil and other wastes in oceans
- **Illegal trades in:**
  - toxic waste
  - timber
  - endangered species; wildlife crime
  - ivory
  - ozone-depleting substances
- **'Food crime':**
  - Related to food production; distribution and sales; use of additives; mis-descriptions; labelling; deceptive packaging.
- **'Anti-social' environmental crimes:**
  - fly-tipping
  - littering
  - vandalism
- **Illegal, unregulated and unreported fishing**
- **Biopiracy:**
  - transport of controlled biological or genetically modified material
  - corporate colonization of nature
  - corporate engineering of nature (GM food)
  - violations of trade restrictions in hazardous chemicals and pesticides
- **Environmental degradation** as a result of wars:
  - Use of depleted uranium; large-scale bombing; chemical weapons
- **Animal abuse:**
  - Dog fights, badger-baiting
  - Factory farming
  - Cruelty to animals

environmental groups such as Friends of the Earth and Greenpeace conduct research and have useful websites, as do international organizations such as UNICRI (United against Crime). Other research includes detailed case studies (Walters 2006; 2007; White 2003; 2009; Beirne and South 2007). Nonetheless, in some areas, such as the trade in endangered species, information remains sparse (Schneider 2008).

The extent of environmental crime

It is therefore impossible to provide any accurate estimate of environmental crime. Box 16.3 outlines some major environmental crimes which have caused mass deaths

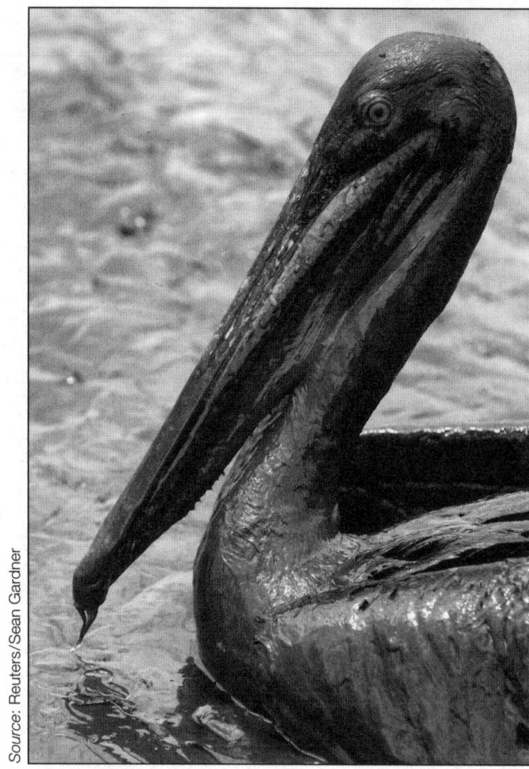

Source: Reuters/Sean Gardner

Major oil spills, such as that in the Mexican Gulf in the early summer of 2010 have a devastating impact on wildlife along with the livelihoods of local people.

or illnesses. Many other offences appear relatively trivial in comparison, although it is vital to recognize that *some*, such as pollution, although invisible, affect the health of all citizens and animals and can seriously affect the quality of life in local areas (Croall 2009b). Moreover, the accumulated effect of seemingly trivial instances can be considerable (South 1998a). Environmental crimes also have many secondary impacts. Green et al (2007), for example, associate illegal logging with deforestation, threatening the biodiversity of areas in which it is common, threatening the natural habitats of species and hastening climate change. It has also been implicated in so-called 'natural' disasters such as landslides and flooding in the Philippines and corporate exploitation of forests can lead to the loss, for producer countries, of legitimate tax revenue. Further examples of the extent of environmental crime will be seen in the specific areas examined below.

Varieties of environmental crime

Toxic crimes

Lynch et al (2001: 109) define 'toxic crimes' as 'illegal or immoral activities that harm the environment and human health through the production and disposal of hazardous waste', which includes pollution and waste 'dumping'. These harms have

Box 16.3 Major cases of environmental crime

Bhopal (December 1984)

What has been described as the world's worst industrial 'accident' took place in the Indian town of Bhopal, where an explosion led to leaks of the poisonous gas, methyl isocyanate. This killed between 3,000 and 5,000 people, with the eventual death tool exceeding 20,000. More than 200,000 were injured and, in the areas most affected, at least 90 per cent of families were affected by the death or severe incapacitation of at least one parent (Pearce and Tombs 1993; Punch 1996). The effects remain today in the form of recurrent stillbirths, birth defects, and a host of illnesses, pain, weakness, anxiety and depression (Sarangi 2002). While the 'cause' has never been fully established, and the company was not successfully prosecuted, it emerged that the plant, run by Union Carbide, was poorly designed and run down and had less adequate safety systems than equivalent plants in the United States. It is also recognized that the location of the plant near shanty towns led to more people being affected than would otherwise have been the case (Pearce and Tombs 1998; Carrabine et al 2004). In June 2010, eight people, including the chairman, managing director and vice president of the Indian arm of Union Carbide were convicted and imprisoned. These were the first successful convictions in the case and were regarded by campaigners as 'too little, too late' (BBC News 2010r).

Minimata

What came to be known as the Minimata disease in Japan (Hatashin 2008; Yokoyama 2006) arose from the discharge of dirty water and, later, vinyl chloride and methyl mercury by the Chisso Manure Company into Shiranui Bay, poisoning marine life and fish along with residents who consumed the fish. After the Second World War, it was noted that cats 'went berserk' after eating contaminated fish and in 1956 the first case was recognized, which eventually led to 543 cases and 17 deaths. While the company continually denied responsibility, after a long campaign on the part of fishermen and victims the former president and the superintendent of the Minimata factory were charged, in 1976, with professional negligence and causing death and bodily injury and were subsequently sentenced to two years' imprisonment. The campaign for compensation continued till 2004 and, by 2005, the number of recognized victims was estimated at 2,955.

North West England

In Britain, one local study explored the extent of explicitly criminal activities in the North West of England (Whyte 2004b; Coleman et al 2002).

- Of a total of 98 Environment Agency prosecutions, 2 were for breaches of radioactive substance regulations, 62 were for waste offences and 32 for water quality and water regulation offences (Whyte 2004b).
- The Mersey Basin, including Warrington, Widnes, Ellesmere Port and Runcorn, is said to be the most concentrated area of chemical production in Western Europe and the most concentrated site of carcinogen production in the UK, with two plants between them annually releasing around four tons of cancer-causing chemicals.
- It also sees some of the most persistent patterns of corporate offending, with ICI topping the list of the worst environmental offenders in relation to toxic air pollution, linked by the local press to high levels of lung cancer.
- This area is also affected by the Sellafield nuclear reprocessing plant.
- Traffic pollution was also a problem with 37 Liverpool streets exceeding government nitrogen limits.

been recognized for centuries with concerns about pollution being evident in the Middle Ages, when burning coal while Parliament was sitting was banned as London air was filled with acrid smoke (Friedrichs 2006a), and throughout the rapid industrialization of the nineteenth century pollution was widespread with adverse effects on health and the environment. The Clean Air Act of 1956 was passed following a number of deaths associated with the 'killer smog' in London in

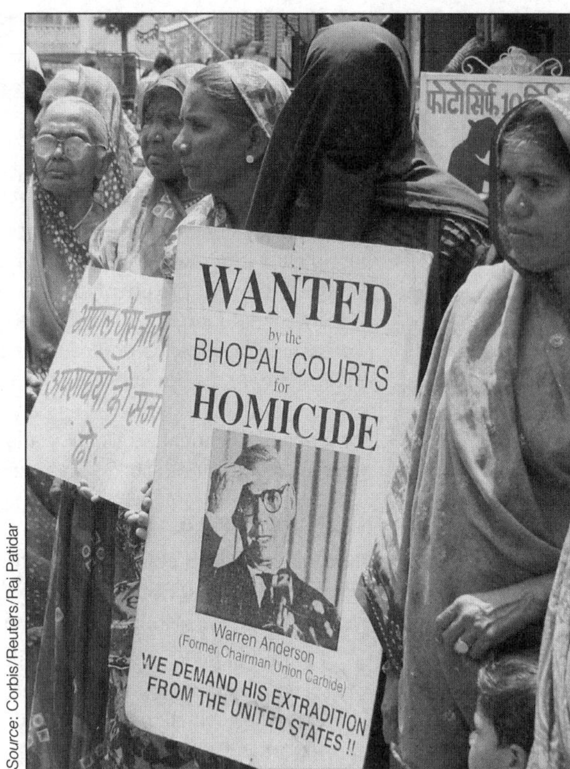

Source: Corbis/Reuters/Raj Patidar

The leak of gas in Bhopal in 1984 affected at least 600,000 people and has been associated with at least 15,000 deaths.

1952 (Carrabine et al 2004). Smog continues to be a problem across the world in cities such as Hong Kong, Beijing and Sydney, and Indonesian forest fires have necessitated closing down businesses and schools (White 2008).

Pollution

Pollution is generally described as involving damage to land, air and water, and some also talk of the noise pollution caused by entertainment venues and building work. It directly affects people's health causing death, injury and disease as shown in the most dramatic examples outlined in Box 16.3. Its effects spread across areas and national boundaries. White (2008: 125) cites the example of a chemical factory explosion in Jilin, China which initially killed five people and injured dozens more. It released toxic chemicals into the Songhua river which virtually destroyed the water supply of Harbin and went on to threaten the water supply of over 10 million people between there and Siberia.

The costs and impact of pollution are not systematically counted although they are known to be considerable. Globally it has been estimated that as many as 800,000 premature deaths can be attributed to ambient air pollution, many in the developing world (Tombs and Whyte 2010). In the UK, Health Department estimates suggest that a total of at least 24,000 human deaths each year can be attributed to environmental air pollution, a figure which may well be an underestimate (Tombs and Whyte 2010), and Walters (2010c) cites DEFRA figures to the effect that life expectancy in the UK was reduced by eight months as a direct result of air pollution, with an annual cost of £20 billion. Walters (2010c) also cites an audit of Scotland's 405 largest industries which found that almost 10 per cent failed an annual SEPA pollution inspection. Waste management was identified as the worst industry. While some pollution is attributed to individuals and motor vehicles, the most deadly pollution is caused by corporations (Tombs and Whyte 2010). A case study of one area, the North West, is included in Box 16.3 illustrating that environmental crime 'hotspots' can be identified, although these are not treated in the same way as those for other crimes (Whyte 2004b; Croall 2009b).

Environmental pollution is also a major issue in the countryside with Environment Agency and SEPA lists of prosecutions revealing a long list of offences associated with farms, including the disposal of farm slurry, the leakage and spillage of regulated substances and sewage into watercourses and the pollution of rivers and fields. This can endanger wildlife and fish – one farmer was fined £20,000 for polluting a beach with slurry and sewage and causing the death of an estimated 2,100 fish (Dube 2005). It can also involve government agencies with almost half of the beaches in England and Wales failing to comply with EU regulations being located in the North West. These have been subject to prosecutions in the European Court of Justice (Whyte 2004b). Seven beaches in Scotland failed to meet minimum European clean water standards in 2009 (Ross 2009) and 2 out of 24 Northern Irish beaches also failed to meet minimum standards (Edie.net 2010).

Agriculture and food production are also responsible for the use of herbicides and pesticides, long-term exposure to which has been strongly associated with cancer and in particular increased risks of breast cancer among women. These have been explored by Lynch and Stretesky (2001). Pesticides are associated with dioxins, chemical waste by-products in the air which biodegrade slowly, steadily accumulating in the environment and, through fatty deposits in animals, into the food chain. They have been linked to immunological diseases and inhibiting normal development. Hazardous waste constitutes a further danger with a variety of chemicals such as pesticides and fertilizers being linked to cancers, birth defects and a variety of diseases, with those living near hazardous waste sites facing higher risks. Despite these well-publicized dangers, the chemical industry continues to advocate the increased use of pesticides and the incineration of toxic waste on the grounds that it reduces the volume of solid waste. Pesticide producers continue to deny their role in causing illness and death, arguing that risks are exaggerated. However, Lynch and Stretesky contest that there are natural alternatives to pesticides and more recycling of toxic waste would avoid many of the harms associated with incineration.

Of particular concern has been pollution associated with the defence and nuclear industries outlined in Box 16.4. Particularly important in this respect is a reliance on self-regulation with some nuclear facilities, including those in Scotland and Northern Ireland (Walters 2007), being exempt from requirements to register for inspections. The MoD is also legally exempt from civil radioactive safety regulations (Edwards and Carell 2009).

Wars are also major sources of pollution and toxic crimes (White 2008: 63). The use of agent orange in the Vietnam war caused long-term environmental damage, contaminated food and affected the quality of life and health of local inhabitants – amounting to 'eco-bio-genocide' (South 2007b: 233). The burning of oil fields in

Box 16.4 British cases of nuclear pollution

- What was hailed as the world's first nuclear accident was a fire at Windscale in Cumbria in 1957, subsequently linked by Greenpeace with approximately 200 fatal cancers and 1300 cases of skin cancers (Whyte 2004b).
- Sellafield has been the site of several leaks, has been associated with poisoning the Irish Sea and has been convicted once or twice a year for health and safety crimes. It was subject to the first European Court of Justice prosecution in relation to an alleged failure to adhere to nuclear safety standards in respect of 30 kilos of deadly plutonium which was 'lost' and remains unaccounted for (Walters 2007).
- The Dounreay nuclear plant in the North East of Scotland was alleged, in 2005 (Walters 2007), to have 'recklessly' released hundreds of thousands of radioactive particles into the environment for over 40 years and attempted to cover it up. It was convicted and fined £140,000 in 2007. A total of 250 safety failures were recorded for the six years up to 2005 including the radioactive contamination of whelks, winkles, rabbits, concrete, soil, water and beaches, and it was disclosed that there had been several fires at the plant between 2001 and 2009. It was closed down in 2009 following a warning letter from SEPA in relation to emissions of radioactive tritium (Edwards 2009).
- SEPA has reported that Dalgety Bay in Fife contained more than a hundred sites contaminated by radioactivity following the dumping by the Ministry of Defence (MoD) of dismantled technology, much of it containing radium (Walters 2007).
- The Hunterstone B plant in North Ayrshire has one of the worst records for safety incidents having recorded 24 fires and leaks since 2001. In one of the most serious, in May 2009, around 2,600 litres of radioactive effluent spilled into the Firth of Clyde as a result of faulty pipe valves. It has also been associated with 24 accidents, leaks, mainly from coolants, and fires from 2001–2009 (Edwards 2009).
- Faslane, on the West Coast of Scotland, which houses nuclear submarines, has been associated with a series of serious safety breaches. There were three leaks of radioactive coolant from nuclear submarines between 2004 and 2008, and a waste plant manager was replaced after it emerged that he had no qualifications in radioactive waste management. The MoD admitted that training is poor, staffing levels are inadequate and maintenance is poor, although it argues that the leaks were minor and had no adverse consequences. Safety breaches are so serious that SEPA has stated that it would close the base down if it had the legal powers to do so (Edwards and Carell 2009).

Kuwait during the first Gulf War also had serious environmental consequences. More recently, the use of depleted uranium (DU) in Iraq during the US invasion exposed Iraqi cities to two thousand times the normal level of radioactive environmental acids (Walters 2007).

A variety of 'low level' environmental crimes also affect the quality of life in local areas. These include littering and 'fly-tipping', the illegal tipping of waste outside legitimate waste disposal sites (Croall 2004). One firm was fined £400,000 after burning tyres caused a dust cloud to 'rain down' on Rugby (Menaud 2006). In an example of 'naming and shaming' and 'zero tolerance', Glasgow city wardens fined major retailers, including Subway, Carphone Warehouse, Evans, Thornton's, River Island, RBS and Lloyds TSB for dumping rubbish, leaving bags and unsecured cardboard boxes on streets and allowing wheelie bins to overflow (*Evening Times* 2008). A total of 2,881 fixed penalty fines were given by Welsh local councils for environmental crimes such as littering, dog-fouling and graffiti (BBC News 2010s). Sony was one of the first companies to receive an ASBO for illegal fly-posting (Whyte 2004a). While some would omit these offences as they divert attention away from the systemic practices of large corporations, these do involve household names, and, as South (1998b: 444) points out, an accumulation of seemingly small-scale local pollution incidents can have 'modest to devastating changes in people's experience of the environment and conditions of life'.

Waste disposal

Hazardous waste must be disposed of and the more stringent regulations surrounding toxic waste disposal have arguably made it more difficult and costly for companies to dispose of waste legally. This has produced a variety of questionable practices such as the domestic and international illegal waste 'dumping' outlined in Box 16.5. White (2008: 117) estimates that the cost of treating one ton of toxic waste in developing nations is around one tenth of that in the United States and Europe. The US is the largest exporter of waste. In contrast, poor countries, often

Box 16.5 Cases of hazardous waste dumping

Somalia

Following the tsunami of early 2005, the United Nations Environment Programme (UNEP) identified hundreds of illegally dumped barrels containing radioactive waste washed up on the shores of Somalia. These included lead, cadmium mercury flame retardants, hospital waste and cocktails of other deadly residues which caused infections, skin diseases and as yet unmeasurable long-term cancers (UNEP 2005, cited in Walters 2007: 190 and White 2008: 117). European companies have struck deals with Somali warlords to dispose of waste, thereby providing them with money for arms.

Trafigura

The Dutch company Trafigura, which has offices in London and its HQ in Switzerland, chartered a boat (Korean built, Greek owned and Panamanian registered with a Russian crew) to carry toxic cargo to the Ivory Coast. The cargo consisted of 'slops', cargo and tank-washing residues, containing hydrogen sulphide, sodiumhydroxide (caustic soda) and chemicals smelling like garlic or rotten cabbages. In August 2006, 600 tons of caustic soda and petroleum residues were dumped at 18 open-air public waste sites in Abidjan, the main city of the Ivory Coast, with 5 million inhabitants, most near the poorest areas. The fumes caused nosebleeds, nausea and vomiting along with a terrible stench. At least 16 died, over 100,000 sought medical attention, and around 75 were hospitalized. A UN representative feared that the pollutants would spread to the food chain, and food crops near rubbish dumps were destroyed, fishing was banned due to contamination, and over 400 pigs were culled and incinerated (White 2008).

E-waste

Generated by computers, television sets and mobile phones, E-waste has been described as the 'fastest growing waste stream' White (2008: 116). It contains toxins such as lead and mercury along with other chemicals which can poison waterways if buried, or release toxins into the air if burnt. Much of this involves transfers from rich to poor countries and it is often not declared as waste but as goods for 'repair' or 'recycling' although much ends up being burnt in huge dumps in Nigeria. In this way, Americans avoid disposal costs and Nigerians find enough to make a profit.

with the involvement of corrupt state officials, may find it financially attractive to offer land for US waste.

Box 16.5 illustrates some of the worst cases along with the global nature of toxic waste disposal which very often involves transferring waste from the affluent West to poorer countries (White 2008). European and North American rubbish is dumped in landfill sites and off the coastline of African states, plastic waste has been dumped in giant pits in the Egyptian desert and German and French radioactive waste has been exported to African states. The disposal of old ships and aeroplanes, which contain metals, chemical and other contaminants is a particular problem in India and Bangladesh (Tombs and Whyte 2010). These examples also illustrate the narrow line between legal and illegal activities and one example of 'lawful but awful' activities is the (legal) agreement between Japan and the Philippines (neither of whom have ratified the Basel Convention) to dispose of Japanese toxic waste rather than treat it in accordance with Japan's own environmental standards (White 2008). Toxic waste disposal is also an example of a criminogenic market in which organized crime services legitimate industry (Chapter 14). Indeed, according to Walters (2007), the transportation and illegal trafficking of toxic waste in Italy is so widely acknowledged than an Italian dictionary has an entry for 'ecomafia' to describe criminal organized networks who profit from dumping or illegally disposing of commercial industrial and radioactive waste.

Pollution and toxic waste disposal involve issues already encountered in relation to organized and corporate crime. The risks associated with contemporary production and pressures for profits at the expense, in this case, of air quality and public health clearly underlie many offences. In some cases legal and regulatory limitations enable offences to flourish although at the same time, ironically, the tightening of regulations in many Western countries has created a criminogenic market in which it is cheaper to dispose of toxic hazards in countries with less stringent regulations. Some of these activities are illegal, and involve organized crime, while others lie on the borderline between the legal and illegal. Yet again the use of the 'spaces between the laws' (Michalowski and Kramer 1987) of different countries is evident. Also evident in this form of environmental crime is the taken for granted 'need' for industry to expand, and a subsequent lack of attention to its damaging consequences.

Food crime

Food, a basic human need, has long been subject to crime. Geis (1988; 2007) recounts examples from pre-biblical times of unscrupulous merchants hoarding food to fix prices, and during the Middle Ages selling underweight or adulterated food could attract draconian penalties including being excommunicated, pilloried, put in the stocks or banished (Harvey 1982; O'Keefe 1966). During the nineteeenth century, food adulteration was rife with the Bradford lozenge scandal in which people were sold adulterated lozenges involving 20 deaths (Paulus 1974). The use of water to expand food is one of the oldest forms of adulteration, and modern food manufacturing technology has led to what some describe as 'legalized adulteration', with thousands of additives, whose long-term impact remains unknown, giving bulk and colour to highly processed food (Lawrence 2004a). There are considerable

Box 16.6 Examples of food crime

Food poisoning

- In 1997, 21 pensioners in Wishaw, Lanarkshire died as a result of contracting E.coli 0157 from contaminated meat. The butcher was subsequently found to have persistently neglected food safety regulations and was convicted (Cox 1998; Croall and Ross 2002).
- In 2007, over 1 million items were recalled and dozens of people, including babies and children, became ill after eating Easter Eggs and other chocolate sweets in an outbreak of *salmonella montevideo*. Cadbury's had not reported the presence of salmonella and took days to comply with a request to withdraw the items. They were subsequently convicted and fined £1 million. They had changed their testing procedures to save money and waste (Tombs and Whyte 2010).

Meat frauds

- *Meat frauds* can involve criminal 'gangs' such as the case of 'Maggot Pete' and his 'gang' from Denby Poultry Products in Derbyshire who were convicted following a 'meat laundering' case in which meat intended as pet food, and unfit for human consumption, was sold to hospitals, schools and local supermarkets and risked passing hepatitis, Staphylocoffi and E.coli septicaemia into the human food chain (Lawrence 2004a).
- *Adding water to meat*: Pork chops sold in major supermarkets have been found to have been injected with water and additives to retain moisture. Some Tesco chops, for example, were found to contain only 80 per cent pork, and in January 2002 the company was convicted for selling 'tender select pork leg' without declaring added water, glucose, syrup and salt on the label (Lawrence 2004b). The FSA, while agreeing that it is 'completely unacceptable for the consumer to be paying for water', does not ban these practices as the meat is not unsafe. According to Tesco the water is added to improve eating quality and Asda blamed customers' 'poor cooking skills' – without water they argued, the meat would dry up.

concerns about the development of genetically modified (GM) food (Walters 2006) and food poisoning can cause death and serious illness. Concerns about food quality have of course been popularly highlighted by the celebrity chef Jamie Oliver in his attempts to improve the standard of school meals. The routinely used but inherently misleading marketing strategies outlined in Chapter 15 also apply to food. This section will follow the 'food chain', briefly exploring offences at all stages, some of which are summarized in Box 16.6.

Food production

The production of food, whether on the farm or the factory involves a range of offences. Some of the toxic crimes outlined above, such as the use of pesticides and herbicides are associated with intensive agricultural processes and also affect food. Other offences associated with farming include:

- *Cruel and inhumane practices*, particularly those associated with the factory farming of chickens and illegal and inhumane practices in slaughterhouses (Lawrence 2004a).
- *Subsidies fraud*: European Union (EU) subsidies have been associated with a variety of frauds (Passas and Nelken 1993), once estimated as amounting to around

10 per cent of its budget (Clarke 1994). These include activities such as claiming for fictitious olive groves, land and, during the 2001 foot-and-mouth epidemic, an investigation in Northern Ireland found that 103 farmers had claimed payments for more sheep than were actually culled (Evans-Pritchard 2002).

- *The use of gangmasters and illegal immigrants*: Using seasonal labour is not itself illegal but has become associated with gangmasters, excise frauds and the exploitation of immigrant labour by requiring them to work beyond maximum hours and below the minimum wage (Lawrence 2004a). This was starkly revealed when 23 immigrant Chinese cockle-pickers drowned in Morecambe Bay in February 2004 following which a gangmaster was convicted (Tombs and Whyte 2007).

A variety of frauds and safety issues have also been associated with fishing, ranging from the use of chemicals in fish farming, the 'fish wars' associated with fishing quotas and breaches of attempts to preserve fishing stocks through black-market fishing. These can create illegal markets in highly desired products such as stolen or poached Australian abalone (Tailby and Gant 2002) and poached Canadian lobster (McMullan and Perrier 2002). In the UK, this has attracted mixed responses, with some sympathy for fishermen's arguments that it is necessary for the survival of families and communities (Mackay 2003).

Food manufacture

Modern food processing technology and the growth of pre-prepared 'convenience' foods have led to many unsafe and fraudulent practices, often lying on the borderline between legality and illegality. So-called 'value adding', altering food by adding cheap ingredients and additives, thereby charging more for basic ingredients (potato crisps being one example) has been associated with 'legalized adulteration'. Food additives are used for a variety of reasons and many have little purpose other than cosmetic, to make the food look more appealing, and a large number are not tested (Millstone and Lang 2003; Lawrence 2004a). Water continues to be added, legally and illegally, to food, as seen in Box 16.6. Many other examples could be provided, including the misleading use of 'sell-by dates', the use of non-organic ingredients in so-called 'organic foods' and cases in which horsemeat has been found in food imports (Lawrence 2004a). Some of these involve a complex chain of production and distribution, evading taxes, and cross-border frauds (Croall 2005). An example of so-called 'food laundering' involves the 'tumbling processes' (Lawrence 2004a) in which Dutch food companies imported cheap frozen chicken from Thailand and Brazil, some salted to avoid EU tariffs on fresh meat. The meat was then defrosted, injected with water and additives and tumbled into giant machines. The water was absorbed, the salt diluted and the meat made palatable. It was then refrozen and shipped for further processing by manufacturers or caterers and much ended up in take-away food. One of the worst cases involving food production in recent years was the contamination of milk in China in 2007 with melamine, used to boost the apparent protein content of milk which had been watered down. At least four babies died and thousands of others became ill. Some of those responsible received a death sentence (see, for example, BBC News 2008).

Food preparation and food poisoning

Hygiene regulations are directed at the prevention of food poisoning. In one survey by the Food Standards Agency (FSA), 13 per cent reported experiences of food poisoning in the last year. At its worst food poisoning can kill or cause serious illness, as illustrated in Box 16.6. Its extent is difficult to estimate as it is often not reported and difficult to trace back to its source. It is often not prosecuted. A *Which?* (2004a) investigation revealed that while 42 per cent of UK food businesses visited by EHOs in 2001 failed to comply fully with food law, less than 0.5 per cent were prosecuted.

Selling and marketing food

Intense competition in the food industry is also associated with a range of inherently misleading marketing strategies. It is significant that labelling regulations are often fiercely resisted by food manufacturers and that labels themselves are often seen by consumers as confusing and misleading (Croall 2007c). Particular concerns have surrounded claims about the health value of foods and a series of *Which?* investigations provide some interesting examples:

- One investigation 'named and shamed' 'offenders' making claims such as 'low-fat', 'nutritious' or 'fortified' for foods containing high amounts of salt, fat or sugar (*Which?* 2005a).
- Another found that of 70 foods tested, only 7 per cent of nutrients matched the label with 17 per cent falling outside an 'agreed' error margin. Many contained more calories and fat than declared. A Bernard Matthews spokesperson, asked about a turkey roll with 22 per cent more fat than indicated on the label, is reported to have commented that 'some natural variation in fat will occur from slice to slice' (*Which?* 2005a).
- 'Cereal offenders' were identified in a study of 100 cereal products. While most were a good source of vitamins and minerals, were low in fat and contained high fibre, as claimed, 85 per cent contained 'a lot' of sugar, including all but one marketed for children; 40 per cent contained 'a lot' of salt, 9 per cent contained 'a lot' of fat and 13 per cent contained hydrogenated oils (*Which?* 2004d).
- A growing number of consumers (60 per cent according to *Which?* 2004b) are worried about GM foods, but they are difficult to avoid. One FSA report found that most processed foods contain elements of GM whether or not declared on the label.

Descriptions and pictures of food used in advertising can also be misleading. The FSA issue guidelines about descriptions such as fresh, natural, pure, traditional, original or authentic, and one study found as many as four out of ten samples breached these guidelines (Rowan and Kellow 2004; Uhlig 2004). For example, around three-quarters of 'farmhouse' products were produced in industrial premises and Tesco was criticized for labelling an Irish Wheaten Loaf as 'traditional', when it was baked in store and used flour treatment agents that were 'unlikely to be part of the Irish tradition'.

Pictorial images have also been criticized, although it is often unclear whether these break any rules. *Which?* (2004e) identifies, for example, the use of 'photographic

Farris, Joseph, Catalog Ref. jfa 3029, www.cartoonstock.com

'It says "An honest product from an honest company . . . 100% artificial.'

tricks' such as blow-torching food to give a 'grilled' or barbecued look and, subject to most complaints, misleading indications of portions – in some cases, small plates are used to indicate a 'full plate'. The Independent Television Commission (ITC), for example, ruled against a McDonald's advertisement in which all the fillings of a burger were pulled to the front making it look fuller than it really was. Packaging can also be deceptive and a *Which?* (2005b) survey reveals a range of arguably deceptive practices such as wrapping small numbers of biscuits into a pack and placing them into one big pack which they liken to 'pass the parcel'. Other practices include selling food in larger packages. Manufacturers claim that some excess packaging is necessary to avoid damaging food, but new rules have been introduced arising from pressures to reduce plastic waste.

Criminogenic aspects of the food industry

As outlined above, food is a highly competitive business, with a high demand for convenience foods and intense competition between food producers and major supermarkets. This can be related to the use of additives and food processing technologies outlined above and food production is concentrated in a very small number of corporations. The widespread use of corn, sugar, soya, palm and rapeseed in food production (much of which is widely seen as a form of adulteration) is associated with subsidies and the food industry, argues Lawrence (2004a), is provided with cheap ingredients by the 'handful of global giants' who dominate trading and processing, and whose subsidies undermine farmers in developing countries. These giants represent powerful political interests – the American Sugar Association, for example, lobbied the Bush administration in an attempt to change World Health Organization advice about the use of processed sugars. Walters (2006) details the illegal and aggressive tactics employed by the 'big four' major food corporations to enforce the use of GM food in Zambia and other African nations.

The concentration of supermarkets can also be regarded as 'criminogenic'. In the UK in 2003, the top ten food retailers accounted for just over 82 per cent of food sales and four retailers (Tesco, Sainsbury's, Asda and Morrison's) enjoyed a 65.3 per cent market share (Jones et al 2005). There have been a number of allegations about the misuse of this power, with allegations of bullying and charging suppliers for shelf space and promotions. Influential groups such as Friends of the Earth have successively called for investigations (Blythman 2004; Lawrence 2004a; Jones et al 2005). This is also associated with the use of gangmasters (Lawrence 2004a) as supermarkets' pressure for 'just in time' production necessitates using casual labour and paying low wages. Wider environmental impacts include the virtual extinction of some crop varieties due to supermarkets' preferences for uniformity of shape and colour.

Globalization is also significant, illustrated in cross-border food 'laundering' and food production can also involve exploiting the 'spaces' between laws (Michalowski and Kramer 1987). Countries in Southern Europe and Africa have been encouraged to intensively produce 'all year round' vegetables for consumption in Northern Europe and the West with adverse environmental consequences (Millstone and Lang 2003; Lawrence 2004a). The production of GM crops also involves pressures on developing nations. Despite protests from the Zambian government, for example, the United States continued to distribute food containing GM maize and exerted pressure on a number of African nations to accept US surplus GM food, to the point where, as one Zambian minister argued, food became a 'weapon of mass destruction' (Walters 2006). The Zambian government particularly feared the contamination of Zambian maize by GM crops.

Biopiracy and the corporate colonization of nature

The globalization of environmental crime features in the exploitation of the natural resources of developing countries by Western countries and corporations, often referred to as biopiracy (South 2007b: 237; Walters 2010a). This can be defined as the

> unauthorised commercial use of biological resources and/or associated traditional knowledge, or the patenting of spurious inventions based on such knowledge without compensation. (Mgbeoji 2006: 13, cited in White 2008: 113)

Many offences are subject to regulation by the United Nations, by CITES, the Convention on the International Trade in Endangered Species of Wild Fauna and Flora and the Convention on Biological Diversity (South 2007b; White 2008). This covers trades in endangered species and other ways of exploiting indigenous resources and knowledge for commercial exploitation.

The trade in endangered species

The illegal trade in wildlife and endangered species is explored by Schneider (2008) who comments on the scarcity and limitations of research on this issue, surprising, she argues, in view of the large profits accrued by offences and their potentially damaging effect on the environment. A large part of the trade in wildlife is legal and provides much needed revenue to source countries, but the illegal market is said to be second only to the drug market. It threatens the survival and conservation of endangered species and offers high rewards and low risks to participants. She outlines some of its main characteristics:

- Estimating costs is extremely difficult. The Metropolitan Police have estimated that around 350 million animals and plants are traded every year with a market value of US$25 billion. Up to one quarter is said to be illegal, with an estimated $25 million worth of caviar being illegally exported from the UAE for the US and UK market.
- Thailand is a major source for birds and orchids and part of the trade is demand led by individuals attracted by the prospect of possessing a rare species.
- The market involves a chain in which the depletion of rain forests contributes to global climate change and to the destruction of natural habitats.
- Increasing controls on legal wildlife markets have provided a fertile environment for illegal markets to develop and scarcer plants or animals are more desirable.
- Participants charge for acquiring the plant or animal from the wild, preparing goods for processing and transporting them to final consumer destinations.
- Major trades include the illegal timber trade, caviar trafficking, specialist specimen collections, and trades in skins, ivory, furs and traditional Asian medicines (TAM), some of which are made from rhino horns or bear gall bladder for which the bear must be dead.
- Each trade has its own specialist markets, trade routes and methods although little is known about the extent to which these are separate or parallel markets and involve organized crime.
- A range of skills are involved with the most skilled trades involving live animals. Less skill is involved in trading in processed parts such as rare timbers, TAM ingredients and processed ivory and dead animals.

Many of these activities are relatively invisible to authorities and, comments Schneider, their 'obscurity, along with fact that these activities are extremely low priority at all government levels, ensures that the illegal trade in wildlife will continue to thrive' (p. 276).

The colonization of nature

Examples of 'piracy' and exploiting the natural resources of less developed countries are provided in South's (2007b) discussion of corporate exploration and exploitation of biodiversity which involves the assertion, by Western interests, of ownership of genetic materials and pharmaceutical products by obtaining intellectual property rights and patents. This has been criticized as a new form of piracy and colonial expropriation and involves Western bio-agricultural corporations and the contested ownership of seeds, plants and indigenous farmers' knowledge. Supporters of these activities describe them as 'bio-prospecting', whereas to critics they are 'bio piracy'. These kinds of activities also include the forcible removal of indigenous populations from the land to which they are spiritually attached to exploit the land for military, agribusiness or other purposes. Local populations are deprived of any control over their own lives, are not given a say and damaging consequences include community dislocation, relationship breakdowns, mental health and substance-misuse problems.

To Walters (2010a) the Zambian case provides a further example of corporate colonization of nature and it can also involve identifying and extracting material from plants for profit. White (2008) cites two further examples. The nut from the greenheart tree in Guyana was patented for a range of medical purposes. The Wapishana tribe had long known of its benefits and objected to the patenting of what they held to be a local resource and traditional knowledge. A lengthy dispute also followed the US attempt to patent the Auhuasca Amazonian vine, used by indigenous people for centuries (White 2008).

A core element of environmental injustice, argues South (2007b: 239), is the commercialization of products incorporating traditional knowledge. Indigenous and local communities suffer a double loss – they cannot share the benefits arising from the new product and at the same time the application of modern biotechnology often eliminates the need to grow the original plant commercially, thus depriving them of income. These practices, he argues, can be viewed from a post-colonial perspective as state-sponsored acts of piracy and neo-colonialist methods of expropriation in which the ethics of the market shape and drive the corporate privatization of environmental resources and indigenous knowledge. They constitute a modern form of empire building, and science and law, he argues, have replaced religion and evolution as justifications. The superiority of Western science and expertise is taken for granted and indigenous or local populations are effectively excluded from having any say. In this form of knowledge transfer the value of knowledge moves from the originating nation state to the West where legal frameworks enable knowledge to be used as property enabling the production of goods for a transnational market. While the enormous health benefits of, for example, pharmaceutical products obtained from these sources cannot be denied, the issue is that what amounts to a 'theft of traditional knowledge' (p. 242) does not benefit the inhabitants of areas of origin.

Understanding environmental crime

Very similar factors to those encountered in relation to corporate crime are involved in analysing environmental crime, much of which is organizational. Environmental justice perspectives are also important along with the conflict between economic development and the environment and the way in which scientific knowledge is used. There are also important issues around regulation.

Environmental justice

The development of 'green criminology' has been closely associated with environmental justice, a movement concerned with relationships between social inequalities and environmental harm. This has tended to focus on the activities of corporations and states, who arguably perpetrate the most serious forms of environmental crime, although it should be recognized that individuals can commit environmental crimes and are complicit in others. The contribution of smaller organizations should also be taken into account (White 2008; Croall 2010). Small vessels can be involved in illegal fishing, small retailers sell short weight or out of date food and small farmers are involved in rural pollution. Indeed, small businesses face higher relative costs of compliance making some offences more likely (Croall 2010). Nonetheless, large corporations are major players, being responsible for deceptive and ecologically damaging production and marketing practices such as the use of additives and chemicals in food and in pollution and waste disposal. They also have a considerable influence over the law itself and its enforcement and, as will be seen below, in controlling scientific knowledge. Environmental crime also illustrates the close relationships between legitimate businesses and organized crime, outlined in Chapter 14. The state and its agencies also feature, particularly in the pollution associated with defence establishments and the destructive effects of weapons of war (see also Chapter 17).

The impact of these activities, whether global or local, falls disproportionately on the poorest. In the United States, a considerable volume of research suggests that more hazardous chemical plants and waste sites are located closer to lower-class communities (Pinderhughes 1996; Pellow 2004). These are often communities populated by people of colour, involving environmental racism, and Lynch and Stretesky (2001) found that chemical accidents were more likely to occur near African-American and low-income census tracts. In the UK, some of the worst cases of chemical pollution have adversely affected lower-class communities (Tombs and Whyte 2010) and those experiencing the poorest air quality tend to live in the most deprived areas (Walters 2010a). Low-income groups are also less able to access healthier food, being more reliant on often expensive corner shops and, as suggested in Chapter 15, are more vulnerable by being less well informed (Croall 2009a). Eco-feminists focus on how these processes adversely affect women, as consumers and as those so often responsible for providing for families.

Globally, citizens in the poorest countries tend to suffer from environmental crimes as seen in the examples of toxic waste disposal, the use of GM food in Zambia and the colonization of nature. According to White (2008), globalization has seen the transfer of dirty industries and waste to the Third World and within countries it is the poorest communities who suffer most – seen most starkly in the cases of Bhopal and toxic waste dumping in Somalia. The 'recycling' of e-waste further exposes Asia's poorer people to poison. Thus, concludes White (2008: 127), 'waste is basically a problem for the poor and something that is generally avoided by the rich'.

The attractions of environmental crime?

Before looking at the structural bases of environmental crime, the motivations of individuals must briefly be mentioned as individual agency cannot be ruled out, also the case with corporate crime. Reference has been made, for example, to the 'macho language' of profiteers, entrepreneurs, cowboys and risk-takers (South 2007b).

There can also be 'thrills' in many environmentally harmful activities such as driving fast in large cars, flying and conspicuous consumption (Halsey 2004), although White (2008) argues that this can overplay the role of agency as the 'seductions' of the marketplace and consumer 'needs' are socially produced and reflected in advertising and subcultures.

It has also been seen that many forms of environmental harm are widely tolerated within cultures and subcultures. Illegal fishing attracts a wide level of support, particularly in communities, like those in Canada, with strong traditions of hunting and fishing (McMullan and Perrier 2002). In such circumstances the 'techniques of neutralisation' (Sykes and Matza 1957) encountered in previous chapters are relevant as harm and injury are denied and the law is questioned. In what amounts to a 'politics of denial' (White 2008: 88) states and corporations can readily legitimate and justify environmentally unfriendly activities through 'greenwashing media campaigns' which misconstrue the nature of harmful business practices and take for granted that the continued expansion of production and material consumption is 'good', irrespective of its damaging effect on animals or nature. It is also argued, in, for example, the chemicals industry, that a certain number of accidents are 'inevitable' (Pearce and Tombs 1998).

Criminogenic practices and globalization

Examples of environmental crime also reveal the existence of the kind of criminogenic industries and markets encountered in Chapters 14 and 15, such as the market in waste disposal in which environmental pressure and more stringent regulations have ironically led to the growth of an illegal market. Quotas, often imposed in the interests of conservation, on fishing have also provided space for markets in illegal fishing. Aspects of the food industry such as intense competition and the dominance of major agribusinesses, food producers and supermarkets can also be seen as criminogenic.

Earlier chapters have also suggested the criminogenic nature of capitalism which is reflected in the tension between environmental protection and the exploitation of natural resources for profit, which can involve stealing these resources from indigenous populations. Globalization and its accompanying ideology of neo-liberalism have also been criticized for a tendency to support economic exploitation which can damage the environment and exploit the inhabitants of poorer countries. This is evident in the construction of dams, the environmental damage brought about by intensive food production and in the market in toxic waste disposal.

A further feature of neo-liberalism is widespread privatization of formerly free basic commodities. What South (2007b: 161) describes as corporate privateers, take what has previously been 'free' and sell it back to consumers for a price. To White (2003; 2008), the privatization of water introduced a profit motive leading to cost-cutting pressures which reduced water quality. This increased the market for alternative sources such as bottled water which further penalizes consumers. Moreover, the transnational privatization of water, also in the hands of a very small number of large corporations, risks disease. In 2000, in Walkerton, Ontario, 7 people died and 2,700 were poisoned in an outbreak of poisoning directly attributable to privatization (Snider 2002). Specialist teams previously responsible for collecting and testing water had been disbanded and the firm to which testing had been outsourced had not carried out its duties. The commodification of water has also, argues White (2003), led to millions across the globe being denied access to clean water as they cannot afford to pay water bills.

The role of scientific 'knowledge'

Technology plays a major role in environmental crime and supposedly 'neutral' scientific knowledge is used to justify particular technologies and deny environmental harm. Yet how impartial is this knowledge, much of it produced with the support and funding of corporations? Corporations also control the dissemination of knowledge and dismiss 'other' 'knowledge', leading Snider (2000) to question '*whose knowledge claims have legs?*' In respect of the chemicals industry, Pearce and Tombs (1998) argue that 'risk assessment', supposedly an objective process, is premised on the need to make enterprises profitable. In, for example, the chemicals industry, chemical engineers claim a monopoly of knowledge and competence to make plants 'safe'. Workers, whose experience might suggest different views, are not seen as 'credible' and thereby disempowered. Similarly, much research on food quality and safety is funded by the food industry, making claims about the safety of products questionable. As outlined above, many additives are inadequately tested, particularly when used in combination, as chemical cocktails (Lawrence 2004a; Croall 2007c). Scientific views about radioactive waste are also polarized by the competing interests of the energy industry and environmental groups whose claims about the long-term dangers of waste disposal have often been overlooked in favour of economic considerations despite scientific disputes (Walters 2007). The examples of bio-piracy also illustrate the lower significance accorded to the indigenous 'knowledge' commodified by capitalist corporations (South 2007b).

These scientific claims prevent potential alternatives being taken seriously. To Pearce and Tombs (1998), so-called accidents are related to mismanagement and the way in which operations are structured is premised on the capitalist need to accumulate. The extensive use of potentially harmful food additives, sugar (which arguably would be banned today if it were introduced), and the use of pesticides and herbicides, all of which have less harmful alternatives, also illustrate the prioritization of corporate interests and the use of corporate 'scientific' knowledge.

Regulation

As with corporate crime, regulatory shortcomings contribute to environmental harms. Not only do, as seen above, corporations resist more stringent regulations and deny the need for them, but not all states are signatories to international conventions and there is no clear set of internationally enforceable environmental laws (White 2008). Disparities between countries also enable the dumping of hazards as the examples above so clearly show. Within countries such as the UK, many offences are subject to environmental forms of criminal regulatory law with all its limitations of scarce prosecutions and low fines, taken as an effective licence to pollute. Few have dedicated specialist environmental prosecution departments, although Scotland has recently introduced a branch of the Procurator Fiscal Service to overcome some of the acknowledged problems of prosecution (Walters 2010c). The relatively narrow scope of these laws has also been illustrated, as have the limitations of some, such as labelling laws, to encompass the full range of commonly used misleading marketing strategies.

Concluding comments

This chapter has illustrated, by drawing together a range of crimes and harms adversely affecting the environment, their serious local and global impact. Environmental crime has been responsible for countless deaths and diseases, for endangering species and the sustainability of the planet. It has an unequal impact, most adversely affecting the poorest both within nations and across the globe. While all are in some ways complicit in environmental damage, some of the most serious harms are caused by corporations and states. Much of it is rooted in the conflict between continued industrial development and extraction of the earth's resources and there is, argues White (2008: 175), a 'basic contradiction between economy and ecology'.

This echoes many themes encountered in Chapter 15, and it could well be asked whether crimes against the environment constitute a special category and what the contribution of a 'green criminology' might be (South 1998a; 1998b). Advocates of this kind of approach argue that it would make criminology relevant in the prevention of environmental harm. It also involves reappraising concepts of 'serious' crime – challenging, for example, the focus of criminological attention on so-called conventional crime. To those adopting an ecological or species justice approach, it also involves challenging the taken for granted assumptions about officially categorized environmental crime along with the anthropocentric or 'speciesist' nature of criminology and victimology which downgrades the victimization of animals (Beirne 1999), and fails to consider the degradation of nature as criminal. The approach should, it is argued (Carrabine et al 2004: 328), document the existence of green crimes and critically evaluate how environmental crimes can be controlled (White 2008). To others, however, issues of environmental harm cannot be separated from corporate power and its links to state crime – the subject of the next chapter – place it firmly in the category of crimes of the powerful. Whichever view is adopted, environmental harm, its generation and control are clearly major issues for criminology.

Review questions

1. List the forms of environmental harm which you would include in crimes of the environment and why. Which harms might you consider including but would reject – and why?
2. Outline some ways in which individuals are complicit in environmental crime.

3 Take any one form of environmental crime and consider how you would go about researching it. Where would you obtain information? How accurate would this be? What major cases would you consider? What theoretical perspectives might be used in its analysis? How can control be improved and how should offenders be punished?

4 To what extent are capitalism, neo-liberalism and globalization criminogenic in relation to environmental crime?

5 Do you think that there should be a 'green' criminology? Why?

Key reading

While crime and the environment is a relatively recent subject of criminological attention, a number of recent texts and collections are of particular use, including:

Beirne, P. and South, N. (eds) (2007) ***Issues in Green Criminology***, Cullompton: Willan Publishing. This is a useful collection of articles on a variety of topics, including animal abuse, food crime and bio-piracy, by some of the leading authors in the field.

White, R. (2008) ***Crimes Against Nature: Environmental Criminology and Ecological Justice***, Cullompton: Willan Publishing. This comprehensive text deals with theoretical and conceptual issues and provides a range of case studies and a critical account of how environmental crime should be controlled.

White, R. (ed.) (2009) ***Environmental Crime: A Reader***, Cullompton: Willan Publishing. An invaluable collection of leading articles in the development of environmental criminology covering theories, concepts and control and a wide range of case studies.

Chapter 17
State crime

This chapter will look at:

- ➜ Defining and constructing state crime
- ➜ The scope of state crime
- ➜ State violence: genocide and torture
- ➜ Police crime and deviance
- ➜ State corporate crime
- ➜ Criminological perspectives on state crime

The state and its agencies perpetrate some of the most serious crimes which cause incalculable harms although they are not generally dealt with as part of criminology, being associated with human rights and international law. It has also been assumed that they happen elsewhere and not in advanced Western liberal democracies such as Britain, although it will be seen that this is far from the case. Indeed the invasion of Iraq, in itself widely regarded as being of dubious legality, has occasioned a 'veritable state crime wave' (Rothe 2009: lx). As for corporate and environmental crime, the definition and concept of state crime are highly contested. As states are responsible for making and enforcing the law, they have the power to prevent themselves being named as 'criminal', to contest counter arguments and withhold information. This chapter will start by outlining the conceptual issues surrounding state crime and at its vast scope. It will then explore selected aspects starting with the most serious forms of state violence: genocide, torture and war crimes. It will then look at police crime and deviance before turning to state corporate crime.

What is state crime?

Defining and constructing state crime involves similar questions to those asked about corporate and environmental crime, particularly in relation to its organizational nature and criminal status, and which activities should be included. Some of the main questions are outlined below.

Legitimate 'force'?

The distinction between illegitimate violence and legitimate force and the difficulties of determining where a line has been crossed were outlined in Chapter 11, where it was seen that, particularly in relation to defining terrorism, what is counted as political violence from above or below is related to whose perspective is being adopted. State agencies such as the police or the army are, in effect, 'licensed to kill' or able to restrain people using 'reasonable force' – but when and in what situations is this 'force' 'reasonable'? This was starkly highlighted in the case of John Charles de Menezes, shot in July 2005 at Stockwell underground station by police who thought he was a terrorist.

Can the state be criminal?

As for corporate crime issues surround individual and organizational responsibility. It has already been seen, for example, that there is a tendency to blame 'rotten apples' for activities which derive from organizational processes. The inquiry into the death of Baha Mousa (see Box 17.4) focuses on the extent to which his killing was primarily attributable to individual soldiers or to more systemic factors. A broad distinction can also be made between crimes which primarily involve individual benefit and gain, often described as political crime, and state crime which arises in pursuit of the aims of the state and its agencies (Friedrichs 1992; Rothe 2009). Chambliss (1989) talked of state organized crime as acts defined by law as criminal and committed by state officials.

State crime or deviance?

A criticism of Chambliss' definition was that it is restricted to the criminal law, illustrating the problems, outlined in Chapters 15 and 16, of using criminal law as a benchmark, particularly since the state passes these laws. State crime also extends beyond domestic to international law, which aims to regulate states. Should all harms caused by the state, as suggested by the social harm approach (see Chapter 5), be included? This might well be seen as too wide – as Ward (2004) points out, virtually all state laws involve restricting activities and while some might regard poverty, social inequalities or discrimination as crimes which the state could alleviate, this could be seen as going too far.

There are nonetheless some widely accepted benchmarks (Green and Ward 2000; 2004). Human rights and international law define activities as war crimes, crimes against humanity or as otherwise unacceptable and the United Nations (UN) has powers to impose economic and other sanctions and to use limited military intervention. Within states, particularly democratic states, questions about state activities by respected organizations reflect widely accepted standards of acceptable and deviant or repressive state policies (Green and Ward 2004). Reflecting these considerations, Green and Ward (2000) define state crime as a form of *organizational deviance* involving *human rights violations* by state agencies and argue that:

- State crime is quintessentially organizational as it involves actors working for state agencies in pursuit of *organizational* goals.
- The label crime should be restricted to behaviour that is both objectively illegitimate and subjectively deviant, including most human rights violations.
- Deviance involves an actor, a rule, an audience (who define the act as breaking a rule) and a potentially significant sanction.
- For state crime, actors are state agencies and rules include international law, domestic law and widely accepted social morality. Audiences include domestic and transnational civil society, international organizations, other states and agencies within the offending state.
- All of these groups can impose sanctions including legal punishments; censure or rebellion by the population; damage to a state's domestic and international reputation; diplomatic, economic and military sanctions.

An example of how these kinds of arguments can be applied to the US invasion of Iraq, with UK support, is outlined in Box 17.1.

The scope of state crime

Research issues

Given its seriousness, state crime has often been neglected by criminology, evidenced in the very small number of articles in journals, sessions at major conferences, funded research projects and space devoted to it in major texts (Tombs and Whyte 2003), although particularly since the Iraq war, it is now receiving more attention (Green 2010). It does, however, pose considerable difficulties for the researcher. Official statistics and victim surveys are of little use and state crimes are particularly invisible, often being shrouded in secrecy. Governments are ideally placed to cover up their activities, to designate sensitive information as 'official secrets', and to use the tactic of 'redacting' (blocking out) as in the case of Binyam Mohammed, outlined in Box 17.4. The academic researcher is in a relatively powerless position vis-à-vis state agencies and it is particularly difficult to obtain access or funding. Indeed, the researcher's legitimacy can be challenged. As Hillyard (2003: 204) points out, allegations of state conspiracies can lead to accusations of 'imagining'

Box 17.1 The case of Iraq: a war of aggression?

Kramer and Michalowski (2005) argue that the invasion of Iraq can be viewed as a war of aggression on the following grounds:

- It involved clear violations of existing human rights standards: a death toll of more than 10,000 innocent civilians; armed attacks on residential neighbourhoods; home invasions, arrests and detention without probable cause; torture and abuse of prisoners.
- Waging an aggressive war is a state crime according to the Nuremberg Charter.
- There was significant censure within countries, from the international community and scholars of international law.
- The United States failed to obtain UN Security Council authorization but attempted to rewrite international law by arguing that they had the right to initiate a 'preventive' war.
- The invasion breached International Humanitarian Law (IHL), including the Hague convention and four Geneva conventions which require parties to armed conflict to protect civilians and non-combatants – violations of these statutes are considered to be war crimes.
- Four types of war crimes were committed under IHL:
  - failure to secure public safety and protect civilian rights
  - illegal transformation of the Iraq economy
  - indiscriminate responses to Iraqi resistance actions
  - torture and abuse of Iraqi prisoners.

crimes, whereas to him conspiracies are imaginative crimes, not crimes of the imagination.

Considerable information can nonetheless be gathered from the reports and investigations of human rights and other pressure groups and from investigative journalism. Government inquiries are also a good source although very often these are partial and biased as government may restrict the scope of inquiries or not publish their full findings. Reports are often contested, new evidence is offered and the full picture may take many decades to emerge. The Saville Inquiry into the shooting and killing of 13 civil rights marchers by British paratroopers in 1972 in Londonderry, known as Bloody Sunday, which found that they were responsible for the killings, was published in June 2010, 38 years after the shootings and 6 years after it was completed, having heard evidence since 1998. The previous Widgery tribunal was widely seen as a 'whitewash' (McDonald 2010). A report into the death of Blair Peach, killed in Southall, west London during an anti-fascist demonstration in 1979, confirming that the fatal blow was likely to have been made by an unnamed police officer, was only made public, with redactions, in April 2010 (Campbell 2010). All material must therefore be critically examined and, as with corporate and environmental crime, would-be researchers must look well beyond criminological sources.

Source: Getty Images/Frederick Hoare/Central Press

The Saville Inquiry report into the shootings in Londonderry on so-called Bloody Sunday in 1972 has been published 38 years after the event.

The extent of state crime

Assessing the extent of state crime is therefore virtually impossible. Box 17.2 lists its main forms, illustrating its massive scope and the enormity of harms with which it is associated, ranging from genocide and war crimes to policies which systematically repress citizens and covertly support or facilitate state-sponsored terror. State crimes can be crimes of omission as well as commission – failing, for example, to ensure that regulations are complied with or to ensure the safety of populations vulnerable to natural disasters. State crimes are said to be increasing (Friedrichs 2010) and Ruggiero (2007: 212) comments that despite a so-called civilization process, the twentieth century saw unprecedented state violence such as massacres, genocides and brutalities, citing a figure of as many as 200 million deaths. While figures of deaths are most often cited, state crimes directly and indirectly cause some of the long-term environmental harms outlined in Chapter 16. They can also destroy a country's social and economic fabric including villages, towns, community centres, hospitals, schools, water or electrical systems, damaged oil refineries, bombed embassies, and have far-reaching effects on health care and mortality rates – all of which is virtually uncountable (Rothe 2009: 80).

Box 17.2 Forms of state crime

- **Political crime**
  - bribery and corruption (for political or personal gain)
  - election frauds
- **State violence**
- **Crimes against humanity**
  - genocide
  - genocidal rape
- **War crimes**
  - crimes of aggression
  - torture
  - use of information obtained from torture
  - state-directed terror (state-sponsored/supported insurgencies; state-sponsored assassinations)
- **Disappearances** extra judicial arrest or abduction – usually followed by torture, secret execution
- **Political repression**
- **Enslavement**
- **Use of child soldiers**
- **Human rights violations**
- **Institutional violence of state agencies** (e.g. police, army)
- **Police crime and deviance** (including violence and corruption)
- **State corporate crime:**
  - Bribery and corruption
  - Awarding of contracts
  - Failure to ensure adequate regulation of corporate activities
  - 'Contracting out' violence
  - Breaching arms embargoes
- **Crimes of globalization**
- **Natural disasters** (failure to protect population from effects – e.g. Hurricane Katrina).

Sources: Green and Ward (2004); Rothe (2009)

Varieties of state crime

State violence

Globally, the scale of state violence is so great that it is difficult to encapsulate it in one section of one chapter. It includes the major cases of genocide and crimes against humanity, outlined in Box 17.2 and 17.3, war crimes such as the unlawful killing of civilians, the ill-treatment or torture of civilians in occupied territory or prisoners of war, the killing of hostages, the plundering of property and the wanton destruction of human settlements and devastation not warranted by military necessity (McLaughlin 1996; 2006c). State-directed terror, as outlined in Chapter 11, involves using death squads to kill terrorists identified by covert means and the use of torture or intimidating interrogation. Combating terrorism also justifies the introduction of 'emergency' powers which undermine citizens' rights and dispense with the normal due process of law. These states of 'emergency' are often 'normalized' and used to criminalize groups assumed to be associated with terrorists. This section will focus on genocide and serious crimes against humanity and torture.

Genocide and serious crimes against humanity

Genocide is generally defined as systematically and deliberately seeking to eradicate, or attempt to eradicate, a national, ethnic, racial or religious group by mass murder and it is state organized (Green and Ward 2004; McLaughlin 2006c). Box 17.3

Box 17.3 Genocides and serious crimes of humanity (twentieth and twenty-first centuries)

Genocide

1933–45, *Germany*: The holocaust involved the killing of 11 million people, 6 million of whom were Jews and 1.1 million children. Gypsies, the disabled and anyone who resisted the Nazis were targets. Up to 1,000 people were transported to death camps where they were kept in appalling conditions and many were killed in gas chambers.

1975–79, *Cambodia*: The Khmer Rouge attempted to totally restructure society by massacring, starving and executing supporters of the old regime, city dwellers and certain ethnic and religious minorities. At least 100,000 people were executed and around one-eighth of the population died from malnutrition, overwork and disease.

1994, *Rwanda*: 500,000–100,000 people, largely Tutsis, were killed in a space of 100 days by largely Hutu perpetrators.

1992–95, *Bosnia*: The so-called 'ethnic cleansing' of Muslim residents of Bosnia by Serb and Croat forces included the destruction of property, forced resettlement, execution and massacres, with around 200,000 victims.

2003–present, *Sudan*: Alleged genocidal intentions on the part of the Sudanese government using the Janjaweed to carry out mass killings of Darfurians. Around 2.7 million people have fled their homes and the UN estimates that around 300,000 have died to 2010.

Other serious atrocities

1976–80, *Argentina*: Following a military coup death squads targeted subversives by disappearances, kidnappings, torture and murder. It is estimated that 10,000–30,000 people 'disappeared' in Argentina between 1976 and 1983 (McLaughlin 1996).

1973–6, *Chile*: Following the fall of the Allende government and the rise to power of the Pinochet regime, supporters of the previous government and others on the left were 'disappeared' or arrested, tortured, exiled and summarily executed.

1981–92, *Iran*: Following the Islamic revolution, the government violently suppressed dissident Muslims, Kurds and prominent Baha'is.

1998–91, *Iraq*: The indiscriminate destruction of Iraqi Kurdish guerrillas by Saddam Hussein's regime through gassing, massacres, disappearances, forced resettlement and demolition of villages.

1967–present, *Israel*: Israel has been accused of violations of human rights and crimes against humanity based on the seclusion of Palestinians, particularly in Gaza, resulting in high levels of poverty and unemployment and successive bombing.

(Based on Rothe 2009; Green and Ward 2004 and other sources as indicated) gives very brief details of some of the major twentieth- and twenty-first century cases along with some of the worst cases of crimes against humanity and serious human rights violations, including the 'disappearances' of thousands of people in South America and the continuing violence in the Middle East which has occasioned many allegations of war crimes. Israel's actions in Gaza, including the construction of a so-called protective wall, deprive Palestinians of means of subsistence, employment, housing and water, and amounts, according to the Goldstone Report, to a crime of persecution (Human Rights Council 2009, cited in Doig 2010). This gives some idea of the massive global toll extracted by these crimes. They have been associated with a range of factors including:

Crime-prone states?

Genocides and other major atrocities almost always occur in one-party states, typically associated with military juntas, communist or theocratic forms of government (Rothe 2009), although fascism is not inherently genocidal (Green and Ward 2004). The economic, cultural and political situation of the specific country is also important as is recent political upheaval (Rothe 2009). In Germany, for example, the trauma of defeat in the First World War, elements of romantic nationalism, anti-semitism and militarism inherited from nineteenth-century German culture and the social and demographic consequences of German conquests of Eastern Europe were all combined (Green and Ward 2004: 168). Cambodia had undergone devastating American bombing and the Khmer Rouge had a profoundly reactionary nationalist agenda (Green and Ward 2004). Charismatic leaders may also play a role as can a history of colonialism (Rothe 2009). Major factors also include pre-existing ethnic, religious or other divisions related to economic and political disadvantage. As Rothe (2009: 147) argues, a 'central element in atrocity-producing environments is a set of intense ethnic rivalries and tensions'. The victim group is also excluded from the perpetrators' 'universe of obligation', creating a 'logic of exclusion and solidarity' (Green and Ward 2004: 71) in which harming 'others' is not regarded as deviant or criminal and elites aim to increase their legitimacy by dividing the population.

Neutralizing genocide

These kinds of factors form the context for using the 'techniques of neutralisation' (Sykes and Matza 1957), encountered in previous chapters, to overcome moral inhibitions. The classic defence in many atrocities is that '*I was only following orders*', reflecting a psychological tendency to obey a 'legitimate' order, particularly in military or police organizations where unquestioning obedience is essential. Like the corporate executives described by Punch (1996; 2000), those engaging in state violence experience 'cognitive' and 'psycho-social dissonance' (Green and Ward 2004: 178), having one self concept at work and another at home. Doctors at Auschwitz were said to have been permitted and even encouraged to express disgust at aspects of their work during drinking sessions – enabling what Cohen (2001) describes as 'interpretive denial' or neutralization, interpreting their actions as merely putting prisoners out of their misery. The 'denial of the victim' is also evident in arguments that 'they' would wreak revenge if not eliminated. Bauman's (1989) analysis of the 'modernity' of the holocaust also stresses how the bureaucratic, quasi-industrial system of camps and the use of gas chambers created physical and emotional distance between killers and victims (cited in Greene and Ward 2004: 175) and so-called 'evil' has been associated with 'banality' (Arendt 1965/1977).

Excessive violence

While many reports of genocide and other atrocities stress the 'banality' or everyday nature of 'evil' acts, there are also elements of excessive and gratuitous violence and economic rewards. To young Hutu men in Rwanda, for example, participation in genocide could enhance their status. In other cases the genocidal ideology is taken to its 'logical' conclusion, and perpetrators demonstrate their commitment to the cause by going beyond what is demanded (Green and Ward 2004). Excessive violence and degrading victims also reinforces victims' inferior status and their exclusion from normal moral concerns and it can also be pleasurable and provide the kind of emotional thrills identified by Katz (Ward 2004).

Torture

Torture can generally be defined as 'the infliction of severe physical and/or mental pain or suffering as punishment and/or as a means of persuasion or confession' (McLaughlin 2006d: 438) and is the 'ultimate form of individualized terror'. It is more than simply a means of making people talk and can be used to prepare 'enemies' or internal dissidents for show trials and public confessions and to deter others by generating fear. Indeed, argue Green and Ward (2004), secrets rarely emerge following torture but it is part of a state strategy of inculcating fear.

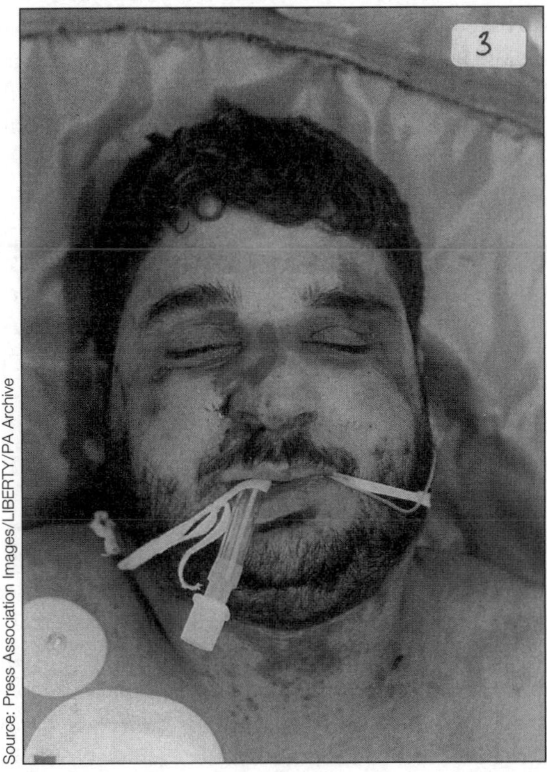

Source: Press Association Images/LIBERTY/PA Archive

The death of Baha Mousa in Basra in 2003 while in British custody has prompted an investigation into the extent to which the abuses from which he suffered were systemic.

Although universally condemned, torture remains common (Crelinsten 2003) and occurs in over 150 countries (Green and Ward 2004: 124). While it is more prevalent in repressive regimes, leading democracies such as the United States, Britain and Israel have all been associated with torture (McLaughlin 1996; Crelinsten 2003; Green and Ward 2004). The United States has covertly used torture for over fifty years and has used a legal loophole by designating Guantanamo Bay detainees as 'enemy combatants' rather than prisoners of war entitled to protection by international conventions (Rothe 2009: 37). It is known to have used hoods, chains, manacles and sedation, along with so-called 'torture lite' – a form of sleep deprivation induced by continuous exposure to bright light – in Guantanamo Bay (Green and Ward 2004: 146). Also notorious were the systematic abuses associated with the Abu Ghraib facility in Iraq which included practices such as keeping prisoners naked and in cruel positions. This was not, argues Rothe (2009: 56), a matter of a few rogue MPs on a night shift but was systemic, not limited to Abu Ghraib, and responsibility went right up to the Pentagon and the White House. British soldiers were also found to have treated prisoners inhumanely in Northern Ireland and Box 17.4 outlines two major cases of British use of and complicity in torture, currently subject to ongoing investigations and legal proceedings. The Baha Mousa case illustrates the use of techniques such as sleep deprivation, hooding and stress positions and, like Abu Ghraib, is unlikely to be dismissed by blaming a few errant soldiers, as serious shortcomings in training and knowledge have been revealed.

States can also be involved in torture 'at a distance'. Green and Ward (2004) identify a 'double discourse' of governments who formally deny engaging in torture but who sell its instruments and offer training expertise to authoritarian regimes. The United States has the largest number of manufacturers, distributors and suppliers of leg irons, shackles, gang chains or thumbcuffs and there are also companies in Germany, the UK, South Africa and Taiwan (Green and Ward 2004: 143). The Iraq war also saw the 'contracting out' or 'outsourcing' (Welch 2009: 359) of torture by the USA through the use of the euphemistically described 'extraordinary renditions' in which suspects were covertly flown to countries such as Syria, Egypt and Jordan where torture is widely practised, and special CIA torture prisons have been established in Poland and Romania. British complicity in these processes was alleged and Prestwick airport was revealed as a crucial staging point, as was the British territory of Diego Garcia (Reprieve 2007, cited in Green 2010: 229). This is illustrated in the case of Binyam Mohammed (see Box 17.4) whose case raises crucial questions about the complicity of British security services who have publicly denied using or being complicit in the use of torture.

Justifying torture

Torture is often denied or re-interpreted by the use of euphemisms such as 'moderate physical pressure'. It is typically justified by appealing to broader goals such as winning a military campaign or the 'war' against terrorism. George Bush, for example, in March 2008 used this to justify vetoing legislation banning the notorious practice of waterboarding, which simulates the experience of suffocation and drowning, on the grounds that 'This is no time for Congress to abandon practices that have a proven track record of keeping America safe' (Green 2010: 220).

Box 17.4 Cases of UK involvement in torture

Baha Mousa, an Iraqi hotel receptionist, died in British custody in Basra in 2003, having sustained 93 separate injuries. Subsequent investigations revealed that he had been subject to techniques of sleep deprivation, hooding and stress positions. Eight or more civilians died in the custody of British troops. Seven members of the Queen's Lancashire Regiment, including the commanding officer, were acquitted in a subsequent court martial but one soldier became the first British serviceman to admit a war crime, treating Iraqi prisoners inhumanely, and was imprisoned for one year. A subsequent inquiry aims to establish the extent to which this abuse was systemic. To date it has revealed that:

- Detainees under interrogation were hooded despite orders to the contrary – Mousa was hooded for 23 hours and 40 minutes during 36 hours.
- This was denied in Parliament by a minister who claimed that hooding was used only in transit.
- One prisoner was held in a container with a barbed-wire door in a temperature of over 40 degrees.
- The head of the army at the time commented that these actions were unacceptable and that the case is a 'stain on the character of the British army'.
- According to an officer of the regiment, soldiers held the view that 'all Iraqis were scum' and that there was an 'arse-covering' exercise after the death.
- Officers were ignorant of the basic rules covering the treatment of prisoners and had received little education.

Sources: Norton-Taylor (2010a; 2010b; 2010c; 2010d) and see Baha Mousa Inquiry http://www.bahamousainquiry.org/baha_mousa_inquiry_evidence/evidencev1.htm

Binyam Mohammed, a UK resident, spent just under seven years in custody, four at Guantanamo Bay camp. He had travelled to Pakistan and Afghanistan and was suspected of being involved in terrorism. He alleges that he was tortured in Pakistan, Morocco and Afghanistan, and subject to waterboarding, sleep deprivation, shackling and threatened 'disappearance'. He further claims that British intelligence agents knew of this torture, were supplying questions and using evidence. The United States subsequently dropped all charges against him. After a hunger strike, he was released from Guantanamo Bay and, along with others held at secret detention centres, is suing the British Government for not taking sufficient steps to ensure they were released or to protect them from ill-treatment and torture. Particularly disputed in the lengthy legal proceedings has been a CIA report about the use of torture which was initially suppressed and then, following appeals, released, after the British Government had attempted to redact key paragraphs on the grounds that intelligence-sharing with the United States would be endangered. Government lawyers also attempted to water down a judge's criticisms of the security services. Also contentious has been the extent to which British security agencies were complicit, and how much they knew about his treatment, with the then Foreign Secretary denying that any officials had acted improperly.

Sources: BBC News (2010t; 2010u); Jenkins (2010); Hirsch (2010)

Torturers, argue Green and Ward (2004) are not sadistic, mentally deranged individuals but emerge from research as ordinary people doing a job. They are trained to accept justifications that, for example, torture saves lives, enables the successful pursuit of a just war, and often cited is the 'ticking bomb scenario' in which information obtained may prevent a bomb exploding. Training also involves a process of 'reality construction' in which the 'enemy' is dehumanized – a process made easier if there are insurgents (Crelintsen 2003: 295). Perpetrators invoke a diffusion of responsibility by using the standard 'only following orders' justification

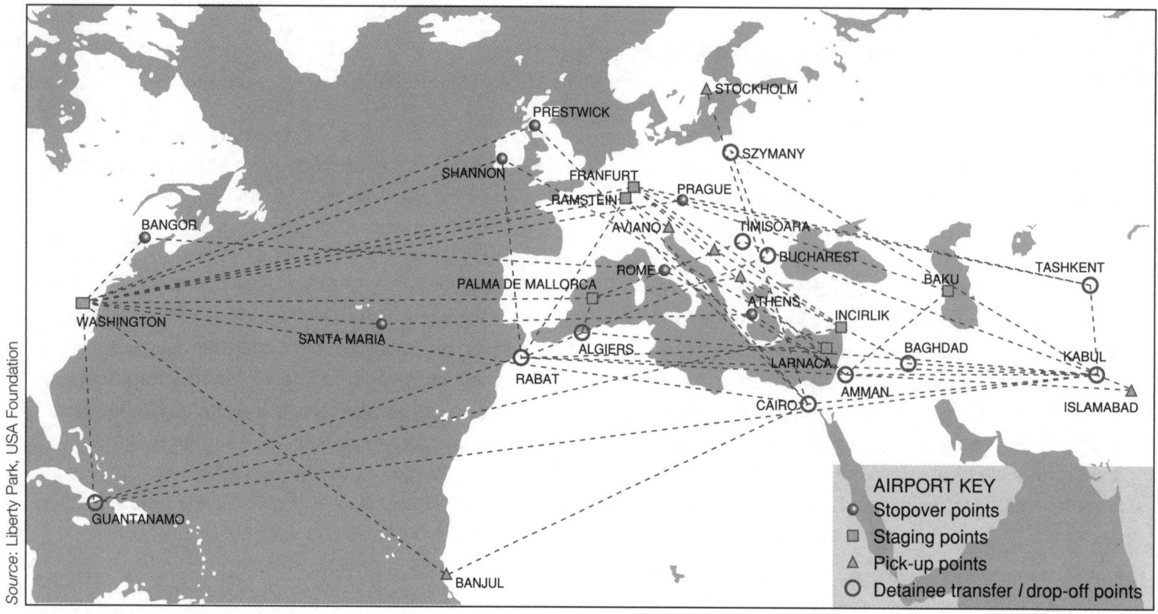

Source: Liberty Park, USA Foundation

The global 'spider's web' of secret detentions and unlawful inter-state transfers.

and also argue that particular techniques are scientifically designed to make it easier for the victim.

Police crime and deviance

Police violence and corruption form a major part of state crime. To Green and Ward (2004: 68) police behaviour can be defined as deviant when

> it is perceived and labelled as brutal or corrupt . . . by others . . . or when the police themselves find it necessary to conceal or lie because they know it would incur some form of censure if it were revealed.

Police deviance encompasses activities such as extra-legal violence, perjury and the fabrication of evidence, bribery, abusing rights, recycling confiscated or stolen drugs, burglary, sexual harassment, co-operating with organized criminals and even murder. Primarily it involves an abuse of the trust vested in a police officer to carry out the law objectively – it is, argues Punch (2009: 31), an abuse of office, of power and of trust. As with other forms of organizational crime, seeking individual benefit can be contrasted with pursuing organizational goals, expressed colloquially as a distinction between cops who are 'bent' for self and 'bent' for the job. Some forms, such as 'fitting up' suspects and doctoring evidence, aim to secure the conviction of a suspect 'known' to be guilty and are described as 'noble cause' corruption (Green and Ward 2004: 82; Punch 2009).

The English police were set up to be an independent, quasi-military body enjoying high levels of legitimacy and have prided themselves on an absence of corruption (Reiner 1992), although there have been recurrent scandals involving issues such as the number of deaths in police custody, miscarriages of justice and covering up abuses. In a recent book, Punch (2009) looks at a number of different cases in the UK, summarized below.

Corruption in the Metropolitan Police

In 1969 *The Times* made a series of allegations against the Metropolitan Police including planting evidence, committing perjury to obtain false convictions, taking money from criminals in return for favours, urging criminals to act as agents provocateurs and selling 'licences' to organized criminals to continue their activities without interference. Close relationships between 'cops, crooks and informants' (p. 131) were alleged in relation to the Drug Squad along with accusations of planting drugs, granting immunity to and rewarding dealers. Six officers were convicted. Offences were primarily motivated by arrests and convictions rather than financial profit. The Obscene Publications Unit or 'Porn' Squad were also found to have informally 'licensed' some premises and to have taken bribes. The new Commissioner, Sir Robert Mark, carried out a series of reforms and between 1972 and 1977 almost 500 officers left the force. Nonetheless, subsequent revelations concerning the Flying Squad led to the extensive Operation Countryman investigation which revealed that bribery was endemic and one chief superintendent and 12 detectives were imprisoned.

Miscarriages of justice

A series of high-profile miscarriages of justice took place in the wake of IRA bombing campaigns across England during the early 1970s which placed heavy pressures on the police to secure convictions. Long campaigns on the part of defendants cast doubt on convictions in the following four cases:

- The Birmingham 6 (accused of involvement in explosions in Birmingham in November 1972 in two pubs which killed 21 people);
- The Guildford 4 (accused of involvement in bombings in Guildford and Woolwich);
- Judith Ward (accused of involvement in several explosions including one resulting in twelve fatalities);
- The Maguire 7 (accused of possessing explosives).

In all cases, including those involving subsequently denied confessions, appeals were successful and all were released. Evidence showed that physical and mental pressure had been applied and that sleep deprivation, persistent questioning and threats had been used. Confessions were fabricated and interrogation notes had been doctored. Important information, particularly about Judith Ward's mental state, had been withheld from the court and forensic evidence in relation to the use of explosives was found to be unreliable. Judges had not always been impartial. In short, argues Punch, these cases indicated a 'collective failure in the system' (p. 139). As the pressure was primarily to secure convictions, they constitute examples of 'noble cause corruption'.

Northern Ireland

The Northern Irish Troubles during which, over 30 years of violence, approximately 3,500 people were killed, generated many examples of serious deviance (Punch 2009; Doig 2010). These included allegations that the British State was implicated in covert activities. Particularly controversial were the so-called revenge killings of those suspected of killing three RUC officers in Lurgan in November 1982. In these cases, seemingly 'ordinary' RUC officers shot apparent suspects although no shots had been fired at them, and in one case 108 rounds were fired. The incidents bore the hallmarks of a 'military style combat operation' (Punch 2009: 145) and it was subsequently discovered that these were special undercover officers; they had been coached to give accounts; vehicle logs had been altered, and officers committed perjury.

This led to the infamous Stalker affair, in which John Stalker, Deputy Chief Constable of the Greater Manchester Police, who had been brought in to investigate the allegations, was subject to a 'dirty tricks campaign' questioning his integrity and was removed from the investigation (Doig 2010). He remained convinced that the allegations against him were timed to coincide with his presentation of a highly critical report and his intention to question very senior officers in Northern Ireland. No action was taken against any RUC officers. To Punch this case demonstrates the involvement of the RUC in a range of deviant activities, including collusion with paramilitaries. They obstructed the external inquiry and the activities of the police, army and intelligence agencies amounted to 'enforcement terrorism'. The British State, he concludes, was 'complicit in police deviance of the gravest sort' (Punch 2009: 149).

The impossible mandate: accounting for police deviance

Sociological and socio-legal studies of policing and police work point to some of the roots of police deviance (Green and Ward 2004). Punch (2009: 2), for example, refers to the 'impossible mandate' of the police who are expected to reduce crime when realistically they can make little difference. Long recognized has been the conflict between *crime control*, the need to bring the guilty to justice, and *due process*, the need to abide by rules of evidence and procedure and to protect the rights of the innocent. Practices such as doctoring evidence represent an 'innovative' response to the strain produced by attempting to secure the conviction of the 'guilty' while conforming to the rules of due process which can be perceived as cumbersome.

The tendency to attribute deviance within organizations to a few 'rotten apples' originated with the police although as seen in relation to other forms of crime, this diverts attention from the 'barrel' or, to Punch, the 'rotten orchard' and from structural and systemic factors. Individual officers learn appropriate attitudes and values through socialization into what has been characterized as a particularly solidaristic and pervasive police culture which can be seen as 'criminogenic' (Green and Ward 2004: 74). 'Nailing villains' is prioritized and those who seek to challenge police activities are regarded as 'bleeding hearts'. The 'Dirty Harry' role stresses the value of securing a conviction and encourages bending and twisting the rules in order to do so (Punch 2009). The 'exceptional' circumstances of the situation in Northern Ireland or the 'war on terror' also lead to the introduction of harder, more paramilitary styles of policing. Punch further suggests that 'good' police officers may start idealistic but slide down a 'slippery slope' to corruption which can become a prerequisite of membership in the occupational group. Indeed, for some deviance can be related to taking policing too seriously.

The police also work within the context of the criminal justice system, which itself can enable police deviance as few errant officers are prosecuted and the law, argues Punch (2009: 227), is 'replete with ambiguity', particularly where prosecutors and the courts accept fabricated or false evidence. In 'exceptional' situations like that in Northern Ireland and in the climate following 7/7 and 9/11 there is more support for increasing police powers. While formally the police are legally accountable, many argue for stronger and more effective policies against police corruption. Too often, argues Punch (p. 228), there is a 'scandal and reform' cycle with only short-lived reforms.

State corporate crime

As seen in Chapter 15, states and corporations may be jointly complicit in crimes, particularly with the tendency in neo-liberal economies for the state to contract out some of its essential functions. This has led to a growing interest in state corporate crime which can be defined as:

> illegal or socially injurious actions that occur when one or more institutions of political governance pursue a goal in direct co-operation with one or more institutions of economic production and distribution. (Kramer and Michalowski 1990: 3)

State corporate crime can be either *state initiated* or *state facilitated*. The former occurs when 'corporations, employed by the government engage in organizational deviance at the direction of, or with the tacit approval of, the government' (Matthews and Kauzlarich 2000: 283) and the latter occurs when the state fails to restrain deviant business activities by, for example, colluding in regulatory failure, passing weak laws or failing to enforce them, associated with forms of corporate crime (Chapter 15).

Corporations were involved in many of the serious examples of state violence outlined above, particularly the Holocaust, supporting Hitler's drive to prevent the rise of communism and reaping the benefits of the Aryanization of companies (Friedrichs 1992). The deadly Zyklon B gas used by the Nazis was provided by IG Farben who also operated a major establishment exploiting slave labour at Auschwitz. IMB and its German subsidiary provided the technology which enabled the Nazi regime to trace Jews, run the railroad network and organize concentration camp labour (Green and Ward 2004: 29/30). Huisman and van Baar (2010) have looked at the 'oven builders' of the Holocaust, for whom providing the technology to dispose of multiple bodies was seen as a challenge unrelated to profit. This section will look at the arms industry and the use of private contractors in Iraq.

The arms industry

The arms industry is particularly criminogenic. For arms manufacturing countries, including Britain, its exports are economically vital to the extent that they have been said to drive foreign policy and overseas development projects, with aid being granted in the expectation of major arms deals (Ruggiero 1996a; 1996b). 'Pariah' governments are subject to arms embargoes which include equipment and technical expertise which could be used for arms manufacture or the development of nuclear or chemical weapons. These governments must rely on illegal supplies. Governments are responsible for implementing these embargoes and co-operating with international inspectors (Ruggiero 1996b).

Deviant and illegal arms deals take many forms. States are involved in condoning, promoting or ignoring arms transfers; failing to institute proper measures to regulate the arms trade; financing the purchase of arms through export credit and as seen above, subsidizing the manufacture and promoting the trade of torture equipment (Green and Ward 2004). International inspectors are part of an international elite closely allied to manufacturers and are exposed to corruption (Ruggiero 1996b). Embargoes can be overcome by exporters making false claims about the purpose of goods or the destination of arms and by misrepresenting the identity of purchasers and sellers. A clandestine market in arms, involving trades in light armaments and second-hand weapons, often destined for countries subject to an embargo, also involves organized crime which is less able to deal with trades involving major quantities of large weapons. There is therefore a large 'grey market' in arms (Ruggiero 1996b: 12), involving government officials and ministers 'innovatively' interpreting official policy which is often characterized by 'confusion'. This was illustrated in the case of the infamous Iraqi 'super gun' (Ruggiero 1996b; Phythian 2000; Doig 2010) and the complex BAE case outlined in Box 17.5.

The Iraqi 'super gun'

Long before the search for weapons of mass destruction triggered off the invasion of Iraq, three executives of the firm Matrix Churchill were prosecuted for illegally exporting defence-related equipment to Iraq in 1988/89, purportedly to be used in the manufacture of an Iraqi 'super gun'. They had used false 'end user certificates' in which the destination country was entered as Jordan, and misrepresented what the equipment was to be used for. The case collapsed when it was revealed that one of the three executives had been working for the intelligence services and that government ministers knew about and had encouraged the exports, despite official guidelines discouraging the sale of defence-related equipment to Iraq. Ministers were also found to have misled Parliament because they feared a public outcry and did not wish to damage relationships with other Arab states. The subsequent Scott Inquiry substantiated claims that ministers had not revealed any shift in export guidelines (Birkinshaw 1996; Doig 2010). They had therefore privately 'relaxed' the rules while publicly insisting they were being complied with (McLaughlin 1996; Ruggiero 1996b). No government ministers were prosecuted, none resigned (Ruggiero 1996b), and the activities were, according to Green and Ward (2004: 41), neither entirely legal or illegal.

Dealing in arms

The BAE case outlined in Box 17.5 illustrates how complex these cases can be, but it is clear that whatever the legal technicalities, pressure was placed on this investigation and that the government were at least complicit in failing to ensure a full

Box 17.5 The case of BAE and the Al-Yamamah arms deals

- The concealment of corruption and prioritizing exports to Saudi Arabia were involved in the £20 billion Al-Yamamah arms deals in 1985 and 1988, said to have involved hundreds of millions of pounds in secret commissions.
- This was subject to inquiries and official denials including the suppression of a National Audit office report by the House of Commons Public Accounts Committee on the grounds of 'Saudi Sensitivities'.
- In 2001, the solicitor of the employee of a travel firm retained by BAE made allegations of corruption to the Serious Fraud Office (SFO) who, after some investigation, sent a report to the MoD and the Ministry of Defence Police (MDP).
- Subsequent leaks of this investigation described several million pounds of travel and hospitality allegedly paid for by BAE to key Saudi officials. Similar allegations from another travel agent covered other BAE contracts in Romania, South Africa and Chile.
- In 2005 and 2006, the Saudi government was negotiating the Typhoon deal worth around £6–10 billion and threatened to switch to a French-built fighter if the inquiries were not halted.
- In December 2006, following a direct threat made to his Chief of Staff, the then Prime Minster Tony Blair terminated the investigation because of its 'negative impact on security' (Holmes 2009: 385).
- Following a judicial review in 2008 ruling that the actions of the SFO were unlawful, the High Court ruled that they had little choice.
- In February 2010, BAE accepted a plea bargain with the US Department of Justice and the SFO in which it accepted that it was guilty of conspiring to make false statements to the US Government (and paid a fine of $400 million) and also paid a £30 million fine to the SFO for an accounting offence relating to the sale of a radar system to Tanzania. The case involving South Africa was dropped (Doig 2010).

investigation. Green and Ward (2004) point to other cases involving British and US companies, including the role played by BAE and Lockheed in arming the Indonesian occupation of East Timor with, at one point, the then foreign secretary claiming that reports of killings in East Timor had been exaggerated (Pilger 1999, cited in Green and Ward 2004: 35). Trade agreements in arms continued even after the new Labour government instituted its ethical foreign policy in 1997. These were not, argue Green and Ward (2004: 41), illegal per se but a breach of the moral rules to which governments profess to subscribe.

An important element in these kinds of offences is the role of personal connections and in some countries corruption is endemic (Green and Ward 2004; Ruggiero 1996a; 1996b). The late Robin Cook, foreign secretary from 1997–2001, referred in his memoirs to the close relationships between Number 10 and BAE (Doig 2010). A further crucial factor is a lack of parliamentary power and oversight and economic considerations are crucial with promoting the arms industry being routinely defended by appeals to export revenues and jobs. Arguably, therefore, profit considerations take priority over foreign policy. As indicated above, embargoes are also criminogenic by providing spaces for illegal trades to flourish.

Contracting out security

The invasion of Iraq and the war in Afghanistan have drawn attention to the use of private contractors. In a study of economic war crime, Whyte (2007b) describes how the rapid transformation of the Iraqi economy, which involved transforming state into private enterprises, created hidden spaces in which corruption and other forms of crime emerged. This implicated the United States and other countries forming part of the Coalition Provisional Authority (CPA). The CPA and the Development Fund for Iraq were intended to facilitate economic development for the benefit of the Iraqi people. Instead, he argues, they benefited a host of companies, primarily from the United States, and granted them immunity from prosecution. Bribery and corruption were said to be 'routinized', contracts were awarded without proper tendering and there were a host of frauds. State-owned enterprises were dismantled to create companies; this allows Iraqi businesses, banks, mines and factories to be owned by foreigners, thus breaching the spirit of international law. It allowed surplus products to be 'dumped', thereby pricing Iraqi industries out of the market and destroying them. Lax regulation and auditing meant that large sums of cash were unaccounted for and contractors complained of 'short tendering' – inviting tenders in impossibly short periods of time – which encouraged bribery and corruption. Payments were made for 'ghost armies' of employees and, in one case, for a fleet of unflyable planes. What Whyte (2007b) describes as 'token' enforcement meant that prosecutions, such as that of Custer Battles for 37 fraudulent acts involved in procurement payments in $100,000 cash bundles, were a minority.

Violence has also been associated with the use of private security companies in Iraq. Welch (2009) explores how the 'contracting out' of security has limited the state monopoly of legitimate force. Over 354 private security firms were involved in Iraq and most controversial was their role in carrying out lethal violence and using CS gas. One firm, Blackwater, was particularly criticized, having been involved in firing into a crowd and, in what came to be known as Baghdad's Bloody Sunday,

Source: Cagle Cartoons

were responsible for 8–20 civilian deaths. Until October 2007, when they came under US military control, they were allowed to operate with little or no supervision, their activities were shrouded in secrecy and they were initially immune from prosecution. Blackwater was seen as particularly prone to violence, were described as 'cowboys' and had close links with the Bush regime (p. 357), again illustrating the importance of close connections between corporations and governments. They were also used in Abu Ghraib, where it was alleged that in a rush for profits, they cut corners in training (p. 359). In December 2009, five Blackwater guards were acquitted of manslaughter and Iraq ordered 250 staff to leave within a week. Blackwater, now called Xe, has made a settlement with Iraqi civilians who took out civil suits. They have also been accused of misconduct in relation to weapons training for the Afghan National Army (BBC News 2010v). The use of these kinds of contractors is an example, argues Welch, of the fragmentation of government and state power and the rise of what is sometimes referred to as 'liquid security'.

Understanding state crime

Similar themes to those identified for white-collar, corporate and environmental crime are relevant for understanding state crime. Individual state agents commit deviant acts within an organizational context, yet scapegoating individuals can divert attention from systemic factors. As with corporate crime, it can be asked how 'good' people embark on the 'slippery slope' to deviant activity (Punch 2009), which can become normalized and justified. State crime involves power, including the power to deny crimes and to fend off efforts at regulation, with regulatory failure being a form of and contributing factor to state crime. This section will focus on some key issues drawing on the above examples.

Normalizing and denying state crime

Although state crime is quintessentially organizational, the role of human agency is important. As Rothe (2009: 105) argues, individuals do not act as automatons and do make decisions to engage in deviant activities, albeit within the context of intense organizational, peer or cultural pressures. While some are 'only' following orders, someone issues these orders and at the top levels of power, 'agency can often be fully revealed and active'. Thus leaders of repressive regimes or particular senior officers can, as is the case in corporations (Clinard 1983), set the tone for others to follow. Individual gratification and career advancement are also important and sexual and other forms of excitement can produce excessive state violence. On the other hand, even extreme forms of violence can be characterized as banal rather than evil.

Creating the enemy

A key question is, therefore, as for corporate crime, under what circumstances 'good', often idealistic, state agents come to regard acts of deviance as acceptable and even 'normal'. The psychological mechanisms through which actors distance themselves from their actions are particularly important. Deviant acts become an almost routine part of the role of the torturers, police officers and war criminals described above, justified as necessary to defeat the enemy. This enemy is 'created', depersonalized and 'othered'. In Vietnam, American soldiers described the Vietnamese as 'gooks', 'dopes' and 'slopes', Serbians described their victims as 'gypsies', 'filth' and 'animals' (McLaughlin 1996; Cohen 1996) and as seen in Box 17.4, Iraqis were depicted as 'scum'. Whole populations have been depersonalized. Jews in Nazi Germany had to wear yellow stars, and coloured labels were used in the killing fields of Cambodia. Military discipline also enables the diffusion of responsibility. Following the My Lai massacre in Vietnam, in which a whole village of between 400 and 500 were killed by American soldiers, one officer, Lieutenant Calley, used the 'only following orders' defence, reportedly commenting that 'it was no big deal' (Cohen 1996: 503). When such acts are ordered, normal principles are replaced by a duty to obey. Once the first step has been taken, soldiers carry on without considering the implications, coming to see it as 'all in a day's work'.

Denying state crime

Cohen (1996; 2001), in his work on strategies of denial, describes a 'litany of denials and justifications' which amount to a spiral of denial:

- The first response of governments is to deny that the event happened at all.
- Faced with proof that it is happening or has happened, they attempt to claim that it is not, or was not, what it appears to be. Negative criticisms are denied by interpreting events in a positive light. Atrocities can be euphemistically described as 'transfers of population', aggressive action as 'self-defence', and killing massive numbers of citizens by bombing described, as in the Gulf wars, as 'collateral damage', caused by 'surgical strikes'.
- Finally governments resort to a tactic summed up as 'even if it's what you say it is, it's justified', arguing that the action is or was necessary to protect national security, to advance the war against terrorism or to serve some other cause (Cohen 1996).

This takes place within a 'culture of denial' employing 'techniques of neutralization':

- Governments *deny injury* by claiming, for example, that 'they exaggerate, they don't feel it, they are used to violence'.
- The *victim is denied* by claims that 'they started it', 'they are the terrorists', 'we are the real victims'.
- *Responsibility is denied* by claiming that individuals were only following orders, that they were cogs in the machine.
- *Condemners are condemned* in what Cohen sees as a vast discourse of official denial – Israel, for example, justifies breaches of international law by claiming that 'the whole world is picking on us', 'everyone is against us' or are anti-semitic. Those who make allegations and criticisms are in turn criticized and states claim that 'it's worse elsewhere' or that criticism amounts to racism and cultural imperialism – often by imposing Western values.

- States and governments also *appeal to higher loyalties* – to the nation, the army, a sacred mission or a higher cause (Cohen 1996). As seen in relation to Iraq, many forms of state deviance flourished in the cultural space provided by the 'war on terror', with appeals variously to 'God' and the 'axis of evil' (Kramer and Michalowski 2005).

Criminogenic states?

As outlined above, state crime occurs in most states although some offences are more characteristic of particular kinds of regimes. A distinction is often drawn (Green and Ward 2004; Rothe 2009) between the crimes committed by different kinds of states.

Advanced democratic states

Less extreme crimes are associated with democratic states which rarely initiate wars against each other or engage in genocide and major crimes against humanity. Human rights violations are more likely to involve reducing or failing to recognize full civil liberties than serious oppression. On the other hand, democratic regimes, including Britain, have been associated with state-sponsored assassinations and terrorism, funding, supporting or initiating coups, insurgencies and counter-insurgencies, supplying arms and training insurgents, conducting covert or low intensity wars, and the kinds of state corporate crimes outlined above (Green and Ward 2004). They are also those most likely to engage in asymmetric wars of aggression, as in Iraq, and before that the US invasion of Grenada, with bombing civilian targets and being directly or indirectly involved with torture (Rothe 2009: 122). Their engagement in other crimes is, however, argue Green and Ward (2004), restricted by the power of strong civil societies who mount serious protests against state excesses.

One-party states

The crimes committed by one-party states, state communist countries, military juntas or 'predatory' states, often cast as 'weak' states, are in general terms more extensive, more direct, larger in scope and indicate a clearer intent of massive harm or death to a significant portion of their own or other populations (Rothe 2009: 135). This can be related, as seen in relation to genocide, to their political, social and cultural history and to factors such as the existence of an 'othered' population. A Durkheimian version of anomie can be relevant in these situations as they are often related to the upheaval brought about by rapid social change, such as the ending of a colonial regime, economic crises or military coups, where moral regulation breaks down. A significant factor in Rwanda, for example, was a collapse in coffee prices (Rothe 2009) and other countries face having to pay large debts to global financial institutions while populations are impoverished. Moreover, ex-colonial regimes, argue Green and Ward (2004), may have inherited military and policing structures from colonial powers without the necessary legitimacy. Also important is the role of religion which can provide the theological, moral and mythical justifications for genocide (Rothe 2009).

Criminogenic wars

Other criminogenic situations can be identified. War can be criminogenic, particularly contemporary asymmetric wars of aggression, which involve a monopoly of force by those who possess highly technological precision instruments, and typically attack not only military targets but the entire infrastructure, aiming at 'demodernization' (Ruggiero 2006; 2007). This not only increases the death toll and arguably breaches international law, but leads to the crimes of contractors involved in security and rebuilding outlined above and also to the emergence of organized crime and a black market (Ruggiero 2010). War also legitimates crimes such as torture and, for some soldiers, killing, and rape and other war crimes can become the norm, a matter of honour, as do predatory and violent acts on the part of police and security agents, armies and paramilitaries. Indeed the 'deviants' are those who do not conform and violence may not need to be 'neutralized' as it is legitimate (Ruggiero 2007: 216).

The 'war on terror' also provides the ideological space in which tougher control measures are justified and many of the examples of British governmental and police deviance outlined above took place in the context of 'states of exception' which justify practices such as banning the publication of incriminating facts on the grounds of 'national security' and a shift from due process towards crime control methods. The Northern Irish situation, seen widely as 'exceptional' (Hillyard 1996), provided the context for many of the most serious examples of state violence and police corruption in Britain outlined above. Britain's involvement in the invasion of Iraq, in itself of dubious legality and subject to the as yet uncompleted Chilcott Inquiry, has also been associated with 'doctoring' or 'sexing up' the so-called 'dodgy dossier' about the threat which Saddam Hussein posed and numerous other forms of misinformation (Doig 2010).

Political economy

To Rothe (2009: 133), a key motivational force underlying state crime is the 'attainment or maintenance of social, economic, or political capital' and Green and Ward (2004) suggest a political economy of state crime. Genocide is most often associated with a group attempting to gain political and economic dominance. Both political and economic factors are involved – arguably political interests took precedence over economic ones in relation to the Al Yamamah arms deal. On the other hand, Western military intervention in the Gulf, the Balkans, Afghanistan and Iraq illustrate the extent to which major imperialist powers are prepared to use force, often of contested legality, where oil or multinational corporate interests are involved, and the 'war on terror' is a key strategic device through which the United States seeks to enforce its hegemony through a series of military incursions.

The close relationships between governments and multinational corporations and the role played by the profit motive is also illustrated in the role of contractors, which, along with arms deals, involved strong personal relationships and 'cronyism' between governments and major corporations, most notably through the well-known association of Vice President Cheney with the Halliburton Corporation. Also important are the effects of globalization outlined in relation to corporate and environmental crime, particularly the activities of international financial institutions and the requirement which they place on debtor nations to institute free market policies. These contribute, argue Green and Ward (2004: 191), to the continued marginalization of much of the developing world and to a crisis of legitimacy in states characterized by poverty, corruption and authoritarianism – the sites of the worst forms of state crime.

Regulating state crime

Asymmetrical power relations also raise questions about the ability of some states to commit crimes with relative impunity due to an absence of effective sanctions. Moreover, states have the power to credibly deny their crime and deviance, to withhold information, to enact or fail to implement laws and to resist revelations of or investigations into covert activities. The state crimes reviewed in this chapter reveal many limitations of domestic and international laws and other controls.

Internally, democratic states and their agencies are accountable through oversight by elected assemblies and the separation of government from an independent legal system and judiciary. At the end of the day, however, the cases outlined above illustrate that the state can override many of these interventions. Information continues to be legally withheld through the use of redactions and other official denials. The need for a stronger independent and external presence in investigating complaints against the police has long been recognized (Reiner 1992; Punch 2009). The state can also undermine internal critics (as allegedly happened with the Stalker Inquiry) and official reports, often with limited resources, all too easily become 'white-washes' (Ross and Rothe 2008). Internal controls are very often lacking in one-party states, and where states rule by fear, state crime can be a means of silencing opposition. Civil society can limit state crime (Green and Ward 2004), although in some cases, the Iraq war being one, British and American political and media opinion failed to challenge successfully false claims about weapons of mass destruction (Kramer and Michalowski 2005).

International controls are also limited and many of the conventions in relation to war crimes and crimes against humanity were developed only after the Second World War and are therefore of relatively recent origin (Robertson 2006). Not all states are signatories to forms of international law, the most glaring example being the failure of the United States to participate in the International Criminal Court. The contested invasion of Iraq in itself arguably demonstrates the ineffectiveness of international opinion and the UN, who did not sanction the invasion despite Britain's attempts to secure a supportive resolution.

Asymmetries of power and the dominance of one superpower enables some nations to proceed with impunity (Green and Ward 2004; Kramer and Michalowski 2005). Israel has consistently disregarded international law by ignoring, for example, a request by the International Court of Justice to dismantle parts of the wall dividing Israel from Palestinian territory (Human Rights Council 2009, cited in Doig 2010). International opinion and sanctions, which can adversely effect civilian populations, are also relatively ineffective against states who continue to perpetrate serious crimes against humanity and genocide. International intervention is limited by the doctrine of non-intervention in the domestic affairs of other nations (Robertson 2006).

Concluding comments

This chapter has only been able to scratch the surface of the vast area of state crime which ranges from the corruption of state agencies to the many crimes associated with wars – both the so-called 'war on terror' and the asymmetric wars in the Middle East and Afghanistan. Many other aspects of state crime could have been explored from the more domestic aspects of political crime and corruption seen in the furore over the expenses claims of Members of Parliament, to more historical and contemporary examples of war crimes, the issue of rape in war, alluded to in Chapter 12, the state's complicity in the failure of regulations and the failure of some states to prevent or prepare for the harms ensuing from sometimes expected natural disasters (Green and Ward 2004). It has, however, looked at sufficient examples of this area of crime to suggest that its global toll dwarfs the conventional crimes more typically studied by criminologists.

While it is often assumed that state and war crimes happen 'elsewhere', in repressive regimes, it has also been seen that they do take place in Britain, have a long history in the development of the British state (Doig 2010), and were endemic in the activities of the army, police and security services during the Northern Ireland Troubles and in the lead up to, and aftermath of, Britain's participation in the Iraq war and in Afghanistan. They are routinely denied, seen most starkly in attempts to 'redact' incriminating paragraphs and suppress evidence of complicity in and the systemic nature of torture. Government reports and investigations can be seen as 'whitewashes' and it takes many many years for investigations to be revealed. In yet other instances, as with arms deals, political interests are prioritized over ethical ones. While some offences are justified as being part of 'exceptional' circumstances such as the war on terror or the Northern Irish Troubles, these states of emergency tend to persist and be associated with more repressive policies.

Some contest that state crime should not be a part of criminology as it is not primarily dealt with by domestic criminal law. Against this it can be argued that it is similar to other crimes, that international law sanctions and criminalizes states, that it involves similar activities to other crimes, and that criminological perspectives can be used, particularly in combination, to analyse it. It involves central criminological themes of harm, risk, seriousness and suffering and it can also be argued that criminologists have a responsibility to point out that for many across the globe, the most serious forms of crime and victimization are those perpetrated by states and their agencies (Cohen 1996; Ward 2004).

Review questions

1 Draw up a list of the main forms of state crime.

2 Locate some current cases in the media.
   (a) How many have been reported in the last month?
   (b) How many in Britain?
   (c) Are they presented and interpreted in the same way as other crimes?
   (d) Detail examples of the 'culture of denial'.

3 Taking any one form of state crime, define it and illustrate how it can be approached using criminological perspectives.

4 List discussion points around the question of whether state crime can and should be part of criminology.

Key reading

While the study of state crime has tended to be neglected in criminology, there has now been a wider recognition of its importance and there are now some extremely good texts and collections on the topic. The best and most recent of these are:

Chambliss, W., Michalowski, R. and Kramer, R. (eds) (2010) ***State Crime in the Global Age***, Cullompton: Willan Publishing. An extremely useful and interesting collection of papers on a variety of state crime topics containing useful case studies and theoretical discussions by some of the leading international authors in the field.

Doig, A. (2010) (**forthcoming**) ***State Crime***, Cullompton: Willan Publishing. A useful text with a specifically British focus covering a range of issues including contrasting definitions of the subject, a detailed examination of the growth of the British state, detailed case studies of many state crimes and a discussion of issues of control.

Green, P. and Ward, T. (2004) ***State Crime: Governments, Violence and Corruption***, London: Polity Press. An interesting and thought-provoking discussion of the definition of state crime, chapters on specific crimes such as genocide, police crime and deviance and torture and a discussion of issues of control.

Rothe, D. (2009) ***State Criminality: The Crime of All Crimes***, Lanham: Lexington Books. This is an engaging and thoughtful text containing many case studies, particularly of genocide and rape, and an excellent review of the major theoretical perspectives on state crime.

Chapter 18
Conclusion

This book has explored many issues involved in the study of crime. It started by looking at how crime is popularly constructed in the media, contrasting this with the more mundane findings of official statistics and victim surveys. These indicators in themselves, however, give only a partial picture, as only some kinds of crime are counted, which in turn necessitates critically exploring which activities are considered to be serious enough to gather information about. Issues surrounding research were therefore explored and the importance of critically evaluating official information about crime was stressed. The many different theories and perspectives used to understand crime were critically reviewed along with the shifting focus from offenders to the victims of crime, and from looking for the 'causes' of crime to a focus on controlling and managing it. The complex relationships between crime and interrelated social inequalities of class, age, race, gender and power have been outlined and it has examined selected patterns of crime. By way of conclusion, this chapter will attempt to draw together some of the main themes and issues encountered throughout the book and return to the questions posed in Chapter 1. It will start by considering how activities are constructed as 'crime' and as crime 'problems'. It will highlight some of the most pervasive themes emerging from attempts to explain or understand crime and consider its relationship to social inequalities. As stated in Chapter 1, the book focused on crime in Britain, in itself raising issues about the role of different historical, cultural and socio-economic factors within cities, regions and jurisdictions across the UK as well as placing crime in Britain within a broader global context. Finally, although the focus throughout has been on crime rather than criminal justice, some points will be raised in relation to wider criminal justice and social policies.

Constructing the crime problem

The socially constructed nature of crime has been illustrated in successive chapters. A major theme in considering white-collar, corporate, state corporate, environmental and state crimes was, for example, the widespread perception that they are 'not really crime' which presupposes some concept of 'real crime'. Yet as seen throughout the book, a very fine line divides 'normal' activities from 'criminal'. When do the dishonest or deceptive activities of a business become defined as 'criminal'? When does misselling financial products or conning consumers become fraudulent? When do 'normal' sexual relationships become 'deviant'? When does drug use become 'abuse' and what determines which drugs are illegal? What is the distinction between legal 'force' and illegal 'violence' and who is defined as a 'terrorist'? Why is corporate, environmental and state violence excluded from representations of violent crime? Why did it take so long for 'abuse' and physical and sexual violence in the family to be recognized as a 'real' crime? Exploration of these and many other questions reveals that the criminal status of activities is often contested and involves political and ideological considerations (see, for example, Muncie et al 2010).

It has also been seen throughout that constructions of the 'crime problems' prioritized by governments, which determine the kinds of questions asked about crime and the thrust of criminological research, are also socially and ideologically constructed. Calls for 'zero tolerance' and to be 'tough on crime' relate to the 'youth crime', gangs, and anti-social behaviour of lower-class young men, some from minority ethnic communities, living in 'dangerous places'. The 'drugs problem' is typically constructed as a problem of recreational drug use among young people. The 'war' on 'organized' crime involved in drugs and human trafficking does not extend to the equally well organized and systemic crimes of corporations and states subject merely to 'regulation'. 'Violent crime' is often portrayed as a problem of public violence and 'stranger danger' – a conception also associated with concepts such as 'real rape'. Criminals are cast as 'others', as 'fiends', 'beasts' and strangers and it has been seen throughout that the media tend to exaggerate some crime problems and ignore others and create 'folk devils'.

The questions asked by academic approaches differ according to whether they accept or challenge these constructions. To early sociological and criminological theories 'the problem' was the pathological nature of or deficits in offenders, families, socialization, subcultures or the structure of society itself. To labelling perspectives and critical criminology, 'the problem' became the activities of social control agents and criminalization. To feminists 'the problem' is male violence and patriarchy, to others it is the inheritance of colonialism and to yet others it is capitalism, globalization and its accompanying neo-liberal ideology. As attention turned from establishing the 'causes' of crime to its control, the 'problem' became an absence of self-control or capable guardians. More recently attention has been drawn to social exclusion, the impact of global social change and some fear the impact of the recession.

Given all these questions, it could be asked if 'crime' remains a useful category at all as it is so difficult to define and encompasses such very different activities. It is distinguished solely by being subject to the criminal sanction, a process which reflects political interests and power rather than the inherent properties of actions. It could be argued, therefore, that 'crime' is a particular form of ideological censure (Sumner 1994; 1997). To the social harm approach, understanding the distribution of harms and their criminalization and means of reducing these harms is more important than staying within a criminology restricted by its relationship to criminal law (Hillyard and Tombs 2004). Harm, nonetheless, could be regarded as too broad and subjective a concept. As seen in relation to corporate, environmental and state crime, alternative benchmarks have been suggested, including activities subject to some kind of legal penalty and seen as deviant by widely respected domestic and international audiences (Green and Ward 2000). These alternative constructions enable the exploration of why only some deceptive or dishonest activities, along with those which cause avoidable harms, are subjected to the criminal law. It also suggests that definitions and depictions of the 'crime problem' have to be looked at critically before researching and studying crime.

Understanding crime and society in Britain

In relating crime and society in Chapter 1, it was argued that individuals' decisions to commit crime are affected by their cultural background and structural position and that crime is strongly affected by technological, economic and social change. These themes have recurred throughout the book, whether looking at how crime can be explained, exploring its relationship to social inequalities or examining specific patterns of crime. Persistent themes have been the contrast between agency – individual characteristics and decisions – and structure, and the importance of looking at both.

Individual, culture and structure

Individualizing crime

A persistent theme throughout criminology has been attempts to attribute crime to individual pathologies and deficits, reflecting popular representations of 'beasts', 'fiends' or 'evil'. Casting the criminal as 'other' has been accompanied by the search for *difference*, whether by looking at atavistic men characterized by biological differences, at 'psychos' suffering from personality or psychiatric deficits, or at 'feral youth' in decaying parts of cities associated with social exclusion. Gender differences were assumed to be 'natural' and violent and sexual crime have been 'medicalized' by relating them to clinical problems, excessive sex drives, cognitive distortions or 'dysfunctional' families. While it is more difficult to pathologize organizational crimes, offenders are typically seen as 'mavericks' or as atypical 'rotten apples' in an otherwise healthy orchard (Punch 2009). More recent theories talk of offenders lacking self-control often as a result of poor parenting.

Individualizing crime has an enormous appeal. It is reassuring to assume that crime is a product of deviant individuals who can be isolated and cured, rather than being a part of normal life. If crimes can be attributed to the deficits of 'others' and related to individual situations 'we' have less to worry about. The promise of the modernist project described in Chapter 4 was that the 'causes' of crime could be identified and a 'cure' developed, and this gave way to arguments that, as crime was a matter of individual choice and responsibility, individuals could be deterred and crime could be reduced by altering the situations in which it took place. Identifying risk factors and risky lifestyles also places the responsibility on victims to protect themselves, forming part of a more general trend towards responsibilization.

While not disputing the role of human agency and recognizing that people choose to commit crime, which can be a rational choice, and that these choices may be affected by an individual's physical characteristics, mental health, temperament and upbringing, it has also been argued that individualized approaches have serious limitations. They do not clearly differentiate between offenders and non-offenders and associating crime with individual pathologies can also involve a circular argument. If 'crime' is seen as deviant, criminals are labelled 'abnormal' and this deviance is then used to explain their behaviour. Violence or sexual abuse in families leads them to be cast as dysfunctional thus explaining the violence (Chapter 11). Moreover, 'blaming' individuals all too often diverts attention from cultural and structural factors. Attributing violent and sexual crime to aberrant men diverts attention from the 'normal' violence in everyday life. Blaming crime on young people's 'natural' tendency to commit crime avoids looking at their structural position. Attributing property crimes and fraud to calculating offenders diverts attention from the narrow line between these crimes and what 'everyone does' and from their roots in a consumer culture promoting the desirability of particular lifestyles and 'must have' goods. Attributing corporate crime to 'pathological' corporations or state crime to 'evil' torturers or 'rogue' states diverts attention from the 'normalization' of crime in many organizations and state agencies.

Crime and culture

Cultures can also be 'blamed' for crime and 'othered'. Chapter 4, for example, outlined classic subcultural theories to which 'sub' cultures, many linked to immigrant cultures, arose out of social strain or social disorganization. Chapter 7 looked at notions of the 'dependency' culture of the underclass and Chapters 2 and 8 pointed to the demonization of successive youth and 'gang' cultures, some associated with ethnic and racial differences. Culture can therefore be used ideologically as part of the criminalization process and can reflect wider structures of domination.

This does not deny the enormous significance of culture. Many crimes are culturally tolerated and not seen as 'real crimes' – a major factor affecting criminalization. This is particularly the case with white-collar and other economic crimes which can be linked to wider cultures of competition or to the enterprise culture. The culture of masculinity has been associated with violent and sexual crime, property crime, car crime, serious crime and aggressive tactics in the world of business. Corporate cultures have been said to be criminogenic, particularly those in which profits take priority over safety, quality or environmental considerations. In turn, this is supported by cultures associated with capitalism or neo-liberalism, particularly during the 'greed is good' era. It has also been seen that the consumer culture, associated with sentiments that 'you are' what you wear or consume can form the basis for the frustration which can give rise to some forms of crime.

The relationship between culture, subculture and structure is therefore complex and fluid. Contemporary cultural approaches, manifested in cultural criminology, have moved away from looking at monolithic cultures and subcultures to the explosion of cultures seen variously in street culture, 'poly drug' culture, the culture of the night-time economy, car culture and other cultural styles. Crime itself can be a cultural commodity and is used to sell films, books and computer games. It forms a key part of the attractions of crime which can, for some, be a means of achieving cultural goals related to achievement, lifestyle, excitement, edge work and masculinity. Culture, and the societal goals which it reflects, is also global and related to wider social and economic factors.

Crime, social structure and social change

Social structure and social change have been major criminological themes from Durkheim's work, written at the end of the nineteenth century, to contemporary work exploring the effects of globalization and de-industrialization. To Durkheim, anomie developed out of the transition from pre-industrial societies to industrial or modern societies which saw the decline of traditional ways of life and the emergence of a society in which economic prosperity was related to unachievable 'boundless aspirations' with insufficient moral regulation (see Chapter 3). To Merton, the strain between society's universal goals and the impossibility, for many, of achieving them through legitimate means generated crime as an innovative or rebellious response. These powerful themes, albeit reworked, restated and remodelled have been applied to contemporary society, particularly in the wake of social and economic change which has brought about globalization and the decline in domestic manufacturing industries on which so many towns, cities and communities were reliant and from which they derived cultural identities and ways of life. The impact of these devastating changes has been seen throughout. Like modernity, globalization has been said to offer prosperity on a global scale but this prosperity is not available to all. Young's (1999; 2003; 2007a) work, invoking a 'globalized anomie', illustrates the lasting relevance of these analyses suggesting that crime is related to the humiliation and degradation of poverty and social exclusion and the insecurity brought about by the increasing casualization of labour.

Many kinds of crime have been related to anomie, relative deprivation and social exclusion, particularly those prevalent in the often neglected spaces characterized by high levels of unemployment in which crime can become a rational economic response and a criminal career can represent an alternative to legitimate work. These also form the context for anti-social behaviour, involvement in serious and 'enterprise' crimes, urban unrest and hate crime, in turn related to the demographic changes in areas which produced invisible boundaries between those most affected by the decline of traditional industries and those (falsely) perceived to be getting more than their 'fair share'. Crime is not only an economic response but can provide a sense of worth and achievement. The innovative 'entrepreneur' seeks out new markets straddling the boundaries between the legitimate and illegitimate economies. Nor are these analyses restricted to the 'poor' or most deprived – the night-time economy with its emphasis on 'partying', drug use and expressive leisure has also flourished in regenerated city centres and involves those with the means to consume, and the desire to participate in more extravagant lifestyles also motivates serious offenders, irregular immigrants, cyber criminals and fraudsters. The more affluent can also experience feelings of relative deprivation and anomie attempting to secure ever greater rewards and bonuses in the 'new' financial economy related to serious corporate frauds or the prioritization of profits – with a lack of regulation also being a factor.

Social change also affects attitudes to and worries about crime as rapid change generates generalized anxieties which focus on crime as an identifiable problem (Jefferson and Holloway 1997). In Chapter 6 it was seen that fears and worries about crime may express more generalized anxieties about other misfortunes, linked to a culture of fear heightened by the media and major incidents such as 9/11 or 7/7. These have also led to the 'othering' of migrant groups and the creation of new folk devils. Rapid social change may also increase anxieties about the antisocial and public activities of the young, with Pearson's (1983) work illustrating the recurrent anxieties of older generations reflected in a tendency to look back to a golden age.

Crime and social inequality

Social change is strongly related to social inequality and successive chapters have looked at the complex relationship between crime and social inequalities such as socio-economic status, age, gender and race and ethnicity. These relationships are not straightforward, are fluid and constantly changing and it was argued that there are great dangers in the essentialism which casts young men, typically from the lower class and in some areas ethnically 'othered' as offenders, and women, older people and children as quintessential deserving victims. These associations, reflected in media images, are so pervasive that they have framed criminological research and policy. They must, however, be critically reviewed and it is important to recognize that inequalities are interrelated.

One of the commonest associations is that between social deprivation, lower-class socio-economic status and crime. This has been disputed from very different perspectives. To critical criminologists, the existence and seriousness of the crimes of the 'powerful' in itself rules out any assumption that crime is restricted to the less well off. To 'conservative' criminologies, linking crime to social deprivation is to 'excuse' it and to deny the role of individual responsibility. Nonetheless, there are strong indications that social inequalities, in particular widening income gaps, are related to crime (Hale 2009) and that this relationship applies to the crimes of most and least affluent. Thus Braithwaite (1991: 40) argues that:

> Inequality thus worsens both crimes of poverty motivated by need for goods for use and crimes of wealth motivated by greed enabled by goods for exchange. Furthermore, much crime, particularly violent crime, is motivated by the humiliation of the offender and the offender's perceived right to humiliate the victim. Inegalitarian societies, it is argued, are more structurally humiliating.

Some forms of crime can therefore be seen as crimes of 'survival' borne out of economic need, such as the crimes of the homeless (Carlen 1996), those arising out of the feminization of poverty or those related to the plight of irregular migrants. The stress of living on low incomes has also been seen to play a part in family and other forms of violence such as homicide which are related to feelings of not being able to live up to the norms expected of parents, mothers or fathers (see Chapter 11). Absolute deprivation is clearly important (Grover 2008).

Many also stress the importance of relative deprivation linked to the feelings of frustration and humiliation outlined above. As Young (2007a) argues, those excluded from the benefits of the consumer society are culturally included and crime can be a means of obtaining the symbols of success. The dynamics of inclusion and exclusion can also be related to perceptions that some are 'better off' than others, to a culture of vindictiveness and can underlie forms of 'hate' crime. Gender and racial inequalities are therefore closely linked and, for young people particularly, feelings of relative deprivation and exclusion can be more acute and crime a more appropriate response.

Deprivation is therefore associated with other inequalities and victimization also illustrates the interrelationships between inequalities with some forms of victimization being gendered, as in sexual violence, related to race and ethnicity, as in racial violence or aged, as in violence towards children or older people. While the more affluent do represent more attractive targets, the poor suffer disproportionately from most forms of crime, from property crime in so-called crime 'hot spots', from living with daily experiences of so-called 'low-level' crimes, living in areas most likely to be polluted, being exploited in dangerous workplaces and, at a global level, to being the recipients of toxic waste dumping and being unable to escape from genocide or ethnic cleansing. These variations can further be linked to culture and structural patterns of domination whether patriarchal, colonial or related to capitalism, neo-liberalism and the political power of state agencies.

Inequalities are therefore important and a large body of work has sought to expose their significance. Feminists played a major role in exposing the victimization of women and the maleness of crime, and other campaigners have exposed the victimization of children and older people, age inequalities and the extent of racial and other forms of harassment and hate crime. Nonetheless, there remain some relatively underexplored aspects of inequality and what Hudson (2007) describes as 'last taboos' to be explored. The connections between crime, victimization and deprivation as they are experienced on a day to day level by women and men, those from different ethnic groups and other groups such as the disabled or faith groups are not well covered by largely quantitative victim surveys with their focus on single incidents. Far more research on the 'lived reality' of continual exposure to crime and victimization needs to be carried out. The focus on men as offenders and women as victims has also meant that the involvement of women in serious crimes, in sexual abuse, violent crime and sex work or economic crime motivated not solely by need is not well researched or understood. Very often female offenders tend to be cast as victims of poverty or men's violence – yet, as Carlen (1988) argues, women can commit crimes for very much the same reasons as men. Male victimization has also been less well researched along with, as seen in Chapters 7–10, the involvement of minority ethnic groups as offenders, non racially motivated 'hate crimes', older offenders and child offenders – often simply cast as 'evil', so much do their crimes challenge stereotypes of innocent children.

Crime in Britain

The focus throughout this book, reflected in its title, has been on Britain, and, while not taking a specifically comparative approach it has revealed important and interesting variations between the three jurisdictions of England and Wales (with some variations between the two), Scotland, and Northern Ireland, which are often overlooked in British criminological writing. In a preface to a collection of articles on Scottish Criminal Justice, Garland pointed out that 'the UK' all too often 'really means England and Wales' (Garland 1999: xiv). In what is regarded as the major British criminology text, the *Oxford Handbook of Criminology*, the index for 'comparative criminal justice' has entries for France, Germany, Holland, Italy, Japan and the United States (Maguire et al 2007: 1144) but not Scotland or Northern Ireland (Croall et al 2010). The 'British' Crime Survey, so often used as a starting point for discussing many crime issues, deals only with England and Wales, and 'official figures' are typically presented in texts with no reference to whether they include or exclude Scotland or Northern Ireland – it is assumed that they include England and Wales. Newburn's (2007) text is one notable exception.

In preparing this book, all too often the author encountered figures which made no mention of whether they included all three jurisdictions, and the words UK or Britain and English are often used interchangeably with little exploration of their significance. Many research reports and journal articles do not specify the location of studies, nor is their application to different parts of Britain or to other cities and regions systematically explored. Some make references to 'British' culture or, indeed, in discussions of race and ethnicity, 'Englishness' which have little relevance to experiences in Scotland (Croall and Frondigoun 2010) or Northern Ireland.

This geographical blindness not only causes considerable confusion for students in Scotland and Northern Ireland, who may use the 'British' Crime Survey (Croall et al 2010) as a starting point, but it also misses an invaluable opportunity to explore the role of local cultures and regional and national differences. It has been seen that, for the crimes represented in official figures, there are important differences and it is significant that some are now including comparisons between jurisdictions, although England and Wales tends to be the benchmark. Also noted were variations between jurisdictions and cities such as Belfast, London or Glasgow in relation to violent crimes, homicides, gangs and serious crime which are worthy of much more research exploring the role of local cultures, traditions and the impact of wider socio-economic factors. Northern Ireland, with its unique history of the Troubles, also has a very unique experience of crime, victimization, policing and social control which are all too often neglected or dismissed on the grounds that it is 'different'.

Regional variations are also significant and successive chapters have indicated variations between urban and rural areas, different regions and individual cities. Chapter 10, for example, drew attention to the way in which social and economic change impacted specifically on northern towns and how local demographic and geographical factors affected urban unrest and ethnically motivated violence. Also neglected has been the relationship between regional and national differences within Britain in relation to aspects of 'hate' crime and criminalization. In Scotland, for example, Highlanders who migrated South were seen as an inferior race by the *Scotsman* in 1846 (Edward 2008: 26) and there were widespread concerns about the influx of the 'barely civilised' Irish (Edward 2008: 38), who have long been associated with crime and were for many years a suspect community (Hillyard 1993). It was also seen in Chapter 7 that the notion of the underclass had 'Celtic' connotations (Bagguley and Mann 1992).

A further 'taboo' subject is the role of sectarianism in Northern Ireland and Scotland, and 'Anglophobic' crimes in Wales, Northern Ireland and Scotland. British criminological research, whether quantitative or qualitative, should therefore be more sensitive to variations across the UK and between different towns and cities. In themselves these could provide extremely revealing comparative work. These differences are also significant in relation to criminal justice policy, particularly since devolution (Croall et al 2010).

Crime in its global context

The avowedly British focus of the book should not detract from the increasingly international nature of crime and its global context. Globalization has been seen to have had a major impact on communications and travel and this has affected crime as it has any other aspect of society or industry. It has had a considerable cultural impact and global inequalities have led to globalized anomie. International forms of crime require international regulation and some crimes have exploited the many spaces between laws. Gaps and weaknesses in regulation can enable many forms of crime to flourish.

International crime industries

Many forms of crime have an international basis, although it was seen in Chapters 2 and 14 that representations of the threat of transnational organized crime with its assumed links to terrorism are overstated. Many forms of crime, however, have been and continue to be international or cross border in that they rely on moving goods from one country to sell in another. As Levi (2007: 771–809) points out, some drugs have to be grown in warmer climates and have to be transported, and, as seen in Chapter 14, variations in revenue duties provide the basis for trades in bootleg items. Many of these trades have been facilitated by improvements in transport and communications. The rise of e-mail and the Internet have also assisted global movements of hot money as well as legitimate transactions and have, as outlined in Chapter 13, made it possible for old-style advance fee and other frauds to be perpetrated on a global scale. Pornography and pirated music, film and other intellectual products can now be downloaded and distributed without the need for 'hard copy' which is so much easier to detect.

Global inequalities and crime

The globalization of telecommunications has also had an enormous impact on culture as many chapters have illustrated. Consumer culture is now global and citizens across the globe receive images of Western affluence. This creates the globalized anomie referred to above which is further related to global inequalities. As outlined in Chapter 7, inequalities between nations are vast and have been linked to international trades such as human trafficking, where the lure of Western lifestyles attracts people from the most impoverished nations to risk their lives by paying smugglers and traffickers. Drugs are often manufactured in poorer countries and provide much needed income, and many kinds of organized, corporate, environmental and state crimes are based on exploiting developing countries' need for inward investment and employment. This means that the poorest of the world are amongst those most victimized by crime. Furthermore, the relative deprivation suffered by the citizens of poorer nations faced with universal images of life in the West can form the basis of fundamentalism and terrorism (Young 2007a).

Many of these crimes exploit the gaps or spaces between laws and the limitations of international regulation seen most vividly in relation to state crime and violence. It was also seen in relation to the 'dumping' of goods banned in the West in the Third World as happened with the drug Thalidomide, exported well after its dangers were known, in the location of factories in countries with less well-developed and enforced safety regimes, as illustrated in Bhopal, and in the trade in toxic waste.

Crime, criminal and social justice

This book has focused on crime rather than criminal justice and this section will not deal with specific policies but will outline some broad issues raised by the study of crime. While it has been seen that the so-called modernist project aimed to establish the causes of and a cure for crime, such grand aims or, to post-modernists, 'meta narratives', have now been abandoned; it was seen in Chapter 5 that many contemporary 'establishment' approaches argue that crime can be prevented without establishing its causes. Against this, however, it can be argued that these policies will inevitably be limited if they neglect the structural roots of crime.

Other sociological perspectives raise other issues. To labelling perspectives, the formal agencies of social control can amplify deviance and demonize specific groups, suggesting less, rather than more, intervention. Critical approaches, criticized for being less directly concerned with policy, nonetheless draw attention to the dangers of exclusion and criminalization, the relativity of the criminal law and serious gaps in regulation. They have also asked serious questions about the extent to which fears about crime have become linked to fears about other policy areas such as social inclusion and housing – amounting in effect to the criminalization of social policy as illustrated in concerns about, for example, anti-social behaviour. Feminist approaches have influenced policies in relation to domestic and sexual violence and prostitution, and the exposure of institutional racism on the part of the police led to fundamental changes in policing and prosecution processes. Taken together these suggest a number of questions.

Can crime be prevented?

Although the formal criminal justice process is often seen as the major vehicle for controlling crime, its role is necessarily limited. It has been seen, for example, that only a small proportion of crimes are detected and reported and even fewer offenders are convicted. This inevitably limits any deterrent effect. Some offences are particularly difficult to detect and prosecute and are relatively impervious to formal controls. Indeed, the success of criminal businesses depends on avoiding detection and capture. While the rational choice approach assumes that offenders will be deterred if the chances of detection and costs of punishment exceed that of offending, not all offenders are rational and many do not accurately calculate their chances of detection. For other offences, such as white-collar or corporate crime, the slim chances of being caught reduce any deterrent value of the law. The criminal justice system on its own is therefore limited in its ability to substantially reduce the total volume of crime, and its more important role is to process offenders who are detected.

These limitations were acknowledged in the growth of crime prevention policies formed on the basis of the situational and lifestyle approaches outlined in Chapter 5. An enormous number of these strategies have now been implemented, including the installation of CCTV in many public spaces. As was particularly evident in Chapter 13, these have had a considerable effect on some property crimes, and simple innovations such as the electronic immobilizer have vastly reduced car theft. Their limitations, however, have also been referred to (see Chapters 5 and 13). While they may reduce some forms of crime in some areas, some offenders have turned to other forms of crime and the Internet has assisted the development of new crimes and made old ones easier. Serious offenders are skilled enough to avoid security and, indeed, the constant challenge of outwitting policing and crime prevention strategies can be one of the attractions of crime. They place considerable responsibility on citizens to take their own precautions, which some cannot afford. This has raised the prospect of the more affluent protecting themselves with locks, bolts and bars and thereby contributing to social exclusion (see Chapter 7). Moreover, an often repeated criticism is that they can do little to address the wider structural roots of crime.

What is the relationship between criminal justice and social policy?

These structural roots lie outside the reach of the formal criminal justice process and it has long been argued that tackling them involves wider economic and social policies, seen most clearly in relation to those addressing social exclusion and inclusion. It was seen in Chapter 7, however, that many of these were based on a 'weak' version of social inclusion which continues to 'blame' the poor and places responsibility on individuals to ameliorate their situation, particularly through work – which may, however, be unavailable for structural reasons. Other developments related to social policy have linked crime, and particularly anti-social behaviour, to wider issues such as housing, and the kind of partnerships seen across Britain dealing with community safety involve the police working with social welfare and other agencies. These have tended, however, to extend the criminal label to 'low-level' crimes such as anti-social behaviour, as outlined in Chapter 8, and cast many social policy areas as assisting the control or management of crime – thus the 'criminalization' of social policy. As seen in Chapter 7, a 'stronger' version of the social exclusion thesis would suggest policies which address the roots of social exclusion which lie in wider social inequalities and the widening gap between the included and the excluded. Criminal justice is therefore related to social justice.

Should the criminal justice process intervene less?

The extension of the criminal label draws attention to the dangers of deviancy amplification, long recognized in the labelling perspective in which punitive and exclusive policies could confirm 'deviant' or criminal identities, stigmatize offenders and lead to secondary deviance or a criminal career. This implied minimal intervention, an approach also advocated by left realists. These ideas have had an impact on diversionary policies and on calls for more victim–offender mediation, along with being supported by writers such as Braithwaite who advocated that offenders be 'shamed' but also 'reintegrated' and warned of the dangers of creating 'outsiders' (Braithwaite 1989a; Braithwaite and Pettit 1990). As seen in Chapter 8, much youth crime is transitory and these kinds of ideas remain influential although the trend of much youth justice policy has been more punitive. Policy towards younger offenders is also a major source of variation between different jurisdictions, with Scotland's more diversionary and welfare-based policy being contrasted with England's more punitive policy although it has been subject to some 'detartanization' in recent years (McAra and McVie 2010).

What is the role of criminal law and prohibition?

These ideas suggest that the formal processes of criminal law, policing and punishment may not be the only, or even the most appropriate, way to deal with some forms of crime, and can indeed 'create' crime by criminalizing activities which can lead to secondary crime. As seen in relation to drug-taking and prostitution, for example, the criminal law is relatively ineffective in reducing illegal markets and has been associated with greater amounts of violence and corruption. It has also been seen that serious crime thrives on trading in prohibited goods – if fewer goods were prohibited this would reduce opportunities for criminal 'enterprises'. The costs of enforcing these laws are also high. Many of the activities in question could be regulated by licensing arrangements which need not involve the criminal law.

Different sets of arguments surround the policing and regulation of corporate, environmental and state crime, often seen to be under-, rather than over-criminalized.

It can be seen as contradictory, particularly for critical criminologists, to advocate reducing intervention and 'legalizing' some kinds of crime while arguing for criminalization and tougher punishment for others (Croall 2001a). Nonetheless, these crimes raise serious issues about the role of the criminal law and differential criminalization. The criminal law, while one amongst other means of regulating harmful activities, remains a powerful form of censure and reflects societal disapproval. Using it more against the serious harms associated with these crimes can be justified as signalling much stronger disapproval, along with providing a greater deterrent, particularly as the economic recession of 2008 has been widely attributed to regulatory 'failure'. As outlined in Chapters 16 and 17 also, the role of international law could also be strengthened.

There are, therefore, no simple or straightforward solutions to crime, just as there are no simple or straightforward explanations of it. Crime is, as has been seen, a vast and complex subject, which can be viewed from the many different perspectives introduced in this book. It involves not one crime problem but many different crime problems, some not widely defined as 'crime'. Many different questions can be asked about crime, reflecting the many different ways in which these problems are constructed. Many of these questions remain unanswered and require further research and analyses.

Bibliography

Aas, K. (2007) *Globalization and Crime*. London: Sage.

Adler, C. and Polk, K. (2001) *Child Victims of Homicide*. Cambridge: Cambridge University Press.

Adler, F. (1975) *Sisters in Crime*. New York: McGraw Hill.

Aitchison, A. and Hodgkinson, J. (2003) 'Patterns of Crime', pp 91–108 in Simmons, J. and Dodd, T. (eds) *Crime in England and Wales 2002/03*. Home Office Statistical Bulletin. London: Home Office. http://rds.homeoffice.gov.uk/rds/pdfs2/hosb703.pdf

Aitken, L. and Griffin, G. (1996) *Gender Issues in Elder Abuse*. London: Sage.

Allen, J., Forrest, S., Levi, M., Roy, H. and Sutton, M. (2005) *Fraud and Technology Crimes: Findings from the 2002/03 British Crime Survey and 2003 Offending, Crime and Justice Survey*, Home Office Online Report 34/05. London: Home Office. http://rds.homeoffice.gov.uk/rds/pdfs05/rdsolr3405.pdf

Amir, M. (1971) *Patterns in Forcible Rape*. Chicago: University of Chicago Press.

Amnesty International (2008) *Scotland's Slaves: An Amnesty International Briefing on Trafficking in Scotland*. Edinburgh: Amnesty International. http://www.amnesty.org.uk/uploads/documents/doc_18605.pdf

Anderson, D., Chenery, S. and Pease, K. (1995) *Biting Back: Tackling Repeat Burglary and Car Crime*. Police Research Group: Crime Detection and Prevention Series. London: Home Office. http://rds.homeoffice.gov.uk/rds/prgpdfs/cdp58bf.pdf

Anderson, S., Grove Smith, C., Kinsey, R. and Wood, J. (1990) *The Edinburgh Crime Survey: First Report*. Edinburgh: Scottish Office (Central Research Unit Papers).

Anderson, S., Kinsey, R., Loader, I. and Smith, C. (1994) *Cautionary Tales: Young People, Crime and Policing in Edinburgh*. Aldershot: Avebury.

Anderson, S. and Leitch, S. (1994) *The Scottish Crime Survey 1993: First Results – Research Findings*. Central Research Unit Paper. Edinburgh: Scottish Office. http://www.scotland.gov.uk/Publications/1999/01/66575548-b5a9-441f-834a-da44182da2af

Arendt, H. (1965/1977) *Eichmann in Jerusalem: A Report on the Banality of Evil*. London: Penguin.

Ariès, P. (1962) *Centuries of Childhood*. London: Jonathan Cape.

Armstrong, D., Hine, J., Hacking, S., Armaos, R., Jones, R., Klessinger, N. and France, A. (2005) *Children, Risk and Crime: The On Track Youth Lifestyles Surveys*. Home Office Research Study 278. London: Home Office Research, Development and Statistics Directorate. http://rds.homeoffice.gov.uk/rds/pdfs05/hors278.pdf

Ashworth, A. and Redmayne, M. (1994) *The Criminal Process*. Oxford: Clarendon Press.

Aubert, V. (1952) 'White collar crime and social structure', *American Journal of Sociology*, 58: 263–71.

Babb, P. and Ogunbor, I. (2008) 'Detection of Crime' in Kershaw, N., Nicholas, S. and Walker, A. (2008) *Crime in England and Wales 2007/8*. London: Home Office. http://rds.homeoffice.gov.uk/rds/pdfs08/hosb0708.pdf

Bagguley, P. and Mann, K. (1992) 'Idle thieving bastards? Scholarly representations of the "Underclass"'. *Work, Employment and Society*, 6(1): 113–26.

Bailey, W. and Peterson, R. (1995) 'Gender Inequality and Violence Against Women: The Case of Murder', pp 174–205 in Hagan, J. and Peterson, R. (eds) *Crime and Inequality*. Stanford: Stanford University Press.

Bangs, M., Roe, S. and Higgins, N. (2008) 'Geographic Patterns of Crime,' pp 143–64 in Kershaw, N., Nicholas, S. and Walker, A. (eds) *Crime in England and Wales 2007/08: Findings from the British Crime Survey and Police Recorded Crime*. London: Home Office. http://rds.homeoffice.gov.uk/rds/pdfs08/hosb0708.pdf

Barak, G. (2001) 'Crime and crime control in an age of globalization: a theoretical dissection', *Critical Criminology*, 10(1): 57–72.

Barclay, G. (ed.) (1995) *Digest 3: Information on the Criminal Justice System in England and Wales*. Home Office Research and Statistics Directorate. London: Home Office.

Barker. M., Geraghty, J., Webb, B. and Key, T. (1993) *The Prevention of Street Robbery: Home Office Police Research Group Crime Prevention Unit, Series Paper 44*. London: Home Office Police Department.

Batchelor, S. (2002) 'The "myth" of girl gangs', pp 247–50 in Jewkes, Y. and Letherby, G. (eds) *Criminology: A Reader*. London: Sage.

Batchelor, S., Burman, M. and Brown, J. (2001) 'Discussing violence: let's hear it from the girls', *Probation Journal*, 48 (2): 125–34.

Bauman, Z. (1989) *Modernity and the Holocaust*. Cambridge: Polity.

Bauman, Z. (1998) *Globalization: The Human Consequences*. Cambridge: Polity.

Bauman, Z. (2000) *Liquid Modernity*. Cambridge: Polity.

BBC News (2001) 'Smugglers Jailed over Chinese Deaths', 11/05/2001. http://news.bbc.co.uk/1/hi/world/europe/1325826.stm

BBC News (2005) 'Sinn Fein leader "backed raids"', 10/02/2005. http://news.bbc.co.uk/1/hi/northern_ireland/4253627.stm

BBC News (2008) 'Why China's milk industry went sour', 29/9/08. http://news.bbc.co.uk/2/hi/asia-pacific/7635466.stm

BBC News (2009a) 'Fall in youth crimes is reported', 6/03/09. http://news.bbc.co.uk/mpapps/pagetools/print/news.bbc.co.uk/1/hi/wales/7925733

BBC News (2009b) 'Madoff fraud investigation widens', 13/03/2009. http://news.bbc.co.uk/1/hi/7941464.stm

BBC News (2010a) 'Crime Row reopens amid Tory claim', 10/03/10. http://newsvote.bbc.co.uk/mpapps/pagetools/print/news.bbc.co.uk/1/hi/uk_politics/85

BBC News (2010b) 'Man to face Milly murder charge', 02/03/10. http://newsvote.bbc.co.uk/mpapps/patetools/print/news.bbc.co.uk/1/hi/england/85938

BBC News (2010c) 'Call to raise age of criminality', 13/03/10. http://newsvote.bbc.co.uk/mpapps/pagetools/print/nedws.bbc.co.uk/1/hi/uk/8565619.st

BBC News (2010d) 'Drop in Homicides for second year', 23/02/10. http://news.bbc.co.uk/1/hi/scotland/8529971.stm

BBC News (2010e) '"One in seven" students attacked', 18/03/10. http://newsvote.bbc.co.uk/mpapps/pagetools/print/news.bbc.co.uk/1/hi/uk/8573368.stm

BBC News (2010f) 'Brady should "consider position"', 17/03/10. http://newsvote.bbc.co.uk/mpapps/pagetools/print/news.bbc.co.uk/1/hi/northern_ireland.stm

BBC News (2010g) 'Pope apology for Irish sex abuse', 20/03/10. http://news.bbc.co.uk/1/hi/world/europe/8577740.stm

BBC News (2010h) 'Priest paid alleged abuse victim', 19/03/10. http://newsvote.bbc.co.uk/mpapps/pagetools/print/news.bbc.co.uk/1/hi/northern_ireland.stm

BBC News (2010i) 'Facebook rules out installing "Panic Button"', 18/03/10. http://news.bbc.co.uk/1/hi/uk/8574727.stm

BBC News (2010j) 'Spanish police arrest masterminds of "massive" botnet', 3/3/10. http://news.bbc.co.uk/1/hi/technology/8547453.stm

BBC News (2010k) 'Hacking "fun" for British teens', 18/03/10. http://news.bbc.co.uk.go/pr/fr/-/1/hi/technology/8574259.stm

BBC News (2010l) 'Banking fraud moves to Internet', 10/03/10. http://news.bbc.co.uk/go/pr/fr/-/1/hi/business/8558535.stm

BBC News (2010m) 'Identity fraud "is set to soar"', 19/03/10. http://news.bbc.co.uk/go/pr/fr/-/1/hi/business/8575936.stm

BBC News (2010n) 'Ash compensation e-mail "is fake" says Wrexham firm', 05/05/10. http://news.bbc.co.uk/1/hi/wales/8662097.stm

BBC News (2010o) 'Sweet firm fined over worker crushed to death', 23/04/10. http://news.bbc.co.uk/1/hi/england/8639707.stm

BBC News (2010p) 'FG Wilson fined over employee death', 26/04/10. http://news.bbc.co.uk/1/hi/northern_ireland/8644099.stm

BBC News (2010q) 'Shops agree to £20m pay-out for "toxic sofas"', 26/04/10. http://news.bbc.co.uk/1/hi/uk/8644156.stm

BBC News (2010r) 'Bhopal trial: Eight convicted over India gas disaster', 07/06/10. http://news.bbc.co.uk/1/hi/world/south_asia/8725140.stm

BBC News (2010s) 'Fines for litter and dog mess top £120,000 in Wales', 03/04/10. http://news.bbc.co.uk/1/hi/wales/8596971.stm

BBC News (2010t) 'Profile: Binyam Mohamed', 12/02/10. http://news.bbc.co.uk/1/hi/uk/7906381.stm

BBC News (2010u) 'Fresh legal challenge over MI5 torture guidance', 23/02/10. http://news.bbc.co.uk/1/hi/uk/8529357.stm

BBC News (2010v) 'Blackwater Iraq allegations prompt US Review', 6/03/10. http://news.bbc.co.uk/1/hi/world/americas/8553104.stm

Beccaria, C. (1963, first English edn 1767) *On Crimes and Punishments*, trans. Paolucci, H. Indianapolis: Bobs-Merrill Educational.

Beck, A., Gill, M. and Willis, A. (1994) 'Violence in Retailing: Physical and Verbal Victimisation of Staff', pp 83–102 in M. Gill (ed.) *Crime at Work: Studies in Security and Crime Prevention*. Leicester: Perpetuity Press.

Beck, M., Cooper, C., Coulson, A., Gorman, T., Howieson, S., McCourt, J., Taylor, P., Watterson, A. and Whyte, D. (2007) *The ICL/Stockline Disaster: An Independent Report on Working Conditions Prior to the Explosion*. Universities of Stirling and Strathclyde. http://www.hazards.org/icldisaster/icl_stockline_report.pdf

Becker, H. (1963) *Outsiders: Studies in the Sociology of Deviance*. New York: Free Press.

Beirne, P. (1999) 'For a nonspeciesist criminology: animal abuse as an object of study', *Criminology*, 37(1): 117–48.

Beirne, P. (2007) 'Animal Rights, Animal Abuse and Green Criminology', pp 55–86 in Beirne, P. and South, N. (eds) *Issues in Green Criminology: Confronting Harms Against Environments, Humanity and Other Animals*. Cullompton: Willan.

Beirne, P. and South, N. (eds) (2007) *Issues in Green Criminology: Confronting Harms Against Environments, Humanity and Other Animals*. Cullompton: Willan.

Bell, D. (1953) 'Crime as an American way of life', *The Antioch Review*, 13: 131–54.

Bennett, C. (2006) 'The Ipswich killings have exposed attitudes to prostitutes that haven't progressed in centuries'. *Guardian* 14 December 2006. www.guardian.co.uk/.../2006/dec/14/suffolkmurders.comment

Bennett, T. (1989) 'Burglars' Choice of Targets', pp. 176–92 in Evans, D. and Herbert, D. (eds) *The Geography of Crime*. London: Routledge.

Bennett, T. and Maguire, M. (1982) *Burglary in a Dwelling: The Offence, the Offender and the Victim*. London: Heinemann.

Bennett, T. and Wright, R. (1984) *Burglars on Burglary: Prevention and the Offender*. Aldershot: Avebury.

Bentham, J. (1970) *An Introduction to the Principles of Morals and Legislation* (eds, Burns, J. H. and Hart, H. L. A.). London: Athlone Press.

Biles, D. (1991) 'Deaths in custody in Britain and Australia', *The Howard Journal of Criminal Justice*, 30(2): 110–20.

Birch, H. (1993) 'If Looks could Kill: Myra Hindley and the Iconography of Evil', pp 32–61 in Birch, H. (ed.) *Moving Targets: Women, Murder and Representation*. London: Virago.

Birkinshaw, P. (1996) 'Government at the end of its tether: Matrix Churchill and the Scott Report', *Journal of Law and Society*, 23(3): 406–26.

Bland, L. (1992) 'The Case of the Yorkshire Ripper: Mad, Bad, Beast, or Male?', pp 233–52 in Radford, J. and Russell, D. (eds) *Femicide: The Politics of Woman Killing*. Buckingham: Open University Press.

Blythman, J. (2004) 'Shopped: The shocking power of British supermarkets'. London: Harper Perennial.

Bottomley, K. and Pease, K. (1986) *Crime and Punishment – Interpreting the Data*. Milton Keynes: Open University Press.

Bottoms, A. (1994) 'The Philosophy and Politics of Punishment and Sentencing', pp 17–49 in Clarkson, C. and Morgan, R. (eds) *The Politics of Sentencing Reform*. Oxford: Oxford University Press.

Bowlby, J. (1953) *Child Care and the Growth of Love*. Harmondsworth: Penguin.

Bowling, B. (1993) 'Racial harassment and the process of victimization: conceptual and methodological implications for the local Crime Survey', *British Journal of Criminology*, 33(2): 216–30.

Bowling, B. (1999) *Violent Racism: Victimization, Policing and Social Context*. Oxford: Oxford University Press.

Bowling, B. and Phillips, C. (2002) *Racism, Crime and Justice*. London: Longman.

Box, S. (1983) *Power, Crime and Mystification*. London: Routledge.

Box, S. (1987) *Recession, Crime and Punishment*. London: Palgrave Macmillan.

Box, S. and Hale, C. (1983) 'Liberation and female criminality in England and Wales', *British Journal of Criminology*, 23(1): 35–49.

Box, S. and Hale, C. (1986) 'Unemployment, Crime and Imprisonment, and the Enduring Problem of Prison Overcrowding', pp 72–99 in Matthews, R. and Young, J. (eds) *Confronting Crime*. London: Sage.

Boyle, J. (1977) *A Sense of Freedom*. London: Pan.

Braithwaite, J. (1984) *Corporate Crime in the Pharmaceutical Industry*. London: Routledge & Kegan Paul.

Braithwaite, J. (1989a) *Crime, Shame and Reintegration*. Cambridge: Cambridge University Press.

Braithwaite, J. (1989b) 'Criminological theory and organizational crime', *Justice Quarterly*, 6(3): 333–58.

Braithwaite, J. (1991) 'Poverty, power, white-collar crime and the paradoxes of criminological theory', *The Australian and New Zealand Journal of Criminology*, 24: 41–58.

Braithwaite, J. (1995) 'Inequality and Republican Criminology', pp 277–305 in Hagan, J. and Peterson, R. (eds) *Crime and Inequality*. Stanford: Stanford University Press.

Braithwaite, J. (2009) 'Restorative justice for banks through negative licensing', *British Journal of Criminology*, 49(4): 439–50.

Braithwaite, J. and Pettit, P. (1990) *Not Just Deserts: A Republican Theory of Justice*. Oxford: Clarendon Press.

Brake, M. (1985) *Comparative Youth Culture: The Sociology of Youth Cultures and Youth Subcultures in America, Britain and Canada*. London: Routledge & Kegan Paul.

Brake, M. and Hale, C. (1992) *Public Order and Private Lives: the Politics of Law and Order*. London: Routledge.

Brand, S. and Price, R. (2000) 'The Economic and Social Costs of Crime', Home Office Research Study 217, Economics and Resource Analysis, Research, Development and Statistics Directorate, London: Home Office.

Brogden, M. and Nijhar, P. (2006) 'Crime, abuse, and social harm: towards an integrated approach', pp 35–52 in Wahidin, A. and Cain, M. (eds) *Age, Crime and Society*. Cullompton: Willan.

Brogden, M., Jefferson, T. and Walklate, S. (1988) *Introducing Police Work*. London: Unwin Hyman.

Brookman, F. (2003) 'Confrontational and revenge homicides among men in England and Wales', *Australian and New Zealand Journal of Criminology*, 36(1): 34–59.

Brookman, F. (2005) *Understanding Homicide*. London: Sage.

Brookman, F. (2010) 'Homicide', pp 217–44 in Brookman, F., Maguire, M., Pierpoint, H. and Bennett, T. (eds) *Handbook on Crime*. Cullompton: Willan.

Brooks-Gordon, B. (2006) *The Price of Sex: Prostitution, policy and society*. Cullompton: Willan Publishing.

Brooks-Gordon, B. (2010) 'Sex work', pp 542–76 in Brookman, F., Maguire, M., Pierpoint, H. and Bennett, T. (eds) *Handbook on Crime*. Cullompton: Willan.

Brown, R. (2010) 'Vehicle Crime', pp 26–47 in Brookman, F., Maguire, M., Pierpoint, H. and Bennett, T. (eds) *Handbook on Crime*. Cullompton: Willan.

Brown, S. (2005) *Understanding Youth and Crime: Listening to Youth?* Maidenhead: Open University Press.

Brownmiller, S. (1975) *Against Our Will: Men, Women and Rape*. London: Secker & Warburg.

Brunsdon, E. and May, M. (1992) 'Absorbing violence? The under-reporting of workplace violence in the care professions', *Criminal Justice Matters*, 8(1): 6–7.

Burman, M. (2004) 'Breaking the Mould: Patterns of Female Offending', pp 38–65 in McIvor, G. (ed.) *Women Who Offend*. London: Jessica Kingsley.

Burman, M., Lovett, L. and Kelly, L. (2009) *Different Systems, Similar Outcomes? Tracking Attrition in Reported Rape Cases in Eleven Countries: Scotland Country Report*. London: Child and Women Abuse Studies Unit (CWASU). http://www.epacvaw.org/IMG/pdf/Summary_Findings.pdf

Burney, E. (2008) 'The ASBO and the shift to punishment', pp 135–48 in Squires, P. (ed.) *ASBO Nation: The Criminalization of Nuisance*. Bristol: Polity.

Burney, E. (2009) *Making People Behave: Anti-social Behaviour, Politics and Policy: The Creation and Enforcement of Anti-social Behaviour Policy*. Cullompton: Willan.

Burr, A. (1987) 'Chasing the dragon: heroin misuse, delinquency and crime in the context of South London culture', *British Journal of Criminology*, 27(4): 333–57.

Cain, M. (1973) *Society and the Policeman's Role*. London: Routledge & Kegan Paul.

Cain, M. (1990) 'Towards transgression: new directions in feminist criminology', *International Journal of the Sociology of Law*, 18(1): 1–18.

Cain, M. and Wahidin, A. (2006) 'Ageing, Crime and Society: An Invitation to a Criminology', pp 1–16 in Wahidin, A. and Cain, M. (eds) *Age, Crime and Society*. Cullompton: Willan.

Calavita, K. and Pontell, H. N. (1993) 'Savings and Loan fraud as organized crime: towards a conceptual typology of corporate illegality', *Criminology*, 31(4): 519–48.

Calavita, K., Tillman, R. and Pontell, H. (1997) 'The Savings and Loan debacle, financial crime, and the State', *Annual Review of Sociology*, 23: 19–38.

Campbell, A. (1986) *The Girls in the Gang: A Report from New York City*. Oxford: Basil Blackwell.

Campbell, Sir A. (2001) *The Report of an Inquiry into Crown Decision-Making in the Case of the Murder of Surjit Singh Chhokar*. http://scottish-parliament.biz/business/committees/historic/equal/reports-01/chhokar-b-01.htm

Campbell, B. (1993) *Goliath: Britain's Dangerous Places*. London: Virago.

Campbell, B. (1994) 'The underclass: regressive re-alignment', *Criminal Justice Matters*, 18(1): 18–19.

Campbell, D. (2010) 'The lessons of Blair Peach', *Guardian* 27/04/2010. www.guardian.co.uk/commentisfree/2010/apr/27/blair-peach-policing-lessons

Campbell, T. C. and McKay, R. (2001) *Indictment: Trial by Fire*. Edinburgh: Canongate.

Cantle, T. (2001) *Community Cohesion: A report of the Independent Review Team*. London: Home Office.

Carlen, P. (1976) *Magistrates' Justice*. London: Martin Robertson.

Carlen, P. (1983) *Women's Imprisonment*. London: Routledge & Kegan Paul.

Carlen, P. (1988) *Women, Crime and Poverty*. Milton Keynes: Open University Press.

Carlen, P. (1992) 'Criminal Women and Criminal Justice: the Limits to and the Potential of, Feminist and Left Realist Perspectives', pp 51–69 in Matthews, R. and Young, J. (eds) *Issues in Realist Criminology*. London: Sage.

Carlen, P. (1996) *Jigsaw: A Political Criminology of Youth Homelessness*. Buckingham: Open University Press.

Carlen, P., Francis, P., Slaughter, P. and Gilligan, G. (1997) 'Homelessness, crime and citizenship', *Criminal Justice Matters*, 2(1): 24–8.

Carlen, P. and Worrall, A. (eds) (1987) *Gender, Crime and Justice*. Milton Keynes: Open University Press.

Carloway, Lord (2005) *Sentencing Statement, HMA v Transco*. Court of Session, High Court Justiciary. http://news.bbc.co.uk/1/shared/bsp/hi/pdfs/26_08_05_transco.pdf

Carrabine, E. (2008) *Crime, Culture and the Media*. Cambridge: Polity.

Carrabine, E., Iganski, P., Lee, M., Plummer, K. and South, N. (2004) *Criminology: A Sociological Introduction*. London: Routledge.

Carson, W. G. (1971) 'White-Collar Crime and the Enforcement of Factory Legislation', pp 192–205 in Carson, W. G. and Wiles, P. (eds) *Crime and Delinquency in Britain: Sociological Readings*. London: Martin Robertson.

Carson, W. G. (1981) *The Other Price of Britain's Oil: Safety and Control in the North Sea*. London: Martin Robertson.

Centre for Social Justice (2008) *Breakthrough Glasgow: Ending the Costs of Social Breakdown*. http://www.centreforsocialjustice.org.uk/client/downloads/BreakthroughGlasgow.pdf

Chadwick, K. and Scraton, P. (2006) 'Critical Criminology', pp 97–100 in McLaughlin, E. and Muncie, J. (eds) (2006) *The Sage Dictionary of Criminology* 2nd edn.

Chahal, K. and Julienne, L. (1999) *We Can't All be White: Racist Victimization in the UK*. York: Joseph Rowntree Foundation.

Chambers, G. and Tombs, J. (eds) (1984) *The British Crime Survey: Scotland*. A Scottish Office Social Research Study. Edinburgh: HMSO.

Chambliss, W. (1989) 'State Organized Crime – The American Society of Criminology, 1988 Presidential Address', *Criminology*, 27(2): 183–208.

Chesney-Lind, M. (2006) 'Patriarchy, crime, and justice: feminist criminology in an era of backlash', *Feminist Criminology* 1(1): 6–26.

Chibnall, S. (1977) *Law and Order News*. London: Tavistock.

Christiansen, K. O. (1974) 'Seriousness of Criminality and Concordance among Danish Twins', in Hood, R. (ed.) *Crime, Criminology and Public Policy: Essays in Honour of Sir Leon Radzinowicz*. London: Heinemann.

Christie, N. (1986) 'The Ideal Victim', pp 17–30 in Fattah, E. A. (ed.) *From Crime Policy to Victim Policy: Reorienting the Justice System*. London: Macmillan.

Christina, D. and Carlen, P. (1985) *Criminal Women*. Cambridge: Polity.

Clarke, J. (1996) 'Crime and Social Order: Interrogating the Detective Story', pp 65–100 in Muncie, J. and McLaughlin, E. (eds) *The Problem of Crime*. London: Sage.

Clarke, J. (2008) 'Looking for Social Justice: Welfare States and Beyond', pp 29–62 in Newman, J. and Yeates, N. (eds) *Social Justice: Welfare, Crime and Society*. Maidenhead: Open University Press.

Clarke, M. (1989) 'Insurance fraud', *British Journal of Criminology*, 29(1): 1–20.

Clarke, M. (1990) *Business Crime: Its Nature and Control*. Cambridge: Polity.

Clarke, M. (1994) *EC Fraud, Issues in Sociology and Social Policy*. Occasional Paper No. 4. Department of Sociology, Social Policy and Social Work Studies, University of Liverpool.

Clarke, R. (1980) 'Situational crime prevention: theory and practice', *British Journal of Criminology*, 20(2): 136–47.

Clarke, R. (1999) *Hot Products: Understanding, Anticipating and Reducing Demand for Stolen Goods*. Police Research Series, Paper No. 112. London: Home Office. http://rds.homeoffice.gov.uk/rds/prgpdfs/brf112.pdf

Clarke, R. V. G. and Felson, M. (eds) (1993) *Routine Activity and Rational Choice*. New Brunswick: Transaction.

Clarke, R. and Mayhew, P. (1980) *Designing Out Crime*. London: HMSO.

Clinard, M. B. (1983) *Corporate Ethics and Crime: The Role of the Middle Manager*. Beverly Hills, CA: Sage.

Cloward, R. and Ohlin, L. (1960) *Delinquency and Opportunity*. New York: Free Press.

Cohen, A. K. (1955) *Delinquent Boys*. New York: Free Press.

Cohen, P. (1972) 'Working Class Youth Cultures in East London', *Working Papers in Cultural Studies*, No. 2. Birmingham University.

Cohen, S. (1972/2002) *Folk Devils and Moral Panics*. Oxford: Martin Robertson/London: Routledge.

Cohen, S. (1979) 'Guilt, Justice and Tolerance: Some Old Concepts for a New Criminology', pp 17–51 in Downes, D. and Rock, P. (eds) *Deviant Interpretations: Problems in Criminological Theory*. Oxford: Clarendon Press.

Cohen, S. (1996) 'Human Rights and Crimes of the State: The Culture of Denial', pp 542–60 in Muncie, J., McLaughlin, E. and Langan, M. (eds) *Criminological Perspectives: Essential Readings*. London: Sage.

Cohen, S. (2001) *States of Denial: Knowing about Atrocities and Suffering*. Cambridge: Polity.

Coleman, C. and Moynihan, J. (1996) *Understanding Crime Data: Haunted by the Dark Figure*. Buckingham: Open University Press.

Coleman, C. and Norris, C. (2000). *Introducing Criminology*. Cullompton: Willan.

Coleman, J. W. (1987) 'Toward an Integrated Theory of white-collar crime', *American Journal of Sociology*, 93: 406–39.

Coleman, R., Tombs, S., Sim, J. and Whyte, D. (2002) 'Power, Politics and Partnerships: The State of Crime Prevention on Merseyside', pp 86–108 in Edwards, A. and Hughes, G. (eds) *Crime Control and Community: The New Politics of Public Safety*. Cullompton: Willan.

Coles, D., Shaw, H. and Ward, T. (1997) 'Deaths, Police and Prosecutions', *Criminal Justice Matters*, No. 29(1): 10–11.

Collier, R. (1998) *Masculinities, Crime and Criminology: Men, Hetrosexuality and the Criminal(ised) Other*. London: Sage.

Collison, M. (1996) 'In search of the high life: drugs, crime, masculinities and consumption', *British Journal of Criminology*, 36(3): 428–44.

Connell, R. W. (1987) *Gender and Power*. Oxford: Polity Press.

Connell, R. W. (1995) *Masculinities*. Cambridge: Polity Press.

Connell, R. W. and Messerschmidt, J. (2005) 'Hegemonic masculinity: rethinking the concept', *Gender and Society*, 19(6): 829–59.

Consumer Law Review (2009) *A Better Deal for Consumers Delivering Real Help Now and Change for the Future*. Presented to Parliament by the Secretary of State for Business, Innovation and Skills, July 2009. London: Department for Business Innovation and Skills. http://www.bis.gov.uk/files/file52072.pdf

Cook, D. (1989) *Rich Law, Poor Law: Different Responses to Tax and Supplementary Benefit Fraud*. Milton Keynes: Open University Press.

Cook, D. and Hudson, B. (eds) (1993) *Racism and Criminology*. London: Sage.

Cook, K. and Jones, H. (2007) 'Surviving Victimhood: The Impact of Feminist Campaigns', pp 125–45 in Walklate, S. (ed.) *Handbook of Victims and Victimology*. Cullompton: Willan.

Cooper, C. (2009) 'Refugees, Asylum Seekers, and Criminal Justice', pp 137–53 in Bhui, H. S. (ed.) *Race and Criminal Justice*. London: Sage.

Copes, H. and Cherbonneau, M. (2006) 'The key to auto theft: emerging methods of auto theft from the offenders' perspective', *British Journal of Criminology*, 46(1): 917–34.

Corbett, C. (2003) *Car Crime*. Cullompton: Willan.

Cornish, D. B. and Clarke, R. V. G. (1986) *The Reasoning Criminal*. New York: Springer-Verlag.

Cowie, J., Cowie, V. and Slater, E. (1968) *Delinquency in Girls*. London: Heinemann.

Cox, G. L. (1998) *Determination in the E-coli 0 157 Fatal Accident Inquiry*. Dumfries and Galloway: Sheriffdom of South Strathclyde.

Crime Concern (1998) *Counting the Cost – A Briefing Paper on Financial Losses Arising from Crime*. Crime Concern: The Thames Valley Partnership.

Crelinsten, R. D. (2003) 'A world of torture: a constructed reality', *Theoretical Criminology*, 7(3): 293–318.

Critcher, C. (2003) *Moral Panics and the Media*. Buckingham: Open University Press.

Croall, H. (1988) 'Mistakes, accidents and someone else's fault: the trading offender in court', *Journal of Law and Society*, 15(3): 293–315.

Croall, H. (1989) 'Who is the White-Collar Criminal?' *British Journal of Criminology*, 29(2): 157–74.

Croall, H. (1992) *White-Collar Crime*. Buckingham: Open University Press.

Croall, H. (1995) 'Target Women: Women's Victimization from White-Collar Crime', in Dobash, R., Dobash, R. and Noaks, L. (eds) *Gender and Crime*. Cardiff: Cardiff University Press.

Croall, H. (1997) 'Business, crime and the community,' *International Journal of Risk, Security and Crime Prevention*, 3(4): 281–92.

Croall, H. (2001a) *Understanding White-Collar Crime*. Buckingham: Open University Press.

Croall, H. (2001b) 'The Victims of White-Collar Crime', pp 35–54 in Lindgren, Sven-Ake (ed.) *White-Collar Crime Research: Old Views and Future Potentials*. Lectures and Papers from a Scandinavian Seminar, The Swedish National Council for Crime Prevention (*Brottsförebyggande rådet*).

Croall, H. (2003) '"Men's Business"? Some gender questions about white-collar crime', *Criminal Justice Matters*, 53: 26–7.

Croall, H. (2004) 'Combating financial crime: regulatory versus crime control approaches', *Journal of Financial Crime*, 11(1): 45–55.

Croall, H. (2005) 'Transnational White-Collar Crime', pp 227–46 in Sheptycki, J. and Wardak, A. (eds) *Transnational and Comparative Criminology*. London: Glasshouse Press.

Croall, H. (2006) 'Criminal justice in post-devolutionary Scotland', *Critical Social Policy*, 26(3): 587–607.

Croall, H. (2007a) 'Social Class, Social Exclusion, Victims and Crime', pp 50–77 in Davies, P., Francis, P. and Greer, C. (eds) *Victims, Crime and Society*. London: Sage.

Croall, H. (2007b) 'Victims of White-Collar and Corporate Crime', pp 78–108 in Davies, P., Francis, P. and Greer, C. (eds) *Victims, Crime and Society*. London: Sage.

Croall, H. (2007c) 'Food Crime', pp 206–29 in Beirne, P. and South, N. (eds) *Issues in Green Criminology: Confronting Harms Against Environments, Humanity and Other Animals*. Cullompton: Willan.

Croall, H. (2009a) 'White-collar crime, consumers and victimization', *Crime, Law and Social Change*, 51(1): 127–46.

Croall, H. (2009b) 'Community safety and economic crime', *Criminology and Criminal Justice*, 9(2): 165–85.

Croall, H. (2010) 'Middle Range Business Crime', pp 678–97 in Brookman, F., Maguire, M., Pierpoint, H. and Bennett, T. (eds) *Handbook on Crime*. Cullompton: Willan.

Croall, H. and Frondigoun, L. (2010) 'Race, Ethnicity and Criminal Justice in Scotland', pp 111–31 in Croall, H., Mooney, G. and Munro, M. (eds) *Criminal Justice in Scotland*. Cullompton: Willan.

Croall, H., Mooney, G. and Munro, M. (2010) 'Criminal Justice in Contemporary Scotland', pp 3–20 in Croall, H., Mooney G. and Munro, M. (eds) *Criminal Justice in Scotland*. Cullompton: Willan.

Croall, H. and Ross, J. (2002) 'Sentencing the Corporate Offender: Legal and Social Issues', pp 528–47 in Hutton, N. and Tata C. (eds) *Sentencing and Society*. Aldershot: Ashgate.

Crow, I. (1989) *Unemployment, Crime and Offenders*. London: Routledge.

Cullen, W. D. (Lord Cullen) (1990) *The Public Inquiry into the Piper Alpha Disaster* (Cullen Report) Cm. 1310. London: Stationery Office Books.

Cullen, F. T., Maakestad, W. J. and Cavender, G. (1984) 'The Ford Pinto Case and Beyond', pp 103–30 in Hochstedler, E. (ed.) *Corporations as Criminals*. Beverly Hills, CA: Sage.

Currie, E. (1991) *International Developments in Crime and Social Policy*. NACRO Crime and Social Policy: 107–20. London: NACRO.

Currie, E. (1996) 'Social Crime Prevention Strategies in a Market Society', pp 369–80 in Muncie, J., McLaughlin, E. and Langan, M. (eds) *Criminological Perspectives: Essential Readings*. London: Sage.

Currie, E. (2007) 'Social Action', pp 326–37 in Vogel, M. E. (ed.) *Crime, Inequality and the State*. London: Routledge.

Daly, K. (1989) 'Gender and varieties of white collar crime', *Criminology* 27: 769–94.

Daly, M. and Wilson, M. (1988) *Homicide*. New York: de Gruyter.

Davidson, J. and Martellozzo, E. (2008) 'Protecting children online: towards a safer internet', pp 338–55 in Letherby, G., Williams, K., Birch, P. and Cain, M. (eds) *Sex As Crime*. Cullompton: Willan.

Davies, A. (2007a) 'The Scottish Chicago: from "Hooligans" to "Gangsters" in Inter-War Glasgow', *Cultural and Social History*, 4(4): 511–27.

Davies, A. (2007b) 'Glasgow's "Reign of Terror": street gangs, racketeering and intimidation in the 1920s and 1930s', *Contemporary British History*, 21(4): 405–27.

Davies, M., Croall, H. and Tyrer, J. (2009) *Criminal Justice: An Introduction to the Criminal Justice System in England and Wales* 4th edn. London: Longman.

Davies, P. (1996) 'Crime, Victims and Criminal Justice Policy', pp 71–89 in Davies, P., Francis, P. and Jupp, V. (eds) *Understanding Victimization*. Gateshead: Northumbria Social Science Press.

Davies, P. (2003) 'Is economic crime a man's game?' *Feminist Theory*, 4(3): 283–303.

Davies, P. (2005) 'Women and Crime for Economic Gain'. Unpublished PhD Thesis, University of Northumbria.

Davies, P. (2007a) 'Lessons from the Gender Agenda', pp 175–202 in Walklate, S. (ed.) (2007) *Handbook of Victims and Victimology*. Cullompton: Willan.

Davies, P. (2007b) 'Women, Victims and Crime', pp 165–201 in Davies, P., Francis, P. and Greer, C. (eds) *Victims, Crime and Society*. London: Sage.

Davies, P., Francis, P. and Jupp, V. (2003) 'Understanding Victimology: Theory, Method and Practice', in Davies, P., Francis, P. and Jupp, V. (eds) *Victimization: Theory, Research and Policy*. Basingstoke: Palgrave Macmillan.

Davies, P., Francis, P. and Jupp, V. (eds) (1996) *Understanding Victimization*. Gateshead: Northumbria Social Science Press.

Davies, P., Francis, P. and Greer, C. (2007) *Victims, Crime and Society*. London: Sage.

D'Cruze, S., Walklate, S. and Pegg, S. (2006) *Murder: Social and Historical Approaches to Understanding Murder and Murderers*. Cullompton: Willan.

Deans, J. (2010) 'TV ratings: 5m gripped by Ipswich serial killer drama', *Guardian* 27/04/10. http://www.guardian.co.uk/media/2010/apr/27/ipswich-five-daughters-ratings

De Haan, W. and Vos, J. (2003) 'A crying shame: the over-rationalized conception of man in the rational choice perspective', *Theoretical Criminology*, 7(1): 29–54.

Dempsey, M. M. (2006) 'What counts as domestic violence? A conceptual analysis', *William and Mary Journal of Women and the Law*, 12(2): 301–33.

Department of Trade and Industry (2002) *Car Servicing and Repairs: Mystery Shopping Research*. London: Department of Trade and Industry. http://www.bis.gov.uk/files/file28064.pdf

Department of Trade and Industry (2004) *Extending Competitive Markets: Empowered Consumers, Competitive Business*. London: Department of Trade and Industry. http://www.cosla.gov.uk/%5Cattachments%5Cexecgroups%5Ces%5Cesoct04item9.doc

Department of Trade and Industry (2005) *Home Accidents involving product fault or contributory behaviour*. London: Department of Trade and Industry. www.dti.gov.uk/homesafety network/gh-rsrch.htm

Di Nicola, A. (2007) 'Researching into human trafficking: Issues and problems', pp 49–72 in Lee, M. (ed.) *Human Trafficking*. Cullompton: Willan.

Ditton, J. (1977) *Part Time Crime: An Ethnography of Fiddling and Pilferage*. London: Macmillan.

Dixon, M., Reed, H., Rogers, B. and Stone, L. (2006) *CrimeShare: The Unequal Impact of Crime*. London: IPPR.

Dobash, R. and Dobash, R. (1992) *Women, Violence and Social Change*. London: Routledge.

Dobash, R., Dobash, R., Cavanagh, K. and Lewis, R. (2000) *Changing Violent Men*. Thousand Oaks, CA: Sage.

Dobash, R. and Dobash, R. (2001) *Homicide in Britain*. Research Bulletin No. 1, University of Manchester.

Dobash, R. and Dobash, R. (2004) 'Women's violence to men in intimate relationships', *British Journal of Criminology*, 44(3): 324–49.

Dodge, M. (2006) 'From Pink to White with Various Shades of Embezzlement: Women who Commit White-Collar Crimes', pp 379–404 in Pontell, H. and Geis, G. (eds) *International Handbook of White-Collar and Corporate Crime*. Irvine, CA: Springer.

Doig, A. (1984) *Corruption and Misconduct in Contemporary British Politics*. Harmondsworth: Penguin.

Doig, A. (1996) 'From Lynskey to Nolan: The Corruption of British Politics and Public Service', *Journal of Law and Society*, 23(1): 36–56.

Doig, A. (2006) *Fraud*. Cullompton: Willan.

Doig, A. (2010) *State Crime*. Cullompton: Willan.

Dorn, N. and South, N. (1990) 'Drugs Markets and Law Enforcement', *British Journal of Criminology*, 30(2): 171–88.

Dorn, N., Murji, K. and South, N. (1992) *Traffickers: Drugs Markets and Law Enforcement*. London: Routledge.

Dorn, N., Levi, M., and King. L. (2005) *Literature Review on Upper Level Drug Trafficking*. Home Office Online Report, 22/05. http://rds.homeoffice.gov.uk/rds/pdfs05/rdsolr2205.pdf

Dowie, M. (1977). 'Pinto Madness', pp 13–29 in Hills, S. (ed.) (1987) *Corporate Violence: Injury and Death for Profit*. Totowa, NJ: Rowman and Littlefield.

Downes, D. (1966) *The Delinquent Solution: A Study in Subcultural Theory*. London: Routledge.

Downes, D. (1997) 'Law and order futures', *Criminal Justice Matters*, 26: 3–4.

Downes, D. (2004) 'New Labour and the lost causes of crime', *Criminal Justice Matters*, 55, Spring 2004, pp 4–5.

Downes, D. and Rock, P. (2007) *Understanding Deviance: A Guide to the Sociology of Crime and Rule Breaking* revised 5th edn. Oxford: Clarendon Press.

Dube, S. (2005) 'Polluting Farmer fined £20,000 as 2,100 fish die', *Western Mail*, 18/10/05. http://www.redorbit.com/news/science/277106/polluting_farmer_fined_pounds_20000_as_2100_fish_die/index.html

Durkheim, E. (1964 (1895)) *The Rules of Sociological Method*. New York: Free Press.

Durkheim, E. (1970 (1897)) *Suicide*. London: Routledge & Kegan Paul.

Earl, S. and Sharpe, K. (2008) 'Intimacy, Pleasure and the men who pay for sex', pp 63–79 in Letherby, G., Williams, K., Birch, P. and Cain, M. (eds) *Sex As Crime*. Cullompton: Willan.

Eaton, M. (1986) *Justice for Women?* Milton Keynes: Open University Press.

Edie.net (2010) 'Northern Ireland's "dirty" beaches slammed by report', 28/05/10. http://www.edie.net/news/print.asp?id=18195

Edward, M. (2008) *Who Belongs to Glasgow?* Edinburgh: Luath Press.

Edwards, A. (2005) 'Transnational Organized Crime', pp 211–26 in Sheptycki, J. and Wardak, A. (eds) *Transnational and Comparative Criminology*. London: Glasshouse Press.

Edwards, A. and Levi, M. (2008) 'Researching the organization of serious crimes' in Edwards, A. and Levi, M. (eds) *The Organization of Serious Crimes: Developments in Research and Theory*. Special issue of *Criminology and Criminal Justice*, 8(4): 363–88.

Edwards, R. (2009) 'Revealed: radioactive waste leak into the Clyde', *Sunday Herald*, 20/09/09. http://www.robedwards.com/2009/09/revealed-radioactive-waste-leak-from-hunterston.html

Edwards, R. and Carell, S. (2009) 'MoD guilty of repeated nuclear safety breaches', *Guardian* 27/04/09. http://www.guardian.co.uk/environment/2009/apr/27/nuclear-mod-clyde-saftey-breaches

Edwards, S. (1981) *Female Sexuality and the Law*. Oxford: Martin Robertson.

Ellingworth, D., Farrell, G. and Pease, K. (1995) 'A victim is a victim is a victim: Chronic victimization in four sweeps of the British Crime Survey', *British Journal of Criminology*, 35(3): 360–5.

Emsley, C. (1996) *Crime and Society in England 1750–1900*. London: Longman.

Ermann, M. and Lundman, R. (eds) (1978) *Corporate and Governmental Deviance: Problems of Organizational Behaviour in Contemporary Society*. New York: Oxford University Press.

European Commission (2001) 'Joint Report from Commission Services and Europol – Towards a European Strategy to Prevent Organised Crime', Commission Staff Working Paper, SEC (2001) 433 (Brussels, 13 March).

Evans, K. and Fraser, P. (2003) 'Communities and Victimization', pp 80–100 in Davies, P., Francis, P. and Jupp, V. (eds) *Victimization: Theory, Research and Policy*. Basingstoke: Palgrave Macmillan.

Evans-Pritchard, A. (2002) 'Financial watchdog discloses EU fraud and error', 06/11/02. http://www.telegraph.co.uk/news/worldnews/europe/1412372/Financial-watchdog-discloses-EU-fraud-and-error.html

Evening Times (2008) '250 Firms fined in blitz on littering', 03/09/08. http://www.eveningtimes.co.uk/250-firms-fined-in-blitz-on-littering-1.962408

Eysenck, H. (1977) *Crime and Personality*. London: Routledge & Kegan Paul.

Farrell, G., Phillips, C. and Pease, K. (1995) 'Like taking candy: Why does repeat victimization occur?', *British Journal of Criminology*, 35(3): 384–99.

Farrington, D. (2007) 'Childhood Risk Factors and Risk-Focused Prevention', pp 602–40 in Maguire, M., Morgan, R. and Reiner, R. (eds) *The Oxford Handbook of Criminology* 4th edn. Oxford: Clarendon Press.

Felson, M. (1998) *Crime and Everyday Life* 2nd edn. Thousand Oaks, CA: Pine Forge Press.

Ferrell, J. (1995) 'Style Matters', pp 169–89 in Ferrell, J. and Sanders, C. (eds) *Cultural Criminology*. Boston: Northeastern University Press.

Ferrell, J. (2006) 'Cultural Criminology', pp 103–6 in McLaughlin, E. and Muncie, J. (eds) *The Sage Dictionary of Criminology* 2nd edn. London: Sage.

Ferrell, J., Hayward, K. and Young, J. (2008) *Cultural Criminology*. London: Sage.

Ferris, P. with McKay, R. (2002) *The Ferris Conspiracy*. Edinburgh: Mainstream Publishing.

Field, S. (1990) *Trends in Crime and their Interpretation: A Study of Recorded Crime in Post War England and Wales*. Home Office Research Study No. 119. London: HMSO.

Field, S. (1996) 'Crime and Consumption', pp 115–20 in Muncie, J., McLaughlin, E. and Langan, M. (eds) *Criminological Perspectives: A Reader*. London: Sage.

Fijnaut, C. (1990) 'Organized crime: A comparison between the United States of America and Western Europe', *British Journal of Criminology*, 30(3): 321–40.

Finley, L. (1996) 'The Pharmaceutical Industry and Women's Reproductive Health: the Perils of Ignoring Risk and Blaming Women', pp 59–110 in Szockyj, E. and Fox, J. G. (eds) (1996) *Corporate Victimization of Women*. Northeastern University Press.

Fisse, B. and Braithwaite, J. (1993) *Corporations, Crimes and Accountability*. Cambridge: Cambridge University Press.

Fitzgerald, G. (2006) 'The realities of elder abuse criminology', pp 90–106 in Wahidin, A. and Cain, M. (eds) *Age, Crime and Society*. Cullompton: Willan.

Fitzgerald, M. (1993) 'Racism: Establishing the Phenomenon', pp 45–63 in Cook, D. and Hudson, B. (eds) *Racism and Criminology*. London: Sage.

Fitzgerald, M. (1995) 'Ethnic Differences', pp 158–74 in Walker, M. (ed.) *Interpreting Crime Statistics*. Oxford: Clarendon Press.

Fitzgerald, M. and Hale, C. (1996) *Ethnic Minorities, Victimization and Racial Harassment: Findings from the 1988 and 1992 British Crime Surveys*. Home Office Research Study No. 154. London: Home Office.

Flood-Page, C., Campbell, S., Harrington, V. and Miller, J. (2000) *Youth Crime: Findings from the 1998/99 Youth Lifestyle Survey*. Home Office Research Study No. 209. London: Home Office.

Fooks, G. (2003) 'In the valley of the Blind the One-Eyed Man is King: corporate crime and the myopia of financial regulation', pp 105–28 in Tombs, S. and Whyte, D. (eds) *Unmasking the Crimes of the Powerful*. New York: Lang.

Foster, J. (1990) *Villains: Crime and Community in the Inner City*. London: Routledge.

Foster, J. (2002) '"People pieces": the neglected but essential elements of community crime prevention', pp 167–96 in Hughes, G. and Edward, A. (eds) *Crime Control and Community: The New Politics of Public Safety*. Cullompton: Willan.

Francis, P. (2007a) 'Race', Ethnicity, Victims and Crime', pp 109–41 in Davies, P., Francis, P. and Greer, C. (eds) *Victims, Crime and Society*. London: Sage.

Francis, P. (2007b) 'Young People, Victims and Crime', pp 202–33 in Davies, P., Francis, P. and Greer, C. (eds) *Victims, Crime and Society*. London: Sage.

Freel, R. and French, B. (2006) *Perceptions of Crime: Findings from the 2005 Northern Ireland Crime Survey*. Belfast: Northern Ireland Office. http://www.nio.gov.uk/perceptions_of_crime_findings_from_the_2005_northern_ireland_survey.pdf

Freel, R., Quigley, D. and Toner, S. (2009) *Experience of Crime: Findings from the 2007/08 Northern Ireland Crime Survey*. Belfast: Northern Ireland Office. http://www.nio.gov.uk/nics_2007-08_experience_of_crime_bulletin.pdf

Friedrichs, D. O. (1992) 'State Crime or Governmental Crime: Making Sense of the Conceptual Confusion', pp 53–80 in Ross, J. (ed.) *Controlling State Crime*. New York: Garland.

Friedrichs, D. O. (2002a) 'State–Corporate Crime in a Globalized World: Myth or Major Challenge?' pp 53–72 in Potter, G. W. (ed.) *Controversies in White-Collar Crime*. Cincinnati: Anderson.

Friedrichs, D. O. (2002b) 'Occupational crime, occupational deviance, and workplace crime: Sorting out the difference', *Criminal Justice*, 2(3): 243–56.

Friedrichs, D. O. (2004) 'Enron et al.: paradigmatic White-Collar crime cases for the New Century', *Critical Criminology*, 12(2): 113–32.

Friedrichs, D. O. (2006a) *Trusted Criminals: White-Collar Crime in Contemporary Society* 3rd edn. Belmont, CA: Wadsworth.

Friedrichs, D. O. (2006b) 'White-Collar Crime in a Postmodern, Globalized World', pp 163–84 in Pontell, H. and Geis, G. (eds) *International Handbook of White-Collar and Corporate Crime*. Irvine, CA: Springer.

Friedrichs, D. O. (2009) 'Exorbitant CEO compensation: just reward or grand theft?', *Crime, Law and Social Change*, 51(1): 45–72.

Friedrichs, D. O. (2010) 'Toward a Prospective Criminology of State Crime', pp 67–82 in Chambliss, W., Michalowski, R. and Kramer, R. (eds) *State Crime in the Global Age*. Cullompton: Willan.

Friedrichs, D. O. and Friedrichs, J. (2002) 'The World Bank and crimes of globalization: A case study', *Social Justice* 29(1–2): 13–36.

Frondigoun, L., Croall, H., Hughes, B., Russell, L., Russell, R. and Scott, G. (2007) *Researching Minority Ethnic Young People in Edinburgh and the Greater Glasgow Area*. Glasgow: Glasgow Caledonian University.

Frondigoun, L., Nicholson, J., Robertson, A. and Monigatti, S. (2008) *Building Safer Communities: An Evaluation of the Enhanced Policing Plan in the Shettleston, Baillieston and Greater Easterhouse Area of Glasgow*. Report prepared for Strathclyde Police Force. Glasgow: Glasgow Caledonian University. http://www.sipr.ac.uk/downloads/Building_Safer_Communities.pdf

Furedi, F. (2003) *Culture of Fear: Risk Taking and the Morality of Low Expectation*. London: Continuum.

Furedi, F. (2007) *Invitation to Terror: The Expanding Empire of the Unknown*. London: Continuum.

Furedi, F. (2009) 'Terrorism and the Politics of Fear', pp 343–62 in Hale, C., Hayward, K., Wahidin, A. and Wincup, E. (eds) *Criminology* 2nd edn. Oxford: Oxford University Press.

Fyfe, N. (1997) 'Crime', pp 244–61 in Pacione, M. (ed.) *Britain's Divided Cities: Geographies of Division in Urban Britain*. London: Routledge.

Gadd, D. (2002) 'Masculinities, Violence and Defended Social Subjects', *Theoretical Criminology*, 4(4): 429–49.

Garland, D. (1999) 'Preface', pp xiii–xvi in Duff, P. and Hutton, N. (eds) (1999) *Criminal Justice Scotland*. Aldershot: Ashgate.

Garland, D. (2008) 'On the Concept of Moral Panic', *Crime Media Culture*, 4(9): 9–30.

Geis, G. (1988) 'From Deuteronomy to deniability: a historical perlustration on white-collar crime', *Justice Quarterly*, 5(1): 7–23.

Geis, G. (2007) *White-Collar and Corporate Crime*. New Jersey: Pearson Prentice Hall.

Geis, G. and Edelhertz, H. (1973) 'Criminal law and consumer fraud: a socio-legal view', *American Criminal Law Review*, 2: 989–1010.

Gelsthorpe, L. (1989) *Sexism and the Female Offender*. Aldershot: Gower.

Gelsthorpe, L. (2002) 'Feminism and Criminology', pp 511–33 in Maguire, M., Morgan, R. and Reiner, R. (eds) *The Oxford Handbook of Criminology* 3rd edn. Oxford: Clarendon Press.

Gelsthorpe, L. and Morris, A. (1988) 'Feminism and Criminology in Britain', pp 93–110 in Rock, P. (ed.) *A History of British Criminology*. Oxford: Clarendon Press.

Gelsthorpe, L. and Morris, A. (1990) 'Introduction: Transforming and Transgressing Criminology', pp 1–6 in Gelsthorpe, L. and Morris, A. (eds) *Feminist Perspectives in Criminology*. Milton Keynes: Open University Press.

Genn, H. (1988) 'Multiple Victimization', pp 90–100 in Maguire, M. and Pointing, J. (eds) *Victims of Crime: A New Deal?* Milton Keynes: Open University Press.

Gilbert, M. and Russell, S. (2002) 'Globalization of criminal justice in the corporate context', *Crime, Law and Social Change*, 38(3): 211–38.

Gill, K., Woolley, A. and Gill, M. (1994) 'Insurance Fraud: The Business as a Victim?', pp 73–82 in Gill, M. (ed.) *Crime at Work: Studies in Security and Crime Prevention*. Leicester: Perpetuity Press.

Gill, Lord (2009) *The ICL Inquiry Report: Explosion at Grovepark Mills, Maryhill, Glasgow*. Edinburgh: The Stationery Office. http://www.theiclinquiry.org/documents/documents/HC838ICL_Inquiry_Report.pdf

Gill, M. and Goldstraw-White, J. (2010) 'Theft and Fraud by Employees', pp 100–19 in Brookman, F., Maguire, M., Pierpoint, H. and Bennett T. (eds) *Handbook on Crime*. Cullompton: Willan.

Gill, M. and Matthews, R. (1994) 'Robbers on Robbery: Offenders' Perspectives', pp 11–28 in Gill, M. (ed.) *Crime at Work: Studies in Security and Crime Prevention*. Leicester: Perpetuity Press.

Gill, P. (2006) 'Organized crime', pp 280–82 in McLaughlin, E. and Muncie, J. (eds) *The Sage Dictionary of Criminology*. London: Sage.

Gillespie, T. (1996) 'Rape Crisis Centres and "Male Rape": A Face of the Backlash', pp 148–65 in Hester, M., Kelly, L. and Radford, J. (eds) *Women, Violence and Male Power: Feminist Research, Activism and Practice*. Buckingham: Open University Press.

Gilling, D. (2001) 'Community safety and social policy', *European Journal on Criminal Policy and Research*, 9: 381–400.

Gilroy, P. (1987a) *There Ain't No Black in the Union Jack: The Cultural Politics of Race and Nation*. London: Hutchinson.

Gilroy, P. (1987b) 'The Myth of Black Criminality', pp 107–20 in Scraton, P. (ed.) *Law, Order and the Authoritarian State: Readings in Critical Criminology*. Milton Keynes: Open University Press.

Glueck, S. and Glueck, E. (1950) *Unravelling Juvenile Delinquency*. New York: Commonwealth Fund.

Goffman, E. (1968) *Asylums*. Harmondsworth: Penguin.

Goodey, J. (2003) 'Migration, Crime and Victimhood: Responses to sex trafficking in the EU', *Punishment and Society*, 5(4): 415–31.

Goodey, J. (2003) 'Recognizing organized crime's victims: the case of sex trafficking in the EU', pp 157–74 in Edwards, A. and Gill, P. (eds) *Transnational Organized Crime: Perspectives on Global Security*. London: Routledge.

Goodey, J. (2005) *Victims and Victimology: Research, Policy and Practice*. London: Pearson, Longman.

Goodey, J. (2007) 'Race, religion and victimization: UK and European responses', pp 423–45 in Walklate, S. (ed.) *Handbook of Victims and Victimology*. Cullompton: Willan Publishing.

Goodey, J. (2008) 'Human trafficking: Sketchy data and policy responses', *Criminology and Criminal Justice*, 8(4): 421–42.

Goodey, J. (2010) 'Human Trafficking', pp 698–734 in Brookman, F., Maguire, M., Pierpoint, H. and Bennett, T. (eds) *Handbook on Crime*. Cullompton: Willan.

Gorgen, T. (2006) '"As if I didn't exist" – elder abuse and neglect in nursing homes', pp 71–89 in Wahidin, A. and Cain, M. (eds) *Age, Crime and Society*. Cullompton: Willan.

Gottfredson, M. and Hirschi, T. (1990) *A General Theory of Crime*. California: Stanford University Press.

Graef, R. (1990) *Talking Blues: The Police in Their Own Words*. London: Fontana.

Graham, J. and Bowling, B. (1995) *Young People and Crime*. Research Study No. 145. London: Home Office Research and Statistics Department.

Graham, P. and Clarke, J. (1996) 'Dangerous Places: Crime and the City', pp 143–81 in Muncie, J. and McLaughlin, E. (eds) *The Problem of Crime*. London: Sage.

Green, S. (2007) 'Crime, Victimization and Vulnerability', pp 91–118 in Walklate, S. (ed.) *Handbook of Victims and Victimology*. Cullompton: Willan.

Green, P. (2010) 'The State, Terrorism and Crimes against Humanity', pp 209–45 in Muncie, J., Talbot, D. and Walters, R. (eds) *Crime: Local and Global*. Cullompton: Willan.

Green, P. and Ward, T. (2000) 'State Crime, Human Rights, and the Limits of Criminology', *Social Justice*, 27(1): 101.

Green, P. and Ward, T. (2004) *State Crime: Governments, Violence and Corruption*. London: Polity.

Green, P., Ward, T. and McConnachie, K. (2007) 'Logging and legality: Environmental crime, civil society, and the state', *Social Justice*, 34(2): 94–110.

Greer, C. (2006) 'Sex Crime', pp 377–80 in McLaughlin, E. and Muncie, J. (eds) *The Sage Dictionary of Criminology*. London: Sage.

Greer, C. (2007) 'News Media, Victims and Crime', pp 20–49 in Davies, P., Francis, P. and Greer, C. (eds) *Victims, Crime and Society*. London: Sage.

Greer, C. (2009) 'Crime and Media: understanding the connections', pp 177–203 in Hale, C., Hayward, K., Wahidin, A. and Wincup, E. (eds) *Criminology* 2nd edn. Oxford: Oxford University Press.

Gresswell, D. and Hollin, C. (1994) 'Multiple Murder: A Review', *British Journal of Criminology*, 34(1): 1–15.

Grover, C. (2008) *Crime and Inequality*. Cullompton: Willan.

Hagell, A. and Newburn, T. (1994) *Persistent Young Offenders*. London: Policy Studies Institute.

Hague, L. (2001) *International Crime Victimization Survey 2000: Key Findings for Northern Ireland*. Belfast: Northern Ireland Office.

Haines, F. and White, R. (2004) *Crime and Criminology* 3rd edn. Oxford: Oxford University Press.

Hale, C. (1999) 'The Labour Market and Post-War Crime Trends in England and Wales', pp 30–56 in Carlen, P. and Morgan, R. (eds) *Crime Unlimited: Questions for the 21st Century*. London: Macmillan.

Hale, C. (2009) 'Economic Marginalization, Social Exclusion and Crime', pp 365–84 in Hale, C., Hayward, K., Wahidin, A. and Wincup, E. (eds) *Criminology* 2nd edn. Oxford: Oxford University Press.

Hall, N. (2005) *Hate Crime*. Cullompton: Willan.

Hall, R. (1985) *Ask Any Woman*. London: Falling Wall Press.

Hall, S. (1996) 'Drifting into a Law and Order Society', pp 257–70 in Muncie, J., McLaughlin, E. and Langan, M. (eds) *Criminological Perspectives: Essential Readings*. London: Sage.

Hall, S. and Jefferson, T. (eds) (1976) *Resistance Through Rituals: Youth Subcultures in Post-War Britain*. London: Hutchinson.

Hall, S., Critcher, C., Jefferson, T., Clarke, J. and Roberts, B. (1978) *Policing the Crisis: Mugging, the State and Law and Order*. London: Macmillan.

Hall, S. (2002) 'Daubing the drudges of fury: Men, violence and the piety of the "Hegemonic Masculinity" thesis', *Theoretical Criminology*, 6(1): 35–61.

Hall, S. and Winlow, S. (2003) 'Culture, gender and male violence: A key problem', *Criminal Justice Matters*, 53(1): 14–15.

Hallsworth, S. (2005) *Street Crime*. Cullompton: Willan.

Hallsworth, S. and Young, T. (2008) 'Gang talk and gang talkers: a critique', *Crime Media Culture*, 4: 175–95.

Halsey, M. (2004) 'Against Green Criminology', *British Journal of Criminology*, 44(6): 833–53.

Hamm, M. (2005) book review: 'After September 11', *Theoretical Criminology*, 9(2): 237–50.

Hancock, L. (2006) 'Urban Regeneration, Young People, Crime and Criminalization', pp 172–86 in Goldson, B. and Muncie, J. (eds) *Youth, Crime and Justice*. London: Sage.

Hansen, K. and Machin, S. (2002) 'Spatial crime patterns and the introduction of the UK minimum wage', *Journal of Quantitative Criminology*, 64(1): 677–97.

Hartless, J., Ditton, J., Nair, G. and Phillips, S. (1995) 'More sinned against than sinning: A study of young teenagers' experience of crime', *British Journal of Criminology*, 35(10): 114–33.

Harvey, B. W. (1982) *Law of Consumer Protection and Fair Trading*, 2nd edn. London: Butterworths.

Hatashin, O. (2008) 'Crime and Culture: Corporate Crime and Criminal Justice in a Different Cultural Environment', pp 141–60 in Minkes, J. and Minkes, L. (eds) *Corporate and White-Collar Crime*. London: Sage.

Hawkins, K. (1984) *Environment and Enforcement: Regulation and the Social Definition of Pollution*. Oxford: Clarendon Press.

Hawkins, K. (1990) 'Compliance Strategy, Prosecution Policy and Aunt Sally – A Comment on Pearce and Tombs', *British Journal of Criminology*, 30(4): 444–67.

Hayward, K. (2002) 'The vilification and pleasure of youthful transgression', pp 80–94 in Muncie, J., Hughes, G. and McLaughlin, E. (eds) *Youth Justice: Critical Readings*. London: Sage.

Hayward, K. (2004) *City Limits: Crime, Consumer Culture and The Urban Experience*. London: Glasshouse Press.

Hayward, K. and Young, J. (2004) 'Cultural Criminology: some notes on the script', *Theoretical Criminology*, 8(3): 259–73.

Hayward, K. and Hobbs, D. (2007) 'Beyond the Binge in "booze Britain": market-led liminalization and the spectacle of binge drinking', *British Journal of Sociology*, 58(3): 437–56.

Hayward, K. and Young, J. (2007) 'Cultural Criminology', pp 102–19 in Maguire, M., Morgan, R. and Reiner, R. (eds) *The Oxford Handbook of Criminology* 4th edn. Clarendon: Oxford University Press.

Hebenton, T. (2008) 'Sexual offenders and public protection in an uncertain age', pp 321–37 in Letherby, G., Williams, K., Birch, P. and Cain, M. (eds) *Sex As Crime*. Cullompton: Willan.

Hebenton, B. and Thomas, T. (1996) 'Tracking Sex Offenders', *Howard Journal*, 35(2): 97–112.

Heidensohn, F. (1968) 'The deviance of women: a critique and an enquiry', *British Journal of Sociology*, 19(2): 160–75.

Heidensohn, F. (1989) *Crime and Society*. London: Macmillan.

Heidensohn, F. (1992) *Women in Control? The Role of Women in Law Enforcement*. Oxford: Oxford University Press.

Heidensohn, F. (1995) 'Feminist Perspectives and their Impact on Criminology and Criminal Justice in Britain', pp 63–85 in Rafter, N. and Heidensohn, F. (eds) *International Feminist Perspectives in Criminology: Engendering a Discipline*. Milton Keynes: Open University Press.

Heidensohn, F. (1996) *Women and Crime* 2nd edn. London: Macmillan.

Heidensohn, F. and Gelsthorpe, L. (1997) 'Gender and Crime', pp 381–420 in Maguire, M., Morgan, R. and Reiner, R. (eds) *The Oxford Handbook of Criminology* 2nd edn. Oxford: Clarendon Press.

Heidensohn, F. and Gelsthorpe, L. (2007) 'Gender and crime' in Maguire, M., Morgan, R. and Reiner R. (eds) *The Oxford Handbook of Criminology* 4th edn. Oxford: Clarendon Press.

Hennessey, J. (1994) in *Scotsman* 8/12/94.

Henry, S. (1978) *The Hidden Economy: The Context and Control of Borderline Crime*. Oxford: Martin Robertson.

Hentig, H. von (1948) *The Criminal and His Victim*. New Haven: Yale University Press.

Herrnstein, R. J. and Murray, C. (1995) *The Bell Curve*. New York: Basic Books.

Hester, M., Kelly, L. and Radford, J. (eds) (1996) *Women, Violence and Male Power*. Buckingham: Open University Press.

Hester, S. and Eglin, P. (1992) *A Sociology of Crime*. London: Routledge.

Higgins, N. and Millard, B. (2009) 'Geographic patterns of crime', pp 143–87 in Walker, A., Flatley, J., Kershaw, C. and Moon, D. (eds) *Crime in England and Wales 2008/2009: Findings from the British Crime Survey and Police Recorded Crime*. Home Office Statistical Bulletin. http://rds.homeoffice.gov.uk/rds/pdfs09/hosb1109vol1.pdf

Hillyard, P. (1987) 'The Normalization of Special Powers: From Northern Ireland to Britain', pp 279–307 in Scraton, P. (ed.) *Law, Order and the Authoritarian State*. Milton Keynes: Open University Press.

Hillyard, P. (1993) *Suspect Community: People's Experience of the Prevention of Terrorism Acts in Britain*. London: Pluto Press.

Hillyard, P. (1996) 'The Stalker Affair and the Quest for Justice: The Failure of the Law in Northern Ireland', Paper presented to the Law Society Association Annual Conference, Strathclyde University, 10 July.

Hillyard, P. (2003) 'Imaginative Crimes or Crimes of the Imagination: Researching the Secret State', pp 201–19 in Tombs, S. and Whyte, D. (eds) *Unmasking the Crimes of the Powerful*. New York: Lang.

Hillyard, P. and Tombs, S. (2004) 'Beyond Criminology?', pp 10–29 in Hillyard, P., Pantazis, C., Tombs, S. and Gordon, D. (eds) *Beyond Criminology: Taking Harm Seriously*. London: Pluto Press.

Hillyard, P., Sim, J., Tombs, S. and Whyte, D. (2004) 'Leaving a "stain upon the silence": Contemporary criminology and the Politics of Dissent', *British Journal of Criminology*, 44(3): 369–90.

Hindelang, M. J., Gottfredson, M. R. and Garofalo, J. (1978) *Victims of Personal Crime: An Empirical Foundation for a Theory of Personal Victimization*. Cambridge: Ballinger.

Hirsch, A. (2010) 'Binyam Mohamed: A victory for open justice and the rule of law', *Guardian* 26/02/2010. www.guardian.co.uk/uk/2010/feb/26/binyam-mohamed-mi5-ruling

Hirschi, T. (1969) *Causes of Delinquency*. Los Angeles: University of California Press.

Hirst, P. (1972) 'Marx and Engels on Law, Crime and Morality', *Economy and Society*, 1(1): 28–56.

Hoare, J. and Jansson, K. (2008) 'Extent of intimate violence, nature of partner abuse and serious sexual assault, 2004/5, 2005/6 and 2006/7 British Crime Survey', pp 58–98 in Povey, D. (ed.) *Homicide, Firearms Offences, and Intimate Violence 2006/7*, Home Office Statistical Bulletin 03/08. London: Home Office.

Hobbes, T. (1968 (1651)) *Leviathan*, ed. Macpherson, C. B. London: Penguin.

Hobbs, D. (1988) *Doing the Business: Entrepreneurship, the Working Class and Detectives in East London*. Oxford: Clarendon Press.

Hobbs, D. (1991) 'A piece of business: The moral economy of detective work in the east of London', *British Journal of Sociology*, 42(4): 597–607.

Hobbs, D. (1994) 'Professional and Organized Crime in Britain' in Maguire, M., Morgan, R. and Reiner, R. (eds) *The Oxford Handbook of Criminology* 1st edn. Oxford: Clarendon Press.

Hobbs, D. (1995) *Bad Business: Professional Crime in Modern Britain*. Oxford: Oxford University Press.

Hobbs, D. (1998) 'Going down the glocal: the local context of organized crime', *Howard Journal*, 37(4): 407–22.

Hobbs, D. (2002) 'The firm: organizational logic and criminal culture on a shifting terrain', *British Journal of Criminology*, 32(1): 549–60.

Hobbs, D. (2010a) 'Stealing Commercial Cash: From Safe-cracking to Armed Robbery', pp 290–308 in Brookman, F., Maguire, M., Pierpoint, H. and Bennett, T. (eds) *Handbook on Crime*. Cullompton: Willan.

Hobbs, D. (2010b) 'Extortion', pp 726–38 in Brookman, F., Maguire, M., Pierpoint, H. and Bennett, T. (eds) *Handbook on Crime*. Cullompton: Willan.

Hobbs, D., Hadfield, P., Lister, S. and Winlow, S. (2003) *Bouncers*. Oxford: Oxford University Press.

Hodgkinson, P. (1997) 'The sociology of corruption – some themes and issues', *Sociology*, 31(1): 17–35.

Holdaway, S. (1983) *Inside the British Police*. Oxford: Blackwell.

Holdaway, S. (1996) *The Racialization of British Policing*. London: Macmillan.

Holdaway, S. (1997) 'Some recent approaches to the study of race in criminological research', *British Journal of Criminology*, 37(3): 383–400.

Hollin, C. (1989) *Psychology and Crime: An Introduction to Criminological Psychology*. London: Routledge.

Hollin, C. (2007) 'Criminological Psychology', pp 43–77 in Maguire, M., Morgan, R. and Reiner, R. (eds) *The Oxford Handbook of Criminology* 4th edn. Oxford: Oxford University Press.

Hollin, C., Hatcher, R. and Palmer, E. (2010a) 'Sexual offences against adults', pp 505–24 in Brookman, F., Maguire, M., Pierpoint, H. and Bennett, T. (eds) *Handbook on Crime*. Cullompton: Willan.

Hollin, C., Palmer, E. and Hatcher, R. (2010b) 'Sexual offences against children', pp 525–41 in Brookman, F., Maguire, M., Pierpoint, H. and Bennett, T. (eds) *Handbook on Crime*. Cullompton: Willan.

Holman, B. (1994) 'A View from Easterhouse', in *Criminal Justice Matters*, 18(1): 12.

Holmes, L. (2009) 'Good guys, bad guys: transnational corporations, rational choice theory and power crime', *Crime Law and Social Change*, 51(3–4): 383–97.

Holmes, R. M. and Holmes, S. T. (1998) *Serial Murder* 2nd edn. London: Sage.

Home Office (2003) *The One-day Count of Anti-social Behaviour*. London: Home Office. http://apps2.suffolk.gov.uk/cgi-bin/committee_xml.cgi?p=doc&id=1_10098&format=pdf

Home Office (2009) *Extending our Reach: A Comprehensive Approach to Tackling Serious Organised Crime*. London: Crime Home Office. www.soca.gov.uk/.../58-extending-our-reach-a-comprehensive-approach-to-tackling-serious-organised-crime.pdf

Hood-Williams, C. (2001) 'Gender, masculinities and crime: from structures to psyches', *Theoretical Criminology*, 5(1): 37–60.

Hope, T. (2000) 'Inequality and the Clubbing of Private Security', pp 83–106 in Hope, T. and Sparks, R. (eds) *Crime Risk and Insecurity*. London: Routledge.

Hope, T. (2001) 'Crime, victimization and inequality in risk society', pp 193–218 in Matthews, R. and Pitts, J. (eds) *Crime, Disorder and Community Safety: A New Agenda?* London: Routledge.

Hopkins Burke, R. (2005) *An Introduction to Criminological Theory*. Cullompton: Willan.

Hopkins Burke, R. (2008) *Young People, Crime and Justice*. Cullompton: Willan.

Hornsby, R. and Hobbs, D. (2007) 'A zone of ambiguity: The Political Economy of Cigarette Bootlegging', *British Journal of Criminology*, 47(4): 551–72.

Houchin, R. (2005) *Social Exclusion and Imprisonment in Scotland: A Report*. Glasgow: Glasgow Caledonian University. http://www.sps.gov.uk/multimediagallery/C1D3FBFB-E123-4643-8D83-AB0F622E7755.pdf

Hough, M. (1996) *Drug Misuse and the Criminal Justice System: A Review of the Literature*. London: Home Office. http://www.scan.uk.net/docstore/HO_DPI_Paper_15__Drugs_Misuse_and_the_Criminal_Justice_System.pdf

Hough, M. and Mayhew, P. (1983) *The British Crime Survey: First Report*. Home Office Research Study No. 147. London: Home Office Research and Statistics Department.

Hoyle, C. (2007) 'Feminism, victimology and domestic violence', pp 146–74 in Walklate, S. (ed.) *Handbook of Victims and Victimology*. Cullompton: Willan.

Hoyle, C. and Zedner, L. (2007) 'Victims, Victimization and Criminal Justice', pp 461–94 in Maguire, M., Morgan, R. and Reiner, R. (eds) *The Oxford Handbook of Criminology* 4th edn. Oxford: Oxford University Press.

Hudson, B. (1993) 'Racism and Criminology: Concepts and Controversies', pp 1–27 in Cook, D. and Hudson, B. (eds) *Racism and Criminology*. London: Sage.

Hudson, B. (2007) 'Diversity, Crime and Criminal Justice', pp 158–78 in Maguire, M., Morgan, R. and Reiner, R. (eds) *The Oxford Handbook of Criminology* 4th edn. Oxford: Oxford University Press.

Hughes, G. and Follett, M. (2006) 'Community Safety, Youth and the "Anti-Social"', pp 157–71 in Goldson, B. and Muncie, J. (eds) *Youth, Crime and Justice*. London: Sage.

Huisman, W. and van Baar, A. (2010) 'The oven-builders of the Holocaust', *Tijsdschrift voor Criminologie*, 52(1): 3–18.

Human Rights Council (the Goldstone Report) (2009) *Human Rights in Palestine and Other Occupied Arab Territories: Report of the United Nations Fact Finding Mission on the Gaza Conflict*. Office of the United Nations High Commissioner for Human Rights. http://www2.ohchr.org/english/bodies/hrcouncil/specialsession/9/docs/UNFFMGC_Report.pdf

Hurley, K. (2005) 'I did not inspire Jodi's killer, says rock star Marilyn Manson', 14/02/05. http://news.scotsman.com/marilynmanson/I-did-not-inspire-Jodix.2603109.jp

Hutter, B. (1988) *The Reasonable Arm of the Law?* Oxford: Clarendon Press.

Hutton, W. (2010) 'Now we know the truth. The financial meltdown wasn't a mistake – it was a con', *Guardian* 18/04/20. http://www.guardian.co.uk/business/2010/apr/18/goldman-sachs-regulators-civil-charges

Iganski, P. (2008) *'Hate Crime' and the City*. Bristol: Policy Press.

Independent Monitoring Commission of Northern Ireland (2006a) *Tenth Report of the Independent Monitoring Commission.* http://www.independentmonitoringcommission.org/documents/uploads/ACFEF3.pdf

Independent Monitoring Commission of Northern Ireland (2006b) *Twelfth Report of the Independent Monitoring Commission.* http://www.independentmonitoringcommission.org/documents/uploads/IMC%2012th%20Report%20pdf.pdf

Independent Monitoring Commission of Northern Ireland (2007) *Seventeenth Report of the Independent Monitoring Commission.* http://www.independentmonitoringcommission.org/documents/uploads/17th_IMC.pdf

Innes, M. (2004) 'Signal crimes and signal disorders: notes on deviance as communicative action', *British Journal of Sociology*, 55(3): 335–55.

Jacobs, P., Brunton, M. and Melville, M. (1965) 'Aggressive behaviour, mental subnormality and the XYY male', *Nature*, 208: 1351.

Jamieson, L., McIvor, G. and Murray, C. (1999) *Understanding Offending Among Young People*. Edinburgh: The Stationary Office.

Jandoo, R. (2001) *Report of the Inquiry into the Liaison Arrangements following the murder of Surjit Singh Chhokar*. Edinburgh: Crown Office. http://www.scottish.parliament.uk/business/committees/historic/equal/reports-01/chhokar-vol01-00.htm

Jansson, K., Robb, P., Higgins, N. and Babb, P. (2008) 'Extent and Trends', pp 21–58 in Kershaw, N., Nicholas, S. and Walker, A. (2008) *Crime in England and Wales* 2007/8. London: Home Office. http://rds.homeoffice.gov.uk/rds/pdfs08/hosb0708.pdf

Jarman, N. and Monaghan, R. (2003) *Racial Harassment in Northern Ireland*. Office of the First Minister and Deputy First Minister: Belfast. http://cain.ulst.ac.uk/icr/reports/jarman03racism.pdf

Jarvis, G. and Parker, H. (1989) 'Young heroin users and crime', *British Journal of Criminology*, 29(2): 175–85.

Jefferson, T. (1990) *The Case Against Paramilitary Policing*. Milton Keynes: Open University Press.

Jefferson, T. (1997) 'Masculinities and Crimes', pp 535–57 in Maguire, M., Morgan, R. and Reiner, R. (eds) *Oxford Handbook of Criminology* 2nd edn. Oxford: Clarendon Press.

Jefferson, T. (2001) 'Hegemonic Masculinity', in McLaughlin, E. and Muncie, J. (eds) pp 201–3 in *The Sage Dictionary of Criminology*. London: Sage.

Jefferson, T. and Holloway, W. (1997) 'The risk society in an age of anxiety: situating fear of crime', *British Journal of Sociology*, 48(2): 255–66.

Jefferson, T. and Walker, M. (1992) 'Ethnic minorities in the criminal justice system', *Criminal Law Review*, 83–8.

Jefferson, T., Walker, M. and Seneviratne, M. (1993) 'Ethnic minorities, crime and criminal justice: a study in a provincial city', *British Journal of Criminology*, 33: 251–66.

Jeffrey, R. (2002) *Glasgow's Hard Men*. Edinburgh: Black and White Publishing.

Jeffrey, R. (2006) *Crimes Past: Glasgow's Crimes of the Century*. Edinburgh: Black and White Publishing.

Jeffrey, R. (2008) *Gangs of Glasgow*. Edinburgh: Black and White Publishing.

Jenkins, S. (2010) 'The torture memos show how illegal wars turn even the nicest people bad', *Guardian* 11/02/10. http://www.guardian.co.uk/commentisfree/2010/feb/11/miliband-mi5-terrorism-war-chilcot

Jewkes, Y. (2004) *Media and Crime*. London: Sage.

Johnson, M. P. (2000) 'Conflict and Control: Symmetry and Asymmetry in Domestic Violence', pp 95–104 in Booth, A., Crouter, A. C. and Clements, M. (eds) *Couples in Conflict*. Hillsdale: NJ: Erlbaum.

Jones, P., Comfort, D., Hillier, D. and Eastwood, I. (2005) 'Corporate social responsibility: a case study of the UK's leading food retailers', *British Food Journal*, 107(6): 423–25.

Jones, S. (2000) *Understanding Violent Crime*. Milton Keynes: Open University Press.

Jones, T., McLean, B. and Young, J. (1986) *The Islington Crime Survey*. Aldershot: Gower.

Jordan, J. (2001) 'Worlds apart? Women, rape and the police reporting process', *British Journal of Criminology*, 41(4): 679–706.

Jupp, V. (1989) *Methods of Criminological Research*. London: Unwin Hyman.

Karstedt, S. and Farrell, S. (2006) 'The moral economy of everyday crime: markets, consumers and citizens', *British Journal of Criminology*, 46(6): 1011–36.

Katz, J. (1988) *Seductions of Crime: Moral and Sensual Attractions in Doing Evil*. New York: Basic Books.

Kearon, T. and Godfrey, B. (2007) 'Setting the scene: a question of history', pp 17–36 in Walklate, S. (ed.) *Handbook of Victims and Victimology*. Cullompton: Willan.

Keith, M. (1993) *Race, Riots and Policing*. London: UCL Press.

Kelly, L. (1988) *Surviving Sexual Violence*. Cambridge: Polity Press.

Kelly, L. (1996) 'When Does the Speaking Profit Us?: Reflections on the Challenges of Developing Feminist Perspectives on Abuse and Violence by Women', pp 34–80 in Hester, M., Kelly, L. and Radford, J. (eds) *Women, Violence and Male Power*. Buckingham: Open University Press.

Kelly, L. (2007) 'A Conducive Context: Trafficking of Persons in Central Asia', pp 73–91 in Lee, M. (ed.) *Human Trafficking*. Cullompton: Willan.

Kelly, L., (2008) 'Contradictions and paradoxes: international patterns of, and responses to, reported rape cases', pp 253–80 in Letherby, G., Williams, K., Birch, P. and Cain, M. (eds) *Sex As Crime*. Cullompton: Willan.

Kelly, L. and Radford, J. (1996) '"Nothing Really Happened": The Invalidation of Women's Experiences of Sexual Violence', pp 19–33 in Hester, M., Kelly, L. and Radford, J. (eds) *Women, Violence and Male Power*. Buckingham: Open University Press.

Kelly, L. and Regan, L. (2000) *Stopping Traffic: Exploring the Extent of, and responses to, Trafficking in Women for Sexual Exploitation in the UK*, Police Research Series, Paper 125. London: Home Office.

Kelly, L., Lovett, J. and Regan, L. (2005) '*A gap or a chasm? Attrition in reported rape cases*', Home Office Research Study 293. London: Home Office. http://rds.homeoffice.gov.uk/rds/pdfs05/hors293.pdf

Kershaw, N., Nicholas, S. and Walker, A. (2008) *Crime in England and Wales 2007/8*. London: Home Office. http://rds.homeoffice.gov.uk/rds/pdfs08/hosb0708.pdf

King, R. and Wincup, E. (eds) (2007) *Doing Research on Crime and Justice* 2nd edn. Oxford: Oxford University Press.

Kinnell, H. (2006) 'Murder made Easy: the final solution to prostitution?' in Campbell, R. and O'Neill, M. (eds) *Sex Work Now*. Cullompton: Willan.

Kinsey, R. (1984) *Merseyside Crime Survey: First Report*. Liverpool: Merseyside Metropolitan Council.

Kinsey, R. and Anderson, S. (1992) *Crime and the Quality of Life: Public Perceptions and Experiences of Crime in Scotland: Findings from the 1988 British Crime Survey*. Scottish Office Central Research Unit. Edinburgh: Stationery Office Books.

Kitsuse, J. and Cicourel, A. (1963) 'A Note on the Uses of Official Statistics', *Social Problems*, 11(2): 132–9.

Kitzinger, J. (2008) 'The "paedophile-in-the-community" protests: press reporting and public responses', pp 356–76 in Letherby, G., Williams, K., Birch, P. and Cain, M. (eds) *Sex As Crime*. Cullompton: Willan.

Knight, S. (2004) *Crime Fiction 1800–2000*. Basingstoke: Palgrave Macmillan.

Kramer, R. and Michalowski, R. (1990) 'Toward an Integrated Theory of State-Corporate Crime', Presented at the American Society of Criminology, Baltimore, MD.

Kramer, R., and Michalowski, R. (2005) 'War aggression and state crime: a criminological analysis of the invasion and occupation of Iraq', *British Journal of Criminology*, 45(4): 446–69.

Lacey, N., Wells, C. and Meure, D. (1990) *Reconstructing Criminal Law: Critical Perspectives on Crime and the Criminal Process*. London: Weidenfeld & Nicolson.

Lacombe, D. (2008) 'Consumed with Sex: The Treatment of Sex Offenders in Risk Society', *British Journal of Criminology*, 48(1): 55–74.

Landau, S. F. and Nathan, G. (1983) 'Selecting juveniles for cautioning in the London Metropolitan area', *British Journal of Criminology*, 23(2): 128–49.

Langan, M. (1996) 'Hidden and Respectable: Crime and the Market', pp 227–65 in Muncie, J. and McLaughlin, E. (eds) *The Problem of Crime*. London: Sage.

Laville, S. (2009) 'The invisible victims: DVD Piracy', *Guardian* 13/07/09. http://www.guardian.co.uk/film/2009/jul/13/dvd-piracy-chinese-workers-london

Law, A., Helms, G. and Mooney, G. (2010) '"Urban disorders", "Problem Places" and Criminal Justice', pp 43–66 in Croall, H., Mooney, G. and Munro, M. (eds) *Criminal Justice in Scotland* (in press). Cullompton: Willan.

Lawrence, F. (2004a) *Not on the Label! What Really Goes into the Food on Your Plate*. London: Penguin Books.

Lawrence, F. (2004b) 'Supermarkets criticised over water in fresh pork', *Guardian* 16/07/04. http://www.guardian.co.uk/uk/2004/jul/16/supermarkets.foodanddrink

Lea, J. and Young, J. (1993) *What is to be Done about Law and Order?* 2nd edn. London: Pluto Press.

Lebov, K. (2010) 'Human trafficking in Scotland', *European Journal of Criminology*, 7(1): 77–94.

Lee, M. (2007) 'Introduction: Understanding Human Trafficking', pp 1–25 in Lee, M. (ed.) *Human Trafficking*. Cullompton: Willan.

Lees, S. (1992) 'Naggers, Whores, and Libbers: Provoking Men to Kill', pp 267–88 in Radford, J. and Russell, D. (eds) *Femicide: The Politics of Woman Killing*. Buckingham: Open University Press.

Lees, S. (1996) 'Unreasonable doubt: the outcomes of rape trials' in Hester, M., Kelly, L. and Radford, J. (eds) *Women, Violence and Male Power*. Buckingham: Open University Press.

Leigh, D. and Vulliamy, E. (1997) *Sleaze: The Corruption of Parliament*. London: Fourth Estate.

Lemert, E. (1951) *Social Pathology*. New York: McGraw-Hill.

Leng, R., McConville, M. and Sanders, A. (1992) 'Researching the Discretions to Charge and to Prosecute' in Downes, D. (ed.) *Unravelling Criminal Justice*. London: Macmillan.

Leonard, W. and Weber, M. G. (1970) 'Auto makers and dealers: a study of criminogenic market forces', *Law and Society Review*, 4(3): 407–24.

Letherby, G., Williams, K., Birch, P. and Cain, M. (2008) 'Problematising Sex: Introducing Sex as Crime', pp 1–18 in Letherby, G., Williams, K., Birch, P. and Cain, M. (eds) *Sex As Crime*. Cullompton: Willan.

Levi, M. (1981) *The Phantom Capitalists*. London: Heinemann.

Levi, M. (1987) *Regulating Fraud: White-Collar Crime and the Criminal Process*. London: Tavistock.

Levi, M. (1988) *The Prevention of Fraud*. Crime Prevention Unit, Paper 17. London: HMSO.

Levi, M. (1989) 'Suite justice: sentencing for fraud', *Criminal Law Review*, 420–34.

Levi, M. (1991) 'Regulating money laundering', *British Journal of Criminology*, 31(2): 109–25.

Levi, M. (1994) 'Masculinities and White-Collar Crime', pp 234–52 in Newburn, T. and Stanko, E. (eds) *Just Boys Doing Business?* London: Routledge.

Levi, M. (1995) 'Serious Fraud in Britain', pp 181–98 in Pearce, F. and Snider, L. (eds) *Corporate Crime: Contemporary Debates*. Toronto: University of Toronto Press.

Levi, M. (1997) 'Violent Crime', pp 841–90 in Maguire, M., Morgan, R. and Reiner, R. (eds) *The Oxford Handbook of Criminology* 2nd edn. Oxford: Clarendon Press.

Levi, M. (2000) 'Transnational White-Collar Crime: Some Explorations of Victimization Impact', pp 341–59 in Pontell, H. N. and Shichor, D. (eds) *Contemporary Issues in Crime and Criminal Justice*. New Jersey: Prentice Hall.

Levi, M. (2006) 'The media construction of financial white-collar crimes', *British Journal of Criminology*, 46(6): 1037–57.

Levi, M. (2007) 'Organized Crime and Terrorism' in Maguire, M., Morgan, R. and Reiner, R. (eds) *The Oxford Handbook of Criminology* 4th edn. Clarendon, Oxford University Press.

Levi, M. (2008a) *The Phantom Capitalists: The Organization and Control of Long-Firm Fraud*. Aldershot: Ashgate.

Levi, M. (2008b) 'White-collar, organized and cyber crimes in the media: some contrasts and similarities', *Crime, Law and Social Change*, 49(5): 365–77.

Levi, M. (2009) 'Suite revenge? The shaping of folk devils and moral panics about white-collar crimes', *British Journal of Criminology*, 49(1): 48–67.

Levi, M. (2010) 'Credit Fraud', pp 153–71 in Brookman, F., Maguire, M., Pierpoint, H. and Bennett, T. (eds) *Handbook on Crime*. Cullompton: Willan.

Levi, M. and Burrows, J. (2008) 'Measuring the impact of fraud in the UK: a conceptual and empirical journey', *British Journal of Criminology*, 48(3): 293–318.

Levi, M. and Nelken, D. (1996) 'The corruption of politics and the politics of corruption: an overview', *Journal of Law and Society*, 23(1): 1–17.

Levi, M. and Pithouse, A. (1992) 'The Victims of Fraud', pp 229–46 in Downes, D. (ed.) *Unravelling Criminal Justice: Eleven British Studies*. London: Macmillan.

Levi, M., Maguire, M. and Brookman, F. (2007) 'Violent Crime', pp 687–732 in Maguire, M., Morgan, R. and Reiner, R. (eds) *The Oxford Handbook of Criminology* 4th edn. Oxford: Oxford University Press.

Levitas, R. (1998) *The Inclusive Society? Social Exclusion and New Labour*. Basingstoke: Macmillan.

Leyland, A., (2006) 'Homicides involving knives and other sharp objects in Scotland, 1981–2003', *Journal of Public Health*, 28(2): 145–47.

Light, R., Nee, C. and Ingham, H. (1993) *Car Theft: The Offender's Perspective*. Home Office Research and Planning Unit: Home Office Research Study No. 130. London: HMSO.

Lilly J. R., Cullen, F. and Ball, R. (2002) *Criminological Theory: Context and Consequences*. 3rd edn. London: Sage.

Lister, R. (2004) *Poverty*. Cambridge: Polity.

Lister, S. and Wall, D. (2006) 'Deconstructing distraction burglary: an ageist offence', pp 107–23 in Wahidin, A. and Cain, M. (eds) *Age, Crime and Society*. Cullompton: Willan.

Lister, S. (2005) 'Secrets and lies of beauty industry laid bare by advertising watchdog' 11/05/05. http://www.timesonline.co.uk/tol/news/uk/article521097.ece

Lombroso, C. (1897) *L'Uomo Delinquente*. Torino: Bocca.

Lombroso, C. and Ferrero, W. (1895) *The Female Offender*. London: Unwin.

Lovbakke, J. (2007) 'Public Perceptions', pp 95–111 in Nicholas, S., Kershaw, C. and Walker, A. (eds) *Crime in England and Wales: A Summary of the Main Figures* 2006/7. Home Office Statistical Bulletin 11/07. London: Home Office. http://rds.homeoffice.gov.uk/rds/pdfs07/hosb1107.pdf

Loveday, B. (1992) 'Right agendas: law and order in England and Wales', *International Journal of the Sociology of Law*, 20: 297–319.

Lynch, M. J., and Stretesky, P. (2001) 'Toxic Crimes: examining corporate victimization of the general public employing medical and epidemiological evidence', *Critical Criminology*, 10(3): 153–72.

Lynch, M. J., Stretesky, P. and McGurrin, D. (2001) 'Toxic crimes and environmental justice', pp 109–36 in Potter, G. (ed.), *Controversies in White-Collar Crime*. Cincinnati: Anderson.

Lyng, S. (1990) 'Edgework', *American Journal of Sociology*, 95(4): 851–86.

McAra, L. and McVie, S. (2005) 'The usual suspects?: street-life, young people and the police', *Criminal Justice*, 5(1): 5–36.

McAra, L. and McVie, S. (2007) 'Youth justice? The impact of system contact on patterns of desistance from offending', *European Journal of Criminology*, 4(3): 315–45.

McAra, L. and McVie, S. (2010) 'Youth Justice in Scotland', pp 67–89 in Croall, H., Mooney, G. and Munro, M. (eds) *Criminal Justice in Scotland*. Cullompton: Willan.

McBarnet, D. (1988) 'Law, policy and legal avoidance: can law effectively implement egalitarian strategies?' *Journal of Law and Society*, 15(1): 113–21.

McBarnet, D. (2006) 'After Enron will "whiter than white collar crime" still wash?' *British Journal of Criminology*, 46(6): 1091–119.

McCullough, D., Schmidt, T. and Lockhart, B. (1990) *Car Theft in Northern Ireland: Recent Studies on a Persistent Problem*. CIRAC Paper No. 2. Belfast: The Extern Organization.

McDonald, H. (2010) 'Bloody Sunday: Saville report to be published at last', *Guardian* 26/05/10. http://www.guardian.co.uk/uk/2010/may/26/bloody-sunday-saville-inquiry-findings

McIntosh, B. (2008) ASBO 'Youth: rhetoric and realities', pp 239–57 in Squires, P. (ed.) *ASBO Nation: The Criminalization of Nuisance*. Bristol: Polity Press.

McIntosh, M. (1975) *The Organization of Crime*. London: Macmillan.

McIntosh, M. (1988) 'Introduction to an issue: family secrets as public drama', *Feminist Review*, 28: 6–15.

McKay, R. (2006) *Murder Capital: Life and Death on the Streets of Glasgow*. Edinburgh: Black and White Publishing.

McKeganey, N. and Barnard, M. (1996) *Sex Work on the Streets: Prostitutes and their Clients*. Buckingham: Open University Press.

McLaughlin, E. (1996) 'Political Violence, Terrorism and Crimes of the State', pp 267–319 in Muncie, J. and McLaughlin, E. (eds) *The Problem of Crime*. London: Sage.

McLaughlin, E. (2006a) 'Broken Windows', pp 27–9 in McLaughlin, E. and Muncie, J. (eds) *The Sage Dictionary of Criminology* 2nd edn. London: Sage.

McLaughlin, E. (2006b) 'Terrorism', pp 432–35 in McLaughlin, E. and Muncie, J. (eds) (2005) *The Sage Dictionary of Criminology* 2nd edn. London: Sage.

McLaughlin, E. (2006c) 'Genocide', pp 183–5 in McLaughlin, E. and Muncie, J. (eds) (2005) *The Sage Dictionary of Criminology* 2nd edn. London: Sage.

McLaughlin, E. (2006d) 'Torture', pp 438–40 in McLaughlin, E. and Muncie, J. (eds) (2005) *The Sage Dictionary of Criminology* 2nd edn. London: Sage.

McLaughlin, E., Muncie, J. and Hughes, G. (eds) (2003) *Criminological Perspectives: Essential Readings*. London: Sage.

McLaughlin, E. and Muncie, J. (1993) 'Juvenile Delinquency', pp 7–37 in Dallos, R. and McLaughlin, E. (eds) *Social Problems and the Family*. Buckingham: Open University Press.

McLeod, E. (1982) *Women Working: Prostitution Now*. London: Croom Helm.

McLeod, M. and Saraga, E. (1988) 'Challenging the orthodoxy: towards a feminist theory and practice', *Feminist Review*, 28: 16–55.

MacLeod, P., Page, L., Kinver, A., Iliasov A., Littlewood, M. and Williams, R. (2009) *2008/9 Scottish Crime and Justice Survey: First Findings*. Edinburgh: Scottish Government Social Research. http://www.scotland.gov.uk/Resource/Doc/296333/0092084.pdf

McMillan, L. (2010) 'Gender, Crime and Criminal Justice in Scotland', pp 90–110 in Croall, H., Mooney, G. and Munro, M. (eds) (2010) *Criminal Justice in Scotland*. Cullompton: Willan.

McMullan, J. L., and Perrier D. C. (2002) 'Lobster poaching and the ironies of law enforcement', *Law and Society Review*, 36(4): 679–720.

MacPherson, Sir W. (1999) *The Stephen Lawrence Inquiry. Report of an Inquiry by Sir William MacPherson of Cluny, CM 4262-1*. London: HMSO.

McRobbie, A. and Garber, J. (1976) 'Girls and Subcultures', pp 67–117 in Hall, S. and Jefferson, T. (eds) *Resistance Through Rituals: Youth Subcultures in Post-War Britain*. London: Hutchinson.

McSweeney, T., Hough, M. and Turnbull, P. J. (2006) 'Drugs and Crime: Exploring the Links', pp 95–107 in Simpson, M., Shildrick, T. and Macdonald, R. (eds) *Drugs in Britain: Supply, Consumption and Control*. Basingstoke: Palgrave Macmillan.

McSweeney, T., Turnbull, P. J., and May, T. (2010) 'Drug Supply and Possession', pp 598–625 in Brookman, F., Maguire, M., Pierpoint, H. and Bennett, T. (eds) *Handbook on Crime*. Cullompton: Willan.

Machin, S. and Meghir, C. (2004) 'Crime and economic incentives', *Journal of Human Resources*, 39(4): 958–79.

Machin, S. and Marie, O. (2004) 'Crime and Benefit Cuts'. Paper presented to the Annual Conference of the Royal Economic Society, Swansea, April. Cited in Hale, C. (2009) pp 365–84 in Hale, C., Hayward, K., Wahidin, A. and Wincup, E. (eds), *Criminology* 2nd edn.

Mack, J. (1972) 'The able criminal', *British Journal of Criminology*, 12(1): 44–54.

Mackay, N. (2003) 'Fishermen Have to Catch Black Fish: Just to survive we have to break the law', *Sunday Herald*, 23 November 2003, p 13.

Mackenzie, S. (2010a) 'Fakes', pp 120–36 in Brookman, F., Maguire, M., Pierpoint, H. and Bennett, T. (eds) *Handbook on Crime*. Cullompton: Willan Publishing.

Mackenzie, S. (2010b) 'Scams', pp 137–52 in Brookman, F., Maguire, M., Pierpoint, H. and Bennett, T. (eds) *Handbook on Crime*. Cullompton: Willan.

Maguire, K. (1993) 'Fraud, Extortion and Racketeering: The Black Economy in Northern Ireland'. Paper presented to the Third Liverpool Conference on Fraud, Corruption and Business Crime. University of Liverpool, March.

Maguire, M. (2007) 'Crime Data and Statistics' in Maguire, M., Morgan, R. and Reiner, R. (eds) *The Oxford Handbook of Criminology* 4th edn. Oxford: Clarendon Press.

Maguire, M. and Pointing, J. (eds) (1988) *Victims of Crime: A New Deal?* Milton Keynes: Open University Press.

Maguire, M., Morgan, R. and Reiner, R. (eds) (2007) *The Oxford Handbook of Criminology* 4th edn. Oxford: Oxford University Press.

Maguire, M., Wright, R. and Bennett, T. (2010) 'Domestic Burglary', pp 3–25 in Brookman, F., Maguire, M., Pierpoint, H. and Bennett, T. (eds) *Handbook on Crime*. Cullompton: Willan.

Mama, A. (1989) *The Hidden Struggle: Statutory and Voluntary Sector Responses to Violence against Black Women in the Home*. London: London Race and Housing Research Unit.

Marchbank, J. (2008) 'War and Sex Crime', pp 238–52 in Letherby, G., Williams, K., Birch, P. and Cain, M. (eds) *Sex As Crime*. Cullompton: Willan.

Marlow, A. and Pitts, J. (1997) 'Taking young people seriously', *Criminal Justice Matters*, 26(1): 12–13.

Mars, G. (1982) *Cheats at Work: An Anthropology of Workplace Crime*. London: George Allen & Unwin.

Mars, G. (2008) 'Rethinking Occupational Deviance and Crime in the Light of Globalization', pp 161–78 in Minkes, J. and Minkes, L. (eds) *Corporate and White-Collar Crime*. London: Sage.

Marsh, I. and Melville, G. (2009) *Crime, Justice and the Media*. London: Routledge.

Marx, G. T. (1995) 'The Engineering of Social Control: The Search for the Silver Bullet', pp 225–46 in Hagan, J. and Peterson, R. (eds) *Crime and Inequality*. Stanford: Stanford University Press.

Mason, D. (1995) *Race and Ethnicity in Modern Britain*. Oxford: Oxford University Press.

Matthews, R. and Kauzlarich, D. (2000) 'The crash of ValuJet Flight 592: a case study in state-corporate crime', *Sociological Focus*, 3: 281–98.

Matthews, R. (1993) *Kerb-Crawling, Prostitution and Multi-Agency Policing*. Police Research Group; Crime Prevention Unit Series Paper 43. London: HMSO.

Matthews, R. (1996) *Armed Robbery: Two Police Responses*. Police Research Group; Crime Detection and Prevention Series Paper 78. London: HMSO.

Matthews, R. and Young, J. (eds) (1992) *Issues in Realist Criminology*. London: Sage.

Matza, D. (1964) *Delinquency and Drift*. New York: Wiley.

Matza, D. (1969) *Becoming Deviant*. Englewood Cliffs, NJ: Prentice Hall.

Mawby, R. (2001) *Burglary*. Cullompton: Willan.

Mawby, R. and Walklate, S. (1994) *Critical Victimology: The Victim in International Perspective*. London: Sage.

Mayhew, P. (1996) 'Researching Crime and Victimization', pp 30–54 in Davies, P., Francis, P. and Jupp, V. (eds) *Understanding Victimization*. Northumbria Social Science Press.

Mayhew, P. and Mirlees-Black, C. (1993) *The 1992 British Crime Survey*. Home Office Research Study No. 132. London: HMSO.

Mayhew P., Elliot, D. and Dowds, L. (1989) *The 1988 British Crime Survey*. London: HMSO.

Measham, F. (1995) 'Young women and drugs', *Criminal Justice Matters*, 19(2): 10–11.

Measham, F. and Brain, K. (2005) '"Binge" drinking, British alcohol policy and the new culture of intoxication', *Crime, Media, Culture*, 1(3): 262–83.

Measham, F. and Moore, K. (2008) 'The criminalisation of intoxication', pp 273–88 in Squires, P. (ed.) *ASBO Nation: The Criminalization of Nuisance*. Bristol: Policy Press.

Measham, F., Newcombe, R. and Parker, H. (1994) 'The normalization of recreational drug use amongst young people in north-west England', *British Journal of Sociology*, 45(2): 287–312.

Menaud, M. (2006) 'Tyre Protestors hit at deadline "sham"' *Coventry Evening Telegraph*, 2/12/06: 5.

Mendelsohn, B. (1947) 'New bio-psychosocial horizons: victimology', *American Law Review*, 13: 649.

Merton, R. K. (1938) 'Social structure and anomie', *American Sociological Review*, 3: 672–82.

Messerschmidt, J. (1995) 'From Patriarchy to Gender: Feminist Theory, Criminology and the Challenge of Diversity', pp 167–88 in Rafter, N. and Heidensohn, F. (eds) *International Feminist Perspectives in Criminology: Engendering a Discipline*. Milton Keynes: Open University Press.

Messerschmidt, J. (2005) 'Masculinities and crime: beyond a dualist criminology', pp 29–43 in Renzetti, C., Goodstein, L. and Miller, S. (eds) *Gender, Crime and Justice: Original Feminist Readings*. Los Angeles, CA: Roxbury.

Mgbeoji, I. (2006) *Global Biopiracy: Patents, Plants and Indigenous Knowledge*. Vancouver: UBS Press.

Michalowski, R. and Kramer, R. (1987) 'The space between laws: the problem of corporate crime in a transnational context', *Social Problems*, 34(1): 113–21.

Miles, R. (1989) *Racism*. London: Routledge.

Mill, J. S. (1963/84) *The Collected Works of John Stuart Mill*, Priestly, F. E. L. (ed.). Toronto: University of Toronto Press.

Miller, M. (1985) *Danger! Additives at Work*. London: London Food Commission.

Miller, P. and Plant, M. (1996) 'Drinking, smoking and illicit drug use among 15 and 16 year olds in the United Kingdom', *British Medical Journal*, 313: 394–7.

Miller, W. B. (1958) 'Lower class culture as a generating milieu of gang delinquency', *Journal of Social Issues*, 14(3): 5–19.

Millie, A. (2009) *Anti-Social Behaviour*. Basingstoke: Open University Press.

Mills, C. W. (1970) *The Sociological Imagination*. Harmondsworth: Penguin.

Millstone, E. and Lang, T. (2003) *The Atlas of Food*. London: Earthscan Books.

Ministry of Justice (2008) *Criminal Statistics: England and Wales 2007*. Statistics Bulletin. London: Ministry of Justice. http://www.justice.gov.uk/about/docs/crim-stats-2007-tag.pdf

Ministry of Justice (2009) *Statistics on Women and the Criminal Justice System*. A Ministry of Justice publication under Section 95 of the Criminal Justice Act 1991. Institute for Criminal Policy Research, School of Law, King's College, London. http://www.justice.gov.uk/publications/docs/women-criminal-justice-system-07-08.pdf

Ministry of Justice (2010) *Criminal Statistics for England and Wales 2008*. Statistics Bulletin. London: Ministry of Justice. http://www.justice.gov.uk/publications/docs/criminal-stats-2008.pdf

Minkes, J. (2010) 'Corporate Financial Crimes', pp 653–77 in Brookman, F., Maguire, M., Pierpoint, H. and Bennett, T. (eds) *Handbook on Crime*. Cullompton: Willan.

Minkes, J. and Minkes, L. (2010) 'Income tax evasion and benefit fraud', pp 87–99 in Brookman, F., Maguire, M., Pierpoint, H. and Bennett, T. (eds) *Handbook on Crime*. Cullompton: Willan.

Mirlees-Black, C., Mayhew, P. and Percy, A. (1996) *The 1996 British Crime Survey: England and Wales*. Home Office Statistical Bulletin Issue 19/96. London: HMSO.

Mitchell, B. (1990) *Murder and Penal Policy*. Basingstoke: Macmillan.

Moley, S. (2008) 'Public Perceptions', pp 117–42 in Kershaw, N., Nicholas, S. and Walker, A. (eds) *Crime in England and Wales 2007/8*. London: Home Office. http://rds.homeoffice.gov.uk/rds/pdfs08/hosb0708.pdf

Moley, S. (2009) 'Property Crime' in Walker, A., Flatley, J., Kershaw, C. and Moon, D. (eds) *Crime in England and Wales 2008/2009: Findings from the British Crime Survey and Police Recorded Crime*. Home Office Statistical Bulletin. http://rds.homeoffice.gov.uk/rds/pdfs09/hosb1109vol1.pdf

Mooney, G. (2008) '"Problem" Populations, "Problem" Places', pp 97–128 in Newman, N. and Yeates, N. (eds) *Social Justice: Welfare, Crime and Society*. Maidenhead: Open University Press.

Mooney, G. (2009) 'The "Broken Society" election: class hatred and the politics of poverty and place in Glasgow East', *Social Policy and Society*, 3(4): 1–14.

Mooney, J. and Young, J. (2005) 'Imagining terrorism: terrorism and anti-terrorism terrorism, two ways of doing evil', *Social Justice*, 32(1): 113–25.

Mooney, G., Croall, H. and Munro, M. (2010) 'Social Inequalities and Criminal Justice in Scotland', pp 21–42 in Croall, H., Mooney, G. and Munro, M. (eds) *Criminal Justice in Scotland*. Cullompton: Willan.

Morawska, E. (2007) 'Trafficking into and from Eastern Europe', pp 92–115 in Lee, M. (ed.) *Human Trafficking*. Cullompton: Willan.

Morgan, J. and Zedner, L. (1992) *Child Victims: Crime, Impact, and Criminal Justice*. Oxford: Clarendon Press.

Morrisey, B. (2003) *When Women Kill: Questions of Agency and Subjectivity*. London: Routledge.

Morrison, S. and O'Donnell, I. (1994) *Armed Robbery: A Study in London*. Centre for Criminological Research, University of Oxford.

Mowlam, A., Tennant, R., Dixon, J. and McCreadie, C. (2007) *UK Study of Abuse and Neglect of Older People: Qualitative Findings*. London: Department of Health.

Muir, R. (2010) 'Crime and Justice after Devolution', pp 166–88 in Lodge, G. and Schmuecker, K. (eds) *Devolution in Practice: Public Policy Differences in the UK*. London: Institute for Public Policy Research. www.ippr.org.uk.

Muncie, J. (1984) *The Trouble with Kids Today*. London: Hutchinson.

Muncie, J. (1996) 'The Construction and Deconstruction of Crime', pp 5–64 in Muncie, J. and McLaughlin, E. (eds) *The Problem of Crime*. London: Sage.

Muncie, J. (2000) 'Decriminalising Criminology', *British Criminology Conference: Selected Proceedings*, Vol. 3. http://www.britsoccrim.org/volume3/010.pdf

Muncie, J. (2003) 'Youth, Risk and Victimization', pp 46–60 in Davies, P., Francis, P. and Jupp, V. (eds) *Victimisation: Theory, Research and Policy*. Basingstoke: Palgrave MacMillan.

Muncie, J. (2009) *Youth Crime* 3rd edn. London: Sage.

Muncie, J., McLaughlin, E. and Langan, M. (eds) (1996) *Criminological Perspectives: Essential Readings*. London: Sage.

Muncie, J. and McLaughlin, E. (eds) (1996) *The Problem of Crime*. London: Sage.

Muncie, J., Talbot, D. and Walters, R. (2010) 'Interrogating Crime', pp 1–36 in Muncie, J., Talbot, D. and Walters, R. (eds) *Crime: Local and Global*. Cullompton: Willan.

Murji, K. (2006) 'Moral Panic', pp 250–53 in McLaughlin, E. and Muncie, J. (eds) *The Sage Dictionary of Criminology* 2nd edn. London: Sage.

Murphy, Richard (2005) *Fiscal Paradise or Tax on Development? What is the role of the tax haven?* London: Tax Justice Network. http://faculty.law.wayne.edu/tad/Documents/Research/Fiscal%20paradise.pdf

Murray, C. (1990) *The Emerging Underclass*. London: Institute of Economic Affairs.

Murray, C. (1996) 'The Underclass', pp 127–41 in Muncie, J., McLaughlin, E. and Langan, M. (eds) *Criminological Perspectives: Essential Readings*. London: Sage.

Mythen, G. and Walklate, S. (2006) 'Criminology and terrorism: which thesis? Risk society or Governmentality?', *British Journal of Criminology*, 46(3): 379–98.

Mythen, G. (2007) 'Cultural victimology: are we all victims now?', pp 464–83 in Walklate, S. (ed.) *Handbook of Victims and Victimology*. Cullompton: Willan.

Naffine, N. and Gale, F. (1989) 'Testing the nexus: crime, gender and unemployment', *British Journal of Criminology*, 29(2): 144–56.

National Consumer Council (2003) *Everyday essentials: meeting basic needs. Research into accessing essential goods and services*. London: National Consumer Council. http://kingsfund.koha-ptfs.eu/cgi-bin/koha/opac-detail.pl?biblionumber=30892

National Organization for the Treatment of Abusers (2006) *Who Commits Sexual Offences and What's the Risk in Northern Ireland?* http://www.nota.co.uk/uploads/NOTA%20briefing%204.pdf

National Society for the Prevention of Cruelty to Children (2002) *Child Abuse in Britain*. London: NSPCC.

Nee, C. and Meenaghan, A. (2006) 'Expert decision making in burglars', *British Journal of Criminology* 46(1): 935–49.

Nelken, D. (2007) 'White-Collar and Corporate Crime', pp 733–69 in Maguire, M., Morgan, R. and Reiner, R. (eds) *The Oxford Handbook of Criminology* 4th edn. Oxford: Oxford University Press.

Newburn, T. (2003) *Crime and Criminal Justice Policy* 2nd edn. London: Longman.

Newburn, T. (2007) *Criminology*. Cullompton: Willan.

Newburn, T. (ed.) (2009) *Key Readings in Criminology*. Cullompton: Willan.

Newburn, T. and Stanko, E. (1994) 'When Men are Victims: The Failure of Victimology', pp 153–65 in

Newburn, T. and Stanko, E. (eds) *Just Boys Doing Business?* London: Routledge.

Newcombe, R. (2007) 'Trends in the Prevalence of Illicit Drug Use in Britain', pp 13–38 in Simpson, M., Shildrick, T. and Macdonald, R. (eds) *Drugs in Britain: Supply, Consumption and Control.* Basingstoke: Palgrave MacMillan.

Newman, O. (1972) *Defensible Space: Crime Prevention through Urban Design.* New York: Collier.

Nicholas, S., Kershaw, C. and Walker, A. (eds) (2007) *Crime in England and Wales 2006/7: A Summary of the Main Figures.* London: Home Office. http://rds.homeoffice.gov.uk/rds/pdfs07/hosb1107.pdf

Nichols, L. T. (1999) 'White-Collar Cinema: Changing representations of upper-world deviance in popular films', *Perspectives on social problems*, Vol. 11, pp 61–84. Amsterdam, JAI Press.

Noaks, L. and Wincup, E. (2004) *Criminological Research: Understanding Qualitative Methods.* London: Sage.

Northern Ireland Office (2006) *The Law on Knives in Northern Ireland: A Consultation.* Criminal Justice Policy Division. http://www.nio.gov.uk/the_law_on_knives_in_northern_ireland.pdf

Northern Ireland Office (2010) *Digest of Information on the Northern Ireland Criminal Justice System.* Statistics and Research Branch: Northern Ireland Office. http://www.nio.gov.uk/digest_of_information_on_the_northern_ireland_criminal_justice_system_5.pdf

Norton-Taylor, R. (2010a) 'Baha Mousa inquiry: eight or more civilians died in British custody', *Guardian* 16/03/10. http://www.guardian.co.uk/world/2010/mar/16/baha-mousa-inquiry

Norton-Taylor, R. (2010b) 'Soldiers viewed all Iraqis as "scum", Baha Mousa inquiry hears', *Guardian* 27/04/10. http://www.guardian.co.uk/world/2010/apr/27/baha-mousa-inquiry-soldiers

Norton-Taylor, R. (2010c) 'Former minister admits misinforming MPs over treatment of Baha Mousa', *Guardian* 02/06/10. http://www.guardian.co.uk/world/2010/jun/02/minister-misinform-mps-baha-mousa

Norton-Taylor, R. (2010d) 'Baha Mousa death "a stain on army's character"', *Guardian* 07/06/2010. http://www.guardian.co.uk/world/2010/jun/07/baha-mousa-death-stain-army-character

O'Brien, M. (2005) 'What is *Cultural* about Cultural Criminology', *British Journal of Criminology*, 45(5): 599–612.

O'Donnell, I. and Morrison, S. (1997) 'Armed and Dangerous? The Use of Firearms in Robbery', *Howard Journal of Criminal Justice*, 36(3): 305–20.

Office of Fair Trading (OFT) (2008) Consumer Detriment: Assessing the Frequency and Impact of Consumer Problems with Goods and Services. http://www.oft.gov.uk/shared_oft/reports/consumer_protection/oft992.pdf

O'Keefe, J. (1966) *Law of Weights and Measures.* London, Butterworths.

O'Neill, M. (1996) 'Researching Prostitution and Violence: Towards a Feminist Praxis', pp 130–46 in Hester, M., Kelly, L. and Radford, J. (eds) *Women, Violence and Male Power.* Buckingham: Open University Press.

O'Neill, M. (2008) 'Sex, violence and work: transgressing binaries and the vital role of services to sex workers in public policy reform', pp 80–98 in Letherby, G., Williams, K., Birch, P. and Cain, M. (eds) *Sex As Crime.* Cullompton: Willan.

Pain, R. (2003) 'Old Age and Victimisation', pp 61–80 in Davies, P., Francis, P. and Jupp, V. (eds) *Victimisation: Theory, Research and Policy.* Basingstoke: Palgrave Macmillan.

Pain, R., Francis, P., Fuller, I., O'Brien, K. and Williams, S. (2002) *Hard to Reach Young People and Community Safety: A Model for Participation, Research and Consultation.* Police Research Series Paper 152, Home Office Research Development and Statistics Directorate. London: Home Office. http://www.dur.ac.uk/resources/cscr/outputs/PRS_152.pdf

Painter, K. (1991a) 'Violence and Vulnerability in the Workplace: Psychosocial and Legal Implications', pp 160–78 in Davidson, M. and Earnshaw, J. (eds) *Vulnerable Workers: Psychosocial and Legal Issues.* New York: Wiley.

Painter, K. (1991b) *Wife Rape, Marriage and the Law: Survey Report, Key Findings.* University of Manchester, Department of Social Policy and Social Work.

Pantazis, C. (2000) '"Fear of Crime", Vulnerability and Poverty: Evidence from the British Crime Survey', *British Journal of Criminology*, 40(3): 414–36.

Pantazis, C. and Gordon, D. (1997) 'Television Licence Evasion and the Criminalisation of Female Poverty', *Howard Journal of Criminal Justice*, 36(2): 170–86.

Paoli, L. and Reuter, P. (2008) 'Drug trafficking and ethnic minorities in Western Europe', *European Journal of Criminology*, 5(1): 13–38.

Paoli, L., Spapens, T. and Fijnaut, C. (2010) 'Drug Trafficking', pp 626–50 in Brookman, F., Maguire, M., Pierpoint, H. and Bennett, T. (eds) *Handbook on Crime.* Cullompton: Willan.

Park, R. and Burgess, E. (eds) (1925) *The City*. Chicago: University of Chicago Press.

Parker, H. (1974) *The View from the Boys*. Newton Abbott: David & Charles.

Parker, H. (1996) 'Young adult offenders, alcohol and criminological cul-de-sacs', *British Journal of Criminology*, 36(2): 282–98.

Parker, H., Newcombe, R. and Bakx, K. (1988) *Living with Heroin: The Impact of a Drugs 'Epidemic' on an English Community*. Milton Keynes: Open University Press.

Parton, N. (1985) *The Politics of Child Abuse*. Basingstoke: Macmillan.

Passas, N. (1990) 'Anomie and Corporate Deviance', *Contemporary Crises* 4: 157–78.

Passas, N. (1995) '"I cheat, therefore I exist?" The BCCI scandal in context', in Passas, N. (ed.) *Organized Crime*. Aldershot: Dartmouth.

Passas, N. (2000) 'Global anomie, dysnomie and economic crime: hidden consequences of neo liberalism and globalisation in Russia and around the world', *Social Justice*, 27(2): 16–35.

Passas, N. (2005) 'Lawful but awful: "legal corporate crimes"', *Journal of Socio-Economics*, 34: 771–86.

Passas, N. and Nelken, D. (1993) 'The thin line between legitimate and criminal enterprises: subsidy frauds in the European Union', *Crime, Law and Social Change*, 19(3): 223–43.

Paternoster, R., and Simpson, S. (1993) 'A rational choice theory of corporate crime', pp 37–58 in Clarke, R. V. and Felson, M. (eds) *Routine Activity and Rational Choice*. New Brunswick: Transaction.

Patrick, J. (1973) *A Glasgow Gang Observed*. London: Eyre Methuen.

Paulus, I. (1974) *The Search for Pure Food: A Sociology of Legislation in Britain*. London: Martin Robertson.

Payne, D. (1992) *Crime in Scotland: Findings from the 1988 British Crime Survey*. Central Research Unit Paper. Edinburgh: Scottish Office.

Pearce, F. (1976) *Crimes of the Powerful*. London: Pluto Press.

Pearce, F. (1992) 'The Contribution of "Left Realism" to the Study of Commercial Crime', pp 313–35 in McLean, B. and Lowman, J. (eds) *Realist Criminology: Crime Control and Policing in the 1990's*. Toronto: University of Toronto Press.

Pearce, F. and Tombs, S. (1990) 'Ideology, hegemony and empiricism: compliance theories and regulation', *British Journal of Criminology*, 30(4): 423–43.

Pearce, F. and Tombs, S. (1993) 'US Capital versus the Third World: Union Carbide and Bhopal', pp 187–211 in Pearce, F. and Woodiwiss, M. (eds) *Global Crime Connections: Dynamics and Control*. London: Macmillan.

Pearce, F. and Tombs, S. (1998) *Toxic Capitalism: Corporate Crime and the Chemical Industry*. Aldershot: Ashgate.

Pearson, G. (1983) *Hooligan: A History of Respectable Fears*. London: Macmillan.

Pearson, G. (1987a) *The New Heroin Users*. Oxford: Blackwell.

Pearson, G. (1987b) 'Social Deprivation, Unemployment and Patterns of Heroin Use', pp 62–94 in Dorn, N. and South, N. (eds) *A Land Fit for Heroin?* London: Macmillan.

Pearson, G. (1994a) 'Youth, Crime, and Society', pp 1161–206 in Maguire, M., Morgan, R. and Reiner, R. (eds) *The Oxford Handbook of Criminology* 1st edn. Oxford: Clarendon Press.

Pearson, G. (1994b) 'Moral blinkers: crime and social exclusion', in *Criminal Justice Matters*, 18(1): 3–4.

Pearson, G. (2007) 'Drug Markets and Dealing: From "street dealer" to "Mr Big"', pp 76–92 in Simpson, M., Shildrick, T. and Macdonald, R. (eds) *Drugs in Britain: Supply, Consumption and Control*. Basingstoke: Palgrave MacMillan.

Pearson, G. and Hobbs, D. (2001) *Middle Market Drug Distribution*. Home Office Research Study 227. London: Home Office. http://rds.homeoffice.gov.uk/rds/pdfs/hors227.pdf

Pease, K. (1997) 'Crime Prevention', pp 963–95 in Maguire, M., Morgan, R. and Reiner, R. (eds) *The Oxford Handbook of Criminology* 2nd edn. Oxford: Clarendon Press.

Peev, G. (2008) 'Teenage gang plague "six times worse in Glasgow than London"', 05/02/08. http://news.scotsman.com/politics/Teenage-gang-plague-39six-times.3742521.jp

Pellow, D. N. (2004) 'The politics of illegal dumping: an environmental justice framework', *Qualitative Sociology*, 27(4): 511–25.

Peters, E. (1996) *Torture*. Philadelphia: University of Pennsylvania Press.

Phillips, C. and Bowling, B. (2003) 'Racism, ethnicity and criminology: developing minority perspectives', *British Journal of Criminology*, 43(2): 269–90.

Phillips, C. and Bowling, B. (2007) 'Ethnicities, Racism, Crime and Criminal Justice', pp 421–59 in Maguire, M., Morgan, R. and Reiner, R. (eds) *The Oxford Handbook of Criminology* 4th edn. Oxford: Oxford University Press.

Phoenix, J. (2007) 'Sex, money and the regulation of women's "choices": a political economy of prostitution', *Criminal Justice Matters*, 70(1): 25–6.

Phoenix, J. (2008) 'Reinventing the wheel: contemporary contours of prostitution regulation', pp 27–46 in Letherby, G., Williams, K., Birch, P. and Cain, M. (eds) *Sex As Crime*. Cullompton: Willan.

Phythian, M. (2000) *'The Politics of British Arms Sales Since 1964: "To secure our rightful share"'*. Manchester: Manchester University Press.

Pierpoint, H. and Maher, J. (2010) 'Animal Abuse', pp. 480–502 in Brookman, F., Maguire, M., Pierpoint, H. and Bennet, T. (eds) *Handbook on Crime*. Cullompton: Willan.

Pilger, J. (1999) 'Death of a Nation: the East Timor Conspiracy' (video), cited in Green and Ward (2004). Available at: http://www.informationclearinghouse.info/article13768.htm

Piliavin, I. and Briar, S. (1964) 'Police encounters with juveniles', *American Journal of Sociology*, 70(2): 206–14.

Pinderhughes, R. (1996) 'The impact of race on environmental quality: an empirical and theoretical discussion', *Sociological Perspectives*, 39(2): 231–48.

Pitts, J. (1988) *The Politics of Juvenile Crime*. London: Sage.

Pitts, J. (1996) 'The Politics and Practice of Youth Justice', pp 284–85 in McLaughlin, E. and Muncie, J. (eds) *Controlling Crime*. London: Sage.

Pitts, J. (2008) *Reluctant Gangsters: The Changing Face of Youth Crime*. Cullompton: Willan.

Plant, M. (1989) 'The Epidemiology of Illicit Drug Use and Misuse in Britain', pp 52–63 in Macgregor, S. (ed.) *Drugs and British Society: Responses to a Social Problem in the 1980s*. London: Routledge.

Plummer, K. (1979) 'Misunderstanding Labelling Perspectives' in Downes, D. and Rock, P. (eds) *Deviant Interpretations*. Oxford: Clarendon Press.

Polk, K. (1994) 'Masculinity, Honour and Confrontational Homicide', pp 166–88 in Newburn, T. and Stanko, E. (eds) *Just Boys Doing Business?* London: Routledge.

Pollak, O. (1961) *The Criminality of Women*. New York: A. S. Barnes.

Povey, D., Prime, J. and Taylor, P. (1997) *Notifiable Offences: England and Wales, 1996*. Home Office Statistical Bulletin. London: Home Office Research and Statistics Directorate. http://rds.homeoffice.gov.uk/rds/pdfs/hosb2397.pdf

Powell, J. and Wahidin, A. (2006) Rethinking criminology: the case of "ageing studies" criminology', pp 17–34 in Wahidin, A. and Cain, M. (eds) *Age, Crime and Society*. Cullompton: Willan.

Presdee, M. (2000) *Cultural Criminology and the Carnival of Crime*. London: Routledge.

Presdee, M. (2006) 'Carnival (of Crime)', pp 33–4 in McLaughlin, E. and Muncie, J. (eds) *The Sage Dictionary of Criminology*. 2nd edn. London: Sage.

Presdee, M. (2009) '"Volume Crime" and everyday life', pp 207–28 in Hale, C., Hayward, K., Wahidin, A. and Wincup, E. (eds) *Criminology*. 2nd edn. Oxford: Oxford University Press.

PSNI (Police Service of Northern Ireland) (2008a) *Annual Statistical Report, Statistical Report No. 3, Hate Incidents & Crimes, 1 April 2007–31 March 2008*. http://www.psni.police.uk/3._hate_incidents_and_crimes_2007-08.pdf

PSNI (Police Service of Northern Ireland) (2008b) *Statistical Report No. 3, Hate Crimes and Incidents, 1 April 2006–31 March 2007*. http://www.psni.police.uk/hate_incidents_and_crimes_2006-07.pdf

PSNI (Police Service Northern Ireland) (2010) *Annual Statistical Report No. 1 Recorded Crime and Detections 1 April 2009–31 March 2010*. http://www.psni.police.uk/1._08_09_recorded_crime.pdf

Pudney, S., Badillo, C., Bryan, M., Burton, J., Conti, G. and Iacovou, M. (2006) 'Estimating the Size of the UK Illicit Drug Market', in Singleton, N., Murray, R. and Tinsley, L. (eds) *Measuring Different Aspects of Problem Drug Use: Methodological Developments*. Home Office Online Report 16/06. London: Home Office. http://rds.homeoffice.gov.uk/rds/pdfs06/rdsolr1606.pdf

Punch, M. (1996) *Dirty Business: Exploring Corporate Misconduct*. London: Sage.

Punch, M. (2000) 'Suite violence: why managers murder and corporations kill', *Crime Law and Social Change*, 33(3): 243–80.

Punch, M. (2009) *Police Corruption: Deviance, Accountability and Reform in Policing*. Cullompton: Willan.

Pyle, D. (1994) 'Crime, unemployment and economic activity', in *Criminal Justice Matters*, 18(2): 6–7.

Pyle, D. and Deadman, D. (1994) 'Crime and the business cycle in post-war Britain', *British Journal of Criminology*, 34(3): 339.

Quayle, E. and Taylor, M. (2003) 'Model of problematic internet use in people with a sexual interest in children', *Cyberpsychology and Behaviour*, 6(1): 93–106.

Quigley, D. and Freel, R. (2010) *Perceptions of Crime: Findings from the 2008/2009 Northern Ireland Crime Survey, Research and Statistics Bulletin 1/2010*. Northern Ireland Office Statistics and Research Branch.

http://www.nio.gov.uk/09_northern_ireland_crime_survey-4.pdf

Radford, J. (1992) 'Introduction', pp 3–12 in Radford, J. and Russell, D. (eds) *Femicide: The Politics of Woman Killing*. Buckingham: Open University Press.

Rafter, N. (1997) Psychopathy and the evolution of criminological knowledge, *Theoretical Criminology*, 1(2): 235–59.

Rafter, N. (2000) *Shots in the Mirror: Crime Films and Society*. Oxford: Oxford University Press.

Rafter, N. (2007) 'Crime, film and criminology: recent sex-crime movies', *Theoretical Criminology*, 11(3): 403–20.

Rafter, N. and Heidensohn, F. (eds) (1995) *International Feminist Perspectives in Criminology: Engendering a Discipline*. Milton Keynes: Open University Press.

Rankin, I. (1999) 'Why crime fiction is good for you', *Edinburgh Review*, 102: 9–16.

Rawlinson, P. (2009) 'Understanding Organised Crime', pp 323–42 in Hale, C., Hayward, K., Wahidin, A. and Wincup, E. (eds) *Criminology*. 2nd edn. Oxford: Oxford University Press.

Ray, L., Smith, D. and Wastell, L. (2004) 'Shame, rage and racist violence', *British Journal of Criminology*, 44(3): 350–68.

Reid Howie Associates Ltd (2002) *Police Stop and Search among White and Minority Ethnic Young People in Scotland*. Scottish Executive Central Research Unit.

Reiner, R. (1989) 'Race and criminal justice', *New Community*, 16(1): 5–22.

Reiner, R. (1992) *The Politics of the Police*. London: Harvester Wheatsheaf.

Reiner, R. (2007a) 'Political Economy, Crime and Criminal Justice', pp 341–81 in Maguire, M., Morgan, R. and Reiner, R. (eds) *The Oxford Handbook of Criminology*. 4th edn. Oxford: Oxford University.

Reiner, R. (2007b) 'It's the political economy stupid! A neo-Clintonian criminology', *Criminal Justice Matters*, No. 70(2): 7–8.

Reiner, R. (2007c) 'Media-made Criminality: The Representation of Crime in the Mass Media', pp 302–40 in Maguire, M., Morgan, R. and Reiner, R. (eds) *The Oxford Handbook of Criminology*. 4th edn. Oxford: Oxford University Press.

Reiner, R. (2007d) *Law and Order: An Honest Citizen's Guide to Crime and Control*. Cambridge: Polity.

Reiner, R., Livingstone, S. and Allen, J. (2000) 'No More Happy Endings? The Media and Popular Concern about Crime since the Second World War', pp 107–25 in Hope, T. and Sparks, R. (eds) *Crime, Risk and Insecurity*. London: Routledge.

Reiner, R., Livingstone, S. and Allen, J. (2003) 'From Law and Order to Lynch Mobs: Crime News Since the Second World War', pp 13–32 in Mason, P. (ed.) *Criminal Visions*. Cullompton: Willan.

Reprieve (2007) *Scottish Involvement in Extraordinary Rendition*. London: Reprieve. http://www.reprieve.org.uk/static/downloads/2009_11_09REPORTONSCOTTISHINVOLVEMENT.__.pdf

Ringham, L. and Wood, M. (2004) 'Property Crime', in Dodd, T., Nicholas, S., Povey, D. and Walker, A. (eds) *Crime in England and Wales 2003/4*. Statistical Bulletin 10/04. London: Home Office. http://rds.homeoffice.gov.uk/rds/pdfs04/hosb1004.pdf

Robertson, R. (1996) 'Teenagers pick up worst kind of habit', *Herald*, 16/8/96: 8.

Robertson, G. (2006) *Crimes against Humanity*. 3rd edn. London: Penguin.

Robb, G. (1992) *White-Collar Crime in Modern England: Financial Fraud and Business Morality 1845–1929*. Cambridge: Cambridge University Press.

Robb, G. (2006) 'Women and white-collar crime: debates on gender, fraud and the corporate economy in England and America, 1850–1930', *British Journal of Criminology*, 46(6): 1058–72.

Robertson, G. (2006) *Crimes Against Humanity: The struggle for global justice*. London: Penguin.

Robinson, A. (2010) 'Domestic Violence', pp 245–69 in Brookman, F., Maguire, M., Pierpoint, H. and Bennett, T. (eds) *Handbook on Crime*. Cullompton: Willan.

Rock, P. (1990) *Helping the Victims of Crime: The Home Office and the Rise of Victim Support in England and Wales*. Oxford: Clarendon Press.

Rock, P. (1991) 'The victim in court project at the Crown Court at Wood Green', *Howard Journal*, 30(4): 301–10.

Rock, P. (1998) *After Homicide*. Oxford: Clarendon Press.

Rock, P. (2007a) 'Sociological Theories of Crime', pp 3–42 in Maguire, M., Morgan, R. and Reiner, R. (eds) *The Oxford Handbook of Criminology*. 4th edn. Oxford: Oxford University Press.

Rock, P. (2007b) 'Theoretical Perspectives on Victimisation', pp 37–61 in Walklate, S. (ed.) *Handbook of Victims and Victimology*. Cullompton: Willan.

Roe, S. and Ashe, J. (2008) *Young People and Crime: Findings from the 2006 Offending, Crime and Justice Survey*. Home Office Statistical Bulletin, 09/08. London: Home Office. http://rds.homeoffice.gov.uk/rds/pdfs08/hosb0908.pdf

Rosoff, S. M., Pontell, H. N. and Tillman, R. H. (2003) *The Looting of America*. Upper Saddle River, NJ: Pearson Education.

Ross, J. (2009) 'Scottish beaches fail clean water test', 12/06/09. http://news.scotsman.com/scotland/Scottish-beaches-fail-clean-water.5359843.jp

Ross, J. and Croall, H. (2010) 'Corporate Crime in Scotland', pp 132–51 in Croall, H., Mooney, G. and Munro, M. (eds) *Criminal Justice in Scotland*. Cullompton: Willan.

Ross, J. and Rothe, D. (2008) 'Ironies of controlling state crime', *International Journal of Law, Crime and Justice*, 36: 196–210.

Rothe, D. (2009) *State Criminality: The Crime of All Crimes*. Lanham, MD: Lexington Books.

Rowson, D. (2008) *The Problem with Fraudulent Solicitors: Issues of Trust, Investigation and Self-regulation of the Legal Profession*. Unpublished PhD Thesis: University of Teeside.

Rowan, D. and Kellow, J. (2004) 'Pack of porky pies', *The Times*, March 20, p 16.

Royal Armouries Museum (2007) *Tackling Knife Crime: A Review of Literature on Knife Crime in the UK*. A Report for the Royal Armouries Museum. Leeds: Royal Armouries. http://www.royalarmouries.org/assets-uploaded/documents/RA_Literature_Review_on_Knife_Crime.pdf

Ruggiero, V. (1993) 'Brixton London: a drug culture without a drug economy?', *The International Journal of Drug Policy*, 4(2): 83–90.

Ruggiero, V. (1994) 'Corruption in Italy: an attempt to identify the victims', *Howard Journal of Criminal Justice*, 33(4): 319–38.

Ruggiero, V. (1996a) *Organized and Corporate Crime in Europe: Offers That Can't be Refused*. Aldershot: Dartmouth.

Ruggiero, V. (1996b) 'War markets: corporate and organized criminals in Europe', *Social and Legal Studies*, 5: 5–20.

Ruggiero, V. (1997a) 'Trafficking in human beings: slaves in contemporary Europe', *International Journal of the Sociology of Law*, 25: 231–44.

Ruggiero, V. (1997b) 'Daniel Defoe and Business Crime', *Social and Legal Studies*, 6(3): 323–42.

Ruggiero, V. (2000) 'Transnational crime: official and alternative fears', *International Journal of the Sociology of Law*, 28: 187–99.

Ruggiero, V. (2006) *Understanding Political Violence: A Criminological Analysis*. Milton Keynes: Open University Press.

Ruggiero, V. (2007) 'War, crime, empire and cosmopolitanism', *Critical Criminology*, 15: 211–21.

Ruggiero, V. (2009) 'Armed struggle in Italy: the limits to criminology in the analysis of political violence', *British Journal of Criminology*, 50(4): 708–24.

Ruggiero, V. (2010) 'Privatising International Conflict: War as Corporate Crime', pp 103–17 in Chambliss, W., Michalowski, R. and Kramer, R. (eds) *State Crime in the Global Age*. Cullompton: Willan.

Ruggiero, V. and South, N. (1995) *Eurodrugs: Drug Use, Markets and Trafficking in Europe*. London: University College London Press.

Ruggiero, V. and Vass, A. (1992) 'Heroin use and the formal economy: illicit drugs and licit economies in Italy', *British Journal of Criminology*, 32(3): 273–91.

Ruggiero, V. and Welch, M. (2009) 'Power crime', *Crime, Law and Social Change*, 51: 297–301.

Ryan, M. (1996) *Lobbying from Below: INQUEST in Defence of Civil Liberties*. London: University College London Press.

Salisbury, H. and Upson, A. (2004) *Ethnicity, Victimisation and Worry about Crime: Findings from the 2001/2 and 2002/3 British Crime Survey. Findings 237*. London: Home Office.

Sampson, A. (1994) *Acts of Abuse: Sex Offenders and the Criminal Justice System*. London: Routledge.

Sampson, A. and Phillips, C. (1992) *Multiple Victimization: Racial Attacks on an East London Estate*. Police Research Group Crime Prevention Unit Series: Paper No. 36. London: Home Office Policing and Reducing Crime Unit Research, Development and Statistics Directorate.

Sampson, R. and Wilson, W. J. (1995) 'Toward a Theory of Race, Crime and Urban Inequality', pp 37–54 in Hagan, J. and Peterson, R. (eds) *Crime and Inequality*. Stanford: Stanford University Press.

Sanday, P. R. (1981) 'The socio-cultural context of rape: a cross-cultural study', *Journal of Social Issues*, 37(4): 5–27.

Sanders, T. and Campbell, R. (2008) 'What's criminal about female indoor sex work?', pp 47–62 in Letherby, G., Williams, K., Birch, P. and Cain, M. (eds) *Sex As Crime*. Cullompton: Willan.

Saraga, E. (1993) 'The Abuse of Children', pp 150–71 in Dallos, R. and McLaughlin, E. (eds) *Social Problems and the Family*. London: Sage.

Saraga, E. (1996) 'Dangerous Places: The Family as a Site of Crime', pp 183–227 in Muncie, J. and McLaughlin, E. (eds) *The Problem of Crime*. London: Sage.

Sarangi, S. (2002) 'Crimes of Bhopal and the global campaign for justice', *Social Justice* 29(3): 47–52.

Scarman OBE, Rt. Hon The Lord (1981) *The Brixton Disorders, 10–12 April 1981: Report of an Inquiry* (Cmnd.; 7648). London: HMSO Books.

SCCCJ (Scottish Consortium on Crime and Criminal Justice) (2000) *Rethinking Criminal Justice in Scotland: Summary and Recommendations from a*

Report of the Scottish Consortium on Crime and Criminal Justice. Edinburgh: SCCCJ. http://www.scccj.org.uk/documents/Cj%20in%20Scotland%203.pdf

Scheff, T. (1966) *Being Mentally Ill*. London: Weidenfeld & Nicolson.

Schneider, J. (2008) 'Reducing the illicit trade in endangered wildlife: the market reduction approach', *Journal of Contemporary Criminal Justice*, 24(3): 274–95.

Schwendinger, H. and Schwendinger, J. (1970) 'Defendants of order or guardians of human rights', *Issues in Criminology*, 7: 72–81.

Scottish Crime and Drugs Enforcement Agency (SCDEA) (2009) *Working in Partnership: Protecting Scotland's Communities from Serious and Organized Crime*. Annual Report 2008–9. Paisley: Scottish Crime and Drug Enforcement Agency. http://www.sdea.police.uk/SDEA-Annual-Report/SCDEA%20Annual%20Report%2008-09.pdf

Scottish Office (1995) *Recorded Crime in Scotland*. Scottish Office Statistical Bulletin CrJ/1995: 2. Edinburgh: the Scottish Office.

Scottish Executive (2004) *News Release: Anti-social Behaviour Measures Come into Force*. 28/10/04. www.scotland.gov.uk/News/Releases/2004/10/28095758

Scottish Executive (2006) *High Level Summary of Equality Statistics: Key Trends for Scotland 2006*. A Scottish Executive National Statistics Publication. Edinburgh: Scottish Executive. http://www.scotland.gov.uk/Resource/Doc/933/0041844.pdf

Scottish Government (2008) *Recorded Crime in Scotland 2007/08*. Statistical Bulletin Crime and Justice Series. Edinburgh: The Scottish Government. http://www.scotland.gov.uk/Resource/Doc/239682/0066121.pdf

Scottish Government (2009a) *Domestic Abuse Recorded by the Police in Scotland 2008/09*. Statistical Bulletin Crime and Justice Series. Edinburgh: The Scottish Government. http://www.scotland.gov.uk/Publications/2009/11/23112407/3

Scottish Government (2009b) *2008–9 Scottish Crime and Justice Survey: Partner Abuse in Scotland*. Findings from the 2008/09 Scottish Crime and Justice Survey. Edinburgh: The Scottish Government. http://www.scotland.gov.uk/Topics/Statistics/Browse/Crime-Justice

Scottish Government (2009c) 'Racist Incidents Recorded by the Police in Scotland, 2004–5 to 2007–8', http://www.scotland.gov.uk/Topics/Statistics/Browse/Crime-Justice

Scottish Government (2010) *Criminal Proceedings in Scottish Courts 2008–9*. Statistical Bulletin, Crime and Justice Series. Edinburgh: The Scottish Government. http://www.scotland.gov.uk/Resource/Doc/304494/0095533.pdf

Scoular, J. and O'Neill, M. (2007) 'Social inclusion, responsibilization, and the politics of prostitution reform', *British Journal of Criminology*, 47(5): 764–78.

Scraton, P. and Chadwick, K. (1991) 'The Theoretical and Political Priorities of Critical Criminology', pp 161–87 in Stenson, K. and Cowell, D. (eds) *The Politics of Crime Control*. London: Sage.

Scully, D. (1990) *Understanding Sexual Violence*. London: Harper Collins.

Scully, D. and Marolla, J. (1993) 'Riding the Bull at Gilleys: Convicted Rapists Describe the Rewards of Rape', pp 26–46 in Bart, P. and Moran, E. G. (eds) *Violence against Women: The Bloody Footprints*. London: Sage.

Seddon, T. (2006) 'Drugs, crime and social exclusion: social context and social theory in British drugs-crime research', *British Journal of Criminology*, 46(4): 680–703.

Semmens, N. (2010) 'Identity theft and fraud', pp 172–89 in Brookman, F., Maguire, M., Pierpoint, H. and Bennett, T. (eds) *Handbook on Crime*. Cullompton: Willan.

Shacklady-Smith, L. (1978) 'Sexist Assumptions and Female Delinquency', pp 74–86 in Smart, C. and Smart, B. (eds) *Women, Sexuality and Social Control*. London: Routledge & Kegan Paul.

Shah, R. and Pease, K. (1992) 'Crime, race and reporting to the police', *Howard Journal*, 31: 192–9.

Shapiro, S. (1990) 'Collaring the crime, not the criminal: re-considering the concept of white-collar crime', *American Sociological Review*, 55: 346–65.

Shapland, J., Willmore, J. and Duff, P. (eds) (1985) *Victims and the Criminal Justice System*. Aldershot: Gower.

Sharp, C. and Budd, T. (2005) *Minority Ethnic Groups and Crime: The Findings from the Offending, Crime and Justice Survey 2003*. Home Office Online Report 33/05. http://rds.homeoffice.gov.uk/rds/pdfs05/rdsolr3305.pdf

Shaw, C. (1930) *The Jack-Roller: A Delinquent Boy's Own Story*. Chicago: University of Chicago Press.

Shaw, C. and McKay, H. (1942) *Juvenile Delinquency and Urban Areas*. Chicago: University of Chicago Press.

Sheen Report (1987) *M.V. Herald of Free Enterprise: Report of the Court No. 8074, Formal Investigation*. Department of Transport. London: HMSO.

http://www.maib.gov.uk/cms_resources.cfm?file=/HofFE%20part%201.pdf

Sheldon, W. (1949) *Varieties of Delinquent Youth*. New York: Harper.

Shelley, L. (2007) 'Human Trafficking as a Form of Transnational Crime', pp 116–37 in Lee, M. (ed.) *Human Trafficking*. Cullompton: Willan.

Shover, N. and Honaker, D. (1992) 'The socially bounded decision making of persistent property offenders', *Howard Journal of Criminal Justice*, 31(4): 276–94.

Shover, N. and Hochstetler, A. (2005) *Choosing White-Collar Crime*. Cambridge: Cambridge University Press.

Silvestri, M. and Crowther-Dowey, C. (2008) *Gender and Crime*. London: Sage.

Sim, J. (1994) 'Tougher than the Rest? Men in Prison', pp. 100–17 in Newburn, T. and Stanko, E. (eds) *Just Boys Doing Business?* London: Routledge.

Sim, J., Scraton, P. and Gordon, P. (1987) 'Crime, the State and Critical Analysis: An Introduction' in Scraton, P. (ed.) *Law, Order and the Authoritarian State*. Milton Keynes: Open University Press.

Simon, D. and Eitzen, D. (1993) *Elite Deviance* 4th edn. Boston: Allyn & Bacon.

Simpson, S. and Elis, L. (1996) 'Theoretical Perspectives on the Corporate Victimization of Women', pp 32–58 in Szockyj, E. and Fox, J. G. (eds) (1996) *Corporate Victimization of Women*. Boston: Northeastern University Press.

Slapper, G. (1994) 'Crime without Punishment', *Guardian*, 01/02/94.

Slapper, G. and Tombs, S. (1999) *Corporate Crime*. London: Addison Wesley Longman.

Smart, C. (1976) *Women, Crime and Criminology*. London: Routledge & Kegan Paul.

Smart, C. (1979) 'The new female criminal: reality or myth?', *British Journal of Criminology*, 19(1): 50–9.

Smart, C. (1990) 'Feminist Approaches to Criminology: Or Post-modern Woman Meets Atavistic Man', pp 453–65 in Gelsthorpe, L. and Morris, A. (eds) *Feminist Perspectives in Criminology*. Buckingham: Open University Press.

Smith, D. J. and Gray, J. (1985) *Police and People in London: The PSI Report*. Aldershot: Gower.

Smith, D. J. (1997) 'Ethnic Origins, Crime and Criminal Justice', pp 703–59 in Maguire, M., Morgan, R. and Reiner, R. (eds) *The Oxford Handbook of Criminology* 2nd edn. Oxford: Clarendon Press.

Smith, D. (2009a) 'Key Concepts and Theories about Race', pp 9–28 in Bhui, H. S. (ed.) *Race and Criminal Justice*. London: Sage.

Smith, D. (2009b) 'Criminology, Contemporary Society, and Race Issues', pp 29–48 in Bhui, H. S. (ed.) *Race and Criminal Justice*. London: Sage.

Smith, K., Flatley, J., Coleman, K., Osborne, S., Kaize, P. and Rose, S. (2010) *Homicides, Firearm Offences and Intimate Violence 2008/09 Crime in England and Wales 2008/09 Supplementary Volume 2 Home Office Statistical Bulletin*. London: Home Office. rds.homeoffice.gov.uk/rds/stats-release.html

Smith, R. (2004) 'Rural rogues: a case story on the "smokies" trade', *International Journal of Entrepreneurial Behaviour & Research*, 10(4): 277–94.

Snider, L. (1996) 'Directions for social change and Political Action', pp 235–66 in Szockyj, E. and Fox, James G. (eds) *Corporate Victimization of Women*. Boston: Northeastern University Press.

Snider, L. (2000) 'The sociology of corporate crime: an obituary (or, whose knowledge claims have legs?)', *Theoretical Criminology*, 4(2): 169–206.

Snider, L. (2002) 'Zero Tolerance Reversed: Constituting the Non-culpable Subject in Walkerton', *Annual Meetings, Canadian Law and Society Association*, Vancouver, 31 May 2002. Vancouver: Canadian Law and Society Association.

Snider, L. (2003) 'Constituting the punishable woman: atavistic man incarcerates postmodern woman', *British Journal of Criminology*, 43(2): 354–78.

Snider, L. (2008) 'Corporate Economic Crimes', pp 39–60 in Minkes, J. and Minkes, L. (eds) *Corporate and White-Collar Crime*. London: Sage.

SOCA (2010) *The United Kingdom Threat Assessment of Organised Crime*. Serious and Organised Crime Agency. http://www.soca.gov.uk/about-soca/library/doc_download/54-the-united-kingdom-threat-assessment-of-organised-crime.pdf

Solomos, J. (1993) 'Constructions of Black Criminality: Racialisation and Criminalisation in Perspective', pp 118–35 in Cook, D. and Hudson, B. (eds) *Racism and Criminology*. London: Sage.

Solomos, J. and Rackett, T. (1991) 'Policing and Urban Unrest: Problem Constitution and Policy Response', pp 42–64 in Cashmore, E. and McLaughlin, E. (eds) *Out of Order? Policing Black People*. London: Routledge.

Soothill, K. and Walby, S. (1991) *Sex Crime in the News*. London: Routledge.

Soothill, K., Francis, B., Ackerley, E. and Collett, S. (1999) *Homicide in Britain: A Comparative Study of Rates in Scotland and England and Wales*. Edinburgh: Scottish Executive Central Research Unit. http://www.scotland.gov.uk/Publications/2000/03/2ff917ae-270d-47d9-acd0-f89c30688868

South, N. (1998a) 'A green field for criminology? A Proposal for a Perspective', *Theoretical Criminology*, 2(2): 211–33.

South, N. (1998b) 'Corporate and State Crimes Against the Environment: Foundations for a Green Perspective in European Criminology', pp 443–61 in Ruggiero, V., South, N. and Taylor, I. (eds) *The New European Criminology: Crime and Social Order in Europe*. London: Routledge.

South, N. (2007a) 'Drugs, Alcohol, and Crime', pp 810–40 in Maguire, M., Morgan, R. and Reiner, R. (eds) *The Oxford Handbook of Criminology* 4th edn. Oxford: Oxford University Press.

South, N. (2007b) 'The "Corporate Colonization of Nature": Bio-prospecting, Bio-piracy and the Development of Green Criminology', pp 230–47 in Beirne, P. and South, N. (eds) *Issues in Green Criminology*. Cullompton: Willan.

Spalek, B., Lambert, R. and Baker, A. (2009) 'Minority Muslim communities and criminal justice: stigmatized UK faith identities post 9/11 and 7/7', pp 170–87 in Bhui, H. S. (ed.) *Race and Criminal Justice*. London: Sage.

Sparks, R., Genn, H. and Dodd, D. (1977) *Surveying Victims*. London: Wiley.

Sparks, R. (1992) 'Reason and Unreason in Left Realism: Some Problems in the Constitution of the Fear of Crime', pp 119–35 in Matthews, R. and Young, J. (eds) *Issues in Realist Criminology*. London: Sage.

Sparks, R. (1997) 'Recent Social Theory and the Study of Crime and Punishment', pp 409–35 in Maguire, M., Morgan, R. and Reiner, R. (eds) *The Oxford Handbook of Criminology* 2nd edn. Oxford: Clarendon Press.

Speed, M. and Burrows, J. (2006) *Sentencing in Cases of Theft from Shops*. Research Report 3 for the Sentencing Advisory Panel. http://www.sentencing-guidelines.gov.uk/docs/researchreport-theft0806.pdf

Spencer, E. (1992) *Car Crime and Young People on a Sunderland Housing Estate*. Home Office Police Research Group Crime Prevention Unit Series, Paper No. 40. London: Home Office Police Department. http://rds.homeoffice.gov.uk/rds/prgpdfs/fcpu40.pdf

Squires, P. (ed.) (2008a) *ASBO Nation: The Criminalization of Nuisance*. Bristol: Policy Press.

Squires, P. (2008b) 'Introduction: why "anti-social behaviour"? Debating ASBOs', pp 1–36 in Squires, P. (ed.) *ASBO Nation: The Criminalization of Nuisance*. Bristol: Policy Press.

Stanko, E. (1990a) *Everyday Violence: How Women and Men Experience Sexual and Physical Danger*. London: Pandora.

Stanko, E. (1990b) 'When Precaution is Normal: A Feminist Critique of Crime Prevention', pp 173–83 in Gelsthorpe, L. and Morris, A. (eds) *Feminist Perspectives in Criminology*. Milton Keynes: Open University Press.

Stanko, E. (1994) 'Challenging the Problem of Men's Individual Violence', pp 32–45 in Newburn, T. and Stanko, E. (eds) *Just Boys Doing Business?* London: Routledge.

Stanko, E. (2000) 'The day to count: a snapshot of the impact of domestic violence in the UK', *Criminal Justice*, 1: 2.

Stanko, E. (2003) 'Introduction: Conceptualising the Meanings of Violence', pp 1–14 in Stanko, E. (ed.) *The Meanings of Violence*. London: Routledge.

Stanko, E. and Hobdell, K. (1993) 'Assault on men: masculinity and male victimization', *British Journal of Criminology*, 33(3): 400–15.

Steffensmeier, D. and Allan, E. (1995) 'Age-Inequality and Property Crime: The Effects of Age-linked Stratification and Status-Attainment Processes on Patterns of Criminality across the Life Course', pp 95–115 in Hagan, J. and Peterson, R. (eds) *Crime and Inequality*. Stanford: Stanford University Press.

Stevens, P. and Willis, C. (1979) *Race, Crime and Arrests*. Home Office Research Study No. 58. London: HMSO.

Sudnow, D. (1965) 'Normal crimes: sociological features of the penal code in a public defender office', *Social Problems*, 12(3): 255–76.

Sumner, C. (1994) *The Sociology of Deviance: An Obituary*. Buckingham: Open University Press.

Sumner, C. (1997) 'Censure, Crime, and State', pp 499–510 in Maguire, M., Morgan, R. and Reiner, R. (eds) *The Oxford Handbook of Criminology* 2nd edn. Oxford: Clarendon Press.

Sutherland, E. (1947) *Principles of Criminology* 4th edn. Philadelphia: Lippincott.

Sutherland, E. (1949) *White-Collar Crime*. New York: Holt, Rinehart & Winston.

Sutherland, E. (1987) *The Professional Thief: By a Professional Thief*. Chicago: University of Chicago Press.

Sutton, A. and Wild, R. (1985) 'Small business: white-collar villains or victims?', *International Journal of the Sociology of Law*, 13: 247–59.

Sutton, M. (1995) 'Supply by theft: does the market for second-hand goods play a role in keeping crime figures high?', *British Journal of Criminology*, 35(3): 400–16.

Sutton, M. (2010) 'Understanding and tackling stolen goods markets', pp 68–84 in Brookman, F., Maguire, M., Pierpoint, H. and Bennett, T. (eds) *Handbook on Crime*. Cullompton: Willan.

Sweeney, C. (2009) 'Glasgow's gang rule imprisons young on their own streets', *The Times*, 03/08/09. http://www.timesonline.co.uk/tol/news/uk/scotland/article6737926.ece

Sykes, G. and Matza, D. (1957) 'Techniques of neutralization: a theory of delinquency', *American Sociological Review*, 22(6): 664–70.

Szockyj, E. and Fox, J. G. (eds) (1996) *Corporate Victimization of Women*. Boston: Northeastern University Press.

Tailby, R. and Gant, F. (2002) 'The illegal market in Australian abalone', *Trends and Issues in Crime and Criminal Justice* No. 225: 1–6. Canberra: Australian Institute of Criminology. http://www.illegal-fishing.info/uploads/AIC-illegal-mkt-in-australian-abalone.pdf

Tappan, P. (1977) 'Who is the Criminal?', pp 50–9 in Geis, G. and Maier, R. F. (eds) *White-Collar Crime: Offences in Business, Politics and the Professions – Classic and Contemporary Views*, revised edn. New York: Free Press.

Taylor, A. (1993) *Women Drug Users: An Ethnography of a Female Injecting Community*. Oxford: Clarendon Press.

Taylor, I. (1997) 'The Political Economy of Crime', pp 265–303 in Maguire, M., Morgan, R. and Reiner, R. (eds) *The Oxford Handbook of Criminology* 2nd edn. Oxford: Clarendon Press.

Taylor, I. (1999) *Crime in Context: A Critical Criminology of Market Societies*. Cambridge: Polity.

Taylor, I., Walton, P. and Young, J. (1973) *The New Criminology*. London: Routledge & Kegan Paul.

Telegraph (2008) 'Ipswich prostitute murders: the victims', *Telegraph*, 16/01/08. http://www.telegraph.co.uk/news/uknews/1575723/Ipswich-prostitute-murders-the-victims.html

Thomas, P. (2001) *Cleaning Yourself to Death: How Safe is Your Home?* Newleaf: Dublin.

Thomas, T. (2005) *Sex Crime: Sex Offending and Society*. 2nd edn. Cullompton: Willan.

Thomas, T. (2009) 'Sex crime', pp 279–300 in Hale, C., Hayward, K., Wahidin, A. and Wincup, E. *Criminology*. Oxford: Oxford University Press.

Thomas, W. I. (1923) *The Unadjusted Girl*. Boston: Little Brown.

Thompson, T. (2010) 'Ruthless and Remorseless: The Shocking Rise of UK's Girl Gangsters', *Observer* 23/05/10: 24.

Thorpe, K., Robb, P. and Higgins, N. (2007) 'Extent and Trends' in Nicholas, S., Kershaw, C. and Walker, A. (2007) (eds) *Crime in England and Wales: A Summary of the Main Figures 2006/7*. Home Office RDS 2007, available from www.homeoffice.gov.uk/res/pdfs07/crime0607summ/pdf.

Thorpe, V. (2010) 'Ridley Scott's new take on the myth of Robin Hood and Maid Marian', *Observer*, *Guardian* 02/05/10. www.guardian.co.uk/film/2010/may/02/ridley-scott-maid-marian-robin-hood

Thrasher, F. (1927) *The Gang*. Chicago: Phoenix Press.

Tierney, J. (2006) *Criminology: Theory and Context* 2nd edn. London: Pearson Education.

Tilley, N. (2010) 'Shoplifting', pp 48–67 in Brookman, F., Maguire, M., Pierpoint, H. and Bennett, T. (eds) *Handbook on Crime*. Cullompton: Willan.

Tilley, N. and Hopkins, M. (2008) 'Organized crime and local businesses', *Criminology and Criminal Justice*, 8(4): 443–60.

Tillman, R. (2009a) 'Reputations and corporate malfeasance: collusive networks in financial statement fraud', *Crime Law and Social Change*, 51(3–4): 365–82.

Tillman, R. (2009b) 'Making the rules and breaking the rules: the political origins of corporate corruption in the new economy', *Crime, Law and Social Change*, 51(3–4): 73–86.

Tillman, R. and Indergaard, M. (2006) 'Corporate Corruption in the New Economy', pp 474–89 in Pontell, H. and Geis, G. (eds) *International Handbook of White-Collar and Corporate Crime*. Irvine, CA: Springer.

Times/Sunday Times (25 April 2010) 'Top Ten paperbacks: Fiction. *Sunday Times* bestseller list at: http://entertainment.timesonline.co.uk/tol/arts_and_entertainment/books/article4304971.ece

Titus, R. M. (2001) 'Personal Fraud and its Victims', pp 57–66 in Shover, N. and Wright, J. P. (eds) *Crimes of Privilege: Readings in White-Collar Crime*. New York: Oxford University Press.

Toch, H. (1969) *Violent Men*. Harmondsworth: Penguin.

Tombs, S. (1990) 'Industrial injuries in British manufacturing industry', *Sociological Review*, 38(2): 324–43.

Tombs, S. (1998) 'Health and Safety Crimes and the Problem of "Knowing"', pp 77–104 in Davies, P., Francis, P. and Jupp, V. (eds) *Invisible Crimes: Their Victims and Their Regulation*. London: Macmillan.

Tombs, S. (2000) 'Official Statistics and Hidden Crimes: Researching Health and Safety Crimes', pp 64–81 in Jupp, V., Davies, P. and Francis, P. (eds) *Doing Criminological Research*. London: Sage.

Tombs, S. (2007) '"Violence", safety crimes and criminology', *British Journal of Criminology*, 47(4): 531–50.

Tombs, S. (2010) 'Corporate Violence and Harm', pp 884–903 in Brookman, F., Maguire, M., Pierpoint, H. and Bennett, T. (eds) *Handbook of Crime*. Cullompton: Willan.

Tombs, S. and Hillyard, P. (2004) 'Towards a Political Economy of Harm: States, Corporations and the

Production of Inequality', pp 30–54 in Hillyard, P., Pantazis, C., Tombs, S. and Gordon, D. (eds) *Beyond Criminology: Taking Harm Seriously*. London: Pluto Press.

Tombs, S. and Whyte, D. (2001) 'Reporting Corporate Crime out of Existence', *Criminal Justice Matters* No. 43, pp 22–3.

Tombs, S. and Whyte, D. (2003) 'Scrutinizing the Powerful: Crime, Contemporary Political Economy, and Critical Social Research', pp 3–48 in Tombs, S. and Whyte, D. (eds) *Unmasking the Crimes of the Powerful*. New York: Lang.

Tombs, S. and Whyte, D. (2007) *Safety Crime*. Cullompton, Willan Publishing.

Tombs, S. and Whyte, D. (2009) 'A deadly consensus: worker safety and regulatory degradation under New Labour', *British Journal of Criminology*, 50(1): 46–65.

Tombs, S. and Whyte, D. (2010) 'Crime, Harm and Corporate Power', pp 137–72 in Muncie, J., Talbot, D. and Walters, R. (eds) *Crime: Local and Global*. Cullompton: Willan.

Travis, A. (1997) 'Crime Fears Lead to Street Anxiety', *Guardian* 26/05/97: 6.

Travis, A. (2009) '"Al Capone-style" plan to curb UK's booming £30bn crime industry', *Guardian* Monday 13 July. www.guardian.co.uk/uk/2009/jul/13/organised accessed 12/02/10

Tseloni, A. and Pease, K. (2003) 'Repeat personal victimization: boosts or flags?', *British Journal of Criminology*, 43(1): 196–212.

Turk, A. (2004) 'Sociology of terrorism', *Annual Review of Sociology*, 30: 271–86.

Turner, J. and Kelly, L. (2009) 'Trade secrets: intersections between diasporas and crime groups in the constitution of the human trafficking chain', *British Journal of Criminology*, 49(2): 184–201.

Tzannetakis, T. (2006) 'Neo Conservative Criminology', pp 259–62 in McLaughlin, E. and Muncie, J. (eds) *The Sage Dictionary of Criminology* 2nd edn. London: Sage.

Uhlig, R. (2004) 'Farmhouse fresh? It's more likely to have been produced on an industrial estate: Government watchdog accuses supermarkets and manufacturers of duping shoppers with misleading labels', *Daily Telegraph* 12/02/04, p 4.

United Nations Environment Programme (2005) 'Somalia'. www.enep.org/tsunami/reports/tsunami_SOMALIA_LAYOUT.pdf

Upson, A., Povey, D. and Gray, A. (2004) 'Violent Crime', in Dodd, T., Nicholas, S., Povey, D. and Walker, A. (eds) *Crime in England and Wales 2003/4 Statistical Bulletin 10/04*. London: Home Office Research, Development and Statistics Directorate. http://rds.homeoffice.gov.uk/rds/pdfs04/hosb1004.pdf

Utting. D., Bright, J. and Henricson, C. (1993) *Crime and the Family: Improving Child Rearing and Preventing Delinquency*. Occasional Paper 16. Family Policy Studies Centre.

Valier, C. (2002) *Theories of Crime and Punishment*. London: Pearson Longman.

Van Dijk, J. and Mayhew, P. (1993) *Criminal Victimization in the Industrialised World: Key Findings of the 1989 and 1992 International Crime Surveys*. The Hague: Ministry of Justice, Department of Crime Prevention. http://rechten.uvt.nl/icvs/pdffiles/key_report_1992.pdf

Van Duyne, P. (1993) 'Organized crime and business crime enterprises in the Netherlands', *Crime, Law and Social Change*, 19(2): 103–42.

Van Duyne, P. C. (2003) 'Organizing cigarette smuggling and policy making, ending up in smoke', *Crime, Law and Social Change*, 39(3): 285–317.

Van Duyne, P. C. and Antonopolous, G. A. (2009) 'Improving Health and Making Crime: An Introduction', pp 1–6 in Van Duyne, P. C. and Antonopolous, G. A. (eds) *The Criminal Smoke of Tobacco Policy Making: Cigarette Smuggling in Europe*. Nijmegen: Wolf Legal Publishers.

Van Duyne, P. C. and Levi, M. (2005) *Drugs and Money: Managing the Drug Trade and Crime-Money in Europe*. London: Routledge.

Vaughan, D. (1998) 'Rational Choice, situated action, and the social control of organizations', *Law and Society Review*, 32(1): 23–61.

Victim Support (2002) *Criminal Neglect: No Justice Beyond Criminal Justice*. London: Victim Support. http://www.victimsupport.org.uk/About%20us/Our%20history%20and%20achievements/~/media/C0DA61EDDFCA4F9D9E0920B3235E654D.ashx

Virdee, S. (1997) 'Racial Harassment', pp 259–89 in Modood, T., Berthoud, R., Lakey, J., Nazroo, J., Smith, P., Virdee, S. and Beishon, S. (eds) *Ethnic Minorities in Britain: Diversities and Disadvantage*. London: Policy Studies Institute.

Waddington, P. A. J. (1986) 'Mugging as a moral panic: a question of proportion', *British Journal of Sociology*, 37(2): 245–59.

Wahidin, A. (2009) '"Ageing" in prison: crime and the criminal justice system', pp 449–70 in Hale, C., Hayward, K., Wahidin, A. and Wincup, E. (eds) *Criminology* 2nd edn. Oxford: Oxford University Press.

Wahidin, A. and Cain, M. (2006) 'Ageing, Crime and Society: An Invitation to a Criminology', pp 1–16 in

Wahidin, A. and Cain, M. (eds) *Age, Crime and Society*. Cullompton: Willan.

Wahidin, A. and Powell, J. (2007) 'Old Age, Victims and Crime', pp 234–50 in Davies, P., Francis, P. and Greer, C. (eds) *Victims, Crime and Society*. London: Sage.

Walby, S. (1989) 'Theorizing Patriarchy', *Sociology*, 23(2): 213–34.

Walby, S. (1990) *Theorizing Patriarchy*. Oxford: Blackwell.

Walby, S. and Allen, J. (2004) *Domestic Violence, Sexual Assault and Stalking: Findings from the British Crime Survey Home Office Research Study 276*. London: Home Office Research, Development and Statistics Directorate. http://rds.homeoffice.gov.uk/rds/pdfs04/hors276.pdf

Walker, A., Flatley, J., Kershaw, C. and Moon, D. (eds) (2009) *Crime in England and Wales 2008/09, Volume 1*. Findings from the British Crime Survey and Police Recorded Crime. Home Office Statistical Bulletin. London: Home Office. http://rds.homeoffice.gov.uk/rds/pdfs09/hosb1109vol1.pdf

Walker, M. (1987) 'Interpreting race and crime statistics', *Journal of the Royal Statistical Society*, 150(1): 39–56.

Walker, M. (1988) 'The court disposal of young males, by race, in London in 1983', *British Journal of Criminology*, 28(4): 441–59.

Walker, M. (1989) 'The court disposal and remands of White, Afro-Caribbean and Asian men in London in 1983', *British Journal of Criminology*, 29(4): 353–67.

Walklate, S. (1989) *Victimology: The Victim and the Criminal Justice Process*. London: Unwin Hyman.

Walklate, S. (1995) *Gender and Crime: An Introduction*. London: Prentice Hall.

Walklate, S. (1996) 'Can there be a Feminist Victimology?', pp 14–29 in Davies, P., Francis, P. and Jupp, V. (eds) *Understanding Victimisation*. Northumbria Social Science Press.

Walklate, S. (1998) *Understanding Criminology*. Buckingham: Open University Press.

Walklate, S. (2004) *Gender, Crime and Criminal Justice*. Cullompton: Willan Publishing.

Walklate, S. (2007a) *Imagining the Victim of Crime*. Maidenhead: McGraw Hill Open University Press.

Walklate, S. (ed.) (2007b) *Handbook of Victims and Victimology*. Cullompton: Willan.

Walklate, S. (2007c) 'Men, Victims and Crime', pp 142–64 in Davies, P., Francis, P. and Greer, C. (eds) *Victims, Crime and Society*. London: Sage.

Walklate, S. (2008) 'What is to be done about violence against women?', *British Journal of Criminology*, 48(1): 39–54.

Wall, D. (2007) *Cybercrime: The Transformation of Crime in the Information Age*. Cambridge: Polity.

Walmsley, R., Howard, L. and White, S. (1992) *The National Prison Survey 1991: Main Findings*. Home Office Research Study No. 128. London: HMSO. http://rds.homeoffice.gov.uk/rds/pdfs05/hors128.pdf

Walters, R. (2006) 'Crime, bio-agriculture and the exploitation of hunger', *British Journal of Criminology*, 46(1): 26–45.

Walters, R. (2007) 'Crime, Regulation and Radioactive Waste in the United Kingdom', pp 186–205 in Beirne, P. and South, N. (eds) *Issues in Green Criminology*. Cullompton: Willan.

Walters, R. (2010a) 'Eco Crime', pp 173–208 in Muncie, J., Talbot, D. and Walters, R. (eds) *Crime: Local and Global*. Cullompton: Willan.

Walters, R. (2010b) 'Eco Crime and Air Pollution', pp 867–83 in Brookman F., Maguire, M., Pierpoint, H. and Bennett, T. (eds) *Handbook on Crime*. Cullompton: Willan.

Walters, R. (2010c) 'Environmental Crime', pp 152–74 in Croall, H., Mooney, G. and Munro, M. (eds) *Crime and Criminal Justice in Scotland*. Cullompton: Willan.

Waquant, L. (2008) *Urban Outcasts: A Comparative Sociology of Advanced Marginality*. Cambridge: Polity.

Ward, T. (2004) 'State Harms', pp 84–100 in Hillyard, P., Pantazis, C., Tombs, S. and Gordon, D. (eds) *Beyond Criminology: Taking Harm Seriously*. London: Pluto Press.

Wark, P. (2010) 'Five Daughters: TV's take on the Ipswich murders', *The Times*, 23/04/10. http://entertainment.timesonline.co.uk/tol/arts_and_entertainment/tv_and_radio/article7104962.ece

Watson, L. (1996) *Victims of Violent Crime Recorded by the Police, England and Wales, 1990–1994*. Home Office Statistical Findings, Issue 1/96. London: Home Office Research and Statistics Directorate.

Webb, B. and Laycock, G. (1992) *Tackling Car Crime: The Nature and Extent of the Problem*. Home Office Crime Prevention Unit Paper No. 32. London: Home Office. http://rds.homeoffice.gov.uk/rds/prgpdfs/fcpu32.pdf

Webster, C. (1996) 'Asian Young People and Drug Use', *Criminal Justice Matters*, 24(1): 11–12.

Webster, C. (1997) 'The Construction of British "Asian" Criminality', *International Journal of the Sociology of Law*, 25(1): 65–86.

Webster, C. (2001) 'Qualitative career research on perpetrators of violent racism', Paper presented to the ESRC Violence Seminar, University of Lancaster. Cited in Francis, P. (2007a).

Webster, C. (2003) 'Race, space and fear: imagined geographies of racism: crime, violence and disorder in Northern England', *Capital and Class*, 27(2): 95–122.

Webster, C. (2007) *Understanding Race and Crime*. Maidenhead: McGraw Hill Open University Press.

Weisburd, D., Wheeler, S., Waring, E. and Bode, N. (1991) *Crimes of the Middle Classes: White-collar Offenders in the Federal* Courts. New Haven, CT: Yale University Press.

Welch, M. (2007) 'Moral Panic, Denial and Human Rights: Scanning the Spectrum from Overreaction to Underreaction', pp 92–106 in Downes, D., Rock, P., Chinkin, C. and Gearty, C. (eds) *Crime, Social Control and Human Rights: From Moral Panics to States of Denial, Essays in Honour of Stanley Cohen*. Cullompton: Willan.

Welch, M. (2009) 'Fragmented power and state–corporate killings: a critique of Blackwater in Iraq', *Crime, Law and Social Change*, 51: 351–64.

Wells, C. (1988) 'The decline and rise of English murder: corporate crime and individual responsibility', *Criminal Law Review*, 789–801.

Wells, C. (2001) *Corporations and Criminal Responsibility* 2nd edn. Oxford: Oxford University Press.

Wells, J. (1995) *Crime and Unemployment*. Employment Policy Institute Economic Report, 9(1): February. London: Employment Policy Institute.

West, D. (1965) *Murder Followed by Suicide*. London: Heinemann.

West, D. (1969) *Present Conduct and Future Delinquency*. London: Heinemann.

West, D. J. (1987) *Sexual Crimes and Confrontations*. Aldershot: Gower.

West, D. J. and Farrington, D. (1973) *Who Becomes Delinquent?* London: Heinemann.

West, D. J. and Farrington, D. (1977) *The Delinquent Way of Life*. London: Heinemann.

Westmarland, L. (2010) 'Gender Abuse and People Trafficking', pp 105–36 in Muncie, J., Talbot, D. and Walters, R. (eds) *Crime: Local and Global*. Cullompton: Willan.

Weston, N. and Innes, M. (2010) 'Terrorism', pp 846–64 in Brookman, F., Maguire, M., Pierpoint, H. and Bennett, T. (eds) *Handbook on Crime*. Cullompton: Willan.

Which? (2004a) 'Food Safety' *Which?* Online: February 2004.

Which? (2004b) 'No to GM' *Which?* Online: September 2004.

Which? (2004c) 'Products Recalls: A Burning Issue' *Which?* Online: March 2004.

Which? (2004d) 'Cereal Offenders' *Which?* Online: April 2004.

Which? (2004e) 'Trick packs?' *Which?* Online: November 2004.

Which? (2005a) 'Nutrition Labelling' *Which?* Online: March 2005.

Which? (2005b) 'Food Packaging' *Which?* Online: April 2005.

White, P. (1995) 'Homicides', pp 130–44 in Walker, M. (ed.) *Interpreting Crime Statistics*. Oxford: Oxford Science Publications.

White, R. (2003) 'Environmental issues and the criminological imagination', *Theoretical Criminology*, 7(4): 483–506.

White, R. (2008) *Crimes Against Nature: Environmental Criminology and Ecological Justice*. Cullompton: Willan.

White, R. (ed.) (2009) *Environmental Crime: A Reader*. Cullompton: Willan.

Whittaker, B. (1987) *The Global Connection: The Crisis of Drug Addiction*. London: Jonathan Cape.

Whyte, D. (2004a) 'Punishing anti-social business', *New Law Journal*, 154: 1063.

Whyte, D. (2004b) 'All that glitters isn't gold: environmental crimes and the production of local criminological knowledge', *Crime Prevention and Community Safety*, 6(1): 53–63.

Whyte, D. (2007a) 'Victims of Corporate Crime', pp 446–63 in Walklate, S. (ed.) *Handbook of Victims and Victimology*. Cullompton: Willan.

Whyte, D. (2007b) 'The crimes of neo-liberal rule in occupied Iraq', *British Journal of Criminology*, 47(2): 177–95.

Whyte, D. (ed.) (2009) *Crimes of the Powerful: A Reader*. Berkshire: Open University Press.

Whyte, W. (1943) *Street Corner Society: The Social Structure of an Italian Slum*. Chicago: University of Chicago Press.

Wilcox, A. and Christmann, K. (2008) '"Getting paid for sex is my kick': A qualitative study of male sex workers', pp 118–36 in Letherby, G., Williams, K., Birch, P. and Cain, M. (eds) *Sex As Crime*. Cullompton: Willan.

Williams, J. and Taylor, R. (1994) 'Boys Keep Swinging: Masculinity and Football Culture in England', pp 214–33 in Newburn, T. and Stanko, E. (eds) *Just Boys Doing Business?* London: Routledge.

Williams, K. (1994) *Textbook on Criminology* 2nd edn. London: Blackstone.

Williams, K. (2008) 'From the oblivious to the vigilante: the views, experiences and responses of residents living in areas of street sex work', pp 172–90 in Letherby, G., Williams, K., Birch, P. and Cain, M. (eds) *Sex As Crime*. Cullompton: Willan.

Williams, M. (2006) *Virtually Criminal: Crime, deviance and regulation online*. London: Routledge.

Williams, M. (2010) 'Cybercrime', pp 191–214 in Brookman, F., Maguire, M., Pierpoint, H. and Bennett, T. (eds) *Handbook on Crime*. Cullompton: Willan.

Williams, J. (2010) 'Elder Abuse', pp 415–26 in Brookman, F., Maguire, M., Pierpoint, H. and Bennett, T. (eds) *Handbook on Crime*. Cullompton: Willan.

Willis, P. (1977) *Learning to Labour: How Working Class Kids Get Working Class Jobs*. Farnborough: Saxon House.

Wilson, D., Patterson, A., Powell, G. and Hembury, R. (2006) *Fraud and Technology Crimes: Findings from the 2003/04 British Crime Survey, the 2004 Offending, Crime and Justice Survey and Administrative Sources*. Home Office Online Report 09/06. London: Home Office. http://rds.homeoffice.gov.uk/rds/pdfs06/rdsolr0906.pdf

Wilson, H. (1980) 'Parental supervision: a neglected aspect of delinquency', *British Journal of Criminology*, 20: 203–35.

Wilson, J. Q. (1975) *Thinking about Crime*. New York: Basic Books.

Wilson, J. Q. and Kelling, G. (1982) 'Broken windows', *Atlantic Monthly*, March pp 29–38.

Wilson, J. Q. and Herrnstein, R. J. (1985) *Crime and Human Nature: The Definitive Study of the Causes of Crime*. New York: Simon and Schuster.

Wilson W. J. (1987) *The Truly Disadvantaged: The Inner City, the Underclass and Public Policy*. Chicago: University of Chicago Press.

Winlow, S. and Hall, S. (2006) *Violent Night: Urban Leisure and Contemporary Culture*. Oxford: Berg.

Winlow, S., Hobbs, D., Lister, S. and Hadfield, B. (2003) 'Bouncers and the Social Context of Violence: Masculinity, Class and Violence in the Night-time Economy', pp 165–83 in Stanko, E. (ed.) (2003) *The Meanings of Violence*. London: Routledge.

Witkin, H. A., Mednick, S. A., Schulsinger, F., Bakkestrom, E., Christiansen, K. O., Goodenough, D. R., Hirschhorn, K., Lundsteen, C. and Owen, D. R. (1977) 'Criminality, Aggression and Intelligence among XYY and XXY Men', pp 165–88 in Mednick, S. A. and Christiansen, K. O. (eds) *Biosocial Bases of Criminal Behaviour*. New York: Gardner Press.

Wolfgang, M. (1958) *Patterns in Criminal Homicide*. Philadelphia: University of Pennsylvania Press.

Wolfgang, M. and Ferracuti, F. (1967) *The Subculture of Violence*. London: Tavistock.

Woodiwiss, M. (2003) 'Transnational Organised Crime: the global reach of an American Concept', pp 13–27 in Edwards, A. and Gill, P. (eds) *Transnational Organized Crime: Perspectives on Global Security*. London: Routledge.

Woodiwiss, M. and Hobbs, D. (2009) 'Organized evil and the Atlantic Alliance: moral panics and the rhetoric of organized crime policing in America and Britain', *British Journal of Criminology*, 49(1): 106–28.

Woods, J. (2005) 'Is make-up making you sick? Britain's £6 billion cosmetics and toiletries industry is facing calls to tighten up safeguards on its chemical ingredients. Just how safe are our lipsticks and moisturizers, asks Judith Woods', *Daily Telegraph*, 18/03/05, p 22.

Wooton, B. (1959) *Social Science and Social Pathology*. London: George Allen & Unwin.

Worrall, A. (1990) *Offending Women*. London: Routledge.

Worrall, A. (1995) 'Troublesome young women', *Criminal Justice Matters*, 19(1): 6–8.

Worrall, A. (2004) 'Twisted Sisters, Ladettes, and the New Penology: the Social Construction of "Violent Girls"', pp 41–60 in Alder, C. and Worrall, A. (eds) *Girls' Violence: Myths and Realities*. New York: State University of New York Press.

Wright, A. (2006) *Organized Crime*. Cullompton: Willan.

Wright, R. and Decker, S. (1994) *Burglars on the Job*. Boston: Northeastern University Press.

Wykes, M. (2001) *News, Crime and Culture*. London: Pluto.

Wykes, M. and Welsh, K. (2009) *Violence, Gender and Justice*. London: Sage.

Yablonsky, L. (1962) *The Violent Gang*. New York: Macmillan.

Yar, M. (2006) *Cybercrime and Society*. London: Sage.

Yokoyama, M. (2006) 'Environmental Pollution by Corporations in Japan', pp 330–50 in Pontell, H. and Geis, G. (eds) *International Handbook of White-Collar and Corporate Crime*. Irvine, CA: Springer.

Young, J. (1971a) *The Drugtakers*. London: Paladin.

Young, J. (1971b) 'The Police as Amplifiers of Deviancy, Negotiators of Reality and Translators of Fantasy', pp 27–61 in Cohen, S. and Taylor, L. (eds) *Images of Deviance*. Harmondsworth: Penguin.

Young, J. (1975) 'Working-Class Criminology' in Taylor, L., Walton, P. and Young, J. (eds) *Critical Criminology*. London: Routledge & Kegan Paul.

Young, J. (1986) 'The Failure of Criminology: The Need for a Radical Realism', pp 4–30 in Matthews, R. and Young, J. (eds) *Confronting Crime*. London: Sage.

Young, J. (1994) 'Incessant Chatter: Recent Paradigms within Criminology', in Maguire M., Morgan, R. and Reiner, R. (eds) *The Oxford Handbook of Criminology* 1st edn. Oxford: Clarendon Press.

Young, J. (1997) 'Left Realist Criminology: Radical in its Analysis, Realist in its Policy', pp 473–98 in Maguire, M., Morgan, R. and Reiner, R. (eds) *The Oxford Handbook of Criminology* 2nd edn. Oxford: Clarendon Press.

Young, J. (1999) *The Exclusive Society: Social Exclusion, Crime and Difference in Late Modernity.* London: Sage.

Young, J. (2003) 'Merton with energy, Katz with Structure: the sociology of vindictiveness and the criminology of transgression', *Theoretical Criminology*, 7(4): 389–414.

Young, J. (2004) 'Voodoo Criminology and the Numbers Game', pp 13–27 in Ferrell, J., Hayward, K., Morrison, W. and Presdee, M. (eds) *Cultural Criminology Unleashed*. London: Glasshouse Press.

Young, J. (2007a) *The Vertigo of Late Modernity.* London: Sage.

Young, J. (2007b) 'Slipping away – moral panics each side of "the Golden Age"', pp 53–65 in Downes, D., Rock, P., Chinkin, C. and Gearty, C. (eds) *Crime, Social Control and Human Rights: From Moral Panics to States of Denial, Essays in Honour of Stanley Cohen*. Cullompton: Willan.

Young, J. and Matthews, R. (eds) (1992) *Rethinking Criminology: The Realist Debate*. London: Sage.

Young, J. and Matthews, R. (2003) 'New Labour, Crime Control and Social Exclusion', pp 1–32 in Young, J. and Matthews, R. (eds) *The New Politics of Crime and Punishment*. Cullompton: Willan.

Zedner, L. (1992) 'Sexual Offences', in Casale, S. and Stockdale, E. (eds) *Criminal Justice Under Stress.* London: Blackstone.

Zedner, L. (1997) 'Victims', pp 577–612 in Maguire, M., Morgan, R. and Reiner, R. (eds) *The Oxford Handbook of Criminology* 2nd edn. Oxford: Clarendon Press.

Names index

Subject index